The Price of Bread

A prime contemporary concern, how to maintain fair market relations, is addressed through this study of the regulation of bread prices. This was the single most important economic reality of Europe's daily life in the early modern period. Jan de Vries uses the Dutch Republic as a case study of how the market functioned and how the regulatory system evolved and acted. The ways in which consumer behavior adapted to these structures, and the state interacted with producers and consumers in the pursuit of its own interests, had major implications for the measurement of living standards in this period. The long-term consequences of the Dutch state's interventions reveal how capitalist economies, far from being the outcome of unfettered market economics, are inextricably linked with regulatory fiscal regimes. The humble loaf serves as a prism through which to explore major developments in early modern European society and how public market regulation affected private economic life.

Jan de Vries is Emeritus Professor of History and Economics and Professor of the Graduate School at the University of California at Berkeley. He is the author of numerous publications, including *The Industrious Revolution: Consumer Demand and the Household Economy, 1650 to the Present*, which won the Ranki Prize. In 2000, he was awarded the Heineken Prize in History, and is a past president of the Economic History Association.

Cambridge Studies in Economic History

Editorial Board

GARETH AUSTIN *University of Cambridge*
STEPHEN BROADBERRY *University of Oxford*
SHEILAGH OGILVIE *University of Cambridge*
ŞEVKET PAMUK *Bogaziçi University*
GAVIN WRIGHT *Stanford University*

Cambridge Studies in Economic History comprises stimulating and accessible economic history which actively builds bridges to other disciplines. Books in the series will illuminate why the issues they address are important and interesting, place their findings in a comparative context, and relate their research to wider debates and controversies. The series will combine innovative and exciting new research by younger researchers with new approaches to major issues by senior scholars. It will publish distinguished work regardless of chronological period or geographical location.

A complete list of titles in the series can be found at:
www.cambridge.org/economichistory

The Price of Bread

Regulating the Market in the Dutch Republic

Jan de Vries

University of California, Berkeley

CAMBRIDGE
UNIVERSITY PRESS

University Printing House, Cambridge CB2 8BS, United Kingdom

One Liberty Plaza, 20th Floor, New York, NY 10006, USA

477 Williamstown Road, Port Melbourne, VIC 3207, Australia

314–321, 3rd Floor, Plot 3, Splendor Forum, Jasola District Centre, New Delhi – 110025, India

79 Anson Road, #06–04/06, Singapore 079906

Cambridge University Press is part of the University of Cambridge.

It furthers the University's mission by disseminating knowledge in the pursuit of education, learning, and research at the highest international levels of excellence.

www.cambridge.org
Information on this title: www.cambridge.org/9781108476386
DOI: 10.1017/9781108639590

© Jan de Vries 2019

First published 2019

Printed and bound in Great Britain by Clays Ltd, Elcograf S.p.A

A catalogue record for this publication is available from the British Library.

Library of Congress Cataloging-in-Publication Data
Names: De Vries, Jan, 1943 November 14– author.
Title: The price of bread : regulating the market in the Dutch Republic / Jan de Vries.
Description: New York : Cambridge University Press, 2019. | Series: Cambridge studies in economic history
Identifiers: LCCN 2018041011 | ISBN 9781108476386 (hardback)
Subjects: LCSH: Bread – Prices – Government policy – Netherlands. | BISAC: BUSINESS & ECONOMICS / Economic History.
Classification: LCC HD9057.N42 D4 2019 | DDC 338.4/36647523094920903–dc23
LC record available at https://lccn.loc.gov/2018041011

ISBN 978-1-108-47638-6 Hardback

Additional resources for this publication at www.cambridge.org/9781108476386 and www.iisg.nl/hpw/data.php#netherlands

Contents

List of Figures	*page* vii
List of Maps	x
List of Tables	xi
Preface	xvii
Note on the Online Database	xviii
Introduction	1

Part I The Regulatory Regime: Protecting the Consumer and Strengthening the State — 5

1	Bread Price Regulation in Europe before the 1590s	7
2	Free Trade in Grain?	39
3	The Dutch *Broodzetting*: The Introduction of a "New System" of Bread Price Regulation	49
4	Administering and Enforcing the New Bread Price Regulations	93
5	The Dutch "Peculiar Institution"	115

Part II Industrial Organization: The Producers in a Regulated Industry — 145

6	Grain: The Interaction of International Trade and Domestic Production	147
7	The Milling Sector: A Trade Harnessed to *Raison d'État*?	165
8	The Baking Enterprise: Efficiency versus Convenience	180
9	The Structure of Bread Prices	224

Part III Consumer Welfare and Consumer Choice   249

10   *Crise de Subsistance*: Did Price Regulation Shelter
     Consumers from Food Crises?   251

11   Choosing What to Eat in the Early Modern Era   282

12   Bread Consumption: A Wheat Bread Revolution?   306

13   Measuring the Standard of Living: A Demand-Side
     Approach   334

Part IV Perspective and Demise   373

14   Dutch Bread Price Regulation in International
     Perspective   375

15   Bread Price Regulation Renewed and Abolished,
     1776–1855   407

     Conclusion   451

     Appendix 1 Old System Bread Price Schedules   456
     Appendix 2 Crisis Periods   463
     Appendix 3 Estimating Bread Consumption from
                 Tax Records   472
     Bibliography   479
     Index   509

Figures

1.1 Wheat bread price schedule: Troyes, Châlons-sur-Marne,
1436; Paris, 1439 *page* 25
1.2a and b Old system bread price schedule 27
1.3 Old system bread pricing: weight-variable 33
1.4 Deventer rye bread, 1509–52 34
3.1 Monthly average rye bread prices calculated using old
and new system rules, January 1590 – December 1600 61
3.2 New system price-based and weight-based schedules 66
5.1a Illustration of the "deadweight loss" incurred through
the imposition of a tax on bread with elastic demand 135
5.1b Illustration of the "deadweight loss" incurred through
the imposition of a tax on bread with inelastic demand 135
5.2 Western average wheat price with and without
Holland's provincial milling excise, 1600–1820 144
6.1 East/West rye price ratios, 1600–1854 159
6.2 East/West wheat price ratios, 1600–1822 163
8.1 Fixed costs of bread production 184
8.2 Average monthly rye bread prices in Haarlem,
1750–69, with and without seasonal charity tax 190
8.3 Bread sector revenue as percentage of GDP in the
western Netherlands, 1597–1799 222
11.1 Potato/rye price ratio relative to rye price, 1763–1853 303
12.1 Estimated taxed bread grain consumption in Holland,
1650–1805 318
13.1 Holland wages, 1550–1822 336
13.2 Eastern wages, 1550–1822 336
13.3 East/west wage ratios, 1550–1822 337
13.4 Average wages for unskilled labor in northern Europe
relative to the western Netherlands, 1500–1799 341
13.5 Cost of an annual supply of bread grain or bread
in the western Netherlands, 1550–1819 357
13.6a Welfare ratios for unskilled labor in Holland, 1550–1689 362

13.6b Welfare ratios for unskilled labor in Holland, 1690–1799   362
13.7 Percentage of journeymen's earnings required for six "bread bundles" plus hypothesized average path of consumption,1550–1839   364
13.8 Journeymen's annual earnings compared to earnings needed to purchase "average" bread bundle using 33 percent of earnings, with and without taxes, 1550–1839   366
13.9 Wage/salary ratio, western Netherlands, 1580–1815   368
13.10 GDP per capita in England/Britain, Holland, and the Netherlands, 1511–1870 in 1700 guilders   369
13.11 Ratio of skilled construction wages to GDP per capita, 1581–1807   370
14.1 London wheat bread prices in relation to wheat prices, 1600–89 and 1710–94   378
14.2a Southern Netherlands/Western Netherlands rye bread price ratios, 1599–1711   388
14.2b Southern Netherlands/Western Netherlands wheat bread price ratios,1608–1712   388
14.3a and b Southern Netherlands/Holland rye and wheat bread price ratios, 1772–1855   389
14.4 Cologne/Netherlands bread price ratios, 1658–1757   390
14.5 Copenhagen/Netherlands bread price ratios,1684–1799   394
14.6 Wheat bread prices: London, Paris, and Holland, 1594–1689   399
14.7 Wheat bread prices: London, Paris, and Holland, 1690–1786   399
14.8 London/Holland wheat bread price ratio, 1599–1855   402
14.9 London and average Netherlands wheat prices, 1594–1855   405
15.1 White bread, wheat bread, and rye bread stuivers per kg, 1840–1913   427
15.2 East/west price ratios for rye bread, coarse wheat bread, and white bread, 1800–99   428
15.3 Price of grains, bread, and potatoes relative to the price of rye bread, 1800–1904   429
15.4 Netherlands GDP per capita, in current and constant (1913) guilders   449
A1.1 Geneva wheat bread price schedule, 1458   457
A1.2 Utrecht wheat bread price schedules, 1374   457
A1.3 Groningen wheat and rye bread price schedules, 1404, 1589   458
A1.4 Groningen rye bread prices: old system and new system, 1404, 1589, 1679   459

A1.5 Brielle rye bread price schedule, 1530   460
A1.6 Brielle wheat bread price schedules, 1530   461
A1.7 Antwerp rye bread price schedule, 1588   462
A2.1 Leiden rye bread prices, 1628–32   464
A2.2 Delft rye bread, 1648–53   465
A2.3 Delft rye bread, 1660–64   466
A2.4 Delft rye bread, 1697–1703   467
A2.5 Delft rye bread, 1704–11   468
A2.6 Delft rye bread, 1739–42   469
A2.7 Delft rye bread, 1770–74   470
A2.8 Delft rye bread, 1794–98   471
A2.9 Leiden rye bread price, 1798–1821   471

Maps

1 Provinces and regions of the Netherlands   *page* xix
6.1 Wheat-growing regions of the Netherlands   155
8.1 Location of Amsterdam bakeries in 1742   196

Tables

1.1 Reconstructed bread price schedule introduced
in Troyes and Châlons-sur-Marne, 1436; Paris,
1439   *page* 24
1.2 Bread price schedule for Groningen, 1404, 1589   28
1.3 The grain-to-bread weight ratios used in fifteenth-
and sixteenth-century bread price regulations in the
Low Countries   29
3.1 Estimated monthly rye bread prices, January 1590
through December 1600   62
3.2 Provincial excise taxes, per last of grain, *c.* 1600   64
3.3 Weight of grains, or specific gravity   75
3.4 Bread yield ratios, 1597–1850   76
3.5 Average yield rates for the period 1596–1800   77
3.6 Cost of fuel and non-grain ingredients and the
revenue gained from the sale of bran, 1826   83
3.7 Summary of Eversdijck's estimates of key parameters
in the pricing of five types of bread   89
3.8 Example from Eversdijck's table "to find what one
pound of bread should cost"   91
4.1 Price change frequency: percentage of months in which
bread prices were changed at least once.   95
4.2 Bread weight tolerances in Leiden, The Hague, and Zwolle   101
4.3 Urban–rural bread price differentials in Holland as
established by ordinance of 1655   107
5.1 Excise on milled grain (*'t gemaal*) in Holland   117
5.2 Holland: public revenue, 1575–1794   118
5.3 Holland's rural milling excise capitation of 1680   120
5.4 Milling excise revenues, in guilders by tax district,
1679–87   123
5.5 The excise on milled grain (*'t gemaal*) in other provinces   126
5.6 Estimated milling excise revenues in the Dutch Republic,
1600–1807   130

5.7   Each region's share of total milling excise revenue,
      1600–1807   131
5.8   Estimated per capita milling excise payments by region,
      1600–1807   132
5.9   The milling excise as a percentage of total tax revenue
      (all provinces), 1600–1807   133
5.10 Milling excise by type of grain at selected dates   139
6.1   The Dutch grain trade with the Baltic, 1562–1783   148
6.2a Imports and exports of all grains at Amsterdam,
      in lasts per year   150
6.2b Imports and exports of wheat and rye at Amsterdam,
      in lasts per year   150
6.3   Consumption of bread grains in the Batavian Republic,
      grain imports and exports, and implied domestic
      production   151
6.4   A model of the Dutch domestic and re-export markets
      for Baltic grain   152
6.5   Coefficients of correlation on first differences of annual
      average rye prices between city pairs in the Netherlands,
      1650–99   161
6.6   Coefficients of correlation on first differences of annual
      average wheat prices on the Amsterdam Grain Exchange,
      1733–79   163
6.7   Coefficients of correlation on first differences of annual
      average wheat prices between city pairs in the
      Netherlands, 1700–49   164
7.1   Industrial census of bakeries and grain mills, 1819   168
7.2   The millers' fee (*maalloon*)   173
7.3   Milling sector revenues, 1600–1850   177
8.1   Constant costs as itemized at several baking trials   181
8.2   Scale of production in bakeries in three cities, 1843   197
8.3   Eversdijck's calculation of bakers' fee based on Goes
      baking trials of 1631–32   203
8.4   Bakers' fee per last of rye in the first decades of the new
      bread pricing policy, compared with 1692   204
8.5   Bakers' fee per last of wheat in the first decades of the
      new bread pricing policy, compared with 1692   205
8.6   Bakers' fee per last of wheat and rye, 1647–1849   206
8.7   The bakers' fees per last of wheat and rye in 1826   206
8.8   Revenue and expenditures per last of grain converted
      to bread   215
8.9   Bakery revenue of a 15-last bakery   218

9.1   Wheat/rye price ratios, 1600–1899   225
9.2   Value of bran per last of milled grain, according to
      baking trials   228
9.3   Weight of one-stuiver wheat bread loaves in Kampen,
      1606–1817   232
9.4   Wheat bread yields and the relative weight of types of
      wheat bread production, according to the baking trials
      of Haarlem and Amsterdam, 1593–1843   235
9.5   Sketch of bread types consumed in Haarlem, 1659–1668   236
9.6   Estimation of the bread price structure using old
      system rules   240
9.7   Three benchmarks for the structure of bread prices   240
9.8a Price structure of bread in the Netherlands, 1596–1854   242
9.8b Structure of bread prices in Dutch cities, 1597–1828   243
9.8c Structure of foreign bread prices   244
9.9   The structure of bread prices in Goes, Zeeland, and
      North Brabant   245
9.10 The structure of bread prices in 1826   247
10.1 Crisis periods in Holland, 1550–1844   255
10.2 Crisis periods in the eastern Netherlands, 1550–1844   256
10.3 The effect of the milling excise on crisis-level bread
      prices   271
11.1 Index of cost per kilocalorie, relative to the average cost
      of the Amsterdam Burghers' Orphanage diet, 1639–1812   285
11.2 Food consumption in three orphanages, 1581–1850   291
11.3 Orphanage diets: the source of calories in percentages
      of the total   293
11.4 Model diets developed by Robert Allen and average
      annual food consumption in the BWH (1639–1812),
      AWH (1683–1795), and Utrecht BWH (1650–1750)   297
11.5 Nineteenth-century diets based on household budget
      studies and orphanage records   300
12.1 Bread and bread grain consumption in three orphanages,
      1562–1899   308
12.2 Per capita grain consumption in Holland, 1798   311
12.3 Bread grain consumption in the Netherlands, 1808   312
12.4 Bread grain consumption in the Netherlands, 1834–37   313
12.5 Bread grain consumption in Holland cities, 1720–1848   315
12.6 Estimates of per capita annual bread grain consumption,
      1500–1850   320
12.7 Model of bread consumption before 1650   322

12.8 Summary estimates of bread grain consumption in the
Netherlands, 1580–1850   325
12.9 Estimated consumption of bread grains in the
Netherlands plus net grain imports, 1600–1850   326
12.10 Per capita bread consumption in four European
countries, 1700–1914   329
13.1 Regional urbanization in the Netherlands, 1550–1840   338
13.2 Silver wages for unskilled labor as a percentage of wages
in the western Netherlands, 1500–1799   339
13.3 Birthplace of brides and grooms in Utrecht, 1721–1800   342
13.4 Migration to Amsterdam as revealed by the marriage
records, 1601–1800   343
13.5 Indicators of rye bread costs in west and east   346
13.6 Annual household bread costs in east and west,
1596–1839   351
13.7a Annual cost of "bread bundles," 1550–1839   356
13.7b Annual cost of "bread bundles," 1550–1839, as
percentage of earnings of journeymen builders   356
13.8 Index of an unskilled laborer's real cost of acquiring
bread and bread grains in 1680–99 relative to 1580–99   363
14.1 Constant costs identified in Parisian bread price
regulations   381
14.2 Estimation of constant costs allowed to Paris bakers,
1745–88, based on actual average annual bread prices   383
14.3 Rye prices in northern Europe   386
14.4 Rye and wheat bread costs in Cologne and the eastern
Netherlands, 1658–1757   391
14.5 Relative prices of Copenhagen bread types   393
14.6 Berlin grain and bread prices in comparison with the
Netherlands, 1757–1805   395
14.7 "Average German" rye bread prices compared with
the western and eastern Netherlands, 1745–1839   396
14.8 French bread prices relative to those of the western
Netherlands, 1724–88   398
15.1 Final provincial milling excise rates (1795–1805)
and the new national rates introduced in 1806–7   411
15.2 Changes in the milling excise (guilders per last) and
the bread price regulatory system from 1806 to 1865   415
15.3 Examples of the central government and municipal
milling taxes   418
15.4a Municipal taxation in North Holland, 1849   419
15.4b Total municipal tax revenue, 1849   419

15.5   Municipal taxes in 1849: average annual taxes in guilders
       per capita   420
15.6   Estimated milling excise revenues, 1807–49   421
15.7   Estimating bakery revenue in the nineteenth century   433
15.8   Wheat as a percentage of total grain consumption, total
       bread expenditure, and total milling tax revenue,
       1804–50   438
15.9   Per capita milling excise for 110 kg of bread grain per year
       under various wheat–rye mixes, 1833–55   439
15.10 The cost of bread, per last of grain, 1840–85   445
15.11 Model of consumer expenditures, 1841–80   446
15.12 Bread grain consumption in the Netherlands, 1580–1993   447
15.13 Changing bread preferences after 1850   448
A1.1   Antwerp rye bread schedule, 1588   462
A3.1   Net and gross revenues of the milling excise and the
       other common means, 1745–53   474
A3.2   Adjusted model of bread consumption in Holland   477

Preface

I gathered the data for this study over many years, and thought about what it all meant for as many. All the while I tried out my ideas at seminars in the US, UK, the Netherlands, and Belgium, and thereby benefited from the questions and suggestions of scores of colleagues. Nuffield College, Exeter College, and the Weston Centre, all at Oxford, the European University Institute and Utrecht University all offered their hospitality as I set out to write this book, and once a draft had been written, I benefited again from the comments of readers and anonymous reviewers. I wish to acknowledge especially: Maxine Berg, Bruno Blondé, Oscar Gelderblom, Philip Hoffman, Maarten Prak, Peter Solar, and Bartolomé Yun. All of this scholarly input and support has certainly made this a better, more insightful book. Indeed, as I look back I cannot but feel blessed by my good fortune in being able to work within an international academic community that is both welcoming and intellectually probing.

My colleagues have made this a better book. But research and writing remain, for the most part, an individual affair. As I contemplated my data and pondered the sparse historiographical signposts, I came to believe that most of those signposts pointed in the wrong direction. Thus, as I ventured into the history of one of the most prosaic aspects of everyday life, the pricing and purchase of bread, it appeared increasingly to be a *terra incognita*. If I lost my way in places, the responsibility is mine alone.

Finally, I can now answer in the affirmative a question my family has been asking for some time: "Is the bread book done?"

Note on the Online Database

This study makes use of newly gathered data on grain prices, bread prices, and excise tax receipts. A full account of the sources and the methods used to assemble the time series of bread and grain prices is presented in the online database at www.cambridge.org/9781108476386, under "Resources." The online database also provides full information on the currencies, weights, and measures used in this study.

Map 1. Provinces and regions of the Netherlands

Introduction

This is a book that needs a few words of explanation. It is, as the title states, about the price of bread. When I embarked on research into bread prices in early modern Europe I believed this would be a straightforward matter of gathering data on prices in order to improve on the cost of living indexes commonly used to study the history of living standards. Most non-farming families bought bread rather than grain, certainly in the highly urbanized Netherlands, so this seemed to be a useful step in improving the measurement of the cost of living. But I discovered soon enough that bread prices, which nearly everywhere were regulated by public authorities, differed in intriguing ways from grain prices, which generally reflected market conditions.

This book is an exploration of discovery into what might be called the political economy of bread pricing. It follows the regulatory practices and their consequences in several directions: into the worlds of the producers, the consumers, and the state. It will examine how the grain and bread markets functioned, how the regulatory system evolved and acted, how consumer behavior adapted to these structures, and how the state interacted with producers and consumers in the pursuit of its own interests. In these ways the humble loaf will serve as a sort of prism through which to channel and study major developments of an early modern European society.

Bread price regulation was a pan-European phenomenon, and I offer an account here of its medieval development and its character in early modern times, but regulation took a particular turn in the Dutch Republic that had far reaching implications for many aspects of Dutch economic and political life. I will identify a new "scientific" approach to the regulation of bread prices that, from its introduction in the 1590s, shaped Dutch bread prices in a distinctive way. The regulatory process then moved from the realm of custom and command, from what Karl Polanyi called "administered trade," to one of measurement and strategic intervention – it became a form of commercial regulation suited to a capitalist, market-oriented, society. The management and enforcement of

1

the new regulatory system over the following centuries required demanding levels of numeracy, familiarity with subtle economic distinctions, and, above all, the amassing and analysis of information on an ongoing basis concerning the behavior of market prices, producers' costs, and consumers' preferences.

Capitalism is commonly defined as an economic order in which outcomes are shaped by markets unfettered by public regulation, where *laissez-faire* rules. But, in fact, regulation is inseparable from modern capitalist economies. Economic actors routinely face often-intrusive regulation by public authorities, and a large body of literature is dedicated to evaluating the efficacy of public regulation of private economic life. This study examines the costs and benefit of regulation and its consequences, intended and unintended, over a long time period – 260 years – in order to achieve a deeper understanding of the place of regulation within a market society as well as its place in the building of state capacity/governmentality – the institutional means to implement, administer, and enforce (and reform) public policy.

The introduction of a technically more demanding form of price regulation in the Dutch Republic was, I discovered, closely associated with innovations in the new state's fiscal regime. Uniquely in early modern Europe, Dutch price regulation and taxation came to be joined closely together as the state learned, step by step over the course of many decades, to tax what Classical economists called the "wage good" (the commodity – bread – whose price defines the living standard of wage earners). The heavy taxation of bread proved to be an exceedingly durable fixture of Dutch fiscalism, outliving the Republic itself. Explaining why this was so – why such a tax could function as an example of "optimal taxation" – will form another objective of this book.

How could a heavy tax on the staff of life (a.k.a. the wage good) long survive the resistance, if not the wrath, of consumers? Indeed, how could the regulatory regime, presumably intended to shelter the humble populace from harsh market forces, become complicit in using bread consumption to collect over 10 percent of the entire public revenue of the Dutch Republic? Nothing in the voluminous history of food riots or in the concept of moral economy prepares one for this striking historical phenomenon. I believe that explaining both the emergence and the longevity of the Dutch regulatory–fiscal complex requires attending closely to the agency of Dutch consumers. They faced bread markets that were shaped in distinctive ways by the regulatory system and state fiscal policy, but they also possessed distinctive options regarding the types of bread they bought and the bread substitutes available to them.

When we examine the consumption of "bread" closely, it quickly becomes apparent that early modern European consumers faced choices among bread grains (wheat and rye, among others), between coarse and fine (bolted) breads, and between bread grains and bread substitutes (such as barley and buckwheat, among others). This realm of choice was not fully accessible everywhere in Europe, but I found that the Netherlands was covered in all but the deepest countryside by networks of grain mills, bakeries, and shelling and grinding mills that could supply consumers with nearly all of these products. This means that consumers faced the tax collectors and bread price regulators with weapons with which to fight back, as it were. That, at any rate, is what an economist would assume. But was it true? Did consumers respond to the fiscal–regulatory regime with their market choices rather than with their bodies in the streets? A major part of this study is dedicated to identifying and explaining the choices made by consumers in this period.

My exploration into the agency of the early modern consumer uncovered a change in preferences that amounted to a "revolution." It also swept through other parts of northwestern Europe, but Holland and its neighboring provinces were early participants. It was a revolution in which a growing portion of consumers switched much of their bread consumption away from the broad range of lesser grains and substitutes and toward wheat bread. This "wheat bread revolution" (a term coined by Fernand Braudel) had far-reaching implications for the task of the regulators and the taxing policies of the state. Just as consumers reacted to changes in the structure of prices presented to them by the authorities, so the authorities adjusted their policies to the unfolding behavior of consumers.

This exploration of regulation, taxation, and consumer behavior also led me to some new insights into the standard of living of early modern Europeans, or, more correctly, into how it should be measured. Once we understand that "bread" is not represented by a single price but represents a category of consumption with a broad range of prices, and that individual choice shifted over time across this range, the standard procedures used by economic historians to measure economic welfare, or wellbeing, present us with a puzzle: price and wage trends seem to enforce reductions in wellbeing while consumer behavior seems to reflect rising incomes. This is a puzzle I uncovered and explored elsewhere (in the realm of colonial goods and manufactures), and proposed to resolve with the concept of the "industrious revolution."[1] Here we will consider

---

[1] Jan de Vries, "Between purchasing power and the world of goods: understanding the household economy in early modern Europe," in John Brewer and Roy Porter, eds., *Consumption and the World of Goods* (London: Routledge, 1993), pp. 85–132; Jan de Vries, *The Industrious Revolution: Consumer Behavior and the Household Economy, 1650 to the Present* (Cambridge University Press, 2008).

whether it is also applicable to consumer behavior in the prosaic core of everyday economic life.

This study pursues these regulatory and fiscal institutions – central to the day-to-day functioning of state and society for well over two centuries – to their dotage, tracking their growing dysfunction, and their sudden and virtually simultaneous abolition. Contemporary debates concerning the stagnation of the nineteenth-century Dutch economy focused much of their attention on these institutions, and they gave rise to historical debates that have continued to this day. The regulatory system devised in the 1590s was sophisticated and beneficial and the associated fiscal policy was successful and perhaps even "optimal." But these same institutions came to be regarded, two centuries later, as an obstacle to modern growth. The ending of this regulatory–fiscal regime will illustrate an issue of substantial contemporary relevance: the "penalties of the pioneer" – the special difficulties preventing an advanced but obsolete economy from reforming its institutions and reorganizing its industrial structure.

Nearly a century ago the eminent British historian Sir William Ashley beseeched patience from those gathered in Oxford for his 1923 Ford Lectures on the topic of bread in the English economy.[2]

I hope you will not be deterred by the limitation of our inquiry to just this one part of the far larger subject of the standard of living generally.

But he promised his auditors, and his readers in the published lectures, *The Bread of Our Forefathers*, a reward for their patience:

We shall have to traverse so large a space of time, to notice such a wide range of evidence, to glance at so many features of English life from a novel point of view, that I think I can promise you that you will not find the road dull.

I am acutely aware that I am addressing myself to an audience accustomed to an even faster pace of life than Ashley faced a century ago. But I, too, feel I can promise you a view of features of Dutch and European life in the early modern era that will offer new perspectives on a series of large questions about the emerging modernity of economy, state, and society, and on problems of markets and their regulators that continue to this day – all through the prism of the price of bread.

---

[2] W. Ashley, *The Bread of Our Forefathers* (Oxford University Press, 1927), p. 1.

Part I

The Regulatory Regime: Protecting the Consumer and Strengthening the State

1 Bread Price Regulation in Europe before the 1590s

The impulse to control the price of bread goes back a long way. Wherever consumers relied on bakers rather than home production for their bread, its price and quality emerged as sensitive social issues. And where they baked their own bread, the cost of grain and the terms of access to mills and ovens attracted the regulatory impulse.

The *Annona*

Europe's early bread price control mechanisms derived from Roman practice, where the emperors established the *annona*, a public bread distribution system. Through a combination of forced delivery and purchase, the *praefectura annonae* of Rome acquired, transported, and stored grain, and made it available to bakers on favorable terms. The famed free distribution of bread was usually restricted to a portion of the population, and a private trade usually existed alongside the *annona*.

The demise of Roman cities as great concentrations of population also brought to an end the long-distance trade that had supplied the *annona* and any hope of maintaining its regulatory apparatus. It survived longer in the Eastern Empire, but the decline of urban population and the loss of Alexandria, first to Persian and later to Arab control, brought the *annona* of Constantinople to an end too, apparently in AD 618.[1]

---

[1] Françoise Desportes, *Le pain au Moyen Âge* (Paris: Oliver Orban, 1987), pp. 146–47; Michael Parlairet, "The descent into a Dark Age: Byzantine Europe, c. 400–800 A.D.," in Philipp Robinson Rössner, ed., *Cities – Coins – Commerce* (Stuttgart: Franz Steiner Verlag, 2012), p. 14; John Teall, "The grain supply of the Byzantine Empire, 330–1025," *Dumbarton Oaks Papers* 13 (1959), 87–139; Barry Cunliffe, *Europe between the Oceans* (New Haven, Conn.: Yale University Press, 2008), p. 426. "[In 618] the free distribution of bread in Constantinople came to an end and was never restored. The arrival of the Arabs in 642 removed Alexandria and the wealth of Egypt from the reach of Constantinople forever. Carthage remained a supplier of corn for a few more years until it too succumbed to the Arabs in 698. The old Roman system of supplying the non-productive centre with an annual levy of corn from the provinces, which had begun with the conquest of Sicily in 212 BC, was now finally at an end" (pp. 426–27).

The memory of this practice may have led Charlemagne to set a maximum price for grain for his empire at the Council of Frankfurt in 794 (in the wake of a period of famine), but no means existed then for the central gathering, storage, and distribution of grain that had characterized the ancient *annona*.[2] Later, with the great urban expansion of the High Middle Ages, the regulatory impulse was again taken up, now usually by cities rather than territorial states.

Medieval cities, as they grew, sought to secure adequate food deliveries to their markets and to that end they developed a range of provisionment policies designed to protect the interests of urban consumers. These sought to maximize and stabilize urban supply by regulating the operation of the markets (prohibiting forestalling, engrossing, and regrating), by restricting regional trade through the assertion of staple rights (forcing the sale of goods in local markets before allowing their removal to more distant markets), and by prohibitions of grain exports in times of dearth.[3] Cities that gained political dominion over their rural districts commonly went on to require farmers and landowners to deliver grain to the city markets and nowhere else (a practice known as *Marktzwang*). In addition, the largest and richest cities devoted public funds to the purchase of grain and the maintenance of public granaries. In short, the medieval towns re-established key features of the *annona* of the ancient world as their officials sought to control grain prices through a combination of market restriction and market participation.

In the thirteenth century, as medieval urban growth accelerated, cities throughout western and central Europe enacted formal rules for the control of bread prices. In northern and central Italy, where the cities struggled to subordinate each other and the rural districts to their rule, *annona*-like policies became the norm, or certainly the ideal. In 1284 Florence established what would later be known as the *Abbondanza*, Venice later establishes the *Proveditori alle Biave*, Genoa its *Magistrato dell'Abbondanza*, and still later, the restored Roman papacy organized a full-blown *annona* regime for the city of Rome.[4]

---

[2] Charlemagne's regulations are recorded in the Frankfurt Capitulary (794). A. Boretius, *Capitularia Regum Francorum* (Hanover, 1897), vol. I, p. 74.

[3] Hans van Werveke, "Les villes belges: histoire des institutions économiques et sociales," in *La ville*, vol. II: *Institutions économiques et sociales* (Brussels: Éditions de la Librairie Encyclopédique, 1955), p. 564.

   Forestallers are those who buy up stocks before they can be offered for public sale at a market. Regraters form corners in order to drive up prices. Engrossers hoard stocks, hoping thereby to force prices upward through artificial scarcity.

[4] A. M. Pult Quaglia, "Controls over food supplies in Florence in the late XVIth and early XVIIth centuries," *Journal of European Economic History* 9 (1980), 449–57; A. M. Pult Quaglia, *"Per provvedere ai popoli": il sistema annonario nella Toscana dei Medici* (Florence: Leo S. Olschki, 1990); E. Grendi, "Genova alla metà del Cinquecento: una politica del

The points to emphasize about these *annona*-style institutions are:

1. They approached the control of bread prices via the grain markets, through some combination of coercion and commercial intervention.
2. Their objective was price *stability*, ideally the maintenance of a fixed price over the long term.
3. All this necessarily involved the cities in public grain storage and in control over the terms on which bakers secured their grain supplies.

The execution of policies designed to secure adequate supplies of grain and maintain stable prices placed the role of the governing classes in high relief. According to Hanlon, they legitimized the governing classes in the eyes of the poor, "who measured the stock and assessed the quality of bread every day … High grain prices by themselves were not enough to unleash popular disturbances. It was the hint of speculation or government indifference that provoked an uprising."[5] He declared this medieval urban world to have been a genuine "'moral economy' aiming to maintain the public good." As an example, he offers Modena, where "every July and August, magistrates issued decrees on grains, forbade their export, and ordered landlords to deliver their harvests into the city. During bad years they ordered hoarders to declare their stocks." Official grain prices, he concluded, were always political. "The city would discourage speculation by dumping reserves on the market at opportune moments."[6]

Were these magistrates motivated by the Scholastic concept of "just price"? It may not have been the pure theory of just price as enunciated by Aquinas or Duns Scotus that guided them, but *annona* practices did appear to recognize an important distinction that was common to just price discourse.[7] That is, somewhere between the "natural price" (the short-term market-clearing price set by supply and demand) and

---

grano?," *Quaderni Storici* 13 (1970), 106–60; I. Mattozzi *et al.*, "Il politico e il pane a Venezia, 1570–1650: camieri e governo della sussistenza," *Società e Storia* 20 (1983), 271–303; Monica Martinat, "Le blé du pape: système annonaire et logiques économiques à Rome à l'époque moderne," *Annales. Histoire, Sciences sociales* 54 (1999), 219–44; Monica Martinat, *Le juste marché: le système annonaire romain aux XVIe et XVIIe siècles* (École Française de Rome, 2004); Volker Reinhardt, *Überleben in der frühneuzeitlichen Stadt: Annona und Getreideversorgung in Rom, 1563–1797* (Tübingen: Max Niemeyer Verlag, 1991). On Naples and Milan, see Lavinia Parziale, "Aspetti della politica milanese in materia annonaria," pp. 321–48 and Brigitte Marin, "Organisation annonaire, crise alimentaire et réformes," pp. 389–417, in Marin and Virlouvet, eds., *Nourrir les cités de Méditerranée: Antiquité – temps modernes* (Paris: Maisonneuve & Larose, 2003).

[5] Gregory Hanlon, *Early Modern Italy, 1550–1800* (Basingstoke: Macmillan, 2000), p. 101.

[6] *Ibid.*, p. 101.

[7] Joseph Schumpeter, *History of Economic Analysis* (New York: Oxford University Press, 1954), pp. 93–97.

the "official price" (set by public authority) one might find the "just price" – a longer-term equilibrium price achieved under conditions of full information, honest dealings, and no coercion. This just price was often – indeed, nearly always – unattainable without official intervention because of market failure and human cupidity. I follow here the approach to the topic developed by De Roover, who went on to note, wryly, that "the Scholastic authors were full of illusions about the omniscience, honesty, and efficiency of public authorities."[8] The just price ideal was difficult for competitive markets to attain, yet somehow, it could readily be known to and enforced by the legislator. This, at any rate, was the view of the influential theologian Jean Gerson (1362–1428), Rector of the University of Paris and a prominent advocate of price fixing. "No one," he intoned, "should presume to be wiser than the lawmaker."[9]

This argument for ongoing public intervention in grain and bread markets might be called the "market failure" justification, and it remains a powerful argument for public intervention in market economies to this day. But *annona*-type regimes also had a second objective: price stability. The "natural price" of grain was more volatile than most other prices; grain prices were far more volatile than wages, but also more than rents, manufactured goods, and capital goods. The association of just price with an immutable fixed price may not do justice to Scholastic philosophy, but it reflects the understanding embraced by the Popes as they re-established their temporal rule over Rome and the Papal States after their return from Avignon. In 1512 Julius II reorganized the Apostolic Chamber to take jurisdiction over grain supply and in 1557 Paul IV created the Prefecture of the Annona, which by 1576, under Gregory XIII, had assumed its definitive powers of comprehensive control over grain supplies and bread prices.

The Papal regime organized the *annona* to defend a constant price (actually a constant weight for a loaf of fixed price) for the *baioccanti*, the loaf intended for the masses that would always cost one *baiocco*, a Roman coin. From 1605 to 1797 the weight of these loaves was adjusted only with great reluctance – it usually remained fixed at its target weight of 8 *once* for years at a time.[10] After 1763, in the face of a long-term rise in grain prices, the Papal *annona* struggled to maintain the loaf weight that generations of Romans had come to regard as proper – and just.

[8] Raymond De Roover "The concept of just price: theory and economic policy," *Journal of Economic History* 18 (1958), 428–29.
[9] Cited in *ibid.*, p. 425.
[10] Reinhardt, *Überleben*, p. 460; Martinat, *Le juste marché*, pp. 245–46.

Papal Rome possessed unique resources, but, as Reinhardt, the Roman *annona's* historian, observes, "the project of decoupling grain and bread prices required a herculean economic power, which, in time, exceeded even the Papal budgets."[11] In 1797, after two decades of continual borrowing to subsidize the *annona*, the old Papal state and the *annona* collapsed together.

Other cities could not hope fully to emulate the Roman *annona*, but they did attempt to stabilize prices over shorter periods.[12] A civic commitment to price stability required the assumption of market risk which, of course, was far from costless, nor was the organization of grain deliveries, buying up grain from afar, storing it for extended periods, and strategically dumping grain on the market to discourage speculation. Who paid for price stability? In the medieval and early modern eras there were four possibilities that singly or in combination financed the *annona*-style regulatory system.

The landlords and/or peasants pay. Through marketing controls, confiscations, and taxation states and especially city-states acted to harness the countryside to their urban priorities. The other side of the coin of low and stable grain prices in the towns was often disinvestment, soil exhaustion, and even famine in the rural districts.[13] "When annonary regulations were efficient," notes Hanlon, "the countryside experienced worse hunger than did the cities, and famished peasants converged on urban charitable institutions."[14] The same point was made by Hilton Root with respect to France: "[P]olicies designed to defend consumer interests produced price distortions that reduced overall income and transferred income from the countryside to the town."[15]

The city pays. Where force was either not feasible or thought undesirable the chief option for a city, or the Crown in a capital city, was to finance the acquisition and maintenance of grain stocks from municipal or royal funds. When magistrates contracted with merchants to purchase grain in distant markets and maintained granaries they understood that they were paying the price of social stability. By the late

---

[11] Reinhardt, *Überleben*, p. 436.
[12] Martinat, *Le juste marché*, p. 243.
[13] The often-predatory economic policies of city-states regarding their rural jurisdictions is described in Stephen R. Epstein, *Freedom and Growth: The Rise of States and Markets in Europe, 1300–1750* (London: Routledge, 2000), and Tom Scott, *The City-State in Europe, 1000–1600* (Oxford University Press, 2012).
[14] Hanlon, *Early Modern Italy*, p. 102.
[15] Hilton Root, *The Fountain of Privilege: Political Foundations of Markets in Old Regime France and England* (Berkeley: University of California Press, 1994), p. 108.

sixteenth century the Grand Dukes of Tuscany were ordering grain from Amsterdam and Venice.[16] City-financed grain distributed at a loss to the bakers and burghers in times of acute need occurred throughout Europe. But, the operation of an *annona* required frequent if not ongoing interventions of this sort. It was a cost no city – not even Papal Rome – could bear indefinitely and this knowledge led to the development of strategies whereby the magistrates sought to recoup their investments in price stability.

The bakers pay. When the *annona* supplied grain to bakers below the market price (because of forced deliveries, sale of old grain acquired at lower prices in the past, or through subsidized sale of expensively purchased grain) it is hard to believe any baker would refuse. But the next step for the *annona* was often to require bakers also to purchase grain from the *annona* at *above market prices* when these were low. In this way the authorities simultaneously pursued their objective of stable bread prices through inter-temporal grain price smoothing (below-market bread prices when they were high; above-market bread prices when they were low) and financed their investments in grain stocks via a stream of payments from the bakers during periods of low grain prices.

It is a clever idea, of course, but could only be enforced for long in an economic island.[17] Bakers had as strong an incentive to evade the obligation to purchase artificially costly grain in the good years just as they had to accept subsidized grain in bad years. Moreover, even if bakers complied with the *annona* rules when grain prices were low, consumers then had a strong incentive to acquire their bread outside the city, where prices would be cheaper. This helps explain why it is a strategy that seems to have endured only in Venice, where the city's *annona*, the Grain Office, allotted grain to bakers at fixed prices.[18] One might argue that the baker did not really pay. He bore some risk in this system, but ultimately, it was the consumer who paid for price stability through high bread prices in periods when grain prices were low.

---

[16] Fernand Braudel, *The Mediterranean and the Mediterranean World in the Age of Philip II*, 2 vols. (New York: Harper and Row, 1972), vol. I, pp. 576–97.

[17] Geneva and nearby Lyon both attempted to operate public granaries coupled with a requirement that bakers purchase a portion of their grain from the granaries. Neither functioned well. W. Gregory Monahan, *Years of Sorrows: The Great Famine of 1709 in Lyon* (Columbus: Ohio University Press, 1993); Karl Gunnar Persson, *Grain Markets in Europe, 1500–1900: Integration and Deregulation* (Cambridge University Press, 1999), p. 138.

[18] Mattozzi *et al.*, 1983; Frederic C. Lane, *Venice: A Maritime Republic* (Baltimore, Md.: Johns Hopkins University Press, 1973), pp. 305–07.

The consumer pays. Stable prices were not necessarily low prices, a fact that is clearly documented for Rome, where bread prices rarely changed for over two hundred years. From 1617 until 1797 consumers paid 1 *baiacco* (100th of a *scudo*) for a wheat bread loaf that the authorities sought to maintain at 8 *once* (226 grams, about half an English pound). At this price bakers earned a net revenue from the bread produced from a *rubbio* of wheat (294 liters) that could pay for the grain twice-over in periods of average wheat prices. At such prices the bakers' net revenue usually exceeded by far their labor and other production costs. Indeed, the Apostolic Chamber, not content to leave the bakers with such large profits, introduced a tax on bread, raised and extended over time, to capture a portion of this revenue, presumably to defray the costs it incurred in the operation of the *annona*. In his exhaustive study of the Roman *annona*, Reinhardt stresses how Rome's stable price policy acted as a social "release valve" shielding the lower classes from high prices. But he felt compelled to add that it also acted to limit "full-blown *abbondanza*."[19] It protected the consumer from dearth, to be sure, but at the price of very costly bread in normal times, thereby denying the consumer the pleasures of easy living – *abbondanza* – when harvests were plentiful.[20] Despite this drawback, *annona*-type bread price regulations – with buffer stocks of grain to intervene in the markets – continued to operate well into the early modern period.[21]

Grain storage and market-moderating policies were also attempted beyond Italy. Geneva's *Chambre des Blés* of 1628 relied on commercial transactions rather than compulsion in the management of its municipal

---

[19] Reinhardt, *Überleben*, p. 68.

[20] A curious example of a long-lived *annona* regime is provided by the island of Malta during its long rule by the Knights of the Order of St. John (1524–1798). Grain was imported by a monopoly agency, the *Università*. Paul Sharp relates that while it bought grain at market prices, it "sold this grain at an inflated price, to cover its costs of inventory, distribution, as well as market losses in years of high prices." When Napoleon's army invaded in 1798, it found the same thing it had found in Rome a year earlier: a bankrupt grain agency. But when, soon thereafter, the British took control of Malta they re-established the *Università* and persisted until 1822 with a regime of high bread prices for the dual purposes of combating idleness and generating state revenue. In their view, only the sharp stick of costly bread would induce the Maltese to industriousness. Bread price regulation has many uses beyond the most obvious one. Paul Sharp, "Malta and the nineteenth-century grain trade: British free trade in a microcosm of Empire?" in J. Chircop (ed), *Colonial Encounters: Maltese Experiences of British Rule 1800–1970s* (Rabat, Malta: Horizons, 2015), pp. 1–13.

[21] Just as Papal Rome followed the traditions of the ancient city, so Ottoman Istanbul embraced the traditions of ancient Constantinople. Rhoads Murphey, "Provisioning Istanbul," *Food and Foodways* 2 (1988), p. 220; Onur Yildirim, "Bread and Empire: the workings of grain provisioning in Istanbul," in Marin and Virlouvet, eds., *Nourrir les cités*, p. 267.

granary, but it, too, sought to maintain reserves whose judicious release on the market would stabilize bread prices.[22] Nearby Lyon moved in this same direction in 1630, and in 1643 established its *Chambre d'Abondance* with the same mission. However, its recent historian admits that it was "at best an occasional institution" and that the grain stocks it held were too small to have the desired effect.[23]

More ambitious was the *Kriegsmagazinverwaltung* (War Granary Administration) of the Prussian kings, beginning with Friedrich Wilhelm in 1719. He funded the establishment – actually the re-establishment – of Berlin's Municipal Granary (*Stadsmagazin*), which then became the Royal Granary (*Koninglichenmagazin*). Under the direction of Berlin's military commandant, a second officer, plus three civil magistrates, its tasks were to maintain grain stocks, sell them in periods of high price below the market rate, supply charitable institutions in normal years, and have grain available for the military when the need arose.[24] This Royal Granary functioned in a period of rapid population growth in Berlin, which may account for its inability to influence the grain markets in any significant way. When, in 1771–72 under Friedrich II (The Great), the release of grain onto the market failed to lower prices, the monarch reacted in fury, sending off a message to Silesian grain traders intended to teach them to fear his wrath: "The high grain price was not caused by bad harvest nor by mice, but by the *Kornjuden* among them, who, if they persist in their Jewish speculation, would provoke him to release grain [again]."[25]

The Prussian granary policy was focused on the provisioning of Berlin, but it was clearly a matter of state rather than only a municipal policy. At the national level, interventions in grain markets, primarily via export controls and supply privileges for the capital cities, continued in many European countries throughout the early modern era.[26] At the

---

[22] Hermann Blanc, *La Chambre des Blés de Genève, 1628–1798* (Geneva: Imprimerie du Journal de Genève, 1939).

[23] W. Gregory Monahan, *Years of Sorrows: The Great Famine of 1709 in Lyon* (Columbus: Ohio State University Press, 1993), p. 33. Jessica Dijkman comes to much the same conclusion in her review of granary policies in England, northern France, and Holland. Jessica Dijkman, "Coping with scarcity: a comparison of dearth policies in three regions in northwestern Europe in the fifteenth and sixteenth centuries," *Tijdschrift voor sociale en economische geschiedenis* 14 (2017), 5–30.

[24] W. Naudé, *Die Getreidehandelspolitik und Kriegsmagazinverwaltung Preussens* (Berlin: Paul Parey, vol. I, 1896; vol. II, 1901; vol. III, 1910; vol. IV, 1931).

[25] Naudé, *Die Getreidehandelspolitik*, vol. IV, pp. 112–16. The Prussian monarch's outburst should be understood not as a claim that grain merchants were Jews but as an accusation that, in Friedrich's eyes, they acted as though they were.

[26] Such controls on the grain trade for the benefit of cities, especially capital cities, were most robust in the Mediterranean region. Grain moved from Sicily to Naples, Genoa, and Spanish cities only via export licences (*tratte*) issued by the Crown. Ringrose describes how both bread (*pan de obligación*) and grain were directed to Madrid as its growth

town level, free grain markets usually had to be taken as an external given; even most Italian city-states ceased to base their bread price regulations on coercion and the management of public grain inventories. While coercive measures long continued in Rome and Naples, the cities of Tuscany and northern Italy lacked either the means or the will to rely on force as a matter of routine.[27] The *annona* continued on in name, but its method of operation was changing – changing in a way that brought it into closer conformity with practices that had spread through the cities of France, Germany, England, and the Low Countries from the thirteenth century onward.

The "Old System" of Price Regulation: Assize of Bread, *Broodzetting, Brottaxe, Tax du Pain, Calmiere*

In most of western and central Europe the urban efforts to control grain markets were modest in scope (they usually involved temporarily forbidding grain exports from a region or county) and could not hope to bend the price of grain to the will of the magistrates for any length of time. Moreover, as urban bread making shifted from household use of public ovens to the purchase of bread from bakers (that is, from bakers as operators of public ovens to bakers as bread makers and sellers) the focus of regulatory interest shifted from grain to bread. The grain markets were, except in times of crisis, relatively free and beyond the effective control of public authorities and the maintenance of grain inventories was recognized as primarily a private matter, left to grain merchants, millers, bakers, and individual households. One might say regulation retreated to a more defensible position.[28] Henceforth the periodic setting of the

strained the supply capacity of central Castile. There a transition from the *annona* style system occurred only after the mid-eighteenth century, when a reforming regime freed the grain trade and came to rely on bread price regulation instead. David Ringrose, *Madrid and the Spanish Economy 1560–1850* (Berkeley: University of California Press, 1983), pp. 144–54; Braudel, *Mediterranean and the Mediterranean World*, vol. I, pp. 570–73.

[27] Reinhardt notes that Florence declared a "*consultum ultimum*" (which suspended normal market operations) only once between 1590 and 1631, while Siena intervened in this way only three times between 1546 and 1776. *Überleben*, p. 432. A far less optimistic view of the Italian situation is presented by Guido Alfani, "Famines in late medieval and early modern Italy: a test for an advanced economy," Dondena Centre, Università Bocconi, Working Paper no. 82, 2015; Guido Alfani, *Calamities and Economy in Renaissance Italy: The Grand Tour of the Horsemen of the Apocalypse* (Basingstoke: Palgrave, 2013).

[28] The distinction I make here is one early modern observers also made. The mid-eighteenth-century French Farmer-General Claude Dupin distinguished between states that secured "abundance" via permanent granaries and comprehensive controls on the grain trade and those, such as France, that refrained from such intervention except in times of dearth. (He thought such temporary measures were insufficient and advocated a return to the comprehensive controls of earlier ages.) See Steven L. Kaplan, *Bread, Politics*

bread price became the primary means by which magistrates sought to demonstrate their ongoing concern for the common weal.

We cannot say with certainty when cities began asserting their authority over bread prices and just where the rules governing price setting were first developed, but we know that Nuremberg, Frankfurt am Main, and Basel established permanent bodies to regulate bread prices, weights, and quality early in the thirteenth century, followed by Liège in 1252 and Lübeck in 1255. In England legislation to guide towns and counties throughout the kingdom in setting prices for bread (and beer) began in 1266. Marseille's regulations date from 1273, while Augsburg, whose city charter of 1156 had specified the Bishop's right to regulate bread price and quality, established in 1276 a set of regulatory policies that would endure as long as Augsburg remained an Imperial city.[29]

In the fourteenth century we can document the introduction of these regulatory regimes in the Low Countries – Antwerp, at an uncertain date, Utrecht in 1341, Arnhem in 1356, Dordrecht in 1367, Zutphen in 1393 – although the archives of several important cities make no mention of them until a century later: Bruges in 1431, Brussels in 1448, Amsterdam in 1479, and Ieper in 1495.[30] Finally, we can note that cities

---

and *Political Economy in the Reign of Louis XV*, 2 vols. (The Hague: Martinus Nijhoff, 1976), vol. I, p. 9.

[29] Desportes, *Le pain*, p. 145; Bernd Roeck, *Bäcker, Brot und Getreide in Augsburg* (Sigmaringen: Jan Thorbecke Verlag, 1987); Kurt Wesoly, *Lehrlinge und Hanswerksgesellen am Mittelrhein*, Studien zur Frankfurter Geschichte 18 (Frankfurt am Main: Verlag Waldemar Kramer, 1985), p. 220; Léon Zylbergeld, "Le prix des céréales et du pain à Liège dans la première moitié du XIIIe siècle," *Revue belge de philologie et d'histoire* 51 (1973), 271–98, 761–85; Léon Zylbergeld "Contribution à l'étude des ordonnances du pain du XIIIe siècle de la Brodtaxe de Lübeck (1255)," *Revue belge de philologie et d'histoire* 60 (1982), 263–304; Léon Zylbergeld, "Les regulations du marché du pain au XIIIe siècle en Occident et l'*Assize of Bread* de 1266–1267 pour l'Angleterre," in Jean-Marie Duvosquel and Alain Dierkens, eds., *Villes et campagnes au Moyen Âge: mélanges Georges Despry*, pp. 791–814 (Liège: Éditions du Perron, 1991); Louis Stouff, *Ravitaillement et alimentation en Provence aux XIVe et XVe siècle* (Paris: Mouton, 1970), p. 33. The Assize of Bread, *Assisa Panis et Cervisiae*, 51 Henry III, 1266. On the old assize (pre-1709), see Alan S. C. Ross, "The Assize of Bread," *Economic History Review*, second series, 9 (1956), 332–42, and Buchanan Sharp, *Famine and Scarcity in Late Medieval and Early Modern England* (Cambridge University Press, 2016), pp. 15–32. More generally, see the classic article by Sidney and Beatrice Webb, "The Assize of Bread," *Economic Journal* 14 (1904), 196–218.

[30] These dates refer to the earliest known documents, not necessarily to the origin of bread price regulation in a city. See E. Scholliers, *De levensstandaard in de XVe en XVIe eeuw te Antwerpen* (Antwerp: Sikkel, 1960), p. 186; E. Scholliers, "De Antwerpse merkuriale van granen en brood (1576–1583)," in Charles Verlinden, ed., *Prijzen en lonen in Brabant en Vlaanderen* (XVIe–XIXe e.), vol. III (Bruges: 1972), pp. 350–58; J. H. van den Hoek Ostende, "Een prijsregeling van de 15e tot de 19e eeuw: de broodzetting," *Maandblad Amstelodamum* 55 (1968), 131–34. R. van Schaïk, "Marktbeheersing: Overheidsbemoeienis met de levensmiddelenvoorziening in de Nederlanden (14de–19de eeuw)," in Clé Lesger and Leo Noordegraaf, eds., *Ondernemers en Bestuurders* (Amsterdam: NEHA, 1999), p. 470.

in northern Italy – Turin, Pavia, Milan, Parma, and Modena – all develop similar bread price regulatory regimes in the fifteenth century.[31] What all these and many other cities developed, mostly between c. 1250 and 1450, came to be known as the *brottaxe, tax du pain, broodzetting,* assize of bread, and *calmiere.* All of these names refer to a policy that differed in spirit from the *annona*-style regime in three fundamental ways:

1. It left the grain trade and grain inventories in the hands of private parties, intervening only in times of distress.
2. It accepted the grain price as an exogenous fact and focused on determining the proper price of bread for any given grain price.
3. It did not hold bread price stability to be its highest priority, focusing instead on bread quality, honest weights, and the maintenance of clear "rules of the game" between producers and consumers.

Theory

How can we explain this refocusing of the objectives of the regulatory system? Certainly, the system that spread across Europe after 1250 represented a substantial retreat. The *annona* aspired to shape, if not totally control, the core of the agrarian economy and the commerce in grain for the benefit of the town and the state. The assize/*broodzetting*/*tax du pain* recognized the centrality of the market and set about regulating the terms on which the bakers, usually organized in guilds, carried out their critical function of supplying bread to the community. Public authority no longer aspired to a command economy; it sought instead to enforce a practical regulation of a primarily market economy. The objective shifted from sheltering consumers from the volatility of the market, to the enforcement of rules that required the price of bread to vary in direct and timely response to changes in the price of grain – and it intervened in the grain markets only exceptionally rather than habitually.

More efficient markets. The timing of this shift in regulatory focus – roughly, the fourteenth and fifteenth centuries – may be related to the gradual achievement of greater market integration in those parts of

---

[31] M. A. Romani, *Nella spirale di una crisi: popolazione, mercato e prezzi a Parma tra Cinque e Seicento* (Milan: Giuffrè, 1975); A. Grab, *La politica del pane: le riforme annonarie in Lombardia nell'età teresiana e giuseppina* (Milan: Franco Angeli, 1986); D. Balani, *Il vicario tra città e Stato: l'ordine pubblico e l'annona nella Torino del Settecento* (Turin: Deputazione Subalpina di Storia Patria, 1987); Gian Luigi Basini, *L'uomo e il pane: risorse, consumi e carenze alimentari della popolazione modenese nel cinque e seicento* (Milan: Dott. A. Giuffrè Editore, 1970);

Europe where monarchs and cities succeeded in extending their jurisdictions and imposing a degree of political centralization over the grain trade, among other things. S. R. Epstein described much of medieval Europe – and especially its more urbanized regions – as zones of fragmented sovereignty. Every city had an interest in protecting its supplies, which led to export bans, import bounties, public storage, and price controls – the characteristic *annona* policies. Ironically, the result of all these local provisionment efforts was higher average prices and greater price volatility than could have been achieved with greater market integration and more efficient markets. Epstein draws on game theory in order to describe the problem facing medieval rulers as one of "coordination failure": If they all liberalized their policies they would all benefit, but in doing so they offered each ruler a strong incentive to renege on the agreement. In Epstein's view, only political events that consolidated power in strong hands could enforce and monitor such a policy change. He saw in the Black Death the external shock that triggered a series of political struggles that brought about greater jurisdictional consolidation and, hence, market integration.[32] Although he did not extend his argument specifically to bread price regulation, the late medieval increase in market efficiency he detects may well have sped the diffusion of the more limited assize/*broodzetting*/*tax du pain* approach and the retreat of *annona*-style regulatory regimes.

Just price. At first glance, this regulatory system appears at odds with the popular understanding of the concept of "just price." But it is consistent with the more sophisticated understanding that Joseph Schumpeter ascribes to Thomas Aquinas and Duns Scotus. The former regarded the just price to be "the normal competitive price," while Duns Scotus, according to Schumpeter, "related just price to cost ... to the producers' or traders' expenditure of money and effort."[33] A regulatory system that keyed the price of bread directly to the price of its chief cost component, that made these prices public, and that inspected the weight and quality of the product to ensure honest dealings certainly conforms to this elevated understanding of just price. Moreover, this interpretation of the just price concept would have aligned nicely with the views of

[32] Epstein, *Freedom and Growth*, pp. 157–67.
[33] Schumpeter, *Economic Analysis*, p. 93. Similarly, De Roover cites Cardinal Cajetan, a sixteenth-century commentator on Aquinas's *Summa Theologica*, as defining just price as "the one, which at a given time, can be gotten from the buyers, assuming common knowledge and in the absence of all fraud and coercion." De Roover, "The concept of just price," p. 423. Bread price regulation could be interpreted as an effort to create these conditions: it policed millers and bakers to suppress fraud and assembled price information to banish informational asymmetry.

the craft guilds that became more influential in many town governments in the fourteenth century. Max Weber called this guild philosophy the *Nahrungsprinzip*, or "livelihood policy," which held that all producers should charge what it takes to maintain their proper station in life.[34] To seek more than this is to commit the sin of avarice, but to receive less is no virtue. One might argue that the *Nahrungsprinzip* is simply just price seen from the perspective of the producer rather than the consumer.

Moral economy. Modern historians concerned with markets and the provision of the staff of life are more inclined to attend to the views of ordinary people than to those of theologians, and this has led to the invocation of "moral economy" as an umbrella term to describe the norms and expectations of common folk regarding the proper regulation of economic relations. If we follow E. P. Thompson's influential use of this concept, moral economy posits a broadly shared set of beliefs (an ideology) about the proper economic roles of market actors and regulators. First, the local community should have direct and primary access to locally produced food (what one might call "the right of first refusal") and second, grain in particular was too important to leave to market forces. The legitimacy of political elites hinged on the public perception that they acted to protect these customs and usages.

Thus, "moral economy" emphasizes localism, the priority of the consumer over the producer, and the obligation of elites to honor popular customs and traditional rights. Historians are divided about the radical, or "progressive" character of moral-economy-style food riots since at their heart one finds an implicit contract where the common folk defer to those in authority in exchange for social patronage and protection. A violation of this understanding erodes the legitimacy of the social hierarchy and justifies violent intervention, but this is an intervention intended to uphold custom and usage; bread riots were intended by the participants to restore an implicit contract with their superiors rather than a "revolutionary" act aiming for their removal.[35]

[34] Max Weber, *General Economic History* (London: Allen Unwin, 1927), pp. 138–43. While this approach to bread price regulation was congenial to guild interests, a rigorous enforcement of price controls apparently was not. A thorough study of late medieval price regulation distinguished between towns under patrician rule (Cologne, Nuremberg, Duisburg …) and those dominated by their guilds (Zurich, Ulm, Strasbourg …). The former imposed strict price controls while the latter were less consistent, focusing more on limiting competition. Ernst Kelter, *Geschichte der obrigkeitlichen Preisregelung* (Jena: Gustav Fischer Verlag, 1935), vol. I, pp. 155–57.

[35] E. P. Thompson, "The moral economy of the English crowd in the eighteenth century," *Past and Present* 50 (1971), 76–136; E. P. Thompson, "The moral economy reviewed," in *Customs in Common* (New York: W. W. Norton, 1991), pp. 259–351. Many historians, sociologists, and anthropologists have invoked and further developed this concept. Thompson presented moral economy as a "structural" feature, or as an aspect of the

State capacity. The historical sociologist Charles Tilly saw the bread riot as an important type of political event for yet another reason. He was less concerned with the rioters than with the authorities, and saw disorders and the threat of disorder as a "learning opportunity": learning to limit and manage these events was central to early modern European state formation.[36]

Far from being impulsive, hopeless reactions to hunger, bread riots and other struggles over the food supply took a small number of relatively well-defined forms. Furthermore they often worked in the short run; crowd action brought prices down, forced stored grain into the public domain, ... Finally, the work of the crowd embodied a critique of the authorities, was often directed consciously at the authorities, and commonly consisted of the crowd's taking precisely those measures its members thought the authorities had failed their own responsibility to take – inventorying grain in private hands, setting a price, and so on.

For the political authorities facing these threats to public order it was essential to develop effective strategies to manage public expectations in order to achieve a polity with the institutional capacity to actually govern. In Tilly's view this interplay of state and populace stood at the heart of early modern state formation,

These "state managers" faced the problem of "balancing the demands of farmers, food merchants, municipal officials, their own dependents, and the urban poor – all of whom caused the state trouble ..."[37] In response, state officials in France – the focus of Tilly's empirical attention – developed the theory and practice of *Police*, which then referred not only, or even primarily, to the suppression of criminal behavior, but to the management of civil society, especially at the local level. And, according to Tilly "The regulation of the food supply was certainly its single largest component."[38]

---

mentalité of common folk, and resisted the view that it was a backward-looking ideology. But others situated moral economy at the intersection of "traditional society" and the technical and commercial changes introduced by market relations or capitalism. In such works, moral economy reflected the worldview of peasants or guild artisans in a changing economy and as a rear-guard defense of an old way of life. See James C. Scott, *The Moral Economy of the Peasant* (New Haven, Conn.: Yale University Press, 1976); William Reddy, *The Rise of Market Culture* (Cambridge University Press, 1984).

[36] Charles Tilly, "Food supply and public order in modern Europe," in Charles Tilly, ed., *The Formation of National States in Western Europe* (Princeton University Press, 1975), p. 386.

[37] Charles Tilly, *Coercion, Capital, and European States, AD 990–1990* (Oxford: Blackwell, 1990), p. 119.

[38] *Ibid.*, p. 119. This was apparent to him from a reading of the multi-volume treatise of Nicolas Delamare, *Traité de la Police*, 4 vols. (Paris, 1707), which "sums up that broad but food-centered conception of the state's police powers."

He emphasized the rationality and even the effectiveness of the bread riot. The participants often succeeded in achieving their immediate goals. But his linkage of the management of public expectations directly to state building suggests something else: the bread riot may have been one of the last efforts of a traditional society to slow the progress of capitalism, but it served simultaneously as a school in which the state learned (or failed to learn) how to enhance "governability."[39]

One thing is certain: if Europe's commoners internalized "moral economy" norms and values in the late medieval and early modern centuries, they did not acquire them from their long exposure to the assize/ *broodzetting/tax du pain*. These regulatory policies were founded on the principle of accepting market prices and they depended, therefore, on a reasonably free trade in bread grains. Moral economy has closer affinities to the spirit of the *annona*, which justified a far-reaching subordination of economic life to public authority, specifically a subordination of food producers to the interests of consumers, and to the immediate goal of stable food supplies at constant prices.[40] In the normal operation of *annona*-style regimes there was no recognition of the value of encouraging production in order to secure future abundance.

However, the assize-type regimes did address the "moral economy" notion that elites should be seen to be actively superintending the food economy – tracking prices, monitoring quality, restraining the avarice of bakers and millers, etc. The ongoing demonstration of elite engagement with honest provisionment is important to both the just price and the moral economy concepts, and the assize-style regulatory regime allowed magistrates to present themselves as guardians of the public weal. But this regulatory regime could not – indeed, was not designed to – shield consumers from high prices. Only its suspension could achieve such a goal.

It might be best not to feel too confident that we understand the minds of the officials who put in place, in city after city over the course of more than two centuries, a set of practical rules that endured to define a key component of Europe's political economy until the early nineteenth

---

[39] Charles Tilly, *The Contentious French* (Cambridge, Mass.: Harvard University Press, 1986), p. 23. The theme of the food riot as anti-capitalist protest is also taken up in the work of Louise Tilly: "The food riot as a form of political conflict in France," *Journal of Interdisciplinary History* 2 (1971), 23–57; "Food entitlement, famine and conflict," *Journal of Interdisciplinary History* 14 (1983), 333–49.

[40] The modern economic concept of distributional coalitions "unmasks" moral economy and most variants of just price as expressions of group interest in which some interests are sacrificed for the benefit of others. See Mancur Olson, *The Theory of Collective Action: Public Goods and the Theory of Groups* (Cambridge, Mass.: Harvard University Press, 1965) and *The Rise and Decline of Nations: Economic Growth, Stagflation, and Social Rigidities* (New Haven, Conn.: Yale University Press, 1982). For historical applications, see Epstein, *Freedom and Growth*, and Root, *The Fountain of Privilege*, pp. 81–112.

century. These officials certainly were cognizant of what we might call "popular opinion," and must have wanted to address it so as to secure the public peace. But the spread of a market-based bread price regulatory system, while it might be reconciled to the just price doctrine, could not have been well received by a populace in the embrace of "moral economy" thinking – if, indeed, such a *mentalité* existed. If ideas of just price and moral economy actually filled the minds of medieval and early modern Europeans, it is hard to explain the adoption nearly everywhere of assize-style price regulation.

Practice

Perhaps the motives behind the regulatory practices of the late medieval period will reveal themselves more clearly if we seek to uncover the actual rules that came to govern the setting of bread prices.

Among the earliest full descriptions of this regulatory system is the English Assize of Bread of 1266. It differed from the other regulations we will consider in being a royal enactment for application throughout the Kingdom of England in what then was an overwhelmingly rural realm. Under its provisions, local magistrates in towns and counties were instructed to determine the prevailing price of grain after each year's harvest (after the Feast of St. Michael – 29 September). The legislation establishing the assize was then consulted to determine the appropriate price for each grade of bread defined in the document. The annual setting of prices in this land with few cities of any size sets the assize apart from the regulations developed by continental towns, which aimed to react to developments in the grain markets on a more frequent basis. Otherwise, the assize conforms to the characteristics listed above: it defined a finite number of bread types, or qualities, it linked grain prices directly to specific bread prices, and it provided that bread prices would rise and fall proportionately with the price of grain.

Two years later, in 1268, Paris adopted a similar regulatory system, although one with more frequent price adjustments than provided for by the English assize. The details of the Paris regulatory system are revealed later, in 1439, when King Charles VII introduced a small modification to what by then was a long-standing practice. His proclamation follows closely the bread price regulations introduced three years earlier in Troyes and Châlons-sur-Marne and which later spread throughout France.[41] The royal proclamation provided the following rules:

---

[41] Desportes, *Le pain*, pp. 149–55. In 1567 Charles IX decreed that the Parisian system of bread price regulation described here was to be applied to all the cities of the kingdom.

When the setier of wheat cost 20 sou, the loaf of bread will cost two denier, plus one maille [0.5 denier] for production costs and profit (*"Les frais, gain et labourage du pain"*). The price of the loaf will rise or decline by one pougeoosie [0.25 denier] for every two-sou rise or decline in the setier [grain] price.[42]

This information is sufficient to develop the price schedule in Table 1.1. We can infer from the statement that the bakers were expected to prepare 120 loaves of bread per *setier* of grain. At a grain price of 20 sou the price of the loaf is 2.5 denier (including the provision for production costs), and we can readily calculate bread prices at 2-sou intervals above and below the initial 20-sou grain price. Grain prices never reached zero, of course, but it is revealing to calculate the notional bread price at that level: it tells us something important about the consistency and rationale of the regulatory system.

A second example, even more straightforward, is provided by the Dutch city of Groningen, which in 1404 established regulations for rye bread pricing that prevailed into the seventeenth century. It declared that the price of a 4-pound loaf of rye bread should cost 4 *grootkens* when a *mud* of grain cost 10 stuivers, and that the bread price should rise or fall by 2 *grootkens* for every 10-stuiver rise or fall in the grain price. From this information one can readily determine that Groningen's magistrates set the bread yield per *mud* at thirty 4-pound loaves, since two additional *grootkens* of revenue per loaf generates the additional revenue needed to defray a 5-stuiver increase in the grain price (thirty loaves * 2 *grootkens* = 60 *grootkens*/12 *grootkens* per stuiver = 5 stuivers).

These two examples can be multiplied by many others, some of which are described in Appendix 1. Some sources provide price tables, others only verbal directives, but the information is nearly always sufficient to determine that the relationship of bread to grain prices is proportional, and that when extended to a notional grain price of zero, the bread price would also be zero. In short, they all bear certain characteristic features of the bread pricing system as it emerged in the Middle Ages – what I will call henceforth the "old system":

1. The bread-grain price schedule, when graphed, passes through the origin. That is, when the price of grain is zero, the price of bread is also zero. The bread price equation takes the form: $Y*b = X$, or $Y = X/b$, where Y = price of bread per loaf; X = price of grain per unit; b = the assumed bread yield, the loaves produced per unit of grain.

---

[42] *Ibid.*, pp. 150–51.

Table 1.1 *Reconstructed bread price schedule introduced in Troyes and Châlons-sur-Marne, 1436; Paris, 1439*

Wheat price per *setier* in sou	Bread price 2-livre loaf in denier	Revenue in sou	Revenue for preparation in sou
0	0.00	0	0
2	0.25	2.50	0.50
4	0.50	5.00	1.00
6	0.75	7.50	1.50
8	1.00	10.00	2.00
10	1.25	12.50	2.50
12	1.50	15.00	3.00
14	1.75	17.50	3.50
16	2.00	20.00	4.00
18	2.25	22.50	4.50
20	2.50	25.00	5.00

and so forth: 0.25 denier rise in the price per 2-livre loaf for every 2-sou rise in the price of a *setier* of grain.

30	3.75	37.50	7.50
40	5.00	50.00	10.00
50	6.25	62.50	12.50
60	7.50	75.00	15.00

Setier = 156 liters
Livre (pound) = 490 grams
Sou = 12 deniers
Prices in **bold**: my calculation of prices based on the relationship described in the documents for wheat prices over the expected range of market prices.
Assumptions made by the regulatory body:

1. The baker can secure 240 livre of bread per *setier*, or 120 2-livre loaves.
2. The preparation costs (other ingredients, fuel, labor, etc.) are provided for by granting the bakers 0.25 per 2-sou rise in the price of wheat.

This rise generates 2.5 sou, or 0.5 sou more than the rise in grain costs. Desportes saw this as "a recognition of a *fixed cost of production*" (my emphasis), but in fact the price schedule provides for extra revenue that rises with the increase in grain prices. Under this schedule preparation costs are a fixed *proportion* (in this case, 20 percent) of the grain price, not a fixed *amount* of revenue.
Source: Desportes, *Le pain*, pp. 150–55.

2. The revenue expected to be generated by the bread price is sufficient to cover the cost of the grain, and only this cost (as in the Groningen example), except:

3. When "preparation costs" are specified (as they are in the French example), these are treated as a proportional addition to the grain costs. The bread price equation then takes the form: $Y = (X^*1.a)/b$, where a = a percentage added to the grain price to defray preparations costs.

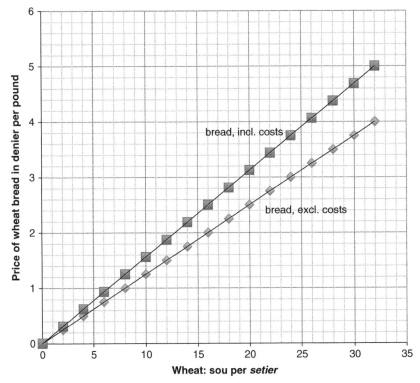

Figure 1.1 Wheat bread price schedule: Troyes, Châlons-sur-Marne, 1436; Paris, 1439

Actual bread prices were not always strictly proportional to grain prices. The relationship sometimes showed irregularity, but deviations from this rule appear to be arbitrary or accidental (for reasons to be discussed below) rather than signals that a different rule inspires the schedule.

When we have sufficient information about the systems of weights and measures being used and the currency system in effect, it is generally possible to calculate the amount of bread that bakers were expected to produce from a measure of grain. This "bread yield" reveals a fourth characteristic of old system bread pricing:

4. Regulators expected a weight of bread output that was approximately equal to the assumed weight of the grain. That is, the old system tended to follow a "pound for pound" rule: a pound of grain was expected to yield a pound of (basic) bread.

This final assumption allowed old system price regulators to apply a simple rule of thumb for the determination of bread prices which was often reduced to the following formula: the loaf will cost as many Y (small coin: pence, denier, penningen, etc.) as the volume grain measure (*setier*, quarter, *zak, malter*, etc.) costs in X (large coin: pound, livre, gulden, etc.). In France, bread prices long continued to be governed in this way. Bread was priced at as many deniers per pound as a *setier* of wheat cost in *livres tournois*.[43] The *livre tournois* contained 240 deniers, and the official output of bread per *setier* was 240 pounds. In Holland a similar rule prevailed: Amsterdam's bread ordinance of 1477 specified that a 12-pound loaf of rye bread will cost in penningen what the last of rye costs in *Rijnse* guilders.[44] The *Rijnse* guilder contained 256 penningen, so the bakers were expected to produce 256 12-pound loaves from a last of rye. Likewise in Friesland the Leeuwarden *Bakkersboek* of 1542 stated that the 11-pound loaf of rye bread should cost as many penningen as a last of rye costs in gold guilders.[45] The gold guilder, a guilder of 28 stuivers, was the customary unit of account for wholesale grain transactions. Thus, if a last of rye cost 100 gold guilders, the 11-pound loaf would sell for 100 penningen, or 6.25 stuivers. Leeuwarden bakers needed to sell 448 such loaves to cover the cost of the grain.

In all these cases, the object was to find a combination of currency system, grain volume unit, and loaf size whereby the grain and the bread would sell for the same number of (different) coins. Figure 1.2a illustrates the relationship of grain prices to bread prices in a classic old system schedule.

---

[43] This venerable relationship is repeated in many sources. Ernest Labrousse, *Esquisse du mouvement des prix et des revenues en France au XVIII siècle* (Paris, 1933), p. 577; Judith A. Miller, "Politics and urban provisioning crises: bakers, police, and parlements in France, 1750–93," *Journal of Modern History* 64 (1992), 227–62; Alain Guerreau, "Mesures du blé et du pain à Mâcon (XIVe–XVIIIe siècles)," *Histoire et Mesure* 3 (1988), 163–219. Long after this pricing system had been superseded in many areas, it continued to reappear in policy discussions. Kaplan cites an official of the Parisian *Police* (which had authority of bread pricing) around 1750: "Bread should be worth as many deniers per pound as the setier of wheat is worth in livres Tournois." In the 1770s Controller General Terray endorsed this formula, as did his successor Turgot. Steven L. Kaplan, *The Bakers of Paris and the Bread Question, 1700–1775* (Chapel Hill, NC: University of North Carolina Press, 1996), pp. 516–17.
   Castile persisted longer than most states in seeking to control grain prices, but its approach to bread pricing followed the same rule: whatever the price of wheat was per *fanega* (a volume measure) in *reales de vellón* would be the price of a 2-pound common wheat bread loaf in *maravedis de vellón*. There were 34 *maravedis* per *real*. Ernesto López Losa and Santiago Piquero Zarauz, "Spanish real wages in the north-western European mirror, 1500–1800: on the timing and magnitude of the little divergence in Europe," AEHE Working Paper, 2016, p. 15.

[44] W. S. Unger, *De levensmiddelenvoorziening der Hollandsche steden in de Middeleeuwen* (Amsterdam, 1916), p. 108.

[45] G.A. Leeuwarden, Bakkersboek, 1542–1802, F 6040; M 506.

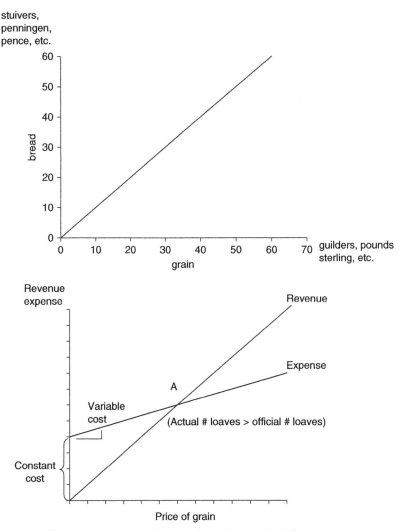

Figure 1.2a and b Old system bread price schedule

The great administrative advantage of this system is its simplicity: once the grain price is established, so is the price of bread. It requires only a minimum of recordkeeping since no conversion tables need to be published and distributed. Consumers might even be attracted to the system's "transparency."

But transparent it was not. At the heart of this regulatory system was a conscious misspecification of the bread yield per measure of grain. The

Table 1.2 *Bread price schedule for Groningen, 1404, 1589*

Rye grain: stuivers per *mud*	Bread: *grootkens* per 4-pound in stuivers per loaf	Revenue per *mud*
0	0	0
5	2	5
10	4	10
15	6	15
20	8	20
25	10	25
30	12	30

A bread price schedule published in 1589 is the same as that of 1404, except that prices were now considerably higher, so the schedule was extended to show bread prices at then-prevailing grain prices.

40	16	40
50	20	50
60	24	60
90	36	90

Mud = 91 liters (33 per last)
Pound = 468 grams
Stuiver = 6 *plakken* = 12 *grootkens*
3,960 pounds (1,853 kg) of rye bread per last of rye.
Sources: Oorkondenboek, no. 1168 (1404); G.A. Groningen, Gilden Archief no. 293, no. 11 (1589).

expected yield was rarely mentioned explicitly. I have derived it in Tables 1.1 and 1.2, and in the examples given in Appendix 1 from the implicit arithmetic relationships between prices and measures. But the available evidence is clear: a pound (kilogram) of grain, when ground and used in its entirety to bake bread, will produce a pound (kilogram) of bread. As late as 1840 this relationship is repeated in the *Dictionnaire du Commerce*, where readers are advised that "le blé rend en pain poids pour poids" [Wheat yields bread, pound for pound].[46]

However, it is easily demonstrated that this is not true. A pound of wheat or rye, when ground into flour, yields well over one pound of bread. The addition of water or milk and the leavening effects of yeast combine to produce between 1.25 and 1.40 pounds of bread for every pound of grain.

A key characteristic of all old system bread price regimes was the use of a much lower grain-to-bread weight ratio than was technically, or naturally, attainable. While bakers could expect to produce 1.25 to 1.40 pounds of bread per pound of grain, the regulatory systems always relied on something close to the "pound per pound" rule of thumb cited above. Table 1.3 lists the implicit grain to bread weight ratio found in Dutch old system rules.

[46] *Dictionnaire du Commerce*, 2nd edn. (Brussels, 1840).

Table 1.3 *The grain-to-bread weight ratios used in fifteenth- and sixteenth-century bread price regulations in the Low Countries*

	Kg bread/liter grain	Kg bread/kg grain*
Rye bread		
Groningen, 1404–1589	0.62	0.886
Zutphen, 1483–1553	0.62	0.886
Deventer, 1509–1552	0.68	0.971
Leeuwarden, to 1542	0.79	1.129
Nijmegen, 1559–85	0.74	0.976
Brielle, 1530	0.77	1.100
Antwerp, 1588	0.69	0.981
Bruges, 1431 – 18th c.	0.79	1.126
Brussels, 1444	0.75	1.068
Wheat bread		
Tiel, 1454	0.85	1.117
Delft, 1546	0.78	1.033
Delft, 1539–96	0.80	1.053
Antwerp, 1621	0.85	1.078

*Assume a specific gravity of 0.70 kg per liter of rye; 0.76 per liter of wheat.
Sources:
Groningen: See Table 1.2.
Deventer: See Figure 1.4.
Nijmegen: P. H. M. G. Offermans, *Arbeid en levenstandaard in Nijmegen omstreeks de reductie (1550–1600)* (Zutphen: De Walburg Pers, 1972), p. 111.
Zutphen: R. van Schaïk, "Prijs- en levensmiddelenpolitiek in de Noordelijke Nederlanden van de 14e tot de 17e eeuw: bronnen en problemen," *Tijdschrift voor geschiedenis* 91 (1978), 249–55.
Antwerp and Brussels: Scholliers, *Levensstandaard*, pp. 25, 186.
Bruges: Pasteboek van Brugge.
Tiel: J. S. van Veen, *Rechtsbronnen van Tiel* (The Hague: Martinus Nijhoff, 1901)
Brielle: H. de Jager, *De Middeleeuwsche Keuren der Stad Brielle* (The Hague: Martinus Nijhoff,1901), pp. 272–75.
Delft: J. Soutendam, *Keuren en Ordonnantiën der stad Delft van den aanvang der XVIe eeuw to het jaar 1536* (Delft, 1870), pp. 174–78; 1539–96 based on price data collected by Dr. R. van Schaïk; kindly made available by Dr. Jessica Dijkman.
Leeuwarden: G.A. Leeuwarden, Bakkersboek, F 6040.
Groningen: G.A. Groningen, Oorkondenboek, no. 1168.
Deventer: G.A. Deventer, Middeleeuws archief, no. 29.

The Old System: Apportioning the Grain

The price of bread was set at a level sufficient to allow the assumed bread yield to cover the cost of the grain. Revenue to compensate the baker for his labor, capital, fuel, and other inputs, and to compensate the miller for transforming the grain to flour, came from the difference between the *assumed* yield and the *actual* yield achieved by the baker. The medieval regulators sometimes spoke of the "mystery" of the bakers' craft, a term used more generally to refer to the special knowledge of guild craftsmen whereby they imparted value to their products. The bakers' mystery was the ability to transform a pound of grain into more than a pound of bread, the exact amount depending on a baker's skill (but also his inclination toward adulteration and fraud). This was the "mystery" that justified the baker in keeping the difference as compensation for his efforts.[47]

In practice, old system bread price regulation relied on a series of proportions and ratios. One began by identifying a common volume measure for grain (quarters in England, *setiers* in France, *viertels* in Flanders, *zakken* and *mudden* in the Netherlands, etc.). First, the miller ground the contents of this measure of grain in return for a share of the resulting flour. In England this was often 1/16th or 1/24th of the flour, while in France 1/16th was the norm into the eighteenth century.[48] In the Southern Netherlands by the sixteenth century, the miller took as his fee (*maalloon* or *molster*) a fixed number of pounds (8 to 10.5) per *viertel* (about 1/12th–1/14th of the grain).[49] The rest of the flour was returned to the baker.

The baker paid for the grain by the sale of a second portion – the largest portion – of the bread, a portion defined by the pound-for-pound rule just discussed. This left a residual third portion. The bread loaves produced from this portion of the grain were intended to defray all the other production costs incurred in the baking enterprise, including the capital costs, labor, fuel, and profits. In effect, bread price regulators assigned a share of a unit of grain to compensate the miller (the millers' fee), a share to pay for the grain (based on the assumed bread yield), and a final residual share to compensate the baker for all other costs. This final share was known in England as the "bakers' advantage." Germans spoke of *Bäckpfunde*; the Dutch referred to *overbroden*.[50]

The old system created a parallelism of bread and grain prices that gives a superficial appearance of transparency and fairness. But most of this system of portions was hidden from the view of consumers, and the "mystery" on which it relied gave rise to what can only be described as

---

[47] Martinat, *Le juste marché*, p. 242.
[48] Christian Petersen, *Bread and the British Economy, c.1770–1870* (Aldershot: Scolar Press, 1995), pp. 51–52; Steven L. Kaplan, *Provisioning Paris: Merchants and Millers in the Grain and Flour Trade during the Eighteenth Century* (Ithaca, NY: Cornell University Press, 1984), pp. 268–69. One-sixteenth equals 6.2 percent of the grain. A similar amount, 6.6 percent of the milled grain, was granted to Istanbul's millers by the Ottoman sultans in the seventeenth and eighteenth centuries. Murphey, "Provisioning Istanbul," p. 218.
[49] Scholliers, *Levensstandaard*, p. 25.
[50] Ross, "Assize," p. 333; August Stalweit, *Die Getreidehandelspolitik und Kriegsmagazinverwalthung Preussens, 1756–1806* (Berlin, 1931), pp. 313–21.

perverse pricing policies. That is, the old system was neither transparent nor reasonable.

Selling Bread by Variable Weight rather than Variable Price

Before turning to these hidden and objectionable features a word needs to be said about an important variant of the old system where the *weight* of the loaf, rather than the *price* varied with the price of grain. Many types of bread – especially wheat bread – were sold not at fixed weights and varying prices, but at fixed prices and varying weights.

Why was this done? It has been suggested that this practice reflected the continuing influence of the *annona* ideal of a fixed, unchanging, price of bread. Since grain prices could not be fixed, so this argument goes, bakers sold bread at a fixed price and concealed the less easily discernible variation in weight, thereby fooling the consumer while appearing to honor a Thomistic notion of just price.[51] A less conspiratorial explanation simply claims that freezing the price while allowing the weight of the loaf to vary with the grain price constituted "a crude form of rationing, common all over Europe."[52] The idea here is that since wages tended to remain stable while grain prices were highly variable, consumers purchased a fixed-price loaf and simply ate less bread in times of scarcity (and, presumably, more in times of glut).[53]

---

[51] Witwold Kula, *Measure and Men* (Princeton University Press, 1986), pp. 71–72. Kula cites M. Bogucka on this, but does not fully embrace this view himself.

[52] De Roover, "The concept of just price," p. 430.

[53] Desportes invokes both of these arguments for the practice of maintaining fixed bread prices while varying the weight of loaves as grain prices changed. This weight-variable system, she argues, "long met with unanimous support. Fixed, immutable prices were advocated at the highest levels by scholastic thinkers drawing support from the nominalist school. Sellers and buyers were usually supportive, notwithstanding the constraints imposed by the unending variation of market conditions." She goes on to concede that fixed prices provided workers with an "illusionary security," but it "allayed their visceral fears for the future" and may have had the practical value of conforming to a natural rhythm of physical exertion, which required long continuous work in times of good harvests and, by implication, required less effort when harvests were poor (and prices high). Desportes, *Le pain*, p. 149. Davis makes the same argument in defense of the English assize of bread. James Davis, "Baking for the common good: a reassessment of the assize of bread in medieval England," *Economic History Review* 57 (2004), p. 469.
Scholliers argues similarly, but stresses the psychological aspect of this policy. "Government was well aware of this. This appears to explain why bread was always sold for a fixed price, for example, one stuiver, which sufficed to purchase a loaf that became smaller as the price of grain rose, and larger as the price of grain fell. The consumer feels the effects of changing grain prices less this way than he would if he had to pay additional coins." E. Scholliers, "Peilingen naar het consumptiepatroon in de pre-industriële samenleving," in J. Hannes, ed., *Consumptiepatronen en prijsindices* (Brussels: Centrum voor Hedendaagse Sociale Geschiedenis, 1981), pp. 11–13.

These explanations are certainly wrong. The sale of bread at variable weights rather than variable prices had nothing to do with social policy and everything to do with the value of the smallest coins in circulation.[54] A bread price schedule gained in accuracy the more sensitively the price of bread varied with the price of grain. If the bread price changes only after large changes in the grain price, the bread will be substantially over- or underpriced at all intermediate grain prices. Only the largest loaves were sold at prices sufficiently high to allow their price to vary promptly by whole units of the smallest available coins as grain prices changed. In the Dutch Republic the smallest coin was the *duit*, equal to two penningen (1/8th of a stuiver; 1/160th of a guilder)[55] Thus, price schedules sought to avoid bread price changes at intervals of less than two penningen. (We will return to the small coin problem in Chapter 4.)

Ironically, it was the poor rye bread eaters who had to lay down large sums at once for their 6- and 12-pound loaves. The alternative was to buy the one-stuiver loaves of the wheat breads (whose per-pound cost, of course, was far higher). These loaves varied by weight because weight could be adjusted more readily than price to small fluctuations in the price of grain. The Dutch pound (*pond*) was divided into 32 *loden*. The *lood* (plural: *loden*) was the normal unit of weight used by bread price regulators. The Amsterdam *lood* was 15.4 grams; where lighter pounds prevailed (as in Haarlem, Leiden, and Delft), the *loden* were correspondingly lighter as well.

Early modern societies resorted to weight-variable bread pricing in order to adjust the price of bread to changing grain prices with an accuracy that exceeded the practical limits of the circulating coinage. But establishing an accurate weight-variable schedule presented problems of its own. The regulators faced an algebraic problem rather more complex than the calculation of a price-variable schedule of bread prices. The relationship of bread to grain prices is linear, but that of bread weight to grain prices is hyperbolic, being derived from a reciprocal equation of the form:

[54] This is not a new insight, but appears to have had difficulty making headway. See, for example, Kurt Wesoly, *Lehrlinge und Hanswerksgesellen am Mittelrhein*, Studien zur Frankfurter Geschichte 18 (Frankfurt am Main: Verlag Waldemar Kramer, 1985). Wesoly rejected arguments that political and/or social factors explained the policy of selling bread on a weight-variable rather than price-variable basis. In the German context he examined, it was clear to him that the motivation was to evade the "small coin problem," p. 220.

[55] By way of comparison, the English penny, in this period, was equal to slightly more than one Dutch stuiver (1.09 st = 1 d). Thus, the smallest English coin, the farthing – one-quarter of a penny – had over double the face value (1.09 st = 17.44 penningen; 17.44/4 = 4.36 penningen) of the Dutch *duit* (2 penningen).

$W = b/X$, where
W = the weight of the fixed-price loaf
b = the official amount of bread produced from the grain measure, and
X = the cost of that grain.

Here, just as in the price-varying schedule, the key to old system regulation was in setting b sufficiently below the true level to allow the millers and bakers to take their (hidden) shares. But since the weight-varying equation generates not a straight line but a hyperbole – a curve that approaches both the x and y axes asymptotically – calculating the correct weight of bread at any given grain price confronted administrators with tedious calculations of numerous fractions (and imposed on the bakers the requirement to make often impossibly fine distinctions in bread weights). Figure 1.3 illustrates the general form of a weight-based bread price schedule.

The Deventer archives preserve an ordinance that reveals the details of the old weight-variable system at work. The ordinance is undated, but appears to have been in effect between at least 1509 and 1552. It ordained

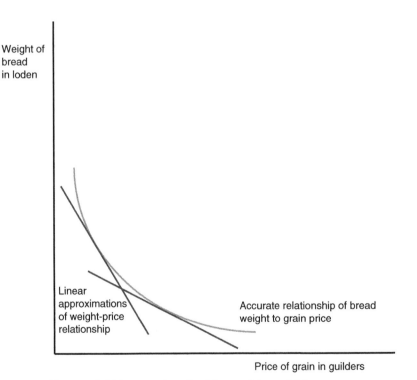

Figure 1.3 Old system bread pricing: weight-variable

that common rye bread be sold at the fixed price of 6 *plakken* (0.75 stuivers) and assumed that bakers would produce 160 pounds of bread per *mud* (26 *mud* = 1 last) of grain. The weight of the 6-*plakken* loaf could be determined for every expected price of grain by dividing the stuiver price for grain into 120 (the 160 pounds to be divided among the loaves multiplied by 0.75, the stuiver price of each loaf). Doing this for each grain price from 15 to 53 stuivers traced out the curved line shown in Figure 1.4. Thus, at every grain price, the city magistrates calculated the number of loaves into which the 160 pounds of bread dough was to be divided in order to generate revenue equal to the price of the grain. For example, at 29 stuivers per *mud* of rye, 38 2/3 loaves were needed. Therefore, the 160 *pond* of bread was to be divided into loaves of 4 pounds 4 and 5/512 *loden*, that is, 4.138 pounds. And so forth.

The claim that a *mud* of rye (115.5 liters) should yield 160 pounds of bread (79 kg) was, of course, far from the full amount, which was closer to 230 pounds. The difference, 30 percent of the total, was allocated, just

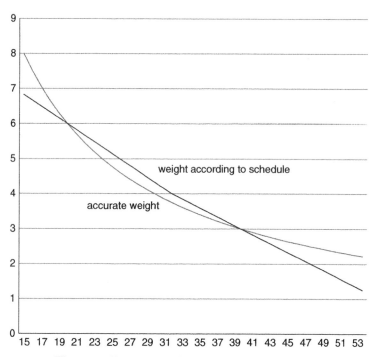

Figure 1.4 Deventer rye bread, 1509–52
Source: G.A. Deventer, Middeleeuws archief, no. 299. Ordonnatie van allen broot te backen geordoneert.

as in the price-variable system discussed above, to defraying the expenses of the miller and the baker: the higher the price of grain the more loaves (because they were smaller loaves) the baker could sell at the fixed price, and the larger was his net revenue (net of grain and milling costs).

The weight-variable schedule solved the small coin problem, but, as noted above, it created a new one. The awkwardness of working with a reciprocal equation (whereby each equal-interval increase in grain price corresponds to a progressively smaller diminution of loaf weight) induced most magistrates to simplify their task by casting the weight schedule in a linear form where each equal-interval increase in grain price corresponds to an equal-interval diminution of loaf weight. Thus, the Deventer magistrates, having determined with care the precise weight of rye bread loaves at each grain price, actually worked with a simplified schedule that is shown in the straight line of Figure 1.4. Loaf weights were altered only at intervals of three and, at higher prices, four stuivers in the grain price, and the weights rose and fell at convenient half-pound intervals. As a result, consumers were given loaves that were slightly overweight at grain prices ranging from 23 to 36 stuivers. Below 20 and above 40 stuivers, the loaves were underweight, and by increasingly larger amounts the further prices rose above 40 or fell below 20 stuivers. It is immediately evident from Figure 1.4 that the adjusted linear schedule offered only a temporary solution to the basic problem posed by reciprocal equations.

The inaccuracy of linear approximations to the hyperbolic curves that related grain prices to bread weights remained a chronic problem. The long-term inflation of the sixteenth-century Price Revolution provoked repeated adjustments in weight-variable regulatory systems, and these adjustments usually took an ad hoc form. This imparts an element of arbitrariness to much of the surviving price/weight evidence, but it does not signify the presence of a new or distinct regulatory philosophy. The weight-variable and price-variable systems are not different in design. They are, literally, two sides of a coin. The weight-variable system introduced a mathematical complication that was usually solved awkwardly, imparting errors that more often than not shortchanged the consumer.

A System of Portions: Actual and Official Loaves

Old system bread price schedules, in both price- and weight-variable forms, allocated to the baker not a fixed income but a fixed quantity of bread. It was the revenue from the sale of this bread that constituted the fund from which the baker covered his production, capital, and labor costs. Under this regime, the size of the baker's net revenue, and hence the profitability of his enterprise, varied directly with the price of grain, with which the price of bread moved in complete sympathy. The higher the price of grain, the higher the baker's revenue per unit of bread sold, but his costs did not rise at the same rate, and for two reasons: first, because the several non-grain costs of production were essentially constant, changing in the short term very little or not at all; second, because the cost of grain was, in fact, spread across a larger number of loaves than was assumed by the bread price schedule. The consequences of these two factors for the baker's income are shown graphically in Figure 1.2b.

Under the variable-price regime, total revenue rises from zero (under the notional situation where the price of grain is zero), while the full cost of producing bread, even when the grain is free, is, of course, positive. Because of the substantial discrepancy between the *actual* number of loaves that could be produced and the *official* number of loaves on which regulators calculated the bread price, the full cost of producing each loaf of bread rises less steeply than the revenue curve set under the old system. Thus, below point A in Figure 1.2b the baker's revenue is inadequate to cover all costs, while above that point, the baker enjoys progressively larger "excess" revenues. Under the variable-weight regime, matters are no different.

The old system, if it sets point A within the range of commonly occurring prices, confronted the baker with a highly uncertain income, but one that will be very high precisely when the consumer faced distress and even famine. Old system bread price regulation, a practice commonly regarded as protecting the humble consumer from hardship, actually sets bread prices systematically too high (relative to total production costs) in times of high grain prices.

Can this feature of old system bread price regulation be justified? Davis, a student of the English assize, takes up the challenge by noting that the high profits are expressed per unit of grain baked into bread, and that the baker's "throughput" was likely to fall in periods of very high prices, as consumers substituted away from bread. Thus, the theoretical windfalls available to the baker *per unit of output* (as illustrated in Figure 1.2b) were not likely, in reality, to generate such handsome *total* revenues. On this basis Davis proceeded to defend this regime as both intentional and necessary:

Bakers would not be selling as much bread (by weight) at high prices. They would be selling the same number of loaves of progressively smaller weights. Since they would sell less bread by weight, the profit per pound of bread needed to rise to cause their total profit to remain constant.[56]

---

[56] Davis, "Baking for the common good," p. 479.

Davis's claim that this regulatory regime left baker's revenue constant as consumer demand responded to short-term changes in grain and bread prices could be true only if the demand for bread were highly elastic with respect to price. At unitary elasticity a one percent rise in price will result in a one percent reduction in demand. Under such circumstances, the baker's sales would fall, but his revenue would remain stable (since his smaller sales would be exactly compensated for by higher prices). This is the response Davis assumes. But no studies of consumer behavior find such a high price elasticity of demand for the staple of the European diet.[57] Demand was not *entirely* inelastic with respect to price, but in most circumstances it was sufficiently inelastic to provide the baker with substantially higher net revenues in periods of high grain prices than when prices were low.

When all mitigating factors are taken into account, the old system of bread price regulation that spread across Europe in the Middle Ages can only be described as crude and socially objectionable. It reinforced

---

[57] The price elasticity of demand e_{Qp} = % change in Quantity/ % change in Price. If a 20% increase in price induces a 20% reduction of demand (unitary elasticity), the baker's revenue begins at, say, 100 units * 10 pence = 1,000 pence and ends at 83.3 units * 12 pence = 1,000. If demand is completely inelastic, the baker's sales do not fall, and his revenue simply rises by 20 percent: 100 units * 12 pence = 1,200 pence.

However, the 20 percent increase in cost applies only to the grain. If this is two-thirds of the total cost of bread, the baker's grain costs at the starting point were 667 pence. They remain the same after a 20 percent reduction of output triggered by a 20 percent increase in grain costs, and rise to 800 pence (that is, by 20 percent) if demand is inelastic. The baker's revenue after subtracting grain costs start at 333 pence, remain at 333 pence if demand elasticity is unitary, but rises to 400 pence under inelastic demand.

Unitary elasticity (-1.0) and complete inelasticity (0) can be considered the extremes of consumer behavior for a necessity such as bread. Gregory King's "political arithmetic" of the 1690s found a relationship between grain prices and consumption, sometimes called "King's Law," that implied a price elasticity of -0.403.

$Q = 1.00P^{-0.403}$

Gunnar Persson's modern calculations settled on an elasticity of -0.6. Robert Fogel argued for an even lower elasticity, -0.183. Any of these elasticities imply that old system pricing provided the baker with a higher total income when grain prices rose. See Persson, *Grain Markets in Europe*, pp. 50–54; Robert Fogel, "Second thoughts on the European escape from hunger: famines, chronic malnutrition, and mortality rates," in S. Osmani, ed., *Nutrition and Poverty* (Oxford University Press, 1992), pp.248–49; Cormac Ó Grada and Jean-Michel Chevet, "Famine and market in Ancien Régime France," *Journal of Economic History* 62 (2002), 706–33.

Studies of the *income* elasticity of demand for food are more plentiful, and they usually measure an elasticity for low income households of 0.6 to 0.7 for food in general; the elasticity for bread grains is nearly always somewhat less than this. Nicholas Crafts, "Income elasticities of demand and the release of labor by agriculture during the British Industrial Revolution: a further appraisal," in Joel Mokyr, ed., *The Economics of the Industrial Revolution* (Totowa, NJ: Rowman and Allenhead, 1985), pp. 151–63; Gregory Clark, Michael Huberman, and Peter H. Lindert, "A British food puzzle, 1770–1850," *Economic History Review* 48 (1995), 216. Carole Shammas, "The eighteenth-century English diet and economic change," *Explorations in Economic History* 21 (1984), 258–59.

the "natural" volatility of grain prices with an even more volatile return to the baker. Instead of protecting consumers from high bread prices in times of scarcity, it set prices at a higher level than was necessary – that is, than was warranted by the underlying total costs of production. It did this by systematically obscuring from view the true costs of bread production. Indeed, the system of grain portions enforced by the regulators seemed designed to preserve the "mysteries" of the millers' and bakers' crafts. The actual bread yield per unit of grain and the actual costs of production (other than grain) were not ordinarily objects of study by the regulators and hence not known with any certainly by either the magistrates or the consuming public.

The old system of bread price regulation lived on long after the Middle Ages in which it arose. When European magistrates did contemplate renovation of their regulatory systems, usually in the eighteenth century, they had before them one clear example of an alternative approach, for the Dutch Republic broke with old system regulatory practices in the 1590s to establish a new, modern set of procedures that endured until bread price regulation itself came to an end in the mid-nineteenth century. But until then, the cities of the Netherlands, in both north and south, had participated fully in medieval old system price regulation. There was nothing to distinguish their practices from those of their European neighbors. There was, however, something that distinguished the supply of bread grain in the Netherlands from its European neighbors.

The following chapter will introduce the distinctive Dutch grain economy, while later chapters will explore how and why a new system of bread price regulation arose, how it functioned, and what its consequences were for both state and society. Toward the end of this study (Chapter 14) we will return to see how regulatory practices evolved in the rest of Europe and compare the course of regulated bread prices in the Netherlands and neighboring countries.

2   Free Trade in Grain?

Grain was produced nearly everywhere in medieval Europe. Even in quite unsuitable districts peasants sought to coax grain from their rocky or boggy soils. They had reason to do so, for a reliance on grain from more favored regions, whereby they could capture the benefits of specialization and comparative advantage, ran the very real risk of being left without this key element of the European diet when harvests were poor or when war threatened. Then territorial and town rulers took steps to secure their own food supply by imposing forced deliveries and export bans, blocking the flows of grain from areas of surplus to areas of deficit. In much of Europe the precautionary measures of rulers interacted with the precautionary measures of farmers to produce both low productivity in agriculture and high volatility in year-to-year tradable supplies.[1]

Still, in normal times, most grain markets were relatively free. To be sure, these markets were often organized to protect urban communities, and farmers were commonly forced to sell their surpluses on the local market. This generally did not prevent the (somewhat distorted) forces of supply and demand from generating useful price signals. But in abnormal times matters could change quickly. Then ordinary market functions were suspended for *raison d'état*; the grain trade became a political rather than an economic activity.

---

[1] Persson, *Grain Markets in Europe*, pp. 1–2. Persson takes the economists' position that free markets achieved a higher level of efficiency, and, hence, greater overall material wellbeing, than regulated markets. An influential defense of restriction and state intervention in markets (the sociologists' position?) was provided by Karl Polanyi, who called it "administered trade." "Polanyi looked on self-regulated markets, outside political intervention or control, as late arrivals in a world where traditional authorities were too afraid of riot and rebellion to play with their double-edged logic: freedom to profit and freedom to starve." Eric Jones, *The European Miracle* (Cambridge University Press, 1981), p. 87; Karl Polanyi, *The Great Transformation* (New York: Farrar and Rinehart, 1944).

Origins of the Dutch Grain Trade

In a world where grain markets were subject to repeated intervention and where an interregional trade in grain was viewed as morally dubious, it took very special circumstances and no small amount of political courage to rely on distant grain markets on a regular, ongoing basis.[2] The coastal provinces of the Low Countries took this step beginning in the fourteenth century, but not without doubts and conflict. It occurred in stages, and by the mid-sixteenth century had assumed a form that would endure until the nineteenth century. Thus, in 1438 the Council of Holland, facing food shortages, issued a prohibition on grain exports saying it "could not think of anything better to provide our poor community with grain."[3] Yet in little more than a century Holland's leaders could not think of anything worse to achieve the same result.

The first steps in this direction were involuntary. The process of reclamation and settlement of the low-lying portions of Holland and coastal Flanders, launched in the eleventh and twelfth centuries, set in motion hydrological processes that made arable farming progressively more difficult. In the century after the Black Death farming in these zones shifted rapidly toward livestock grazing, which, in turn, sent redundant labor (grazing is less labor-intensive than arable agriculture) to the towns, where migrants sought their fortunes in fishing, cloth making, brewing, and shipping. In the course of the fifteenth century the region became highly urbanized at the same time that local grain production fell sharply: there was little choice but to import grain from distant production centers.[4]

[2] Long-distance trade in grain was not unknown, of course, but it generally took place within an imperial context: the supply region was under the direct and coercive control of a dominant state. One thinks of ancient Rome and its North African granary, Constantinople and Egypt, or, in later times, Spain and Sicily. The distinction of concern here is well analyzed by Immanuel Wallerstein. His world-systems theory distinguishes between world empires, where trade is embedded in command structures, and world economies, where markets form the ligaments of the international political and economic structure. Immanuel Wallerstein, *The Modern World-System*, vol. I (New York: Academic Press, 1974), pp. 15–16, 180–82.
[3] Unger, *De levensmiddelenvoorziening*, pp. 492–93. Medieval market organization is studied in detail in Jessica Dijkman, *Shaping Medieval Markets: The Organization of Commodity Markets in Holland, c. 1200 – c. 1450* (Leiden: Brill, 2011).
[4] This brief summary of the profound and enduring structural change in the region's maritime economy is discussed in more detail in: D. E. H. de Boer, *Graaf en grafiek. Sociale en economische ontwikkelingen in middeleeuws 'Noordholland' tussen 1345 en 1415* (Leiden: New Rhine Publishers, 1978), pp. 211–50; Jan Luiten van Zanden, "A third road to capitalism? Proto-industrialization and the moderate nature of the late medieval crisis in Flanders and Holland, 1350–1550," in Peter Hoppenbrouwers and Jan Luiten van Zanden, eds., *Peasants into Farmers?* CORN Publication Series 4 (Turnhout: Brepols, 2001), pp. 85–101; Jan de Vries and Ad van der Woude, *The First Modern Economy* (Cambridge University Press, 1997), pp. 16–20; Wim Blockmans, *Metropolen aan de Noordzee* (Amsterdam: Bert Bakker, 2012), pp. 282–95; Jan Luiten van Zanden and Bas van Bavel, "The jump-start of the Holland economy during the late medieval crisis, c. 1350 – c. 1500," *Economic History Review* 57 (2004), 503–32.

Grain entered the coastal Netherlands from all directions: East Anglia supplied wheat and, especially, barley; Hansa ships from northern Germany, Denmark, and the Baltic Sea brought rye; river vessels floated down the Rhine from the German lands (principally Gelre, Cleves, and Jülich) with wheat and rye; and river and coastal vessels brought wheat and rye from northern France (Artois and Picardy). France was usually the most important of these suppliers, but all were subject to disruption and diversion to alternative centers of demand.[5] Most of these grain supplies entered the Dutch delta region: the German supplies at Dordrecht, the French and English supplies at Delft and its outports.[6] North Sea and Baltic sources of grain normally entered the Zuider Zee, where Amsterdam was consolidating its position as the dominant port – and, simultaneously, was emerging as the principal trading rival to the commercial networks of the cities united in the Hanseatic League.

The luxury of drawing on grain surpluses from multiple regions did not last long. The low population levels in the century after the Black Death had created a favorable supply and demand setting for the newly import-dependent Low Countries, but the revival of population growth and the growth of the great metropoles of London and Paris turned England and France into less dependable suppliers. Indeed, those countries and others in western Europe threatened to become net grain importers as their populations grew in the sixteenth century. But the retreat of these suppliers from the international market was also influenced by the competition of lower-cost Baltic grain supplies, and here is where the role of Dutch traders became decisive.

Threat and opportunity often go hand in hand, and while the Dutch grain markets of Dordrecht and Delft felt acutely the diminution of their supplies after the 1450s, the grain traders of the Zuider Zee ports, Amsterdam foremost among them, sensed the prospect of large gains if they could secure regular access to the Baltic grain ports (Konigsberg, Elbing, Stettin, and particularly, Danzig), where price levels were half those prevailing in western markets. If they could break the control of the Hansa merchants over this region and maintain good relations with the kings of Denmark, the gatekeepers to the Baltic, the low costs of their

---

[5] Milja van Tielhof, *De Hollandse graanhandel, 1470–1570: koren op de Amsterdamse molen,* Hollandse Historische Reeks 23 (The Hague:Stichting Hollandse Historische Reeks, 1995).

[6] Until the mid-sixteenth century, Dordrecht remained the chief market for grain shipped by river "from above" the German *bovenlanden.* Most grain reaching Dordrecht was sent further to consuming markets in the Southern Netherlands. The volume of this trade fell substantially after the 1550s. Job Weststrate, *In het kielzog van moderne markten: handel en scheepvaart op de Rijn, Waal en IJssel, ca. 1360–1560* (Hilversum: Verloren, 2008), pp. 237–42.

shipping services would not only dominate existing markets but create new ones as well. The movement of a bulky commodity such as rye over a distance of 1,500 km (Danzig–Amsterdam) could equal the purchase price of rye, thereby doubling the price at which it could be offered in the Low Countries. Merchants who could reduce these shipping costs stood to gain in two ways: by securing the trade from competitors (in this case, the Hansa) and by enlarging the western market for Baltic grain.

The story of how ship captains and merchants from the Zuider Zee towns gained their dominance in the Baltic in the course of the century after the 1430s cannot be told here in any detail.[7] However, developments in ship design, access to off-season fishing vessels, and a growing labor supply in the half-agrarian, half-maritime villages of North Holland, all contributed to the lowering of Dutch shipping costs. By the 1470s Amsterdam's Baltic grain supplies competed head on with the other suppliers (England, France, Germany); in the first forty years of the sixteenth century Baltic grain imports rose by 50 percent while imports from others sources declined. Amsterdam now stood at the center of a trading system that dominated grain supplies in the Low Countries. Between 1539 and 1564 Baltic grain shipments through the Danish Sound more than doubled, from 24,400 to 60,000 lasts, and Dutch ships moved over 70 percent of it.[8] In 1564 Amsterdam was still not an enormous city (perhaps 30,000 inhabitants vs. Antwerp's 100,000), but it was highly specialized in the Baltic trade, which came to be known as the city's "mother trade" [*moedernegotie*]. This tells us that Amsterdam merchants saw it as foundational to the commercial advantages that would lead them into many other branches of trade. But, it was also foundational to the Dutch domestic economy, which could now rely on distant grain supplies and go on to pursue its comparative advantage in specialized agriculture, industry, and trade, and support a large, urbanized population.

Liberating the Grain Trade

On the eve of the Dutch Revolt a key feature of the specialized economy of the later Dutch Republic was already in place. By then 60 to 70,000 lasts of foreign grain entered the region annually, forcing adjustments to domestic agriculture, sustaining an intense urbanization, and encouraging

---

[7] For a brief account, see De Vries and Van der Woude, *The First Modern Economy*, pp. 350–59; for a full account, see Van Tielhof, *De Hollandse graanhandel.*

[8] Richard Unger, "Feeding Low Countries towns: the grain trade in the fifteenth century," *Revue Belge de philologie et d' histoire* 77 (1999), 329–58; Van Tielhof, *De Hollandse graanhandel*, pp. 98, 125.

the broader commercial development of Dutch ports. But, how secure were these grain supplies, in fact? Holland and the city of Amsterdam had established their political status among the northern powers and the old Hansa cities largely on their own, and sought to maintain their de facto autonomy in the conduct of their commercial policies. Yet they were part of the Habsburg Netherlands and of the larger Habsburg Empire, where the inclination toward command and control was strong. The Habsburg monarchs' surrogates in the Netherlands sought to impose in Holland what was customary elsewhere in the empire: a system of grain re-export licenses known as the *congiegeld*, or "release payments." This involved the appointment of a royal official who would monitor grain inventories, gain information about trade flows, issue the export licenses (for a fee), and when conditions warranted refuse to issue them, thereby bringing the grain trade to a standstill.[9] Efforts to impose this invasive oversight in Holland were made repeatedly, in 1527,1531, 1540–41, and again in 1545–46. Amsterdam, usually with the support of the States of Holland, resisted and sought to defend its autonomy in this matter. To be sure, it sometimes intervened on its own to limit or prohibit grain exports in times of crisis, which were severe and frequent in the mid-sixteenth century, especially 1553–54, 1557, and 1566. But it made a distinction between acting in its local self interest and subordinating its trade practices to imperial policy.[10]

This point of tension, which greatly complicated Amsterdam's internal politics and its relations with the Habsburg state, remained until 1578, when Amsterdam joined in the revolt against Habsburg rule. Thereafter, with the effective independence of the seven provinces that allied to form

[9] James D. Tracy, "Habsburg grain policy and Amsterdam politics: the career of Sheriff Willem Dirkszoon Baerdes, 1542–1566," *The Sixteenth Century Journal* 14 (1983), 293–319. The control of grain trade by export licenses was also practiced in England and France. It is more than likely that the chief purpose of this policy was royal revenue rather than consumer protection. The license fees enabled the crown to share in the profits available to merchants in periods of scarcity. Sharp, *Famine and Scarcity*, pp. 91–97; Usher, *Grain Trade in France*, pp. 224–30; Unger, *Levensmiddelenvoorziening*, pp. 55–56.

[10] In 1545 the States of Holland remonstrated against an Imperial prohibition of grain exports. It defended Amsterdam's commercial interests by claiming that it could not understand why the emperor sought to prohibit a trade that imported six times as much grain as it exported. Milja van Tielhof, "Grain provision in Holland, ca. 1490 – ca. 1570," in Peter Hoppenbrouwers and Jan Luiten van Zanden, eds., *Peasants into Farmers? The Transformation of Rural Economy and Society in the Low Countries (Middle Ages – 19th Century) in Light of the Brenner Debate* (Turnhout: Brepols, 2001), p. 207.

However, in the crisis of 1556–57 it was Amsterdam, supported by the States of Holland, that invoked Habsburg trade policy to embargo all grain shipments from the city. As Tracy notes, in this instance it was the central government that was seeking to "pry loose" its grain in order to supply towns elsewhere in the Low Countries. Tracy, "Career of Sheriff Baerdes," p. 312.

the Dutch Republic in 1579, the international grain trade centered on Amsterdam was largely free of political interference. This is not to say that famine conditions did not elicit official concern and intervention, but that intervention now exhibited a sensitive awareness of the "unintended consequences" of trade prohibitions and price controls, and was always designed to minimize such consequences.

The magistrates now acted to prohibit or limit grain exports only as a last resort. They were always acutely aware of the fact that news of such prohibitions could discourage the grain *imports* on which the Republic always depended. Thus, an export prohibition in 1596 lasted but fleetingly and those of 1630 and 1698 were both lifted after two months. Thereafter, general prohibitions on grain exports were not contemplated until the (political) crisis of 1789. The problem then was not inadequate grain supplies in the Republic, but extraordinary demand for grain elsewhere in Europe, especially France, then on the cusp of revolution.

Grain markets elsewhere in Europe continued to be subject to intervention, especially when prices rose. "Letting go" of the crutch of controls over grain deliveries, exports, and prices proved to be very difficult, as was famously illustrated by the oscillations between liberal and command policies in the final decades of *ancien régime* France.[11] However, throughout the seventeenth and eighteenth centuries, grain sellers and buyers throughout western Europe had access to a free-market reference point in the form of the Amsterdam Grain Exchange [*Korenbeurs*]. There, Baltic and other grain was bought and sold freely, was held in storage by specialized merchants, and was freely sold again to final customers both foreign and domestic.

This transition was rendered dramatically visible for all to see in 1590–91, when 26 ships laden with grain sailed from Holland's Zuider Zee ports to Italy, risking capture as enemy vessels by Spain. Grain from the Baltic could be sold profitably in distant Italy only under exceptional circumstances – famine conditions. But such conditions persisted through much of the 1590s, and recurred periodically thereafter, such that at

---

[11] France's comprehensive controls on the internal grain trade were ended by the free market reforms of Controller General Bertin in 1763–64. By 1770 nearly all of this liberalization had been rescinded by his successor, the Abbé Terray. In 1774 a second reform attempt was made, led by Controller General Turgot. No sooner had his free trade policies been implemented but grain shortages, or feared shortages, led to the "flour war," the dismissal of Turgot, and a rollback of his decrees. In 1787, yet another Controller General, Calonne, tried to implement free trade policies. Within a year he was replaced by Jacques Necker, who earlier had brought an end to Turgot's reforms and now ended those of Calonne. Kaplan, *Bread, Politics and Political Economy*; Miller, *Mastering the Market*, pp. 43–49; Karl Gunnar Persson, "On corn, Turgot, and elasticities: the case for deregulation of grain markets in mid-eighteenth-century France," *Scandinavian Economic History Review* 41 (1993), 37–50.

least 1,419 Dutch grain ships sailed for Italy in the period 1591–1620.[12] Amsterdam was now not only the granary for the Low Countries, but for western Europe more generally.

The new understanding that freedom of trade offered a better guarantee of abundant supplies than a system of licenses and prohibitions was widely shared by the eve of the Revolt, but it would take time before it could be articulated as a theory in support of free trade in both the domestic and international markets. In 1651 Dirck Graswinckel, scion of a Delft regental family, wrote a remarkable treatise with the prosaic title *Proclamations, ordinances, and regulations on the theme of foodstuffs* [*Placcaten, ordonnantien ende reglementen op 't stuck vande lijf-tocht*]. The first of its two volumes did, indeed, consist of a compilation of edicts concerning the regulation of the grain trade introduced from 1501 to 1634. But the second volume offers Graswinckel's analysis of these policies and his conclusions that a policy of free trade, including the domestic freedom of grain brokers to purchase and store grain for speculative purposes, was the only reasonable guarantor of price stability and adequate supplies. His incisive dismissal of arguments that adequate food supplies required an interventionist state, ever ready to block the free flow of grain and force down prices, is worth dwelling on for a moment.[13]

Just as water flows toward the lowest level, without need of windmills [pumps] to achieve its goal, so, in the opposite way, grain flows toward the highest market without the need of state regulations.

It is high prices that attract grain, not edicts. Graswinckel was an unapologetic advocate of high prices for agricultural products, whose benefits he

---

12 P. C. van Royen, "The first phase of the Dutch Straatvaart (1591–1605); fact or fiction," *International Journal of Maritime History* 2 (1990), 69–102; J. I. Israel, "The phases of the Dutch *straatvaart* (1590–1713): a chapter in the economic history of the Mediterranean," *Tijdschrift voor geschiedenis* 99 (1986), 1–30; J. G. van Dillen, *Van rijkdom en regenten* (The Hague: Martinus Nijhoff, 1970), pp. 69–71. The 1590 fleet was, indeed, captured by Spain (on its return voyage, once the cargo had been delivered), but the much larger fleet of 1591 was granted safe passage in light of the Mediterranean famine conditions. Even larger fleets delivered grain to Italy in later years, reaching a peak in 1597–98. Altogether, Dutch ships delivered 175,100 lasts of grain in the period 1591–1620.

13 Dirck Graswinckel, *Placcaten, ordonnantien ende reglementen op 't stuck vande lijf-tocht*, 2 vols. (Leiden: Elseviers, 1651), vol. II, p. 133. Gunnar Persson places Graswinckel's contribution in historical perspective: "The argument that price stability and supply adequacy are best served by free trade rather than state-administered trade is usually associated with figures such as the French Physiocrats François Quesnay and A. R. J. Turgot and other Enlightenment-era political economists, such as Salustio Bandini in Tuscany and Charles Smith in England. However, over a century earlier Graswinckel had made the intellectual case that soon thereafter was applied to the French Colbertian regime by Pierre de Boisguilbert (whose more polemical work, *Le detail de la France, ou la France ruinée sous la règne de Louis XIV*, was first published abroad, in Cologne in 1696)." Persson, *Grain Markets in Europe*, pp. 1–8.

saw in a distinctly non-Malthusian way. High prices encourage investment in land improvement, reclamation and drainage. He noted how the preceding seventy years (that is, since the effective independence of the Republic) had witnessed an enormous increase in population and of commercial life. It had also witnessed investment in polders (land reclamation), drainage, and farm improvements. In his estimation, this had not yet achieved a growth in the grain supply that could fully keep pace with the growing demand for foodstuffs, but he argued that securing the benefits of agricultural improvements required patience and the continued encouragement given by high prices. The Republic, in his view, was on the right path.

But what about the poor? Was the state to leave them to their fate in its dogmatic adherence to free trade? Graswinckel's answer went to the heart of the problem with the age-old tradition of state control of the trade in foodstuffs:[14]

If one desires to subsidize [the consumption of the poor], these resources should be drawn from the common funds [public revenues] and not from those who happen to own grain.

The owners of grain were farmers and grain merchants. Graswinckel's work is noteworthy for its early recognition that the medieval "pro-consumer" policies that restricted and channeled the grain trade were more correctly "anti-producer" in their impact; they discouraged the very production that offered the best hope of reducing the incidence of food shortages.

Graswinckel did not stop here. He went on to defend vigorously the long-demonized practices of the grain merchant and speculator. Most of Europe then shared the French view enunciated in a sixteenth-century statute: The merchants' aim was "to profit from public misfortune"; they were "justly suspect" because they had "no view other than their own interests."[15] But Graswinckel saw their role as essential and, therefore beneficial, and was able to articulate this in a manner few of his age were capable of.[16]

Grain brokers must be tolerated because they are as necessary as the baker or the farmer, who is the first seller of grain. In the event that the whole world had the ability to take in their provisions for a full year, then no grain merchants would be necessary. But just as the farmer needs to sell [grain] and acquire ready cash, so the common people cannot acquire their provisions except for a short time,

[14] Graswinckel, *Placcaten*, vol. II, p. 148.
[15] Cited in Kaplan, *Bread, Politics*, vol. I, p. 55.
[16] Graswinckel, *Placcaten*, vol. II, pp. 115–16.

indeed, weekly or even daily. [In the absence of grain brokers] others would have to be found to furnish the farmers with cash and supply the common people with foodstuffs.

Here Graswinckel illustrates with a crystalline clarity the social need for grain storage and for a financial mechanism to assemble the farmers' grain and to distribute it to consumers both over space and over time. The farmers need their payment before the ultimate consumers have purchased and consumed their foodstuffs. He who financed this inter-mediate role is not a parasite and monopolist, to be despised, but the provider of a socially useful service.[17]

Graswinckel's defense of free markets in grain were both insightful and pungently expressed, but in the Dutch Republic, he was preaching to the choir, for the political elite of urban regents already embraced the policy he advocated. In this the Republic was unusual; more than a century later Adam Smith could still observe that "the freedom of the corn trade is almost everywhere more or less restrained, and, in many countries, is confined by such absurd regulation as frequently aggravate the una-voidable misfortune of dearth into the dreadful calamity of a famine." He accounted for this backwardness by drawing a mischievous analogy between laws regulating the grain trade and laws regulating religion:[18]

The people feel themselves so much interested in what relates either to their sub-sistence in this life, or to their happiness in a life to come, that government must yield to their prejudices, and, in order to preserve the public tranquility, establish that system which they approve of. It is upon this account, perhaps, that we so seldom find a reasonable system established with regard to either of these two capital objects.

To this Graswinckel would have said: amen!

The Republic embraced free trade in grain far in advance of any other European state, but this did not lead it to embrace a free trade in bread. On the contrary, the same state that was in the vanguard in rejecting

---

[17] Schumpeter, *History of Economic Analysis*, p. 368 fn. Graswinckel's views on the harm done by prohibiting grain exports and speculative purchases were not new, Schumpeter claims, but "Graswinckel had a keener sense of the price mechanisms involved, espe-cially of the function of forestalling." Usher's pioneering study of the French *ancien régime* grain trade breathed the spirit of Graswinckel's analysis. Usher insisted that speculation was inherent in the ownership of grain, but that speculation would dimin-ish in scope and violence the more perfect and transparent the markets. As he put it, "Increased freedom to speculate has in fact narrowed the range of speculation." Abbott Payson Usher, *The History of the Grain Trade in France* (Cambridge, Mass.: Harvard University Press, 1913).
[18] Adam Smith, *Inquiry into the Causes of the Wealth of Nations* [1776], ed. Edwin Cannon (London: Methuen & Co., 1904), book IV, ch. 5, pp. 48–49.

controls on the grain trade simultaneously pioneered in transforming the medieval regulations of bread prices into a far more comprehensive and invasive set of regulatory policies. Did this represent a deep contradition at the heart of Dutch political economy or was there perhaps a functional relationship between the freedom of trade in grain and the comprehensive regulation of trade in bread?

3   The Dutch *Broodzetting*: The Introduction of a "New System" of Bread Price Regulation

Bread was the basis of the diet in the Netherlands as it was throughout Europe and in the late Middle Ages the Dutch towns regulated the price of bread in the same manner as the rest of Europe. In this chapter we will seek to understand why and how the young Dutch Republic, in the 1590s, came to introduce a significant innovation to what by then was a venerable tradition of civic economic regulation. But before delving into the regulatory innovation and its motivations we need to become familiar with the focus of these regulatory concerns – the bread itself.

Dutch Bread

Bread is a familiar foodstuff, and the custom of modern bread makers to advertise their dedication to old artisanal traditions can give us a false confidence that we know more than we do about the breads of the past. While I cannot recreate the smells and taste of the breads of the early modern era, I will begin here with a brief introduction to the several types of bread that were widely available in the Netherlands, and also the most important bread substitutes available to consumers in the period of this study, which begins in the 1590s and ends with the abolition of regulated bread prices in 1855. More than in most European regions, Dutch consumers faced a wide realm of choice, concerning both the available types of bread and the available alternatives to bread. This realm of choice influenced both the distinctive Dutch regulatory policies and the behavior of consumers.

Rye Bread

Rye bread is the place to start, since it is commonly held to have formed the basis of the diet and to have been the only bread that common people routinely ate.[1] The price of rye is nearly always used as the primary if not the only item in cost of living indexes used to determine the purchasing power of the bulk of the population.[2] It was, indeed, a universally available and, by the standards of the time, standardized product. The rye grain usually was milled in its entirety, without sifting, and baked into loaves. A dense rye loaf could keep, allowing consumers to buy at intervals of several days. For this reason, rye loaves tended to be very large. Many cities quoted the prices for rye bread in loaves of 12 pounds (nearly 6 kg), although it was generally possible to purchase smaller loaves (or, were they portions of these large loaves?) of 6 or 3 pounds.

In the eastern regions of the Netherlands, where rye was the dominant field crop, rye figured in several sorts of bread. There one encountered, in addition to the normal large loaves, small loaves prepared with more finely milled rye flour often mixed with some wheat called *kleyn rogge, schoon rogge,* and *huisbakken.* For example, in the Overijssel city of Kampen rye was milled into fine flour, coarse flour, and a rough residual substance

---

[1] According to I. J. Brugmans, in his history of the working class in the nineteenth-century Netherlands, "Bread was not consumed in large quantities. Wheat bread was out of the question ... the working man simply ate rye bread ... or bread made of ground barley – or potato meal." I. J. Brugmans, *De arbeidende klasse in Nederland in de negentiende eeuw,* 2nd edn. (The Hague: Martinus Nijhoff, 1929), pp. 151–52. The social historian Leo Noordegraaf thought much the same: "Bread, rye bread in particular, was the chief food of low-income families in the preindustiral era." Leo Noordegraaf, "Levensstandaard en levensmiddelenpolitiek in Alkmaar vanaf het eind van de 16de tot in het begin van de 19de eeuw," in M. van der Bijl *et al.* (eds.), *Van Spaans beleg tot Bataafse tijd: Alkmaars stedelijk leven in de 17 de en 18 de eeuw,* Alkmaar Historische Reeks 4 (Zutphen: De Walburg Pers, 1980), p. 62. Agricultural historian Jan Bieleman follows in this tradition: "Rye was the quintessential grain of ordinary folks, and rye bread more than any other foodstuff formed the basis of the daily diet in the Republic. This was particularly the case for the low-income city-dweller and others who could not produce their own food and needed to purchase it." Jan Bieleman, *Boeren in Nederland Geschiedenis van de landbouw, 1500–2000* (Amsterdam: Boom, 2008), p. 48. In the same way food historian Anneka van Otterloo described "the pre-industrial rhythm of life": "Good times were followed by bad with the rise and fall of grain prices. The cheapest kind, rye, was, with potatoes, the chief food of the largest part of the population." Anneke H. Van Otterloo, *Eten en eetlust in Nederland* (Amsterdam: Bert Bakker, 1990), p. 18. Fellow food historian Jozien Jobse-van Putten was of the same opinion: "The most common bread in our country in earlier centuries was ryebread. Even in the western provinces, the more highly valued refined wheat bread was regarded as a luxury, whose consumption conferred status. Only in the course of the nineteenth century did rye bread lose, rather quickly, its dominant position [in the Dutch diet]." Jozien Jobse van Putten, *Eenvoudig maar voedzaam: cultuurgeschiedenis van de dagelijkse maaltijd in Nederland* (Nijmegen: SUN, 1995), p. 301.

[2] Wim Blockmans and Walter Prevenier, "Armoede in de Nederlanden," *Tijdschrift voor geschiedenis* 88 (1975), 501–38; Noordegraaf, "Levensstandaard"; Jan Luiten van Zanden, "Wages and the standard of living in Europe, 1500–1800," *European Review of Economic History* 3 (1999), 175–97; Robert Allen, "The great divergence in European wages and prices from the Middle Ages to the First World War," *Explorations in Economic History* 38 (2001), 411–47; Robert Allen, Tommy Bengtsson, and Martin Dribe, *Living Standards in the Past: New Perspectives on Well-being in Asia and Europe* (Oxford University Press, 2005).

called *kort* or *kortmeel* (middlings, or shorts). The coarse flour was used to make standard rye bread (which elsewhere, where the rye was milled into a single, uniform meal, will have been of a higher quality). The fine rye flour that remained was combined with coarse wheat flour to produce the mixed grain *huisbakken*, which was the lightest, softest bread many inhabitants of the eastern regions ordinarily ate.[3] In the western provinces, in contrast, breads made of grain mixtures generally were forbidden.[4]

With these exceptions, rye bread was a standard product, similar in preparation and quality throughout the Netherlands, and generally sold in large loaves sufficient to feed an entire family for several days. It was ubiquitous, but, as we will see, not everywhere the universal food that historians have tended to assume.

Wheat Bread

Wheat bread is often described as a luxury product in the Netherlands, available to ordinary people only on special occasions, if at all. Easter brought round loaves of *paasbrood* and at Christmas some workers could expect to receive from their employers small loaves of fine wheat bread, called a *duivekater*. Also called *wiegbrood* [cradle bread], it gave its corrupted name, *weggen* to small fine wheat bread loaves generally.[5] The first weeks of a couples' marriage – their honeymoon – came to be called the *wittebroodsweken* [white bread weeks] just as the week following Christmas was known as the *weggeweek*. This emphasis on wheat bread as an exceptional foodstuff or holiday treat exaggerates its luxury character, but it is certainly correct to emphasize wheat bread's urban associations and its strong links to commercial bread making. Wheat bread quickly becomes stale, requiring the frequent purchase of fairly small loaves. It requires either a homemaker prepared to bake frequently, or convenient access to a bakery.

[3] G.A. Kampen, Oud Archief, no. 2206–2208. Documents from as early as 1606 distinguish ordinary *roggebrood* and *"cleyn roggen van claren rogge gebacken"* and continue to do so into the nineteenth century. G.A. Deventer, no. 27 Republiek, 1629 and G.A. Zwolle, no. 488 [no date, mid-seventeenth century], also refer to the small rye loaves. G.A. Deventer, 1784 Concordat, refers to *Oortjes roggens*. At this date it was baked exclusively with wheat flour, its name notwithstanding. However, in earlier times it had been a rye–wheat mixture, similar to Kampen's *huisbakken*. Breads of this type were also common in Germany and Denmark. In Berlin coarse rye bread took the name *Hausbackbrot*, while the fine rye bread was called *Scharnnbrot*.

[4] For example, the 1626 ordinance of the Utrecht bakers' guild stipulated in clause 42: "No one may bake or sell *masteluyn* [mixed] bread of half wheat–half rye, or any other bread grain mixed together with bran, on penalty of 10 guilders." G.A. Utrecht, Backersgilde ordonnantie, no. 461, deel 1, no. 8.

[5] J. L. de Jager, *Volksgebruiken in Nederland* (Utrecht: Het Spectrum, 1981), pp. 64, 83; L. Burema, *De voeding in Nederland van de middeleeuwen tot de twintigste eeuw* (Assen: Van Gorkum, 1953), p. 140.

If rye bread was with minor exceptions a uniform product in the Netherlands, wheat bread was always characterized by variety. Wheat alone among the bread grains contains sufficient gluten to allow a raised loaf of aerated dough that enabled the differentiation of several distinct grades and styles of bread. At least four basic types of wheat bread were commonly on offer in the time of the Republic and well into the nineteenth century.[6] These wheat loaves differed from each other according to whether they were made of bolted or unbolted flour and by how finely the wheat flour was milled. Bakers typically offered their customers:

> Coarse, unbolted wheat bread [grof, ongebuild tarwebrood]
> White bread [wit brood]
> Fine, bolted wheat bread [fijn, gebuild tarwebrood, later "Franschbrood"]
> Coarse, bolted wheat bread [grof, gebuild tarwebrood; bruin tarwebrood; rode tarwebrood, ruygbrood]

The first, coarse unbolted wheat bread, was produced from flour as it came from the mill, with no further processing. Where no further processing was intended, the miller might grind the "whole wheat" so finely that the bran and coarse middlings, [zemelen and kortmeel] which otherwise would be sifted out, were inseparably ground into the flour. This form of milling, known as krop uit de zak, yielded the largest amount of flour for every unit of grain. It produced a coarse, brown bread.

When the milled grain was devoted to the production of bolted breads, the remaining three types listed above, the bran first needed to be removed from the ground meal. The meal then could be further separated into a fine flour (bloem), a second grade (middelmeel), coarse meal (kortmeel), and any remaining rough materials.[7] The fine flour, often mixed together with milk and eggs, produced the finest, white breads, which were variously known as schoon brood, weggen, fijn brood, witte bollen, and, most commonly, wit brood. Such bread was sold in small units (rolls and small loaves) and usually by weight.

The baker devoted the middle quality flour to a bolted wheat bread that went by many names: middelbroot, tarwen timpen, Franschbrood, fijn

---

[6] In other European countries, baking regulations usually distinguish two and sometimes three types, or grades of wheat bread. The eighteenth-century English assize of bread identified wheaten, standard wheaten, and household bread. French documents always refer to pain blanc (white bread) and pain bis (dark, coarse wheat bread), and usually a middle grade referred to variously as pain bourgeois, pain de tout, and bis-banc. Petersen, Bread, p. 100.

[7] For details on the milling and sifting process, see Burema, De voeding. For an account of the similar process in England, see A. Edlin, A Treatise on the Art of Bread-Making (1805; reprinted London: Prospect Books, 2004).

tarwebrood. The most dependable distinction in nomenclature was that the finest bread was *wit brood* or "white bread" while the middle quality bread was identified as *tarwebrood* or "wheat bread." This bread was darker in color and somewhat coarser than white bread. Beginning in the 1670s, these breads often acquired the name "French bread," often with the predicate *luchtig,* or light, fluffy.[8] This may signify the introduction of techniques to make this bread take on some of the color and texture qualities otherwise identified exclusively with white bread.

Finally we come to the bolted *coarse, or brown wheat bread* made partly from the coarsest flour and residual materials of the milling process. This coarse flour was mixed in varying proportions with a higher quality flour to produce breads named: *bruin tarwebrood, achterlingsbollen, grove bollen, ruychbrood.* The name *achterling* (literally, left behind or last [in the sifting process]) is evocative of this category. Although the term is certainly older, Haarlem's bread commissioners turned to it in 1643 when they found it necessary to forbid the sale of a mixed-grain bread: *mastelluyn, mescelin,* or maslin. They took this step out of concern that the bakers dumped various inferior materials into breads to which they gave this name. The bakers complained that they now had no legal means of using their lower quality flour, which led the commissioners to approve a new category, *achterlingen brood,* "to accommodate the bakers and the poor." Bakers could mix the coarsest flour, *kortmeel,* into this bread, but, the commissioners added: "it must be baked in a long form so that the community will not mistake it for [fine] wheat bread ... "[9] In the eighteenth century this type of bread is sometimes specified as being made from red wheat, a cheaper grade of wheat that yielded a soft dark flour, rather deficient in gluten, that produced a dense bread.

Of the four wheat bread types described here, the three bolted wheat breads form something like a continuum. Bakers exercised some discretion in the sifting and separating of their flour, and the relative demand for each grade of bread must have affected their exact composition. The bakers faced trade-offs in determining their assortment of wheat breads:

[8] Utrecht introduces *Franschbrood* in 1674 (as the French occupation of the city ends). Some cities soon follow, but others introduce this name much later: Kampen in 1784 and Dordrecht in 1800. *Luchtigbrood* is introduced in Dordrecht in 1748 and in Haarlem in 1750.

[9] G.A. Haarlem, Broodzettingsboek. 14 January 1643. "In order to accommodate the bakers and poor community [*den onvermoogende gemeente*] a type of bread, named *achterlinge,* may now [be produced]. It must take an elongated or pear-shaped form so that the community does not mistake this new product for wheat bread." In Leiden, the 1596 ordinance provided for "a third type of wheat bread, in which they [the bakers] can use their *kortmeel.*" But the new rules for wheat bread of 1648 put an end to this, much as Haarlem had intended to do in 1643. G.A. Leiden, Secratarie archief, no. 2099, Ordonnantie van 1596; no. 2250, Concept rapport, 4 Oct. 1803.

the more fine white bread they produced, the less bread they extracted from a unit of grain; the more fine white bread they produced the more low-grade flour would remain as a by-product, which could be used only in coarser wheat breads. This trade-off played out somewhat differently from place to place and over time.

It appears that the wheat bread assortment typically available up to the late sixteenth century was simpler than this. But by the early seventeenth century the four wheat bread types discussed above were all in common use. The Dutch consumer faced a considerable choice of breads, each with its own characteristics and its own price.

Bread Substitutes

The Boiled Grains

For most early modern Dutch households, certainly in the towns and the western provinces, wheat and rye breads were not an either-or proposition. Both had a place in the diet. But that did not exhaust their options. In both city and country Dutch consumers also had access to a variety of lesser grains – barley, oats, and buckwheat – distinguished by their lower gluten content, or, in the case of the pseudo-grain buckwheat, the total absence of gluten. Barley breads and oatcakes were widely consumed in northern Europe, but they were flat, dark, dense, and difficult to digest.[10] In the Netherlands none of these grains were used by bakers; indeed, except in times of famine bakers were explicitly forbidden from mixing them into their breads.

These alternatives, or substitutes, all required a milling process for shelling or hulling, and for the grinding, or breaking, of the grain kernels. Specialized mills, known as *grutmolens* or *pelmolens* performed these tasks and supplied networks of retailers, who, in turn, supplied consumers with these grains, and also with legumes, peas, and beans, known collectively as *grutten*, or *grutterswaren*. De-husked barley and oat groats (*gort*), and buckwheat formed the "boiled grains" as distinct from wheat and rye, the "baked grains," and were widely used to prepare porridges (*pap, brij, potje-beuling*) and (when mixed with some rye flour) pancakes. They were typically soaked in water, boiled, and then served in buttermilk, to which sweeteners (raisins and, especially, *stroop*, or treacle, a molasses-like by-product of sugar refining) might be added.

---

[10] The kernels of barley and oats, unlike wheat and rye, do not thresh out, but remain enveloped in the husk. When milled the resulting meal contains particles of husk, which makes for a very coarse bread. E. J. T. Collins, "Why wheat? Choice of food grains in Europe in the nineteenth and twentieth centuries," *Journal of European Economic History* 22 (1993), 26–27.

Buckwheat, the most important of these bread alternatives, was grown on a large scale on the thinner sandy soils in the east and south of the Netherlands. Measure for measure, buckwheat provides about as much protein as the bread grains, although it is notably deficient in the B vitamins. As we shall see in more detail later, buckwheat was widely consumed in both city and country, in the east where it was grown as well as in the west. It was not simply a survival from an earlier time of self-provisioning.[11]

This does not exhaust the alternative foods widely available in the Netherlands, but the others – rice and potatoes – came to play a significant role only in the eighteenth century, and will be discussed later. The town authorities which concerned themselves with establishing bread prices in the early years of the Dutch Republic focused on wheat and rye, but they knew that a largely unregulated alternative, what I will call, collectively, the boiled grains, was readily available to most consumers.

The Decision to Change the System of Bread Price Regulation

In Chapter 1, I explained the traditional method of regulating bread prices. I called it the "old system" in anticipation of introducing a break with these venerable practices that I will refer to as the "new system."

This new system was nowhere announced as such, and the archival evidence, which is abundant in describing its ongoing operations, is all but silent on explaining why it was introduced. Consequently, some inference and speculation must be added to the available evidence in order to understand why Dutch towns introduced a new approach to the regulation of bread prices and why it quickly displaced the traditional approach throughout the profoundly decentralized Dutch Republic.

We have already established that nearly all Dutch cities had been regulating bread prices since at least the fifteenth century, and had been doing it in the same way as the rest of Europe – following the old system. Ordinances confirming and updating this regime continued to be promulgated through the 1580s (in Leeuwarden in 1582, and Groningen in 1589).

---

[11] In 1812–13, just as in 1850, buckwheat accounted for about 20 percent of the total arable land in the Netherlands planted to wheat, rye, and buckwheat. J. L. van Zanden, *De economische ontwikkeling van de Nederlandse landbouw in de negentiende eeuw, 1800–1914*, AAG Bijdragen 25 (Wageningen: Afdeling Agrarische Geschiedenis, 1985), pp. 91–92; Merrijn Knibbe, *Agriculture in the Netherlands, 1851–1950* (Amsterdam: NEHA, 1993), pp. 55, 294.

But two other provincial towns, Nijmegen and Deventer, then introduced bread price schedules that appear as harbingers of a new approach. Nijmegen bread prices, which are known from 1559, followed the old system until 1587, when the magistrates introduced a new ordinance that contained a constant cost provision (14 guilders per last) at every grain price. Yet actual rye bread prices in the years thereafter did not actually follow the new ordinance. In practice Nijmegen's bakers continued to rely on the revenue from advantage loaves until at least the early seventeenth century. Deventer's new regulatory practices of 1593 – two years after its release from Spanish occupation – represented a more decisive step in the direction of new system principles. Only in 1629 do Deventer's magistrates document this change, but in the interval their rye bread prices followed a consistent new system price schedule.[12]

What is only implied in the price schedules of these towns became explicit in Holland beginning in 1596. Amsterdam introduced the new system as of 21 April 1596 and several other cities soon followed Amsterdam's example. We know this innovation primarily from the records of other cities, especially Leiden, which immediately established a commission to inform itself of Amsterdam's actions. The Leiden city council minutes of 21 November 1596 tell us of the commission's findings:[13]

Report of a commission of *burgemeesters*, Jan Janssen van Baersdorp, Claes Adriaensz, plus the *schepen* [councilman] Jan Gysbrechtsz, concerning the reform of the bakers.

[This commission] has met and consulted together to read through and consider revisions to the ordinances concerning bread baking in order properly to reform them and improve them and, with regard to the heaviness or weight of bread, apart from rye bread, to make them equal to the ordinances of the city of Amsterdam with the aim that the same [bread price regulation] will be put into effect in this city ...

Alkmaar took similar action, since we know its bread prices followed those of Amsterdam as of 1597.[14] The city of Haarlem appears to have

---

[12] Nijmegen price data provided in Offermans, *Arbeid en levenstandaard in Nijmegen*, pp. 111–13; G.A. Deventer, Middeleeuws archief, no. 299. Both cities endured severe, war-induced crises in 1586–88 that appear to have been the catalyst for a change in policy. Conflicts with the bakers led the Nijmegen town council to permit private citizens to trade in bread they baked privately. This attempt to increase competitive pressure on the bakers was followed in the same year with the "proto-new system" regulations discussed above. On Nijmegen's crisis, see Jan Kuys and Hans Bots, eds., *Nijmegen: geschiedenis van de oudste stad van Nederland*, vol. II (Nijmegen, n.d.), pp. 377; on Deventer, see Paul Holthuis, *Frontierstad bij het scheiden van de markt. Deventer: militair, demografisch, economisch, 1578–1648* (Deventer: Arko Uitgeverij, 1993), pp. 39–42.
[13] G.A. Leiden, Secretarie archief, no. 48, Gerechtsdagboeken, 21 Nov. 1596, fol. 79.
[14] Noordegraaf, "Levensstandaard," p. 61, fn. 11.

been preparing for such a move with ordinances on wheat bread in 1592 and a baking trial to determine the constant costs appropriate for wheat bread in the following year. Price records have survived only from 1610 for rye bread and 1612 for wheat bread, but they probably began earlier. When in 1659 the commissioners reviewed their archive to resolve a dispute with the bakers, they found documents recording constant costs reaching back to 1 April 1597.[15] Rotterdam's archives preserve a fragment of a bread price register that starts up in 1599.[16] In the case of Utrecht we can be more confident that the new system was introduced in 1599 (on 6 January), since a bound volume of weekly price notations (the *Rijdingboek*) begins then.[17] Finally, Delft introduced its new ordinance for rye bread (which until then had remained unregulated) in 1600.[18]

In sum, the new system was essentially the creation of a brief period beginning in the early 1590s, but taking a definite form in April 1596. By 1600 it had been widely adopted throughout Holland and the rest of the Republic, and the rules and practices established then would continue to characterize the Dutch *broodzetting* until bread price regulation was abandoned in 1855.

What motivated the regents of Amsterdam and the other cities to establish the new system in and shortly after 1596? The fullest contemporary statement I have uncovered that addresses this matter is a proclamation found in the first pages of Leiden's new bread price register, dated 8 December 1596:[19]

Whereas in past times various ordinances have been made concerning bread baking, with the aim of assuring that the bread is made of good and honest ingredients, and that the honest citizens, and especially the poor, may receive the full weight [of bread], and

[Whereas] the insights of the present times, especially given the great increase and expense of the price of grain, require changes so that the poor may buy their bread for an assured and established price and [so that] the excessive greed of certain persons with regard to the baking and selling of bread may be reigned in and as far as possible prevented,

Therefore, the *schout* [sheriff] and *burgemeesters* resolve ...

This proclamation invokes commonplaces that recur elsewhere, both before and after this date, about the *raison d'être* of price regulation: that

---

[15] G.A. Haarlem, Stadsarchief 1581–1795, R 413
[16] G. A. Rotterdam, Oud Stadsarchief, no. 2122–27.
[17] G.A. Utrecht, Oud Archief, no. 2023. Rijdingboek.
[18] G.A. Delft, Keurboek, ordonnantie op roggebrood, 1600, fol. 95.
[19] G.A. Leiden, no. 2536, Broodzettingregister, p. viii.

it will guarantee honest, wholesome bread and that it will serve the interests of the poor. But it also makes two important additional claims:

1. That bread price regulation is nothing new; it is a practice of long standing.
2. That the present time is one of both *new insights* and of *a pressing need* to reform the setting of bread prices.

The "great increase and expense of the price of grain" in 1596 is clear enough. Political, religious, and military disturbances beginning in the 1560s, and the general inflationary trend of the sixteenth-century "price revolution" had made grain price volatility a chronic problem and the region suffered full-blown subsistence crises in 1557, 1565–66, and 1571–74. But the price rise of the mid 1590s was greater than anything the young Republic had experienced since it had set out to assert its independence some twenty years earlier.[20]

By November of 1595 the price of rye at the Amsterdam market stood 80 percent above the average level that had prevailed in the decade 1582–91. The States General took the extraordinary step of placing a six-month moratorium on grain exports effective on 19 November of that year and individual cities took a variety of measures to secure sufficient grain for themselves. On 3 November, Alkmaar's city council simultaneously ordered its well-to-do burghers to ensure that they had grain stocks that would last until the following Pentecost (i.e., a six-month supply), and ordered that all grain stocks (presumably, in excess of a personal six-month supply) be taken into custody and sold at their acquisition prices. The city had already resolved to purchase 100 lasts of rye directly in Baltic ports.[21]

Prices fell back a bit in the months thereafter, but new political tensions then threatened access to the Danish Sound, the vital artery for Baltic grain supplies and Dutch trade more generally. Once again, the States General proposed a prohibition on grain exports, especially the large-scale exports to the Mediterranean markets that had become a conspicuous new feature of the Republic's trade beginning in 1591. Amsterdam's protestations put an end to this threat to its trade but not to the short

---

[20] For an English perspective on these years, see R. B. Outhwaite, "Dearth, the English crown and the 'crisis of the 1590s'," in Peter Clark, ed., *The European Crisis of the 1590s* (London: George Allen & Unwin, 1985), p. 28; Andrew Appleby, *Famine in Tudor and Stuart England* (Liverpool University Press, 1978), pp. 109–54. Appleby went to great pains to distinguish famine mortality from mortality caused by epidemics. He was convinced that the crisis of 1596–99 was a true famine, perhaps the last true *crise de subsistance* ever experienced in England (p. 135).

[21] J. H. Kernkamp, *De handel op den vijand, 1572–1609* (Utrecht: Kemink en Zoon, 1931), vol. II, pp. 157, 179; Noordegraaf, "Levensstandaard," pp. 80, 77.

supplies of grain. By July 1597 both rye and wheat sold for double the 1582–91 average and they remained abnormally high through 1598. Only in the course of 1599 did grain prices begin to drift down toward more normal levels. Thus, Amsterdam's 1596 initiative in introducing the new system and its prompt adoption elsewhere in Holland took place in a prolonged period of supply uncertainty and elevated prices.

What is more, this period of scarcity hit Holland as it was in the grip of a veritable urban explosion. For at least the previous decade, certainly since the fall of Antwerp to the Spanish army of the Duke of Parma in 1585, Holland's cities had received a flood of refugees from Flanders and Brabant in addition to migrants from many other places sensing new opportunities in the fledgling Republic and a safe haven from religious persecution. Amsterdam in 1596–97 was bursting at the seams. Its population had doubled since it joined the Revolt in 1578, and the small physical extensions of the city in 1585 and 1597 did more for harbor expansion than for the accommodation of new residents. Leiden received thousands of textile workers in these same years, causing severe crowding since the city did not expand its physical size until 1611. This was a period of crisis for residents seeking housing and food, but it was simultaneously a boom time. Two fleets of ships set out for Asia in 1595 – one via the Cape of Good Hope to confront directly the Portuguese claim to monopolize this route, and another via the North Cape in search of a Northeast Passage to Asia. The survivors of these ventures both returned in the course of 1597, and while they had been far from triumphant (indeed, Willem Barentsz's venture to the Arctic had been a disaster, albeit a heroic one), plans were made immediately to follow through with new fleets to Asia. In short, the food crisis hit Holland at a time of great expansion, innovation, and improvisation.[22] The introduction of a new approach to the venerable task of bread price regulation in this setting is, perhaps, not altogether surprising.

What, then, was the "new insight" alluded to in Leiden's preamble, and how could it offer solace in this time of great need? Just what was new about it? I have found no documents that offer an explicit answer to this question, but I believe it is implicit in the design of the new system. In Chapter 1 it was established that the old system bread price schedules allocated to the baker not a fixed income but a fixed quantity of bread. It was the income from this bread that constituted the revenue from which the baker covered his production, capital, and labor costs. The size of this revenue, and hence the profitability of the baker's enterprise, varied

---

[22] For more on life in Amsterdam in this period, see Gabri van Tussenbroek, *Amsterdam in 1597: kroniek van een cruciaal jaar* (Amsterdam and Antwerp: L. J. Veen, 2009).

directly with the price of grain, with which the price of bread moved in lock step: the higher the price of grain, the higher the baker's revenue per unit sold. Yet, in the short term, his non-grain costs were constant. Consequently, when grain prices were high, so were the bakers' profits; they rose with the rising price of grain. Conversely, when grain prices were low, bakers' earnings were also low, perhaps too low to cover the constant costs of production.

Those charged with bread price regulation had long been aware of the distinction between constant and variable costs of production. Many documents mention constant costs and claim to take them into account in the design of the bread price schedules. But very little came of these intentions. A few bread price schedules specified a constant cost but simply added this cost to the price of grain from which the bread price was derived. The French price schedules described in Table 1.1 followed this practice, which only intensified the undesirable feature of old system regulation. Recognizing the theoretical importance of constant costs was one thing; acting effectively and consistently upon it was something else altogether.

When the Holland towns introduced a rigorous distinction between constant and variable costs they took upon themselves a significant new administrative burden, which included itemizing and measuring the admissible constant costs, drafting the new price schedules, and establishing the true bread yield from a measure of grain. In return for this effort they secured a tangible benefit: by tethering the bakers to a fixed amount of revenue to defray their constant costs, the bread price rose less rapidly (in percentage terms) than the grain price. This, I believe, is what the Leiden preamble had in mind when it alluded to the need for "assured prices" and reigning in "the excessive greed of certain persons."[23]

We can demonstrate that the new system had precisely the effect intended by the magistrates. No extended records exist of the bread prices in effect under old system regulation, but we can calculate them with considerable confidence by exploiting the handy central feature of that system: that grain and bread prices were directly related, and could be determined without elaborate calculation. Figure 3.1 presents estimates of the old system prices for a pound of rye bread, and estimates of

---

[23] The reformed system of regulation applied, of course, to all bakers, not to "certain persons" guilty of "excessive greed." Earlier ordinances on this topic, which usually introduced measures to strengthen enforcement of the existing rules, customarily invoked the bad behavior of "certain persons." I believe that this language appears here more out of habit than because of an actual effort to restrain particular bakers.

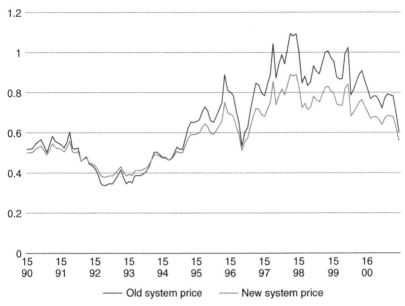

Figure 3.1 Monthly average rye bread prices calculated using old and new system rules, January 1590 – December 1600 (stuivers per kg)

new system prices for the same rye bread.[24] Over the entire decade, the new system yielded bread prices that averaged 10.4 percent below those generated by the old system. But, as Table 3.1 shows, the old system yielded lower bread prices until the price of rye exceeded 106.50 guilders per last, which was the case before September 1594, and would again be the case in 1601.

In the 1594–1600 period, when grain prices were high, the new policy reduced bread prices by 11.2 percent overall, and when the grain price reached its peak, in October–December 1597, the new system bread price was 18.6 percent lower than it would have been had the old system continued in effect. In exchange for some tedious arithmetic and an ongoing commitment to monitoring the costs of the baking enterprise, the magistrates of Holland's towns delivered a tangible and substantial benefit to the

---

[24] Both time series are based on monthly rye prices in Utrecht for the period 1591–1600. The old system prices are calculated on the assumption that 3,850 pounds of bread (1,900 kg) are dedicated to covering the cost of a last of rye. This bread yield is drawn from old system evidence from Groningen, Zutphen, Deventer, Utrecht, and Antwerp, which all set the rye bread yield between 3,652 and 4,160 pounds. The new system price estimates assume constant costs of 43 guilders (equal to Leiden, slightly above that of Utrecht) and a bread yield of 5,700 pounds.

Table 3.1 *Estimated monthly rye bread prices, January 1590 through December 1600 (prices in stuivers per pound, using both old system and new system methodologies)*

		New system		
	Old system	Estimated	Actual	Difference
Jan. 1590 – May 1594	0.461	0.463		+0.002
June 1594 – Dec. 1600	0.808	0.696		-0.112
May 1596 – Dec. 1600	0.869	0.738		-0.131
Using actual Leiden prices		0.738	0.727	-0.019

Old system rye bread price estimate = rye price per last / 3,850 pounds
New system rye bread price estimate = rye price per last + 43 guilders constant costs/ 5,700 pounds.
Beginning in May 1596 actual new system bread prices are available (for Leiden) to test the adequacy of this estimation procedure. The overall level of estimated prices is only 1.9 percent higher than actual Leiden prices.

swelling population that was gathering in their jurisdictions. They were visibly fulfilling their sworn duty to serve their communities as good regents.

This was a signal achievement, but it was not the only achievement; they also provided a tangible benefit to themselves. Besides the immediate problem of high bread prices, the magistrates also faced a second, long-term problem – securing additional tax revenue – and the new system provided a taxing opportunity that they were quick to exploit. To better understand this second attractive feature of the new system we need to pause for a brief review of the new Republic's tax policies.

The *Gemene Middelen* / the Common Means

Shortly after the Dutch Revolt began, the province of Holland, scrambling to secure revenue to conduct its war against Spain, introduced a series of excise taxes: on beer, wine, peat, slaughtered livestock, soap, fish, and milled grain. Excise taxes had long been a familiar feature of municipal finances, especially excises of beer. But now, in 1574, provincial levies would be added to the municipal excises and these would be considerably larger than anything that had been collected by the towns.[25]

---

[25] This early initiative of a rebel state had a pre-history. Urged by the Duke of Alva to supply a large contribution (*bede*) to the Spanish authorities, the States of Holland had agreed in 1570 to introduce new excises on milling, slaughtered livestock, butter, cloth, foreign beer, and herring. But implementation of these new levies was stopped with the onset of hostilities. Thus, the true beginning of these excise taxes came in 1574, when the Prince of Orange requested a large war subsidy. James Tracy, *The Founding of the Dutch Republic: War Finance and Politics in Holland, 1572–1588* (Oxford University Press, 2006), pp. 44, 102–07.

The new tax on milled grain (called *impost op 't gemaal*, or simply *het gemaal*) was collected, as the early ordinances put it, "in the manner and after the usage observed earlier by the cities," but now by the Receiver of the Common Means, a provincial official.[26] It was paid by the owner of the grain at or near milling sites, and the tax varied according to the grain sort and the use to which the grain was to be put: more for wheat than rye, more for bread grain than brewers' grain. This new tax was a cost born by the owner of the grain being presented for milling (bakers, but also private individuals who had grain milled for personal use). Millers themselves were forbidden from producing flour on their own account and from trading in flour. Thus, the baker paid the miller his fee and in addition paid, or demonstrated by written document that he already had paid, the applicable tax. The new milling excise of 1574 was set at 3 guilders per last of wheat and 1.5 guilders per last of rye.

At the outset, the milling excise was a minor source of public revenue and represented a modest addition to the cost of bread.[27] It added about 1.5 to 2.0 percent to the baker's grain cost. The procedures used to set bread prices made no provision to add these costs to the calculation of bread prices; bakers were expected to absorb this new cost together with all their other non-grain costs in the old system manner described in Chapter 1.

But what began as a small levy gradually grew larger. In 1579 when seven Low Countries provinces joined together in the "Union of Utrecht" to form what would become known as the United Provinces of the Netherlands, they resolved to defend themselves by raising a common tax – known as the *gemene middelen* or common means – for the purpose of financing their war effort. These taxes were the excises Holland had already been levying, including the milling excise. The Union of Utrecht issued an ordinance setting a common rate of 5 guilders per last for wheat and 1.5 guilders per last for rye.[28] In fact, this milling excise was never levied at the same rate across the Republic's provinces, but they all proceeded to introduce such a tax.[29]

The excises proved to be a flexible device to tap into the market-based consumption of Holland's growing urban population. Over time,

---

[26] Manon van der Heijden, *Geldschieters van de stad. Financiële relaties tussen stad, burgers en overheden, 1550–1650* (Amsterdam: Bert Bakker, 2006), pp. 95–96.

[27] James C. Tracy, "Holland's new fiscal regime, 1572–1576," in Oscar Gelderblom, ed., *The Political Economy of the Dutch Republic* (Farnham, Surrey: Ashgate, 2009), pp. 44–45.

[28] *GPB van Utrecht*, vol. II, p. 725. Ordonnantie van de Geünierde Provintieën, 1579.

[29] A set of common means excises, always including the milling excise, were introduced in Holland in 1574, in Zeeland in 1576, and in Utrecht in 1578. Gelderland and Groningen introduced them in the 1590s, Overijssel in 1601, and Friesland, definitively, in 1602.

new goods became subject to an excise and the rates were repeatedly increased. In 1574 the States of Holland hoped to raise 540,000 guilders via its new excises; by 1578 those excises raised 818,000 guilders. By 1586 this had risen to 1.5 million guilders, and by 1599, to at least 2.7 million.[30] Holland raised its milling excise faster than the average of its other excises: it was doubled in 1583, and doubled again in 1597. That is: the excise on a last of rye rose from 1.5 guilders to 3 guilders in 1583, and to 6 guilders in 1597. The tax on wheat was always double the tax on rye.

By the end of the sixteenth century Holland's milling excise added approximately 6 to 8 percent to the cost of rye and 8 to 10 percent to the cost of the wheat that entered into the production of bread. The other provinces followed the same general course as Holland, as can be seen in Table 3.2.

An important characteristic of the common means in general and the milling excise in particular was its broad base. Its focus on basic necessities touched very nearly everyone, and these were taxes that needed to be paid in ready money. Early ordinances emphasized the broad embrace of the milling excise with an expansive phrasing: The Union of Utrecht's ordinance specified that "No one is exempt, be he banner lord, noble or commoner, clergy or layman, or whatsoever he may be, excepting only hospitals, leper houses and houses of charity."[31]

With the common means the state had identified a powerful instrument for raising revenue on a wide and expandable range of basic commodities from a broad base of taxpayers that excluded only the indigent. The details of these taxes were now to be defined by the provinces separately,

Table 3.2 *Provincial excise taxes, per last of grain, c. 1600 (guilders per last)*

		Wheat	Rye	Barley	Buckwheat
Holland	1597	12	6		
Utrecht (city)	1601	13.75	5		
Friesland	1602	21.6	5.4	1.8	1.8
Overijssel	1597	6.75	2.7	2.7	2.7
Groningen	1602	6.00	3.00	2.00	
States Brabant	1580	n/a	4.00		

[30] R. Liesker and Wantje Fritschy, *Gewestilijke financiën ten tijde van de Republiek der Verenigde Nederlanden. Holland, 1572–1795,* vol. V (The Hague: Instituut voor Nederlandse Geschiedenis, 2004; hereafter *GWF – Holland*), p. 160.
[31] *GPB van Utrecht,* vol. II, p. 725. The wording in Holland's ordinance of 1597 is similar: No one is exempt, whether noble or commoner, or whatever state, quality or condition he may be, excepting only the Mint of Dordrecht, the hospitals, leper houses, and houses of charity and other houses for the poor that are sustained by alms. *GPB van Holland,* vol. I, 20 October 1597, p. 1769.

a necessary concession to the heterogeneity of the commercial life of the provinces at that time, but every province levied a broad range of excises, and in all of them the excise on milled grain, *het gemaal*, figured prominently. What was effectively a tax on bread is central to the entire history of Dutch bread price regulation, and we will devote more attention to it in later chapters, especially in Chapter 5. Here, it is sufficient to know that by the last decade of the sixteenth century this tax was emerging as a significant factor in the cost of bread.

Holland's plan to double the milling tax in 1597 may not have been known with certainty by the first town magistrates to introduce the new system of bread price regulation. But they must have recognized that the milling excise would, in time, lead to endless problems with the bakers' guilds unless some means was devised to remove this burden from the general revenues of the bakers and incorporate its cost explicitly into the official bread prices.

Thus, the excise on milled grain, and the expectation that it would be raised over time, was, I believe, the second catalyst to reform. By introducing the new system of price regulation, with its clear distinction of constant costs (such as the milling excise) and variable costs, the magistrates removed a source of friction with the bakers and established a mechanism by which this tax could be incorporated directly into the price of every type of bread. This set the stage for a fiscal policy unique to early modern Europe: the heavy taxation of "the staff of life."

Implementation of the New System

Once the Republic's magistrates broke with tradition and established their new system, they faced the task of developing administrative procedures that would be up to the task of administering it on a week-by-week basis. If the old system relied primarily on rules of thumb and direct relationships between grain and bread prices, the new system would require elaborate and continuous information gathering, recordkeeping, and monitoring. Moreover, the bread price commissioners found soon enough that however much the new system demystified bread pricing and established a rational basis for price regulation, they could never hope to remove their function entirely from the realm of debate and controversy. The "economics of regulation" is invariably enveloped in the larger terrain of political economy. Every one of the commissioners' tasks, even the most prosaic, involved some element of discretion and judgment and had the potential to spark controversy. Here we will consider these tasks one by one as they were carried out for more than 250 years in the dozens of price-setting cities that dotted the Netherlands.

We can begin by considering Figure 3.2, which offers a graphic representation of new system price/weight schedules. The equations that determine the position and slope (or curvature) of the graphs also describe fully every Dutch price or weight table ever developed under the new system. They depend on two elements which it was the sworn duty of the bread price commissioners to define on the basis of careful observation and measurement: the amount of the *constant costs* legitimately incurred by bakers in transforming a unit of grain into bread, and

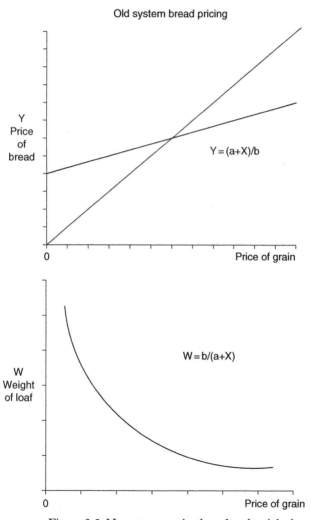

Figure 3.2 New system price-based and weight-based schedules

the *amount of bread* (the bread yield) produced by the milling and baking of a volume measure of grain. Those two factors uniquely determined the price of bread *for any given price of grain*, and can be represented in the equation:

$$Y = (a + X)/b$$

Where Y = the price of a loaf of bread of fixed weight

a = the constant costs per unit of grain
b = the number of loaves of a given weight per unit of grain
X = the price of a unit of grain

The weight-based formula, displayed in panel b of Figure 3.2, is:

$$W = b/(a + X)$$

Where W = the weight of a loaf of bread of fixed price

a = the constant costs per unit of grain
b = the weight of bread produced from a unit of grain
X = the price of a unit of grain

A visual display of the effects of the two factors is more complex in the case of the reciprocal equation, but when it is recalled that W is simply the inverse of Y in the earlier equation, it will be apparent that the issues are no different.

The bread price commissioners had three distinguishable tasks: to determine X, the "prevailing price" of the bread grains, wheat and rye, in the relevant markets; to measure a, the constant costs incurred by bakers in transforming grain into bread; and to settle on b, the amount of bread the bakers could extract from a measure of grain. For the first task they met weekly; for the second and third they met less frequently, often only after the passage of many years. But revising a and b required the assembly of a great deal of information, much of which the bakers regarded as proprietary – what they would have called the "mysteries" of their craft.

The *burgemeesters* of the Dutch towns usually appointed a commission of *broodzetters* or *broodwegers* [bread price setters or bread weighers] to act as their representatives. The appointees were burghers close to the regental families of the towns sometimes supplemented by representatives of the bakers' guild. They met weekly (the Amsterdam commissioners convened every Saturday at 2 pm at the town hall) to determine the prevailing prices of wheat and rye, consult the price schedules then in force, and announce and publicize the new bread prices. They posted the price lists at various public places: in Amsterdam at the *Oude Kerk, Nieuwe Kerk, Stadhuis,* and *Korenbeurs* (the Old and New Churches, the largest in the city, the town hall and the Grain Exchange).[32] In Leiden, the commissioners met on Tuesdays before 1 pm to set prices that would go into effect the following day at noon. They posted the prices at the *Raadhuis*, the *St. Pieters Kerk, Pancras Kerk, Vrouwen Kerk*, and *Saaihal* (the town hall, three churches, and the Cloth Hall, the economic heart of this textile town).[33] In The Hague, the ordinance of 1669 ordered the commissioners to post a signed announcement of prices at the town hall ever Monday morning.[34] Alkmaar also posted prices weekly, but went further, dispatching a boy to run past every bakery so that no baker could plead ignorance of the latest price change.[35] In 1689 Amsterdam took a similar step, distributing the weekly price announcements to every baker, who was now obliged to post this information in a conspicuous place in his shop.[36] Utrecht announced new prices every Saturday. The 1626 ordinance governing its bakers' guild stipulated that the newly announced prices would become effective on Sunday mornings. Until then the bakers were obligated to continue selling bread at the previous week's price. They faced severe penalties for withholding bread in this time interval.[37]

Determining the Market Price of Grain: Setting X

How did the commissioners determine the "prevailing price" of wheat and rye? Amsterdam was known throughout the seventeenth and eighteenth centuries as "the granary of Europe"; the inventories of grain stored in its warehouses were available for shipment to wherever local market conditions made this profitable, and, as a consequence, its grain prices were highly correlated with many other markets.[38] One might suppose, then, that monitoring the price of grain would be among the

[32] *Handvesten van Amsterdam* (Amsterdam, 1748), Ordonnantie voor de Brootwegers, M fol. 179, 24 Dec. 1653, pp. 882–92.

[33] G.A. Leiden, Stadsarchief tot 1816, no. 2550, "Rapport omtrent broodzetting en maalloon, 1803." The report states that these posting requirements had been in effect since 1596.

[34] G.A. Den Haag, Oud Archief, no. 5741 Ordonnatiën, publicatiën en andere stukken. 5 Okt 1669, "Ordonnatie op het broodbakken." "From now on, a signed poster will be displayed at the town hall every Monday."

[35] G.A. Alkmaar, Stadsarchief voor 1815, no. 1969, "Ordonnantie op het bakken."

[36] A. J. M. Brouwer Ancher, *De Gilden* (The Hague: Loman en Funke, 1895) pp. 150–51.

[37] G.A. Utrecht, Stadsarchief, no. 461, deel 1, no. 8. "Backergilde ordonnantie," 30 October 1626, article XXXVI. *GPB van Utrecht*, vol. III, p. 789.

[38] W. Achilles, "Getreidepreise und Getreidehandelsbeziehungen europäischer Räume im 16 und 17 Jahrhundert," *Zeitschrift für Agrargeschichte und Agrarsoziologie* (1959), 32–55; Persson, *Grain Markets in Europe*; Robert Allen and Richard Unger, "The depth and breadth of the market for Polish grain, 1500–1800," in J. Ph. S. Lemmink *et al.*, eds., *Baltic Affairs* (Nijmegen: Institute for Northern and Eastern European Studies, 1990), pp. 1–18.

simpler tasks of the Dutch regulators. In fact, this task presented several challenges, as will become apparent as we consider separately the market structures of the two major bread grains, rye and wheat.

Rye from the Baltic region, usually identified as Prussian rye, was Amsterdam's biggest grain import by far, and much of it was distributed from Amsterdam to towns and villages throughout the maritime zone of the Dutch Republic. Consequently, throughout this region and beyond, the price of Prussian rye on the Amsterdam Grain Exchange was determinative. Nearby Haarlem, for example, stated that its rye price "is always based on Prussian and Danziger rye" while Leiden and Delft received weekly reports on the Amsterdam rye market from a correspondent. Delft's bread regulation instructions of 1640 stated directly that rye bread "is regulated absolutely and simply according to the price in Amsterdam." Dordrecht, likewise, specified in 1709 that its rye prices were based on the Amsterdam market for Prussian rye.[39] Indeed, this was the case in all the cities of Holland, and is confirmed by the high correlation of rye bread prices among these cities discussed in Chapter 6.

But as soon as one moves inland a short distance, the question of which market to consult becomes more complicated. Very little rye was grown in the western regions of the Republic, but in the eastern provinces rye was the dominant bread grain. Thus, in its 1626 baking trials Utrecht specified the use of *Stichtsche rogge* (rye from the province of Utrecht – known from its earlier history as an ecclesiastical polity as *Het Sticht*). It used local rye in later trials as well, but also referred to *bovenlandsche rogge* (rye from "the lands above" – the higher-lying lands to the east, including neighboring German lands).[40] Further east, in Nijmegen, the magistrates stipulated in 1601 that the market price of rye would be determined by "*hierlandschen en overmaeschen rogh*," or rye from the region around the

---

[39] G.A. Haaarlem, Gewestelijk bestuur, no. 587, 1807 report; G.A. Delft, Stadsarchief voor 1795, no. 980. Broodzettingsboek; G.A. Leiden, no. 2536 Broodzettingsregister, p. viii. In its first entry, for 9 December 1596, one reads, "First, in setting (grain prices) he was required to follow exactly the price setting of Amsterdam, where Pieter Stevensz, broker, was tasked to record the market [prices], which he did beginning on 1 April 1596." G.A. Dordrecht, no. 4763. Alkmaar: Noordegraaf, "Levensstandaard," p. 96, fn. 11. Noordegraaf found only two (possibly three) occasions between 1596 and 1815 when the magistrates of Alkmaar found reason not to follow Amsterdam's lead in this matter.

[40] G.A. Utrecht, no. 2025. Aantekeningen van genomen bakproeven, 1601–1653. 11 Maart 1626. In 1672, when a French army of invasion had entered the city, the magistrates announced price controls on grain. The proclamation distinguished the following sorts of wheat: local (*stichtsche*), eastern (*bovenlandsche*), and coastal (*voorlandsche*), from Zeeland and Holland. The types of rye were: local (*hierlandsche*) and Prussian (*Pruyse*), supplied from the Amsterdam market. These price controls made further distinctions between new and old grain stocks (current harvest and inventoried grain from a previous harvest). *GPB van Utrecht*, vol. III, 17 December 1672.

city and from across the river Maas, in the German borderlands.[41] To the north, in Groningen, the magistrates instructed that the rye price be "computed from the market reports (*marktbrieven*) of foreign (Baltic) rye together with *Hooglandsche*, and *Drentsche rogge* (rye from nearby Drenthe and German lands)," brought to the Groningen markets.[42] Thus, in normal times the orbit of Amsterdam's rye shipments did not extend far beyond Holland, while, to the east, the provincial towns were supplied by locally produced rye and by rye coming downstream from rural areas of the Republic and the German lands. Year-by-year, the supply zones shifted, and the price regulators periodically redefined which rye – local, eastern, or Baltic – should be preferred for defining the prevailing price.

Wheat presents us with a rather different story. At the same time that Holland's cities looked to Amsterdam for guidance on rye prices, they usually looked in a different direction for information about wheat prices. In the fifteenth and sixteenth centuries, the Delft market played the leading role in supplying Holland with wheat, which came from the Zeeland islands and further south, especially the French provinces of Artois and Picardy.[43] The importance of the Delft market had already declined before the mid-sixteenth-century introduction of Baltic wheat via Amsterdam. But Delft continued to play a role in wheat trading, if not as a physical market. The Haarlem price registers contain a marginal comment concerning an error in pricing in 1636 that blames it on "the error of our correspondent Jan Willemsz van Stenenbergh in Delft." Thus, they still drew their wheat market information from Delft. But in 1657 one finds the following marginal notation: "Now the market [price] is from Rotterdam, because there is, indeed, no longer a market in Delft."[44] Rotterdam – not Amsterdam – had assumed the role of primary wheat market much earlier than 1657. In 1640 even the Delft regulators had announced that "with regard to wheat bread, we regulate simply according to the [loaf] weight in Rotterdam." The Hague later declared that "The rise and fall of the bread [price] is regulated following [the example of] Delft, and both cities [Delft and The Hague] base themselves on the Rotterdam grain market ... " In 1803 a report on Leiden's bread pricing regime noted that "Leiden generally follows the Rotterdam market for wheat bread and the Amsterdam market for rye bread."[45]

[41] G.A. Nijmegen, Oud Archief, no. 3113, Politie Boeck der Stadt Nijmegen. 9 December 1601.

[42] G.A. Groningen, Oud Archief, no. 394. 6 May 1771.

[43] Van Tielhof, *De Hollandse graanhandel*, pp. 12–14.

[44] G.A. Haarlem, Archief der Stad, R 412–417, Broodzettingregisters, 1611–1795. 6 October 1636; 19 March 1657

[45] G.A. Delft, Stadsarchief voor 1795, no 980; G.A. Den Haag, Oud Archief, no. 5780, Report on the *broodzetting c.* 1780; G.A. Leiden, no. 2550, 1803 report.

The prices for rye of different origins did not differ greatly, but wheat differed considerably in price – from 10 to 20 percent – because of perceived quality differences, and this brings us to a second decision the commissioners faced. In deciding which type of wheat to use in setting prices, the commissioners were also making decisions about the quality of the wheat bread produced in their towns. In 1659 the Haarlem bread price commissioners stipulated that the governing wheat price would be an average of three market prices: that for Polish, Stettin, and Cleves wheat. The first two were from the Baltic, the third was a *bovenland* wheat, from the German borderlands.[46]

It is curious that the commissioners made no mention of Zeeland wheat despite the fact that we have already noted Haarlem's 1657 decision to seek its wheat price information from Rotterdam, where Zeeland wheat was sold. The resolution of this archival puzzle is, I believe, the following: the Baltic and German wheat was used to produce the luxurious wheat bread, bolted white bread; Zeeland wheat was then used exclusively to produce the coarser wheat bread. This explains why the wheat price for the coarse loaf was always expressed in schellingen, the Flemish monetary unit that remained customary in Zeeland price notations, while the wheat price for the luxury bread was expressed in gold guilders, the monetary unit used for large-scale grain transactions at the Amsterdam market.[47] The eighteenth-century records are consistent with this explanation. Then, the bread price registers routinely identify the coarse wheat bread as made from Zeeland wheat and the luxury bread (*fijn luchtig wittebrood*) as made from Polish wheat. A middle-quality bread was made from half-Zeeland half-Polish wheat.[48]

In 1807, as the Batavian regime began implementing major changes to the regulatory system, the Haarlem bread price commissioners were asked to draft a report justifying their policies. They used the opportunity to provide the new reform-minded government with some historical background. Wheat bread, they explained, was once based on the price of Polish wheat. Later, Polish and Zeeland wheat were both used, and now it has been determined that the wheat price should be an average of Polish, Zeeland, and *bovenland* (German) wheat. The commissioners explained

---

[46] G.A. Haarlem, Gildenarchief, no. 2068. The document refers to "*Poolse, Statynse en Kleefse tarwe.*"

[47] G.A. Haarlem, S.A. 1581–1795, Broodzettingsregisters, II 1930a (R 412–417)

[48] A similar "division of labor" appears in the baking trials conducted in Utrecht, at least through the first half of the seventeenth century. The wheat for fine, bolted bread is measured by the Amsterdam *mud*, suggesting it was Polish wheat bought on the Amsterdam market, while the wheat used in making the coarse, unbolted bread is measured by the Utrecht *mud* suggesting that it was drawn from local sources. G.A. Utrecht, no. 2025.

that they had long followed Amsterdam practice, but recently had come to the conclusion that by using a mix of equal parts of the wheat from these three regions the bakers could produce bread of an acceptable quality at a price lower than that prevailing in Amsterdam. According to their example, the price difference was about 7 percent. They went on to state that Leiden and Rotterdam had long based their wheat price entirely on wheat from Zeeland and Germany (i.e., no Baltic wheat), and that their wheat breads were even cheaper than in Haarlem.[49] This is confirmed for Leiden by its own report on their bread price regulations, drafted in 1803. The Leiden commissioners reported that they generally follow the Rotterdam grain market for wheat bread and the Amsterdam prices for rye bread. The city reported using Prussian rye and Zeeland wheat.[50]

Determining the "prevailing price" for the grains that went into the bread loaves purchased and consumed by the Dutch public was not the straightforward affair it might have been in less commercialized regions of Europe. The commissioners had choices to make, and could be misled in any number of ways about which market prices were truly representative.[51] But this task was at least a familiar one, one that also had preoccupied their predecessors under the old system. When they turned to their new tasks – defining the yield rate and the constant costs of bread production – they entered into unfamiliar terrain and needed new methods to fulfill their new responsibilities.

The Baking Trial (Bakproef)

The bread price commissioners met to set the official grain prices every week. They gathered much less frequently to establish the constant costs of bread production. When they did so, often only after repeated

---

[49] G.A. Haarlem, Gewestelijk bestuur, no. 587.
[50] G.A. Leiden, no. 2550, Report of 1803.
[51] An ongoing concern of price commissioners, especially in provincial markets, was the problem of outliers. The market masters reported the transactions, yielding a range of prices that sometimes included a few very high or very low prices. This could lead the correspondents on whom the commissioners relied to report distorted calculations of the *middelmarkt*, or median market price. The bakers were most concerned with very low prices, of course, and often complained that such price notations referred to low quality grain suitable only for animal fodder. The commissioners often suspected the correspondents of conspiring with the bakers to inflate "prevailing" market prices. The bakers' complaints are discussed in W. Tijms, *Groninger graanprijzen: de prijzen van agrarische producten tussen 1546 en 1990. Historia Agriculturae* 31 (2000), 209. The commissioners' suspicions are voiced without reservation in Leiden's 1803 report on the overall operation of the regulatory system: "We must add here that the grain brokers, who have a strong interest in the welfare of the bakers, always convey the very highest market prices to the city governments, and that the true market for the high-quality wheat is always one or two schellingen lower, which profits the baker." G.A. Leiden, no. 2550.

requests from the bakers' guild imploring them to adjust these costs to reflect altered circumstances, they began their deliberations by ordering a baking trial, or *bakproef*. The commissioners met with representatives of the bakers, usually on "neutral ground" – the ovens of a municipal institution, such as an orphanage or hospital. There, a measure of grain was prepared and baked in the presence of the commissioners, who took careful notes of the proceedings.

The resulting documents reporting on these baking trials make for interesting reading. They take the form of "laboratory reports," recording the results of each step of the milling and baking process. These baking trials represented efforts to "demystify" the baker's craft, indeed, to turn an art into a science. The bakers, of course, could always protest that such baking trials were artificial, unrepresentative, and unrealistic – and they often did so. But throughout the long life of the new system *broodzetting* the commissioners never ceased to rely on them for guidance in revising the coefficients of the equations on which the bread prices rested. Specifically, they relied on the baking trials to determine the yield rate and the constant costs.

The Yield Rate: Setting *b*

The yield rate is the amount of bread of a given type that can be baked from a volume measure of grain, and conflict over this rate became the first test of the new system's integrity. As we have seen, a deliberate understatement of the true yield rate stood at the heart of the old system; the new system sought to replace this indirect manner of compensating bakers for their production costs with a defined monetary provision: the bakers' fee, or *bakloon*. Thus, it sought to replace an understated yield rate (which generated "advantage loaves") with an accurate assessment of the constant costs.

But, just how much bread could a measure of grain reliably be expected to yield? What about failed bakings and other wastage? What about light grain harvests and sub-standard grain? The bakers had many arguments in support of their view that the yield ratio used for price setting should be well below the theoretical limit; the commissioners countered with baking trials whereby they sought to determine the truth of the matter via careful observation of the baking process in a controlled environment.[52]

---

[52] In ordering an early baking trial in 1604 the Utrecht commissioners stated it was their intention "to study how much each grain type will produce in order thereby to instruct the bakers every week as to the proper price." G.A Utrecht, Oud Archief, no. 2023, Rijdingsboek.

Leiden. The Leiden bread price account book, or *broodzettingregister*, recorded the official prices of bread, week-by-week, begininning on 8/9 December 1596. It devoted its first page to a *Staet dienende tot de broot-settinghe*, a "table to serve in setting the bread price," which offers us a glimpse into the earliest efforts to define the rules under which bread prices would henceforth be set.[53] This table carefully lists all constant costs associated with the transformation of a last of rye into bread, which included the cost of buying, measuring, transporting, and storing the grain, the municipal and provincial excise taxes, fuel cost, a milling fee, and a baking fee. The commissioners reckoned all these costs to total 41.29 guilders per last of rye. The commissioners then set an assumed rye price (154 guilders per last) and went on to calculate the price of a six-pound loaf under two assumptions about the number of such loaves that could be secured from a last of rye: 924 and 968.

We must pause here for a moment. In taking this step, Leiden's commissioners were departing for the first time from a foundational assumption of all old system price regulation. We are present here at the dawn of the new system and, unsurprisingly, the commissioners acted with some hesitation, in the knowledge that a hostile reception from the bakers' guild was sure to await them.

Brief Technical Excursus: The Bread Yield

The bread yield can be a confusing topic. Some of the confusion can be dispelled by making a distinction between the "natural" yield – or the maximum extraction rate of bread from grain – which we might regard as a ceiling on what is attainable, and the yield rates established by policy, intended to guide pricing decisions.

How much bread, expressed by weight, can be produced from a given volume of grain? The first step is to observe the weight of the grain, or its specific gravity. The weight of a liter of wheat could vary from year to year, depending on the state of the harvest. Overall, the weight of the bread grains fluctuated around a fairly steady level, showing no long-term increase until the early nineteenth century,[54] but short-term changes in harvest conditions sometimes led the bakers to petition the commissioners for compensatory adjustments to their pricing policy.[55]

---

[53] The discussion that follows is based on: G.A. Leiden, Stadsarchief 1575–1816, Secretarie archief no. 2536.

[54] G.A. Leiden, Stadsarchief tot 1816, no. 2550. Leiden's 1803 report compares recent, higher, grain weights with those prevailing in earlier times.

[55] At least one city, Utrecht – which held its bakers to a high yield rate and also depended more than the cities of Holland on local grain harvests – attempted to adjust official

Table 3.3 *Weight of grains, or specific gravity*
(weight in kg per 100 liters of grain)

	Rye	Wheat
Seventeenth–eighteenth-century observations	69–74	72–78
1826 survey: eastern provinces	70–72	72–74
western provinces	72–74	75–76
1800–50 average	72	75
Average weight of a last of grain	2,100–2,200	2,250–2,325

The next step is to determine how much bread can be baked from a given weight of grain. This could be affected by milling technology and, especially for wheat, by the specific types of bread most in demand. The bread-to-grain ratios revealed by baking trials and surveys of local practice fall mostly within a relatively narrow range throughout the seventeenth and eighteenth centuries. After 1800 they are mostly higher, probably reflecting some combination of changed milling technique (securing more usable flour per pound of grain) and bread-quality deterioration (other things remaining equal, bread quality falls as the bread yield rises).[56]

bread price schedules to variations in the weight of grain. In 1653 the magistrates took this step in order to put an end to constant bickering with the bakers. The Utrecht city council [*Vroedschap*] explained the problem as follows: "Every year much effort and expense is taken in conducting baking trials, and yet there are always difficulties with one thing or another, even when conditions are favorable. Moreover, [we have] discovered in the notations of the bread price book that since 1600 wheat has never weighed as much as 200 pounds [per *mud*] nor ever less than 182 pounds. Therefore, the magistrates have agreed to the drafting of a permanent table, consisting of three price schedules, which will guide the setting of bread prices from year to year: for 185 pounds, or 190 pounds, or 195 pounds. Each year the wheat will be weighted to determine which one of these lists will be followed." Thus the Utrecht commissioners took on the added task of establishing every year an average weight for the standard volume measure of wheat, and then consulting the appropriate table for the weekly determination of the bread price/weight. The commissioners noted with some irritation that these annual differences rarely amounted to much, but tracking them seemed to be the price for maintaining peace with the bakers. G. A. Utrecht, Stadsarchief III, no. 2023 Rijdingboek, 1599–1818. Vroedschapsresolutie van 12 April 1653.

[56] According to Collins, "it seems probable that in north-west Europe baking quality deteriorated during the Agricultural Revolution [late eighteenth – early nineteenth centuries] with the switch to more prolific varieties [of wheat], higher in starch but lower in gluten than the older varieties." Collins, "Why wheat?," p. 30. The development of milling techniques may also have played a role. A more thorough grinding (and regrinding) process yielded a flour that incorporated the previously separated *kortmeel* (middlings). This innovation was called "economic milling" in France, and is discussed in some detail in Kaplan, *Provisioning Paris*, pp. 393–465.

Table 3.4 *Bread yield ratios, 1597–1850*
a. Yield ratios for types of wheat bread (kg bread per kg wheat)

		Unbolted wheat	Bolted coarse	Bolted fine	Bolted white
Amsterdam–Haarlem	1597–1676			0.89–0.98*	
Kampen	1606			0.97–1.08*	
Arnhem	1625–1720				0.72
Deventer	1629				0.69
Goes	1632	1.31	1.06	0.90	0.73
Utrecht	1640	1.27			0.65
Utrecht	1653	1.30			0.71
Nijmegen	1693–99		1.07		
Deventer	1784				0.75
Zwolle	1785				0.68
Leiden	1803	1.20	0.99		0.75
Holland	1826		0.95		
Amsterdam	1847	1.20–1.38			0.75
Netherlands	1800–50	1.24		1.00–1.04	0.78

*Yield for a varying mixture of coarse and fine bolted breads.

b. Yield ratios for basic rye bread (kg bread per kg of rye)

		Rye bread
Deventer	1597	1.23
Goes	1622	1.28
Utrecht	1626	1.26
Deventer	1639	1.28
Amsterdam BWH	1793	1.31
Holland	1790	1.31
Amsterdam BWH	1816	1.45
Holland	1826	1.39
Netherlands	1800–50	1.43

On the basis of the data summarized in Tables 3.3 and 3.4, the follow-ing grain weights and bread yields *per last* are used in this study. Slightly different figures are used for the period after 1800, reflecting slightly higher average wheat weights per unit of volume, and increased bread yields per kg of grain.

This overview of bread yields helps put in perspective the issue facing the magistrates and bakers as they implemented the new system. To return to Leiden's pioneer efforts of 1596: Leiden's magistrates began

Table 3.5 *Average yield rates for the period 1596–1800*

1 last grain	Rye	Wheat
Volume	3,003 liters	3,003 liters
Weight grain	2,100 kg (0.70)	2,300 kg (0.766)
Weight bread	2,900 kg (1.38)	2,900 kg (1.26) unbolted
		2,438 kg (1.06) bolted wheat
		2,070 kg (0.90) fine wheat
		1,679 kg (0.73) white bread
Average yield rates used in this study for the period 1800–50		
1 last grain (= 30 hl)		
Volume	3,000 liters	3,000 liters
Weight grain	2,100 kg (0.700)	2,340 kg (0.780)
Weight bread	3,000 kg (1.430)	3,000 kg (1.282) unbolted
		2,340 kg (1.00) bolted wheat
		2,035 kg (0.87) white bread*

*By 1800 the finest white bread in most places had become a less luxurious commodity than it had been earlier. It probably more resembled the "fine wheat bread" category that tended to fall into disuse in the late eighteenth century.

by calculating bread prices using two different estimations of b, the bread yield, 968 six-pound loaves and 924 loaves. The first (968 loaves = 5,808 pounds per last = 2,798 kg of rye bread) came fairly close to the limit of the realistically achievable. The second was significantly more lenient (924 loaves = 5,544 pounds per last = 2,671 kg of rye bread), and would certainly have been preferred by the bakers. Perhaps the high yield standard was proposed as an opening bid, or bargaining chip. We are not told how this debate unfolded, but in the end the regulators split the difference with the bakers, setting the official bread output at 946 6-pound loaves (2,734 kg), and went on to calculate the rye bread price schedule accordingly: the price of a 6-pound loaf (Y) would be:

Y = [f. 154.00 (110 gold guilders, the assumed grain price per last) + f. 41.29 (the constant cost)] / 946.

They then repeated this calculation for every gold guilder increase or decrease in the price of a last of rye,[57] calculating the bread price to a fraction of a penning. Thus, at a grain price of 140 guilders per last (100 gold guilders), the total cost would be fl 181 5 st 13 penn. Cast in penningen (16 penn. = 1 st) and divided by the number of pounds of bread to be

[57] The "gold guilder" (*goudgulden*) consisted of 28 stuivers in contrast to the standard *carolusgulden*'s 20 stuivers. It was the customary monetary unit for large-scale grain transactions. Grain prices in this study are converted to standard unit of account, the guilder of 20 stuivers.

derived from a last (946 × 6 = 5,676 pounds per last), they determined that the correct price for a pound of bread would be 10 1253/5676 penn. and a 6-pound loaf would thus cost 3 st 13 1846/5676 penn.

All of this detail was necessary, I suspect, in order to assist the magistrates in making decisions about the minimum change in the grain price that would trigger a revision of the bread price. Too large an interval, and bakers might enjoy undue profits (or suffer losses) as grain prices fluctuated within the band without any change in the bread price; too small an interval and the bread price would be changed constantly and by amounts too small to be accommodated by the smallest available coins (recall that the smallest coin, the *duit*, equaled 2 penningen). In the event, Leiden developed a price schedule that responded very sensitively to changing grain prices through the expedient of doubling the size of the rye bread loaf for which official prices would be set. The standard loaf was now set at 12 pounds. This mega-loaf could be adjusted in price by a single *duit* (2 penningen) for every 2.80 guilders (2 gold guilders) rise or fall in the cost of a last of rye. At price levels then prevailing, a grain price change of about 2 percent was sufficient to trigger a revision in the bread price.[58]

The Leiden commissioners found themselves very busy with their initial new system bread price schedule. They issued a new price for rye bread in 109 of the 159 weeks between December 1596 and the end of 1599. Often a small increase in one week was reversed the following week. In addition, in this same three-year period they felt pressure to adjust their calculation of constant costs six times, even though the cumulative increase of all these adjustments amounted to only a 7.4 percent increase in these costs. Each of these revisions required the drafting of a new price schedule.

Underlying the unceasing pressure from the bakers to increase the constant costs was their continuing dissatisfaction with the yield rate. The magistrates had initially decided to calculate bread prices on an assumption that bakers could extract 946 6-pound loaves of rye bread. This number reflected a concession to the bakers (their opening bid had been 964 loaves), but five months after the inauguration of new system pricing the magistrates yielded ground again, setting a still lower standard of 924 loaves per last (or 21 loaves per sack).

But then, almost immediately, the city's magistrates returned to the offensive. Rising grain prices created a crisis atmosphere that forced them to consider costly measures to alleviate distress. They ordered the commissioners to hold new baking trials in order to take another look at

---

[58] Consumers retained the ability to buy rye bread in 6-pound and even 3-pound loaves, paying proportionately. For these smaller loaves, the small change problem reasserted itself, of course. For more on how this problem was handled in practice, see Chapter 4.

the question of bread yield. Three bakers, identified as Gerrit, Thunnes, and Herman, were observed to produce between 22 and 22.5 6-pound loaves per sack of grain. These results (equal to 968 and 990 loaves per last, respectively) strengthened the magistrates' resolve to return to their original 968 loaf standard. The commissioners incorporated this standard into their next revision of constant costs, which, of course, reduced the price per loaf across the board, at every grain price. The new level of bread output comes fairly close to the maximum amount of rye bread that can be extracted from a last of average-quality grain. It left only a small margin for error and must have become a source of profound unhappiness among the bakers.

By 1599 the magistrates – tiring of the constant redrafting of the bread price schedules – allowed themselves to be persuaded that their decision of two years earlier had been excessive, and, in a significant concession to the bakers, they based their next revision of the price schedule on the much lower standard of 896 6-pound loaves per last (5,376 pounds per last, or 2,590 kg). This decision (taken as grain prices were falling) had the effect of raising the price per loaf across the board, and gave the bakers a generous margin for profitable "error." The new schedules required less frequent adjustments to changing grain prices, and the schedules themselves were altered at longer intervals. Clearly, the magistrates and commissioners had gone through a learning process in which they made several concessions to the bakers and to practicality.

Kampen. Leiden was not alone in struggling to make the new system both tolerable to the bakers and practical in its week-by-week implementation. The small port city of Kampen, at the mouth of the IJssel River, launched its new system around 1600 with a schedule of rye bread prices that expected bakers to extract 5,832 pounds (2,881 kg) from a last of grain.[59] Kampen divided the last into 108 *schepel*, each of which was to yield 54 pounds of rye bread. Almost immediately the bakers complained that this was an unrealistically large amount and the commissioners, for their part, also found reason to be unhappy with the system they had just

[59] G.A. Kampen, Oudarchief, no. 2208, undated. The first *broodzetting* document introducing the "new system" to Kampen is, unfortunately, undated. It was certainly drafted before 1606 (when its provisions were superseded by a new schedule), and after 1597. In what follows, I date it as "*c.* 1600." In the preamble to each price schedule this founding document describes the underlying assumptions about the costs of baking bread with great precision, making explicit mention of a recent rise in production costs including the new excise tax on milled grain introduced by Overijssel in 1597. The "*c.*1600" document provided a full account of the arithmetic calculations required to set the bread prices under the new system based on the distinction of constant from variable costs, which supports my view that this approach was, indeed, new.

designed: it offered no simple way to adjust the price of a 12-pound loaf to changes in the grain price. Since the *schepel* yielded 4.50 such loaves, a one-stuiver (= 16 penningen) rise/fall in the *schepel* grain price would require a 16 penning/4.5 loaves = 3.6 penning rise/fall in the price of a 12-pound loaf. But, of course, the commissioners were constrained by the size of the smallest coin to alter the bread price in 2-penning increments. If they raised the price 2 *duiten* for every stuiver rise in the grain price, they would overcharge consumers. Their initial solution was to raise the bread price by 2 *duiten* the first four times the grain price rose by one stuiver and by one *duit* the fifth time, and then begin the cycle over again. In this way, the average rise of 3.6 penningen per stuiver in rye prices would be achieved over the course of a 5-stuiver increase in the *schepel* price of rye. This solution was mathematically correct, but ran into predictable problems in implementation. Just which price rise was the fifth one? Moreover, a 5-stuiver price rise per *schepel*, or 27 guilder rise per last, was substantial, and might occur only over many years – while consumers overpayed for their bread while waiting for the compensatory correction.

In 1606 Kampen replaced its original schedule with a new one that incorporated revisions that proved more workable – so workable that its principles remained in effect for nearly two centuries. It established the 6-pound loaf as the basis for price setting and reduced the bread yield expected from a *schepel* of rye by 11 percent, from nine loaves (of 6 pounds each) to eight. The estimation of 48 pounds of bread per *schepel* surely recommended itself less because of its accuracy (54 pounds was certainly closer to the true yield), than because it is neatly divisible by the 16 penningen of the stuiver. Every one-stuiver change in the price of a *schepel* of rye could now be covered by a one *duit* (2 penningen) change in the price of a 6-pound loaf.

The attentive reader will note, as the attentive burgher of Kampen surely would have done, that with this decision Kampen's magistrates made a strategic retreat. The yield rate they would now use in setting prices provided the bakers with an extra 6-pound loaf of bread for every *schepel* they baked, thereby supplementing the bakers' incomes with the revenue of 108 loaves for every last of grain they baked. These extra loaves, or *overbroden*, represented a slackening of the rigor of the new system. But the magistracy of Kampen then took one extra step, clawing back a portion of the windfall they had just conceded to the bakers: in exchange for the reduced yield rate, which left extra loaves for the benefit of the baker, Kampen's magistrates imposed a reduction of the constant costs (from 7.5 to 6 stuivers per *schepel* of grain) used in the calculation of bread price. This reduction removed 3 penningen (1.5 st = 24 penn.; 24 penn./8 loaves = 3 penn.) from the price of every 6-pound loaf, regardless of the price of grain.

One might say that what the magistrates gave to the bakers with one hand they took back with the other. Unfortunately for Kampen's consumers these two moves were not equal in their effects. The net result was an increase in the cost of rye bread at every likely price of grain.[60] The virtue of the new 1606 price schedule was not to be found in its accuracy, but rather in its arithmetic friendliness, yielding a simple rule for the adjustment of bread prices, and in offering plenty of "slack" for the bakers.

Utrecht. Not every city followed this downward course in adjusting the yield rate. Utrecht began in 1601 with a rather high 5,700 pounds-per-last standard which they adjusted upward in 1607 to 5,850. In 1613, for reasons that are not revealed, a new schedule reduced the yield rate significantly, to 5,432 pounds. But by 1630 Utrecht's magistrates reversed course again, approving a new price schedule that required the bakers to extract 6,000 pounds per last. This is as high a yield rate (2,987 kg) as one observes until the nineteenth century, and Utrecht stuck with it throughout the early modern era.[61]

Overall, the Republic's cities varied considerably in setting the yield rate. Arnhem joined Kampen and Leiden in allowing their bakers to extract less than 5,300 pounds of rye bread per last, while Utrecht, Nijmegen, Zwolle, Dordrecht, and Haarlem all expected at least 5,700 pounds. Cast in kilograms, the new system regulations set the "official" rye bread yield in a range of 2,600–2,940 kg per last, while the old system had based their prices on an assumed bread yield of 1,900–2,000 kg.

The Constant Costs: Setting *a*

The baking trials also supplied the information essential to carrying out the third and final task of the bread price commissioners: setting the level of constant costs. Actually, the constant costs signified by *a* in the new system bread price equation consisted of five distinct components:

The excise tax (provincial and municipal)
The millers' fee
Non-grain inputs (fuel, yeast, salt, oil, milk, etc.)
Sale of by-products (bran removed in the preparation of bolted wheat bread)
The bakers' fee (labor, rent, capital costs]

---

[60] For example, when a 6-pound loaf of rye bread cost 4 stuivers, the bakers could earn an additional 21.60 guilders per last (selling 108 extra loaves). For this they had conceded 8.10 guilders in the reduction of the bakers' fee.

[61] G.A. Utrecht, Oud Archief, no. 2023, Rijdingboek.

The first two components were not "discovered" via the baking trials: both were set by provincial and municipal magistrates independently.

Excise taxes. When the provincial states changed the excise tax and the town magistrates altered the municipal excise on milling (or added local surcharges, usually for the benefit of the poor), the bread price commissioners had no choice but to adjust their constant costs and recalculate their bread price schedules. From their perspective the milling excise was an exogenous fact, but for the public officials who turned repeatedly to this tax to raise public revenue, it was a policy decision of great importance. We will examine the evolving level of these taxes and consider just what motivated the Republic to burden the staff of life in this way in Chapter 5.

The millers' fee (*Het maalloon*). The millers performed their service for a monetary fee that was usually set by the city magistrates. One might suppose that the bread price commissioners would take charge of this along with their responsibilities for the bakers' fees and prices. Their advice and expertise were regularly sought, but setting the millers' fee was, it appears, too important for the magistrates to countenance its delegation.

The millers formed a corporate body whose number and income was of great concern to the authorities since milling was the stage of production at which the provinces and cities levied the excise tax. The fiscal importance of the milling sector led public authorities everywhere in the Republic to reserve for themselves decisions about their compensation. We will consider the milling sector in more detail in Chapter 7.

Non-grain inputs to the baking process and the sale of by-products. The baking trials supplied the commissioners with detailed information about the amounts and costs of fuel for the ovens and ingredients, mainly yeast, milk, salt, eggs, and oil, for the various types of bread. The cost of local transportation services (carrying sacks of grain to the bakery) were also taken into account. These were minor costs relative to the other categories of expense, but weighed more heavily on wheat bread, especially fine white bread, than on rye bread. Consequently, they were usually itemized with some care.

The baking trials also addressed the question of bran and other waste materials. Dutch millers ground the grain delivered to them by their customers, but it was the customers' task to sift out the bran and rough materials from this meal if they wished to bake with fine flour. Indeed, millers were forbidden from performing this task; they were enjoined to deliver back to their customers everything they had been given for milling. The bakers were, thus, the owners of bran that they were forbidden to mix with any other breads. They were expected to sell the bran, usually as animal feed, and the expected revenue from this sale was deducted from the bakers' constant costs. Some calculations of constant costs were rather sloppy, asserting with false confidence that the (unitemized) cost of ingredients was cancelled out by the (unspecified) income from the sale of bran, but most baking trials were quite specific, and careful to allocate these costs and revenues to the relevant types of bread. Table 3.6 offers an overview of these costs as summarized in a survey of municipal practices in 1826.

The bakers' fee (*Het bakloon*). By far the largest portion of the constant costs that were under the authority of the bread price commissioners was the bakers' fee, which was intended to compensate the baker for his labor costs and his equipment, buildings and other invested capital. Occasionally the constant costs distinguished labor costs *stricto senso* from the baker's capital costs and profit, but more commonly the bakers' fee was presented as a lump sum per unit of grain processed into bread. How did the commissioners go about setting this fee? The size of this cost component depended sensitively on the scale of bakery operations and could not be derived directly from the information generated by the baking trials. Important goals of the regulatory enterprise were involved in setting this fee, and they will be examined in detail in Chapter 8.

Table 3.6 *Cost of fuel and non-grain ingredients and the revenue gained from the sale of bran, 1826*

	Fuel	Yeast	Milk	Salt, eggs	Oil	Local transport	Total	Sale of bran
Rye bread, guilders per last of grain								
7 Holland cities	5.10	1.59	–	1.11	1.14	2.31	11.25	–
5 Holland towns	5.67	2.25	–	0.45	1.35	1.23	10.95	–
2 Utrecht cities	4.56	1.80	–	0.69	1.35	0.54	9.09	–
3 IJssel cities	2.58	–	–	0.99	–	0.57	4.14	–
Bolted wheat bread, guilders per last of grain								
6 Holland cities	4.02	3.96	8.43	0.99	1.35	2.31	21.06	-6.06
5 Holland towns	3.18	3.87	7.47	1.17	1.20	1.44	18.33	-4.71
2 Utrecht cities	5.79	4.05	10.59	0.57	0.69	0.54	22.23	-7.20
3 IJssel cities	5.40	9.69	9.60	0.45	0.24	1.65	17.43	-6.39

Source: A.R.A. The Hague. Ministerie van Binnenlandse Zaken, 1813–64, no. 1366, Bestuur B, 1824–31.

To summarize, the commissioners drafted bread price schedules once they had determined the full constant costs of bread production and established a realistic estimate of the bread yield. They then declared the price of the various types of bread after determining, each week, the prevailing market prices of wheat and rye. This elaborate system was not intended to regulate prices in the sense of holding them below the market level, or to protect consumers in periods of high prices. The resulting bread price was not a "just price" in a moral or theological sense any more than old system pricing could have made such a claim. But just what was this new regulatory regime trying to accomplish? This was not a system designed for direct *intervention* in the market; instead, it appears designed to allow the commissioners to *discover* the market. But many questions remain about just what the Dutch achieved with their new, more sophisticated, regulatory apparatus. Whose interests did the regulators seek to serve? Did they actually achieve their goals?

In later chapters we will investigate in greater detail the public policies that motivated the setting of milling excises (Chapter 5), millers' fees (Chapter 7), and bakers' fees (Chapter 8). There we will follow their evolution over the 260 years during which this regulatory system remained in place. Here, our chief concern was to examine the steps needed in order to break with the venerable and ubiquitous old system of bread price regulation and introduce and institutionalize a new system. What the Dutch towns introduced in the course of the 1590s found followers elsewhere in Europe, but not many, and not for nearly a century.[62] Indeed, even two centuries later, in 1781, a French *savant* could feel he was making a scientific breakthrough worthy of his enlightened times by proposing to the Paris Academy of Sciences nothing more than the regulatory procedures described in this chapter.[63]

This new regulatory science emerged at the hands of practical, commercially astute town magistrates. They were not inclined to philosophical reflection, and for this reason much of my account of it is based on "reverse engineering." But shortly after its introduction, the Dutch new system did find its theoretical voice and this chapter closes with a discussion of the remarkable treatise that sought to theorize the Dutch new system of bread price regulation.

---

[62] The international diffusion of the new system is discussed in Chapter 14.

[63] Mathieu Tillet presented a learned paper to the Paris Academy of Sciences describing the principles for a scientific bread price schedule. Kaplan relates that Tillet's enlightenment approach was endorsed by Controller General Calonne and adopted by a number of provincial towns. Yet even Calonne was ultimately unwilling fully to embrace this regulatory science. He complained that "An infinity of motives and circumstances can make inadmissible the arithmetic calculation that serves as a base [of Tillet's pricing formula]." Cited in Kaplan, *Bakers of Paris*, p. 498.

The Science of Bread Price Regulation: Cornelis Françoiszoon Eversdijck's Amazing Price-Setting Machine

Regulating the price of bread was understood to be an obligation of town governments everywhere in the Dutch Republic, where the cities enjoyed a high degree of autonomy. To be sure, the town magistrates and their appointed commissioners kept themselves informed about developments in other cities, if only to defend themselves against complaints that they had unjustifiably set the price of bread higher than in a neighboring town. And, as we have seen, the towns of Holland quickly followed Amsterdam's lead in adopting the new system in 1596. Soon, bread price commissioners in every city of any size reorganized their routines, conducting baking trials, drafting new price schedules, and adjusting their policies in the face of practical realities.

These towns all maintained their own local sets of weights and measures. The Amsterdam grain last was the national, indeed the international volume measure for wholesale transactions in wheat and rye, but every city subdivided the last into its own sub-measures: the *zak* (sack), the *mud*, the *schepel* (akin to the bushel), etc. Similarly, every town maintained its own standard of weight. The Amsterdam *pond* was adopted by many places, especially around the Zuider Zee, but a lighter *pond*, apparently derived from the Cologne weight system, was also common. Table 0.2 (see the online Database at www.cambridge.org/9781108476386) gives an overview of the variety that existed in the weight and volume measures used at the municipal level for trade in grain and bread.

Finally, cities varied in the specific types of bread they allowed in their jurisdictions. For all these reasons, the regulatory regime of each city was a little world of its own: its own types of bread, its own weights, its own grain measures. A necessary and often frustrating aspect of this study, has been reducing all these differences to the metric system, which was not fully adopted by the Kingdom of the Netherlands until 1821.

Despite the Republic's extreme and lovingly nurtured decentralization, its well-integrated grain markets (described in Chapter 6) and the strong commonalities of municipal new system regulatory practices yielded bread prices that were highly correlated from place to place. One might suppose that the small army of commissioners charged with regulating bread prices would be receptive to the development of a simple mechanism for acquitting their responsibilities. It happens that one of these magistrates, Cornelis Françoiszoon Eversdijck, felt that this was precisely what his colleagues needed and he produced a short treatise intended to reduce their regulatory task to a science, a farine science. He summarized this science in two simple, easy-to-use tables that would, he claimed, be "very useful for all magistrates and regents in order to establish good order to the baking and selling of bread." This remarkable volume spells out the essentials of the new system and reduces it to a universal formula. It makes explicit what those who established the new system beginning in 1596 usually left unsaid. As a theoretical statement and as a display of an estimable arithmetic sophistication it deserves a moment of our attention.

Eversdijck, scion of a prominent regental family of the city of Goes – then as now the market town of the Zeeland island of Zuid Beveland – published his *Paste-boeck vanden Broode* in 1663. This is long after the introduction of the new system of price regulation. But Eversdijck's text is based on his personal role in establishing the new system in Goes in 1622. His treatise begins as follows:[64]

The honorable magistrature of the city of Goes, always interested in making sound laws, rules, and ordinances for the peace and wellbeing of its burghers, did not stand idly by [in the matter of bread regulation], but with great energy and determination assembled bread price ordinances from several nearby cities in order to select from among them that which, in its judgment, was the best and most reasonable, and to apply it to their city. But, seeing soon enough that these tables were not at all as perfect as the task required, it pleased them in 1622 to examine the matter further by appointing several commissioners from their honorable council, namely Eversdijck, Van Stapelen and Secretary Brune, to conduct (baking) trials.

This preamble raises more questions than it answers. By 1622 the cities of Holland and nearly all in the rest of the Republic had plenty of experience with the new system, and they could easily have supplied the magistrates of Goes with sound examples of a well-founded regulatory regime. Goes and its neighboring Zeeland cities (Middelburg, Vlissingen, and Zierikzee being the largest) were the last cities of the Republic, so far as I can tell, to break with the old system. The trade of Zeeland's towns depended on the estuary of the river Schelde, the old merchant center of Antwerp, and the even older center of Bruges. The grain measures and the currency system of these old metropoles continued in use in Zeeland long after the Revolt and despite the erection of formidable trade barriers between the new Republic and the Spanish Southern Netherlands. Thus, when Eversdijck speaks of "seeking the advice of nearby cities," he is referring to the cities to his south, not to his north. And, what he and his fellow commissioners found there were unreconstructed regulatory practices, untouched by the north's new system.

[64] Cornelis Fr. Eversdijck, *Paste-boeck vanden Broode* (Middelburg, 1663).

Eversdijck begins his review of "best practice" by examining the earliest known French pricing regime, introduced for Paris by King Philippe II in 1316 and renewed, with little revision, by monarchs up to his own time. He then examined the price schedules "from a nearby city" – almost certainly Bruges. Both the Paris and the Bruges tables provided for three grades of wheat bread, each to sell for a fixed price – 2 sous in Paris, 1 Flemish *groot* in Bruges – with bread weights varying according to the price of wheat. Eversdijck then calls attention to two features of these tables: the loaf weights fall as the grain price rises, but more than is required to generate the revenue needed to match the rise in the grain price, and they fall irregularly (the French table, especially). "The knowledgeable reader can readily see," he noted, "how impertinent and disproportional these tables are." Indeed, "the imperfection and irregularity of this list [referring to the Bruges data] is evident from all its parts; nowhere does one observe a reasonable regularity or proportionality."[65] These, and the other ordinances on bread pricing examined by his commission were, he concluded, all "built on a faulty foundation" (*op een quaet fondament gebout*).

He summarized the problem of all these old system price tables as follows:[66]

It is obvious and certain that the weight of baked bread should not vary in direct proportion to the price of the wheat, because this would take no account of the costs of baking and the profit of the baker, which do not change, even while the price of wheat rises or falls.

This, of course, was the key insight of the new system that had spread through Holland in the 1590s. But Eversdijck and his Zeeland colleagues make no reference to Holland's experience. Instead, their attention remained fixed on the cities of the Southern Netherlands. In Bruges, the pricing regime established in 1431 remained in force well into the eighteenth century. Throughout, it was based on the old rule of thumb that the price of grain and of bread should be the same per unit of weight.[67] In 1588, shortly after Spain had re-established its control over the Southern Netherlands, both Brussels and Antwerp reviewed and updated their bread price systems without breaking with the old system. Scholliers, in his study of the standard of living in Antwerp, describes an old system price schedule in effect until 1620, and notes, elsewhere, that the

---

[65] *Ibid.*, p. 3.

[66] *Ibid.*, p. 4.

[67] E. Scholliers and C. Vandenbroeke, "Structuren en conjuncturen in de Zuidelijke Nederlanden, 1480–1800," *Algemene geschiedenis der Nederlanden* (Haarlem: Fibua-Van Dishoek, 1980), vol. V, p. 293.

Brussels price schedules were highly irregular.[68] Coeckelberghs' study of the standard of living in Brussels confirms the justice of Eversdijck's critique. Indeed, he expresses surprise and outrage that the system caused bakers' revenue to rise, as he put it, exponentially when grain prices rose arithmetically.[69]

Eversdijck was just the man to bring order to this unreasonable system. He brought more than just the good intentions of an upright regent to the Goes commission, having earlier cultivated an intense interest in applied mathematics.[70] In order to establish once and for all (or so Eversdijck asserted) the terms on which grains were transformed into breads of various types, and the production costs associated with each, he assembled data from the results of the 1622 baking trials held in Goes, which he describes as follows:[71]

[The Commissioners] ordered trials for every type of bread that was customarily consumed in the city, taking note of everything with the greatest curiosity, and observing everything with their own eyes: as in the measuring of the grains and in the weighing thereof; likewise with the milling, sifting, kneading, baking, etc., and in assiduously recording the weights of the grain, flour, bran, dough, and of the baked bread; likewise the quantities of the milk, water and other ingredients necessary thereunto. And from all this [the commissioners] prepared a consistent ordering on which basis, from that time onward, the price/weight of bread has been governed.

From the careful observations of these baking trials – which, of course, commissioners in cities throughout the Republic were also conducting periodically – Eversdijck established to his satisfaction exactly how much of each type of bread could be produced from a given weight of grain. He also established the constant costs of production: the costs of fuel and ingredients (yeast, milk, salt, oil), the compensating revenue from the sale of milling by-products (primarily bran), the cost of the excise tax on milling, and a more global insight into the cost of labor involved in the

---

[68] Antwerp's revised bread price schedules of 1620 did introduce the principles of the new system. But one could say that they continued to breathe the spirit of the old system. Constant costs were taken into account, but they were miniscule, and the assumed bread yields differed little from those that had prevailed under the old system. The result was a price schedule difficult to distinguish from the old system. Scholliers, *Levensstandaard*, pp. 25–27; Scholliers, "De Antwerpse merkuriale van granen en brood," pp. 350–58.

[69] H. Coeckelberghs, "Lonen en levensstandaard te Brussel in de 16e eeuw," *Bijdragen tot de geschiedenis* 58 (1975), 169–207.

[70] Eversdijck (1586–1666) also wrote *Tafelen vande Wanne-mate*, which presented a practical method for estimating the volume of barrels and other containers ("*kantige vaten*"), and *Tractaet van roeden en landmaten*, which was incorporated in Matheus van Nispen, *De Beknopte Landmeet-konst* (Dordrecht, 1665), a work on surveying. He offered the *Paste-boeck* as "Very useful for all magistrates and regents to put in good order the (regulation of) the baking and selling of bread."

[71] Eversdijck, *Paste-boeck*, pp. 5–6.

Table 3.7 *Summary of Eversdijck's estimates of key parameters in the pricing of five types of bread*

Bread yield per 100 pounds of grain (based on Goes baking trials, 1622)

White bread	71 317/359 pounds, after subtracting waste
Fine bolted wheat bread	88 22/359 pounds cold bread
Coarse bolted wheat bread	104 2353/6400 pounds cold bread
Unbolted wheat bread	128 199/256 pounds cold bread
Rye bread	127 64/125 pounds cold bread

Grain weight per last in kilograms (based on summary data from Table 3.5)

Goes pound = 437.2 grams	5,260.7 pounds wheat = 2300 kg
	4,803.3 pounds rye = 2100 kg

Bread produced per last of grain	Goes pounds	Kilograms	Kg bread/Kg grain
White bread	3,848	1,682.5	0.73
Fine bolted wheat bread	4,713	2,061	0.90
Coarse bolted wheat bread	5,588	2,443	1.06
Unbolted wheat bread	6,893.6	3,014	1.31
Rye bread	6,124.2	2,677.5	1.28

Constant costs, Goes 1631–32 (guilders per last)

	Wheat bread				Rye bread
	White	Fine	Coarse	Unbolted	
Transport to/from miller	3.75	3.75	3.75	3.75	3.75
Excise taxes	37.5	37.5	37.5	37.5	18.75
Millers' fee	3.75	3.75	3.75	3.75	3.75
Sale of bran	[no provision made]				
Yeast	18.75	18.75	18.75	18.75	9.375
Milk	33.75	45.00			
Stryt					11.25
Eggs		3.75	3.75	3.75	
Bakers' fee	22.50	18.75	18.75	18.75	22.50
Profit and distribution	37.5	26.25	26.25	26.25	26.25
Total	157.5	157.5	112.5	112.5	95.625
Kg bread per last	1,683	2,061	2,443	3,014	2,678
Price per kg	1.872	1.528	0.921	0.747	0.714
Avg. grain price 1630s	220	220	220	220	150
Total cost	377.5	377.5	332.5	332.5	245.625
Price per kg (in stuivers)	4.486	3.663	2.722	2.206	1.834
Index (rye bread = 100)	245	2.00	148	120	100

various phases of production. Table 3.7 offers a summary of the bread yield and cost estimates reported by Eversdijck.

So far, Eversdijck and his fellow commissioners had done no more than their counterparts in other cities. But Eversdijck aspired to create tables that, once established, would be *"generael en perpetual"* – applicable universally (regardless of the specific weights and measures used in a given place) and in perpetuity (regardless of future changes in taxes and other costs).

His first step was to establish a coefficient, A, for every likely weight of a sack of grain and for each of five bread types.

(1) $A = c * (b/a) * 12$

a = the bread yield in pounds per 100 pounds of grain
b = a root (*wortel*): 10,000
12 = conversion from *schellingen* to *groten* (from the currency unit in which grain prices are quoted to the smaller unit in which bread prices are quoted).
c = the reciprocal of the weight in pounds of a unit of grain multiplied by 100 pounds. $c = 1/(g * 100)$, where g = weight of grain

Once Eversdijck calculated A for every weight of a grain sack and for each bread type, he arrayed this in a table (partially displayed as Table 3.8) from which one can determine the proper price for one pound of each type of bread.

Then, one only needs to know:

d = the price of grain in *schellingen*
e = the constant costs in *schellingen*
g = the weight of the relevant measure of grain.

With these three pieces of information, the commissioner – in whatever city, with whatever local weights and measures – added d plus e together, and multiplied this sum times the coefficient, A, found in the table for the type of bread in question and the weight, g, of the grain measure used locally.

(2) $(d+e) * A = B$

Having found B, the final step is to divide by 10,000 (remember the root, b, in equation 1) and the desired result is achieved: B/b = the price per pound in *groten* (or, for 2 pounds, expressed in stuivers).

Consider the case in which a magistrate wants to know the appropriate price for a pound of white bread in a town where a sack of wheat weighed 140 pounds, the current price of such a sack of wheat is 23 *schellingen*, and the constant costs per sack total 14 *schellingen*: First, Eversdijck has already made the following calculation, using equation 1:

Table 3.8 *Example from Eversdijck's table "to find what one pound of bread should cost"* (Tafelen om te vinden wat een pond gebacken broot costen moet)

	Witte broot	Fijn tarwe	Grof tarwe	Crop tarwe	Rogge broot
	[white bread]	[fine wheat]	[coarse wheat]	unbolted wheat]	[rye bread]
Een sack in ponden [pounds per sack]					
100	1,669	1,339	1,150	932	941
101	1,653	1,349	1,138	923	932
102	1,633	1,336	1,127	914	923
103	1,621	1,323	1,116	905	914
130	1,284	1,048	884	717	724
131	1,274	1,040	878	711	718
132	1,265	1,032	871	706	713
133	1,255	1,025	865	701	708
140	**1,190**	972	820	665	671
207	806	658	555	450	455
208	803	655	553	448	452
209	799	652	550	446	450
210	795	649	548	444	448

Note: **1,190**, in bold, identifies the number the user of this table needed to find in the example provided in the text.

$$A = 100/140 * 10,000/71.8830 * 12 = 1190$$

which we, using the decimal system, can express as:

$$A = 0.71429 * 139.115 * 12 = 1190$$

The magistrate locates this number, 1190, in Eversdijck's table, under the column for white bread and the row for 140 pounds. He then plugs this value for A into equation 2:

$$(23+14) * 1190 = 44,030/10,000 = 4.403$$

4.403 is the correct price of white bread, expressed in *groten* per pound. If one wishes to use stuivers instead of *groten*, one divides this result by 2.[72]

Equations 1 and 2 are my interpretation of his verbally described procedures, and the calculations using decimals were, in the original text,

---

[72] Eversdijck went on to devise a second table to assist magistrates seeking to determine the proper *weight* of a loaf of bread.

expressed as fractions. Thus, the yield of white bread per 100 pounds of grain was 71 317/359 pounds. But by using a root of 10,000, Eversdijck converted many of his calculations to an approximation of decimalized fractions. This strategy simplified the computations somewhat, but one cannot avoid concluding that Eversdijck's tables involved a formidable amount of heavy-duty number crunching.

Eversdijck believed his booklet and its two amazing tables would lighten the administrative burden of bread price regulators throughout the Republic, yet there is no evidence that anyone actually adopted it.[73] His contribution is of interest to us, first, because it reveals at once a perceptive critique of old system price/weight tables and a clear explanation of the principles of the new system, and, second, because of its demonstration of the advanced mathematical techniques available to a seventeenth-century administrator seeking to systematize the task of calculating proper bread prices and weights in a world of multiple systems of weights, measures, and currencies. The old system of bread price regulation, with its rules of thumb and proportions, had placed relatively few demands on the numeracy of its users. The new system clearly was designed for a highly numerate society.

[73] Why not? Once the magistrates in a city had gone to the trouble of establishing new system price schedules for the various types of bread, they only needed to revise the schedules for two reasons: when the constant costs rose, and when they determined that the amount of bread that could, or should, be baked from a given volume measure required a change. The first happened frequently, but adjusting the price schedules for this purpose was relatively straightforward and quickly accomplished. The second happened infrequently and triggered a comprehensive recalculation of bread prices. But Eversdijck's tables offered no real escape from this burden. His tables were based on a fixed bread yield *per 100 pounds* of grain for each type of bread. The municipal regulators always based their tables on a fixed bread yield *per volume measure* of grain. Eversdijck's assumed bread yields were on the modest side, especially in the case of rye bread, and they could not be altered without completely redoing his tables. Thus, when all is said and done, his contribution to farine science was very clever, but not quite as useful to the busy magistrate as he claimed.

4   Administering and Enforcing the New Bread Price Regulations

Getting the new system of bread price regulation up and running required a concerted effort on the part of the bread price commissioners. Old rules of thumb gave way to careful measurement via the baking trials, accurate observation of market behavior, and the drafting of carefully calibrated price schedules. The new system demanded of the commissioners a higher level of arithmetic skill and administrative discipline than before – or than was long common elsewhere in Europe. Eversdijck's treatise on the subject stands as a testament to this fact.

But it was also Eversdijck's belief that a price schedule, once properly established, could live on indefinitely, could be in his words "general and perpetual." In this he was mistaken. Translating a regulatory regime from the realm of theoretical perfection to the real world – full of inconvenient practical limitations, recalcitrant bakers, and consumers seeking ways to circumvent the rules and "play the system" – required both vigilance and adaptability. Even today, the visions we have of needful regulation are nearly always separated by a great chasm from the realities of actual regulatory practices. In this chapter we will examine how the *broodzetting* commissioners confronted a series of practical problems.

Setting Prices

Bread price commissioners throughout the Netherlands met weekly to declare the prices (or weights) for a list of bread types that bakers were to charge within their towns and, usually with a small adjustment, in the surrounding rural areas. But, how large a change in grain prices was required to trigger new bread prices? The commissioners began, certainly in Leiden, Amsterdam, and Haarlem, with price schedules that were highly sensitive to even small fluctuations in grain prices. Leiden's original schedule of 1596 triggered the proclamation of new rye bread prices nearly every week, and even after some relaxation Leiden altered bread prices at least once in 72 percent of the months from 1600 until 1609. Experience taught the commissioners to loosen the price schedules:

Leiden had begun by altering rye bread prices with every gold guilder (1.4 guilders) change in the price of a last of rye (a price change of about 1 percent), but they quickly decided to change prices only after a 2 gold guilder (2.8 guilder) change. Haarlem in 1610 also used the 2 gold guilder standard, but by the 1630s had relaxed the price schedules further, changing bread prices only after a 4 gold guilder (5.60 guilder) change in the grain price. At prevailing price levels, this amounted to about a 3 percent price fluctuation. Later, the price intervals at which bread prices and weights were changed lengthened further. Kampen altered its bread prices only after a 10.80 guilder change in rye prices and a 16.20 guilder change in wheat prices. Much later, in 1816, Haarlem altered them after a 9 gold guilder (12.6 guilder) change in rye prices and a 13 gold guilder (18.20 guilder) change in wheat prices, which was approximately the standard used by Zaltbommel. The grain prices now needed to change by 8–12 percent in order to trigger a new bread price.

Under these standards, bakers and consumers could expect their commissioners to proclaim price adjustments to rye bread at least once in one-third of all months and adjustment to wheat bread prices at least once in nearly a quarter of all months. Wheat bread prices were adjusted less frequently not because the underlying grain prices were less volatile but because of the "technical" difficulties of finding a viable price for the typically small wheat bread loaves.

Bread price changes were, of course, not randomly distributed. They were concentrated in periods of crisis, as commissioners made repeated adjustments in response to persistently rising grain prices, and again as grain prices made their retreat to more normal levels. They were also concentrated in July through October for rye bread, and August through November for wheat bread, as market-moving harvest information had its effects. There were also long periods when bread prices changed little if at all. Utrecht's rye bread price remained unaltered from March 1730 through October 1733. After a small increase in November, the price remained constant again from December 1733 to January 1736. Table 4.1 provides an overview of the frequency of bread price changes in several cities. Obviously, these price changes were triggered by changes in the underlying grain prices, and the volatility of these prices varied over time.

Maximum and Minimum Prices

One might think that there were long periods in which the commissioners had little to do, but the enforcement of the prices and weights that they set was a never-ending task, and one made doubly difficult because the prices set by the commissioners week-by-week were not

Table 4.1 *Price change frequency: percentage of months in which bread prices were changed at least once*

Rye bread	Leiden	Utrecht	The Hague
1596–1609	72		
1610–49	63	39	
1650–99	36	33	43
1700–49	19	19	27
1750–89	20	28	31
1790–1819	30	50	51
1820–44	21		
Wheat bread	Haarlem	Zaltbommel	The Hague
1610–49	23	30	
1650–99	28	22	26
1700–49	19	16	22
1750–89	20	24	16
1790–1819	44	40	71

Overall percentage of months in which prices are changed at least once

	Wheat bread
Haarlem, 1611–1801	20.7
The Hague, 1650–1811	25.3
Zaltbommel, 1629–1819	24.6
	Rye bread
Leiden, 1596–1844	34.3
The Hague, 1650–1811	34.5
Utrecht, 1599–1819	32.8

simply price maxima, nor were the weights established for bread sold at fixed prices only minimum weights. The commissioners everywhere were clear that their price and weight declarations were to be followed exactly. In Haarlem, the 1646 ordinance (an amplification on earlier ordinances) declared that "all the *bakkers en baksters* [male and female bakers] shall commit to selling bread at the specific price established by the bread price commissioners."[1] Utrecht, noting that the (temporary) abolition of the excise tax on milling in 1748 had led the bakers to neglect other rules pertaining to the bread trade, used the occasion to lay out its long-established policy in clear, forceful language: "The [members of the] bakers' guild must conform exactly to, and honor, the bread price as that is set from time to time by the Deputized Gentlemen

---

[1] G.A. Haarlem, Stadsarchief 1581–1795, II-1926, Ordonnantie op 't bakken van brood, 1646.

[the commissioners] according to their determinations of the grain price and its weight, without violating this by selling bread for either a higher or lower price, or a lower or even higher weight ... "[2]

This insistence on selling at neither a higher nor a lower price was not unique to the new system. Already in the mid-sixteenth century Leeuwarden had insisted that "no one may sell his bread for more nor less than the price set by the Council ... "[3] But in the course of the seventeenth century, these regulations became rather more comprehensive in scope. Not only could bakers not charge less than the established price, but, as Delft's commissioners put it, "the bakers shall ... not sell under the set price, nor give [to the customer] any small items, *timpen* [sweet rolls], crusty rolls, flour, Easter breads, *duivekaters* [fine wheat flour, or small breads made from such flour], nor anything else, neither directly, nor at the time of settlement of accounts, nor by settlement by the sack, nor by any other indirect manner whatsoever."[4]

The practice of offering a "baker's dozen" appears to have been widespread, and the commissioners' battle against it was unrelenting. The 1680s may have been a period of particularly desperate competition among bakers. The large milling excise increase of 1680, increasing bread prices, and the economic slump of this period could be expected to depress demand. Compounding this problem was the influx to the Dutch towns of thousands of French Huguenot refugees, including a fair number of bakers who were exempted by magnanimous magistrates from the normal guild regulations and who, the complaint went, proceeded to "bake bread according to their own fantasies, with respect both to the form and weight [of the loaves]."[5]

---

[2] G.A. Utrecht, Stadsarchief, no. 2023, Rijdingboek. Resolutie van 28 April 1749.

[3] G.A. Leeuwarden, Bakkersboek. No date, mid-sixteenth century.

[4] G.A. Delft, no. 2030, Broodkeure van 1717. Leiden's ordinance of 1658 had language to the same effect, as did The Hague's ordinance of 1669. "No bakers may give to or honor their clients, or deliver to their houses, any *deuvecaters*, egg-bread, or flour, or any *koeckjes* or pretzels (*kraeckelinge*), or biscuits or any money or [items of] monetary value, whether under pretext of New Years, Christmas, Easter, or Shrove Tuesday [*Vastenavond*] gifts, on pain of a twelve guilder fine for the first offence and banishment from the trade ... for the second." G.A. Leiden, Ordonnatie van 1658. Cited in D. H. [Hartevelt], "Ons dagelijksch brood. Voorheen en Thans," *De economist* 19 (1870), p. 220. "Bakers may not [sell] at a higher or a lower price, nor may they add anything, be it *koekjes*, flour, or egg-bread, or whatever it may be, on penalty of 25 guilders." G.A. Den Haag, Oud Archief, no. 5741. Ordonnatie op het broodbakken, 5 October 1669.

[5] Cited in Erika Kuijpers, *Migrantenstad: immigratie en sociale verhoudingen in 17de-eeuws Amsterdam* (Hilversum: Verloren, 2005), p. 236. In this crisis period the bread price commissioners of Amsterdam, under pressure from a bakers' guild facing this combination of threats to their financial viability, issued a ringing defense of the importance of the social and economic necessity of their regulatory work. Absent their price fixing, consumers would be exposed to adulterated bread as bakers engaged in ruinous competition. G.A. Amsterdam, Archief 5028, Archief van de Burgemeesters, no. 516, "Redenen door de brootwegers ende Ed. Achtb. Heeren overgegeven," 1683.

Nijmegen's *politieboek* – a record of bread prices and their enforcement – recorded in 1685 that the *burgemeester* had been made aware that "nearly all the bakers" were evading the price rules by giving with each rye bread some small wheat rolls, and that some of them sold their wheat bread loaves at two and even four penningen under the official price. In response, the city council resolved to enforce the rules with a heightened severity.[6] In 1698 Alkmaar's council resolved similarly to battle against the gift-giving practices of certain "evil intentioned" bakers.[7] By 1747 they were again on the warpath, this time to bring an end to "the continuing practice of divers bakers to sell bread far below the official price under the pretext that it is being sold to retail peddlers."[8] (Those hawking bread through the streets, called *slijters*, sold bread at the official price but acquired the bread from the bakers at a lower "wholesale" price.)

At first glance, a regulatory system that claimed to protect consumers yet forbade low prices might seem perverse.[9] But the insistence that bakers neither overcharge nor undercharge gave expression to a second important goal of the regulatory regime, what the documents refer to repeatedly as guaranteeing "honest" (pure, unadulterated) bread. Thus, Delft's renovated law on bread of 1717 declared that its purpose was "supplying the city with honest, nutritious bread of proper weight," while Dordrecht's magistrates, when defending the price-setting regime against criticisms in 1800, defined its mission, first and foremost, as "to insure bread of good quality and to prevent adulteration [*vervallsching*] as much as possible *by securing for everyone working in this trade a reasonable profit [taamlijke winst]*."[10] The italicized phrase points to a second meaning of "honest" bread: providing a "reasonable" living for the bakers. This was important for the general peace and stability of the towns, to be sure, but the

---

[6] G.A. Nijmegen, Oud Archief, no. 3114. Politieboek. 4 February 1685. Utrecht's commissioners were similarly vigilant, forbidding the bakers "to provide any additional goods, whether directly or indirectly" to their customers. G.A. Utrecht, Stadsarchief, no. 2023, Rijdingboek, 28 April 1749.

[7] G.A. Alkmaar, Archief vóór 1815, no. 34, fol. 261v. 28–1–1698.

[8] G.A. Alkmaar, Archief vóór 1815, no. 1969. "Various bakers persist in selling bread from their houses at prices far below the official level. They do so under the pretext that this concerns bread sold to the distributors [*slijters*] (who in fact have never in any way been registered under the relevant regulations [*plakkaten*], let alone been examined)."

[9] In fact, many modern regulatory systems also prohibit selling below the official price. The American Interstate Commerce Commission set all railroad tariffs from 1887 until its reform in 1980. Its concern extended to low prices in order to protect weak railroads, small shippers, and geographically remote locations. More generally, it was intended to protect the industry from itself, given the "temptation" faced by firms in a high fixed / low variable cost industry to engage in fare wars. Richard D. Stone, *The Interstate Commerce Commission and the Railroad Industry: A History of Regulatory Policy* (New York: Praeger, 1991).

[10] G.A. Delft, Stadsarchief vóór 1795, no. 2030. Broodkeure van 1717; G.A. Dordrecht, Archief Bataafse Tijd, no. 389.

magistrates thought it essential in order to neutralize the natural temptation of sinful man to seek his own profit at the expense of the consumer,
the state, and/or other bakers. The system set maximum prices to prevent
overcharging (or short-weighting); it made these simultaneously serve
as minimum prices to prevent false and ruinous competition that would
tempt bakers to adulterate their goods, which was understood broadly, as
any reduction of a standard quality. Thus, using lower grades of flour than
specified for a particular type of bread was seen as culpable in the same
way as was the introduction of foreign materials into the dough.

How far did the bread price commissioners think they had to go in
order to inoculate bakers against temptation? They protected them from
"outside" bakers – bakers from the countryside who tried to sell bread at
lower prices in the town markets – and they protected them from each
other, by prohibiting prices beneath the official level and gifts such as
bonus loaves and treats. In addition, as just noted, they saw it as their duty
to secure the bakers a "reasonable profit." What did they mean by that?
This is a question we will consider in more detail in Chapter 8, below.

Speculating on Grain Prices

Bread prices were established on the basis of weekly changes in grain
market conditions, and the commissioner insisted that prices reflect
those market realities precisely. Correspondents at these markets com-
municated the relevant price information and the commissioners developed rules to establish what they regarded as a representative price.
These rules were of particular concern in the case of wheat, since prices
varied considerably according to quality and source.

The commissioners sought to use the prices of grain types actually
purchased by the bakers and they generally chose the "middle price"
from the range of quotations supplied by their market correspondents for
a given week. Moreover, they were disinclined to engage in hypotheticals.
When the correspondents provided fresh price information, but frozen
canals prevented grain at these prices from actually reaching the town
markets for local distribution, they preferred to retain the prices (usually
lower prices) established in earlier weeks, since these presumably determined the actual grain costs incurred by the bakers.[11]

---

[11] In Haarlem, usually supplied via nearby Amsterdam, the commissioners made notations
in the margins of their record books, which allow us to follow their decision-making
process closely. Consider the following entries:25 January 1644: "Amsterdam has raised
the six-pound loaf by one *duit* (2 penn.), since rye there was 136 g.gl. [per last], yet it
remains here [at the old price] because the waterways are frozen."26 December 1649:
"Amsterdam raised [the rye bread loaf'] by two penningen, but because the waterways

Prices were set week-by-week, but bakers were under no obligation to purchase their grain on a weekly basis. They were free to purchase in larger quantities when prices seemed attractive, maintain inventories of wheat and rye, and have portions thereof milled as needed.[12] That is, they could speculate on future grain prices in the hope of achieving a lower overall grain cost than would result from a policy of "buy-as-you-go" – buying only what is needed week-by-week, or month-by-month.[13] The commissioners never intervened in this dimension of the bakers' business.

It takes money to make money. A baker hoping to profit from strategic purchases of grain needed to have a capital stock to invest in grain that he might hold for many months, if not years. In addition, the baker needed to store this grain, or pay someone to do so. If he was to profit from holding grain, his strategic purchases had to produce a yield that exceeded his "carry cost": the physical cost of storage, the loss due to spoilage, and the opportunity cost of his capital (the prevailing interest rate). Little is known about the grain purchase behavior of bakers but many of them, the larger bakers especially, must have engaged in strategic purchasing since, in times of stress, they were often found to hold substantial stocks relative to their short-term use. However, it is doubtful that "playing the market" – whether to exploit seasonal or inter-year

---

are frozen, it remains here at the former price."4 March 1658: "Because of closed canals, no change [in price] such as occurred in Amsterdam."26 February 1663: "In Amsterdam, the price is reduced by four penningen, but because of closed canals, no change [here]."7 December 1676 and 12 December 1678: Frozen canals prevent deliveries; hence, no price change is allowed. 22 January 1685: In an extreme case of a major price change and a long period of canal closure, the matter went before the *burgemeesters*, who relented: "In Amsterdam twelve-pound [rye bread] raised by twelve penningen, but since it is here an old usage that no price change is made while canals are closed, the *burgemeesters* have approved, since the market for rye during the canal closures rose too much, and the bakers cannot endure it for so long, that they should enjoy a four-penning increase."24 January 1691: The old practice is restored: "On 20 January Amsterdam raised the rye bread by four penningen, but here the canals are frozen." The freezing weather continued, and on 11 February the bread commissioners noted that "the bakers complain that prices should be raised, but we resolve to keep to the old custom of no new price setting during canal closures."G.A. Haarlem, II, no. 1930a, R 412 – 417. "'t Boeck van de settinge van 't Broot."

[12] This was a freedom denied to the bakers of Paris. They were supposed to purchase the grain and flour they needed for their bakeries, but no more. "Let the baker bake and let the commercial specialists and professional suppliers take care of furnishing the raw materials." Kaplan, *Provisioning Paris*, p. 466.

[13] The "speculation" described here involves purchase and storage in advance of need. An alternative, relied upon today, is purchasing futures contracts: purchase now at an agreed price for delivery in the future. Such contracts might then be sold again in advance of the delivery date, in which case the market actor is engaged in pure speculation on prices, without ever holding, let alone using, the commodity in question. Futures trading was certainly not unknown in the Dutch Republic, but was confined to wholesale brokers.

price fluctuations – could have been a source of consisitent profit to the bakers. The grain markets were well integrated and monitored by professional traders (see Chapter 6), leaving little opportunity for more than occasional profit opportunities for bakers.[14]

Monitoring Weights

Besides monitoring the prices charged by the bakers, and the bonus products thrown in to attract and secure the patronage of their customers, the commissioners also monitored weights, periodically visiting bakeries to weigh the loaves. If the loaves fell outside a range of tolerances the bread baker faced a punishment. For example, Utrecht's 1626 rule provided for an 8-guilder fine plus the confiscation of all bread of the type found to be in violation. A second infraction resulted in a doubled fine of 16 guilders; and the third time the baker was caught the fine rose higher still, to 50 guilders plus the risk of expulsion from the bakers' guild.[15]

Many cities required bakers to keep a hanging scale and weights at their premises for the use of customers.[16] One would like to know how the use of this convenience worked in practice. Some of the municipal ordinances went on to warn the bakers not to make difficulties with customers who actually wished to use the scales. This provision notwithstanding, the first line of defense for all but the most thick-skinned customers must have been the unannounced visits of the municipal bread weighers.

When Leiden established its new style bread price system in 1596, it also laid out the margins of error to be observed for each type of bread sold by price. Their table of weight tolerances shows that the

[14] This doubt is based on my analysis of grain market fluctuations and the speculative behavior of institutional buyers in: Jan de Vries, "Playing the market: grain prices, inventory formation, and speculation in the Dutch Republic," unpublished paper.

[15] G.A. Utrecht, Backergilde ordonnantie no. 461, deel 1, no. 8, 30 October 1626. Ord. no. 31. This pattern was common throughout the Republic. Two centuries later, Zaltbommel's renovated ordinance provided for a 5-guilder fine at first offense and 10 guilders plus confiscation of bread at the second offense. G.A. Zaltbommel, Archief 1816–1928, no. 19–1226. Ordinance of 12 December 1820.

[16] G.A. Den Haag, Oud Archief, no. 5741. Ordonnatie op het broodbakken, 5 October 1669. "The bakers' sales rooms [voorhuysen] must [be furnished with] hanging scales and correctly calibrated weights, with which anyone who wishes to may weigh their bread, or have it weighed." G.A. Dordrecht, Archief 4, no. 389. 1804 "At all times the shops of bakers and bread distributors must have a hanging scale and calibrated weights, which must be available to anyone who desires it to have their bread weighed." According to Burema, Leiden's "bakers were always required to have scales and correct weights available in their shops for anyone who desired it to weigh their bread without suffering abuse [from the baker]." Burema, De voeding in Nederland, p. 108. Brouwer Ancher noted that the ordinances guiding the bakers' guild of Amsterdam, in 1689 and again in 1741, required the bakers to provide a hanging scale at the sales counter to allow customers to check the weight of loaves. Brouwer Ancher, De Gilden, p. 150.

commissioners had given considerable thought to their task. Large 12-pound loaves of rye bread could not fall short by more than 1 percent before triggering a fine, but the commissioners tolerated progressively larger margins of error for progressively smaller loaves, whether of wheat or rye bread. Small luxury white bread rolls could be up to 16 percent underweight before falling foul of the inspectors. The commissioners appear to have recognized the practical limits of fairly identifying violations involving less than 2 *loden*, or 30 grams (1.06 oz). They also punished the bakers for overweight loaves, but for the basic rye and wheat bread loaves they tolerated a larger excess weight than under weight.

Leiden and The Hague, whose tolerance limits are laid out in Table 4.2, established a bright line, and punished violators with fines that rose with repeated violations. However, Zwolle's eighteenth-century rules, also displayed in Table 4.2, took a different approach. There the size of the penalty varied with the size of the violation, although even the smallest fine, one gold guilder, was substantial: approximately ten times the value of the offending loaf.

Table 4.2 *Bread weight tolerances in Leiden, The Hague, and Zwolle*

a. Leiden
Over- and underweight margins of tolerance allowed in Leiden's bread price ordinance of 1596 (*pond* = 481 grams; 32 *loden* per *pond*; 1 *lood* = 15 grams)

	Permitted tolerance			
	By weight		By percentage of weight	
Weight in pounds	plus	minus	plus	minus
Rye bread				
12	12 *loden*	4 *loden*	3.1%	1.0%
6	8	4	4.2	2.1
3	6	4	6.3	4.2
Wheat bread				
6	12	4	6.3	2.1
3	6	4	6.3	4.2
1.5	6	4	12.5	8.3
0.75	4	2	16.7	8.3
White bread rolls				
1.5	4	4	8.3	8.3
0.75 (24 lood)	2	3	8.3	12.5
0.375 (12 lood)	2	2	16.3	16.3

Table 4.2 *(cont.)*

b. The Hague

The bakers of The Hague were held to a constant and symmetrical standard by an ordinance of 1669.

| Weight in pounds | Permitted tolerance | |
	By weight	By percentage of weight
12	+/- 8 *loden*	2.1%
8	6	2.3
4	3	2.3
2	1.5	2.3

c. Zwolle

The 1753 ordinance of Zwolle provided for penalties that rose with the severity of the violation. A 4-pound rye loaf faced no penalty until it was 3 *loden* (2.8 percent) over- or underweight. Then the penalties began at one gold guilder (28 stuivers), but rose from there with the size of the violation. Note that the penalties were not symmetrical. Underweight loaves faced steeper penalties than overweight loaves for the same weight-discrepancy.

Penalties for over- and underweight rye bread, per 4-pound (128 *loden*) loaf

| Overweight by penalty | | Underweight by penalty | |
loden	gold guilders	*loden*	gold guilders
3	1	3	1
4	1	4	2
5	2	5	3
6	2	6	4
7	3	7	5
8	3	8	6
9	4	9	7
10	4		
11	5		
12	5		

Penalties for over- and underweight wheat bread, per one-stuiver loaf

| Overweight by penalty | | Underweight by penalty | |
loden	gold guilders	*loden*	gold guilders
1	0	1	1
2	1	2	2
3	2	3	3
4	3	4	4
5	4	5	5
6	5		

Sources: G.A. Leiden. Secretarie archief, no. 2536, 1596 ordonnantie op 't backen. 9 December 1596; G.A. The Hague, Oud Archief, no. 5741. Ordonnatie op het broodbakken, 5 October 1669; G.A. Zwolle, no. 488, Besluiten van de Keurmeesters, 1651–1822.

Enforcement beyond the Town Walls: Rural Competition

The *broodzetting* was in its origins an urban institution. But it could not be kept a strictly urban affair under the new system, for town burghers could then evade the fixed urban prices by purchasing bread from bakers operating outside the town's jurisdiction, just as rural bakers could attempt to smuggle their bread into the towns.

But why should burghers seek to evade the policies of regulators dedicated to protecting them from market forces? In fact, unregulated bread prices could be lower, and for two major reasons. First, rural bakers typically operated at lower costs, especially for fuel, rent, and labor. If this differential was sufficient to compensate the consumer for the inconvenience of distance for a product purchased nearly every day, the urban bakers faced serious competition from which they were likely to seek relief from the bread price commissioners.

Most towns had long made some provision to allow rural suppliers to compete with the town bakers. Utrecht, for example tolerated bread from outside the city at its markets on Friday, but only after 12 noon, and all day on Saturday. This ordinance dated from 1484, and appears to have continued in force into the seventeenth century.[17] Amsterdam similarly forbade outside bread, with the exception of Mondays, the free market day. Then *caveat emptor* was the rule; on Mondays "everyone must decide for themselves what they buy and from whom."[18]

These fifteenth-century ordinances reflect a common urban policy of tight regulation paired with a "safety valve" exception – a well-defined zone of toleration – designed to manage the discontents of producers and consumers alike.[19] Weekly free markets (free to suppliers from outside the town; free from price controls) proved socially and politically useful to the town magistrates. Indeed, in the Southern Netherlands non-guild bakers operating outside the cities supplied a large fraction of the urban bread in the seventeenth and eighteenth centuries. Based on the example of Leuven, De Wilde and Poukens argue that the town magistrates used

---

[17] Ordinance of 23 September 1484. J. C. Overvoorde and J. G. Ch. Joosting, *De Gilden van Utrecht tot 1528* (The Hague: Martinus Nijhoff, 1896).

[18] Amsterdam 1484 "ordonnancie op 't Brood." Art. IX. Neither Poorters nor outsiders may sell any bread forbidden by this ordinance except on Mondays, which is a free market day, "wanneer een ieder voor zich moest weten van wie en wat voor waar hij kocht." Brouwer Ancher, *De Gilden*, p. 145.

[19] Such "zones of toleration" continue to exist in Dutch cities. Known as *gedoogzones*, they seek to channel formally illegal activities, usually concerning drug use and commercial sex transactions, to places and times that minimize disamenity to the citizenry.

these low-cost suppliers as a check – a countervailing force – on the town guilds, especially in times of distress and high prices.[20] Standing behind such a municipal practice one detects the "provisionment policies" of the medieval cities, designed to keep prices low via an abundant supply of goods, even at the expense of the local guilds.[21] While such provisionment policies could remain useful to magistrates in the Southern Netherlands throughout the early modern era, they quickly became untenable in the new fiscal environment of the Dutch Republic.

From 1574 onward the Dutch milling excise was no longer strictly an urban affair. This provincial excise was higher than the municipal levies and it was intended to be collected at rural and urban mills alike, and at the same rate. But enforcement of this tax posed a special challenge in a rural setting. While urban grain mills were sufficiently few to be effectively monitored, this was not often the case in rural areas, where mills were generally smaller and widely scattered. Provincial laws sought to prevent "informal" milling by prohibiting the ownership of hand mills and querns; they also forced the destruction of old millstones, and ordered the dismantling of disused mills.[22] But the elaborate controls on millers were inherently difficult to enforce in the countryside, especially in districts where the bread grains were produced and locally traded.

The provinces acted cautiously in introducing the new milling excise in rural areas. Utrecht enacted the new tax in 1578, but waited until 1601 to enforce it outside the towns; Friesland began collecting the milling tax in 1585, but disagreement between the urban and rural chambers of the provincial States delayed its collection in the countryside until

---

[20] Brecht De Wilde and Johan Poukens, "Bread provisioning and retail dynamics in the Southern Low Countries: the bakers of Leuven, 1600–1800," *Continuity and Change* 26 (2011), 405–38. In Leuven the guild bakers faced such a competitive environment that many of them supplemented their baking trade with other retail activities. Many became "members of multiple guilds, allowing them to offer a range of non-bakery goods for sale in their bakeries." Scholliers describes a similar policy in sixteenth-century Antwerp. Outside bakers (*buitenbakkers*) were normally limited to supplying the city at the Saturday market, but in periods of high prices they were welcomed on a daily basis. Scholliers, *Levensstandaard*, p. 53.

[21] A classic example of this policy, one that undermined the power of the bakers of Paris, is found in Martha Howell, *Commerce before Capitalism in Europe, 1300–1600* (Cambridge University Press, 2010), pp. 283–84.

[22] Ordinances prohibiting the ownership of hand-operated mills, *GPB van Holland*, vol. III, p. 894, 19 July 1675. Placaet tegen querns, handmolens, enz. It did not escape the notice of Holland's fiscal authorities that ship captains commonly owned these small grinding mills for use on board their ships while at sea. An ordinance of 1676 required them to take an oath that these devices would never be used while their ships were in port. *GPB van Holland*, vol. III, p. 986, 17 July 1676.

1602.[23] The early enforcement history of the milling excise in Holland is not known, but until after 1600 this tax generated revenues that are inconsistent with even very low estimates of per capita bread consumption, suggesting a limited enforcement outside the towns.

This state of affairs put pressure on both the price regulation policy and the excise tax. The underpayment of the tax depressed revenue while the success of rural millers and bakers in evading this cost increased their competitive advantage over their urban counterparts and threatened to undermine the regulatory regime in the cities. This, in turn, reduced the amount of grain brought to urban mills for processing and, hence, reduced tax revenues further.

As the milling excise was periodically increased to become a weighty element in the total cost of bread these two problems migrated from nuisance status toward becoming a significant threat to the integrity of the entire edifice of bread regulation and taxation. In response, municipal rules restricting or prohibiting the importation of bread from the countryside multiplied in the first half of the seventeenth century.

Amsterdam's free Monday market continued into the seventeenth century, but it threatened to overwhelm the town-based bread supply when specialized bakeries emerged in the nearby Zaan region to produce ships' biscuits (*beschuit*). Concentrated in the villages of Wormer and Jisp, these large-scale bakeries supplied ships in Amsterdam's harbor, but they also produced cheap wheat and rye bread that they supplied to Amsterdam's citizenry. The city first limited these large bakeries to the Monday market, then forbade them from storing supplies within the city between market dates, and finally, in 1626, banned them altogether.[24] Rural bakeries could continue to supply bread and biscuits to ships in the harbors, but a provincial ordinance insisted that these producers be located within the tax-collection jurisdiction of the city being supplied.[25]

In addition, ordinances designed to patrol the areas just beyond town jurisdictions proliferated. Soldiers residing in the garrison towns appear

[23] Verstegen, *GWF – Utrecht*, p. 16; Trompetter, *GWF – Friesland*, pp. 12–24.

[24] Diederik Aten, *"Als het gewelt comt ... ": politiek en economie in Holland benoorden het IJ* (Hilversum: Verloren, 1995), pp. 232–38.

[25] *GPB van Holland*, vol. I, p. 1772. Much later, in 1808, the tradition of the Monday "free" bread market appears to have lived on in Amsterdam. The market was said to be supplied by rye bread producers in Harderwijk, Meppel, and Zwartsluis (all on the eastern shore of the Zuider Zee), but the market was limited to the hours of 8 am to 1 pm, and was said to sell approximately 3,000 pounds per week. Diederiks, who cites this information, thought it must have threatened the city's bakers, but 1,500 kg per week in a city that then consumed 70,000–75,000 kg of bread daily, hardly seems to pose a real danger. Herman Diederiks, *Een stad in verval: Amsterdam omstreeks 1800* (University of Amsterdam, 1982), p. 308.

often to have had time on their hands, which some used to engage in a type of arbitrage, buying bread from rural bakers and bringing it into the cities for resale. Holland forbade this explicitly by a 1677 ordinance, while in 1689 Utrecht forbade rural bakers from selling bread to any soldier garrisoned in the city (lest he resell in the city). Similarly, in 1708 Utrecht forbade bread hawkers and peddlers (*broodslijters*) from residing in villages that bordered on the city of Utrecht and went on to forbid any inhabitant of such villages from possessing more than two *mud* (240 liters) of grain, unless they were bakers.[26] This obsessive concern with the multitude of ways citizens might evade the letter and spirit of the tax system seems to have had no natural limits.

Tailoring Regulation to Rural Conditions

Bread Prices in the Countryside

The problem of rural competition and rural tax evasion called for a more comprehensive remedy than patrolling city gates for contraband loaves. The States of Holland tackled the problem directly in 1655, when it issued an ordinance, apparently instigated by Leiden's magistrates, that began by noting that it was their experience that ever more fraud was being schemed and carried out at the expense of the milling excise and that bread in the countryside often was not sold at the regulated price. It went on to declare that rural bread was to be subject to the same price controls as urban bread.

To this end, the States granted to each of the seventeen cities vested with tax-collecting responsibility the power to enforce its own bread prices, with appropriate adjustments, in its rural tax jurisdiction.[27] The "appropriate adjustments" the States of Holland had in mind were not described, nor did this provincial ordinance grant cities the right to be the judge of what was "appropriate." The States instructed them to make the adjustments described in Table 4.3.[28]

---

[26] *GPB van Utrecht*, 1689; 1 July 1708.

[27] G.A. Haarlem, Gilden archief no. 2068; G.A. Dordrecht, Stadsarchief 3, no. 4767. Settinge van 't broodt ten plattenlande. This policy is renewed by Placaat van 1749, when the excise tax was re-established.

[28] The bread price registers of Haarlem, Leiden and Rotterdam follow the price differentials decreed by the States of Holland, while Dordrecht's and Haarlem's records show some deviations from these rules. Dordrecht's rural price differential is known only from 1750. Rural consumers paid one penning less per pound of rye bread, a discount that rose to 2 penningen in 1787, when the wheat bread differential rose to 2.5 penningen per pound. G.A. Dordrecht, Stadsarchief 3, no. 4764. In Haarlem's jurisdiction there was no rural differential for breads sold by weight (small loaves and buns of white bread). G.A. Haarlem, Stadsarchief 1581–1795, R 414, Broodzettingsregisters; G.A. Leiden, Stadsarchief, no. 2546, Reglement, 20 July 1655.

Table 4.3 *Urban–rural bread price differentials in Holland as established by ordinance of 1655*

	City price per pound	Rural price per pound
Rye bread	X	X minus 0.667 penn.
Coarse wheat bread	X	X minus 1.333 penn.
Fine white bread	X	X plus 5.333 penn.

Source: GPB van Holland, vol.II, p. 1366. Ordinance of 8 December 1655.

The urban-rural differential established in 1655 remained unaltered until at least the late eighteenth century, and it can only be described as minimal. Over the entire period 1656–1790 the average urban price of rye bread was 0.943 stuivers per pound; rural consumers paid only 4.4 percent less while the rural discount for the more costly coarse wheat bread was nearly the same. Put differently, the rural baker charging the official prices earned only about 12 guilders less than his urban counterpart for the sale of bread from one last of rye and 24 guilders less for bread from a last of wheat. Yet rural bakers' total production costs were lower by considerably more than these amounts. And what are we to make of the "appropriate adjustment" for fine white bread? Rural consumers of such bread may have been few, but they were expected to pay a *premium* of some 15 percent over the urban price for the privilege.

The cities now had the authority to set rural bread prices at levels that minimized the competitive advantage of rural bakers. The lower production costs of rural baking were, it appears, not among the "appropriate adjustments" the magistrates included in their bread pricing policies. To the extent that their price controls were enforced, there now could be little incentive for urban consumers and rural bakers to seek each other out.

But what powers did the towns possess to enforce their bread pricing in rural jurisdictions? Apart from the small number of rural jurisdictions under direct town control, the magistrates depended on the cooperation of rural sheriffs, whose motivation to cooperate with the towns in enforcing their price edicts may be doubted.[29] As the fiscal role of

---

[29] This is a topic about which little is known. Rural enforcement of the bread price regulations certainly was not altogether lacking. But, after the fall of the old Republic, such enforcement mechanisms as existed may have broken down until a new system of rural municipalities could be established. In 1806 it was possible for the bakers of several villages near Leiden to send a joint letter to the bread price commissioners of Leiden, who long had informed them, week by week, of the official bread prices, which read: "[This is] a friendly request to stop bothering us about this, now and in the future, [*om ons nu en in het vervolg, met dezelve niet meer lastig te vallen*] for we are resolved no longer to be governed by the *broodzetting*." G.A. Leiden, Gilden Archief, np. 180, Bakkers van Alphen, Oudshoorn, Oudewetering, en Alkemade, letter of 18 July 1806.

the bakers – who, after all, were the actual collectors of the milling excise – became steadily more critical to both city and province, the motivation of regulators to enforce strictly the official prices became stronger. Deviations from official prices hinted at the possibility that this important tax was also being evaded, and nearly all the provincial governments give abundant evidence of their obsessive concern with the problem of enforcing the milling excise in rural areas. This concern soon led to a second, more comprehensive, reform, to which we will turn in the following chapter, where we examine the fiscal dimensions of the new regulatory regime.

At this point, if not much earlier in this study, the reader might wonder whether the regulation of rural bread prices had much point. Did much of the rural population actually purchase bread from bakers?

Home Baking in the Countryside

One must concede at the outset that home baking was certainly not unknown in the rural areas of the Republic, but it appears to have been a distinctly minority pursuit in most areas. In rural Zeeland home baking may long have remained the rule. When Zeeland converted its rural milling excise to a head tax in 1687, the new provincial ordinance anticipated an evasive maneuver on the part of rural folk:

> Refusing to pay the head tax by claiming to pay the excise to the baker cannot serve as an excuse "since the rural people have no need to depend on bakers, every [farm] house having its oven, and there are ovens enough in the villages to serve the needs of households, as is everywhere the custom."[30]

Indeed, the first occupational censuses offer confirmation of Zeeland's exceptionality. The industrial survey of 1819 found the province of Zeeland to be supplied with bakeries at a rate (2.7 per 1,000 inhabitants) about equal to the Netherlands as a whole. But the 1807 occupational census reveals that these bakeries were concentrated in Zeeland's cities, where there were 4.3 bakers per 1,000 inhabitants. Rural Zeeland supported only 1.5 baker per 1,000 inhabitants, which is as low a rate as could be found at that time anywhere in the Netherlands.[31]

---

[30] *GPB van Holland*, vol. IV, pp. 1110–13; Ordonnantie, Quotisatie ten plattenlande, article XII.

[31] I. J. Brugmans, *Statistieken van de Nederlandse nijverheid uit de eerste helft der 19e eeuw*, Rijks geschiedkundige publication, Grote serie, 98–99 (The Hague: Martinus Nijhoff, 1956); J. D. H. Harten, "De verzorging van het platteland van de Zeeuwse eilanden in de Franse Tijd," *Bulletin Geografisch Instituut Rijksuniversieit Utrecht* 3 (1971), 31–73.

In Holland and Utrecht the new regulations reveal that home baking was seen as something quite exceptional. In Holland, "those who declare they will bake at home ... " were accommodated with a special tax form for their use in documenting compliance when they brought grain to the millers.[32] In fact, most rural areas did not differ fundamentally from the towns with respect to the supply of bakeries, although, of course, the average distance between consumers and bakers was much greater. (The density of bakeries in both urban and rural districts is examined in detail in Chapter 8.)

The greatest concentration of home bakers must be sought in the rural districts of the eastern and southern provinces. Twentieth-century folkloric investigations conducted by the P. J. Meertens Instituut found evidence of home baking among farmers in "significant portions" of Drenthe, the Achterhoek of Gelderland and North Brabant. Among the many cottagers of these regions self-provisioning was a seasonal practice. Their small plots of land yielded only enough rye to last from harvest time, in August, into the beginning of the next year. By April most of these householders were again dependent on the baker for their bread. In these regions many bakers served the dual functions of selling bread and selling the use of their ovens to householders who prepared their own dough, at least on a seasonal basis.[33]

Home baking was far from being the norm, even in the rural Netherlands. Already in the seventeenth century, bakers supplied most consumers in both town and country. Developing effective mechanisms for enforcement of the bread price regulatory system in the countryside was therefore important to both the stability of the baking sector and the fiscal health of the state.

Tailoring Prices to the Money Supply

Paying for Bread

The regulatory system's chief concerns were establishing and enforcing a fair price for bread and ensuring that the bakers sold honest – unadulterated and full-weight – loaves to their customers. But it also had to pay heed to the practicalities of retail trading, chief among which was what has come to be known as the "small change" problem.

---

[32] *GPB van Holland*, vol. IV, 6 March 1680, Ordonnantie op het gemael ten plattelande, article V.
[33] Jobse-van Putten, *Eenvoudig maar voedzaam*, pp. 305–06; Vincent Tassenaar, *Het Verloren Arcadia: de biologische levensstandaard in Drenthe, 1815–1860* (Capelle a/d Ijssel: Labyrint Publications, 2000), p. 135.

We have encountered this problem already. In order to avoid it most medieval bread pricing set a fixed bread price and adjusted the weight of the loaf as the grain price varied. This practice continued, mainly for the finer grades of wheat bread, which were usually sold in relatively small loaves. The coarser wheat loaves and especially rye loaves were purchased at longer intervals and in larger units of weight, and it is these loaves that were sold in fixed weights at prices that varied with grain prices. But even with these large loaves, the problem was not entirely solved. If the loaf price was to reflect the changing grain price without great distortion, there had to be an adequate supply of small coins. The smallest Dutch monetary unit was the penning (1/360th of a guilder), but there was no such coin. The smallest coin was the *duit*, worth two penningen. Compounding the payment problem were the dubious quality of the smallest coins and seasonal fluctuations in the availability of coins of many kinds.

Bakers and regulators pursued two solutions to the "small coin" problem. One was a "work around" – adjusting bread prices to the available coins; the second emphasized avoidance, relying on credit to limit the need to use small coins and to time payments to accommodate seasonal availability. Both approaches were used throught the early modern period.

Cash. Efforts to devise "work arounds" illustrate by their awkwardness why the weight-variable system remained in use for so long. In 1635 the Leiden commissioners sought to maintain even-numbered penning prices by alternately raising and lowering the price of large rye loaves every week *in the absence of a change in the grain price sufficient to trigger a price change.* They tired of this by 1655 and ended the practice. Nearby Haarlem changed the bread price every three months beginning in 1687: first up by 4 penningen, then, three months later, down by 4 penningen, and so on. The commissioners revealed their motive in a marginal comment in the Haarlem *broodzettingsboek* for 4 August 1687. The bakers complain ("again" the commissioner notes wearily) that they mostly sell loaves of 3 pounds, i.e., half the size of the 6-pound loaf whose price varied in 2-penning increments. Since the price of the 6-pound loaf is often not divisible by two into an even number of penningen, the bakers must over- or undercharge. Therefore, the commissioners "approved an arrangement whereby the price of the 6-pound loaf [then selling for 4 st 6 penn.] will be set at 4 st 8 penn. for a period of three months, at the end of which it will be set at 4 st 4 penn., and every three months it will rise and fall in this manner."[34] In short, the price was adjusted at intervals

[34] G.A. Haarlem, Archief der Stad Haarlem, II, no. 1930a, R 412. 4 August 1687; 15 December 1691.

to retain the "true" average while allowing 3-pound loaves always to be priced in an even number of penningen. At the end of 1692, wearied by these constant price adjustments, the commissioners resolved to discontinue this cumbersome policy.

The currency system of the Dutch Republic, like those of many European countries, featured three broad categories of coinage. As a major trading nation, a large portion of the output of Dutch mints consisted of trade coins (*negotiepenningen*). These were large-denomination coins made of gold or silver intended for use in long-distance trade. The mints also produced smaller silver coins intended for domestic circulation (*standpenningen*). In the seventeenth and eighteenth centuries the smallest of these coins were 1- and 2-stuiver silver coins. They joined *schellingen*, coins valued at 6 stuivers, and, by the end of the seventeenth century, 20-stuiver (1-guilder) coins.[35] Coins of this size – 2 to 20 stuivers – were suitable for making weekly wage payments, paying house rents, and purchasing clothing. But they were not suited to making payments for daily necessities such as bread. This brings us to the third category of coinage.

The mints produced small copper coins, fractional currency, with values expressed in penningen, the subunit of the stuiver: the *groot* (8 penn.), *oord* (4 penn.), and the *duit* (2 penn). Here is where the small change problem was most acute. Mint masters found little profit in producing these coins, leading to shortages that encouraged private entities to supply token substitutes.[36] Moreover, the holder of both tokens and official copper coins faced an exchange risk, in that these "coppers" did not have an intrinsic value equal to their face value. That is, 16 penningen did not equal 1 stuiver in metallic value. The coppers were a sort of fiat money circulating in societies in which a coin's acceptance still usually depended on its intrinsic value.

The cash held by householders generally came to them via weekly wage payments or, as in the case of soldiers, sailors, fishermen, and the like, at longer – often much longer – intervals. Farmers, of course, came into cash primarily at harvest times and at seasonal livestock markets, while the wide assortment of craftsmen and service providers found in Dutch towns and villages were generally paid most of their income on a seasonal basis, often tied to the six-month rental and servant contract

---

[35] Foreign coins, primarily from the Southern Netherlands, also circulated in the Republic, especially before the 1650s. Jan Lucassen, "Loonbetaling en muntcirculatie in Nederland (1200–2000)," *Jaarboek voor munt- en penningkunde* 86 (1999), 1–70.

[36] For a discussion of the causes of this problem, see Jan Lucassen, "Deep monetisation: the case of the Netherlands, 1200–1940," *Tijdschrift voor sociale en economische geschiedenis* 11 (2014), 73–121.

dates of 1 May and 1 November – which were the clearing dates for the settlement of debt.[37]

Wage earners paid on a weekly basis could expect pay packets of between 5 and 8 guilders (100–160 stuivers), which would be paid in some combination of 1, 2, 6, and, after 1700, 20-stuiver silver coins plus the smaller copper coins. Repeated ordinances forbidding employers from paying wages in small foreign and clipped coins suggest that this was a temptation to which employers often succumbed.[38] In 1689 the state even forbade employers from using its own sound domestic copper coins as wage payments beyond a value of 10 stuivers, which would have been about 10 percent of an unskilled worker's weekly wage.[39]

One can see that the small coins were something like a "hot potato" passed from hand to hand as quickly as possible.[40] No one wanted to be caught holding a large amount of such coins given their doubtful standing. Bearing silent testament to this fact were charity collection boxes, which became the destination for many of the poorest quality coins.[41]

This brings us to our bakers. They were among the retail traders most exposed to this problem, since their loaves almost always sold at prices requiring the use of copper penningen and the smallest, most dubious silver coins. They could hope to pass some of these coins on to other customers as they made change, but ultimately could not avoid accumulating them. Their own payments to grain merchants, millers, and tax collectors were invariably for much larger sums, requiring the use of larger silver coins. Indeed, the millers turned to the state to protect themselves from bakers using copper coins as payment for the millers'

---

[37] Jan deVries, "The Republic's money: money and the economy," *Leidschrift* 13 (1998), 23; Clé Lesger, *Huur en conjunctuur* (Amsterdam: Historisch Seminarium van de Universiteit van Amsterdam, 1986), pp. 23–31.

[38] *Nederlandsche jaarboeken* (May 1750), pp. 696–706. This article reviews the *Generaliteitsmuntordonnaties* [Mint ordinances of the central government] of 1606, 1659, and 1694, all of which forbid the use of foreign coins in making wage payments.

[39] Ordinance of 27 October 1689. W. L. Korthals Altes, *Van £ Hollands tot Nederlandse f.: de geschiedenis van de Nederlandse geld eenheid* (Amsterdam: Boom, 1996), p. 117f.

[40] Philipp Robinson Rössner, "Mercantilism as an effective resource management strategy," in Moritz Isenmann, ed., *Mercantilismus: Wiederaufnahme einer Debate* (Stuttgart: Fritz SteinerVerlag, 2014), pp. 39–64. Rössner notes that the velocity of circulation (how often a coin changes hands per unit of time) was inverse to its value: low for high-denomination silver coins (V), higher for smaller silver coins (V'), highest for small coppers (V"). Thus V">V'>V, which can lead to the effects of Gresham's Law, or a long-term tendency for small coins to lose value relative to large coins.

[41] In 1643 a Delft Poor Relief Office sold an estimated 37,600 copper coins contributed in weekly door-to-door collections for just over half their face value. D. Teeuwen, "A penny for the poor: the widespread practice of monetary charitable donations in Dutch towns, 17th–18th century," *Tijdschrift voor sociale and economische geschiedenis* 11 (2014), 15–38.

services. A Utrecht resolution of 1658 ordered bakers to pay at least three-quarters of their milling fees in silver coin.[42] This leaves open the question of how bakers consolidated the small payments from customers, laden with small coppers, into the larger coins suitable for making payments for grain, fuel, milling fees and taxes. Was there any banking service that stood ready to perform this function?[43]

Credit. Bakers, just like other retail traders, could attempt to sidestep the small coin problem by extending credit to their customers. This was not the only reason to extend credit, of course. Many customers faced severe cash flow problems, receiving payment, as we have just noted, irregularly or seasonally. But the incentive to resort to credit seems to have come from both sides: the customer could acquire bread on a regular basis despite being paid irregularly and the baker bound to himself customers dependent on his credit while minimizing payments in small coin.[44] A bakery of average size sold bread at a rate that – depending on the mix of wheat and rye bread, and coarse and fine wheat bread sold – generated 10 to 15 guilders of revenue per day, most of which had to be set aside to pay for grain, milling, and taxes. If customers paid cash at every transaction, the baker might find that 2 to 3 guilders of his daily takings consisted of dubious coins. But if most customers bought on credit – or as contemporaries put it "*op het korfstok*," a tally stick recording every loaf purchased with a notch – the baker could hope to be paid primarily in silver coins, and he evaded the problem of finding expedients to make change in units smaller than the *duit*.

The extension of credit was the more widespread and enduring solution to the problem of making payment under the coinage regime of early modern times. It solved a coinage problem for both bakers and consumers and it appealed to bakers as a means of binding their customers to them. But it also exposed the baker to a credit risk. How large was this risk? Did bakers customarily expect to write off some portion of the revenue due them as uncollectable?

We do not have an answer to this question. Probate inventories reveal that bakers often died with a long list of "receivables" from their

---

[42] *GPB van Utrecht*, 22 November 1658. Resolutie op het maalloon by de backers te betallen.

[43] There might have been. Recipients of small copper coins are said to have assembled them in paper-wrapped rolls representing a fixed silver coin value, and these are said to have circulated at their supposed face value. Teeuwen, "A penny for the poor," pp. 15–38.

[44] For a detailed study of the role of credit in eighteenth-century retail trades, see Bart Willems, *Leven op de pof: krediet bij de Antwerpse middenstand in de achttiende eeuw* (Amsterdam: Aksant, 2009).

customers, just as they reveal deceased citizens with substantial debts to their bakers.[45] The ubiquity of such debts should caution us not to associate them too quickly with poverty or economic distress. The observation of a Parisian, cited by Kaplan, that "the baker is something like the treasurer of the indigent" seems to misconstrue the functional role of this type of retail credit.[46] Many of the deceased who left debts for bread and many other ordinary purchases had simultaneously extended credit and/or had accounts receivable of their own. As often as not, their credits exceeded their debts. Credit and debt were essential elements of market society in the early modern era and bakers were deeply enmeshed in the credit networks of their communities.

Still, the credit risk borne by bakers must have imposed a cost, one that could vary by baker and over time. When bakers complained that the cost measurements and calculations of the bread price regulators were unrealistic, they were thinking of more than the probability that some of their bakings might fail or that their grain might be underweight. They also had to worry about underweight coins and defaulting customers.

The bakers were among those traders who literally stood between two commercial worlds. The conversion of the copper and clipped coins they received into the larger silver coins their suppliers expected in payment identified a boundary line marking the limit of full monetary integration in the early modern economy. Similarly, the baker faced two worlds of contract. The grain dealers and other suppliers with whom they dealt operated in a world governed by contract law, where time limits and interest charges applied to credit, and notarial contracts and law courts stood ready to resolve disputes. The bakers, in contrast, extended book credit without interest to customers who expected flexibility concerning repayment dates. For such debts courts were a costly last resort for the resolution of disputes and even a favorable court ruling did not assure that the creditor would be paid.[47]

---

[45] Bakery accounts in probate inventories are discussed in A. Th. van Deursen, *Een dorp in de polder: Graft in de zeventiende eeuw* (Amsterdam: Bert Bakker, 2006), pp. 111–12; Jan de Vries, "Peasant demand patterns and economic development: Friesland, 1550–1750," in William N. Parker and Eric L. Jones, eds., *European Peasants and their Markets* (Princeton University Press, 1975), p. 225. A database of such inventories is maintained by the Meertens Instituut: www.meertens.knaw.nl/boedelbank/index.

[46] Kaplan, *Bakers of Paris*, p. 148.

[47] Bakers brought cases of non-payment to the courts, but they served as an "ultimate recourse." Kaplan's account of the use made by Parisian bakers of the courts emphasizes its cost and the difficulty of actually securing compensation in successful suits. Kaplan, *Bakers of Paris*, pp. 137–51. However, Muldrew sketches a more hopeful picture for the seventeenth-century English town of King's Lynn. There, bakers made regular use of the courts to collect debts. Craig Muldrew, "The importance of the food trade in urban credit networks in early modern England: the example of King's Lynn," in Piet Van Cruyningen and Erik Thun, eds., *Food Supply, Demand and Trade* (Turnhout: Brepols, 2012), pp. 173–87.

5   The Dutch "Peculiar Institution"

Bread and Taxes

From the beginning of the new system, the regulation of bread prices in the Dutch Republic became intertwined with the levying of a tax on bread. Such a tax was not altogether unique in Europe, but nowhere else was it so long lasting, so comprehensive, and so large.[1] I argued in Chapter 3 that this tax, the milling excise, could not have functioned as it did without an alteration in the method of setting bread prices, the new system, and we shall soon see (in Chapter 9) that the tax regime, in turn, did much to shape the level and the structure of relative bread prices facing Dutch consumers. For some 260 years, bread and taxes were bundled together, and their interaction formed a major pillar of Dutch political economy.

Early economic theorists debated the wisdom of this "peculiar institution" and since its dismantling in 1855 economists and historians have continued to debate its effects. While the importance of the tax on bread is often acknowledged, knowledge of its inner workings remains limited. This chapter seeks to remedy that lacuna. It will demonstrate that this tax was resilient, perhaps uniquely resilient, in extracting a large and growing revenue from the Dutch population over more than two centuries, and I will argue that the source of this resilence lay in the milling excises' approximation of an "optimal" tax – one that minimizes distortions to economic behavior. We will see how the Dutch state learned over time to tax effectively the "wage good" by exploiting the inelastic demand for wheat bread revealed by a growing share of the population while, simultaneously, crafting tax and pricing policies that offered poorer consumers a partial escape from what became the largest single source of public revenue in the entire Republic.

---

[1] See Chapter 14 for a discussion of bread taxation in other European countries.

115

The Milling Excise in Holland

The Republic faced recurring needs to raise additional revenue throughout the seventeenth century. Financing wars with Spain (to 1648), England (1651–53, 1664–67, and 1672–74), and France (1672–78, 1689–97, and 1702–13) claimed the great bulk of public revenue, either as direct expenditures or as interest payments on public debt incurred, invariably, for military defense. Holland felt this need acutely. Its quota in the Republic's central budget was about 60 percent throughout the seventeenth and eighteenth centuries, and it often contributed even more to compensate for shortfalls in payments by other provinces.

As requirements rose, every province sought additional revenue but turned first and foremost to the common means – the indirect taxes levied on consumption. They added new excises to the initial array of taxed goods and increased rates on those already existing. In Holland these strategies accounted for nearly all – 95 percent – of the growth of total revenues between 1584 and 1650.

Among the many excises on consumption, the milling excise gradually rose in importance. When Holland introduced it as a provincial levy in 1574 it was a small burden, one the bakers were forced to absorb given the limitations of old system bread price regulation. But, as discussed in Chapter 3, the post-1596 new system provided a mechanism for incorporating the milling excise in the bread price. This simultaneously removed a major souce of friction with the bakers and opened a promising new revenue-raising opportunity.

The States of Holland found reason to increase the milling excise eight times in the seventeenth century. After the doubling of the tax in 1597, the tax rose as shown in Table 5.1. Holland's leaders developed an appreciation for this source of revenue that was shared – and put into words – by the States of Groningen, which said of the milling excise in 1623 that "it is beyond debate the greatest and best tax levied in this province."[2]

The milling excise, which accounted for only 4 percent of the common means in the 1580s, grew to become at least 20 percent by 1650; by itself it accounted for a quarter of the growth of the excises as a whole, as shown in Table 5.2, which offers an overview of the course of Holland's total tax revenue from 1575 to 1794.

Holland's common means revenue taken as a whole ceases to grow rapidly after 1650. This led the States of Holland to order a comprehensive review of the entire panoply of excise levies in 1679 – all forty-two

---

[2] Cited in T. B. M. Matthey, *Westeremden: het verleden van een Gronings terpdorp* (Groningen, 1975), p. 280.

Table 5.1 *Excise on milled grain (*'t gemaal*) in Holland*
(guilders per last of grain milled for bread baking)

	Wheat	Rye
1597	12	6
1605	32.4	16.2
1618	38	19
1625	40.5	20.25
1627	47.7	23.85
1636	63.6	31.8
1680	95.40	47.70
1683	104.9375	52.4685
1748–49	0	0
1750	104.9375	42.35
1806	National excise replaces provincial excises.	

See Table 15.2.

of them – with a view to identifying new taxing possibilities, abolishing taxes with excessive collection costs, and improving the enforcement of those that remained.[3] In the following year the States of Holland took action with a flurry of new ordinances. It abolished sixteen excises and increased substantially the tax rates of three of the most promising of those that remained: the excise on wine and brandy, the *herengeld* ("gentleman's tax"), a tax on servants, and *het gemaal*, the milling excise.[4] The first two were clearly targeted at the well-to-do – drinkers of wine and employers of servants – while the milling excise, of course, focused on the staple food of nearly everyone, who now suddenly faced a 33 percent increase of the tax incorporated in their bread prices, both wheat and rye. In addition, the 1680 reforms introduced new measures to monitor the conduct of bakers and millers, limited more strictly the movement of bread and flour across tax jurisdictions, and altered radically the method by which the States collected the milling excise in rural areas.[5] As if that were not enough, in 1683 the States levied an additional 10 percent surcharge (the *tiende verhoging*) on this and all other excises, a surcharge that remained in effect as long as the Republic endured.

---

[3] Wantje Fritschy, "The efficiency of taxation in Holland," in Oscar Gelderblom, ed., *The Political Economy of the Dutch Republic* (Farnham: Ashgate, 2009), pp. 64–74.

[4] *Ibid.*, pp. 65–66. The abolished excises included those on necessities such as salted fish, candles, shoes, woolen cloth, herring, soap, and salt.

[5] *GPB van Holland*, vol. IV, 6 March 1680, Ordonnatie op het gemael ten platte Lande; 19 March 1680, Ordonnatie tot vermeerderinge van impost op 't gemael; 29 March 1680, Placaet tot weeringe van sluykeryen en fraudatien in 't middel van 't gemael, pp. 888–99.

Table 5.2 *Holland: public revenue, 1575–1794 (thousands of guilders per year)*

	Total revenue	Common means	CM as % of total rev.	Milling excise	Milling excise as % of common means
	Net revenues (excluding tax farmers' margins)				
1575	800	280	35%	24	8.6%
1578–82	1,008	820	45	[33]	4.0
1590	2,900	1,797	62	76	4.2
1599	4,600	2,700	59	216	8.0
1608	5,844	4,344	74	698	16.1
1620–29	8,438	5,863	70	1,006*	17.2
1630–39	10,584	7,367	70	1,344**	18.2
1640–49	11,966	8,386	70	1,439	17.2
1650–59	11,544	7,774	67	1,672	21.5
1660–69	13,884	8,001	58	1,687	21.1
1670–79	15,946	7,890	50	1,625	20.6
1680–89	15,638	9974	64	2,417	24.2
1690–99	23,035	10,107	44	2,400	23.7
1700–09	22,356	9,353	42	2,156	23.1
1710–19	21,712	8,973	41	2,050	22.8
1720–29	21,205	9,281	44	2,083	22.4
1730–39	21,854	9,285	42	2,103	22.6
1740–47	22,173	8,588	39	2,104	24.5
	Gross revenues (including collection costs)				
1750–59	26,306	11,120	42	2,485	22.3
1760–69	26,865	11,843	44	2,581	21.8
1770–79	26,280	11,479	44	2,631	22.9
1780–89	27,171	11,501	42	2,720	23.7
1790–94	31,472	11,497	37	2,566	22.3

* 1624 only
** 1635–39 only
[] Estimate based on contemporary statements.
Sources: Tracy, *Founding*, 102–05, 176, 247–48, 267; Fritschy and Liesker, *GWF – Holland*, table II 1.1 (total revenue); table II 1.2 and III 2.1 (common means); table III.4.a(2) (milling excise).

How did the renovated excises perform? When the reforms to the common means were proposed, Grand Pensionary Fagel, the Republic's highest executive officer, reckoned each of the three excises selected for major increases would yield an additional 400,000 guilders annually. The wine and brandy tax disappointed, raising less than half that amount. The *herengeld* [Gentleman's tax] met the goal, and then some, but only after being refashioned into a directly collected head tax whose rate depended on the tax payers' outward signs of wealth (such as the number of servants and the value of real property). In short, it ceased to be an excise tax based on actual consumption.[6]

Fagel had estimated that a 33 percent rise in milling excise would increase revenue by about 25 percent. The milling excise had secured a reputation as a dependable generator of revenue based on the experience of earlier seventeenth-century tax increases, especially in 1605, 1625, and 1636. But such a large increase, coming on top of so many earlier increases, led Fagel to suppose that consumers would reveal a fairly elastic demand for bread as its price rose further. In fact, the milling excise out-performed them all. Consumer demand for bread, especially wheat bread, remained highly inelastic. The milling excise alone accounted for 40 percent of the total revenue increase achieved by this comprehensive renovation of the common means. From 1680 to 1805 the milling excise served as the backbone of Holland's common means, accounting single-handedly, year-in and year-out, for nearly one-quarter of Holland's common means revenues.

The excellence of the milling excise – from the point of view of a revenue-hungry state – rested on the behavior of consumers, who did not allow increased prices to reduce their bread consumption, but also on a change in the way this tax was collected in the countryside.

Tailoring Taxation to Rural Conditions

The collections of the milling excise in rural areas had always fallen well short of projections. In its early years many rural areas were in practice exempted from this quintessentially urban levy. When rural enforcement was sharpened, this took the form of increasing surveillance of rural grain mills, and reducing the number of such mills (see Chapter 7). But the fiscal authorities continued to complain of evasion and fraud, and the 1680 excise reforms provided an opportunity to introduce a new, hopefully more effective, approach to rural enforcement.

The States resolved to cease levying this tax at rural grain mills, and to replace it with a capitation tax on rural households. Each rural household was assessed a fee that represented an assumed per capita consumption of either wheat or rye: 1/28th of a last of bread grain per head (above 10 years of age), half this amount for those aged 4 to 10, and nothing for children under four. (See Table 5.3 for details.) The amount due was equal to the milling excise that would otherwise be payable on an equal amount of grain brought to the mill for grinding. For example, an adult

---

[6] *Ibid.*, p. 71. Renamed the *zout-, zeep-, heren- en redemptiegeld* (salt, soap, gentleman's and redemption tax) it eventually generated about 540,000 guilders more than the excises it replaced.

Table 5.3 *Holland's rural milling excise capitation of 1680*
Per capita milling excise. The capitation is based on an assumed adult consumption of
1/28th of a last of bread grain, which equals 107.35 liters or 78.6 kg (capitation in guilders)

Age	Wheat	Rye
Above 10	3.75	1.875
Children, aged 4–10	1.875	0.938
Children under 4	0	0

Estimate of maximum capitation revenue, c. 1680s
Rural population *c.* 1680: 328,000; assumed bread consumption: 60% wheat; 40% rye

Age	% of rural population	Average tax per capita	Total revenue
Above 10	76%	2.97	740,362
Aged 4–10	14%	1.485	68,191
Under 4	10%	0	0
Total			808,553
Deduct 10% for exempt populations			727,698 gross revenue
Deduct 15% for tax farmers' revenue			618,543 net revenue

paid 3.75 guilders per year for wheat (half that amount for rye). These amounts were 1/28th the excise due for milling one last of grain in the cities. Having made this payment, due in quarterly installments, a household could send 1/28th of a last of grain to the mill for conversion to flour (if it planned to bake bread at home) or it could purchase 200 pounds of wheat bread or 192 pounds of rye bread from the baker.[7]

The conversion of the excise on milling into a capitation tax appears at first glance to represent an effort to simplify tax collection in the countryside. Everyone was to pay for an assumed level of consumption – a very low level: approximately 70 kg per capita (including children). In return for this modest level of compliance, rural folk would, one assumes, be left alone in their buying and selling of grain and flour. In the rural province of Drenthe, where such a conversion had been made already in 1630, this was certainly the intention.[8] In Utrecht and

[7] The capitation tax assumed that a last of wheat could be expected to yield 5,600 pounds (2,766 kg) of coarse wheat bread and a last of rye could yield 5,376 pounds (2,655 kg) of rye bread. These are reasonable estimates, typical of the yields assumed by the towns, although well below what bakers could actually achieve. In 1750 the bread quantities were adjusted slightly to incorporate a small change in the milling excise on rye. *GPB van Holland*, vol. VII, 26 November 1749.

[8] *Tegenwoorde Staat van Drenthe* (Amsterdam, 1795), p. 186. The capitation sum was collected directly and the bakers, now free of entanglement in the administration of the milling excise, were required to reduce the bread price by 8 percent.

Zeeland, which turned to a rural capitation tax on milling around the same time as Holland, in 1675 and 1687, respectively, the price for being left alone was high since they assumed a higher level of per capita consumption than Holland. But in Holland the administration of the capitation tax was in fact remarkably invasive; it was intended to be a *minimum* tax, not a total substitution for the milling excise, and required extensive recordkeeping.[9]

It operated – or was supposed to operate – as follows:[10] Each rural tax jurisdiction supplied its tax farmers with lists (*kohieren*) of households, with details on household size and age composition. The tax farmers were to present each household with a form (*biljet*) specifying the size of the household and the type of grain consumed (which could be wheat, rye, or a combination of both). This form was a tax bill. For example, a household of four full and two half adults, consuming a 50–50 mix of wheat and rye bread was to pay 14.0625 guilders.[11] The tax farmer then left this document with the household, which gave it the right to purchase 500 pounds of wheat bread and 480 pounds of rye bread from the bakers, free of further taxation. The household members took their form to the baker, who held it and deducted their bread purchases over the course of the year.[12] (The ordinance specified that households retained the right to change bakers, and ordered bakers to return the tax form on request.) If the household consumed less bread in a year than provided for by the capitation tax, it was not entitled to any refund; if, however, its consumption exceeded the amounts specified on the form, the excess bread was to be purchased at the bread price that incorporates the excise

---

[9] Folkert Nicholaas Sickenga, *Bijdrage tot de geschiedenis der belastingen in Nederland* (Leiden, 1864), pp. 397–98; *GPB van Utrecht*, vol. II, p. 759; *GPB van Holland en Zeeland*, vol. IV, pp. 1110–13.

[10] In what follows I am guided by the 6 March 1680 Ordonnantie op het gemael ten Platte Lande, which set out the details of the new policy under twenty headings. It was later amended in minor ways, but remained in effect until 1806. In 1796 an ordinance of the new Provinciaal Committé van Holland, "Over de belasting op tarwe en rogge d.d. 23 juni 1796," repeated these same procedures, with an added provision requiring those subject to the *verponding*, the property tax, to pay at least one-third of their tax at the rate applicable for wheat.

[11] What if household contained a seafarer or soldier who spent part of each year away from home? The ordinance provided that persons who could demonstrate an absence of at least two consecutive months would be taxed at half the normal rate. What if the household divided its time between the city and a country residence? The 1796 review of the enforcement procedures required such households to pay the rural capitation for six months of the year.

[12] What if the household baked its own bread? These households were supplied with a special form giving them the right to have their quota of grain milled, without being subjected to further taxation, at a specified mill.

tax, just like urban consumers.[13] The baker, for his part, used these forms to demonstrate to the grain miller that his grain was covered by head-tax-paying consumers, since grain milled to produce bread in "excess" of the base consumption level was subject to direct payment of the milling tax, as in the cities.

The rural head tax that replaced the milling excise in 1680 remained in use until the introduction of a national tax policy in 1806.[14] Those responsible for Holland's fiscal system must have regarded it as an improvement over direct collection in the countryside. But it was in no sense a simplified system designed for a rustic society of self-providers. On the contrary, it required tax collectors to possess detailed information about every rural household, required that bakers maintain records of every household's bread purchases, and forced millers to verify the tax status of every grain parcel brought for milling. Did the head tax regime really function as specified in the ordinances? One would like to see some of the household lists and tax forms that must have been produced in the millions in order to comply with the requirements of this cumbersome policy. But, here as elsewhere with the administrative procedures of Holland's tax farmers, nothing remains of their local recordkeeping.[15]

Did the 1680 reforms succeed in getting rural bread consumers to pay their fair share of the milling excise? How serious had underpayment actually been before 1680? A glance at the annual milling excise revenues from 1679 on gives a positive impression – revenues do, indeed, jump upward in 1680 and the years thereafter. But how much of that increase was attributable to the rural reform and how much to the rise in rates? An added complication is the fact that our only information on milling tax receipts until 1750 is the amounts paid by the tax farmers as they bid on the collection rights. To the extent that the bidding process was competitive, this should leave us with a fair idea of the *net* revenues (the

---

[13] The poor who received distributions of bread from charitable institutions were not subject to the head tax, just as charitable institutions in the cities were exempt from the milling tax. But such households received the same form, which they were to place in the hands of the charitable institution that supplied them, giving these institutions the right to acquire bread (up to the 200 pound limit!) free of tax. The 1796 review of these procedures added a monitoring procedure, requiring the tax collectors to submit lists of those eligible for exemption to the magistrates of their rural jurisdictions for review and approval.

[14] It was last renewed and described in detail on 1 December 1790, but continued in effect until 1806. *GPB van Holland*, vol. IX, pp. 904–22, Ordonnantie in vordering van 't gemaal.

[15] In Zeeland these detailed village-level household head counts have survived. They were first prepared in 1680 in preparation for the conversion to the rural capitation regime begun in 1687. Peter Priester, *Geschiedenis van de Zeeuwse landbouw circa 1600–1910*, AAG Bijdragen 37 (Wageningen: Afdeling Agrarische Geschiedenis, 1998), pp. 487–88.

Table 5.4 Milling excise revenues, in guilders by tax district, 1679–87

	1679	1680	1681	1682	1683	1684	1685	1686	1687
Dordrecht	92,230	125,110	145,060	149,580	172,749	160,550	164,680	165,840	
Brielle	45,343	27,680	45,927	50,895	59,848	56,910	60,614	62,840	
Gorinchem	31,219	43,217	39,205	34,347	50,150	48,092	48,255	52,969	
Rotterdam	115,200	169,800	172,500	172,200	191,400	171,000	172,000	160,700	
Gouda	80,800	110,697	119,405	121,105	135,839	118,365	118,780	112,665	
Delft	177,950	253,950	265,950	258,450	281,710	256,525	257,475	261,475	
Leiden	181,500	269,800	279,400	272,900	306,130	278,700	283,800	278,800	
Haarlem	202,890	271,230	299,688	302,663	335,029	309,262	294,950	288,775	
Amsterdam	376,225	385,030	408,615	601,440	661,818	626,475	625,400	624,880	
South Holland	130,3357	1,656,514	1,775,750	1,963,580	2,194,673	2,025,879	2,025,954	2,008,944	2,008,631
North Holland	263,990	341,890	354,540	352,438	382,122	335,510	335,065	337,815	326,360
Direct collection	251,959		*						233,509
Total	1,567,347	2,250,363	2,130,290	2,316,018	2,576,795	2,361,389	2,361,019	2,346,759	2,568,500
		Rate increase			Surcharge introduced	Surcharge rescinded			Surcharge reintroduced
Increase in rates		33.30%			10.00%	−10.00%			10.00%
Actual increase in revenues		43.60%			11.30%	−9.10%			9.45%
Index model	100	133.3	133.3	133.3	146.6	133.3	133.3	133.3	146.6
Index actual	100	143.577842	135.9169348	147.7667677	164.4048829	150.6615319	150.6379251	149.7281074	163.88
Difference		10.27784205	2.61693479	14.46676767	17.8048829	17.36153188	17.33792511	16.42810743	17.28

* direct collection unreported in 1681

gross revenue collected minus collection costs). But it is reasonable to expect that bidders would have been cautious in their assessments of the added revenue that they might actually collect in the initial years of the reforms. By how much would a 33 percent increase in the tax rate reduce the consumption of bread? Would the capitation system increase revenue more than it would increase administrative costs?

Answering our questions about the impact of the shift to the capitation system requires that we take some care in sorting out several simultaneous changes as they unfold in each of Holland's tax districts, year by year, just before and after 1680. Table 5.4 shows the annual milling excise payments for each tax district in South Holland and a total for the seven small North Holland districts beginning with 1679, the last pre-revision year. The tax farmers increased their milling excise payments by 27.5 percent in 1680, rather less than one might have hoped from a 33 percent increase in the tax rate (and close to Fagel's prediction!). But marginal comments in the revenue collection document provide some interesting clarification: they list a series of subdistricts that the treasury had not succeeded in leasing to tax farmers, among them Brielle, Amsterdam, and the rural jurisdictions of these towns.[16] In these places provincial officials had to take on the direct collection of taxes. When their collections are added to the tax farm revenues, the total raised by the revised milling excise in 1680 came to 2.25 million, or nearly 44 percent more than in the previous year.

In the following year matters still had not settled down completely. Returns for Amsterdam and Brielle remain anomalous and the tax documents refer again to the need for direct collections, although in this case we do not know how much was ultimately collected in this way. Perhaps 1682 can be regarded as offering a fair reflection of the net effect of the changes introduced in 1680. Total collections then were 48 percent above the 1679 level. If the 33 percent increase in the tax rates had led to no changes in consumer behavior (they neither consumed less bread nor shifted from more heavily taxed wheat to less heavily taxed rye) and the capitation system was "revenue neutral" in its effects, we could not expect more than a 33 percent increase in revenue. The remaining 15 percent (at least) can be attributed to the introduction of the capitation system in the rural areas.

In 1683, the entire panoply of excises, the milling tax included, was subject to the *tiende verhoging* or 10 percent surcharge. This surcharge on existing rates was a more straightforward tax change to implement, and

---

[16] A.R.A. Den Haag, Financien van Holland, no. 826. This matter is discussed in Liesker and Fritschy, *GWF – Holland*, p. 319.

revenues immediately reflect the added tax burden: total revenues rise by 11.3 percent overall and in nearly every tax district.[17] From 1683 onward, the milling excise generated 270–280,000 guilders more in annual revenue than can be accounted for under the most optimistic assumptions about the price elasticity of demand for bread (i.e., that it was zero – that consumers did not alter their consumption at all in the face of the tax-induced rise in price). The capitation tax, if fully collected from the rural population, could have raised approximately 600,000 guilders (Table 5.3 supplies a justification for this estimate), which suggests that the capitation system succeeded in increasing rural revenue by 40–50 percent over what had been collected from rural consumers before its introduction. The 1680 renovation of the common means succeeded in securing a sharp increase in revenue, and the reformed milling excise proved crucial to this success.

The Milling Excise in Other Provinces

As we have seen, the Republic's founding document envisioned that the common means – including the milling excise – would be levied uniformly in all the provinces. In practice, nothing was ever uniform in the Dutch Republic. Every province and every town found reasons to select and shape public policies to local needs and interests. But they all introduced a milling excise. The rates varied by province and city but no portion of the Republic escaped this tax, as Table 5.5 reveals.

At the risk of a bit of oversimplification, one can gather the remaining provinces into two groups. One comprises Zeeland, Utrecht, and Friesland. The first two are often grouped with Holland to form the "west" referred to so often in this volume. Its highly urban population shifted toward wheat bread consumption in the course of the seventeenth century. I add Friesland to this group here, even though it remains predominantly rye-bread-eating, because it shared with Zeeland and Utrecht a common set of taxing policies.[18] The second group comprises the remaining provinces of the "east": Groningen, Drenthe, Overijssel, Gelderland, and States Brabant, a territory administered directly by the States General. These more rural provinces all remained predominantly rye-bread-eating and pursued a distinctive taxing policy.

---

[17] The surcharge was removed the following year but reinstated, now permanently, in 1687. *Ibid.*, p. 112.

[18] The shared policies of interest here concern the milling excise, but the fiscal commonalities of these provinces went much further than this. See De Vries and van der Woude, *First Modern Economy*, pp. 98–102.

Table 5.5 *The excise on milled grain ('t gemaal) in other provinces (guilders per last of grain milled for bread baking)*

Overijssel	Wheat	Rye	Friesland	Wheat	Rye
1597	6.75	2.7	1602	21.6	5.4
1603	12	3	1605	25.2	5.4
1623	24	8	1608	32.4	10.8
1627	24	12	1624	36	10.8
1675–1805	36	18	1649	46.9	16.8
			1673	72	27
			1691	90	36
Gelderland (Zutphen and Veluwe Quarters)			1741	99	39.6
			1750–1805	72	39.6
1618	17.6	14.3			
1623	24				
1642	30	14	**Utrecht**		
1700	30	14			
1750–1805	30	14	1579	5	1.5
			1599	10	2.2
			1601	13.125	2.813
			urban rates		
Gelderland (Nijmegen Quarter)			1627	30	10
1625	58.85	24.75	1629	40	13.4
1692	54		1640	60	24.7
1700	45	21	1665	62.5	32.5
1750–1805	45	21	1679	75	38.75
			1689	110	60
			1750–1805	115	53.75
Groningen					
1594	6	3	rural rates		
1602	24	12	1629	26.5	4.1
1623	33	13.2	1640	53.125	22.5
1665	49.5	9.9	1689	87.5	40
1678	39.6	16.5			
1716	66	24.75	**Zeeland**		
1786–1805	82.5	24.75			
			1586	11.25	5.75
			1599	22.5	11.25
			1623	30	15
			1627	37.5	18.75
			1666	45	22.5
			1668	52.5	26.25
			1681	63.75	31.875
			1688	69.275	34.69 (urban)
			1692–1805	75	37.5 (urban)

West. The States of Utrecht and Zeeland followed Holland's pattern fairly closely, taxing wheat at double the rate for rye, and increasing their rates frequently in the course of the seventeenth century. Friesland taxed wheat much more heavily than rye, at five times the rye rate at first. The average tax per last of grain in these three provinces began lower than Holland's – about two-thirds Holland's rates – but rose faster, converging on Holland's milling excise by the 1680s.

In the 1680s both Utrecht and Zeeland shifted rural consumers to a head tax in order to address tax evasion, just as in Holland. Utrecht left the local taxing authorities with a degree of discretion. They could charge from 2.0 to 2.5 guilders per head "according to circumstances," although they were to be guided, much as in Holland, by detailed written registers of household size.[19] But even the minimum charge, 2 guilders, was more than a poor Hollander consuming only rye bread was asked to pay. In Zeeland, a wheat-producing province, everyone above 12 years of age was levied 4.25 guilders, again, well above Holland's levy for wheat-bread eaters, albeit for an assumed consumption double the amount in Holland, 1/14th of a last, or about 165 kg of wheat bread.[20] States Flanders (a jurisdiction under the direct rule of the States General that would later be known as Zeeland Flanders) also saw its excise tax converted to capitation in 1687. Holland's rigorous enforcement rules found application there: the tax farmer was instructed to keep a register at each mill, tracking the milling ordered by each household, which, for its part, could exercise its right to shift its patronage to another miller only once per year.[21]

As a result of these measures, Utrecht and Zeeland succeeded in collecting nearly as much milling excise per capita as Holland. Since Friesland's population ate relatively little wheat, its revenue potential was necessarily lower. But, perhaps because it lacked the broad range of excises levied in Holland, the States of Friesland exploited the milling excise with special vigor. Successive tax increases caused it to account for 72 percent of the total increase in Friesland's common means revenues between 1634 and 1640, when comprehensive data first become available, and between 1694 and 1702. By the latter period the milling excise

---

[19] *GPB van Utrecht*, vol. II. 1 Aug. 1675, gerenoveerd 11 July 1676, p. 759.
    "Ordonnantie, waar na het middel op het gemaal in plaatse van verpachting, over alle ingesetenen deser prov. ten plattenlande by omslag, of quotisatie ..." The tax farmers were instructed to maintain an "inner proportionality" regarding the number of heads in each household and regarding their consumption. Then, each household was to be given a billet informing it of its yearly tax, to be paid in quarterly installments.
[20] Veenstra, *GWF – Zeeland*, p. 159; Verstegen, *GWF – Utrecht*, pp. 119–20.
[21] *GPB van Holland* (Zeeland), vol. IV, p. 1162.

accounted for 40 percent of Friesland's total common means revenues, and the population paid at the per capita rate of at least 2.4 guilders.[22] Overall, the rise in milling excise rates and their improved enforcement in rural areas succeeded in increasing per capita payments in Utrecht, Zeeland, and Friesland nearly threefold over the course of the seventeenth century while they more than doubled in Holland. All of these provinces raised their milling excises repeatedly in the course of the seventeenth century to reach a plateau of high taxation that endured into the nineteenth century.

East. The inland or eastern provinces also introduced the common means, including the milling excise, and initially their tax rates were comparable to the "high tax" provinces of the west. Around 1600–05 both the wheat and rye taxes in the east stood at approximately 60 percent of Holland's level. The States of these provinces increased their milling tax rates until the 1620s, but thereafter practiced forbearance. Further increases were few and those quite modest, the protestations of Holland and the States General notwithstanding.[23] By the 1680s the milling excises in the east had fallen to only 33–40 percent of Holland's level.

The total revenue raised in the eastern provinces by the milling excise was much smaller than even these tax rates would suggest, since their inhabitants consumed little of the more highly taxed wheat bread. Groningen (with higher milling excises than the other provinces with which it is grouped here) secured about 1.60 guilders per capita from the 1680s onward, but Overijssel was more typical of the region, raising only 0.72 guilders per head in 1700–09 and only two-thirds of this amount by the 1790s.[24] In sum, the eastern provinces decided early on not to rely heavily on the milling excise. Rates remained low, especially for the rye bread that accounted for the bulk of total bread consumption, such that the per capita milling excise paid in the region as a whole barely rose at all over the entire period 1600–1805.

In the more rural eastern provinces the introduction of taxation by capitation seems to have served not so much to combat evasion as to shelter the rural population from the full brunt of the already low milling tax rates prevailing there. Gelderland, which introduced rural capitation

---

[22] Trompetter, *GWF – Friesland*, p. 82.
[23] In 1640 the States General urged all provinces to adopt the high excise rates of Holland. Nothing came of this. Griet Vermeesch, *Oorlog, steden en staatsvorming* (Amsterdam University Press, 2006), p. 157
[24] Tax revenue data from Van der Ent and Enthoven, *GWF – Groningen*, p. 120, digital post a002; Fritschy, *GWF – Overijssel*, pp. 124–35.

only in 1724, charged a fairly robust 1.8 guilders per head (above age 10), but Drenthe effectively exempted a large portion of the population (students, soldiers, the lower orders, the poor, and peat diggers) from this excise, and levied 1.6 guilders per head on the rest.[25] States Brabant, governed directly by the States General, levied a capitation tax in the eighteenth century that did not exceed 1.0 guilders per adult (above age 14), although the actual revenue generated fell well below that level.[26] Later, in the early eighteenth century, Overijssel took a somewhat different approach. It gave towns and rural districts the option of paying a negotiated "redemption" fee. In exchange for this "buyout" local governments collected the milling excise – or not – for their own benefit.[27] The stagnation in provincial excise collections in eighteenth-century Overijssel (where the rural population was growing steadily) is most likely a product of this policy.

Total Milling Excise Revenue

Direct evidence of the revenue raised by this provincial milling excise is fairly abundant, but contains many gaps.[28] Still, our knowledge of the tax rates applied plus the incomplete revenue data that are available suffice to estimate the milling excise revenue at benchmark periods for the three zones into which I have divided the country: Holland; Z-U-F (Zeeland, Utrecht, and Friesland); and the east (Groningen, Drenthe, Overijssel, Gelderland, and States Brabant). These estimates, plus an account of the estimation procedures, are presented in Table 5.6

These revenue estimates for the Republic as a whole cannot be regarded as exact, but the overall levels and their regional distribution appear to be fairly reliable. Table 5.7 shows the proportional division of milling excise revenue by region. Holland always accounted for the lion's share, to be sure, while its "high-tax" neighbors gradually increased their relative effort; the eastern provinces, in contrast, accounted for less and less until the eighteenth century, when their growing populations brought about some increase in the absolute size of their contributions.

---

[25] *Tegenwoordige Staat van Drenthe*, I: 84.

[26] *GPB van Holland*, vol. VI, 27 October 1729. Four rural districts comprising the Meijerij of 's-Hertogenbosch paid 40,504 guilders annually, well under 0.50 guilders per head (of total population).

[27] Fritschy, *GWF – Overijssel*, pp. 174–75.

[28] The invaluable data collections assembled and published in the *Gewestelijke financiën* series (*GWF* volumes on the fiscal histories of the Republic's provinces) are the best source for annual revenue data. www.huygens.knaw.nl/gewestelijkefinancien. Holland's milling excise revenues are known from 1650 onward (before then, only for isolated years); Groningen's are available for the entire period; Friesland's are available, with

Table 5.6 *Estimated milling excise revenues in the Dutch Republic, 1600–1807 (in thousands of guilders per annum;* **boldface** = *based on direct evidence)*

	Holland	Z-U-F*	East	Total
1600–04	**700**	174	212	1,086
1625–29	**1,000**	312	280	1,592
1650–54	**1,672**	**533**	259	2,464
1680–84	**2,670**	**782**	330	3,782
1700–04	**2,702**	790	351	3,843
1750–54	**2,661**	**838**	393	3,892
1780–84	**2,720**	876	448	4,044
1790–94	**2,515**	**900**	467	3,882
1806	2,927	1,252	1,187	5,462
1807	2,767	1,151	849	4,767
Actual revenues				
1806	**2,950**	**1,256**	**1,256**	**5,462**
1807	**2,720**	**1,170**	**878**	**4,768**

* Z-U-F = Zeeland, Utrecht, and Friesland
I estimated total revenue as follows: I calculated average milling excises in guilders per last for wheat and rye for each benchmark period: 1600–04, 1625–29, 1650–54, 1680–84, 1700–04, 1750–54, 1780–84, and 1790–94. I inflated these tax rates by the population of each zone, and then estimated total revenue. I then discounted this "maximum attainable revenue" for each zone collected in proportion to the actual revenues realized by Holland at each benchmark period. This "potential" revenue was then reduced further by the assumption that tax evasion was greater than in Holland by 5 percent in Zeeland-Utrecht-Friesland and by 20 percent in the eastern provinces. In summary, the estimates above are based on the tax rates and populations of each zone, and calibrated to Holland's actual revenues with an adjustment for greater avoidance in less urban regions. The bold figures in the Z-U-F column indicate dates for which direct evidence is available for all provinces. Except for 1790–94, the estimation procedure yielded revenue estimates within 10 percent of the actual revenues.

In 1806 the Batavian Republic replaced the provincial excises with uniform national tax rates, and centralized collection. Thus, we know the actual revenues generated by the milling excise beginning in 1806, shown in bold in the table. The 1806–07 revenue estimates are based on the same procedure used for the earlier period, with the exception that the evasion rates have been raised from 5 to 10 percent for Z-U-F and from 20 to 30 percent for the east. For these provinces the new national tax regime introduced a large and sudden increase in rates. The jump in revenues in the east reflects a sharp rise in tax rates but if tax evasion had not risen the revenue jump would have been greater still. See Chapter 15 for more detail on the effects of the new tax regime.

many gaps from the 1630s to 1680s, whereafter the series is continuous. Overijssel provides continuous data only from the 1750s. Data for Zeeland and Utrecht are available only for the chief towns until late in the eighteenth century. Elsewhere (Drenthe, Gelderland, and the special case of States Brabant) the evidence is incidental.

Table 5.7 *Each region's share of total milling excise revenue, 1600–1807*

	Holland	Z-U-F	East
1600–04	64%	16%	20%
1625–29	63	20	18
1650–54	68	22	11
1680–84	71	21	8
1700–04	70	21	9
1750–54	68	22	10
1780–84	67	22	11
1790–94	65	23	12
1806	54	23	23
1807	58	24	18

For comparison, consider the tax quota each of these provincial groupings was committed to pay to the Republic's central government budgets:

1612	57	27	18*
1616	58	26	16
1792	65	18	17
1807**	57	23	20

The population was distributed across these regions as follows:

1600	43	21	36
1680	50	18	32
1795	41	19	40

*The milling excise revenues in Table 5.5 include collections from the Generality lands, the most important of which was States Brabant. These regions, since they were administered directly by the States General, were not included in the tax quota regime described here. Consequently, total revenues from the "east" will have been somewhat larger than the quota percentages shown here.
**The figures for 1807 do not reflect a quota, since this had been abolished by the new unitary tax regime. They reveal the actual revenues collected in each region.
Source: De Vries and van der Woude, *First Modern Economy,* p. 99.

In 1806–07 the Batavian Republic replaced the decentralized provincial excises with a new uniform national milling tax. This brought a sudden change to these long-stable proportions: Holland's relative effort became a bit smaller; Zeeland, Utrecht, and Friesland's position remained essentially as it had been; while the eastern provinces now suddenly faced a much higher burden.

The revenue estimates of Table 5.7 also allow for a calculation of the regional differences in tax burden placed by the milling excise on the average consumer. Table 5.8 expresses the total revenue estimates in per capita terms. Holland's inhabitants, facing high rates and displaying a strong propensity to consume the heavily taxed wheat breads, always paid the most: 1.24 guilders per capita in 1600–14, rising to 3.40

Table 5.8 *Estimated per capita milling excise payments by region, 1600–1807*

	In guilders per capita			Index, relative to Holland		
	Holland	Z-U-F	East	Holland	Z-U-F	East
1600–04	1.24	0.64	0.44	100	52	35
1625–29	1.39	0.98	0.57	100	71	41
1650–54	2.09	1.56	0.50	100	75	24
1680–84	3.02	2.40	0.58	100	79	19
1700–04	3.16	2.50	0.57	100	79	18
1750–54	3.40	2.52	0.60	100	74	18
1780–84	3.47	2.46	0.60	100	71	17
1790–94	3.21	2.41	0.60	100	75	19
1806	3.69	3.14	1.57	100	85	43
1807	3.40	2.93	1.10	100	86	32
Total per capita taxation by region (in guilders)						
1795	22.84	18.55	7.21			
1807	29.78	23.40	9.80			
Milling excise revenue as percentage of total tax revenue						
1790–94	14.1	13.6	8.5			
1807	11.4	12.5	11.2			

Source: Total taxation by province from I. J. A. Gogel, *Memoriëen en correspondentien betreffende den staat van 's Rijks geldmiddelen in den jare 1820* (Amsterdam, 1844), pp. 510–11.

guilders by the mid-eighteenth century, but the inhabitants of Zeeland, Utrecht, and Friesland were not far behind. Their per capita milling excise payments more than tripled over the two centuries, reaching over 2.50 guilders. The eastern provinces reveal a fundamentally different pattern: low per capita taxes that rise only slightly over the entire two centuries of the old Republic's existence. In these provinces the shock of the Batavian fiscal innovations is plainly evident. While consumers in the other regions faced per capita tax increases of 10–20 percent, the eastern provinces suddenly paid 2.6 times more in tax (in spite of their many evasive efforts) in 1806.

Finally, this estimation exercise allows for an overall assessment of the place of the Dutch Republic's peculiar practice of taxing bread in its overall fiscal regime. How large a contribution did the milling excise make to the total revenues of the Republic? The results, shown in Table 5.9, are surprising in their consistency, both over time and across the provinces. The milling excise alone generated 10–12 percent of total provincial revenues in every region. (The eastern provinces appear to have avoided heavy reliance on the milling excise, but they avoided most other forms of taxation as well!) Moreover, the milling excise contributed this

Table 5.9 *The milling excise as a percentage of total tax revenue (all provinces), 1600–1807 (in thousands of guilders)*

	Milling excise	Total revenue	Milling as % of total
1600–04	1,086	9,300	11.7
1630	1,592	15,500	10.3
1650	2,464	19,000	13.0
1680	3,782	24,500	15.4
1700	3,843	28,500	13.5
1750	3,892	37,100	10.5
1780	4,044	37,800	10.4
1790–94	3,882	39,000	10.0
1800–04		34,300	
1806	5,462	42,700	12.8
1807	4,768	44,600	10.7
1814–16	5,446	33,000	16.5
1822–25	2,571 3,850*	37,000	7.0–10.3
1826–30	3,496 5,100*	38,000	9.2–13.4
1833–39	4,529 7,250*	50,300	9.0–14.4
1845–49	4,832 6,932*	55,000	8.8–12.6
Municipal taxes only		Total municipal revenue	
1845–49	2,100	11,500	18.3

*National and municipal milling excises combined.
Milling excise estimates, see Table 5.5.
Total tax revenue refers to the total tax revenue of each of the provinces, plus the generality lands. It does not include direct central government revenues, primarily customs revenues (*convooi en licentien*). These estimates to 1794 are based on provincial tax data assembled in the GWF volumes. Thereafter, they are drawn from the following: Wantje Fritschy and René van der Voort, "From fragmentation to unification: public finance, 1700–1914," in 't Hart *et al.*, eds., *Financial History of the Netherlands*, pp. 68, 84, 87; T. J. E. M. Pfeil, "Nederlandse bezuinigingsbeleid, 1795–1810," in Wantje Fritschy, J. K. T. Postma, and J. Roelevink, eds., *Doel en middel. Aspecten van financieel overheidsbeleid in de Nederlanden van de zestiende eeuw tot heden* (Amsterdam: NEHA, 1995), p. 135.

substantial share of total public revenues throughout the seventeenth and eighteenth centuries.[29]

A steady percentage may suggest that the bread excise remained a fairly constant burden. But the Republic – so often at war with its neighbors – found it necessary to double the total per capita tax burden over the course of the seventeenth century – from about 11 to 22 guilders. After a pause at

[29] The Republic also raised the equivalent of customs revenues (*convooien en licentien*) collected by the admiralties. In addition property owners paid drainage taxes to polder authorities and urban residents were subject to municipal taxes (which everywhere included an additional milling excise). None of these revenues are included in this exercise. Together, these taxes raised an additional 8–10 million guilders annually.

that level, it rose further to 25 guilders by the 1780s. To achieve these revenue needs the Republic's provinces introduced new taxes and transformed extraordinary (temporary) taxes into permanent levies. In this setting the milling excise stands out as uniquely capable of keeping pace with the pressure for ever more revenue throughout the old Republic's existence. What gave this tax its resilience? Was the milling excise, perhaps, an example of that elusive ideal of economists, an "optimal tax"?

Optimal Tax Theory

If a given revenue must be raised via taxes on consumption then, as Ramsey originally demonstrated, such taxes should be imposed in inverse proportion to the representative consumer's price elasticity of demand for those goods.[30] Focusing taxation on commodities with inelastic demand is therefore "optimal" in the sense that it minimizes the deadweight loss to the consumer resulting from the tax's distorting effect on behavior (that is, buying less of the taxed commodity).

Figure 5.1 helps explain what is at issue here. If a good (say, bread) faces demand curve A, then Q_0 will be sold at price P_0. The addition of a tax, t, will raise the price to $P_0 + t$, inducing consumers to cut back on consumption to Q_1. Just how much consumption is reduced by an increase in price depends on the price elasticity of demand for the good in question. The demand curve in Figure 5.1a portrays a fairly elastic demand. The imposition of the tax generates revenue for the state represented by the rectangle $P_0 \, B \, E_1 \, P_0 + t$. However, the welfare loss to consumers is larger than the state's gain by the size of the triangle $E_1 \, B \, E_0$. This space, known as the Harberger triangle, measures the deadweight loss to consumers – a loss uncompensated for by gains to others. When demand is elastic with respect to price, this triangle is large, suggesting that the imposition of the tax has imposed a welfare-reducing distortion in consumer behavior. If demand for the taxed good is price inelastic (Figure 5.1b), the demand curve would be nearly vertical and the triangle very small, implying minimal distortion to consumer behavior and, hence, little welfare loss (beyond the burden of the tax itself). Bread represented the largest single expenditure and by far the largest source of calories in the diet of nearly all Europeans in the early modern period. If the States of Holland and its neighboring provinces understood the demand for bread to be inelastic with respect to price, they may have fastened onto the milling excise as a reliable "cash cow" – an optimal way to fill the treasury, year after year, without materially altering consumer behavior.

---

[30] F. P. Ramsey, "A contribution to the theory of taxation," *The Economic Journal* 37 (1927), 47–61.

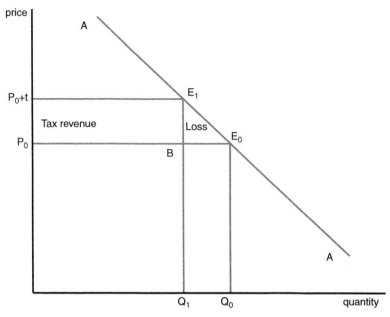

Figure 5.1a Illustration of the "deadweight loss" incurred through the imposition of a tax on bread with elastic demand

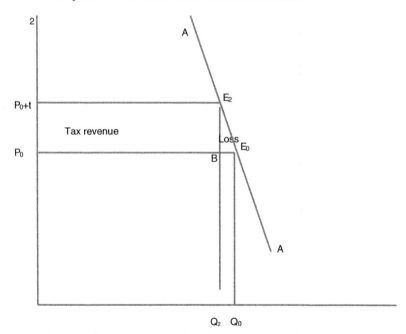

Figure 5.1b Illustration of the "deadweight loss" incurred through the imposition of a tax on bread with inelastic demand

But tax optimality does not end here. The optimality of tax policy is evaluated not only by its *efficiency* (the minimization of distortion), but also by whether it is seen to be *equitable*. There is no simple test of equitability comparable to that for efficiency, but there is historical reason to believe that even absolutist regimes were sensitive to popular understandings of just rule. Tax policies that violated notions of so-called "moral economy" could meet with resistance, tax revolts, and food riots that, at the very least, would make tax collection very costly.[31] Did Dutch consumers object to – and resist – the milling excise as inequitable?

The milling excise was levied primarily on bakers (who "passed on" this cost via the regulated bread price) and until 1748 it was collected by tax farmers. The tax farms consisted of the right to collect a specified excise tax in a single tax district (a city and its surrounding countryside), usually for a six-month period. Prospective tax farmers bid for this right at auction, the highest bidder paying the province (usually in installments) and then proceeding to collect the tax required by law from the inhabitants of the tax district. The tax farmer hoped his gross receipts would exceed the amount of his bid, since the difference had to cover his expenses (setting up offices and hiring assistants to collect the taxes and monitor compliance), provide a return on the capital he had paid in advance to the provincial treasury, and supply him with a profit. The farms were numerous and relatively small: up to 41 separate excises divided among 17, later 19, tax districts.[32]

It has been argued that this arrangement tended to diffuse opposition to the common means in general, since ordinary consumers did not pay most excises directly and could direct their ire, when the occasion arose, at the small-fry tax farmers, who were easily replaced.[33] But these arguments, while not without force, hardly seem sufficient to account for Dutch quietude and the general lack of resistance to the milling excise. After all, the States of Holland raised the tax on wheat bread from 1 or 2

---

[31] Thompson, "The moral economy," and *Customs in Common*; Tilly, "Food supply and public order," pp. 380–455.

[32] Tax farming practices are described in some detail in W. F. H. Oldewelt, "De Hollandse imposten en ons beeld van de conjunctuur tijdens de Republiek," *Jaarboek Amstelodamum* 47 (1955), 48–80.

[33] Van Deursen described the class of men bidding for these tax farms as "*kleine scharrelaars*" – small-time operators or punters – bereft of public stature. He reasoned that this suited the regent class of the towns well, since public opprobrium was directed against these "publicans" rather than against the elites who set the tax rates and received the bulk of the revenue. A. van Deursen, *Plain People in a Golden Age* (Cambridge University Press, 1991), pp. 171–81. J. M. F. Fritschy shares in this assessment in *De patriotten en de financiën van de Bataafse Republiek*, Hollandse Historische Reeks 10 (The Hague: Stichting Hollandse Historische Reeks, 1988), p. 52. See also R. M. Dekker, *Holland in beroering: oproeren in de 17de en 18de eeuw* (Baarn: Ambo, 1982), pp. 134–35; R. M. Dekker, "Oproeren in de provincie Holland, 1600–1750. Frequentie en karakter, relatie met de conjunctuur en repressie," *Tijdschrift voor sociale geschiedenis* 3 (1977), 299–329.

percent of the cost of the bread in the 1580s, to an average of 4.1 percent in 1599–1604, then 10.5 percent in 1605–35, 15 percent in 1636–82, and finally 24 percent from 1683 until 1747. That is, from 1683 onward one quarter of the total price of a loaf of wheat bread consisted of provincial tax, and in most cities a separate municipal milling tax added a few percent to these figures. The percentage burden on rye bread was only slightly less. The milling excise may have been efficient, but it was far from equitable.

How did consumers, especially the most vulnerable ones, respond to this "optimal tax"? Very quietly, it seems. This is not to say that the Republic's inhabitants voiced no objections at all. Rudolf Dekker compiled a list of all riots (*oproeren*) and disturbances (*rellen*) related to taxation in Holland during the seventeenth and eighteenth centuries. He found over 30 riots and an additional 80 disturbances. But very few of them were focused specifically on the milling excise: one in 1616, two in 1680 – the year of the major increase in this tax – and one in 1747, shortly before all the excises were temporarily abolished. The others concerned taxes on other items of consumption, while two or three were focused on the excise system as a whole.[34]

Taking this all into account, one is left with the strong impression that the public authorities had succeeded in placing a heavy tax burden on a prime necessity without facing much public resistance. Were they just lucky, or had they succeeded in developing a tax policy that sidestepped opposition and mitigated its most inequitable features?[35] That is, had they succeeded in crafting a tax that was truly optimal – both efficient *and* equitable?

Perhaps consumers confronted with higher taxes did not exercise "voice" (rebel) because they exercised "exit" instead, shifting their consumption away from bread.[36] But, this implies a highly elastic demand with respect to price, which contradicts the efficiency argument made

---

[34] The 1696 *Aansprekersoproer* (undertakers' riot) in Amsterdam, and the 1748 *Pachteropro-eren* (tax farmers' riot) in at least eight towns and villages evolved to voice a generalized discontent with the excise tax regime. Otherwise, the incidents Dekker lists were localized, took place in small places rather than large cities, and were focused variously on the excises levied on beer, peat, butter, wine, and brandy. Dekker, *Holland in beroering*, pp. 28–38. It is probable that popular resistance to the common means tended to take the form of smuggling and intimidation of the tax farmers' agents rather than the open revolts that most interested Dekker. A recent study of seventeenth-century Gorinchem, situated near Holland's provincial borders, finds that tax evasion and intimidation was common. Vermeesch, *Oorlog*, pp. 190–93.

[35] The handful of food riots in Holland can be compared to the over 700 food riots counted in England between 1580 and 1850 in John Bohstedt, *The Politics of Provisions: Food Riots, Moral Economy, and Market Transition in England, c. 1550–1850* (Farnham: Ashgate, 2010).

[36] Albert O. Hirschman, *Exit, Voice, and Loyalty* (Cambridge, Mass.: Harvard University Press, 1970).

above. Just how inelastic relative to price was the demand for bread really? Did the provincial authorities pay any heed to the response of consumers as they turned repeatedly to the milling excise for additional revenue? It will come as no surprise that no seventeenth-century documents discuss the concept of price elasticity of demand or invoke optimal tax theory. But the provincial States left silent evidence that they were cognizant of consumer behavior and also sensitive to the problem of equity, and in what follows I will argue that these concerns are reflected in the overall design of the milling excise as well as the timing of increases in the rates.

Thus far I have discussed "bread" in general, but as we have seen, Dutch consumers could choose between several grades of wheat bread and rye bread. They also had ready access to a variety of bread grain substitutes. Each of these foodstuffs was subject to a unique excise tax. In seventeenth-century Holland wheat always bore a tax double that of rye, while in the eastern provinces the tax on wheat often exceeded this two-to-one ratio. Other grains and grain substitutes were also subject to the milling tax, primarily beans, barley groats (*gort*), and shelled buckwheat (*grutten*). None of these was used in commercial bread baking; they were consumed primarily in a boiled form, as porridge, or as pancakes.[37] Table 5.10 shows the broad range of tax rates that applied to these competing foodstuffs in Holland, Utrecht, and Overijssel.

Immediately apparent from Table 5.10 is the fact that in 1583 and 1605 the non-bread grains in Holland were subject to distinctly lower tax rates than wheat and rye. The buckwheat rate rose in harness with the bread grains until 1636, but thereafter, as the tax on all other grains continued to rise, the excise on buckwheat remained fixed and even declined. In the eighteenth century the tax on barley and beans was also rolled back to the 1636 level. By then, the bread substitutes bore much lower taxes than wheat and rye. In Utrecht rye, barley, and buckwheat were at first taxed nearly equally, but after the 1627 rate hike, further increases did not touch barley and buckwheat. While excise rates on wheat and rye did not increase as steeply in Overijssel, much the same pattern is observed there.

The design of the milling excise, as it evolved in the early seventeenth century, offered consumers a choice: their tax burden varied directly with their choice of diet. All of these grains were widely consumed in the Republic, and most households made use of all of them to some degree. The mix varied by income level and urban residence, with wheat bread

---

[37] Barley was milled primarily for brewing and distilling. Special, very low, milling tax rates applied for these purposes, presumably because beer and spirits bore heavy excise taxes of their own.

Table 5.10 *Milling excise by type of grain at selected dates*
(guilders per last)

Holland

	1583	1605	1636	1683	1723	1750
Wheat	6	32.4	63.6	104.938	104.938	104.938
Rye	3	16.2	31.8	52.469	52.469	42.35
Barley & beans	2	10.8	21.2	34.931	21.2	23.1
Buckwheat	2	6.0	11.788	11.00	9.825	8.275

Utrecht, city only

	1579	1601	1627	1640	1682	1750
Wheat	5	13.125	30	60	82.5	123.75
Rye	1.5	2.813	10	24.688	41.25	62.50
Barley & beans	2	2	6.25	8.438	10	27.50
Buckwheat	2	2	6.25	8.438	10	6.25

Overijssel

	1597	1603	1623	1675	1750	
Wheat	6.75	12	24	36	36	
Rye	2.7	3	8	18	18	
Barley & beans	2.7	3	4	12	12	
Buckwheat	2.7	2.4	4	9	9	

held in the highest esteem and buckwheat in the lowest, but, as I will show in Chapter 10, it was rarely the case that households consumed only wheat or only rye.

Over the course of the seventeenth century, the States of Holland and the other maritime provinces increased the milling excise rates mightily. But the States also crafted the milling tax so that consumers could avoid some or even most of its burden by consuming rye bread (taxed at half the rate of wheat) or buckwheat (taxed at 18.5 percent, and from 1683 at 10 percent of the rate of wheat). Later, after 1740, another option became available. The potato, which required no milling or other processing, escaped taxation altogether.[38]

This gradation of tax rates puts the application of optimal tax theory in a somewhat different light. The demand for bread *in general* may be highly inelastic with respect to price, but the Dutch economy offered several types of bread and several boiled grains. There was considerable scope for substitution at the margin, which suggests that the demand for wheat bread (the most heavily taxed) might have been quite elastic with

---

[38] Potato consumption escaped provincial taxation everywhere except in Groningen. The province introduced an excise on potatoes – actually a tax on the acreage planted to potatoes – beginning in 1743, but it was very small and raised little revenue. Van der Ent and Enthoven, *GWF – Groningen*, pp. 230–31.

respect to price. This raises two questions: how did Dutch consumer behavior actually respond to the evolving tax policies of their leaders, and did those leaders revise the milling excise in response to the behavior of consumers – which they were capable of observing since the milling excise itself supplied them with the necessary information to assess the "efficiency" of their periodic adjustments.

We can be fairly certain that the elasticity of demand for commodities subject to increased taxation was a matter of ongoing concern because of the periodic adjustments made to the broad range of goods subject to excise. Besides the original set of excises of 1574 (beer, wine, milling, peat, salt, soap, and woolen cloth) Holland added over time new excises on meat, silk, vinegar, candles, firewood, building supplies, oils, fish, coal, tobacco, butter, coffee, and tea, as well as several services. Most of the newly added taxes raised nowhere near the revenue of more basic items of consumption and they often incurred heavy collection costs. Moreover, experience taught that the added revenue collected when the excise levels were raised varied considerably. Indeed, in one very important case increased tax rates were paired with a major decline in consumption. A brief examination of this case – the beer excise – will help put the growing importance of the milling excise in context.

The Beer Excise: An Optimal Tax No More

Municipal finances in medieval Europe are said to have floated as a cork in a barrel of beer. Beer was the major source of indirect tax revenue in cities throughout northern Europe, and when Holland first introduced provincial-level excise taxes, beer accounted for nearly half of the common means as a whole. In 1608 it accounted for 42 percent, and by 1650, after many new excises had been introduced and the tax rates repeatedly raised, beer continued to be the largest single source of revenue, at 26 percent of the common means. By then, the absolute amount of revenue raised from the beer excise had risen steadily to over 2 million guilders annually. But from 1650 on, the amounts collected began to drift downward. Increases in the rates slowed the decline temporarily, but never stopped it: by 1680 the beer excise accounted for only 16 percent of the common means, and by 1747 it had shrunk further to 8.5 percent.

The central role of Holland's beer excise had revolved around the attractive combination of ease of collection (at a small number of urban breweries) and inelastic demand. But, consumer behavior changed after the mid-seventeenth century as distilled spirits began to compete directly with beer, and even more after 1700, when tea and coffee quickly rose in public acceptance. Consequently, the demand for beer became more elastic relative to price and no adjustments made to the beer excise in this period (primarily altering the tax differentials for beers of different quality/strength) succeeded in stopping the revenue decline.[39] The centrality of the common means to the Republic's fiscal system made the development of some effective response to this growing problem a pressing necessity. The most obvious response was to follow consumers toward their new, preferred beverages. They acquired taxes of their own, of course, but they never generated revenue comparable to that lost from declining beer consumption. In 1650, the excises on beer, wine, and spirits (*brandewijn*) combined (there was not yet a tax on coffee and tea) was 2,941,000 guilders, 82.5 percent of which was accounted for by beer. By 1747 these excises plus the new excise on coffee and tea, added in 1690, yielded half this amount, 1.5 million guilders, but beer accounted for only 49 percent. Under the post-1750 regime of direct collection, the revenues from these beverage taxes stabilized. By 1800 total revenue stood at 1.6 million guilders, but beer now accounted for only 17 percent of the total. Thus, in the long run, from 1650 to 1800, new taxes on spirits, tea, and coffee compensated for only 40 percent of the decline in beer tax revenues. Since the Republic's import duties on coffee and tea were negligible (unlike other European nations), there certainly was considerable scope for substantial excises on these fashionable beverages. But packets of tea and bags of coffee beans were apparently more difficult to track and tax than barrels of beer. When Holland introduced its tax on coffee, tea, and chocolate in 1690 it was not a true excise, but a capitation tax levied only on households listed in the property tax registers. In short, it was treated as a sort of luxury tax.[40]

No revisions to the provincial beer excises succeeded in stemming the decline in beer consumption. It was bread that proved to be the savior of the common means. But bread, as we have seen, was also not a single, standardized product. People had to eat, but most consumers faced several options in the satisfaction of this requirement. When the provincial states set the excise rates – and periodically revised them – they anticipated that consumer behavior would follow a certain pattern. They did not use the economics vocabulary of income and substitution effects, price and income elasticities of demand, and cross-elasticities, but they

---

[39] The decline of the brewing industry is discussed in detail in Richard Unger, *A History of Brewing in Holland, 900–1900: Economy, Technology, and the State* (Leiden: Brill, 2001), pp. 222–84. The successive changes to the level and structure of the beer excise are described in Leisker and Fritschy, *GWF – Holland*, pp. 305–11.

[40] Leisker and Fritschy, *GWF – Holland*, pp. 304–05. Beginning in 1701, Utrecht also taxed tea and coffee in this way, but it allowed householders to escape payment on the declaration under oath that they abstained from the consumption of either of these fashionable hot drinks. Verstegen, *GWF – Utrecht*, p. 129.

revealed an appreciation of the underlying reality of these concepts as they crafted – with considerable success – a complex set of excise rates that varied by province, by urban and rural location, and by type of grain.

A battle of elasticities: income elasticity, price elasticity, cross-elasticities. When the States of Holland seized upon the milling excise to generate a major increase in revenue, notably in 1605, 1618, 1625–27, and 1636, they did so in a period of generally rising grain prices. The milling tax had the effect of intensifying the long-term rate at which grain prices rose in this period, and this – other things remaining equal – will have encouraged consumers to *substitute away* from bread and particularly from the more costly wheat bread toward cheaper alternatives. But that is not the end of the story, for other things did not remain equal. Real earnings in this period appear to have risen (except for a sharp reversal in the 1620s), which could have induced a shift toward wheat bread via an *income effect*.[41] In short, two contradictory forces appear to have worked on Dutch bread consumers in the course of the seventeenth century, a substitution effect in response to changing relative prices and an income effect reflecting rising real earnings.

If, over time, consumers revealed a preference for wheat bread made stronger by rising incomes, fiscal officials could exploit that marginal propensity to spend on the finer types of bread by raising the tax on wheat, expecting that the normal tendency to substitute away from the heavily taxed wheat bread would be held in check, and more, by a positive income effect. Simultaneously, the same fiscal officials could gesture their concern for equity by offering lower taxes on "inferior" grains, confident that this option would not be taken up by so many consumers that it would negate the goal of increasing public revenues. Thus, consumers who did not aspire to the luxury of fine breads could avoid at least some of the pain inflicted by the Republic's "peculiar institution."

This is all hypothetical, one might object, and perhaps just a bit too clever. Yet the milling excise itself gave magistrates the means to observe consumer behavior after each rate increase. Only a minor part of the tax data at their disposal survives, but I will analyze it in Chapter 11 to test my hypothesis that consumers acted on their preferences and their rising incomes to purchase more of the most heavily taxed bread, and that the provincial States responded to that behavior as they periodically raised the excise rates.

After the 1660s, when neither the Republic's population nor nominal wages rose much further, this dynamic ceased to function. Yet the States of the maritime provinces continued to increase the milling excise

---

[41] On real earnings, see De Vries and van der Woude, *First Modern Economy*, pp. 627–31.

rates: Holland in 1680 and 1683; Zeeland in 1668, 1680, and 1687; Utrecht in 1679 and 1689; Friesland in 1673 and 1691. It was in this period that the problem of falling beer tax revenues became most acute, but it was also the period in which the States were able to exploit a new opportunity. Grain prices peaked around 1663 and began a long-term decline that persisted, albeit with several sharp reversals, until the mid-eighteenth century. It would strain credulity to argue that fiscal officials understood this immediately, but the deflationary trend was clearly evident and much discussed by 1680.[42]

A further increase in regressive excise taxes then seemed highly undesirable, and, indeed, the new taxes introduced in Holland between 1670 and 1715 fell almost entirely on owners of property and financial assets.[43] Except for the milling excise. The comprehensive revisions to the common means of 1680 led to the abolition of several excises on necessities (salted fish, candles, shoes, woolen cloth, herring, soap, and salt) and a moderation of the beer taxes (in the hope of stemming the declining revenues), but, as we have seen, they brought a major rise in the milling excise: in 1680 and 1683 Holland's excise on wheat rose by 41.34 guilders per last; Utrecht's rates rose by 48 guilders between 1679 and 1689; Zeeland's rates rose by 37.5 guilders between 1668 and 1687. In all these cases the excise on rye rose by half as much. Why was the milling excise the great exception to the general policy of sheltering the common man from further tax increases in this period?

An answer is found in the price of grain. The average market price of wheat fell from 244 guilders per last in 1636–61 to 152.12 in the decade beginning in 1683, that is, by 92 guilders per last. The fiscal policies of Holland, Zeeland, and Utrecht – adding 38 to 48 guilders per last to the price of wheat – filled, so to speak, a large part of the economic "space" vacated by falling grain prices, as shown in Figure 5.2. Since nominal wages did not decline with agricultural commodity prices, the effects of the rising taxes on the demand for bread (as opposed to their effect on the demand for many other goods) may have been minimal. Once again, it appears, the Republic's leaders showed a capacity – a cynical capacity,

---

[42] A particularly insightful analysis of the dangers of the deflationary environment in which the Dutch economy found itself was prepared in 1684 by the Amsterdam city council in order to argue against the military adventures then being advocated by the stadholder, Willem III. What the country most needed, they argued, was peace, lower taxes, and a reduction of the public debt, so that production and trading costs could be reduced and international competitiveness restored. See De Vries and van der Woude, *First Modern Economy*, pp. 679–80.

[43] *Ibid.*, pp. 111–13; Marjolein 't Hart, "The merits of a financial revolution: public finances, 1550–1700," in Marjolein 't Hart et al., eds., *A Financial History of the Netherlands* (Cambridge University Press, 1997), pp. 33–34.

guilders per last

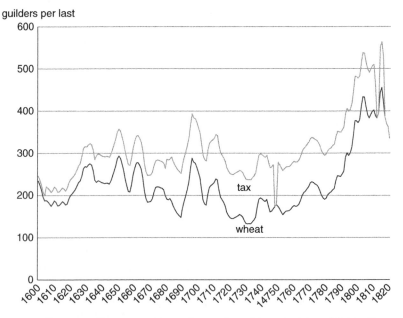

Figure 5.2 Western average wheat price with and without Holland's provincial milling excise, 1600–1820 (seven-year moving average; guilders per last)

perhaps – to exploit price and income elasticities to extract a large and rising revenue stream from bread consumers.

In the Dutch golden age, the state learned to tax the "wage good." It exploited a growing preference for wheat bread, and the inelasticity of demand exhibited by many consumers. Simultaneously, it dampened criticism of this regressive excise by offering tax concessions to consumers willing or needing to consume lesser grains. Then, when grain prices fell, it forced bread consumers to share their windfall with the state. Overall, the seventeenth-century milling excise, the Republic's "peculiar institution," offers a striking example of optimal tax policy.

If the seventeenth century was one of frequent manipulation of the milling excise rates and the methods of enforcement in order to raise additional revenues, the eighteenth century breathed the spirit of caution and preservation. There were no further increases in the milling excise rates in Holland and no net changes of consequence elsewhere. This is not to say that all was smooth sailing. The aim now was to preserve what had been achieved in a much less expansive economic environment. We will return to this theme in Chapter 15.

Part II

Industrial Organization: The Producers in a Regulated Industry

6 Grain: The Interaction of International Trade and Domestic Production

In most regions of early modern Europe, what is consumed can be inferred, to a first approximation, from what is produced. In the Netherlands matters are more complicated; indeed, the one piece of historical information that most readers will bring to this study is that the Netherlands' food supply depended, from an early date, on imports. In this chapter we interrogate this commonplace, with the aim of learning how imports, exports, and domestic production combined to shape the supply of bread grains in the Netherlands over the course of time.

The Volume of Trade

The Netherlands became a major grain importer in the fifteenth century as its economy became more specialized and more urbanized. As we noted in Chapter 2, merchants originally imported grain from all neighboring countries, but these multiple sources gradually narrowed to one, the Baltic region, which dominated Dutch supplies by the sixteenth century. In an average year in the first half of the seventeenth century, 1200 Dutch ships sailed westward through the Danish Sound annually, carrying, among other goods, 50,000 lasts of grain, nearly 90 percent of which was rye.[1] Over the entire period 1580–1750 Dutch ships carried at least three-quarters of all the grain passing through the Sound. Some of these ships by-passed Dutch ports, sailing directly to customers elsewhere in Europe, but most of them entered the Zuider Zee and the harbor of Amsterdam, which came to be known as Europe's granary. This quantity of grain represented the annual bread grain consumption for some 800,000 people. This is not an enormous supply relative to the 10–15 million inhabitants of the cities and coastal regions of western and Mediterranean Europe that this grain might

---

[1] J. A. Faber, "Het probleem van de dalende graanaanvoer uit de Oostzeelanden in de tweede helft van de zeventiende eeuw," *AAG Bijdragen* 9 (1963), 7.

Table 6.1 *The Dutch grain trade with the Baltic, 1562–1783*

	Baltic grain in Dutch ships		Annual averages			
	Rye	Wheat	Rye	Wheat	Total lasts	Wheat as % of total
1562–69	377,792	33,869	47,224.0	4,233.6	51,457.6	0.0827
1574–79	186,776	19,753	31,129.3	3,292.2	34,421.5	0.0963
1580–89	311,499	36,895	31,149.9	3,689.5	34,839.4	0.1066
1590–99	464,566	66,017	46,456.6	6,601.7	53,058.3	0.1241
1600–09	473,715	51,527	47,371.5	5,152.7	52,524.2	0.0987
1610–19	522,439	61,266	52,243.9	6,126.6	58,370.5	0.1054
1620–29	418,812	68,215	41,881.2	6,821.5	48,702.7	0.1403
1630–39	315,158	68,753	39,394.8	8,594.1	47,988.9	0.1791
1640–49	578,415	160,541	57,841.5	1,6054.1	73,895.6	0.2171
1650–57	207,690	52,026	25,961.3	6,503.3	32,464.5	0.2001
1669–70	77,709	28,679	38,854.5	14,339.5	53,194	0.2706
1671–80	221,879	89,620	22,187.9	89,602.0	31,149.9	0.2889
1681–90	389,026	161,226	38,902.6	16,122.6	55,025.2	0.2933
1691–1700	279,897	97,008	27,989.7	9,700.8	37,690.5	0.2577
1701–10	162,303	61,611	16,230.3	6,161.1	22,391.4	0.2757
1711–20	153,524	45,433	15,352.4	4,543.3	19,895.7	0.2286
1721–30	226,181	87,471	22,618.1	8,747.1	31,365.2	0.2794
1731–40	174,110	90,644	17,411.0	9,064.4	26,475.4	0.3424
1741–50	98,540	51,623	9,854.0	5,162.3	15,016.3	0.3449
1751–60	130,043	81,449	13,004.3	8,144.9	21,149.2	0.3852
1761–70	192,345	101,588	19,234.5	10,158.8	29,393.3	0.3468
1771–80	221,600	119,287	22,160.0	11,928.7	34,088.7	0.3509
1781–83	49,260	13,072	12,315.0	3,268.0	15,583.0	0.2106
1789–93					42,400.6	

Sources: W. S. Unger, "De Sonttabellen," *Tijdschrift voor geschiedenis* 41 (1926), 136–55; "De publikatie der Sonttabellen voltooid," *Tijdschrift voor geschiedenis* 71 (1958), 147–205; supplement V, p. 154; supplements VIII and X; J. A. Faber, "Scheepvaart op Nederland in een woelige periode: 1784–1810," *Economisch- en social-historisch jaarboek* 47 (1984), 67–78.

have supplied.[2] But it was easily Europe's largest concentration of freely tradable grain and while its influence in most markets was usually marginal, it was periodically of strategic importance. In the Netherlands itself, it was much more than this.

The transportation of grain to Amsterdam, its storage there and its further distribution to final markets at home and abroad, was a large

[2] Baltic grain was potentially sent to all western European coastal regions, and up-river to large cities. It could also supply Mediterranean coastal areas of Spain and Italy. Some 50 million people lived in Low Countries, Britain, France, Portugal, Spain, and northern Italy in 1600–50. But, economically, Baltic grain could usually reach only a portion of this population.

industry in its own right. In the first half of the seventeenth century the ships sailing back and forth from the Baltic employed some 4,000 seamen. In the harbor of Amsterdam another army of workers specialized in the handling of the grain.[3] Hundreds of grain lightermen, organized in their guild (*korenlichtermansgilde*), transferred grain from the ships to barges. On the quays, the even more numerous members of the grain porters' guild (*korendragersgilde*) carried the grain sacks to the storage lofts and the markets. A guild of grain weighers and measurers (*korenmeters en zetters*) ascertained weight and volume, while an unorganized army of grain turners (*verschietsters*), primarily women, monitored the grain storage lofts, turning the sacks periodically to prevent overheating and spoilage. All of this grain was bought and sold at a specialized grain exchange (*Korenbeurs*) by sworn brokers.[4]

Over two thousand workers found regular employment in Amsterdam's grain trading and storage sectors, receiving mainly Baltic grain, and sending much of it out again to domestic and foreign markets.

How Much of This Grain Was Required in the Netherlands?

While the Sound Toll Registers give us continuous but incomplete data on the total flow of grain moving toward the Dutch Republic, we have only incidental information about the re-export of grain.

The years for which re-export data have been preserved were not randomly selected; most of them were years of high prices, when interest in these trade flows was acute and when the scope for profitable re-export will have been greater than normal. Until the 1660s, it appears to have been good harvests in eastern Europe (and low prices there) that motivated merchants to buy grain for sale in the west, but thereafter –

---

[3] Estimates of seamen employed in the Baltic trade for 1610, the 1630s, and 1680 all stand at 4,000. Jan Lucassen "Zeevarenden," in L. M. Akveld *et al.*, eds., *Maritieme geschiedenis der Nederlanden*, vol. II (Bussum: De Boer Maritiem, 1977), pp. 131–32; P. C. van Royen, *Zeevarenden op de koopvaardijvloot omstreeks 1700* (The Hague: De Bataafse Leeuw, 1987), p. 25.

[4] In the 1640s some 250 lightermen, 700 grain porters (they could not exceed 38 years of age), 42 weighers (plus an equal number of assistants, mostly women), and nearly 400 official brokers found employment in Amsterdam's grain trade. The women who turned the grain sacks had no guild and remained uncounted, but there must have been many hundreds of them. M. Heijder, *Amsterdam, korenschuur van Europa* (Stadsdrukkerij van Amsterdam, 1979), pp. 251–90; Milja van Tielhof, "Stedelijke regulering van diensten op de stapelmarkt: de Amsterdamse korengilden," in Lesger and Noordegraaf, eds., *Ondernemers en bestuurders*, pp. 492–523.

Table 6.2a *Imports and exports of all grains at Amsterdam, in lasts per year*

	Import	Export	Net import
1649	112,900	46,000	66,900
1667	63,800	1,900	61,900
1680	64,500	8,400	56,100
1692	76,400	57,100	19.300
1710	74,400	68,000	6,400
1717, 1723	45,250	26,300	18,900
1740*	63,356	27,877	34,479
1753	23,100	11,100	12,000
1766–74	31,280	12,260	18,820
1789–92	35,230	28,500	6,730

*From 1 January through 22 November 1740.

Table 6.2b *Imports and exports of wheat and rye at Amsterdam, in lasts per year*

	Imports			Exports		
	Wheat	Rye	Total	Wheat	Rye	Total
1710–23	13,600	20,530	34,130	9,700	17,450	27,150
1741–73	17,670	15,840	33,510			
1769–83	22,540	20,930	43,470	13,180	16,520	29,700
1789–92	16,550	13,630	30,180	17,430	3,450	20,880
1793–99	9,720	12,880	22,600			

Sources: J. G. van Dillen, "Stukken betreffende den Amsterdamschen graanhandel omstreeks het jaar 1681," *Economisch-Historisch Jaarboek* 3 (1917), 84; H. Brugmans, "Statistiek van den in- en uitvoer van Amstserdam, 1 Oct 1667 – 30 Sept 1668," *Bijdragen en mededelingen van het Historisch Genootschap* 19 (1898), 125–83; Heijder, *Korenschuur, passim.*

including most of the observations of Tables 6.2a and b – Baltic grain moved west when west European production fell short and high prices there stirred the merchants to action.[5] From a position of dominance in western grain markets, Baltic supplies gradually became marginal. But

[5] In the period 1624–65 a rise in grain shipments from the Baltic brought about a *decline* in the Amsterdam price, with an elasticity of –0.30; from 1693 to 1720 a rise in grain shipments was associated with *higher* prices, the elasticity was now +0.16. However, the volatility of both shipments and prices was now much higher than before, making the measured relationship statistically not significant. P. W. Klein, "Kwantitatieve aspecten van de Amsterdamse roggehandel in de 17e eeuw en de Europese economische geschiedenis," in Johan de Vries, ed., *Ondernemende geschiedenis* (The Hague: Martinus Nijhoff, 1977), pp. 75–89.

what about the Dutch domestic market? Did Baltic grain not continue to dominate there?

By the late sixteenth century Baltic grain and the Amsterdam entrepôt had reached a position of peak influence, and they would remain highly influential in the domestic Dutch market into the nineteenth century. However, the grain imports from neighboring countries that had declined in the face of Baltic competition did not disappear altogether, and by the eighteenth century they had grown to again achieve a large importance.

The place of grain imports *from all sources* in the Dutch domestic market can first be examined in the early years of the nineteenth century. This is not an ideal period to serve as a benchmark, since grain prices were unusually high and volatile, and trade was subject to serious political disruption. But the overall picture given by data from several sources and gathered in Table 6.3 can serve as a rough sketch of the grain economy around 1800–10.

Table 6.3 *Consumption of bread grains in the Batavian Republic, grain imports and exports, and implied domestic production*

a. Bread grain consumption in the Netherlands, 1808 (in thousands of lasts)

Bread grain	Wheat	Rye	Total
West	32.0	17.3	49.3
East	7.2	44.5	51.7
Total	39.2	61.8	101.0

b. Grain imports, re-exports, net imports (averages per year)

1803–09	Wheat	Rye	Total
Imports	8.99	28.49	37.48
Re-exports	5.69	2.38	8.06
Net imports	3.31	26.12	29.42
1810 net imports	**5.20**	21.40	26.60

c. Estimated domestic production (thousands of lasts per year)

	Wheat	Rye	Total
Domestic production:	34–36	36–40	70–76
Percentage of consumption imported:	10–13%	35–42%	27–29%

Sources: 1808: Gogel, *Memoriën en correspondentiën.* The bread grain estimates are based on the taxed grain increased by 10 percent to account for untaxed grain. 1803–09: F. J. B. d'Alphonse, *Aperçu sur la Hollande* (1811), reprinted in Centraal Bureau voor de Statistiek, *Bijdragen tot de Statistiek van Nederland,* n.s., no. 1 (The Hague, 1900), p. 457; 1810: Van Zanden, *De economische ontwikkeling,* p. 373.

The chief characteristics of the Dutch grain market at this time can be summarized as follows:

1. The Batavian Republic's 1.9 million inhabitants consumed about 95,000–100,000 lasts of the bread grains (wheat and rye). Other grains – such as buckwheat, barley, and oats – are excluded from this analysis. Nor do these estimates consider the non-bread uses of grain, such as brewing, distilling, starch making, and animal fodder.
2. Grain imports accounted for some 30 percent of total consumption, with the Netherlands depending much more heavily on foreign suppliers for rye than for wheat.
3. In these years the grain re-export business was of minor importance: only about 20 percent of imported grain was re-exported.

If we take this as a baseline, how might conditions have differed in the preceding two centuries? We know that grain imports from the Baltic had been much larger – twice as large – in the seventeenth century than in the eighteenth. The portion of these shipments retained for domestic consumption is not known with certainty, but grain re-exporting was definitely a much bigger and more regular business before the 1680s than thereafter. As a thought experiment (displayed in Table 6.4), we might assume that half the Baltic grain entering Dutch ports up to 1690 was re-exported. Contemporary accounts of Amsterdam's warehousing function, while sometimes highly colored, are not inconsistent with such an estimate. Thereafter, as the Great Northern War and Polish succession crisis choked off the flow of grain and western demand fell as a joint result of revived domestic production and population stability, the Dutch re-export function certainly diminished.

Under these assumptions we find that grain imports from the Baltic destined for Dutch domestic consumption remain quite stable, at the

Table 6.4 *A model of the Dutch domestic and re-export markets for Baltic grain (annual averages in lasts)*

	Gross imports					
	Rye	Wheat	Total	Wheat as % of total imports*	Retained imports	Re-exported
1574–1629	42,461	5,423	47,884	11.3%	23,900	23,984
1630–90	35,798	11,217	47,014	12.9	23,500	23,514
1691–1730	20,548	7,288	27,836	26.2	22,400	5,436
1731–83	16,035	8,475	24,510	34.6	19,600	4,910

*See text for explanation.

20,000–24,000 last level. But the Baltic was not the only source of grain. Its low cost may have marginalized other suppliers in the 1560–1660 period, but they returned thereafter. We know, for instance that England shipped wheat and, especially, barley to Dutch ports in growing quantities from the 1680s until the 1760s. Merchants in the East Anglian ports exported as much grain in the 1730–60 period as had the entire Baltic in its heyday. They were encouraged in this by an export bounty paid by the British state. Adam Smith held this trade up as a prime example of a "forced export," and the trade's modern historian concurs that "English grain would not have found a market in Europe" in its absence.[6] Most of the barley went to Rotterdam and neighboring ports, the centers of gin (*genever*) distilling. Most of the wheat and other grains found markets in other countries (thereby undercutting the Dutch re-export trade), but the amount sent to the Dutch Republic averaged 5,500 lasts per year over the period 1700–59, and considerably more than this in the 1740s and 50s.

After 1760 England's accelerating population growth increased the domestic demand for grain, which brought a sudden end to its career as a grain exporter, but by then the Southern, then Austrian, Netherlands emerged as a significant grain exporter. It was, perhaps, not a dependable exporter, since the nervous authorities imposed bans on grain exports in 1767, 1770, 1775, 1780, 1784, and 1789, but it appears to have exported, on average, some 15,655 lasts per annum in the 1760–89 period.[7] Unfortunately, the Austrian customs administration did not specify the destination of its exports. Not all was shipped to the Northern Netherlands; some must have gone east, to Liège, and south, to France. But, for a decade beginning in 1784, grain imports into the jurisdiction of the Admiralty of the Maas (Rotterdam, Dordrecht, and their hinterlands) are known, and they reveal a lively importation from Austrian Brabant, both by land and by internal waterways.[8]

---

[6] David Ormrod, *The Rise of Commercial Empires* (Cambridge University Press, 2003), pp. 216–17. Gross exports of British wheat averaged 9,500 lasts in 1697–1731, rising to 30,700 lasts in 1732–66. Thereafter Britain became a net importer of grain.

[7] Ann Coenen, *Carriers of Growth? International Trade and Economic Development in the Austrian Netherlands* (Leiden: Brill, 2015), pp. 247–48, 251; Chr. Vandenbroeke, "Landbouw in de Zuidelijke Nederlanden, 1650–1815," in *Algemene Geschiedenis der Nederlanden*, vol. VIII (Haarlem: Van Dishoek, 1979), pp. 83–85. Vandenbroeke estimated grain exports at about 5 percent of domestic production.

[8] Johan de Vries, "De statistiek van in- en uitvoer van de Admiraliteit op de Maaze, 1784–1793," *Economisch-historisch jaarboek* 29 (1961), 188–259; 30 (1963), 236–310. The import data distinguish imports by sea and via inland waterways from Brabant and Germany. In 1784–88 over 17,000 lasts entered Rotterdam annually, 13,000 from Brabant. In 1789–93 about 11,000 lasts entered annually, nearly all of it by sea.

Rotterdam and the nearby river port of Dordrecht played increasingly important roles in the grain markets of the Netherlands. Rotterdam received grain from England, France, and the Southern Netherlands. Likewise, nearby Dordrecht received grain sent down the Rhine and Maas from the German lands. The size of these inflows is not known in any detail. Moreover, it is hard to distinguish these grains from the domestic interregional grain shipments with which they were mingled – and these domestic supplies became substantial.

Domestic Grain Production

The grain markets of Rotterdam and Dordrecht gained their new stature much more from domestic grain sent there for further distribution in Holland than from foreign shipments, which waxed and waned over time.

The knowledge that the Netherlands was a major grain importer and a specialist in livestock and dairy production has led many to conclude – too quickly – that domestic grain production was a marginal activity, certainly in the western provinces. Once Amsterdam had consolidated its place as the granary of western Europe, domestic producers faced a massive flow of low-cost imports from the Baltic and a state that had no interest in protecting them.[9] Yet, against all expectations, commercial grain farmers found sufficient market opportunities in this unpromising economic environment to expand their acreage (partly via land reclamation), increase their yields, and so gradually regain a significant share of the domestic grain market.

The major source of this grain was the southwestern zone of the Republic, consisting of the entire island province of Zeeland, the adjacent South Holland islands, States Flanders (a portion of Flanders bordering the Schelde estuary held by the Dutch Republic and today a part of Zeeland) and the westernmost portion of North Brabant.[10] See Map 6.1 for identification of the Republic's grain regions. The clay soils of

[9] Grain imports faced a specific tariff for the first time in 1725, but at 6 guilders per last of wheat and 4 per last of rye it was too low to have much effect on domestic prices. The United Kingdom of the Netherlands of 1815–30 included modern Belgium, and had to pay more heed to agricultural interests than its predecessor polities, but until 1825 tariffs remained very close to the 1725 level. Only in 1835, after the departure of Belgium, did the state strike out in a new direction, introducing a new corn law similar in design to the famous British Corn Laws. It provided for a sliding scale of tariffs that could rise to 61.20 guilders per last when wheat prices were very low. But, after its first year of operation, grain prices rose to levels sufficiently high to deactivate this tariff trigger, and by 1845 the law was abolished. Jan Luiten van Zanden and Arthur van Riel, *The Strictures of Inheritance: The Dutch Economy in the Nineteenth Century* (Princeton University Press, 2000), pp. 155–56.

[10] Wheat production on certain polders of the South Holland islands is discussed in C. Baars, *De geschiedenis van de landbouw in de Beijerlanden* (Wageningen: Centrum voor landbouwpublikaties en landbouwdocumentatie, 1973). Baars found that throughout

these lands in the heart of the Rijn–Maas delta made them well suited to wheat production. Since Zeeland itself had a large urban population to feed, achieving substantial grain surpluses depended on a long process of land reclamation and improvement. Wheat shipments to the markets of Holland could not have been large in the early days of the Republic. Priester estimated that the wheat surplus available for export from the province of Zeeland alone amounted to some 4,300 lasts *c.* 1600–10,

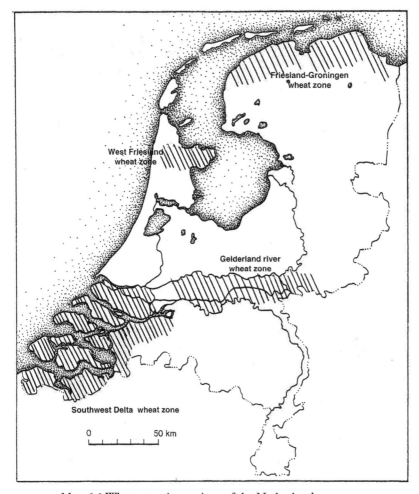

Map 6.1 Wheat-growing regions of the Netherlands

the eighteenth century wheat was planted on over 30 percent of the arable land. An even higher specialization in wheat is documented for western North Brabant in W. J. Dewez, "De landbouw in Brabants Westhoek in het midden van de achttiende eeuw," *Agronomisch-historisch bijdragen* 4 (1958), 1–65.

rising to 6,667 by the 1660s, and perhaps 7,500 lasts, a century later.[11] A study of the western half of States Flanders, another center of wheat production, found that most of its surplus was directed toward the nearby Flemish cities of Bruges and Ghent in the seventeenth century. After 1700 the region became even more focused on wheat production and redirected its wheat northward, toward Rotterdam. Its annual exports more than doubled over the course of the eighteenth century, from 1,000 to 2,200 lasts. Adding the other half of States Flanders could double these volumes.[12] When the wheat production of the South Holland Islands and western North Brabant are added to these estimates, it is possible that the Rotterdam and Dordrecht markets received some 8,000 lasts of wheat annually in the seventeenth century, rising to 15,000 lasts in the eighteenth.[13] A relatively small corner of the Dutch Republic had developed into a major wheat producer.

A second zone of specialized wheat production, the Betuwe, or Gelderland river region, stretched eastward from the markets of Dordrecht and Rotterdam, along the tributaries of the Rijn and Maas rivers that encapsulated numerous clay-soiled polders, nearly to the border with Germany. Just one of its districts, the Over-Betuwe, annually shipped some 2,700 lasts of wheat to Dordrecht in the late eighteenth century. Its farming population appears to have consumed imported rye, sent in from the sandy soil districts further to the east, so that more of its wheat could be sent on to markets to the west.[14]

Elsewhere in this riverine region, respondents to Gelderland's 1808 statistical survey reported a similar dedication to wheat production

---

[11] Note that these figures refer to shipments beyond the province. To these figures we must add the wheat supplied to the population of the province itself, half of which was urban. Priester estimated eighteenth-century production after deduction of seed corn at about 14,000 lasts. Priester, *Zeeuwse landbouw*, pp. 299–302, 305–09. Zeeland wheat yields were unusually high (18 to 25 hl/ha) in the first half of the seventeenth century. Output growth was made possible by land reclamation, which augmented Zeeland's cultivated area by 50 percent between 1600 and 1676. Bieleman, *Boeren in Nederland*, pp. 48, 75. Paul Brusse, *Gevallen stad* (Zwolle: Waanders, 2011), p. 120.

[12] P. J. van Cruyningen, *Behoudend maar buigzaam. Boeren in West-Zeeuws-Vlaanderen, 1650–1850*, AAG Bijdragen 40 (Wageningen: Afdeling Agrarische Geschiedenis, 2000), p. 200; Piet van Cruyningen, "Farmers' strategies and the West-Zeeland-Flanders grain trade, 1648–1794," in Piet van Cruyningen and Erik Thoen, eds., *Food Supply, Demand and Trade* (Turnhout: Brepols, 2012), pp. 161–72.

[13] Jan de Vries, "The production and consumption of wheat in the Netherlands, with special reference to Zeeland," in B. de Vries, *Het platteland in een veranderende wereld: Boeren en het process van modernisering* (Hilversum: Verloren, 1994), pp. 218–19. There, I estimated the exportable wheat surplus at the end of the eighteenth century at approximately 18,000 lasts. This now appears somewhat too high in light of the research of Priester and Van Cruyningen.

[14] Paul Brusse, *Overleven door ondernemen. De agrarische geschiedenis van de Over-Betuwe, 1650–1850*, AAG Bijdragen 38 (Wageningen: Afdeling Agrarische Geschiedenis, 1999), pp. 273, 279.

for external markets. In the district of Buren, it was reported that half the wheat went to markets in Utrecht, Culemborg, and Tiel; in the Tielerwaard, likewise, "probably about half" of the wheat was shipped out; in the Bommelerwaard, an "annually variable" amount left the district. The inhabitants of Maas and Waal consumed their farm output locally, "except for wheat, which is sold in the nearby cities." The respondent for this district went on to observe: "the local inhabitants consume mostly rye bread, which is not produced sufficiently here, so they secure their bread from neighboring districts." Still further to the east lay yet another district of this type, the Liemers. Its inhabitants consumed all of the buckwheat and nearly all the rye that they harvested, but exported 83 percent of their wheat, which was the district's largest crop.[15] All of these observations date from the beginning of the nineteenth century and our knowledge is insufficient to be able to say how the region's dedication to wheat production for sale elsewhere evolved over time.[16]

A third region also specialized in wheat production, this time directed toward the Amsterdam market. Farms on the clay soils of northern Friesland and Groningen, to which we can add "West Friesland," the northernmost district of Holland, regularly produced wheat surpluses from at least the sixteenth century. Here, as in the Gelderland river region, farmers bought rye from nearby production regions for their own use in order to direct their wheat production to the market.[17] And, as in Zeeland, the outflow of wheat appears to have risen over time. Frisian probate inventories in the grain growing districts, which specified the acreage put to crops on the lands of the deceased, showed only about 12 percent of the arable land planted to wheat around 1600. Over half of the arable was then devoted to barley production. By the 1660–90 period, farms in the same area devoted at least one-third of their land to wheat, and only one-sixth to barley.[18] In Groningen and northern Holland

---

[15] *Statistische beschrijving van Gelderland van 1808*, vol. III: *Kwartier van Nijmegen* (Arnhem: Vereniging Gelre, 1986), pp. 69, 175, 181, 202, 214–15, 221–22.

[16] Bieleman's account of early modern agriculture emphasizes the substantial hydrographic barriers to agronomic improvement in this region, prone to dike seepage and, especially in the eighteenth century, flooding. On the other hand, he also demonstrates how the region responded with alacrity to market opportunities over time – especially for hops, hemp, fruit, potatoes, and livestock breeding. *Boeren in Nederland*, pp. 185–200.

[17] As early as 1570, the Frisian farmer Rienck Hemmema's account books show that he devoted his arable land to wheat, barley, and oats. He sold 92 percent of his wheat crops and 63 percent of his barley. He purchased rye for feeding his family and servants. B. H. Slicher van Bath, "Een landbouwbedrijf in de tweede helft van de zestiende eeuw," *Agronomisch-historisch bijdragen* 4 (1958), 97.

[18] Jan de Vries, *The Dutch Rural Economy in the Golden Age, 1500–1700* (New Haven, Conn.: Yale University Press, 1974), p. 148. These data are based on a limited sample of farms in Leeuwarderadeel, het Bildt, Barradeel, and Franekeradeel: 24 farms in 1582–1605 and 34 farms in 1662–95.

seventeenth-century land reclamation increased substantially the land devoted to arable production. Thus, in this region, just as in Zeeland, the flow of wheat toward the consumer markets of Holland almost certainly grew over time, although wheat was never as important as oats and barley, the chief export crops. By the early nineteenth century Groningen sent out 2,850 lasts of wheat annually.[19] Friesland's shipments may have been somewhat smaller than this, and West Friesland's smaller still.[20]

By the eighteenth century the Dutch Republic produced roughly equal amounts of rye and wheat but little of the rye entered into interregional trade. Production was concentrated on the lighter, sandy soils of the eastern and southern provinces where nearly all of it was also consumed. These provinces were distinctly more rural in character than the maritime provinces, but it is important to recognize that they all had large urban populations by contemporary European standards. In the seventeenth century the urban population of Friesland, Groningen, Drenthe, Overijssel, Gelderland, and North Brabant, taken as a whole, reached 30 percent of the total. Producing a sufficient surplus to supply this local market and also export to the west would have been a challenge in most of Europe, but, in fact, eastern farmers rarely had an incentive to send rye to the markets of Holland, where prices, dominated by Baltic rye supplies, offered no long-term price difference that might induce a regular east-to-west trade.[21]

---

[19] It deserves emphasizing that Groningen's wheat exports were not so much a reflection of massive production as of minimal local consumption. For the period 1815–21, Priester offers the following overview of provincial production and consumption of the bread grains:

	Wheat	Rye
Consumption per capita in kg	20	90
Total consumption in 1816 in lasts	904	5,804
Average harvest, 1817–21 in lasts	3,756	6,946
Surplus production in lasts	2,852	1,142
Exported surplus as % of output	76%	16 %

Peter Priester, *De economische ontwikkeling van de landbouw in Groningen, 1800–1910*, AAG Bijdragen 31 (Wageningen: Afdeling Agrarische Geschiedenis, 1991), p. 364.

[20] But, perhaps, not much smaller. Amsterdam maintained a separate weekly market dedicated to West Frisian grain, and the Alkmaar market – famed for its cheese – managed to receive some 3,000 lasts of grain (mainly wheat and barley) in 1757–59, despite complaints that Zaan region merchants bought up West Frisian grain supplies directly at the farm gates for use in their large ships' biscuit (*beschuit*) bakeries. On Amsterdam's markets see Jan Wagenaar, *Amsterdam* (Amsterdam: Isaak Tirion, 1765), vol. II, p. 424. On the Alkmaar market: G.A. Alkmaar, no. 1326.

[21] Jan Luiten van Zanden *De economische ontwikkeling van de Nederlandse landbouw in de negentiende eeuw, 1800–1914*, AAG Bijdragen 25 (Wageningen: Afdeling Agrarische Geschiedenis, 1985), p. 177. In the same period, neighboring Westphalia (part of the *Bovenlanden* to which Dutch sources referred) was also a major producer of rye, but not a major exporter. "By far the larger part of the agricultural production of the interior of North-west Germany remained within local boundaries, if not within the farm or holding itself." Michael Kopsidas and Klaus-Joachim Lorenzen-Schmidt, "North-west Germany, 1000–1750," in Leen Van Molle and Yves Segers, eds., *The Agro-Food Market: Production, Distribution and Consumption* (Turnhout: Brepols, 2013), p. 276; Michael

This survey of the international and interregional grain trade has many gaps and there is much that remains to be known about both. But these fragments of information do allow us better to understand developments in what is our chief interest here: the efficient functioning of the Dutch Republic's internal grain markets.

Domestic Grain Markets

Rye

From the beginnings of the Dutch Republic until the nineteenth century the trade in rye was characterized by a striking dualism: it was the dominant crop of the inland provinces and the *bovenlanden*, the German lands that bordered on the Republic. Rye was the basis of the diet in these regions and in normal times production sufficed to supply regional demand. In the maritime provinces very little rye was produced and the population depended on external sources for nearly all of the rye it consumed, yet very little of this supply came from the large rye-producing zone immediately to its east.

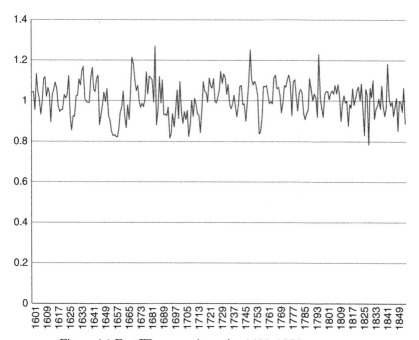

Figure 6.1 East/West rye price ratios,1600–1854

Kopsidas, "The creation of a Westphalian rye market, 1820–1870: leading and following regions: a co-integration analysis," *Jahrbuch für Wirtschaftgeschichte* (2002/2), 85–112.

In the east the bread price commissioners periodically altered the specific markets from which they sought price guidance, but these were nearly always located within the region. In Holland, rye prices were governed by Baltic supplies on the Amsterdam market.[22] The rye produced in the inland provinces did not ordinarily penetrate to the zone of Amsterdam's dominance.

Despite this bifurcation, differences in absolute price level among Dutch domestic markets were rarely large by the late sixteenth century. Price shocks were dissipated fairly quickly, restoring via arbitrage a stable long-term relationship. Thus, the average price of rye in eastern markets (the unweighted mean annual price for Utrecht, Zaltbommel, Kampen, Deventer, Zwolle, Arnhem, and Groningen) was less than 1 percent above that prevailing on the Amsterdam market over the very long period 1596–1855. There were, however, years, and occasionally multi-year periods, with larger price differentials, as displayed in Figure 6.1. Overall, rye was slightly costlier in the east, where it was locally produced, than in Holland, where most supplies came from distant, East-Elbian production zones. This western advantage disappeared in the period 1648–67, and again in 1689–1717 – both periods of frequent warfare – and yielded to a period of great volatility after 1795 – another period of frequent warfare. But underlying these disruptions was a persisting, small absolute price differential in favor of the western provinces.

Despite the lack of physical commodity flows between them, eastern market prices show a high degree of price integration with Amsterdam, as revealed by coefficients of correlation. Table 6.5 shows these for twenty-one city pairs in 1650–99. The rye markets were integrated by information flows and a latent commercial capacity to act on arbitrage opportunities.

Wheat

Wheat markets differed from rye in the relative concentration of both production and consumption. Our first comprehensive overview of bread grain consumption in the Netherlands, in 1808, showed that wheat was consumed everywhere but that the provinces of Holland, Utrecht, and Zeeland accounted for 85 percent of the total. Wheat cultivation, as just noted, was similarly concentrated in a small number of zones of specialized, commercial wheat farming.

On the other hand, wheat imports came – at one time or another – from all directions: northern France (Picardie and Artois), the Southern

---

[22] A review of the evidence for this claim is found in H. K. Roessingh, *Inlands Tabak*, AAG Bijdragen 20 (Wageningen: Afdeling Agrarische Geschiedenis, 1976), pp. 280–84.

Table 6.5 *Coefficients of correlation on first differences of annual average rye prices between city pairs in the Netherlands, 1650–99*

1650–99	A'dam	Utrecht	Zaltbommel	Kampen	Deventer	Arnhem
Utrecht	.930					
Zaltbommel	.883	.932				
Kampen	.931	.942	.889			
Deventer	.972	.983	.959	.964		
Arnhem	.725	.820	.789	.859	.865	
Groningen	.908	.902	.862	.918	.958	.730

Additional correlation data, for the entire period 1596–1799, is available in Jan de Vries, "Dutch bread and grain prices, 1594–1855," www/iisg.nl.hpw/data.php#netherlands

Netherlands (Brabant and Hainault), the German borderlands (especially Cleves), East Anglia, and the Baltic region. In short, there were many potential suppliers, and none was overwhelmingly dominant in the manner of Baltic rye.

Over time, wheat assumed a larger place in the Baltic grain trade. Table 6.1 shows that it accounted for only 11–12 percent of grain shipments up to 1690, but rose to account for 35 percent after 1730. And, as noted earlier, by then wheat had begun to flow in again from other sources – England, the Southern Netherlands, Germany, and France. We cannot attach firm numbers to most of these flows, but a cautious estimate of foreign wheat shipped to the Republic would begin by noting that in the period 1590–1630 the 5,000 lasts of Baltic wheat may have been augmented by smaller shipments from German and French sources. By the 1730–60 period, Baltic and English sources sent 8,500 and 5,500 lasts, respectively, for a total of 14,000. This figure was supplemented by German wheat, and after 1760, as England falls away, the Southern Netherlands stepped in to fill the gap until 1789.[23] Against these inflows, we must remember the re-export trade. Surely, not all of this wheat remained in the Republic for domestic consumption. But, it is not impossible that gross imports rose from 6,000–7,000 lasts to 14,000–16,000 lasts between the early seventeenth and eighteenth centuries.

This multi-sourced wheat market faced severe disruptions after the outbreak of the French Revolution. In that year wheat shipments from the Southern Netherlands came abruptly to an end. Shortly thereafter, when French armies took control of States Flanders in 1794, they forced this region's substantial wheat exports to flow south, toward France and its armies. After 1800 Napoleon's imposition of the Continental System periodically brought the Baltic trade to a standstill, and, finally, with

---

[23] Brusse, *Gevallen stad*, pp. 71–72.

the incorporation of the Batavian Republic into the French Empire in 1810, Zeeland itself was prohibited from shipping wheat to Holland as the French requisitioned its grain surpluses for imperial needs.[24] As a result of all these shocks to normal market relations, the domestic markets became much less integrated than before. The relative price of wheat rose abruptly in 1795; wheat prices in Holland rose above those of eastern markets; and the co-movement of prices among cities became less highly correlated. These events also disturbed the rye markets, of course, but wheat was more severely affected.

The 1808 survey of the Dutch grain economy found that the Netherlands then consumed some 40,000 lasts of wheat, which is probably the approximate level of consumption throughout the eighteenth century as well. The Republic's retained imports of wheat are unlikely to have covered more than one-fifth of domestic consumption in the eighteenth century. (Table 6.3 shows retained imports accounting for only 8–13 percent of consumption.) Whatever the exact percentage, it is safe to conclude that domestic production supplied a much larger portion of wheat consumption than was the case for rye, and the locations of domestic production allowed Rotterdam, in concert with the river port of Dordrecht, to serve as the centers of the wheat trade. Wheat from the Baltic, just as its rye, went to Amsterdam, but this supply never loomed so large in the domestic market as to make Amsterdam the Republic's central market for wheat.

Wheat was a far less homogeneous product than rye. As noted in Chapter 3, wheat from each producing region was associated with distinct qualities and this led to the maintenance of significant price differentials. The bread price commissioners had frequent occasion to discuss these differentials, and they add an element of complication to the integration of regional grain markets – or, more correctly, to our effort to measure this integration. Moreover, while production areas were associated with enduring quality differences, the wheat of a given region could also vary considerably in quality from year to year, causing the transactions at a given market to reveal substantial price spreads for what was, ostensibly, the same grain.[25] In general, wheat prices more than rye reflected persisting quality differentials that render the "law of one price" an elusive benchmark for assessments of market integration.[26]

---

[24] Priester, *Zeeuwse landbouw*, p. 311; Van Cruyningen, *Behoudend maar buigzaam*, p. 206.

[25] For instance, weekly price notations for Polish wheat at the Amsterdam Grain Exchange in the period 1709–87 exhibited an average price spread of 24 percent. The spread for Prussian rye was 14.4 percent.

[26] This problem is explored in detail in Liam Brunt and Edmund Cannon, "Variation in the price and quality of English grain, 1750–1914: quantitative evidence and empirical implications," *Explorations in Economic History* 58 (2015), 74–92.

Table 6.6 *Coefficients of correlation on first differences of annual average wheat prices on the Amsterdam Grain Exchange, 1733–79*

	Polish	Konigsberg	Frisian	Zeeland
Konigsberg	0.969			
Frisian	0.841	0.887		
Zeeland	0.854	0.878	0.908	
Mean price:				
guilders per last	193.36	172.15	177.53	198.29
Coeff. of variation	24.2	24.3	23.3	26.1

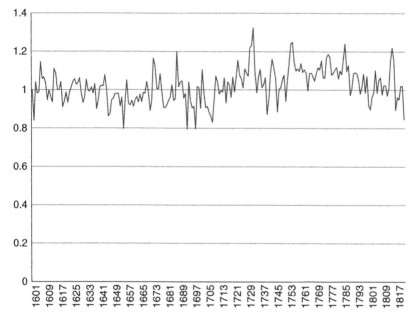

Figure 6.2 East/West wheat price ratios, 1600–1822

Price correlations between markets were always a notch lower for wheat than for rye. Eighteenth-century price notations at the Amsterdam Grain Exchange show that the two Baltic grades (Polish and Konigsberg) were well correlated, and two domestic grades (Frisian and Zeeland) were also, but the correlation between imported and domestic grades of wheat on the same market were a bit lower (see Table 6.6). Moreover, the price differentials between the costliest grades of wheat – Polish and Zeeland – and the cheaper Konigsberg and Frisian grades was on the order of 12–13 percent.

Table 6.7 *Coefficients of correlation on first differences of annual average wheat prices between city pairs in the Netherlands, 1700–49*

	A'dam (Polish)	Haarlem	Dordrecht	Utrecht	Zaltbommel
Haarlem	.875				
Dordrecht	.873	–			
Utrecht	.927	.944	.936		
Zaltbommel	.918	.804	.925	.976	
Kampen	.804	.898	.848	.942	.937

Additional correlation data, for the entire period 1596–1799, is available in Jan de Vries, "Dutch bread and grain prices, 1594–1855," www/iisg.nl/hpw/data.php#netherlands

Wheat prices beyond the maritime zone reveal somewhat larger market price differentials with Holland's markets than do those for rye. At first glance, higher wheat prices in the east are unexpected since, measure for measure, wheat – about 50 percent more expensive than rye – could more easily bear the transport and other transaction costs. In the seventeenth century these differentials were not large, but they became larger in the eighteenth century, especially after 1750. After 1800, these differentials reverse, and wheat prices in provincial markets fell below the Amsterdam market. Then, the war-induced contraction of foreign supplies to the major western markets had the effect of increasing inter-regional price spreads.

The price differentials rose, but the year-to-year price correlation among markets – the co-movement of prices – did not, as Table 6.7 shows for the period 1700–49. A full study of price correlations reveals that Dutch grain markets for both wheat and rye were already highly integrated at the beginning of our period, and remained so at its end.[27] Consumers nearly everywhere had access to supplies of both bread grains, and to several grades of wheat, on broadly equal terms. Very little of the regional differences that emerged in bread prices that we shall observe in later chapters can be attributed to the underlying grain prices.

[27] Jan de Vries, "Bread and grain prices, 1594–1855," www.iisg.nl/hpw/data.php#netherlands

7   The Milling Sector: A Trade Harnessed to *Raison d'État?*

An Intensely Regulated Industry

The new system of setting bread prices and the emergence of the excise tax on grain milling as a major source of public revenue combined to create a unique regulatory setting for the milling sector. Under the old system, millers were compensated primarily in kind: they kept a portion of the milled grain in payment for their services, which necessarily put them in the business of selling flour to bakers and private parties. The new system brought this entrepreneurial character of the milling enterprise to a sudden end. Under the new system the millers were paid in money for their services, and all of the milled grain belonged to the customer. The miller was no longer in the business of selling flour. Indeed, the magistrates now regarded any private trade in flour to be a threat to the new tax regime since it opened the door to tax avoidance.

The principal excise on milled grain was a provincial levy, but most cities levied supplementary excises of their own. Consequently, nearly every town had an interest in preventing the importation of milled grain from outside since this reduced its tax revenue. Millers were even forbidden to bolt and sift the milled grain; bakers had to do this themselves. Millers were enjoined to return to their customers – who were, after all, the owners of the grain – everything that survived the milling process, including the bran and any waste materials.

Under the new excise tax regime the grain mill became the control point for tax collection – one that became vital to the Republic's fiscal wellbeing. This fact shaped profoundly the structure of milling as an industry, for the state now had a direct interest in a milling sector that was stable, concentrated, and contented – and thereby easily supervised.

To minimize tax avoidance and fraud, the provincial governments placed a multitude of restrictions on millers and their families. Utrecht's ordinance of 1632 is typical: millers were forbidden from owning their mills in partnership with individuals from outside the city or anyone involved in baking or bread distribution. Neither they nor their wives or children (still living at home) could have any interest in a bakery, nor could they keep livestock (lest they be tempted to fatten them with bran and other residuals of the milling process).[1] In order to render the milling process transparent, millers were required to work by batch, that is, to process each delivery of grain separately, so that it could be identified with a tax certificate bearing the name of the owner. In this way, grain intended for brewing (which paid a lower tax) could be distinguished from that intended for baking, which, in turn, could be distinguished from that intended for starch making, or use as livestock feed, which, since it paid no tax, had to be mixed with a bit of sand to discourage misuse.[2] Overseeing all this were tax farmers and their agents (after 1750, provincial tax officials, the *chercher*, or *toeziender*) who eased their oversight role by requiring millers to operate only in daylight hours and never on Sundays.[3] Millers were forbidden from milling on their own account or receiving payment in kind for their services (which long remained common elsewhere in Europe).[4] All these prohibitions, intended to assist in the enforcement of the milling excise, rendered suspicious every sack of grain found at the mill without an attached ticket documenting tax payment and ownership. Some ordinances went so far as to forbid any grain from remaining at the mill overnight.

These cumbersome requirements certainly lowered the productivity of the mills. Batch milling, in particular, forced them to operate well below their theoretical capacity. On the other hand, the same fiscal imperative that prevented efficient operation led to increased scale in the milling sector since the provinces worked to minimize the number of mills in order to ease their enforcement task. The province of Groningen pursued this goal with singular determination when, in 1628, it ordered the "rationalization" of the province's 125 grain mills, reducing their number to 90. Mills at locations that made fiscal oversight difficult were closed and torn down. Two centuries later, when Groningen's population had nearly doubled, the number of grain mills had increased only to 98. Friesland acted to limit the number of mills in 1637, ordering any mill not generating at least 300 guilders in excise revenue per six-month period to shut down. A few years later such low-volume mills were ordered to be

---

[1] *GPB van Utrecht*, vol. III, Ordonnanatie op de molenaars, 12 August 1632.
[2] Holland's ordinance of 1790 specified that grain milled for fodder be mixed with 1/32nd part sand.
[3] Tax law in Holland forbade private possession of querns (hand-operated grinding mills). Sickenga, *Geschiedenis der belastingen*, pp. 394–95; J. A. de Jonge, *De industrialisatie in Nederland tussen 1850 en 1914* (Amsterdam: Scheltema en Holkema, 1968), p. 217.
[4] This rule appears to have been evaded in some rural settings. In 1642 the province of Utrecht found it necessary to remind rural millers that they were to receive their milling fee in cash and not in kind, "just like the urban millers." *GPB van Utrecht*, vol. II, p. 758.

dismantled. Later still, in 1677 Friesland continued its pressure: mills vulnerable to closure and demolition were now those that generated less than 500 guilders (sometimes adjusted to 400 guilders). In 1748 it forbade the construction of new mills and the placement of additional millstones at existing mills. Utrecht embarked on this same path in 1640. It compiled a list of rural grain mills, closed down two small ones and assigned every village to one of the 46 that remained, a number that now could not be increased without permission from the provincial States.[5]

Elsewhere, it was usually municipal officials working with the self-interest of the millers' guilds who acted to limit the number of mills by denying permission to erect new ones and providing financial support to tear down redundant mills. In this way the number of wind-powered grain mills in Holland was gradually reduced from 365 in 1630 to 306 by 1800.[6]

The result of two centuries of state interest in such consolidation is revealed in the industrial census of 1819, which recorded the number of grain mills in every province of the United Kingdom of the Netherlands. This new state embraced both the former Dutch Republic and the Southern Netherlands (modern Belgium). Table 7.1 shows two distinct patterns. In the north, where the milling excise had then been in effect for over two centuries, there were only 0.5 grain mills per 1,000 population, with each mill serving on average 4.4 bakeries. In the south, where no such provincial-level tax had ever been levied, the grain mills were far more numerous, and operated at a much smaller scale.[7] There were 1.4 mills per 1,000 population, and only 1.3 bakeries per mill.[8]

The distinctive structure of the Dutch milling sector is thrown into even sharper relief when compared to the German lands to the east.

---

[5] Matthey, *Westeremden*, pp. 281–82 Urban mills were left undisturbed, but rural mills, the most difficult to monitor, were reduced in number from 112 to 77. Trompetter, *GWF – Friesland*, p. 146 (A mill needed to process at least 28 lasts of rye annually to meet the 500 guilder threshold.) *Tegenwoordige Staat van Friesland*, vol. IV, p. 404; *GPB van Utrecht*, vol. III, p. 756. "Lyste van graan molens ten platte Lande van Utrecht waar verpachting van 't gemaal sal worden gedaan," 16 July 1640.

[6] Karel Davids, "Innovations in windmill technology in Europe, c. 1500–1800," *NEHA-Jaarboek* 66 (2003), 43–63.

[7] The Spanish and Austrian regimes in the Southern Netherlands did not follow the Republic in imposing provincial-level excises, but some towns did impose taxes of this sort. Leuven levied excises on milling and baking in 1609–10 that amounted to about 6.5 guilders per last of wheat and 1.95 guilders per last of rye. De Wilde and Poukens, "Bread provisioning," p. 411.

[8] In Britain milling and baking bore a strong resemblance to the situation in the Southern Netherlands. Between 1830 and 1870 there were not quite two bakers for every miller in Britain. Per 1,000 population, mid-nineteenth-century Britain maintained 1.6 millers (three times the Dutch density!) and 2.8 bakers (approximately the Dutch density). Petersen, *Bread*, pp. 66, 81.

Table 7.1 also presents the results of the Prussian state's industrial census, taken in 1822. By then Prussia had consolidated under its control most of the lands to the west of the Netherlands (roughly, the modern *Land* of Rhineland-Westphalia). This zone, with over 3 million inhabitants counted 2.3 master bakers and 1.6 grain mills per 1,000

Table 7.1 *Industrial census of bakeries and grain mills, 1819*

	Bread bakeries	Pastry bakeries	Grain mills	Groats grinders (*grutterijen*)
Province				
North Holland	1,000	88	146	45
South Holland	800	102	154	110
Zeeland	308	25	111	20
Utrecht	271	14	54	58
Friesland	494	28	82	70
Groningen	442	26	98	102
Drenthe	97	6	41	33
Overijssel	388	42	117	87
Gelderland	542	42	193	54
North Brabant**	793	53	200	186
Northern Neth*	5,135	426	1,196	765
Southern Neth	5,427	129	4,079	116
Prussia, Western Prov.***	7,189	389	4,982	
Prussia, Eastern Prov.****	12,462	869	17,921	

Province	Shelling mills (*pelmolens*)	Bakeries per 1,000 pop.	Mills per 1,000 pop.	Bakeries per mill
North Holland	57	2.64	0.39	6.85
South Holland	18	2.04	0.39	5.19
Zeeland	7	2.73	0.98	2.77
Utrecht	4	2.51	0.5	5.02
Friesland	19	2.78	0.46	6.02
Groningen	47	3.25	0.72	4.51
Drenthe	4	2.06	0.87	2.37
Overijssel	14	2.62	0.79	3.32
Gelderland	18	2.13	0.76	2.81
North Brabant**	30	2.71	0.68	3.97
Northern Neth*	218	2.50	0.58	4.29
Southern Neth	151	1.90	1.43	1.33
Prussia, Western Prov.***		2.29	1.59	1.44
Prussia, Eastern Prov.****		1.12	2.14	0.70

*excludes Limburg, which is included in the Southern Netherlands totals.
**North Brabant grain mills estimated from 1827 count of mills.
***Prussia's western provinces in 1822: Rhineland and Westphalia.
****Prussia east of the river Elbe in 1822.

inhabitants – a pattern that corresponds closely with that of the Southern Netherlands. East of the Elbe, as we might expect, matters were different. There bakers were much less numerous – just over one per 1,000 inhabitants – while grain mills were more numerous than bakeries. This suggests that most mills were very small in scale and served a largely self-baking population.[9]

In cities that suffered population decline, the millers' guilds shared the state's interest in consolidation, and the existence of a municipally enforced millers' fee provided the regulatory mechanism to finance such consolidation. Leiden, which in the mid-seventeenth century had grown to a population of 60,000–70,000, came to possess fourteen grain mills, standing as sentinels along its town walls. As its population declined to 30,000 by the end of the eighteenth century, many of these mills became redundant. The guild bought out the surplus mills, stopped production in them, and eventually tore them down. Three were torn down in 1731 alone. Eight mills remained in operation in 1752 and a ninth mill, then idle, was dismantled three years later. One more was shut down in the 1780s, leaving seven in operation in 1803. Every mill taken out of operation was purchased by the millers' guild, usually from the widow or heirs of a deceased miller. The guild financed the purchase by taking out loans secured by an increase in the millers' fee (*maalloon*) agreed to by the city. That is, the redundant mills were treated as "stranded assets" and became a "ratable charge," in the parlance of modern utilities regulation. In this way, the millers who faced ruin were bailed out at the expense of the consumer, whose bread long continued to embody in its price interest on debts incurred perhaps decades earlier for the benefit of the owners of redundant mills. For this reason, Leiden, whose population decline was particularly severe, charged among the highest milling fees of any city in Holland in the eighteenth century.[10]

The operation of the fiscal system and the regulation of milling fees together encouraged the consolidation of the grain milling industry. The surviving Leiden millers each served an average of ten bakers, and each apparently processed an average of some 260 lasts of bread grain (plus, of course, grain for brewing and other purposes). Amsterdam's thirty-one grain mills in 1765 (there were about this number throughout the period 1670–1850)[11] operated on an even larger scale, with an average

---

[9] Stadsarchiev Münster, Landratsamt, *Munsterlander Heimatskalender*, 2 (1939). Gewerbetrabelle der Preussischen Monarchie für das Jahr 1822.

[10] G.A. Leiden, Stadsarchief tot 1816, no. 2550. Rapport omtrent broodzetting en maalloon, 1803.

[11] Diederiks, *Stad in verval*, pp. 202–05. Amsterdam's grain mills numbered 34 in 1730 and 32 in 1808.

throughput of some 300 lasts annually.[12] Overall, around 1820, the average scale of operation in Holland and adjacent Utrecht, Zeeland, and Friesland – taking urban and rural mills of all sorts together – stood at 105–15 lasts per year. In the more rural eastern provinces mills operated on the distinctly smaller average scale of 65–70 lasts.[13] Yet the 65–70-last average in the eastern provinces far exceeded the average output of all mills in the Southern Netherlands as well as the national average for English grain mills (500 quarters, or about 47 lasts) later in the nineteenth century. French grain mills in the vicinity of Paris also appear to have worked below the level of eastern grain mills in the Netherlands.[14]

Dutch grain mills differed from most of Europe in being predominantly wind-powered. In 1850, when comprehensive information is available, the Netherlands possessed some 1,800 wind-powered grain mills and only 200 water-powered mills, the latter located in the eastern regions. In addition, there were some 1,200 horse-powered mills (*rosmolens*) that ground grain and other substances. They were located almost exclusively in rural, inland locations, and many of these small mills appear to have served as a back-up facility for the wind-powered mills. This was certainly their role in the small city of Zaltbommel, whose bread price registers on 21 October 1695 noted the following:[15]

Because of the great and lengthy stillness, whereby no grain can be ground with the wind, use had to be made of the *Rosmolen* [horse-powered mill]. The honorable magistrates – noting that agents of the bakers' guild said they [at first] paid eight stuivers per sack [for milling] and now pay six stuivers – have approved a rise in the price of bread by four penningen per loaf, which rise will cease as soon as the wind once again begins to blow.

[12] *Ibid.* In Amsterdam and other large cities, the mills were much larger than average and many were owned by multiple millers. The 30–34 mills were owned and operated by twice as many millers. What concerns us here is the unit of production and the resulting possibility for economies of scale in production.

[13] Estimates based on the 1819 and 1827 industrial censuses of grain mills and bread grain milling of 1.3 hl per capita. Milling for other purposes is excluded from these estimates. 1819–27. Total grain milling (including non taxed) 100,000 lasts / 1,196 to 1,298 mills = *c.* 84–77 lasts per mill.
In the west: milling: 52,000 lasts / 465–489 mills = 112–106 lasts.
In the north and east: milling 48,000 lasts / 731 – 809 mills = 71–64 lasts.

[14] Petersen, *Bread*, p. 66. According to Kaplan, *Provisioning Paris*, p. 315, French water mills had a capacity 60–70 percent greater than windmills, Kaplan set the daily output of these mills (when water flow and wind allowed full operation) at 6 *setier* for water mills and 4 *setier* for wind-powered mills. If they operated at this rate for 200 days per year, their total output would be approximately 63 lasts and 42 lasts, respectively.

[15] G.A. Zaltbommel, o. a., 20–1079, Broodzettingsregisters, 21 October 1695. The same problem is noted again on 8 September 1718: the bread price is raised temporarily "On account of the stillness [lack of wind] since the grain must be ground by *rosmolen*."

These "emergency" milling fees were approximately double the fees normally charged at the wind-powered mills (and incorporated in the official bread price).[16]

Setting the Millers' Fee

The state had a special interest in minimizing the millers' temptation to engage in fraud; through its substantial control over the number of mills and the power of the municipal authorities to set the fee collected by the millers, it certainly had the tools in hand to win the millers' loyalty. Yet, as already noted, the state never took the honesty of the millers for granted. Its deep and abiding suspicion was on display in the ordinance of 1680, which altered the tax collection system in rural Holland. The preamble to the ordinance states flatly that the numerous frauds undermining collection of the milling excise could not occur without the complicity of the millers. The tax authorities had hoped that greater vigilance and heavier fines would suppress this behavior, but since this had proven to be an insufficient deterrent, the States of Holland now declared that future fraud would be punishable with a fine of 1,000 guldens (an enormous sum). The ordinance went on to express the official conviction that most fraud was committed by millers who leased rather than owned their mills. Such millers now were required to pay two bonds (*borgsom*), of 500 guilders each, in order to continue in their business.[17] This requirement, which later became a single 500-guilder bond, continued into the nineteenth century. The renovated ordinance of 1790 exempted millers who owned their mills free and clear, but required them to pledge their mills in lieu of paying the bond.[18]

---

[16] The notation in the bread price register speaks of temporary milling fees of 14.40 guilders and 10.80 guilders per last of grain (whether rye or wheat is not stated). The normal milling fee at this time (1695) in Zaltbommel is not known, but provincial milling fees were then approximately 5 guilders per last of rye and 7 guilders per last of wheat. Zaltbommel's normal milling fees could not have been appreciably higher than this. Therefore, the emergency millers' fee was about double the normal fee – that payable when there was sufficient wind.

[17] *GPB van Holland*, vol. III, 29 March 1680, "Placaet van de Staten van Holland tot weeringe van sluyckeriyen en fruadatien in 't middel van 't gemaal."

[18] *GPB van Holland*, vol. IX, pp. 904–22. When Zeeland adopted the rural capitation tax in 1687, the accusation of endemic fraud perpetrated by the millers was, if anything, even more forceful. Article XIV states that "most fraud involving the milling excise has been introduced by the wicked practices and maliciousness of the [rural] millers." *GPB van Holland*, vol. IV, pp. 1110–13. "Quotisatie ten platen lande (buyten de gemelde zes steden)." Art. XI: In Friesland, the authorities apparently believed the threat of physical punishment was more effective than heavy fines. "When the tax authorities are convinced that the millers or other persons have conspired to evade collection of the milling excise they will be punished with thrashing, branding, and five years banishment in prison." *Tegenwoordige Staat van Friesland* (Amsterdam, 1789), vol. IV, p. 409.

Besides wielding a stick the provincial and municipal authorities also offered a carrot: the millers' fee (*maalloon*) that they set and incorporated into the constant costs of the regulated bread price. Did they try to buy the loyalty of the millers by setting the millers' fee at a level higher than elsewhere in Europe, where the old system of compensating millers with a share of the grain was long retained, and where millers were free to trade in grain and flour?

The available evidence does not support this hypothesis. In old system Europe, millers were compensated in kind, their "toll" typically being 1/16th of the flour produced. In the case of wheat, any further "dressing" of this meal into bolted/sifted flour was done in exchange for the remaining bran and middlings.[19] In Flanders and Brabant, until at least 1620, the millers' fee was not a share, but a fixed number of pounds of the grain delivered for milling: from 8 to 10.5 pounds of grain per *setier* of rye or wheat.[20] The customary share grants the miller 6.3 percent of the grain while the fixed-weight system gives the miller between 7 and 8 percent of the grain.[21]

Evidence I have found on the millers' fees established in the Dutch Republic is assembled in Table 7.2. The cities almost always granted the millers a larger fee for milling wheat than rye, usually between 10 and 25 percent more. Dutch millers were forbidden to "dress" the flour – to sift and separate the bran and rough materials from the whole grain. This task was left to the baker, who then was free to sell the bran and pollards himself. Since the basic milling of wheat was not appreciably more complex than that of rye, the reason for this price premium is not evident.

---

[19] Kaplan, *Provisioning Paris*, pp. 268–69; Petersen, *Bread*, pp. 51–2. According to Petersen, this practice remained common in England until the end of the eighteenth century. Only in 1796 were English millers required to levy a monetized fee for their services. In this the French were ahead of the English, but according to Kaplan, the law of 1719 requiring French millers to charge a monetary fee was not widely enforced.

[20] Scholliers, *Levensstandaard*, p. 25.

[21] According to Eversdijck's *Paste-boek*, Goes and the other Zeeland cities compensated the miller with a mix of payment in kind and in money. They received 3.75 guilders per last for both rye and wheat plus 3.5 percent of the grain. Overall, the millers received between 6 and 8 percent of the value of the grain, depending on the price level of grain. Presumably, Goes ended this practice after adopting Eversdijck's new system pricing regime. But there are exceptions to every rule. Roessingh reports on an 1805 survey of rural grain mills in the Veluwe district of Gelderland where a distinction was made between *geldmolens* and *schepmolens*: mills that performed their services for cash (*geld*) and those that took measures of grain (*schep* = a shovelful) – the practice presumably abolished more than 200 years earlier! The millers who operated *schepmolens* took 1/16th of the grain in payment. Roessingh found that payments in kind persisted only at mills in the deepest countryside, located away from the larger towns and the main routes of travel. H. K. Roessingh, "Beroep en bedrijf op de Veluwe," *AAG Bijdragen* 13 (1965), 221–22.

Table 7.2 *The millers' fee* (maalloon)

a. Average millers' fee per last in the west, for wheat and rye

Millers' fee	Millers' fee guilders per last		Grain price guilders per last		Millers' fee as % of grain price	
	Wheat	Rye	Wheat	Rye	Wheat	Rye
Estimated share fees						
1585–95: 1/24ᵗʰ	*6.80*	*3.86*	*162*	*94*	*4.2%*	*4.2%*
1/16ᵗʰ	*10.21*	*5.92*	*162*	*94*	*6.3*	*6.3*
Money fees						
1596–1603	4.95	4.40	212	154	2.3	2.9
1603–33	7.23	5.28	207	136	3.5	3.9
1633–49	9.45	7.38	239	146	4.0	5.1
1650–64	10.33	7.71	250	182	4.1	4.2
1665–1718	10.33	7.71	201	136	5.1	5.7
1719–54	10.50	8.00	171	113	6.1	7.1
1755–88	10.82	8.80	238	147	4.5	6.0
1789–1802	10.82	8.80	337	223	3.2	3.9
1803–06	14.20	10.97	403	261	3.5	4.2
1826	19.40	17.90	236	150	8.2	11.9
1820–39	20.34	16.44	232	152	8.8	10.8

b. Average milling fee per last in the east, for wheat and rye

	Millers' fee guilders per last		Millers' fee as % of west fee		Millers' fee as % of grain price	
	Wheat	Rye	Wheat	Rye	Wheat	Rye
1593–1620	5	3	100%	68%	2.4%	2.1%
1670–1748	7.5	5	73	65	4.0	4.0
1826	10.8	8.6	57	49	4.6	5.7
1855	12	9	59	55	5.0	5.6

However, it appears to be a step in the right direction when compared to the old practice of payments in kind, where the miller would have taken possession of milled wheat that was on average 50 percent more valuable than an equal quantity of rye.

The millers' fees established by the municipal authorities in the first years of the new system were no more than half as much as had been provided by the old system practice of payment in kind. At the (rather high) grain prices prevailing in those years, the millers' fees of 1596–1603 equaled no more than 3 percent of the price of rye, and even less, 2.3 percent, of the price of wheat. I have found no direct evidence of the payment system prevailing in the Dutch towns directly before the introduction of new system price regulation. If they did collect 1/16th or 1/24th of the grain as their fee in the decade preceding 1596, the milling fee would have stood at a level well above that set from 1596 onward in Leiden, Haarlem, and Utrecht, for which we have the earliest evidence. Table 7.2, panel (a), offers an estimate of the monetary value of milling fees under the old system, based on the average grain prices for the decade 1586–95. They are 50 to 100 percent above the new fixed fees for wheat and from 0 to 50 percent above the rye fees.

The new system of bread price regulation began in most towns by setting rather severe norms for the bakers (discussed in Chapter 3), from which the magistrates retreated to some degree in subsequent years. Something comparable seems to have occurred with the millers. We can follow this closely in the case of Leiden, where major upward adjustments were made to the millers' fee in 1603, 1633, and 1652. By then the millers' fee for wheat had more than doubled while the rye fee rose by 70 percent. Much the same thing occurred in Utrecht, where the millers' fees for both grains stood at 4 guilders per last until 1621, but were raised in 1628, 1632, and 1647, by which date the wheat fee had more than doubled (to 10 guilders per last) and the rye fee had been raised by 88 percent.[22]

By the 1650s the millers' fees stood at a level equivalent to about 4 percent of the then-prevailing price of grain. Thereafter, the millers' fee changed little until the beginning of the nineteenth century, but after 1665, grain prices usually stood at much lower levels. As a consequence, the millers' fee expressed as a percentage of the grain price reached a peak level in the first half of the eighteenth century, when wheat milling cost the equivalent of 6 percent of the grain and rye milling cost 7 percent. After the mid-eighteenth century, as grain prices tended upward, the millers' fee became relatively lighter and this was especially so after 1780. By 1789–1802 the fees had fallen back to the 3 to 4 percent range common to the first two-thirds of the seventeenth century.

The course of Dutch millers' fees might be compared to those of neighboring countries. The English assize as reformulated in 1709 retained a payment in kind of 1/16th to 1/24th of the grain until 1796, or about 5 percent of the price of grain. At the wheat prices prevailing in the 1770s, this gave millers £1.215, or fl13.70 per last. The monetized millers' fee of 1796 amounted to £1.42, or fl16, which was raised in 1816 to £2.13, or fl25.50.[23] These fees also rose sharply in the nineteenth century, and were

[22] W. A. G. Perks, *Zes eeuwen molens in Utrecht* (Utrecht: Het Spectrum, 1974), pp. 30–31.
[23] Petersen, *Bread*, pp. 26, 52.

always somewhat higher than millers' fees in the maritime Netherlands. In France, the 1/16th rule was also common, but millers around Paris levied a higher milling fee of 1/12th of the grain.[24]

One might object that charting the evolution of the millers' fee as a percentage of the grain price is misleading. The cost of operating a grain mill does not vary with grain prices, but with the costs of capital and labor. Indeed, it was an achievement of the new system to recognize this fact and place the compensation of millers on a rational basis. But, in making this shift the regulators also altered the nature of the miller's business. They had been dealers in grain and flour and part of their income came from trade; now they were barred from any participation in the grain and flour trade and their income rested entirely on a fee-for-service basis. Coupling this suppression of the millers' profit opportunities as traders with a significant reduction in the absolute size of their fee would seem to be a recipe for trouble – an encouragement to evasion and fraud. And yet, as emphasized at the beginning of this chapter, the magistrates had a strong interest in maintaining a contented corps of millers, since their cooperation was essential to the efficient operation of the tax regime. Perhaps this connection was less apparent to the magistrates in the new system's first years, when the milling excise was still a minor tax, but by 1618 and 1625, when Holland's milling excise rose sharply, its importance would have become more evident, and it is then that we see the magistrates making mollifying adjustments to the millers' fee.

Yet their corrective action seems not to have been excessive. The state's interest in coddling the millers did not lead to millers' fees higher than had prevailed before the introduction of the new system, or higher than in neighboring countries. Just the opposite took place, as millers' fees in Holland and Utrecht – which were always higher than in the eastern provinces – declined from the old system norm of 6.3 percent of the grain price to as little as half that level.

Millers' Earnings

The new system seems to have imposed a significant reduction on the milling revenues of Dutch millers. Cash payments now replaced the share of the grain that had been the customary compensation for the millers' services. Not only were these cash payments lower in value than the payments in kind they replaced, but the millers were denied the

---

[24] Kaplan, *Provisioning Paris*, pp. 456–57. The Parisian baking trials of 1700, on which Nicolas Delamare based the bread price schedules that were to govern Paris for the next forty years, set milling costs at 20 sous per *setier*, then the equivalent of about 15 guilders per last, which was at least 50 percent above the level of the Dutch millers' fee.

entrepreneurial profits that they had enjoyed when they had been free to trade in grain and flour. And, not only was this trade denied them but they were now subject to a multitude of restrictions that affected the efficient operation of their mills.

However, we have also seen that the same regulatory regime that hobbled the efficient operation of grain millers also enforced a consolidation of mills that tended to increase the millers' scale of operations. What was the overall impact of the new regulatory system on millers' earnings?

We can approach this question from a macroeconomic perspective, by multiplying the volume of grain milled for bread-making purposes by the millers' fees. My estimates of per capita bread grain consumption, provided below in Chapter 12, and the millers' fee averages assembled in Table 7.2, provide the necessary information to make the estimates shown in Table 7.3, which provides separate estimates for the western Netherlands (Holland, Zeeland, and Utrecht), the northern and eastern Netherlands (all other provinces), and for the Dutch Republic as a whole at fifty-year intervals from 1600. For the Republic as a whole, milling bread grain generated approximately 377,000 guilders per annum around 1600. Revenue nearly doubled, to 700,000 guilders in the course of the seventeenth century, and rose further to over 800,000 guilders by 1800. Shortly thereafter milling revenues rose sharply. Major increases in the millers' fees beginning in 1803 led to revenue of some 1,500,000 guilders by 1826 and 2,200,000 guilders by the 1840s. The total revenue of the milling sector will have been higher than these estimates since they do not include milling services performed for other grains and for brewers, distillers, ships' biscuits, pastry bakers, and other non-bread-making purposes.[25]

These figures, if they fairly reflect the general course of the sector's revenues, raise three questions. First: did the millers' revenue really double in the first half of the seventeenth century, or was it restored to something like its pre-1596 level? I have interpreted the large increases in the milling fees in this period as largely a "correction" to an overzealous reform of the millers' fee introduced with the new system of bread price regulation. It does appear that the new system regulators got off on the

---

[25] Jansen estimates "value added" in the milling sector at 2.5 million in 1850. The inclusion of milling revenue for purposes other than bread baking can account for most of the difference in our estimates. Michael Jansen, *De industriële ontwikkeling in Nederland, 1800–1850* (Amsterdam: NEHA, 1999), pp. 162–66. Most wind-powered grain mills were designed to serve as "general purpose" mills, capable of grinding groats, oil seeds, barley malt, etc. De Jonge attributes the ability of these mills to compete with steam-powered flour mills in the nineteenth century to this flexibility. It can also help account for the gap between the apparent earnings of millers and the revenue generated by their work for the bakers. De Jonge, *De industrialisatie in Nederland*, p. 218.

Table 7.3 *Milling sector revenues, 1600–1850*
(revenue in thousands of guilders per annum)

	West	East	Total
1600	257	120	377
1680	487	207	694
1750	503	227	730
1800	521	299	830
1800–04	594	322	916
1810–14	417	225	642
1825–29	996	544	1,540
1845–49	1379	830	2,209

1600–1800: Grain milling volume from Chapter 12, milling fees from Table 7.2.
1800–50: Grain milling volume from Jansen, *De industriële ontwikkeling*, pp. 164–65.
Milling fees from Table 7.2. Jansen estimates the value added of the milling sector in the
Netherlands for 1850 as a whole by two methods, arriving at estimates of 2.5 million and
1.9 million guilders.

wrong foot with the millers, but I have found no direct evidence of a
conscious policy to undermine their economic status.

Second: How could these revenue levels supply millers with the
handsome incomes recorded in income tax registers of 1742 (*Personele
Quotisatie*), which provide a comprehensive picture of the income of millers in urban Holland found to have a taxable income of at least 600 guilders? The surviving registers (for sixteen cities) listed 158 taxable millers.
Since all of Holland had not many more than 300 grain mills, and at
least 100 of these were in rural areas and small towns, there could not
have been many urban millers whose incomes fell short of the 600 guilder threshold. Thus, the vast majority of Holland's urban millers earned
over 600 guilders per year (placing them in the top 20 percent of Dutch
urban income earners). In fact, as a group they stood far above the 600
guilder income threshold: the average annual income of all 158 taxable
millers was 1,125 guilders, which placed them within the top 10 percent
of urban income earners – and well above the income level suggested by
my macroeconomic estimates.[26]

These high millers' incomes were concentrated in the western provinces. This region accounted for just over half of the Republic's population
until 1800, while it accounted for at least two-thirds of milling revenue
and – in 1819, our first opportunity to observe the Republic's grain mills
province by province – only 39 percent of the grain mills. If that 1819

[26] For a fuller discussion of the 1742 *Quotisatie Kohier*, see De Vries and Van der Woude,
First Modern Economy, pp. 564–69.

ratio held earlier, as seems likely, some 450 grain mills in 1800 divided about 452,000 guilders in revenue, or 1,182 guilders each. Of course, the larger urban mills will have generated more revenue and the rural ones (and particularly the numerous small mills of Zeeland) considerably less. An Amsterdam grain mill (where we noted annual production to have averaged some 300 lasts of bread grains) took in nearly 3,000 guilders in gross revenue, and Leiden's mills about 2,500. It was the rural mills that brought the averages down. In the northern and eastern provinces, where the remaining 750 mills divided about 300,000 guilders, the resulting average revenue of some 400 guilders per mill seems too low.

The operating costs of a grain mill cannot be estimated here in any detail. None of the bread price regulation documents gives any insight into this question. While the bakers' fees were determined only after baking trials had investigated the costs faced by the baker, the millers' fees were never accompanied by the equivalent of "milling trials." But millers faced substantial capital costs and a mill of any size hired labor as well. In order to generate an income in excess of 1,000 guilders per year to the miller, his mill would have needed to generate a gross revenue of at least twice that amount. Our Amsterdam and Leiden millers certainly enjoyed such revenues, and many other urban millers did too. But most millers in smaller town and rural locations – notwithstanding their large scale of output relative to the rest of western Europe – faced a millers' fee that sharply limited their incomes.

Third: If magistrates kept millers' fees at a low level throughout the era of the Dutch Republic – lower than in neighboring countries or in the Netherlands itself before 1596 – their successors under the Batavian Republic and the Kingdom followed a very different course. Why?

After the fall of the old Republic the Batavian reformers abolished the guilds, including the millers' guilds in 1805. They presented themselves as advocates of a liberal, competitive economy. Therefore it is surprising and puzzling to find sudden and large increases in the publicly sanctioned millers' fees. Beginning in 1803 these fees rose by some 25–30 percent, and rose again around 1815. By 1826, when comprehensive information is available, they were nearly double the pre-1803 levels: 19.40 guilders per last of wheat and 17.90 guilders per last of rye. Grain prices by the 1820s had then fallen significantly from the high levels of the Napoleonic Wars, causing the milling fees to weight more heavily in the cost of making bread than ever before: they now added 9 percent to the cost of wheat and 11 percent to the cost of rye. Rising production costs cannot explain this sharp rise in the milling fee, but perhaps a fall in per capita bread grain consumption in the crisis-ridden 1810s can. Milling has high fixed costs, and a fall in output well below capacity could be expected to generate pressures for a compensatory rise in fees.[27] If this is the cause, it may also help explain the simultaneously sharp rise in milling fees in England in this same period (from 16 guilders per last as late as 1808 to 24 guilders after 1812).[28] Yet in neither Holland nor England did millers' fees fall when consumers returned to a more normal pattern of bread consumption as grain prices fell back from their elevated Napoleonic war levels. Nineteenth-century millers earned a good living.

Overall, the macro approach to estimating millers' incomes has significant limitations. Milling for bread production was their chief activity, but certainly not the only one, and the heterogeneity of mill capacity, particularly between urban and rural mills, limits the value of average earnings estimates. However, before 1800 there is little evidence that regulators curried favor with the millers. They consistently voiced suspicions about their honesty and held their fees at levels well below those found before 1596 or in other countries.

---

[27] It is possible that the upward pressure on milling fees stemmed from the need of millers to recover investment costs in improving their mills. In the city of Utrecht the millers requested an increase in these fees to enable them to build larger, taller mills (*stelling-molens*) on the city walls. These more powerful mills, it was argued, could grind more finely, reducing the amount of bran that bakers needed to remove from their flour in the preparation of bolted white bread. The increase in the millers' fee, they argued, would "pay for itself." Perks, *Zes eeuwen molens in Utrecht*, p. 45.

[28] Petersen, *Bread*, p. 52.

8   The Baking Enterprise: Efficiency versus Convenience

Constant Costs and Fixed Costs

The records left by the bread price commissioners are extensive and detailed, and, as we found in Chapters 3 and 4, they reveal a sophisticated understanding of the economics of bread making and a readiness to engage in tedious, if not advanced, mathematics. But the baking trials possessed one notable analytical weakness: while they specified and measured the *constant costs*, often in great detail, they did not directly address the *fixed costs* of operating a bakery. The constant costs, once set, continued in force for years, sometimes decades, until new trials or new tax rates led to a revision. When added to the grain costs, which, of course, could vary from week to week, they established the total allowable costs, and, hence, the revenue that needed to be generated by the sale of bread baked from a last of grain.

Table 8.1 displays several examples of the itemization of constant costs. Consider one drawn up by the Haarlem commissioners in 1659 for wheat bread: items 1 through 5 were raw materials and fees payable to boatmen and porters, while items 6 and 7 were externally determined by municipal and provincial governments. All of these costs were introduced in earlier chapters and are fairly straightforward. But item 8, the bakers' fee, is not. It was intended to compensate the baker for all labor costs and for the capital value of the bakery and oven. A few cost accounts distinguished between the bakers' fee proper (for labor) and what was usually called the bakers' profit, which was intended to cover the capital costs and the managerial services of the baker, but most documents simply lumped them together.[1]

---

[1] The 1826 national survey of baking costs prompted the municipalities to use standard categories of expense that distinguished labor costs from bakers' profit. The returns from the cities of Holland provided a suspiciously uniform response. The total of labor plus capital costs varied from town to town, and the costs attributable to wheat production were always much higher than for rye. But with one exception all towns set the labor portion, the bakers' fee, at 40 percent for both wheat and rye.

Table 8.1 *Constant costs as itemized at several baking trials (in guilders, stuivers, and penningen per last of grain)*

	Haarlem	1642 wheat	1659 wheat
1.	Transport costs	7.01.12	8.14.00
2.	Milk	20.05.00	17.08.00
3.	Yeast	13.10.00	26.02.00
4.	Fuel	15.04.00	11.12.00
5.	Eggs	3.07.08	2.18.00
6.	Excise taxes	57.12.06	67.15.12
7.	Millers' fee	8.02.00	8.02.00
8.	Bakers' fee	45.04.08	75.04.06
	Total	170.07.02	217.16.02
	Bran (proceeds from sale of)	-20.12.04	
		149.15.08	
	Dordrecht	**1709 rye**	**1709 wheat**
1.	Transport costs	5.12.00	6.08.00
2.	Yeast	0	16.00.00
3.	Fuel	12.16.00	12.16.00
4.	Excise taxes	58.00.00	111.00.03
5.	Other taxes	8.008.00	8.08.00
6.	Millers' fee	10.00.00	10.00.00
7.	Bakers' fee	36.00.00	58.12.00
	Total	130.16.00	223.04.03
	Leiden	**1597 rye**	**1603 wheat**
1.	Transport costs, measuring, drying	2.02.01	
2.	Fuel, yeast, other ingredients		14.10.00
3.	Excise taxes	4.19.00	11.12.00
4.	Millers' fee	4.08.00	8.14.00
5.	Bakers' fee	25.16.00	43.10.00
	Total	37.05.01	78.06.00
	Utrecht	**1647 rye**	**1653 wheat**
1.	Transport	2.10.00	2.10.00
2.	Ingredients	2.10.00	
3.	Excises	28.08.12	65.00.00
4.	Millers' fee	7.10.00	10.00.00
5.	Bakers' fee	46.11.04	67.10.00
	Total	87.50.00	145.00.00
	Zaltbommel	**1806 rye**	**1806 wheat**
1.	Transport costs	1.16	1.16
2.	Fuel	14.08	14.08
3.	Yeast		10.16
4.	Oil	3.12	3.12
5.	Excises	45.00	108.00
6.	Other taxes	3.12	7.04
7.	Millers' fee	?	?
8.	Bakers' fee	27.00	27.00
	Total	96.06	174.03

Sources: G.A. Haarlem, Stadsarchief 1581–1795, R. 413; G.A. Dordrecht, no. 4763; G.A. Leiden, Gilden archief, no. 180; G.A. Utrecht, no. 2023, Rijdingboeken; G.A. Zaltbommel, 20: 1079–80, Broodzettingsregisters.

From an economist's perspective the new system of bread price regulation had taken an important step forward in distinguishing constant from variable costs, but it had stopped short of clarifying the distinction between constant costs (constant per unit of output – such as items 1 through 7 above) and fixed costs (constant regardless of the level of output). If these fixed costs – the bakers' oven, shop, and equipment most notably – were a trivial part of the cost of baking bread, this omission may have had little practical effect, but if a substantial portion of what the bakers' fee was intended to defray was an expense that was indeed fixed, then this fee, which varied with the volume of output, was likely to over-compensate large bakers and under-compensate small ones. In other words, the presence of fixed plant and equipment creates the possibility of exploiting economies of scale, since production costs per unit of output decline the closer one comes to fully utilizing the capacity of the production facility.

Information about the capital costs of bakeries is not abundant, and what we have cannot usually be related to the production capacity of the firm. Seventeenth-century Amsterdam bakeries seem to have sold for between 1,000 and 3,000 guilders, and were leased for some 300 guilders per year. The tools of the trade – forms, kneading troughs, bolting sieves, copper kettles and pails, scales – easily cost another 200–300 guilders.[2] Grain storage areas and equipment to transfer grain, fuel, and other ingredients from place to place added further costs, as did a residence sufficient to house both the baker's family and his apprentices and journeymen.[3] All told, it was easily possible for an urban bakery of some size to incur annual fixed costs (via depreciation and rent) of 400–600 guilders.

The chief fixed cost and constraint on output was the oven. A larger oven saves on both labor and fuel with each firing, while multiple firings per day represent a capital saving. In addition, the full use of the labor of the baker and his family can also be considered as a fixed cost in the context of the artisanal organization of this industry. Consequently, a key assumption of the *broodzetting* – that all constant costs rise proportionately with the volume of output – is in conflict with the tendency for unit costs to fall with an increasing scale of operation, at least up to the limit of full capacity utilization.

The commissioners' records occasionally reveal some appreciation of this fact. Their baking trials typically made use of the ovens of charitable

---

[2] Examples are provided in Kuijpers, *Migrantenstad*, pp. 231–32.
[3] Bakers, more than other artisans, tended to house their single workers on the premises, since their work was primarily at night and in the early morning.

institutions, which were larger than those of most bakers. The guilds regularly complained that the resulting calculations of fuel and labor costs based on these large ovens were unrealistically low. Leiden's 1803 report on all aspects of the milling and baking sectors compared the then-prevailing bakers' fee (66 guilders per last for rye bread) to the fee paid by the city to bakers at the poorhouse bakery (*armenbakkerij*). They were paid 19.80 guilders per last. They also received free housing and bread and purchased their fuel tax-free, all of which was thought to have a monetary value of another 20 guilders per last. Of course, these benefits would have had nearly a fixed monetary value per year, not per last. Old habits of mind were difficult to shake! The report went on to claim that these bakers "could survive on this [at most, 40 guilders per last] because of their high volume of production" and concluded that: "the profits of the [commercial] bakers must be described as exorbitant." But this exorbitant profit did not so much enrich the bakers as it allowed too many of them to survive in the trade. The authors of the Leiden report caught the nub of the matter, even if their calculations were inexact, by concluding with this question: "should the city government set a bakers' fee at which a very few people [the large bakers] earn 50 percent profit while the good burghers of the city pay at least 32,000 guilders more [the cost of keeping the small bakers in operation] than necessary?"[4]

A Dordrecht commissioner in 1826 complained similarly that the bakers' fee had been set too high "with respect to bakeries of any importance."[5] But what is most striking is the silence on this matter.

What (unspoken) assumptions did the commissioners make when setting the bakers' fee? Figure 8.1 offers a sketch of what was at stake. It assumes that the cost of baking bread from a measure of grain declined over a broad range, up to the full utilization of a large baking oven. Bakeries varied in the volume of their output. If the commissioners set a low bakers' fee, they reduced the price of bread but undermined the financial viability of small bakeries (fee A in the figure). In some areas

---

[4] G.A. Leiden, no. 2550. The high volume was made possible by the large-capacity ovens of the poorhouse, the restricted range of bread types supplied to the charity-dependent orphans, and, of course, to their large number. In the 1770s the commissioners in The Hague nearby had also attempted to use the cost of maintaining the bakers of the city's poorhouse to come to a better understanding of the proper bakers' fee. Their report concluded that "the costs of the baker cannot really be calculated" because of the many incommensurabilities with commercial bakers, but they did recognize that the costs of the baker and his labor "should be calculated over as many thousand loaves produced by a baker in a year in order to know what costs should be charged per loaf." They grasped the issue, but did not have the information to proceed to a proper calculation. G.A. The Hague, O.A. no. 5741, no date.

[5] G.A. Dordrecht, no. 741.

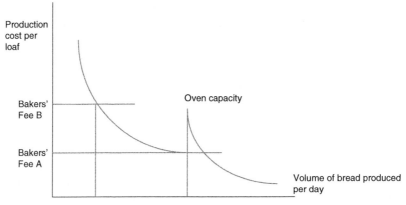

Figure 8.1 Fixed costs of bread production

this might deny consumers convenient access to a bakery.[6] If the commissioners set it high, they inflated the bread price and enriched the largest, most efficient, bakers (fee B). They also supported, more modestly, a large number of half-idle bakers.

By now it will be clear that setting the baking fee was not simply an innocent or purely technical activity; a larger public policy objective – or set of possibly conflicting policy goals – was affected by this decision. As we have noted, the sources do not speak directly to this issue. However, one historian has ventured to explain the intent of Republican bread price regulation. In a study of the impact of bread prices on the cost of living in the Netherlands, Jan Luiten van Zanden took note of a large difference in rye bread prices between Holland and the eastern Netherlands (we turn to this issue in Chapter 12), and determined that this difference was only partly accounted for by the difference in provincial taxation. He concluded, without much further discussion of alternative explanations, that most of the observed difference in rye bread prices reflected a policy of Holland's bread price commissioners "to protect the bakers' income! ... Once an instrument to protect the interests of the consumer,

---

[6] That is, if regulators adopted the American standard of "universal access" for telephone and electricity service, prices would need to be sufficiently high to allow very small rural bakeries to be financially viable. A similar problem arose in setting the milling fee. Millers probably faced larger fixed capital costs than bakers. In this case, we know that the provinces of Holland and Utrecht, at least, offered subsidies to small rural mills as an alternative to raising the milling fee paid by the customers of all mills, large and small. *Groot Placaat-boek van Holland*, 1 December 1790, pp. 904–22; Ordonnantie in vordering van 't Gemaal. R.A. Noord Holland, Gecommitteerde Raden van West Friesland en het Noorderkwartier, no. 1228, "Douceur van getrouwheid," Uitbetaling van provisie aan korenmolenaars.

the assize (*broodzetting*) thus became an instrument to effect cartel agreements between the bakers."[7] Why would the commissioners, sworn to regulate bread prices for the public good, manipulate their procedures – by inflating the bakers' fee, in this case – for the private benefit of the bakers? Van Zanden offered little evidence or argument in support of his claim that Holland's regulatory system had been hijacked by the bakers and turned into a conspiracy against the public. But his argument is consistent with a well-known and widespread phenomenon in modern economic life: regulatory capture.

Regulatory Capture and the Economics of Guilds

"Regulatory capture" refers to the tendency for a public agency established to regulate an industry in order to protect the public interest to be "captured" by that industry. That is, the industry, directly or through its lobbyists, persuades the regulatory body to enact policies that subordinate the public interest to that of the industry itself. Regulatory capture is widespread – some argue unavoidable – not simply because of the regrettable corruptibility or gullibility of public servants, but because of three specific, structural, problems that affect the operation of most regulatory bodies.[8]

1. Information asymmetry. The regulatory agency knows less about the industry than do the firms within it. It comes to depend on those it regulates for information essential to its mission.

The bread price commissioners engaged in periodic baking trials in order to inform themselves about the "mysteries" of the bakers' craft. We have seen how they struggled to determine the true bread yield (pounds of bread per measure of grain) achievable by the bakers, and how they pondered which of the several grain prices to use in setting bread prices week-by-week. In these matters they had independent access to the

---

[7] Jan Luiten van Zanden, "Kosten van levensonderhoud en loonvorming in Holland en Oost-Nederland, 1600–1815: de voorbeelden van Kampen en Alkmaar," *Tijdschrift voor sociale geschiedenis* 11 (1985), 317–18. Quote from English translation in *Rise and Decline of Holland's Economy*, p. 34. Nineteenth-century critics of the *broodzetting* were also of the view that regulation allowed the bakers' guilds "to sell their labor above its actual value." From their classical-liberal perspective this was not an unintended result of regulation; it was its purpose. J. van Kuijk, *De broodzetting: onnut, schadelijk, ongeoorloofd* (Amsterdam: J. H. Gebhard en Comp.,1852), p. 22.

[8] On the first problem, see George Stigler, "The theory of economic regulation," *Bell Journal of Economics and Management Science* 2 (1971), 3–21; on the second, Mancur Olson, *The Theory of Collective Action* (Cambridge, Mass.: Harvard University Press, 1965); on the third, Mancur Olson, *The Rise and Decline of Nations* (New Haven, Conn.: Yale University Press, 1982).

needed information. But the bakers' fee required information much of which was proprietary to the bakers and varied considerably from one baker to the other. The commissioners must have felt far less confident about setting the bakers' fee than about any of the numerous other matters on which they ruled.

2. The public interest may be diffuse and vague, while the industry's interest is specific and clear. The industry is concentrated and makes its position clear while the public is large and diverse in its interests and does not focus on the issues of the industry with any intensity or consistency

The public had an interest in low bread prices, to be sure, but segments of the public may also have been concerned with other issues, such as ready access to bakeries, the availability of a broad range of bread types, and bread of high quality. Meanwhile, the bakers, organized in guilds, usually spoke with one voice to the commissioners.

3. The regulatory agency's *stated* charge is to advance a public interest, but this overlooks its *unstated* charge. The sovereign authority has an interest of its own that is distinct from that of the public at large. If regulation creates an economic rent (a revenue in excess of the economic costs of production), the sovereign will wish to share in it. More generally, the sovereign (in our case the town magistrates) can use the regulatory agencies to bind regulated groups to it through an accommodating regulatory posture and thereby strengthen its political position.

In setting the prices of all significant bakery products, the bread price commissioners not only affected the wellbeing of consumers, they affected the very economic fate of a large, organized artisanal group (thousands of bakers, their families and employees, plus ancillary trades, from millers to grain porters). In their desire to maintain municipal peace among the broad middle class of artisans, the magistrates could use the bread price commissioners as part of a politics of "pacification."[9] This most closely aligns with Van Zanden's claim concerning the perverse operation of bread price regulation in Holland – although it remains odd that in his telling regulators in the other Dutch provinces remained immune to these temptations.

---

[9] Maarten Prak, "Corporate politics in the Low Countries," in Maarten Prak, ed., *Craft Guilds in the Early Modern Low Countries: Work, Power and Representation* (Aldershot: Ashgate, 2006), pp. 74–106.

Regulatory capture is generally treated as a problem confined to the political economy of modern industrial societies. But before concluding that we have here one more way in which the Dutch Republic was ahead of its time – the "first modern economy" – we should note how closely the third channel for the propagation of regulatory capture is related to a classic problem in the study of pre-industrial economies: why was so much of urban economic life organized in guilds?

The bread price regulators almost always confronted bakers not as individual operators of private firms but as a corporate body – a guild – that was the exclusive representative of the bread producers. If the producers had "captured" the regulators, then it was the guild rather than the individual producers that had done the capturing. This directs our attention to the identification of some common interests shared by the political authority and the guilds that animated the policies of both. If "what do bosses do?" is a question that has long divided students of the modern capitalist economy, "what do guilds do?" has similarly been a bone of contention among medieval and early modern economic historians.[10]

One approach is to emphasize the positive: besides the religious, social, and insurance functions they perform for their members, guilds helped enforce contracts, insure product quality, develop human capital via apprenticeship training, and even stimulate technological innovation – all in exchange for the security offered by a local monopoly on supply. In the case of bakers, it is clear that the regulatory regime enforced by the public authorities gave the bakers an unusually encompassing security, and that, *in theory*, the public authority held powerful levers to use that security in order to regulate product quality, support training, and even finance productivity-enhancing investments.[11]

Another approach, influential ever since the classical economists launched their attack on guilds in the eighteenth century, emphasizes the negative: guilds, in the words of Sheilagh Ogilvie's recent overview of the subject, "are a mechanism whereby guild members and political elites

[10] Stephen Marglin, "What do bosses do? The origins and functions of hierarchy in capitalist production," *Review of Radical Political Economy* 6 (1974), 60–112; 7 (1975), 20–37; Sheilagh Ogilvie, "The economics of guilds," *Journal of Economic Perspectives* 28 (2014), 169–92. Marglin and Ogilvie probably differ on most things, but they both see corporate hierarchies and guilds, respectively, as rent-seekers.
[11] Stephan R. Epstein, "Craft guilds, apprenticeship, and technological change in preindustrial Europe," *Journal of Economic History* 58 (1998), 684–713; Stephan R. Epstein and Maarten Prak, eds., *Guilds, Innovation and the European Economy, 1400–1800* (London: Routledge, 2008); Avner Greif, Paul Milgrom, and Barry Weingast, "Coordination, commitment and enforcement: the case of the merchant guild," *Journal of Political Economy* 102 (1994), 912–50.

could collaborate in capturing a larger slice of the economic pie and redistribute it to themselves at the expense of the rest of the economy (that is, at the expense of consumers of guild products or services and all the potential competitors excluded from guild membership)."[12] From this perspective the regulatory bodies established by the town magistrates to control bread prices were not primarily intended to "protect" consumers or even the "public weal" more generally. Rather, they were, first and foremost, the mechanism whereby the guild bakers extracted rents (above-market returns) from consumers, which then would be shared with the public authority as the "price" for its cooperation.

To put it bluntly, guilds were a conspiracy against the public in which the state and the producers colluded to divide the spoils. But, to return to the Dutch bakers' guilds and their regulators: just how much of a rent were the bakers granted and what did they give the public authorities in return? We should be able to answer the first question, for we have most of the information needed to reconstruct the profitability of the baking enterprise, a topic we will address below. But where should one look to find the *quid-pro-quo* in this bargain? What did the bakers and their guilds do for the public authorities? Unlike French guilds of the period, they did not make payments and loans to the state in return for their charters and privileges.[13] Nor is there evidence that their rent-sharing took the form of gifts and bribes or other corrupt practices. If, as Van Zanden suspected, Holland's price regulation system unjustly enriched the bakers, the regulators seem to have gotten precious little of a tangible nature in return for their essential cooperation.

What the town magistrates *did* need from the bakers – increasingly in the course of the seventeenth century – was cooperation in the use of the bread price as a mechanism for the generation of public revenue. As we have seen, every loaf of bread included in its price a large provincial tax, a smaller municipal tax, a stamp tax, and, in some places, special surcharges for poor relief. These taxes were "buried" in the bread price to be "passed through" to the consumer, the ultimate payer. But the bakers had good reason to doubt that the pass-through of taxes incorporated in the bread prices would be smooth and complete and, hence, of no cost to them. To the extent that consumers resisted the higher prices (that their demand for bread with respect to price was not completely inelastic) the bakers stood to suffer from reduced custom. In a free market, the bakers might have felt compelled to moderate their prices (to pass through less than 100 percent of the tax) in order to retain their customers. The

---

[12] Ogilvie, "The economics of guilds," p. 169.
[13] Root, *The Fountain of Privilege*, pp. 121–27.

regulatory system forbade this. They could charge neither more nor less than the official price, which led many bakers, as we have seen in Chapter 3, to offer consumers other inducements in the form of small rolls, specialty breads, and extra buns – the proverbial " baker's dozen." If the regulators succeeded in suppressing these measures, and they certainly tried, all that was left for the baker was to endure a reduced demand for his product. What could the baker expect from the regulator in return for this damage to his economic interests?

The tax regime to which the bakers were harnessed made them, in effect, the unpaid collectors of one of the Republic's chief revenue sources. They were required to set aside revenues for periodic payments to several tax farmers and municipal fiscal agents. This led to a serious recordkeeping obligation and the inevitable disputes with public authorities. Consider the case of Haarlem's municipal tax for the benefit of its orphanage for the poor (*Armekinderhuis*). In 1715 this declining industrial city's magistrates hit upon the sort of brilliant idea that only occurs to the desperate. Grain and bread prices, they observed, generally followed a seasonal pattern, with higher prices in winter than in summer. They reasoned that the hard-pressed inhabitants of the city could more easily bear an additional tax on their bread if it was imposed only when the price was likely to be lower than average. Arguing thus, they ordered the bakers to add 4 penningen to the price of the 6 pound rye loaf, but only in the six months from May through October, when experience had taught them that grain prices were usually lower than the annual average. This countercyclical tax had the desired effect; the seasonal pattern of bread prices that had prevailed before 1715 became a bit smoother, as shown in Figure 8.2. The bakers charged an additional 4 penningen (0.25 stuivers) per loaf of rye bread, and the city collected from the bakers 5.40 guilders for every last of rye used during the six months each year the tax was levied.[14]

The city fathers could congratulate themselves on having rather cleverly exploited a recurring seasonal pattern in bread prices in order to squeeze a bit of extra revenue (about 5,000 guilders per year) from Haarlem's burghers, and they kept the new tax in place for the rest of the century. But in doing so they had placed yet another administrative burden on the bakers. Which brings us back to our question: what did they offer the bakers by way of compensation?

Provincial fiscal officials were acutely aware of the strategic position of the millers, and spoke often of the need simultaneously to mollify them and to monitor their actions with an especially sharp eye. Expressions

[14] G.A. Haarlem, Broodzettingregisters no. 1930a, R412–417.

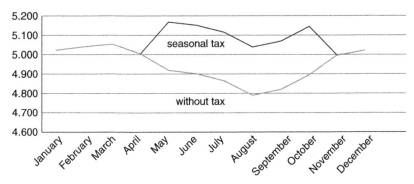

Figure 8.2 Average monthly rye bread prices in Haarlem, 1750–69, with and without seasonal charity tax (stuivers per 6-pound loaf)

of concern over the civic loyalty of the bakers were much less common. On the rare occasions when the magistrates articulated a justification for the regulation of bread prices, they commonly cited the wisdom of securing for the bakers the means to achieve a decent standard of living ("to maintain themselves as burghers" [*zich als een burger te handhaven*] as they expressed it); to do otherwise would incite bakers to adulteration of bread, fraud, and ruinous competition with fellow bakers.

The guilds and the political authorities both had interests that converged in the system of bread price regulation, but by itself this does not imply that the two conspired directly to secure and share rents in the direct manner suggested by Ogilvie's definition of the purpose of guilds. Still, this leaves considerable room for more subtle forms of regulatory capture, and the single most important place to look for evidence of it is in the bread price commissioners' decisions about the bakers' fee – the component of the constant costs allocated to the bakers to defray their expenses for labor and capital.

Setting the Bakers' Fee: Scale and Location

The Scale of Operation

The bakers' fee was the regulated cost that was most difficult for the commissioners to set with confidence and yet, simultaneously, it was critical to both the structure and prosperity of the baking sector as a whole. Before we can assess the merits of the charge that the commissioners' mission had been hijacked via regulatory capture we need to know more about the actual size of bakeries, the actual level of bakers' fees, and, thus, the revenues earned by bakers.

The number of bakeries per 1,000 population can offer a first approximation of the average scale of bakery operations. No comprehensive information is available until the nineteenth century, but several mid-eighteenth-century provincial and regional tax registers provide occupational information that offers some insight into the typical size of a bakery's potential circle of customers, and, hence, of its likely level of production.

The most comprehensive insight is provided by the *Personele Quotisatie*, the 1742 effort to establish an income tax in Holland. Its intention was to tax every household head with an annual income of at least 600 guilders.[15] The tax collectors identified 472 taxable bakers in Amsterdam and another 413 such bakers in fifteen other cities for which the tax rolls have been preserved.[16] In addition there were poorer, non-taxable bakers, just over 100 in Amsterdam and probably more in the other cities.[17] Thus, these sixteen cities with about 450,000 inhabitants in 1742 supported 885 taxable bread bakers (plus 167 pastry bakers) and at least 200–250 bakers with annual incomes below 600 guilders – altogether, about one bread baker per 400 inhabitants, or 2.5 per thousand.[18]

Elsewhere, the density of urban bakeries was even higher: 3.4 per thousand in two Overijssel cities, 5.5 in the eleven cities of Friesland, and 4.2 in the six cities of Zeeland.[19] Small-city bakers may have served rural customers, uncounted in the population estimates, but overall, the Republic's towns, large and small, appear to have supported rather more than the 2.5 bakeries per 1,000 of population that prevailed in the towns of Holland.[20] Still, the 1819 industrial survey for all of the Netherlands

---

[15] An annual income of 600 guilders was well above average – double the annual earnings of building laborers. In 1742 it appears that only 20 percent of urban households in Holland had incomes that subjected them to the *Personele Quotisatie*. See De Vries and Van der Woude, *First Modern Economy*, pp. 561–69, for details.

[16] These data from W. F. H. Oldewelt, *Kohier van de personele quotisatie te Amsterdam over het jaar 1742*, 2 vols. (Amsterdam, 1945).

[17] G.A. Amsterdam, Archief v. d. Burgemeesteren, P.A. 5028, Stukken betreffende de broodzetting. Similar numbers were counted in the first decade of the nineteenth century. See Diederiks, *Stad in verval*, pp. 202–05.

[18] The tax collectors drew up registers of taxable inhabitants (*kohieren*) which included persons whose incomes, based on external attributes, *may* have reached the 600-guilder threshold. If their incomes were found to fall short their names were scratched out. One can see from this that the incomes of bakers as a group straddled the 600-guilder mark. Most had higher incomes (the 885 taxable bakers of the sixteen cities averaged 874 guilders in annual income), but at least a quarter of them had lower incomes. In the smaller cities, the percentage with lower incomes is likely to have been higher still. De Vries and Van der Woude, *First Modern Economy*, pp. 518, 566–69.

[19] *Ibid.*, pp. 516–18; Faber, *Drie eeuwen Friesland*, vol. II, pp. 444–48.

[20] The density of bakers in the Netherlands can be compared to England. In London, about 1,500 "assized" bakers operated in 1797–98, about one per 682 inhabitants. In Southampton, a much smaller city, the number of bakeries varied irregularly between one per 400 and per 600 inhabitants in the 1783–1861 period. More generally, in London

reveals a bakery density that comes close to the evidence we have for Holland in 1742. It counted 4,800 bakeries in the Netherlands (excluding Limburg) plus an additional 440 pastry bakeries, or 2.4 bakers per 1,000 inhabitants at that date – one bakery per 417 inhabitants (see Table 7.1).[21]

One bakery per 400 inhabitants is a norm that also seems to have prevailed in Holland's cities in earlier times. Haarlem's guild of bakers numbered about 95 in 1668, when the city's population stood at its peak size of 43,000, resulting in a ratio of one baker per 453 inhabitants. After 1700 the city suffered from a substantial long-term decline of population. The bakers responded to this decline by agreeing in 1714 to let their numbers "die out" – decline by attrition – to 80. By that date Haarlem's population had fallen from its seventeenth-century peak to 33,000. Eighty bakers would have been one per 412. The city's downward slide did not end here. By the 1750s the population stood at 27,000, and in 1759 the bakers agreed to a further reduction in their numbers to 70 – one per 385. In 1786 the bakers again resolved to reduce their numbers by attrition, this time to 50 – again, about one per 400 inhabitants at the time.[22]

Unlike Haarlem, The Hague was a growing city, but in 1790 its magistrates decided that its 130 bakers were too many, and that their number should "die out" to 100. At that level there would be one baker

---

and environs, there was one bakery *worker* per 200 inhabitants in 1851. This density declined markedly as one moved north. The one-per-200 density was reached again in the urban lowlands of Scotland. Petersen, *Bread*, pp. 67–72, 81–82. In the German regions closest to the Netherlands, the population per *master baker* in 1849 stood at 380 in the Prussian *Rheinprovinz*, and 515 in *Westfalen*. Few of the 10,354 bakers in these two large provinces could have operated at more than the traditional artisanal scale, for together they employed only 4,843 journeymen and apprentices. Wolfgang Köllmann, *Bevölkerung in der industriellen Revolution* (Göttingen: Vandenhoeck & Ruprecht, 1974), pp. 226–27.

[21] The pastry bakers (*koekbakkers*) escaped the embrace of the bread price regulatory regime. So long as they paid the excise tax on milled grain, they were remarkably free to arrange their own affairs. Their own guild leaders set their prices and enforced them among the members. Their numbers grew, especially in the eighteenth century, and their appearance in rural locations drew the suspicious gaze of the magistrates. In 1739 the States of Holland resolved to clamp down by forbidding the establishment of new rural pastry bakeries and allowing existing ones to continue in operation only until the death of the current owner's son or daughter. If this rule was enforced it did not prevent Holland from having some 300 pastry bakeries eighty years later. The States did not spell out the nature of their suspicions, but it is probable that they suspected pastry bakers of supplying normal breads outside the price control regime. *GPB van Holland*, vol. VI, 14 March 1739, Publicatie tegen Koekebakkerijen ten Platteland; Keure op de Koeckenbakkers gilde, *Keuren der Stad Haarlem* (Haarlem, 1749).

[22] G.A. Haarlem, Stadsarchief 1581–1795, R 413, Memoire van de brootsetting, 29 Okt. 1668; Ambachtsgilden, deel 16, no. 22. Population data from Jan de Vries, *European Urbanization, 1500–1800* (London: Methuen, 1984), p. 271.

per 390 inhabitants. Rotterdam numbered 147 bread bakers (plus 26 pastry bakers) in 1674, or one per 330 inhabitants, while Amsterdam in 1611 counted 169 bakers. This snapshot was taken in the midst of the city's very rapid expansion. If its population then had reached 80,000 (105,000 would be counted in 1622), Amsterdam then possessed one baker per 473 inhabitants.[23]

When we turn our attention to bakeries in rural areas, a substantial regional variation presents itself. In 1742–49 the highly commercialized region north of Amsterdam, the Noorderkwartier, supported 5.4 bakers per 1000 inhabitants, or one baker per 192 people. Rural Friesland supported 2.8 bakers per 1000 inhabitants, half the density of North Holland, but sufficient to blanket with bakeries a countryside where home baking was uncommon.[24]

Adjacent Groningen was little different. Its rural districts counted over three bakeries per 1,000 population throughout the eighteenth and early nineteenth centuries and "home baking of bread did not exist, or barely existed, in [Groningen's] clay soil regions."[25]

Elsewhere bakeries were somewhat less numerous. In rural Overijssel there were 2.0 bakers per 1,000 in 1795. In the adjacent Veluwe, a rather thinly populated district of Gelderland, the figure rose to 2.6 per 1,000. There we can locate the bakers by village: of the 24 "church villages" (*kerspels*) that dotted the Veluwe 17 possessed a baker. Yet 22 of these villages had a miller, which suggests that some portion of the rural population here baked its own bread. Indeed, one of the villages, Renkum, listed the presence of a *broodschieter*, someone who maintained an oven for use by self-baking households. Finally, rural Zeeland, its highly commercial farm economy notwithstanding, appears to have been particularly partial to home baking (see Chapter 3). In 1811 it supported only 1.5 bakers per 1,000 population. Thus, the density of bakeries in rural areas varied considerably, but an overall average probably falls in the 2.5 to 3.0 per 1,000 range, or one bakery per 333 to 400 inhabitants – very similar to the average for urban places.[26]

---

[23] G.A. The Hague, O.A. no. 5741; Hans Bonke, *De kleyne mast van de Hollandse coopsteden. Stadsontwikkeling in Rotterdam, 1572–1795* Amsterdamse Historische Reeks 32 (Stichting Amsterdamse Historische Reeks, 1996), p. 154. D. Daamsma *et al.*, eds., *Statistiek van de Nederlandse nijverheid uit de eerste helft der 19de eeuw, Supplement*, Rijks geschiedkundige publication, Grote serie 168 (The Hague: Martinus Nijhoff, 1979); Erika Kuijpers, *Migrantenstad. Immigratie en sociale verhoudingen in 17de-eeuws Amsterdam* (Hilversum: Verloren, 2005), p. 238.

[24] Van der Woude, *Noorderkwartier*, vol. I, pp. 270, 290; Faber, *Friesland*, vol. II, pp. 445–46. Reassuringly, an industrial census of 1855 recorded 534 bakeries in rural Friesland, or 2.7 per 1,000 of the population. *Provinciale Verslag van Friesland*, 1855.

[25] Richard Paping, *Voor een handvol stuivers* (Groningen: NEHI, 1995), p. 85.

[26] Roessingh, "Beroep en bedrijf op de Veluwe," pp. 212–14, 222–24; Priester, *Zeeuwse landbouw*, p. 300.

We now have an idea of how many bakeries served the Dutch population, which allows for a rough estimate of how much grain the average bakery must have processed in order to supply that population with bread. At one baker per 400 inhabitants, the 1.9 million inhabitants of the Netherlands in 1795 would have been served by some 4,750 bakeries. In 1807–08 about 90,000 lasts of rye and wheat were taxed for use in bread production, which yields an average throughput per bakery of 19 lasts of grain. This estimate overstates the case, since it does not allow for home provision of bread. We cannot measure the extent of this practice with any precision, but the evidence reviewed does not suggest home baking was widespread. If one-third of the rural population did not purchase bakery bread, this would reduce the overall average bakery throughput to 15.5 lasts per year.

An average annual bakery production of 15–16 lasts gives us a reference point. Of course, a great deal of important information may hide behind this average figure. Amsterdam and other large cities will have had more large bakeries than small cities, let alone villages.[27] And, within the towns, there may also have been a wide dispersion of bakery sizes. Did the bread price commissioners face a world in which most bakeries clustered around the mean size – where the mean was also the mode (the most common size) – or did bakeries form a bi-modal distribution, with some very large and many very small operations?

The organization of bakers into guilds and the operation of the *brood-zetting* both acted to check the ability of large bakers to exploit their cost advantage fully. Since their unit costs were lower than those of small bakers, they could profit more at any given level of the bakers' fee, but they could not readily deploy that higher profitability to compete *directly* with smaller bakers via lower prices. Moreover, the distribution of bread by a baker far beyond the location of his premises was both costly (requiring hired street sellers) and hobbled by local regulations.

Bakery Location

Bakeries were located close to their customers; indeed, geographers hold them up as a classical example to illustrate a core teaching of location theory: the location of an economic activity is determined by "range" and "threshold." The range of a product is the maximum distance consumers are prepared to travel to acquire it; the threshold is the minimum

---

[27] For example, Haarlem's bread price commissioners assumed the city's 95 bakeries of 1668 processed 1,916 lasts of bread grain, which gives us a mean size of 20.2 lasts. G.A. Haarlem, Stadsarchief 1581–1795, R 413, Memoire van de brootsetting, 29 October 1668.

demand required to support a producer at a given location.[28] For bread and many other daily necessities the distance consumers will travel is very limited since they must repeat the trip often – almost daily. The threshold demand, to judge from the information reviewed above, may be close to 400 consumers (about 100 households), although it could be considerably less if bakery operation was a viable part-time undertaking. Here is where regulatory policy becomes critical: the bakers' fee set by the bread price commissioners directly affected the size of the threshold level of demand.

Clé Lesger's geographical analysis of retailing in eighteenth-century Amsterdam offers some insights into the locational pattern of the city's bakeries.[29] Exploiting information on nearly every Amsterdam bakery available in the *Personele Quotisatie* of 1742, Lesger first reveals what theory leads us to expect: that bakeries were located near their customers, spread fairly evenly across the city, as shown in Map 8.1. Of the 446 bakeries that could be located, at least one could be found on 226 of the city's 880 streets. Everywhere one turned, there was another bakery, which suggests that bakery size was constrained at the upper end by geography as well as by policy (the prohibition of price competition).

At the other end of the size distribution of bakeries were small operators, perhaps in rural locations or on the fringes of a town, whose customer base was secure (no other baker nearby) but small, falling short of an economically viable threshold size. Here, location theory predicts there will be no supplier. But in a regulated industry the minimum threshold can be influenced by public policy, which might seek to guarantee access to bakers. Did the Dutch regulators set the bakers' fee – and, hence, bread prices – with an eye to protecting small bakers and the convenience of the customers they served?

Size Distribution

The only detailed information available about the size distribution of bakeries dates from 1843. The *broodzetting* was then still in operation and factory-scale baking operations had not yet disrupted the artisanal structure of the baking enterprise. One could still say of it what Karl Marx

[28] The key theorists of location theory are Walter Christaller and August Lösch. See J. A. Dawson, *Retail Geography* (London: Croom Helm, 1980).
[29] Clé Lesger, "Patterns of retail location and urban form in Amsterdam in the mid-eighteenth century," *Urban History* 38 (2011), 24–47. This is part of a larger study of retail location in Amsterdam: Clé Lesger, *Het winkellandschap van Amsterdam. Stedelijke structuur en winkelbedrijf in de vroegmoderne en moderne tijd, 1550–2000* (Hilversum: Verloren, 2013).

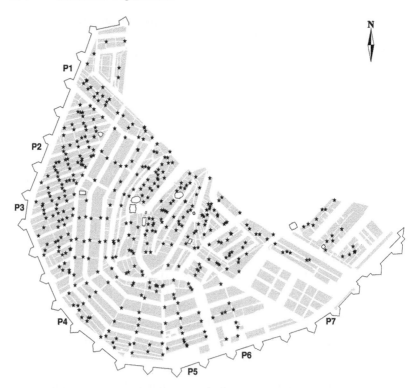

Map 8.1 Location of Amsterdam bakeries in 1742
Source: Clé Lesger, "Patterns of retail location and urban form in Amsterdam in the mid-eighteenth century," *Urban History* 38 (2011), 32. © Cambridge University Press 2011.

said in 1867 of England's baking sector, long in the embrace of the assize of bread: "No other branch of industry in England has preserved up to the present day a method of production as archaic, as pre-Christian (as we see from the poets of the Roman Empire) as baking has."[30]

The industrial survey of 1843 required each firm to reveal the number of its adult and child employees and the physical volume of its output. In the case of bakeries this was expressed in kilograms of rye and wheat flour processed annually. Regrettably, the detailed records for bakeries have been preserved for only three cities. Table 8.2a shows the overall

---

[30] Karl Marx, *Capital* (1867; London: Penguin, 1967), vol. I, p. 358.

Table 8.2 *Scale of production in bakeries in three cities, 1843*
a. Bakeries by lasts of grain baked annually

Output	Schiedam	Utrecht	Zwolle	Total	Total production in lasts
Over 45 lasts		2		2	100
41–45		1	1	2	86
36–41		3	1	4	152
32–36	2	3	1	6	204
28–32	3	7	4	14	406
23–27		6		6	150
18–23	6	8	1	15	300
15–18	3	15	6	24	384
9–14	8	17	12	37	407
4.5–9	2	31	16	49	343
under 4.5	1	9	12	22	88
Total	25	102	54	181	2,670

b. Percentage of bakeries and bread output by bakery size

	Number of bakeries	Total production
Output >27 lasts	15%	36%
Output 15–27 lasts	25	32
Output <15 lasts	60	32

c. Average production (in lasts per year) of bakeries according to workforce size (number of bakeries in parentheses)

Employed workers				
Adult	Child	Schiedam	Utrecht	Zwolle
3+			(6) 35.0	(2) 40.9
2	0	(4) 27.2	(12) 29.1	(4) 30.5
1	1		(3) 19.6	(7) 23.5
1	0	(13) 17.5	(40) 13.1	(17) 11.0
0	1	(5) 15.7	(2) 11.7	(2) 10.8
0	0	(2) 4.5	(39) 9.1	(20) 5.2
Average production		(24) 17.4	(102) 14.9	(52) 11.6

Source: Daamsma *et al.*, eds., *Statistiek,* pp. 290–91, 919–21.

distribution of bakery size (in lasts of grain worked annually), while 8.2c shows average output according to the number of workers employed by the bakery.

In the small industrial city of Schiedam the bakeries clustered rather tightly around the mean size. Half of the town's 25 bakeries employed one worker and processed an average of 17.5 lasts of grain. There were few very small bakeries. In the larger city of Utrecht, with 102 bakeries, matters were rather different. No fewer than 39 bakeries had no hired employees at all and processed, on average, only 9 lasts of grain per year. The city was also home to 16 bakeries, all with at least two adult employees, that worked at double and triple the 15-last average for the city's bakeries as a whole and that together produced 40 percent of the city's bread. Different from either of these was the Overijssel city of Zwolle. There three-quarters of all the bakeries were small, processing on average only 7.3 lasts per year and hiring, at most, one adult worker. But Zwolle was also home to two of the largest bakeries in our entire sample, each working over 40 lasts of grain with at least three adult workers.

If we pool the data from these three cities, each with a distinctive bakery-size distribution, three observations present themselves. First, the overall average bakery size of the 178 bakeries is 14.5 lasts, not far from the 15.5 last average we had estimated on the basis of national-level data. Second, even in these urban centers one-third of all bakeries operated on a very small scale, employing no labor outside the baker's household. Many of their operators may not have been full-time bakers. Finally, most bakers "of any importance" (as the Dordrecht commissioner put it in 1826), with one or more adult employees, produced on a scale that exceeded the national average.[31] More data are needed to confirm this impression, but it appears that two models for the operation of a bakery coexisted: one a (probably part-time) family operation; the other a full-time business requiring hired labor.[32] The range of their scales of operation overlapped, creating the illusion of a roughly normal distribution, but the pooled data of Table 8.2b reveals that 60 percent of all the

---

[31] More limited information on the structure of the baking sector is available for Dordrecht. The 1843 industrial census found 67 bakeries (including pastry and waffle bakers). This suggests a bread bakery for about 400 inhabitants and an average bakery throughput of 18 lasts. But 36 of the 67 bakeries were one-person operations; the proprietor claimed to hire no additional personnel. The remaining 31 bakeries employed 38 men and boys. The Dordrecht commissioner may have had this dichotomy in mind when he spoke of bakeries "of any importance." Data from Caroline Koopmans, *Dordrecht, 1811–1914* (Hilversum: Verloren, 1992), pp. 178–79.

[32] The 1855 industrial survey of Friesland also hints at such a bifurcation. The survey says nothing about the volume of production of individual bakeries, but it does record, per town and rural district (*grietenij*), the total number of bakeries and employees. The urban bakeries (some in very small cities), averaged 1.24 hired workers per bakery; the rural bakeries averaged only 0.30, suggesting that at least 70 percent of rural bakeries operated without the assistance of hired labor, depending solely on the labor of the baker and his/her family. *Provinciale Verslag van Friesland*, 1855.

bakeries produced less than one-third of the bread, while, at the other end, 16 percent of the bakeries accounted for 36 percent of the bread consumed in Schiedam, Utrecht, and Zwolle. The intermediate group – a quarter of the bakers producing a third of the bread – was "average," but it was not really "typical."[33]

A Typical Bakery?

The "modal" bakery may not have existed, which must have presented a challenge to the bread price commissioners when they gathered to set the bakers' fee. Yet they appear, nevertheless, to have developed some notional standard for the "typical" bakery. I have found only one clear articulation of this notional standard, athough it comes not from a city but from the South Holland village of Zegwaard. The central government's 1826 request for information on the broodzetting inspired the respondents from this village to supplement their submission of the requested data on their baking and milling costs with a written justification for the level of these charges:[34]

The labor cost is equal to the daily wage of a laborer under the assumption that it takes one man-day to carry out all the activities associated with transforming one mud (one hectoliter) of milled grain into bread. The profit is set at 700 guilders calculated on a yearly basis, and spread over the 250 mud of wheat and 125 mud of rye processed in a year. This amount is needed for a baker seeking to maintain himself as a burgher [wil hij in eenen burgerlyken kring staande blyven], in order to pay rent, maintain his tools, cover credit risks, support his family, and for the maintenance of a horse, which is necessary in the pursuit of his occupation.

Zegwaard's response assumed a modest annual throughput of 12.5 lasts of grain: two-thirds wheat and one-third rye. It further assumed that a baker would need to hire one full-time laborer (costing about 260 guilders per year) and would need 700 guilders to maintain his capital stock and support his family. The family income (needed to maintain a burgerlijk standard of living) would have been only a portion (unspecified in the document) of this 700 guilders, perhaps 400–500 guilders. A rural baker's income under the "Zegwaard model" would almost certainly

---

[33] If my reading of these data is correct, it may help in interpreting the fact that when Amsterdam's magistrates called together all the city's bakers in 1789 (to consider how best to prepare for a possible grain shortage) it divided the 572 bakeries into two roughly equal groups: large bakers and small bakers. The magistrates gave no definition of these categories, but the large bakers were found to hold in storage, on average, three times as much grain as the small bakers. G.A. Amsterdam, Archief v. d. Burgemeesteren, P.A. 5028, "Stukken betreffende de broodzetting."

[34] A.R.A. Den Haag, 2de Afdeling, Binnenlandse Zaken, Binnenlands Bestuur B, no. 1366.

have fallen short of the level attained by the large majority of Holland's urban bakers as revealed by the income tax of 1742.

The only other direct statement I have found on the scale of production of a "normal bakery" comes from the 1791 petition of Rotterdam's bakers' guild to increase the bakers' fee. After complaining about all the increases in costs the bakers had had to endure since 1680 (increased wages, bakery rents, fuel, etc.) they sought to show how little was left to the baker as annual income after subtracting all these costs from the revenues of a "typical" bakery that processed one last of grain monthly – or 12 lasts per year.[35] It was very little, of course. We now know from the bakeries in Holland's cities in 1742 and in Rotterdam's neighbor, Schiedam, in 1843 that a 12-last-per-year operation was far below average. Did the guild members use this example because they thought the commissioners had a duty to set the bakers' fee – and hence bread prices – at such a level that even small 12-last bakers could "live as burghers"?

If *broodzetting* commissioners generally had internalized the norms expressed by Zegwaard in 1826 and the Rotterdam bakers' guild in 1791, they would have set the bakers' fee at such a level that 12.5 lasts of grain would have generated the necessary 960 guilders needed to cover operating costs and maintain a baker at a respectable – burgher's – standard of living. Zegwaard's commissioners would be driven by the considerations cited above to the conclusion that the bakers' fee should be 960/12.5 = 76.80 guilders per last of grain. But what if the commissioners wished to "nudge" the village bakers toward some rationalization of their trade, whereby a smaller number of larger bakeries, processing an average of, say, 16 lasts per year, worked at a bakers' fee of 960/16 = 60.00 guilders? The Royal Decree of 1826, which set in motion the assembly of local evidence we have been drawing on here, may have had such a "nudge" in mind. It admonished local authorities to set their bakers' fees "without taking any regard of the number of bakers present in the municipality." That is, it was thought important to instruct the commissioners not to place the cart before the horse, by setting the bakers' fee at a level needed to support the existing number of bakers.[36]

If commissioners set the bakers' fees at a level designed to encourage rationalization of the baking trade, what factors might stand in the way of achieving this goal? Perhaps one full-time employee would be insufficient to process the larger volume of flour (although evidence from Table 8.2c suggests that bakeries with one adult employee routinely processed considerably more than 12.5 lasts of grain). A more likely constraint on

[35] G.A. Rotterdam, no. 2125. "Van de overlieden van het broodbakkersgilde."
[36] Koninklijk Besluit van 25 januari 1826 (Staatsblad no. 5).

increasing the scale of output was the size of a baker's oven. We noted earlier that when urban commissioners used institutional ovens to conduct their baking trials, the issue arose that most bakers' ovens were smaller. In Utrecht, they rarely exceeded a capacity of one *mud* (120 liters) of grain. Bakers who fired such an oven once per day (and never on Sundays), could process 12.5 lasts of grain per year.[37] They might hesitate to fire a second time unless they could utilize most if not all of the oven's capacity, whereby they would suddenly become a sizeable bakery, processing 25 lasts per year and employing (to judge from the evidence of Table 8.2c) at least two workers. In sum, the baker faced *thresholds* in the pursuit of scale economies that could reduce his/her production costs per unit of output. These barriers to a smooth, incremental growth of scale were real, but not insurmountable. A baking fee of 76.80 guilders might have removed the pressure to make the investments needed to increase scale; a lower fee – 60.00 guilders in this example – could have induced small operations to either grow or quit the business – since it no longer assured the small baker a "burgher's standard of living."

Setting the Bakers' Fee: Rye vs. Wheat; East vs. West

Production Costs for Wheat and Rye Bread Compared

So far I have treated the production costs of a bakery as though it produced a single product. But we know that Dutch bakeries routinely turned out both rye bread and wheat bread, the latter in three or four distinct qualities. Moreover, we have found that the bread price commissioners always set distinct bakers' fees for the two chief bread sorts, wheat and rye. Thus, while a single bakers' fee applied to all bakers regardless of their scale of operation, distinct bakers' fees applied to the major types of bread they produced.

We might suppose that the commissioners were guided in setting these distinct fee levels by differences in the labor and capital costs involved in the production of each bread sort. If so, what were these differences and how did the commissioners come to know their magnitudes? To keep matters simple our concern here is a cost comparison of wheat

---

[37] Amsterdam commissioned a report on the city's bakeries in 1903. The report described bakeries with small beehive-shaped (*wulfvorminge*) brick ovens fired by peat and sawdust. Unfortunately, the actual capacity of these small ovens was not noted. Only after 1855 did bakers introduce larger, convection-heat ovens fueled by coal. *Het bakkersbedrijf te Amsterdam* (Amsterdam, 1903). As for Sunday baking, the ordinances of bakers' guilds generally prohibited this. Utrecht's ordinance of 1626 forbade baking or stoking ovens after 10 pm, or on Sundays and declared days of prayer (*bededagen*). G.A. Utrecht, no. 461, Backergilde ordonnantie, 30 October 1626.

bread prepared from flour "as it comes from the mill" – with the coarse materials and bran still included – with rye bread, which was nearly always prepared in this same way. Which of them involved more labor time and baking time; which would have required more fuel, or additional equipment?

The reflections on this matter left by the bread price commissioners are not numerous, but they are unanimous on one point: the labor and capital costs involved in preparing wheat and rye bread were about equal. When, in 1659, the bakers' guild of Haarlem complained to the *burgemeesters* that their earnings were too low the city's bread price commissioners responded with a historical survey of the bakers' fee from its inception in 1597. "The bakers should be satisfied [with what they now enjoy]" they concluded, "all the more because the *bakloon* since 1597 weighs so much more heavily on white bread than on rye bread." They expressed puzzlement at the premium originally allowed for wheat in 1597, and could only guess at the possible explanation:[38]

Considering that the fee for rye originally was 14.85 guilders [per last] while for white bread it was 62.50, the only explanation must be that the cost of milk and yeast was incorporated in the *bakloon*, since the labor in making rye bread is much more arduous, and the time required about the same.

Nearly 150 years later, Leiden's commissioners were of the same opinion. In their investigation of 1803 they found that the labor time required to produce equal quantities of wheat and rye breads was basically the same, although they, too, judged the work of preparing rye to be more laborious. Wheat dough was kneaded by hand, while the heavier rye dough was kneaded by foot, after the manner of Sicilian wine makers.[39] The heavy work of preparing the dough for rye bread seems, eventually, to have attracted the attention of inventors. In 1819 the Groningen respondents to a survey of industrial conditions looked forward to the broad dissemination of the "recently invented rye bread kneading machine, so that the disgusting [*walgelijke*] kneading by foot will no longer be necessary for this daily necessity of the people in this and the other northern provinces."[40]

These impressions are confirmed by the meticulous 1631–32 baking trials in Goes on which Cornelis François Eversdijck based his science

---

[38] G.A. Haarlem, Stadsarchief 1581–1795, R 413. 1659–61.
[39] G.A. Leiden, Gilden Archief, no. 180.
[40] Quoted in Daamsma *et al.*, eds., *Statistiek*. In 1829 an Amsterdam bakery advertised that its dough was kneaded "by machines and not by hands or feet." But this mechanical bakery seems to have failed soon thereafter. Diederiks, *Stad in verval*, p. 204.

of bread pricing (discussed in Chapter 3). These trials distinguished between labor and capital costs, although "distribution costs" (payments to bread hawkers and other sales expenses) were added to the latter. The Goes commissioners thought that higher labor costs were justified for both rye bread (because it was laborious) and the finest white bread (because of the extra steps involved in sifting the flour and forming the small loaves). Otherwise costs were equal for all bread types except for a substantially higher cost for the distribution of the luxury white bread. Overall, the Goes commissioners deemed an 8 percent premium to be justified for rye bread and a hefty 33 percent premium for luxury white bread relative to the other wheat breads.

A similar pattern is found in the river town of Zaltbommel. From 1628, when we are first informed of bread prices here, the constant costs assigned to basic wheat bread (which includes fuel and ingredients which, unfortunately, cannot be separated out) were 43 guilders per last, compared to 51 guilders for rye bread. In 1646 the allowable costs were made equal for both grains, 54 guilders, and they remained equal until 1682, when the town began to conform more closely to the prevailing practices elsewhere and raised the bakers' fee for wheat bread above that for rye.

These examples and the opinions of contemporaries demonstrate that there was no objective reason for large differentials in the bakers' fees for the preparation of rye bread and wheat bread (except for the finest white bread). Yet they *did* differ almost everywhere – and by a great deal.

To divine what policy objectives could have guided the bread price commissioners in their differential treatment of wheat and rye bread costs, I will proceed by describing how much the bakers' fees for wheat and rye bread differed by place and over time, then to a consideration of possible motives behind these differentials, and, finally, to an examination of the financial consequences of these regulatory policies for the bakers. In later chapters, I will turn to the consequences for consumers.

Table 8.3 *Eversdijck's calculation of bakers' fee based on Goes baking trials of 1631–32 (guilders per last)*

	White bolted	Fine bolted	Brown bolted	Coarse unbolted	Rye unbolted
Baking costs (labor)	22.50	18.75	18.75	18.75	22.50
Profit and distribution	37.5	26.25	26.25	26.25	26.25
Total	60.00	45.00	45.00	45.00	48.75

Source: Eversdijck, *Paste-boeck vanden broode*, pp. 40–41.

Rye. When the Leiden commissioners established their new system regime in 1596 they allowed a bakers' fee of 16.60 guilders per last of rye. In the same year, Amsterdam and Haarlem allowed 14.85 guilders, while Utrecht set its initial bakers' fee at 17.5 guilders in 1599. Within a few years all of these cities raised these fees by 3 to 5 guilders. Further east, in Kampen, the bakers' fee was not specified as such, but the allowance provided in the 1606 price schedule after deducting the excise taxes and millers' fee was 19.70 guilders, which, in turn, was similar to Arnhem. After subtracting an amount for fuel and other ingredients, the bakers in both places will have cleared approximately 16 to 17 guilders per last.

This is enough to show that the cities of the Dutch Republic began their new system of bread pricing with a surprisingly uniform idea of the fixed costs incurred by a baker in the production of rye bread. In 1597 Leiden was a boomtown, receiving migrants from near and far who were attracted by its prospering textile industry. The city was literally bursting at the seams, and in desperate need of expansion. Tight housing and labor markets must have made Leiden a costly place for a baker to do business.[41] At this time Kampen's glory days as a Hansa port were firmly in the past and it was a demographically stagnant provincial town. Labor and housing costs must have been significantly lower here, but the bakers' fees allowed by the two cities for rye bread production (Leiden in 1599, Kampen in 1606) were equal and the totality of constant costs (including taxes, milling costs, fuel, and other inputs) allowed by Kampen stood at 93 percent of the Leiden level (43 vs. 41 guilders per last).

Table 8.4 *Bakers' fee per last of rye in the first decades of the new bread pricing policy, compared with 1692 (guilders per last)*

	Amsterdam and Haarlem	Leiden	Utrecht	Kampen	Zaltbommel	Arnhem
1597	14.85	16.60				
1599		19.80	17.50			
1601	18.90		22.50			
1606				19.70		17.60
1618						22.00
1629					27.00	
1692	36.00	45.50	46.56	19.70	27.00	27.50

[41] House rents in Leiden rose by 62 percent between 1580–84 and 1595–99. In Amsterdam, the cost of housing – and presumably shop rentals – rose even more, 2.3-fold, between 1586–7 and 1596/7. N. W. Posthumus, *De geschiedenis van de Leidse lakenindustrie*, 3 vols. (The Hague: Martinus Nijhoff, 1908–1939), vol. II, pp. 207–09; Lesger, *Huur en conjunctuur*, p. 77.

The economically dynamic decades that followed brought price inflation, rising wages, and rising rents in the Republic's rapidly growing cities, and the commissioners periodically adjusted the bakers' fees upward, each city making its own assessment of costs. In Amsterdam and Haarlem, the bakers' fee doubled in the course of the seventeenth century and in Utrecht and Leiden it rose even more. But in Kampen the bakers' allowance remained unaltered; at the end of the seventeenth century it stood where it had begun, which was then only half what was provided to the bakers in Amsterdam and even less than half of Utrecht's bakers' fee. Other eastern towns increased their bakers' fee, but only modestly. As a result, the seventeenth century witnessed a major divergence in the constant costs faced by the bakers – or, more correctly, in the costs that the bread price commissioners allowed to be incorporated in the bread price, what modern utility regulators call the "ratable charges."

Wheat. When we turn our attention to wheat bread, a very different situation presents itself, one that places the entire enterprise of price regulation in a new light. The early years of new system bread price regulation are poorly documented with respect to wheat bread. It is possible, as we have seen in the case of Leiden, that efforts to apply the new system got off to a rocky start. Regulating wheat bread was simply more complicated than rye, given the several grades of wheat bread and the common practice of selling it at fixed prices and variable weights. Table 8.5 assembles the available evidence. Utrecht's commissioners set a baking fee of 25 guilders per last of wheat in 1599, which they quickly raised to 35 guilders in 1601. They rewarded the baker with about 50 percent more revenue to defray all production costs of wheat bread than they did for rye bread. In 1603 Leiden's (apparently unimplemented) price schedules for

Table 8.5 *Bakers' fee per last of wheat in the first decades of the new bread pricing policy, compared with 1692 (in guilders per last)*

	Amsterdam and Haarlem	Leiden	Utrecht	Kampen	Zaltbommel	Arnhem
1597	62.50 [45.00]					
1599			25.00			
1601	75.00 [57.00]		35.00			
1603		43.50				
1606				c. 47.00		
1618						26.40
1628				27.00		
1692	104.00	99.00	67.5	47.00	54.00	33.00

Table 8.6 *Bakers' fee per last of wheat and rye, 1647–1849*

		Rye	Wheat
Amsterdam and Haarlem	1692–1795	36.00	104.00
Dordrecht	1709–95	36.00	58.60
Utrecht	1647–1795	46.56	67.50
Arnhem	1650–1720	27.50	33.00
Zaltbommel	1648–1785	27.00	32.00
Utrecht	1806	81.00	114.75
Zaltbommel	1808	27.00	27.00
Leiden	1806	99.00	66.00
Amsterdam	1815	54.00	
Amsterdam	1849	69.00	120.00

Table 8.7 *The bakers' fees per last of wheat and rye in 1826*

	Rye	Wheat	Ratio
Brielle	66		
Delft	66	96	1.45
Gorinchem	42		
Gouda	63	51	0.81
The Hague	72	108	1.50
Haarlem	45	88.8	1.97
Leiden	66	99	1.50
Dordrecht	57.6	86.4	1.50
Leerdam	45		
Oudewater	48	75	1.56
Rotterdam	67.5	76.8	1.14
Schoonhoven	39	60	1.54
Woerden	45	64.5	1.43
Amersfoort	58.5	78	1.33
Deventer	46.5	186	4.00
Zwolle	34.5	90	2.61
Kampen	24	82.5	3.44
Groningen	28.5		
Summary			
7 large Holland cities	64.50	90.30	1.40
7 small Holland cities	45.00	71.40	1.59
3 Overijssel cities	35.00	119.50	3.41

Towns and villages throughout the Netherlands were ordered to conduct baking trials and report their findings in a standardized format for ease of comparison and compilation. Unfortunately, the results survive for only three provinces. Moreover, the state requested data for only two types of bread, rye bread and bolted wheat bread. Thus, we cannot directly compare the two *unbolted* bread types.
Source: A.R.A. The Hague. Ministerie van Binnenlandse Zaken, 1813–1864, no. 1366, Bestuur B, 1824–31.

wheat bread allowed the bakers even more: 43.5 guilders per last, which was double what the city allowed for rye bread. Amsterdam, followed by Haarlem, set the bakers' fee for wheat bread even higher. They probably include compensation to the baker for ingredients, fuel, and milling costs that should be excluded to render them comparable to other figures. The likely "pure" bakers' fees are shown in brackets in Table 8.5. But even these are three times the fees allowed for rye bread. In the east, Kampen awarded its bakers 2.4 times as much revenue for baking wheat as for baking the same quantity of rye, and its fees were comparable to those in the large western cities.

The more abundant evidence for later decades (see Table 8.6) does not alter the general pattern revealed at the outset of the new system. Much of Holland followed Amsterdam's lead in setting the bakers' fee for wheat bread at three times the level they set for rye bread; many towns in the eastern provinces, where wheat was little eaten, raised their fees for wheat even higher while holding down the bakers' fees for rye; towns stretching from Utrecht to Rotterdam and Dordrecht held to a lower wheat bread premium, at approximately 50 percent. Finally, there was a small zone where the premium was lower than this: Goes (and probably all of Zeeland) and Zaltbommel and Arnhem, where the bakers' fee for wheat was held to a 20 percent premium over rye.[42]

These general patterns persisted until the nineteenth century, when the survey of all bread-making costs ordered in 1826 by the central government shows some moderation of the differentials, as shown in Table 8.7. Still, even then bakers almost everywhere earned more, often much more, for working up a given volume of wheat into bread than they earned for preparing rye bread, despite the absence of a significant difference in the underlying production costs. Why did the regulatory bodies establish these large differentials?

Explaining the Large Differences in Bakers' Fees

The Persistence of Old Practices?

The pattern of large bakers' fee differentials revealed itself from the onset of new system price regulation in most places. This suggests the hypothesis that these differentials were simply attempting to perpetuate long-existing practices under the old system of price regulation.

---

[42] G.A. Arnhem, Oud Archief, Archieven der Gasthuizen en Fundatiën, Gilden, Schutterijen en Vendels, no. 1513, Stukken op den broodzetting, 1693; G.A. Zaltbommel, Oud Archief, 20–1079–80, Broodzettingregisters.

Recall that the old system had provided for the baker's non-grain costs by allocating a portion of the bread produced for this purpose. In Chapter 1 we saw that bakers received the revenue from the sale of approximately one-third of the bread they produced from both wheat and rye, while the rest went to pay for the grain and the services of the miller. Since the price of wheat bread was at least 50 percent higher, pound per pound, than rye bread, the baker secured a correspondingly higher revenue to cover his non-grain costs. By this hypothesis, the new system sought only to perpetuate a feature of the old system, irrational though it might have been. But, if true, it accounts for only a part of the actual differentials, which in most places were far larger than 50 percent.

Cross-subsidization?

A second hypothesis, and the one I believe to be preferred, is that the new system – by exposing the constant costs of bread making to examination and rendering those costs malleable to public policy objectives – invited the inauguration of a policy of "cross-subsidization." This concept can be grasped intuitively by recalling the claims made by the magistrates of Zegwaard, discussed above. They had described a bakery that produced both wheat and rye bread, and incurred costs for an employee, the bakery, its oven and equipment, a horse and wagon, and, of course, the baker and his family. They reckoned the total annual cost of operating this bakery and supplying the baker with a socially acceptable income at 960 guilders, to be defrayed by bakers' fees on 12.5 lasts of annual output. But they did not describe how they allocated these costs across the types of bread. This is, perhaps, understandable. Assigning the fixed costs among the divisions of a firm is, even today, a fraught undertaking. How much of the cost of the baker's oven, the rental cost of his premises, or the upkeep of his horse and wagon are attributable to rye bread as opposed to wheat bread? In the Zegwaard example I evaded this issue by simply dividing the total constant costs by the total amount of grain processed by the bakery – wheat and rye together. But in reality Zegwaard's bread price commissioners assigned their bakers a specific bakers' fee for each grain. They did not describe their procedure, but we can infer from the justificatory statement appended to their report that the commissioners set the bakers' fees for the two grains by solving an algebraic equation.

Recall that the average Zegwaard bakery processed 250 hl of wheat and 125 hl of rye, and that the objective was to supply the bakery with revenue, after deducting all grain and input costs, of 960 guilders per year. X = the bakers' fee for rye bread, here expressed in guilders per hectoliter (30 hl = 1 last).

(250 hl wheat * 1.5 X) + (125 hl rye * X) = 960 gld
500 X = 960
X = 1.92

The bakers' fees for wheat bread and rye bread are, therefore:

Wheat fee: 1.92 * 1.5 per hl *30 = 86.40 per last
Rye fee: 1.92 * 1.0 per hl *30 = 57.60 per last

One might ask where the wheat coefficient of 1.5 came from? The Zegwaard commissioners seem not to have inquired into the actual labor and capital expenses attributable to wheat versus rye, but to have set a cost differential that suited their larger goals. They set it at 50 percent. Consequently, wheat, which accounted for two-thirds of the bread produced, supplied three-quarters of the Zegwaard bakers' revenue. To the extent that the assignable costs for the two grains were equal, the regulatory regime shifted a portion of the joint production cost onto the consumers of wheat bread by burdening the price of such bread with a larger portion of the costs of general bakery operation. Correspondingly, they removed some of that burden from the consumers of rye bread. This is what is meant by cross-subsidization: wheat bread consumers paid for a part of the cost of producing rye bread, allowing the latter to be sold at a lower price than would otherwise have been the case. In this case the bakers' fee for rye bread was set at only 75 percent of what it would have been if all bread had shared the fixed costs equally.

Zegwaard's nineteenth-century wheat bread premium was modest – near the low end of all the examples I have found. As noted above, in Table 8.6, cross-subsidization was much more extreme in Amsterdam, Haarlem, Leiden, and the many towns that followed their example throughout the seventeenth and eighteenth centuries. If Amsterdam's threefold difference between the wheat and rye bakers' fees were applied to the Zegwaard example just discussed, the fees, using the same algebra, would have been 99 guilders per last for wheat bread and 33 guilders for rye bread. Wheat bread, which accounted for two-thirds of the bread sold, would now generate 85 percent of bakery revenue, while rye bread – one-third of total output – would have accounted for only 15 percent of revenue.

The cross-subsidization hypothesis is amply supported by evidence, but it has one serious problem: we can easily see how it could work at the level of the entire baking industry of a province or even a city, but how could it work at the level of the individual bakery? The baker can capture the bakers' fees only through the sale of bread, whose price includes its portion of these fees. It follows that bakery revenue depends not only on the *volume* of output but also on the *mix*. That is, if a bakery generated two to three times more revenue from the sale of wheat bread than from rye, its fortunes would seem to depend on its ability to attract wheat-bread-eating customers. Is it reasonable to believe that most bakeries sold the two bread types in roughly the proportions of their region or province? Only then could the cross-subsidy strategy work as intended.

There is no doubt that nearly all bakers sold both rye and wheat breads. The distinction made in the German lands between wheat and rye bread bakers (*Weisbäcker* and *Schwarzbäcker*) had no counterpart in the Netherlands.[43] One might say that what was forbidden in Germany (selling both types of bread) was required in the Netherlands.

Still, it is one thing to establish that nearly all bakeries produced both rye and wheat breads; it is another to be confident that they did so in roughly similar proportions. It stands to reason that bakers in poor neighborhoods will have sold less wheat bread than their better-situated brethren. The Dordrecht commissioners were sensitive to this point when they argued against an explicit cross-subsidization scheme proposed by the Provisional Council of Dordrecht in the tense early months of the Batavian Revolution. The Council had resolved, on 10 July 1795, to sell wheat to the bakers at a below-market price if they committed themselves to reducing the price of their rye bread by one quarter to one half stuiver per loaf. The bread price commissioners took a dim view of this scheme. On 18 July they wrote:[44]

To sell our wheat, purchased on the city's account, at a reduced price to the bakers in exchange for their moderation of the price of rye bread is totally impossible, since some bakers will gain a large advantage from this while others will be

---

[43] "The distinction made in Germany between rye bread bakers and wheat bread bakers is not observed in Holland. Both types of bread were produced by the same bakers." Unger, *Levensmiddelenvoorziening*, p. 95. The only exception to this rule I have found is from the North Holland city of Alkmaar, which followed Amsterdam's lead in all things pertaining to bread price regulation, yet differed from it – and all other Dutch towns – in insisting, in the words of its 1697 ordinance on baking, that "the bread bakers must declare which type of bread they choose to bake, whether rye or wheat, and may not switch from the one to the other without the permission of the *burgemeesters*." Neither the purpose of this restriction nor the length of time it remained in effect is known to me. G.A. Alkmaar, Stadsarchief vóór 1815, no. 1969, Ordonnantie op het bakken. The city of Würzburg offers an example of German practice. Its 26 bakeries of 1679–1708 were divided between 18 *Weisbäcker* and 12 *Schwarzbäcker*. In addition, the city maintained separate market halls for the public sale of *Schwartzbrot* and *Weisbrot*. Ulrich Wagner, ed., *Geschichte der Stadt Würzburg*, 2 vols. (Stuttgart: Konrad Weiss Verlag, 2004), vol. II, p. 196.

[44] G.A. Dordrecht, Archief 3, Stadsarchief Bataafse tijd, no. 387, 18 July 1795.

disadvantaged. Two examples in support of our claim will suffice: consider F. v. d. Hoeg, who reported using 570 Z[eeland] sacks of wheat but only 74 sacks of rye from 1 January to 30 June, and L. van Buul, who in the same period reported only 84 Z[eeland] sacks of wheat and 268 sacks of rye.

The Dordrecht commissioners presumably chose their examples for maximum effect. At the extremes we find a bakery where wheat accounted for 89 percent of sales and another where it was only 24 percent. A complete view of the distribution of bakeries by their sales of wheat and rye breads is available only in 1843 from the industrial survey discussed above. The survey not only specifies the bread output per bakery, but also the division between wheat and rye bread. We have these detailed data for only two western cities, but they reveal only a few bakeries – some of the smallest bakeries in Utrecht – where rye bread sales were far above the average for the town as a whole. In view of the relatively small circle of customers served by most bakeries, this suggests that even plebeian customers did not purchase only rye bread and that maintaining a healthy mix of both bread sorts was possible for most bakers because even at the level of the individual, consumers purchased both types of bread.[45] This sparse evidence sustains the plausibility of the cross-subsidization hypothesis, but we must concede it could never have been wholly equitable to the bakers.

In the eastern provinces the problem with the cross-subsidization hypothesis is different. How could higher burdens on a bread grain that accounted for only about 15 percent of total production contribute to a significant reduction of the cost of producing the dominant rye bread? The answer has two parts. First, the dominance of rye bread in these provinces generally was less pronounced in the towns. Most of the larger cities of the region recorded wheat consumption in the late eighteenth – early nineteenth centuries at between 25 and 31 percent of the total.[46] Second, many of the eastern towns pursued a much more aggressive policy of cross-subsidization than prevailed in the west. This is revealed in the analysis of overall bakery revenues below, and also, in more detail

---

[45] *Productie der broodbakkerjen* in Daamsma *et al., Statistieken.* Utrecht bakers without employees, on average, produced a 40–60 rye–wheat mix while bakers with employees (usually one or two) produced, on average, at a 24–76 rye–wheat mix.

[46] The evidence I have assembled is incidental, but quite consistent (only Kampen and Zwolle are exceptions) in showing that wheat accounted for 25–31 percent of total bread grain consumption in the larger eastern towns. Gogel, *Memorieën*, Bijlage B, p. 414; G.A. Zwolle, Oud Archief, no. 4427–28, 484; *Statistische beschrijving van Gelderland van 1808*, vol. III: *Kwartier van Nijmegen*, pp. 17, 22; Matthey, *Westeremden*, p. 283; B. D. H. Tellingen, "Het verbruik van tarwe en rogge in de stad Groningen in de jaren 1821 en 1822, en in de jaren 1827–1856," *Staathuishoudkundig jaarboekje* 9 (1857), 320–21; Ton Kappelhof, "Laverend tussen mars en Mercurius," in A. Voss, ed., *'s-Hertogenbosch: de geschiedenis van een Brabantse stad, 1629–1990* (Zwolle: Waanders, 1997), p. 77.

for the city of Kampen, in the analysis of the evolution of the structure of bread prices in Chapter 9, and especially in Table 9.4. Here, it will suffice to note that Kampen's bakers' fees c. 1600 were much as in Holland: the fees allowed for wheat bread were about double those for rye bread. Thereafter, the bakers' fees for rye bread remained constant while those for wheat bread rose step by step to become triple and ultimately over four times the level for rye bread. Kampen's case was extreme, but many eastern towns followed this general pattern of intensifying the policy of burden-shifting over time.

Bakery Earnings

What we have learned about bakery operations and regulatory policies counsels modesty regarding our ability to measure bakery earnings in any detail. For any individual bakery, the gross revenues will be related to the volume of sales, of course, but it will depend even more on the mix of wheat bread vs. rye bread sold, the mix of fine white bread vs. unbolted wheat bread sold, and the allowance provided by local regulators for extra loaves (the loaves produced per unit of grain in excess of the yield assumed in setting the bread prices). However, what cannot be known at the micro-level of the bakery can be measured at least approximately at a more aggregated level, and these macro-level estimates can then be used to estimate earnings over time for "average" bakeries – those producing bread in an amount and mix that was average for a particular region.

My procedure will be to estimate the bakers' net revenue (approximating the bakers' "value added" in the overall production process). This net revenue equals the gross revenue (proceeds from the sale at official prices of each type of bread) after deduction of all the external costs incurred by the baker. Thus, from his/her gross revenue the baker must pay for the grain purchased, the miller for converting the grain to flour, the tax collectors for the excises on milling, and a variety of suppliers for fuel, yeast, milk, eggs, and other ingredients and local services. Happily, the baking trials and other regulatory documents provide sufficient information about these costs to approximate how much of the gross revenue is left as the baker's net revenue (or value added) per last of grain converted into each of the main bread types. This net revenue does not equal the baker's personal income. Rather, it is the fund from which the baker pays for the fixed expenses of bakery operations (the labor and capital costs) and receives his entrepreneurial profit.

As we have seen, the bread price commissioners had the task of defining this net revenue when they set the bakers' fee (*bakloon*). However, we have also seen that these commissioners provided for some number of extra loaves ("advantage loaves" or *overbroden*) per last of grain that served to supplement bakery earnings. We should expect the calculation of net revenue as a residual to equal the calculation of net revenue as the official bakers' fee plus the revenue from extra loaves. In practice, the revenue derived from extra loaves can never be directly observed; it must be inferred from the assumed difference between the officially stated number of loaves per last of grain and the actual bread yield achievable. Here, too, there is scope for considerable intra-bakery variability; bakers varied in the number of failed bakings they endured, in the quality of the bread they produced, and in the general efficiency of their operations. This is why the establishment of the bread yield was always such a contentious matter. Still, evidence concerning the bakers' fees as they were set over time can serve as a check on the reasonableness of net bakery revenues calculated via the residual method.

The estimates that follow are based on annual bread and grain price data and the excise taxes for the western and eastern regions of the Netherlands. These annual data are then averaged in twenty-year periods, and it is for these periods that the less abundant evidence concerning millers' fees and the costs of fuel and ingredients are estimated.

This procedure is used to calculate net revenue per last of rye and wheat processed by bakeries in the two regions. Since most rye was converted into a single, standard type of bread, the estimation of gross and net revenues is straightforward. With wheat, matters are more complicated since bakers commonly produced three or four distinct types of bread, each with its own price, and also with somewhat different ingredient costs. I have simplified this estimation procedure by assuming that bakers produced half unbolted wheat bread (the cheapest type) and half fine white bread (the costliest type), and used the prices and production costs relevant to each. Fortunately, the net revenue achieved from the sale of a last-worth of fine white bread or of coarse wheat bread usually did not differ by much, so our results are not highly sensitive to variations in the grades of wheat bread sold.

This multi-step procedure generates estimates of bakers' net revenue per last of rye and wheat for both the western and eastern regions in twenty-year periods stretching across the entire era of new system bread price regulation. These per-last revenue estimates can then be used in two ways: to estimate average revenues per bakery, under assumptions about the volume of production of an average bakery, and to estimate the regional and national gross and net revenues of the baking sector, which can then be used to assess its place in the Dutch Republic's gross domestic product.

Table 8.8 displays the results of this exercise. In the first period, 1596–1619, bakers in Holland and the other western provinces could expect to collect 184.25 guilders for every last of rye they converted to standard rye bread. After paying for the grain, the taxes due, the millers' fee and the cost of other inputs, the baker cleared approximately 40 guilders. We saw earlier, in Table 8.4, that the bakers' fees incorporated in the bread price schedules of this period did not exceed 20 guilders per last in the first years of this period. But we also noted that most price schedules established an official bread yield well below the full attainable yield. The resulting extra loaves (the difference between the 2,900 kg assumed in my calculations in Table 8.8 and the 2,700 kg commonly set by regulators) accounts for most of the difference (13 guilders in our example).

These revenue estimates are not utterly precise, but the resulting patterns of revenue by grain type, by region, and over time tracks well with changes in the bakers' fees over time. In the west the bakers' revenue per last of grain processed into bread rose period by period – faster before 1680, more gradually thereafter – until it had doubled by the 1780–90s.[47]

In the eastern provinces, Table 8.8 reveals a rather more dramatic pattern: net revenue per last of rye rose in the early decades (to 1640–59), but remained stable, or even declined thereafter, so that it ended near where it had begun. But bakers fared much better with wheat: the bread price commissioners increased the bakers' fees for wheat bread substantially, especially in the 1660–1719 period. Even when we set aside the very high revenue calculation for 1800–19, eastern bakers earned nearly 2.5 times as much per last of wheat in the nineteenth century as they had at the beginning of the seventeenth century. This dichotomous pattern is, of course, not surprising in view of what we have already learned about eastern cross-subsidization efforts. But it remains striking nonetheless that while western bakers could expect net revenue per last of wheat that was double that for rye throughout the seventeenth and eighteenth centuries, eastern bakers began earning nearly three times as much from the production of wheat breads and ended earning four to six times as much.

What did all this mean for the earnings of a bakery? Earlier in this chapter we established that a bakery processing 15 lasts of grain per year stood near the statistical average throughout the seventeenth and eighteenth centuries. Evidence on the size distribution of bakeries around this

[47] However, one should note that the least reliable estimates are certainly those for the 1800–19 period. This was an era of sharp price increases, innovations and frequent changes in tax policy, and new price schedules that sharply reduced the scope for income from "extras loaves." While it is possible that the enlarged bakers' net revenues shown for this period were real (perhaps to compensate for diminished bread consumption in at least part of this period), it may also be that our methodology fails to capture accurately the effect of the multiple changes on the bakers' costs.

Table 8.8 *Revenue and expenditures per last of grain converted to bread (in guilders)*

	Total revenue	Grain	Taxes	Milling	Ingredients	Bakers' rev.	Index bakers' rev.	Real index bakers' rev.	CPI
West: rye									
1597–1619	184.25	117.61	13.75	5.01	8.09	39.79	100	100	100
1620–39	258.18	160.96	26.25	5.4	10.5	55.07	138.401608	107.336591	128.941685
1640–59	274.464	159.75	34.98	6.04	12.46	61.234	153.892938	104.725233	146.949244
1660–79	273.1	153.39	34.98	7	13.06	64.67	162.528273	109.968591	147.795176
1680–99	281.03	137.69	56.88	7.85	13.23	65.38	164.312641	109.207612	150.458963
1700–19	285.87	136.74	57.67	8.05	13.98	69.43	174.491078	117.904826	147.993161
1720–39	254.78	101.1	57.67	8.5	14.43	73.08	183.664237	130.000446	141.279698
1740–59	265.23	121.35	48.19	8.5	14.43	72.76	182.86015	121.65123	150.314975
1760–79	285.53	137.84	46.59	8.5	15.35	77.25	194.144257	120.723614	160.817135
1780–99	333.31	176.74	46.59	8.5	16.93	84.55	212.490576	120.028227	177.033837
1800–19	429.59	270.3	27.82	11	31	89.47	224.855491	105.537243	213.057955
1820–39	301.3	159	16.7	14.9	25	85.7	215.380749	141.081754	152.663787
1840–55	359.25	217.2	23	17	25	77.05	193.641618	127.647011	151.700864
West: wheat									
1597–1619	328.99	190.69	28.49	6.53	20.21	83.07	100	100	
1620–39	442.11	236.83	51.89	8.1	28.99	116.3	140.002408	108.578082	
1640–59	469.64	241.27	69.6	10	33.01	115.76	139.352353	94.8302622	
1660–79	482.84	222.08	69.6	10.33	40.99	139.84	168.339954	113.900845	
1680–99	517.14	209.94	113.85	10.33	40.13	142.89	172.011557	114.324566	
1700–19	502.68	197.72	114.85	10.33	39.09	140.69	169.363188	114.439875	
1720–39	462.54	142.3	114.85	11	43.43	150.96	181.726255	128.628712	
1740–59	486.49	173.66	106.99	11	43.48	151.36	182.207777	121.217315	
1760–79	540.55	202.14	114.85	11	46.6	165.96	199.783315	124.230118	
1780–99	608.9	254.35	114.85	11	51.01	177.69	213.903936	120.826583	
1800–19	784.75	415.5	93.06	16	64.36	195.83	235.740941	110.646392	
1820–39	589.48	233.1	73.72	20.55	60.77	201.34	242.373902	158.763192	
1840–55	619.61	295.5	100	22.1	60	142.01	170.952209	112.690333	

Table 8.8 (*cont.*)

	Total revenue	Grain	Taxes	Milling	Ingredients	Bakers' rev.	Index bakers' rev.	Real index bakers' rev.	CPI
East: rye									
1597–1619	165.06	125.57	3.91	3.17	5.71	26.7	100	100	100
1620–39	216.02	161.91	12.35	3.25	6.88	31.63	118.464419	91.8744157	128.941685
1640–59	225.01	155.65	15	3.25	8.82	42.29	158.389513	107.785184	146.949244
1660–79	221.29	152.33	16.5	4	8.51	39.95	149.625468	101.238397	147.795176
1680–99	208.86	133.71	21	5	8.7	40.45	151.498127	100.690663	150.458963
1700–19	201.52	130.49	21	5	8.05	36.98	138.501873	93.5866713	147.993161
1720–39	175.74	105.73	21	5	7.76	36.25	135.76779	96.098585	141.279698
1740–59	183	120.64	19.65	5	6.65	31.06	116.329588	77.3905515	150.314975
1760–79	206.32	143.83	21	5	6.53	29.96	112.209738	69.7747402	160.817135
1780–99	240.18	177.85	21	5	7.05	29.28	109.662921	61.9446107	177.033837
1800–19	325.94	240.9	21.45	8	13	42.59	159.513109	74.8684124	213.057955
1820–39	226.9	147.3	14.7	8	11	45.9	171.910112	112.607001	152.663787
1840–55	283.65	203.1	21	9	11	39.55	148.127341	97.6443621	151.700864
East: wheat									
1597–1619	315.14	190.69	13	5.5	21.19	84.76	100	100	
1620–39	392.36	241.39	27.2	5.5	23.654	94.616	111.628126	86.5725671	
1640–59	425.03	247	30	5.5	28.506	114.024	134.52572	91.5457038	
1660–79	384.58	225.78	33	6.5	23.86	95.44	112.600283	76.1867105	
1680–99	421.63	203.49	42	7.5	33.728	134.912	159.16942	105.789257	
1700–19	440.13	203.11	42	7.5	38.944	155.776	183.784804	124.184661	
1720–39	385.33	164.01	34.8	7.5	35.804	143.216	168.966494	119.597151	
1740–59	430.37	195.85	36.96	7.5	38.012	152.048	179.386503	119.340407	
1760–79	505.22	242.16	42	7.5	42.712	170.848	201.566777	125.339117	
1780–99	576	292.17	42	7.5	46.866	187.464	221.170363	124.931124	
1800–19	782.8	392.02	66.23	11	66.81	246.74	291.104294	136.631507	
1820–39	555.36	214.8	51.37	11	66.51	211.68	249.740444	163.58529	
1840–55	617.47	278.1	71.5	12	55.47	200.4	236.432279	155.854274	

mean production volume was not abundant, and mostly from the very end of our period, but it left open the possibility that most bakeries were either smaller or larger than the 15 last standard – in short, the distribution of bakeries may have been bi-modal, making the 15 last bakery "average" but not "typical." Still, I will use this standard to calculate the annual revenues of a bakery, with the understanding that most bakers probably earned considerably less and a smaller but significant number earned considerably more.

Table 8.9 shows the gross earnings, the expenses, and the net earnings of a 15-last bakery in both the western and eastern regions. The calculation is highly sensitive to the assumed rye–wheat mix per bakery. We must draw here on findings presented in Chapter 11 and summarized in Table 11.11. There I show that consumers in the west shifted gradually from a bread diet where rye predominated to a diet dominated by wheat in the course of the seventeenth century, while in the east rye's position of dominance remained unchanged. Taking the period 1720–39 as an example, the table shows that a 15-last bakery in the west, processing 10 lasts of wheat and 5 lasts of rye, took in some 5,900 guilders of gross revenue annually from the sale of bread. Only one-third of this revenue represented the cost of grain. This was partly a reflection of the historically low grain prices of this period, but also partly a consequence of the important role bakers played as tax intermediaries. Nearly a quarter of the baker's gross revenue was, in effect, passed on to the collectors of the milling excise. After paying the miller and various suppliers of fuel, yeast, and other inputs the 15-last bakery yielded 1,875 guilders in net revenue. From this revenue the baker covered his labor and capital costs, primarily the wages of a journeyman, the rental value of the premises, and the depreciation of the oven and equipment. While these expenses cannot be determined with precision it is likely that they accounted for no more than half of the net revenues. Table 8.9 shows what was left as the bakers' earnings under the assumption that labor and capital costs were 40 percent of net earnings – in this case, 1,126 guilders per annum. These results fit comfortably in the range of taxable incomes of urban bakers in Holland as revealed by the *Personele Quotisatie* of 1742 discussed above.

Bakers in the eastern provinces earned much less. Their customers purchased primarily rye bread from which bakers derived little profit. They earned much more from the sale of wheat bread – far more than their western counterparts – but unless this rose well above the 15 percent level of all bread consumption assumed for the region as a whole (which it certainly did in the larger towns), the 15-last baker could expect a net revenue of only 750–850 guilders from the 1640s to the 1790s, and

Table 8.9 *Bakery revenue of a 15-last bakery (in guilders per year)*

	Composite CPI	Total revenue	Grain	Taxes	Milling	Ingre-dients	Bakers' rev.	Bakers' rev. index	Bakers' rev. real index	Bakers' income if labor and cap. were 40% of rev.	Total revenue if mix grain and wheat always 67% wheat	Bakers' rev.	Bakers' rev. index	Bakers' rev. real index	Bakers' income if labor and cap. were 40% of rev.
West															
1597–1619	100	3,632.19	2202.63	294.69	84.27	194.07	856.53	100	100	513.918	4,211.15	1,029.65	100	100	617.79
1620–39	128.941685	5,390.1225	3040.3275	605.28	103.275	310.0425	1,331.1975	155.417,499	120.533169	798.7185	5,712	1,438.35	139.6931	108.3382	863.01
1640–59	146.949244	5,873.544	3129.93	836.28	111.03	371.85	1409.244	164.529,439	111.963447	845.5464	6,068.72	1463.77	142.1619	96.7421,783	878.262
1660–79	147.7,95176	6,193.9	2987.75	870.9	128.8	475.2	1721.75	201.014559	136.008876	1,033.05	6,193.9	1721.75	167.217015	113.141051	1,033.05
1680–99	150.458963	6,576.55	2787.85	1422.9	138.35	467.45	1,755.8	204.989901	136.243064	1,053.48	6,576.55	1,755.8	170.523964	113.335863	1,053.48
1700–19	147.993161	6,456.15	2660.9	1436.85	141.25	460.8	1,754.05	204.785588	138.375035	1,052.43	6,456.15	1754.05	170.354004	115.109376	1,052.43
1720–39	141.279698	5899.3	1928.5	1436.85	152.5	506.45	1875	218.906518	154.945489	1,125	5,899.3	1875	182.100714	128.89376	1,125
1740–59	150.314975	6,191.05	2343.35	1310.85	154.7	506.95	1877.4	219.186719	145.818285	1126.44	6191.05	1877.4	182.333803	121.301156	1,126.44
1760–79	160.817135	6,833.15	2710.6	1381.45	163.5	542.75	2,045.85	238.85328	148.524771	1,227.51	6,833.15	2,045.85	198.693731	123.552588	1,227.51
1780–99	177.033837	7,755.55	3427.2	1381.45	163.5	594.75	2,199.65	256.809452	145.062354	1,319.79	7,755.55	2,199.65	213.630845	120.672324	1,319.79
1800–19	213.057955	9,995.45	5506.5	1069.7	215	798.6	2,405.65	280.859982	131.823278	1,443.39	9,995.45	2,405.65	233.637644	109.659197	1,443.39
1820–39	152.663787	7,401.3	3126	820.7	280	732.7	2,441.9	285.092174	186.745121	1,465.14	7,401.3	2,441.9	237.158258	155.346767	1,465.14
1840–55	151.700864	7,992.35	4041	1115	306	725	1,805.35	210.774871	138.941114	1083.21	7992.35	1,805.35	175.336279	115.580277	1,083.21

East

1597–1619	100	2,813.58	2030.07	79.1025	52.7925	120.48	531.135	100	100	318.681
1620–39	128.941685	3,637.065	2607.48	218.6625	53.8125	140.9415	616.1685	116.009772	89.9707273	369.7011
1640–59	146.949244	3,825.195	2540.2875	258.75	53.8125	176.5935	795.7515	149.820949	101.954216	477.4509
1660–79	147.795176	3,686.7525	2450.2125	284.625	65.625	162.1875	724.1025	136.331159	92.2433073	434.4615
1680–99	150.458963	3,611.6325	2162.655	362.25	80.625	186.813	819.2895	154.252591	102.52137	491.5737
1700–19	147.993161	3,559.6725	2120.745	346.05	80.625	190.2615	821.991	154.761219	104.573224	493.1946
1720–39	141.279698	3,107.6775	1717.08	346.05	80.625	179.499	784.4235	147.688158	104.53601	470.6541
1740–59	150.314975	3,301.5825	1978.8225	333.6975	80.625	170.3145	738.123	138.970883	92.4531194	442.8738
1760–79	160.817135	3,767.325	2378.6925	362.25	80.625	179.3595	766.398	144.29388	89.7257552	459.8388
1780–99	177.033837	4,358.295	2924.97	362.25	80.625	195.336	795.114	149.700923	84.5606274	477.0684
1800–19	213.057955	5,917.035	3860.55	422.505	126.75	316.0725	1191.1575	224.266429	105.260763	714.6945
1820–39	152.663787	4,142.535	2361.375	303.0075	126.75	289.8975	1061.505	199.855969	130.912493	636.903
1840–55	151.700864	5,005.845	3215.25	428.625	141.75	265.0575	955.1625	179.834223	118.545286	573.0975

a personal income of perhaps 450–500 guilders – about half the expected income of western bakers producing at the same scale.[48] At this point we have the information needed to return to a question raised in the discussion of the applicability of the concept of "regulatory capture" to the baking sector. Did the regulation of bread prices serve to enrich the bakers? Did the regulators set the bakers' fees at levels that caused bakers to become distinctly better off than they would have been under old system pricing or under a regime of competitive markets?

Table 8.9 shows that net revenues rose substantially from their initial level in 1596–1619. The eastern bakery saw net revenues rise by some 50 percent by the 1640s, only to remain at this level until after 1800, but the net revenues of the western bakery rose much more, doubling from their initial level by the 1660s and rising further, to some 2.5 times the initial level by the 1780s. On the face of things, this was a golden age for Holland's bakers.

Before jumping to conclusions, we need to adjust these net revenue trends for changes in the cost of labor, rents, and the overall cost of living. That is, the current guilders of Table 8.9 need to be converted to constant guilders. House rents in Amsterdam rose by 57 percent in the century after 1596–1619 and had nearly doubled by 1780–99. Amsterdam may be thought to have experienced a stronger rental market than most Dutch towns, but a more comprehensive index of house values for Holland as a whole rose by nearly as much over these two centuries.[49] A comprehensive consumer price index (CPI) for Holland rose by 45 percent in the first half of the seventeenth century and, after a century-long hiatus, climbed again after 1750. By 1780–99 the CPI was 75 percent above the level of 1597–1619, and prices would rise sharply higher thereafter, during the volatile Napoleonic era.

Column 6 of Table 8.8 shows the development of a bakers' net revenue *per last of wheat and rye* in both west and east. Column 10 of Table 8.9 calculates the course of real net earnings of *15-last bakeries* in west and east. The regulatory regime in the west set prices in such a way that bakers' real earnings per last of both bread grains rose by approximately 20 percent over the course of the seventeenth century, whereafter any further

---

[48] In the larger cities of the north and east, such as Groningen, Zwolle, Arnhem, Nijmegen, and Den Bosch, eastern bakeries working on a 15-last scale could expect a net revenue between 25 and 30 percent higher than estimated in Table 8.9 – about 1,000 to 1,100 guilders – with a personal income around 600 guilders, from 1640 to 1799.

[49] Lesger, *Huur en conjunctuur*. House values for Holland are based on taxes on real property, which were adjusted only at long intervals. See Lee Soltow and Jan Luiten van Zanden, *Income and Wealth Inequality in the Netherlands, 16th – 20th Century* (Amsterdam: Het Spinhuis, 1996); P. M. A. Eichholz and M. A. J. Theebe, "Zo vast als een huis," *Economisch-statistisch berichten* 84 (1999), 132–34.

gains were temporary. (The more volatile pattern after 1800, about which I am less confident, will be discussed separately in Chapter 15.) Regulatory policy in the east led to very different results. Bakers' earnings from rye bread rose just enough to keep pace with the price inflation of the early seventeenth century, but they failed to keep pace with the CPI thereafter. This decline was compensated for by wheat bread, which became steadily more remunerative for the bakers: after 1680 real earnings from the production of wheat bread rose by 35 percent.

These results are combined to form estimates of the total real earnings of 15-last bakeries in Table 8.9. In the eastern region bakers' real earnings were essentially trendless, fluctuating around the index of 100 in 1597–1619, until the nineteenth century. What the bakers lost in the production of rye bread they gained from the more generously priced wheat breads. A policy of cross-subsidization kept rye prices "artificially" low and kept the bakers on a very short leash. The details of regulatory policy differed from province to province in the east, but there is no evidence that the regulatory system served to enrich the bakers in any of them

In Holland matters are more complex. From Table 8.8 we noted that real earnings per last rose by about 20 percent for both wheat and rye. But the changes in consumer behavior, concentrated in the first two-thirds of the seventeenth century, resulted in the "average" bakery selling a richer mix of wheat and rye breads, which lead to a rise in net income even when net income per last of wheat and rye individually remained unaltered. The small rise in earnings per last of grain (granted by the regulators) combined with a shift toward the production of the more lucrative wheat breads (granted by consumers) to raise real bakery earnings by 40 percent by the 1660–79 period and often by slightly more than that through the following 120 years.

Did Holland's bread price commissioners enrich the bakers at the expense of the consumers they were pledged to protect? They had a motive to increase the earnings of these artisans that grew stronger over time, as the bakers came to serve as important front-line tax collectors, and the timing of their growing prosperity corresponds with the timing of the rise of milling excise to its key place in Dutch fiscalism. Still, the 20 percent increase in net bakers' revenues per last of grain does not rise to the level of scandalous enrichment in the more general context of seventeenth-century prosperity. Many other Hollanders also experienced rising real incomes in this period; indeed, Holland's per capita GDP is estimated to have risen by 20–22 percent. It was the good fortune of Holland's bakers that this rising prosperity led to an increasing preference for wheat bread. Consumers willingly paid the higher prices placed by the regulatory system on wheat bread, and this shift in consumer preferences increased the earnings of bakers by an additional 20–25 per cent.

Another approach to assessing the effects of regulatory policy on both bakers and consumers – and one that can be described much more briefly – is to calculate the total annual revenue of the bread sector (the total volume of bread produced times the regulated prices at which rye and wheat bread was sold) and express it as a percentage of gross domestic product (GDP). Before 1800 GDP estimates (discussed in more detail in Chapter 13) exist only for Holland. I have estimated GDP in the other western provinces, Utrecht and Zeeland, at 85 percent of Holland's per capita level and calculated the portion of the regional economy accounted for by bread costs – grain, taxes, the bakers' revenues, and other costs (milling and other production costs) – for successive twenty-year periods from 1597 to 1799. The results, shown in Figure 8.3, reveal that the bakers' revenue remained fairly steady throughout the period, hovering between 3.0 and 3.5 percent of GDP, while the other constant costs (for milling and the baker's non-grain inputs) added an additional 0.5 percent. Grain costs fell relative to GDP, such that total pre-fisc bread costs declined from 11.5 to a low of 8 percent of GDP, before rising grain

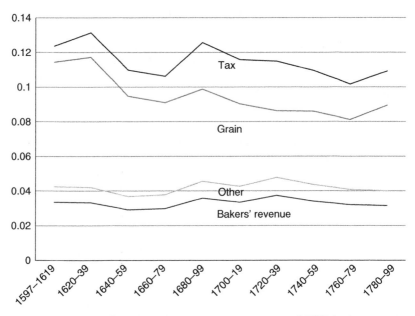

Figure 8.3 Bread sector revenue as percentage of GDP in the western Netherlands, 1597–1799

costs pushed the weight of the bread sector upward after 1780. When the excise tax is added, a substantial portion of this decline is removed. But for current purposes, this exercise reveals bakers' revenues rising with the overall growth of the economy. On this evidence, the bakers do not appear as scandalous beneficiaries of the regulatory system. On the other hand, the bread sector does not decline in relative size with the rise of per capita income, as Engel's law has taught generations of economists to expect. This is a puzzle we will examine in some detail in Chapter 13.

The study of regulatory policy gets us only so far in understanding this industry; our effort to reconstruct the earnings of bakers has revealed that consumer choice also plays a large role. It is time now to look into this in greater detail. We begin with an examination of the evolving structure of bread prices faced by Dutch consumers (Chapter 9), followed by an examination of the "revealed preferences" of consumers, as they responded to these prices, in Part III.

9   The Structure of Bread Prices

The new system of bread price regulation introduced by the Dutch towns in the 1590s replaced old rules of thumb and their frequently unreasonable bread prices and weights with a regime based on careful measurement of the constituent costs of bread production. As discussed in Chapter 3, the resulting distinction made between constant and variable costs led to a "scientific" calculation of official bread prices. But, as demonstrated in Chapters 5 and 8, it also presented the regulators with new opportunities to intervene in defining the constant costs of the major bread types. The same new methodology that removed what might charitably be called technical distortions from the price-setting process for each type of bread separately, introduced policy-driven distortions to the relative prices of the different bread types.

The millers' fees and the costs of non-grain ingredients were calculated with care, but they were minor elements in the totality of the constant costs. The bakers' fee and the excise tax were by far the two largest contributors to the constant costs. The level, indeed the existence, of the tax had nothing to do with production costs; more surprisingly, we found that the bakers' fee, which was obviously an essential element of production, also was set much more as a matter of policy than as a result of measurement. The combined impact of these two major elements of constant costs is revealed in the price differentials that arose among the several types of bread commonly sold in the Netherlands. The new system of bread price regulation confronted consumers with patterns of relative bread prices that constituted a major departure from both earlier Dutch pricing patterns and those prevailing elsewhere in Europe.

In order to appreciate what the regulators managed to impose, we will begin by establishing the actual differences in the production cost of the two major bread types. These will serve as a "baseline" for the interpretation of the actual prices established by the bread price commissioners over the course of the new system's 260-year run.

"Intrinsic" Relative Bread Prices

Wheat and rye were both available throughout the Netherlands as well as in most parts of northwestern Europe. A measure of wheat was more costly than the same measure of rye and, correspondingly, wheat bread always cost more than rye bread, pound per pound. But how much more should the consumer have expected to pay? This is a more complex question than it appears, but the place to start is with the principal cost component, the price of grain. Table 9.1 displays the wheat/rye grain price differentials in the Netherlands over time, revealing that the price of wheat usually exceeded that of rye by 45–55 percent.

A volume measure of wheat is 45–55 percent more expensive than rye, but it is also heavier. The weight of a last of grain will vary from harvest to harvest, but wheat usually exceeded rye by nearly 10 percent (c. 2,300 kg wheat vs. c. 2,100 kg rye per last) in our period.[1] Therefore, on a pound-per-pound basis, the wheat/rye price ratios shown at the bottom of Table 9.1 are reduced as follows:

Wheat/rye price ratio per kilogram of grain: 1.32 – 1.42

A more difficult matter is the yield rate: the weight of the bread produced from a given weight of grain. Here, much depends on the quality of the bread. We will confine ourselves here to basic rye bread and basic unbolted wheat bread (*krop uit de zak* = baked from milled grain "just as it comes from the miller"). The many baking trials performed over the years to inform the price commissioners of the true bread yield always found that wheat yielded more bread per kilogram of grain than did rye. For example, Eversdijck's 1622 baking trials in Goes found wheat's advantage to be 5.3 percent, while Nieuwenhuis reported on baking

Table 9.1 *Wheat/rye price ratios, 1600–1899*

1599–1619	1.69
1620–99	1.54
1700–99	1.49
1800–19	1.52
1820–49	1.45
1850–99	1.37
Range of 20-year averages, 1620–1819	
Per volume measure of grain	1.44 – 1.56

These ratios are based on the composite time series for wheat and rye prices.

[1] This weight difference is also expressed in terms of specific gravity. That for wheat is generally in the range of 0.76–0.78 kg per liter; for rye the range is 0.70–0.72.

trials in Amsterdam that gave wheat a 8.8 percent advantage in 1793 and 9.7 percent in 1816.[2] If, on average, the yield for wheat bread is 6 percent greater than for rye bread, the price ratios can be adjusted again:

Wheat/rye price ratio per kilogram of bread: 1.25 – 1.34

Finally, we must consider the nutritional value of wheat and rye bread. A kilogram of whole grain wheat bread contains about 2,100 kcal compared to rye bread's 1,906, a 10 percent difference, while wheat bread has an even larger advantage with respect to protein: 76 grams per kg of wheat bread compared to 54 grams for rye bread.[3] If we adopt Jasny's concept of "net energy value," rye bread scores 15 percent below wheat bread. Thus, the price differential between the two breads can be expressed in terms of cost per unit of nutritional value:[4]

Wheat/rye price ratios per unit of nutritional value: 1.09 – 1.17

In sum, even though a liter of wheat cost, on average, 45–55 percent more than rye, wheat could supply nutritional value at a cost very little above that of rye: on average, about 10 to 15 percent. Of course, this final adjustment would not appear in market prices but it could be reflected in the budgets of consumers, via the purchase of smaller quantities of wheat bread than rye bread.[5]

Relative Production Costs

Unbolted wheat bread would sell at more than a 25–35 percent premium over rye bread if the bakers' production costs in converting a measure of grain into bread were higher for wheat than for rye. But we have just found in Chapter 8 that this was not the case. Contemporary testimony was unanimous in judging the labor costs of the two bread types to be about equal, and the cost of non-grain ingredients for both breads to be a minor factor.

---

[2] For Goes, see Eversdijck, *Paste-boeck vanden Broode*; for Amsterdam, see Cs. Js. Nieuwenhuijs, *Proeve eener geneeskundige plaatsbeschrijving der stad Amsterdam* (Amsterdam, 1816).

[3] Anne McCants, "Monotonous but not meager: the diet of burgher orphans in early modern Amsterdam," *Research in Economic History* 14 (1992), 69–116, p. 91; Nutritional values from FAO, *Technical Conversion Factors for Agricultural Commodities* (Rome: Food and Agriculture Organization of the United Nations, 1972).

[4] N. Jasny, *Competition among Grain* (Stanford University, 1940) p. 30.

[5] Petersen engaged in a similar exercise using eighteenth-century English sources and reached the same conclusion as I do here. Petersen, *Bread*, p. 22.

Ratio of wheat to rye costs at 1770s prices in England:

	Grain per bushel	Grain per pound	Bread per pound
Wheat/Rye	1.47	1.39	1.19

Matters are more complex in assessing the production costs of the finer grades of wheat bread. Because they were made from bolted flour, their yield ratios were substantially below those for unbolted wheat bread. Table 3.4 offers an overview of data drawn from town baking trials and contemporary declarations. While they vary in detail, they are consistent in showing that grain baked as bolted wheat bread yielded approximately one pound of bread per pound of grain: somewhat more for coarse bread, somewhat less for fine. The table also makes clear that white bread was a distinct product; its yield fell in the range of 70–75 pounds per 100 pounds of grain. All of these expected yield rates were sensitive to quality standards, which varied from place to place and over time, but the basic pattern remained constant: the grain cost of producing bolted wheat breads was 25–45 percent greater than for unbolted wheat bread, depending on quality, and the finest white bread's grain cost was 70–75 percent greater.

This is not quite the end of the matter. The lower yields of the bolted wheat breads were, of course, caused by the removal of the bran from the ground wheat grains. The bran belonged to the bakers, and the regulators expected the bakers to sell the bran they captured via the bolting process, primarily to livestock fatteners. They were continually on guard against the temptation facing bakers to mix the bran into their bolted bread, which was regarded as a form of adulteration. To this end, numerous ordinances prohibited bakers from storing bran on their premises. If not sold immediately, it had to be removed to storage attics.[6]

The proceeds from the sale of bran figured in the calculation of the constant costs for wheat bread. Some baking trials measure the amount of bran removed from a last of wheat (18–24 pounds was common), and assigned it a market value that then stood as a credit against other constant costs. Amsterdam in 1597 supposed that the bran was worth 12.50 guilders; Haarlem in 1609 set it at 8.10 guilders. But in 1618 Haarlem simply allowed the sale of bran to cancel out the cost of yeast (see Table 9.2). More commonly, nothing was said about the value of the bran, or the commissioners noted that any revenue from the sale of bran was for the (additional) profit of the baker. Its sale had the effect of reducing the net cost of wheat by 5 to 10 percent, dampening somewhat the cost differentials between unbolted and bolted wheat bread types stated above.

We have established that the cost differential of producing basic wheat and rye breads was much smaller than suggested by the price differential of the two bread grains. Wheat's greater weight per volume measure and its higher bread yield per kilogram reduce this differential, and the greater nutritional value of wheat bread reduces it further. The production costs

---

[6] Brouwer Ancher, *De Gilden*, p. 155.

Table 9.2 *Value of bran per last of milled grain, according to baking trials*

Amsterdam	1593	10 st per Utrecht *mud* = 12.50 gld
Haarlem	1609	6 st per A'dam *mud* = 8.10 gld
Haarlem	1618	"Sale of bran covers the cost of the yeast."*
Utrecht	1653	"[The revenue from the sale of] bran is left for the profit for the baker."**
Haarlem	1668	5.70 gld
National Survey	1826	
Holland, six large cities		20.20 gld
Holland, four small cities		16.125 gld
Utrecht, two cities		24.00 gld

In general, the sale of bran covered between 5 and 10 percent of the cost of wheat.
*"zemelen tegen de gist"
**"Latende de zemelen tot profijt van de Backer."

of these breads seem also to have been roughly equal, as revealed by contemporary comments and the costs identified in detailed baking trials. Presumably, in a competitive market setting, unbolted wheat bread and basic rye bread would have sold at prices that, depending on the prevailing grain price differentials, generally would have differed by between 25 and 35 percent.

But the regulated prices of wheat and rye bread almost never fell within this range; wheat bread regularly sold at a larger premium than rye bread, and this premium tended to rise over the course of the seventeenth century.[7] That is to say, the regulatory process intervened to establish price differentials that would not have occurred in a competitive market, that did not occur under old system forms of regulation, and that would disappear once the regulatory system was abolished in 1855.

Shaping the Structure of Bread Prices

The bread price commissioners announced the price of bread every week, week-in-week-out, year-by-year, from the introduction of the new system, in the late 1590s, until the abolition of the *broodzetting* in 1855. Bread prices had been regulated before then, but, as already noted, the old system left few price records. Few records were kept, I believe,

---

[7] Almost never, but not never. The Gelderland river town of Zaltbommel was unique in the sources I have examined in desisting – until 1680 – from burdening wheat bread with differential production costs, while further upriver, Arnhem imposed only a modest differential. These exceptions demonstrate the validity of the cost calculations made at the beginning of this chapter.

because bread prices followed a simple rule of thumb that required little recordkeeping. It is also likely that regulators concerned themselves with only one or two basic types of bread, leaving the more "luxurious" breads to be governed by the market.

With the introduction of the new system, this changed, and the commissioners began making their weekly price announcements public via printed forms listing all the bread types permitted in the city. For example, beginning in 1612 Haarlem's form listed the following bread types:[8]

Roggebrood, 6 pond	Rye bread, 6-pound loaves
Grof tarwebrood, 6 pond	Coarse wheat bread, 6-pound loaves
Fijn tarwebrood, 4 stuiver brood	Fine wheat bread, 4 stuivers
Wittebrood, 4 stuiver brood	White bread, 4 stuivers
Mascheluynebrood, 3 stuiver brood [to 1643]	Mixed grain bread, 3 stuivers
Achterlingenbollen, 3 stuiver brood [from 1643]	Lowest quality wheat bread, 3 stuivers

Haarlem introduced a revised form in 1750:

Roggebrood, 6 pond	Rye bread, 6-pound loaves
Zeeuwse tarwebrood, 3 pond	Zeeland (coarse) wheat bread, 3-pound loaves
Luchtig Poolse tarwebrood, 2 pond 26 lood	Light Polish wheat bread, 2.81 pounds
Wittebrood bollen, 6 stuivers per boll	White bread rolls, 6 stuivers
Fijn Franschbrood, 5 stuiver brood	Fine French bread, 5 stuivers
Achterling, 3 stuiver brood	Lowest quality wheat bread, 3 stuivers

Whenever grain prices changed enough to warrant a change in bread prices, the commissioners filled out these forms, entering the new price (in stuivers and penningen) or the new weight (in *loden* – 32 per pound) for each type of bread. Haarlem, like most Holland towns, recognized but one sort of rye bread. But there were four or five grades of wheat bread, which sold variously by weight and price. One price schedule sufficed for all wheat breads sold by price; the second bread sort was simply priced at a constant differential to the first, say, 8 penningen less per loaf: whatever the price of type A, type B sold for 8 penningen less. Likewise for breads sold by weight: whatever the new weight of a 3-stuiver loaf of bread type C, type D would weigh an additional, say, 6 *loden*, while type E would weigh 10 *loden* more than C.

In this way fixed price/weight differentials characterized the various types of wheat breads, but the differentials did not remain unchanged. Most towns made occasional adjustments that made particular bread

[8] G.A. Haarlem, Stadsarchief 1581–1795 R 412, 414.

types more costly or cheaper relative to the other breads. In this way the commissioners could adjust the cross-subsidization policy *within* the wheat bread sector. That is, not only did the regulatory system's specification of constant costs create an opportunity to shift costs from rye to wheat (as discussed in Chapter 8), it also allowed costs to be shifted from, say, the consumer of unbolted coarse wheat bread to fine white bread.

For example, when Leiden (re)established its regulation of wheat bread in 1648, it provided for a 4 penning (0.25 stuiver) differential between the prices of 3-pound loaves of its two grades of bolted wheat bread, known simply as *het beste* (the best) and *het minste* (the least). In 1703 it raised this differential to 8 penningen (0.50 stuiver; in 1794 the differential rose further to 12 penningen, and in 1796 it rose to 16 penningen – a full stuiver.[9] By then the costs of wheat bread production had shifted considerably toward the purchasers of "the best" bread.

When Utrecht introduced *Franschbrood* in 1674, this "French bread" sold at the same price as ordinary bolted wheat bread but weighed 10 *loden* less. Thus, its price per pound was considerably higher. In 1680 the weight differential was raised to 11 *loden*. The commissioners reversed their previous policy in 1692, reducing the weight differential to 8 *loden*, but then, in 1736, they greatly increased the relative price of *Franschbrood* by ordering that it always weigh 15 *loden* less than the ordinary wheat loaf of the same price. Perhaps the quality of *Franschbrood* was also increased since its price now nearly equaled that of fine white bread, which ceased to be sold after 1748.[10]

In these examples from Leiden and Utrecht, costs shifted toward the more luxurious bread. In the eastern city of Kampen, the costs shifted in the opposite direction. From 1606 on, the city's bakers produced three grades of wheat bread – fine white, fine wheat, and coarse wheat – all available in loaves costing one stuiver. For example, the 1606 schedule ordained that when wheat cost 162 guilders per last the finest loaf would weigh 21 *loden*, the middle quality loaf 25 *loden*, and the coarse loaf 35 *loden*. As the price of grain rose or fell, one *lood* would be removed or added to the weight of all of these loaves, always preserving the 4-*lood* differential between the fine and middle quality loaves, and the 10-*lood* differential between the middle and coarse types of bread.

Kampen, like other eastern towns, never increased the constant costs allowed for rye bread pricing, but this led them to load costs onto the wheat breads with a notable vigor: they raised the bakers' fees for wheat

<hr />

[9] G.A. Leiden, Stadsarchief, 1574–1816, Secretariearchief, no. 2536, Registers van de broodzetting.
[10] G.A. Utrecht, Oud Archief. Stadsarchief III, no. 2023, Rijdingboek.

bread from about 60 to 120 guilders between 1675 and 1708 and further to at least 130 after 1768, before scaling it back a bit after 1800. The commissioners could translate higher constant costs into the bread prices in two ways: they could decrease the weight of all three types of wheat bread loaves at a given grain price and they could change the weight differentials between the three grades of wheat bread. Kampen's commissioners used both, and on numerous occasions. The complex story is summarized in Table 9.3, which displays the official weight of the three wheat breads for a single wheat price – 210.60 guilders per last, or 39 stuivers per *schepel* – at each year in which the schedules were revised from 1606 to 1817.

A number of "general adjustments" – in 1675, 1682, 1708, 1806, and 1815 – shifted the entire bread weight schedules downward. At a given grain price, all wheat loaves were reduced in weight. In other years – 1631, 1661, 1673, 1677, 1768, and 1817 – the commissioners made "specific adjustments" affecting the relative loaf sizes of the three bread types. They invariably reduced the size differentials, which reduced the amount of lower-quality breads a consumer got for her stuiver. Over two centuries, the weight of the coarse loaf (at a fixed grain price) fell by half, the fine wheat loaf fell by 30 percent, and the weight of the white bread loaf, so long as it lasted, fell by only 15 percent. This was achieved by compressing the weight differentials step by step until there was very little difference in effective prices of the wheat breads.

The total revenue accruing to the baker from the sale of bread produced from of a measure of wheat depended on the relative shares of the three types of wheat bread. Having no direct information about this, the revenue calculations in Table 9.3 are based on the assumption that one-third of the grain was devoted to each of the three bread types. Under this assumption a last of wheat generated approximately 75 guilders of revenue net of the cost of the grain in the early seventeenth century, which corresponds to the constant costs provided in Kampen's earliest bread price ordinance.[11]

Finally, note two years marked in bold lettering in Table 9.3: 1748 and 1812. In those years the milling excises were abolished – temporarily – resulting in a sudden 3-*lood* increase in loaf weights at a constant grain price. This illustrates the substantial practical impact of the milling excise, even in a lightly taxed eastern province. It also serves as a rough check on the accuracy of the estimated revenue left to the baker after deducting the cost of grain and the excises.

What had Kampen's bread price commissioners achieved with all of these adjustments to the weight of the three types of wheat bread? Until 1675 consumers sacrificed a portion of the size of their wheat bread loaves

---

[11] G. A. Kampen, Oud Archief, no. 2206, Ordinances over de broodzetting, 1606–61.

Table 9.3 *Weight of one-stuiver wheat bread loaves in Kampen, 1606–1817*
The weight of each bread type is given in *loden* when the market price for wheat is set at
210.60 guilders per last. 32 *loden* = 1 pound = 494 grams

	Fine white	Fine wheat	Coarse wheat	Revenue per last after subtracting the grain cost	Revenue per last after subtracting the milling excise
1606	16.5	20.5	30.5	76	59
1631	18	20	29	74	45
1661	18	20	26	84	55
1673	18	20	24	92	63
1675	17	19	23	107	60
1677	17	18	22	118	71
1682	16	17	20	143	96
1708	15	16	19	164	117
1748	18	19	22	107	107
1750	15	16	19	164	117
1768	15	16	17	180	133
1784	*	16	17	205–180	158–133
1806		15	16	231–204	117–90
1812		19	20	141–124	119–102
1815		15	16	231–204	121–93
1817		14.5	15	254–224	126–96

The revenue per last is estimated under the following four assumptions:

1. One-third of the grain is devoted to each of the three bread types.
2. The total output of fine white bread is set at 1,574 kg per last, which Kampen established
   as the expected bread yield in 1600. The total output of coarse bread is set at 2,300 kg per
   last, which was the average yield in many cities. In the absence of direct information, the
   fine wheat bread yield is assumed to be the average of the other two, or 1,937 kg per last.
3. The cost of a last of wheat, 210.60 guilders, is subtracted from the total revenue
   generated by the sale of the three bread types.
4. The provincial milling excise levied in Kampen began at 12 guilders in 1603; rose to 24
   guilders from 1624, and further to 36 guilders in 1675. It remained at that level until
   the provincial excises were replaced by a national levy in 1806, which was 108 guilders
   per last of wheat until lowered to 60 guilders in 1815.

In addition, the city levied a municipal surcharge. From 1675 this was 11 guilders. Before
then, the level is not known, but is assumed here to have been 5 guilders.

Bold: Periods in which the milling excise was temporarily abolished.

* In 1784 Kampen's bread price/weight registers cease listing weights for fine white
bread. From then on only the weights of the two remaining wheat breads are recorded.
Consequently, the revenue estimates from 1784 onward are based on the assumption that
the two remaining bread types were produced in equal amounts.

It is probable that the quality of the two remaining wheat breads was altered, affecting
the total bread yield. Total revenue is estimated under two assumptions: that the overall
bread yield remained as before, and that the bread yield of the two remaining bread types
remained as before. Under the latter assumption, total revenue will have fallen somewhat.
Source: G.A. Kampen, Oud Archief, no. 2207, *broodzetting* registers, 1661–1821.

in order to pay the increased milling excises (the provincial excise rose from 12 guilders per last in 1606 to 36 guilders in 1675). Thereafter, the continued erosion of loaf weights served to increase the bakers' revenues. What were the commissioners seeking to achieve? In a town where rye dominated the diet and wheat bread was consumed primarily by a well-off minority, they may have had less hesitation to burden the wheat breads with more of the bakers' general overhead costs. The revenue raised in this way had its limits, but if Kampen's wheat bread consumers were truly confirmed in their preferences, the commissioners seemed intent on pressing them all the way to the limit.

"Soaking the rich" was certainly not the only motive for adjusting the wheat bread price differentials. They also needed adjustment in order to manage consumer demand for the various types of wheat bread. To a large extent, the bread types were the joint outputs of a single production process. The bolting of grain yielded fine and middle-grade flours, a coarse residual flour, middlings or shorts (*kortmeel*) plus bran. The bakers were obligated to sell the bran, and they used the fine and middle-grade flours for fine white bread and middle-grade wheat bread, respectively. The coarsest material posed a challenge for both the bakers and regulators. Mixed with a better grain, it produced edible bread, but to the commissioners this practice stood on a fine line between adulteration and honest baking.

Bakers commonly used their coarsest wheat flour to prepare *mestulijn*. This was a wheat–rye mixture in Holland, but (unlike in the eastern regions) it was always treated as a type of wheat bread. The regulators viewed it with distaste, suspecting the bakers of dumping their worst wheat flour, even waste materials that should have been discarded, with the rye. Leiden approved its production in the new ordinance of 1596, which stated that "the bakers may bake a third type of bread [i.e., a mixed rye–wheat bread, or *mestulijn*] in which they may mix their *kortmeel*, shaping it in the fashion of wheat rolls."[12] Haarlem tolerated *mestulijn* until 1643, when the magistrates forbade its further production. However, within months, after listening to the entreaties of the bakers' guild, the magistrates agreed to establish (actually, revive) a type of bread named *achterlingen*. This would be prepared from the coarsest wheat flour, "in order to accommodate the bakers and the poor inhabitants," but could only be baked in elongated double loaves, "so that the consumers will not mistake it for proper wheat bread." They went on to specify that it would be sold at a fixed price, with the weight varying, at a suitable differential to the other wheat bread loaves.[13]

---

[12] G.A. Leiden, Stadsarchief, 1574–1816, Secretariearchief, no. 2536, Registers van de broodzetting; 1596 ordonnantie.
[13] G.A. Haarlem, Stadsarchief 1581–1795, R 412.

One important task of the bread price commissioners, thus, was setting the relative prices of the various grades of wheat bread in a way consistent with the supply of these breads relative to the demand. Bakers could alter the mix of their breads, of course, and the fineness of the flour supplied by the millers also played a role in this matter. But with every shift of the mix there was a trade-off: more luxury bread implied a lower overall bread yield and higher bread prices; it also implied that the coarsest wheat bread would become coarser still. Thus, we cannot assume that the bread types, whose names remained remarkably stable over the centuries, always represented breads of a constant quality.[14]

Beginning in the 1670s a "middle-class" wheat bread – sufficiently white and light, but with a higher bread yield than the finest white bread (*witbrood*) – gained favor, known as French bread (*Franschbrood*) or light/fluffy bread (*luchtigbrood*). The bread price commissioners assigned it a price roughly in the middle of the existing range of prices for the wheat breads. But in many cities its relative price was adjusted significantly over time and in some it came to replace the most costly white bread altogether.[15]

The records of the bread price commissioners rarely provide much insight into the quantitative side of these adjustments, even though they are alluded to in many of the baking trials. Happily, Amsterdam and Haarlem's baking trials form an exception to this rule, since they specify the amounts of three grades of bolted wheat bread produced as the joint output of a last of grain. Table 9.4 shows the results of trials held over the period 1593–1843. For each trial, the total amount of bread produced per last of wheat is noted, in kilograms, as well as the distribution of this bread among the three grades of bolted wheat bread: fine, middle, and *achterling*, the coarsest grade. Demand for a fine, white loaf appears to have risen, causing bakers to reformulate their methods so as to produce

[14] The juggling of quality and price differentials was also a preoccupation of the English magistrates charged with the administration of the assize of bread. In 1757 an Act of Parliament ordered that the finest white breads cease to be produced (with minor exceptions), that the middle-grade "wheaten" bread be improved in quality, and that the lowest grade, "household" bread, also be improved in quality and sold at a 25 percent discount to the price for wheaten bread so as to encourage its consumption. Indeed, the new price structure implied some cross-subsidization of household bread by the purchasers of wheaten bread. These measures failed to bend consumer preferences to the will of Parliament, which hoped that a shift toward coarser breads would economize on grain. In London the price incentive was inadequate to induce consumption of household bread, while in the provinces, the increased cost of wheaten bread provoked riots. Petersen, *Bread*, pp. 102–03.

[15] Kampen: in 1784 *fijn witte* was abolished. From then on *fijn tarwe*, the middle grade of bolted wheat bread, which came to be called *Fransche tarwe*, was the costliest bread. Utrecht: in 1747 *wegge*, the finest white bread, was abolished. *Franschbrood*, which had been introduced in 1674 (during the French army's occupation) as a bread quality between *wegge* and bolted wheat bread, increased in price in 1736, and became the costliest bread in 1747. Dordrecht: in 1750, *luchtbrood* was introduced, which became the costliest bread in 1768. In 1799 *Franschbrood* was introduced to assume that position.

Table 9.4 *Wheat bread yields and the relative weight of types of wheat bread production, according to the baking trials of Haarlem and Amsterdam, 1593–1843*

Year	City	Total bread output per last, in kg	Percentage of each bread type		
			fine white	middle	lowest
1593	Haarlem	2,339 kg	49.2	31.9	18.9
1609	Haarlem	2,207	78.2	10.6	11.2
1618	Haarlem	2,270	86.6	–	13.4
1659	Haarlem	2,150	83.2	–	16.8
1676	Haarlem	2,269	55.5	27.7	16.8
1733	A'dam	2,266	69.2	–	30.8
1782	A'dam	2,169	74.6	–	25.4
1789	A'dam	1,930	88.4	–	11.6
1826	Haarlem	2,310	69.5	–	30.5
1843	Haarlem	2,370	82.4	–	17.7
		Unbolted wheat bread			
1636	Haarlem	2,816			
1789	A'dam	2,934			
1843	Haarlem	3,105			

Sources: G. A. Haarlem, Archief der stad Haarlem II, no. 1930a (189); III, no. 2068, Broodbakkersgilde. Stukken betreffende de broodzettingen, 1593–1676; G. A. Amsterdam, Arch. 5028, Archief van de Burgemeesters, no 603; Arch. 5243, no. 3.

a larger amount of sufficiently white bread and, of necessity, a small amount of coarse wheat bread.

From 1676 the mix appears to shift back a bit toward the cheaper wheat breads. But perhaps one should not attempt to read too much into these baking trials; they do not show what bakers actually produced, but only what the commissioners were prepared to accept as the basis for setting prices. And what they accepted was that bolted wheat would be transformed primarily – from 66 to 88 percent – into fine white bread. Correspondingly, they accepted that a last of wheat, when bolted, would yield no more than 2000–2200 kg of bread in total.

But even if the bakers did devote 66 to 88 percent of their bolted wheat to the production of fine white bread this would not describe the *total* demand for wheat bread. Unbolted wheat bread was not part of the joint production process of the bolted breads. Unfortunately, I have found only scattered evidence that can shed light on the relative market shares of bolted and unbolted wheat breads. A 1668 Haarlem report to the *burgemeesters* estimated that the weekly output of the city's bakers required 400 sacks of bolted and 200 of unbolted wheat flour (plus 800 sacks of rye).[16]

[16] G. A. Haarlem, Stadsarchief, II, no. 1926 (R 412), Memoriën en rapporten, 1644–1795. Memorie van de brootsetting, 29 October 1668.

Table 9.5 *Sketch of bread types consumed in Haarlem, 1659–1668*

Bread type	Weekly production (kg)	Percentage of total	Price stuivers per kg	Index	Weekly revenue gld	Percentage of total revenue
Rye bread	63,158	62.2	1.47	100	4,642.11	43.2
Achterling	3,802	3.7	1.90	129	361.20	3.4
Unbolted wheat bread	15,790	15.5	2.68	182	2,115.86	19.7
Bolted wheat bread	0	0	3.53	240	0	0
White bread	18,830	18.5	3.85	262	3,624.78	33.7
Total	101,580	100.0	2.12	144	10,743.95	100.0

Source: G.A. Haarlem, Stadsarchief, II, 1926 (R 412), Memoriën en rapporten, 1644–1795.

This may have been a rough estimate, but if we refer to Haarlem's 1659 baking trial summarized in Table 9.4, it can give us some insight into the sensitive role bread pricing played in the behavior of consumers. Table 9.5 summarizes the amount of each type of bread produced by Haarlem's bakers per week, based on the number of sacks of grain processed in 1668, the proportions of the types of bolted bread produced in the baking trial of 1659, and the yield rates for each type of grain established earlier for the Netherlands as a whole. The prices for each bread type, expressed in stuivers per kg, are found in Haarlem *broodzetting* records, from which one can readily calculate the total revenue generated by the sale of each bread type in the city. Overall, the finest white bread accounted for half of total wheat bread consumption, although less than a fifth of the bread consumption of all types. The baking trials implied that the middle grade of wheat bread was not produced at all. This may seem unlikely, but the commissioners priced this bread only slightly below the finest bread. Perhaps this differential was not large enough to attract much custom. If the 1668 report is to be believed, Haarlemmers then still relied on rye bread for the bulk of their diet. Unbolted wheat bread would have been the chief alternative for most people, but the price differential was sufficiently large to deter them. A few decades later this was no longer the case, since Haarlem's tax records of 1733 show that wheat had replaced rye as the dominant bread grain. Finally, the coarse *achterling* sold for little more than rye bread, but this did not attract much interest, presumably because of its low quality.

Historians of living standards customarily focus their attention exclusively on the price of the cheapest foodstuffs under the assumption that most early modern people struggled to secure a basic diet, but the interplay of quality and price appears to have been important to Republican consumers, and not only to elite consumers. We have just seen that in 1668 Haarlem's residents, in the aggregate, spent at least 44 percent more on bread than was "necessary" (if they had confined themselves to basic rye bread). Delft's commissioners revealed their sensitivity to the interplay of quality and price in 1640, when they offered a justification for their pricing policy. Delft's wheat bread prices follow the nearby Rotterdam market, they noted, but they saw fit to deviate from Rotterdam's practices in one particular: in Rotterdam the 3-pound loaf of bolted bread sold at a 4-penning premium over the 3-pound loaf of unbolted bread. However, as the Delft commissioners explained, "Our bolted bread of 3 pounds is 8 penningen higher in price than our unbolted bread, so that the bargain price [*door de goede koop*] will cause the unbolted bread to be eaten more than would otherwise be the case."[17]

This sensitivity to consumer preferences appears to have been important even when consumers faced difficult economic conditions. In 1744 Rotterdam's bakers proposed changes in the milling and bolting of wheat bread in order to achieve economies that presumably could be passed on to consumers. This provoked the opposition of Floris van Weersel, the collector of the milling excise [*impostmeester*] for the Rotterdam tax district. He petitioned the *burgemeesters* to reject the proposed changes – which would yield a darker wheat bread – for both fiscal and political reasons. He attributed the growing preference for wheat bread among consumers to the high quality of Rotterdam's bread, and especially its whiteness [*blankheid*]. In his view this preference stood behind a notable rise in milling excise revenue over the previous decades: from 112,000 guilders per year in 1711–12 under his predecessor Kinkenberg, to 160,000 guilders in 1744. A reduction in bread quality and whiteness, he feared, "would bring much dissatisfaction to the impoverished citizenry, which is very attached to white bread, and which because of the high cost of the other foodstuffs now offers them [their only] bit of comfort." Making bread less white, he warned, will not only provoke great dissatisfaction but will also encourage the smuggling into the city of white bread produced elsewhere.[18]

A final clue as to the place of the various wheat breads in the Dutch diet comes from an investigation into Amsterdam's bread consumption in 1850, on the eve of the abolition of the entire structure of bread price regulation. It revealed that the city's residents consumed bolted wheat bread

---

[17] G.A. Delft, Stadsarchief voor 1795, no. 980, Broodzettingsboek.
[18] G.A. Rotterdam, Oud Archief, no. 2124. Van Weersel attributed the pleasing whiteness of Rotterdam's bread to a 1719 regulation requiring the bakers to use only Zeeland wheat, the costliest grade available.

almost exclusively. There was little demand for unbolted wheat bread. Given the price differentials then prevailing, Amsterdammers stuck with rye bread rather than unbolted wheat bread as their cheap, basic bread. But soon thereafter the price controls were abolished along with the milling excise. We will investigate the consequences of all this in Chapter 15 (see, especially, Table 15.13), which will confirm what our scraps of evidence show for the pre-1855 period: consumers viewed rye and unbolted wheat bread as substitutes, while fine bolted wheat bread did not compete directly with either of these breads – it was in a class of its own.

These examples should suffice to demonstrate that bread price commissioners in the Netherlands devoted as much of their attention to the *structure* of bread prices as to their *absolute level*. They were simultaneously involved in adjusting bread prices to the evolution of the grain markets and adjusting them to the evolution of consumer preferences for breads of differing qualities. But, in the latter case, whose interests were they serving?

The Evolving Structure of Bread Prices

In view of the many types of bread and the varying names by which these breads were locally known, a summary of the structure of bread prices and its long-term development calls for a bit of simplification. An adequate accounting can be achieved by focusing on four basic price ratios:

1. **The price of rye bread relative to the cost of rye.** This measures the price of one kilogram of rye bread relative to the cost of one kilogram of rye, assuming a bread yield of 2,100 kg per last of rye.[19] This measure calibrates the remaining three price ratios to the price of grain, revealing the extent to which rye bread is burdened by costs in excess of the requirements of production.
2. **The price of the finest bolted white bread relative to rye bread.** This measures the widest price spread, between the cheapest and costliest bread, pound-per-pound and suggests the overall scope for cross-subsidization.
3. **The price of unbolted wheat bread relative to rye bread.** This measures the premium that consumers must pay to consume the closest substitute for rye bread.

---

[19] A last of rye weighed approximately 2,100 kg and could yield up to 3,000 kg of unbolted rye bread. The standard of 2,100 kg of rye bread is used here much as it was often used in the old system's "pound-per-pound" rule, in order to establish a rough standard for the basic, unavoidable costs of producing rye bread.

4. **The price of the finest bolted white bread relative to unbolted wheat bread.** This measures the extent of the price spread between the cheapest and costliest wheat breads. Everywhere, one or more intermediate quality wheat breads (*fijn tarwe brood, Fransche brood ...*) stood between these wheat bread price extremes. This price spread may reveal cross-subsidization *within* the wheat bread category.

It is my argument that the new system of bread pricing enabled regulators to impose a price structure that differed significantly from what had gone before, what continued to prevail elsewhere in most of Europe into the eighteenth century, and that re-emerged in the Netherlands once bread prices were deregulated after 1855. Interpreting the pattern of relative bread prices in the Netherlands under the new system of price regulation requires some benchmarks for what the price structure would look like under the old system and in a competitive market environment.

One such benchmark relies on "intrinsic," or physical, cost differentials. The analysis of these production costs with which this chapter began supplies the needed information. Based on grain and production costs alone, we found that basic, unbolted, wheat bread would have cost between 25 and 34 percent more than rye bread. We can set the long-run average price difference at 30 percent.

A second benchmark for this cost differential is the price structure that prevailed before the introduction of the new system of price regulation. Direct price evidence is lacking, but our knowledge of old system procedures allows the construction of a simple model of the likely pre-1596 price structure.

Under the old rules of thumb, bread prices were based entirely on variations in grain prices. Since no separate account was taken of the constant costs of production, there was no opportunity for the regulators to shift costs from one bread type to another. Old system bread pricing was based on the assumption that all bread produced over and above the weight of the grain from which it was baked "belonged" to the baker. The bread yield per kilogram of grain was slightly larger for wheat than for rye, but in both cases regulators set this portion at the average weight of each grain. (See Chapter 1 for details.) In the case of bolted wheat bread, this simple rule offered no clear guidance, since a sizeable portion of the grain was discarded in the preparation of white flour. However, old system data for Deventer, Groningen, Brielle, and Antwerp all set the assumed output of fine white bread at approximately 1,400 kg per last, which is about two-thirds of the 2,000 kg commonly observed in later – new system – baking trials. The information summarized in Table 9.6 forms the basis for my estimate of the price structure prevailing under the old system before 1596.

A third benchmark that can guide us is provided by the price ratios prevailing in the Netherlands once the regulation and taxation of bread was ended in the period 1855–65. Thereafter bread markets became more competitive, while new milling and baking technologies only gradually influenced relative prices. We can consider bread prices in the period 1876–1913 as reflecting "free market" conditions, to a first approximation.

Table 9.7 summarizes the three benchmarks. They are reassuringly similar, and justify the conclusions that the "normal" price structure was characterized by an overall price spread of two-to-one between the costliest white bread and the cheapest rye bread, a 30 to 50 percent premium for basic unbolted wheat bread over rye bread, and a rather less certain

Table 9.6 *Estimation of the bread price structure using old system rules*

Assumptions	Price of grain per last	Assumed bread yield per last
Rye bread	100 gld	2,000 kg
Unbolted wheat bread	150 gld	2,200 kg
Fine wheat bread	150 gld	1,400 kg
Estimated price of bread per kg:		
Rye bread	100 gld per last/2000 kg = 0.050 gld = 1.00 st	
Coarse wheat bread	150 gld per last/2200 kg = 0.068 gld = 1.36 st	
Fine white bread	150 gld per last/1400 kg = 0.107 gld = 2.14 st	

Table 9.7 *Three benchmarks for the structure of bread prices*

	1. Rye bread / rye grain	2. White bread / rye bread	3. Coarse wheat bread / rye bread	4. White bread / coarse wheat bread
Cost analysis			1.30	
Old system, pre 1596*	1.00	2.14	1.36	1.57
1876–1913	1.01	1.91	1.50	1.28
Old system price structure, from published price/weight schedules				
	1.	**2.**	**3.**	**4.**
Utrecht, 1374				1.50 – 1.55
Tiel, 1454				1.60
Brielle, 1530	0.91			1.69
Delft, 1591–96				1.39

* Based on Table 9.6.

30 to 65 percent differential between basic wheat bread and fine white bread.

In the light of these benchmarks, the structure of bread prices developed and upheld by Dutch regulators under the new system, revealed in Table 9.8, shows several striking features. The first is one we have already had occasion to discuss: the introduction of the new system allowed – but did not require – the insertion of new costs into the price of a loaf of bread. In the case of rye bread, Table 9.8 shows how Holland and its neighboring provinces added taxes and increased allowances for labor and capital, the bakers' fee, in the course of the seventeenth century. A kilogram of rye bread cost no more than a kilogram of rye grain in 1596–1603, and 15 percent more for the longer period 1596–1619. Thereafter, the relative cost of rye bread rose in every twenty-year period to 1680–99, when it cost some 50 percent more than the grain, a level held until the late eighteenth century, when rising grain prices diluted somewhat the relative weight of the constant costs with which rye bread had by then long been burdened. The ratio of the bread-to-grain price in the eastern Netherlands also began at unity, but in contrast to the west, the ratio rose only slightly above its initial position, reflecting the very different policy objectives of the eastern commissioners.

The price of fine white bread was always well above that of the basic rye loaf. Our benchmarks suggest that the extra costs involved justified a price differential of approximately two-to-one. But everywhere, regulators set the price of the luxury bread far above that level. In seventeenth-century Haarlem and in Delft, to 1660, the ratio stood near 2.5, but elsewhere fine white bread sold at between 2.75 to nearly three times the price of rye bread. Here, too, one sees a distinctive policy in the eastern provinces. The same regulators who kept rye bread prices unburdened by extra costs set fine white bread prices at three times the rye bread price, and raised that even higher in the eighteenth century, to 3.5 times the price of rye bread.

The white bread – rye bread price ratio can be divided into two constituent parts: the price ratio of coarse unbolted wheat bread to rye bread, and the ratio of fine white bread to the coarse wheat bread. The first of these is of particular importance since these two breads were close substitutes for each other. Where the poorest people routinely consumed wheat bread, it is the brown, unbolted wheat bread that they purchased, and we have seen that such bread can be sold for considerably less than the typical 50–60 percent grain price premium of wheat over rye; in Holland the bread premium could have been in the 25–35 percent range. But Table 9.8 shows clearly that Holland's regulators did nothing to encourage consumers to switch from rye bread to wheat bread. They

Table 9.8a *Price structure of bread in the Netherlands, 1596–1854*

1. Rye bread to rye grain price ratio. The price of 1 kg of rye bread relative to the price of 1 kg of rye grain.
2. Fine white bread to rye bread price ratio.
3. Unbolted wheat bread to rye bread price ratio
4. Fine white bread to unbolted wheat bread price ratio

	1	2	3	4
West				
1596–1619	1.152		1.85	
1620–39	1.172	2.45	1.72	1.4
1640–59	1.268	2.56	1.70	1.51
1660–79	1.347	2.82	1.66	1.7
1680–99	1.566	2.80	1.79	1.56
1700–19	1.494	2.65	1.69	1.57
1720–39	1.703	2.83	1.69	1.68
1740–59	1.528	2.87	1.73	1.66
1760–79	1.458	2.88	1.84	1.57
1780–99	1.401	2.85	1.72	1.66
1800–19	1.348	2.58	1.69	1.53
Van Riel database				
1820–39	1.30	2.69	1.51	1.53
1840–55	1.11	2.38	1.53	1.55
1856–69		2.32	1.52	1.52
1870–89		2.08	1.52	1.37
1890–1913		1.48	1.20	1.23
East				
1596–1619	1.008	3.28	1.69	2.00
1620–39	0.995	3.15	1.52	2.07
1640–59	1.035	3.03	1.66	1.84
1660–79	1.094	2.61	1.74	1.51
1680–99	1.159	2.85	2.12	1.35
1700–19	1.072	2.99	2.3	1.29
1720–39	1.172	2.90	2.40	1.21
1740–59	1.037	3.16	2.56	1.24
1760–79	1.028	3.31	2.66	1.25
1780–99	1.003	3.25	2.61	1.24
1800–19	1.001	3.41	2.64	1.30
Van Riel database				
1820–39	1.09	3.74	2.45	1.53
1840–55	1.01	3.24	2.07	1.56
1856–69		2.71	1.78	1.52
1870–89		2.28	1.74	1.31
1890–1913		1.92	1.54	1.25

Table 9.8b *Structure of bread prices in Dutch cities, 1597–1828*

	2. White bread	3. Coarse wheat	4. White bread
	Rye bread	Rye bread	Coarse wheat
Haarlem, 1613–33		1.73	
1634–60	2.40	1.74	1.38
1661–78	2.41	1.75	1.48
1680–1702	2.52	1.84	1.37
1703–49	2.57	1.75	1.47
1750–1800	2.85	1.88	1.51
Leiden, 1648–1702		1.70	
1703–1793		1.76	
1794–1801		1.55	
1820–1828		1.89	
The Hague, 1650–71	2.76	1.66	1.66
1672–89	2.79	1.81	1.55
1690–1768	2.77	1.86	1.48
1769–89	2.91	2.22	1.31
1789–1811	2.78	1.81	1.54
Delft, 1640–59	2.58	1.59	1.62
1660–79	2.71	1.54	1.76
1680–99	2.92	1.74	1.68
1700–19	2.60	1.54	1.69
1720–39	2.77	1.61	1.72
1740–59	2.82	1.68	1.68
1760–79	2.89	1.78	1.62
1780–1800	2.82	1.65	1.71
Rotterdam, 18th century			1.92
Dordrecht, 1710–47*		1.65	
1748–1799*	1.87	1.67	1.12
1800–16*	1.84	1.67	1.10
1800–16	2.56	1.54	1.39
Zaltbommel, 1629–59		1.26	
1660–79		1.27	
1680–1749		1.32	
1750–94		1.43	
Utrecht, 1599–1619	2.98	1.74	1.71
1620–99	2.86	1.55	1.85
1700–40	3.00	1.62	1.85
1740–79**	2.78	1.61	1.73
1780–99**	3.04	1.70	1.79
1800–18**	3.18	1.78	1.79
Zwolle, 1650–1666	3.03	2.38	1.27
1731–1758	3.55	2.85	1.25
1763–1784	3.63	2.72	1.30
1785–1820	3.55	2.55	1.42

Table 9.8b *(cont.)*

	2. White bread	3. Coarse wheat	4. White bread
	Rye bread	Rye bread	Coarse wheat
Deventer, 1594–99	2.79		
1606–61	3.01		
1684–98	3.05	2.44	1.37
1699–1708	3.18	2.02	1.59
1709–1818	3.10	2.17	1.40
Kampen, 1662–76	2.87	1.92	1.50
1677–82	3.05	2.29	1.34
1683–1764	3.19	2.55	1.25
1765–83	3.48	3.01	1.16
1784–1820	3.52	3.18	1.10

* Dordrecht. From 1710 to 1799, the costliest wheat bread is *luchtbrood*. From 1800, *Franschbrood* prices are quoted, which was likely the finest bread available. The periods indicated with * use *luchtbrood* prices for "white bread," but it was actually an intermediate grade of wheat bread.
** Utrecht. From 1740 the costliest wheat bread is *Franschbrood*.

Table 9.8c *Structure of foreign bread prices*

	White / rye bread	Coarse wheat / rye bread	Fine/coarse / rye bread	White / coarse white bread
Copenhagen, 1684–1712	2.14		1.59	
1776–99	2.62		2.18	
Berlin, 18th century		2.40		1.33
Cologne, 1658–1757		2.20		
Mâcon, 1369				1.75
Mâcon, 1692				1.42
Paris – Rouen, 1700–25				1.65*
Bayeux, 18th century				1.40
Caen, 1778				1.17
London, 1757				1.25
Antwerp, 1450–59	2.05	1.37		1.44
Antwerp, 1594–1600	2.00	1.33		1.50

* The price differential between *pain blanc* and *pain bis* is high at low grain prices (1.85) and low at high grain prices (1.43). The ratio shown is for an average grain price.

set prices on coarse wheat bread at least 50 percent above that of rye bread, and more often 70 to 80 percent higher. In the eastern provinces the disincentive to consume coarse wheat bread was stronger still. There seventeenth-century consumers paid at least twice as much for a kilogram of coarse wheat bread as for a kilogram of rye bread, and a century later they paid even more, sometimes three times the rye bread price.

There is one place that stands as a major exception to this pattern. In the small river town of Zaltbommel consumers paid only 26 percent more for coarse wheat bread than for rye bread in 1629–59, and while this premium rose thereafter it was always distinctly below the level in all other locations. Was this small city really unique in charging no more for wheat bread than required by the actual costs of production?[20] In fact it reveals the structure of bread prices characteristic of a larger area that had long relied on wheat for basic consumption needs. Zeeland, a wheat-producing province, was such a region, and while we have no time series of bread prices in Zeeland before the nineteenth century, we do have Eversdijck's baking trial data for the small city of Goes. The trials specified the constant costs assigned to each of five types of bread. When the grain costs are added, we can calculate the bread prices for each of the following ten years, which yield the structure of prices shown in panel (a) of Table 9.9.

Goes, like Holland's towns, already assigned fairly heavy costs to rye bread (column 1). Unlike them – but like Zaltbommel – it set a price for unbolted wheat bread that was only 20 percent above that of rye bread

Table 9.9 *The structure of bread prices in Goes, Zeeland, and North Brabant*
a. Bread prices in the Zeeland town of Goes, 1633–42

	Rye bread / rye grain	Rye bread / white bread	Rye bread / unbolted wheat bread	Unbolted wheat bread / white bread
Goes	1.28	2.45	1.20	2.04

b. Bread prices in Zeeland and North Brabant, 1823–49

Zeeland	1.30	2.14	1.33	1.61
North Brabant	0.98	2.66	1.84	1.45

Source: Eversdijck, *Paste-boeck vanden broode*, pp. 40–41; panel (b) Van Riel database: www.iisg.nl/hpw/data.php#netherlands

[20] Culemborg, another river town, priced its bread much as did nearby Zaltbommel, as shown by its 1658 bread price schedule. G.A. Zaltbommel, no. 20–2079, 20–2080.

(column 3). Consumers of the luxury white bread, on the other hand, faced a steep premium, paying two times the price for unbolted wheat bread (column 4).

The same basic pattern is directly observable two centuries later. Then we can compare the structure of average bread prices for the entire province of Zeeland, a predominantly wheat-eating area, with neighboring North Brabant, which can stand for the larger eastern zone where rye bread remained dominant. In the period 1823–49, wheat sold at an average 40 percent premium to rye in the markets of both provinces. Panel (b) of Table 9.9 shows that Zeeland's price commissioners continued to favor coarse wheat bread (colmn 3), while placing significant cost burdens on rye bread (column 1). In North Brabant the opposite is the case: rye bread was relatively cheap and coarse wheat bread relatively expensive.

The new system of bread price regulation gave the cities and provinces a powerful tool with which to shape the structure of bread prices, and they all made use of that tool, although not all in the same way. The result of the regional policy differences can be examined in some detail in 1826, when the central government began to concern itself with provincial and municipal bread prices and launched an inquiry into local regulatory practices. The surviving returns are partial, but they can be compared with provincial data for the same period – all displayed in Table 9.10 – and they suffice to give some insight into the strategy behind the pattern of regional variation.

The towns and villages all faced very similar grain prices but the 1826 price ratios of the two types of bread varied enormously. At the provincial level, coarse wheat bread was priced at 3.2 times that of rye bread in Groningen and 2.7 times in Overijssel, while in Zeeland the ratio was only 1.2. At the town level, where we are comparing rye bread with the higher-priced *bolted* wheat bread, the ratios range from 4.0 in Kampen and Deventer to 1.7 in Rotterdam and Delft. These large differences were almost entirely the product of policy. By 1826 the various provincial taxes had been replaced by a common national milling excise, but local decisions about how the bakers' fees and municipal taxes, where they existed, should be distributed over the bread grains could still make an enormous difference in the set of relative prices faced by consumers.

The bread price commissioners appear to have used their regulatory authority to advance a public purpose: in assigning the constant costs for wheat and rye they acted to reduce the price of rye bread at the expense of wheat bread. Towns varied in the extent to which they shifted costs in this way and the speed with which they moved in this direction. The IJssel

Table 9.10 *The structure of bread prices in 1826*

	Prov.	Rye bread cents per kg	Bolted wheat bread cents per kg	Wheat/rye ratio
Kampen	OV	5.5	22.5	4.1
Deventer	OV	6.5	26	4.0
Amelo	OV	6	22	3.7
Steenwijk	OV	5.5	20	3.6
Haarlem	NH	8.5	24.5	2.9
Zwolle	OV	6.5	17.97	2.8
Dordrecht	SH	8.42	22.94	2.7
Leiden	SH	9.08	22.81	2.5
Oudewater	SH	8.44	21.17	2.5
Gouda	SH	9.17	22.72	2.5
Schoonhoven	SH	8.26	20.02	2.4
The Hague	SH	9.83	23.56	2.4
Amersfoort	UT	8	18.5	2.3
Alphen a/d Rijn	SH	7.72	17.36	2.2
Woerden	SH	10	20.84	2.1
Utrecht	UT	9	18.5	2.1
Zegwaard	SH	8.33	16.84	2.0
Montfoort	SH	7.9	15	1.9
Rotterdam	SH	8.87	15.73	1.8
Delft	SH	9.2	15.5	1.7
Mean		8.036	20.22	2.5

The structure of provincial average bread prices, 1824–29

Province	Rye bread cents per kg.	Coarse wheat bread cents per kg	Wheat/rye ratio
Groningen	7.3	23.5	3.2
Overijssel	7.24	19.7	2.7
North Brabant	6.56	14.9	2.3
Utrecht	8.38	17.3	2.1
South Holland	9.13	15.9	1.7
North Holland	8.58	14.5	1.7
Gelderland	7.75	11.8	1.5
Zeeland	9.51	11.8	1.2
Weighted avg.	8.1	16.3	2.0
Unweighted avg.	8.06	16.18	2.1

Source: A.R.A. The Hague, Tweede afdeling, Binnenlandse Zaken, Binnenlands Bestuur, no. 1366. Provincial data: Van Riel database: www.iisg.nl/hpw/data.php#netherlands

towns (Kampen, Zwolle, Deventer), where wheat bread always remained a luxury food, supported a large differential, one that grew over time. They kept the bakers' fees for rye bread low, so low that it is hard to see how the bakers could have earned a living from the sale of rye bread. The commissioners sought to compensate the bakers for these unremunerative fee levels by raising the bakers' fee for wheat bread. But Amsterdam, Haarlem, and other towns of Holland also placed very high bakers' fees on wheat bread, triple the level of the fees on rye bread, even though it was – or soon came to be – the dominant bread type consumed by most social classes in these places. In South Holland cities such as Rotterdam and Dordrecht and the towns of Zeeland, the differentials were smaller. Here, wheat bread – coarse, unbolted wheat bread – held the place in the diet for many people that rye held elsewhere, and the case for cross-subsidization as a social policy was less compelling. Yet, even in this region, the bakers' fee for wheat bread was generally double that for rye bread. Nearly everywhere, the regulatory regime defined the non-grain costs attributable to the production of wheat bread in such a way that it cost far more than was required by actual production costs. Dutch consumers endured this imposed structure of bread prices as long as the new system *broodzetting* and milling excises lasted. How did consumers respond to these pricing policies? This question is the focus of Part III.

Part III

Consumer Welfare and Consumer Choice

10   *Crise de Subsistance*: Did Price Regulation Shelter Consumers from Food Crises?

Price Regulation in Times of Crisis

We have established that the regulation of bread prices in the Netherlands was not designed to constrain bread prices when grain prices rose. Its technical superiority corrected the tendency of old system regulations to set inflated bread prices in periods of high grain prices, and, as we have just seen in Chapter 9, the new system also allowed regulators to pursue cross-subsidization policies. But these were structural features of the new system; they were not instruments of intervention in times of crisis.

These facts have not prevented most historians from simply assuming as self-evident that the regulatory regimes actually did what those who controlled them claimed was the chief intention: to protect the poor in times of distress and famine, to stand as a bulwark against pre-industrial Europe's recurring *crise de subsistance*.[1] When the actual price evidence contradicted this ingrained assumption, most scholars let their beliefs override the evidence. N. W. Posthumus revealed this habit of mind in his monumental study of the Leiden textile industry. In that work he published the first, and until now the only, time series of Dutch rye bread prices. His pioneering work was the starting point for this study – as was his account of the purpose and animating spirit of regulation. He began his analysis of Leiden's rye bread prices from 1596 through 1620 with the observation that bread prices rose less rapidly than grain prices. He

---

[1] The "subsistence crisis" as a chronic condition of pre-industrial life was anatomized in a series of influential "Annales school" studies. See Jean Meuvret, "Les crises de subsistance et la démographie de la France d'Ancien Régime," *Population* 1 (1946), 643–50; Pierre Goubert, *Louis XIV et vingt millions de Français* (Paris: Fayard, 1966); François Lebrun, "Les crises démographiques en France aux XVIIe et XVIIIe siècles," *Annales. Économies, sociétés, civilisations* 35 (1980), 205–34. See also Wilhelm Abel, *Massenarmut und Hungerkrisen im vorindustriellen Europa: Versuch einer Synopsis* (Hamburg and Berlin: Parey Velag, 1974). For critiques see Jacques Dupâquier, "Demographic crises and subsistence crises in France, 1650–1725," and David Weir, "Markets and mortality in France, 1600–1789," both in John Walter and Roger Schofield, eds., *Famine, Disease and the Social Order in Early Modern Society* (Cambridge University Press, 1989), pp. 189–200, 201–34.

acknowledged that Leiden's magistrates were guided by price quotations for Prussian rye on the Amsterdam market but he felt confident to add that they did so "without slavishly following every steep price increase. They sought to achieve some stability in the price in order to prevent bread from becoming too expensive for the poor population."[2] As we have seen, he was mistaken in this: bread prices actually rose in a linear relationship to grain prices, but Posthumus did not pause to investigate the relationship.

He returned to this issue in his third volume. In the section focused on the seventeenth century, which included several episodes of sharply higher grain prices, he observed that bread prices rose and fell more moderately than the underlying grain prices – the amplitude of the bread price time series was smaller – and quickly concluded from this that the vigilance of Leiden's magistrates again had suppressed the usurious pricing that would have prevailed if market actors had been free of regulation. The actual cause of moderation in bread price fluctuations was the increased size of the constant costs embedded in the bread price, especially the increased excise tax, that acted as a "ballast" on bread prices.[3] Indeed, it did not escape Posthumus's notice that bread prices were "higher than what was required by the price of rye."[4] But he did not allow this to raise troubling questions.

Finally, in his account of the eighteenth century, Posthumus completed his analysis of Leiden's regulated bread pricing. Here, too, he was struck by the greater stability of the bread price than the grain price. This "was due in part," he supposed, "to the government's more pronounced determination to maintain a stable price for bread." And again, he noted that this price level seemed higher than required by the cost of grain, but he concluded nonetheless with a ringing endorsement of

---

[2] N. W. Posthumus, *De geschiedenis van de Leidse lakenindustrie*, 3 vols. (The Hague: Martinus Nijhoff, 1908–39), vol. II, pp. 204–06.
[3] This point can be made most simply by comparing the coefficients of variation for grain prices and bread prices in Holland for the same periods:

	Rye grain	Rye bread	Bread/ grain%	Wheat grain	Unbolted wheat bread	Bread/ grain%
1596–1649	25.6	20.6	81	18.6	18.6	100
1650–99	34.0	24.1	71	28.1	15.8	56
1700–49	24.7	14.6	59	27.4	13.4	49
1750–99	25.6	18.9	74	24.7	14.6	59
1800–54	31.8	21.8	69	26.8	14.9	56

[4] *Ibid.*, vol. III, p. 1004.

Leiden's regulatory policy: "with this [policy] the price of this essential foodstuff did not rise excessively for most of the century and speculation was prevented from gaining control of it."[5] In short, high prices – relatively stable though they might have been – did not prevent him from supposing that the bread price commissioners had somehow protected the consumer from a greater evil.[6] Absent the magistrates' steady hand and steely eye, speculators and usurers surely would have driven bread prices even higher.

This study has gone to some lengths to demonstrate that the rules guiding Europe's bread price regulators – whether under the old or the new system – were not designed to soften the effects of rising grain prices on the bread consumer. Indeed, a social policy designed to protect consumers from high prices in times of shortage required not the *operation* of the Dutch *broodzetting* but its *suspension*. In its defense one can certainly say that the ongoing operation of a regulatory system endowed public authorities with both the information and a mechanism to intervene in the bread markets when distress threatened, but this intervention constituted a (temporary) abandonment of normal policy; it was an initiative reserved for the town councils and the *burgemeesters* and was well beyond the ordinary authority of the bread price commissioners.

Thus, the regulatory regime was meant to function in normal times, while it might be suspended or modified in times of crisis. But the definition of "crisis" was far from uniform; in some countries interventions were frequent, even incessant, while in others, among them the Dutch Republic, they were highly exceptional. French towns prepared *tarifs* – price schedules showing the price of bread for every price of grain – just as in the Dutch towns, but the municipal *police* officials charged with administration and enforcement, no less than the royal *intendants* who monitored their work, treated the *tarifs* more as a point of orientation than a definitive guide to pricing.[7]

---

[5] *Ibid.*, vol. III, pp. 1082–83.

[6] The conviction that the *broodzetting* was designed to shelter consumers from sharp upswings in the grain price and "forced bakers," in such periods "to take satisfaction with lower profits" is also expressed in a major recent study of the social safety net in the Netherlands. Moreover, the author bases this conviction on the same type of evidence as invoked by Posthumus: in crisis periods bread prices rose by a smaller percentage than did grain prices. Marco van Leeuwen, *De rijke Republiek, 1500–1800*, vol. I, pp. 189, 207, and Marco van Leeuwen, *De eenheidsstaat, 1800–1890*, vol. II, p. 225, in Jacques van Gerweren and Marco van Leeuwen, *Zoeken naar zekerheid: risicos, preventive verzekering en andere zekerheids regelingen in Nederland, 1500–2000* (The Hague and Amsterdam: NEHA, 2000).

[7] The French official mind long continued to reflect this position, as revealed by the prefect of the Seine-Inférieure in 1812: "It is important for the prosperity of the state and for public tranquility that the government become the supreme regulator of prices." Miller, *Mastering the Market*, pp. 39, 94–95.

Periods of High Bread Prices Anatomized

The issue of periodic food scarcity and its consequences has been studied many times in the past, although less thoroughly in the Netherlands than elsewhere in early modern Europe because of a general consensus that grain shortages were less severe and less frequent, at least in the time of the Dutch Republic, than in other European countries.[8] These studies have focused almost exclusively on the prices of grain rather than bread. Since most Dutch consumers, and nearly all urban consumers, purchased bread rather than grain this simplification prevents us from examining the impact of the *broodzetting* on their economic circumstances. Another weakness of many earlier studies is their reliance on annual grain prices and, often, on price and wage data for even longer periods, such as five-year averages. While this is perfectly suitable for the study of trends and multi-year cycles, it is not ideal for our present concern; we want to know the prices actually faced by consumers in the course of an episode of scarcity.

Here we will examine Dutch crisis periods on the basis of monthly average bread prices in two regions: Holland (standing for the maritime region) and the inland provinces (with data drawn primarily from Overijssel, Gelderland, and Groningen). For each of these regions – west and east – I have assembled annual wage data for both unskilled labor (mainly construction and dike- and canal-maintenance workers) and skilled construction labor (journeyman construction workers). By constructing a consistent measure of purchasing power, we can identify the exposure to periods of scarcity in the western relative to the eastern provinces, and among unskilled relative to skilled workers.

I extend the estimation of monthly bread purchasing power back to 1550 by estimating bread prices from monthly average rye prices as recorded in the Utrecht market. Before 1596 bread prices are estimated following "old system" rules, as described in Chapter 3. This procedure generates a single set of bread prices that must be applied to both Holland and the east, which may slightly overstate bread prices in the east. The pre-1596 data are less precise than those thereafter, but will serve to illustrate general patterns.

[8] J. A. Faber, "Dure tijden en hongersnoden in preïndustriëel Nederland," (University of Amsterdam, 1976); P. C. Jansen, "Armoede in Amsterdam aan het eind van de achttiende eeuw," *Tijdschrift voor geschiedenis* 88 (1975), pp. 613–25; Noordegraaf, "Levensstandaard," pp. 72–96.

Later, in Chapter 13, the investigation will be expanded to include the full range of food purchases and allow for changes in diet over the course of time in order to achieve a fuller understanding of the standard of living. Here interest is focused on access to basic bread. I measure that access in Tables 10.1 and 10.2 with a simple calculation of bread

Table 10.1 *Crisis periods in Holland, 1550–1844*
The percentage of an unskilled laborer's income required to purchase 2.2 kg. of rye bread per day in the costliest month of the period (col. 2), the number of months in which the purchase of 2.2 kg required at least 50 percent (col. 3) and 45–49 percent (col. 4), and the total duration, in months, of the crisis period (col. 5). Columns 6, 7, and 8 show the months of elevated bread prices for journeymen building craftsmen.
    Periods of prolonged or deep crisis are shown in **bold**. Lesser crises are shown in *italics*. Brief episodes of elevated prices are shown in normal font.

Period	Peak	Unskilled labor			Journeymen		
		50+%	45–49%	Duration	50+%	45–49%	Duration
1551–54	**62.8**	**21**	**8**	**29**			
1555	53.9	1	1	2			
1556–57	**130.5**	**14**	**1**	**15**	**8**	**1**	**9**
1562–63	54.8	5	1	6			
1565–66	**83.8**	**8**	**5**	**13**	**5**	**0**	**5**
1571–75	**99.0**	**41**	**9**	**50**	**26**	**11**	**37**
1576–77	58.2	4	1	5			
1577–78	66.6	3	10	13			
1579–80	53.5	2	5	7			
1587	49.4	0	5	5			
1595–1600	48.5	0	7	7			
1623–25	56.5	2	1	3			
1629–31	**78.5**	**19**	**10**	**29**	**5**	**1**	**6**
1649–51	49.6	0	28	28			
1661–63	*56.1*	*16*	*4*	*20*			
1692–95	46.3	0	2	2			
1697–1700	**64.8**	**15**	**7**	**21**	**0**	**5**	**5**
1708–10	*57.8*	*10*	*4*	*14*			
1740–41	47.2	0	2	2			
1756–58	45.0	0	2	2			
1771–73	*58.7*	*9*	*10*	*19*			
1788–90	47.2	0	7	7			
1794–96	**88.3**	**16**	**11**	**27**	**8**	**3**	**11**
1799–1807	**73.0**	**100**	**4**	**104**	**11**	**30**	**41**
1811–13	**64.3**	**22**	**6**	**28**	**0**	**8**	**8**
1816–18	**62.2**	**12**	**14**	**26**	**0**	**1**	**1**

purchasing power that is based on two assumptions. First, I assume that annual household income consists of 250 days of work at the average

Table 10.2 *Crisis periods in the eastern Netherlands, 1550–1844*
The percentage of an unskilled laborer's income required to purchase 2.2 kg of rye bread per day in the costliest month of the period (col. 2), the number of months in which the purchase of 2.2 kg required at least 50 percent (col. 3) and 45–49 percent (col. 4), and the total duration, in months, of the crisis period (col. 5). Columns 6, 7, and 8 show the months of elevated bread prices for journeymen building craftsmen.Periods of prolonged or deep crisis are shown in bold. Lesser crises are shown in italics. Brief episodes of elevated prices are shown in normal font.

1.	2.	3.	4.	5.	6.	7.	8.
			Unskilled labor			Journeymen	
Period	Peak	50+%	45–49%	Duration	50+%	45–49%	Duration
1550–54	88.5	42	7	49	0	8	8
1555–58	**160.8**	**29**	**2**	**31**	**10**	**2**	**12**
1562–63	65.3	11	6	17			
1565–67	**109.3**	**26**	**6**	**32**	**6**	**1**	**7**
1568–69	60.3	11	9	20			
1570–82	**136.4**	**142**	**12**	**154**	**41**	**8**	**49**
					10	**12**	**22**
1583	50.2	1	3	4			
1586–88	66.5	19	2	21	0	3	3
1588–92	54.2	12	18	30			
1594–99	**64.4**	**35**	**9**	**44**	**1**	**1**	**2**
1608–09	45.3	0	3	3			
1611–13	49.0	0	17	17			
1616–17	48.5	0	13	13			
1622–26	52.8	9	20	29			
1628–32	**79.7**	**29**	**8**	**37**	**6**	**9**	**15**
1649–52	63.0	34	10	44			
1661–63	65.0	17	2	19	9	0	9
1675	46.3	0	7	7			
1693–94	51.9	3	13	16			
1697–1700	**80.1**	**16**	**16**	**32**	**1**	**6**	**7**
1709–10	64.2	10	3	13	0	1	1
1771–72	49.7	0	5	5			
1793–96	**80.3**	**15**	**6**	**21**	**6**	**1**	**7**
1799–1809	**78.0**	**102**	**16**	**118**	**3**	**24**	**27**
1811–13	**72.8**	**23**	**6**	**29**	**0**	**4**	**4**
1815–19	**85.6**	**36**	**9**	**45**	**2**	**5**	**7**

summer wage for unskilled or skilled (adult male) labor.[9] This income must be spread over 365 days of bread consumption.

The second assumption concerns the amount of bread an average household consumed. In Chapter 12 we will examine this issue in detail, and find important changes in the level and composition of bread consumption. Here the purpose is to examine the frequency and intensity of distress caused by high bread prices across the period 1550–1850, and for this purpose it is best to use a single standard to measure the economic accessibility of a basic diet. To this end I make the simplifying assumptions that bread consumption consisted entirely of rye bread and stood at 200 kg per adult per year. Under these assumptions an average household of 4.0 "adult-equivalents" (yet another assumption, which generously estimates the average size of a family, especially in Holland and in urban settings) purchased 803 kg of bread annually, or 2.2 kg per day. This bread allowance suffices to supply 61 percent of a daily intake of 2,100 kcal per adult. This is well above the highest bread consumption levels suggested for the Netherlands, but allows comparison with numerous studies of the standard of living elsewhere in Europe and beyond.[10] In making these assumptions I have sought to err on the side of modesty in estimating household income and generosity in estimating household bread consumption.

I calculate the cost of 2.2 kg of rye bread at its average price, month by month, and compare that to the annual income at the average wage

---

[9] Wage workers in most places earned a summer wage for eight or nine months of the year and were paid less (from 67 to 80 percent of the summer wage) in the shorter days of winter. The potential days of labor per year stood at about 250–260 before the Revolt and the abolition of saints' days that was one of the first acts of the newly empowered Reformed Church. After 1572 the theoretical work year was lengthened to 307 days. Here I make a simplifying assumption of 250 days of summer wages as an approximation of the achievable annual earnings of a wage laborer, and do not adjust this standard for the probable effects of the reformed calendar. For details, see Jan de Vries, "How did pre-industrial labor markets function?" in George Grantham and Mary MacKinnen, eds., *The Evolution of Labour Markets* (London: Routledge, 1994), pp. 39–63; Jan de Vries, "An employer's guide to wages and working conditions in the Netherlands, 1450–1850," in Carol Leonard and Boris Mironov, eds., *Hours of Work and Means of Payment: The Evolution of Conventions in Pre-industrial Europe. Proceedings of the XI International Economic History Congress, Milan, September 1994* (Università Bocconi, 1994), pp. 47–63.

[10] Robert Allen's widely used model for calculating standards of living across countries is based on a "respectability basket" that contained foodstuffs sufficient to supply 2,100 calories. The 2.2 kg per day per household level, which corresponds to about 200 kg per adult per year equivalent, is adopted to be comparable with the international standards developed by Robert Allen, his "respectability basket" and the "barebones basket." These were introduced in Allen, "The great divergence in European wages and prices." The 2.2 kg per day standard also conforms to earlier studies of the standard of living in the Low Countries such as Blockmans and Prevenier, "Armoede in de Nederlanden," and Noordegraaf, "Levensstandaard."

(separately for unskilled and skilled labor), year by year, divided by 365 days.[11] This procedure yields two large tables showing the percentage of workers' earnings needed to secure 2.2 kg of bread per day for every month of every year from 1550 to 1843 – one for Holland and one for the eastern provinces.

Normal years. In the long period 1580–1790 we can set aside 85 percent of the years as "normal." Grain prices, and bread prices, varied in the narrow range of seasonal fluctuations and did not vary in multi-year periods by more than 10 percent. In these periods, which sometimes lasted for decades, an unskilled laborer could acquire 2.2 kg of bread per day with less than one-third (31.3 percent) of the annual income secured by 250 days of labor.

Crisis years. The definition provided here of "normal" times helps us define the abnormal – the crisis periods. The thirty-three "abnormal" years between 1580 and 1790 were spread among thirteen distinct episodes in which bread prices rose above the normal levels prevailing before and after by at least 20 percent. In these years unskilled laborers had to part, on average, with 44.7 percent of their income in order to secure 2.2 kg of bread per day. While the long-term average expenditure in "normal" times (31.3 percent) is useful in describing the accessibility of bread, the use of averages in times of crisis is not: it is in the nature of a crisis that prices rise to a peak, which will be far above the average. What we want to know about these periods is their intensity and duration: *how far* above normal levels did bread prices rise, and *how long* did consumers have to endure these extraordinary burdens?

To address these questions, I have summarized the intensity and duration metrics from the monthly data in Tables 10.1 for Holland, and 10.2 for the eastern provinces. Each identifies the crisis periods, defined as consecutive months in which the purchase of 2.2 kg of rye bread per day required at least 45 percent of the wage laborers' daily income as defined above. Besides the duration of each crisis in months, the table

---

[11] For example, in July 1648, the average price of rye bread in Holland was 1.845 stuivers per kilogram. The average wage for unskilled labor in Holland in 1648 was 17.125 stuivers per day. The daily cost of rye bread: 1.845*2.2 = 4.059 stuivers. The daily household income: 17.125/(250/365) = 11.729 stuivers. Thus, in July 1648 the household of an unskilled laborer needed 4.059/11.729 = 34.6 percent of its income to secure a daily supply of 2.2 kilograms of rye bread.

At the same time in the eastern provinces (based on Deventer weekly prices), rye bread cost 1.392 stuivers per kilogram while the average wage for unskilled labor was 12.167 stuivers per day. Following the same procedure as above: (1.392*2.2) / (12.167 * (250/365)) = 36.7 percent.

also reveals the number of months in which 2.2 kg of rye bread required over 50 percent of daily income, and the percentage of income required in the month of peak severity.

These tables reveal several important features of the threats to the Dutch standard of living over a period of nearly three centuries.

1. **The pre-1580 era of severe and frequent crises.** This analysis was extended back to 1550, well before the introduction of the new system *broodzetting* (and the availability of detailed bread price data) in order to remind us of the very frequent and often severe food crises experienced in the Netherlands in the years leading up to the Dutch Revolt and, of course, during the years of active warfare.[12] In Holland, nearly 40 percent of all months from 1550 to 1579 reached crisis levels by the definition used here, including true famine conditions in 1556–57 and 1565–66 and an extended era of elevated bread prices that stretched throughout the eventful 1570s.

In the eastern provinces matters were far worse. Warfare and occupation continued longer there and eastern wages were then at their lowest level relative to wages in the west. Consequently, rye bread was rarely affordable: in the entire period 1550–79, a daily allowance of 2.2 kg of bread required over 50 percent of an unskilled worker's wage in 64 percent of the months, as it did in 40 percent of the months in the remaining two decades of the sixteenth century. Here, "normal" conditions were, in fact, quite uncommon.

2. **The Republican era of infrequent crises.** By beginning this analysis in 1550, the distinctiveness of daily life during the two-century existence of the Dutch Republic is revealed clearly. After 1580 in the west price spikes and periods of elevated bread prices were certainly not unknown; as we have seen, the rising prices of 1596–97 provoked the reformation of the bread price regulatory system itself. But after 1580 (after 1600 in the east) serious, extended periods of distress were few until the onset of the political and economic crisis into which the nation was plunged – with most of Europe – in 1795. If we define famine as "a

---

[12] Rye bread prices before 1596 are estimated using the method described in Table 3.1. Using Utrecht monthly rye prices from J. A. Sillem, "Tabellen van markt-prijzen van granen te Utrecht, 1393–1644," *Verhandelingen der Koninklijke Akademie van Wetenschappen, Afd. Letteren*, n.s., 3 (Amsterdam, 1901). Rye bread prices are calculated with the formula: rye price in stuivers per last/2,000 kg rye bread = price per kg. The 2,000 kg figure is typical of old system pricing formulas, as discussed in Chapter 9. The pre-1596 estimated bread prices used in this analysis are not region-specific and are somewhat less reliable than the direct observations available thereafter. They may overstate slightly the severity of sixteenth-century food crises in the east.

widespread lack of food leading directly to excess mortality from starvation or hunger-induced illnesses," then only the crisis of 1629–31 had the potential to qualify in the long period 1580 to 1795.[13]

3.   The relative improvement of bread purchasing power in the east. Nominal wages in the eastern provinces were always lower than in Holland and the west, from 25 to 33 percent lower (see Figure 13.3 for details). Yet, as late as 1600, bread prices in the east were little different from those in Holland, causing bread purchasing power to be distinctly lower than in Holland. After 1600 a gap emerged between eastern and western bread prices and grew steadily as both the price and tax policies in the two regions diverged. Unskilled workers in the east continued to face a significantly higher incidence of crisis episodes in most of the seventeenth century. In the 1594–1675 period, one-fifth of all months were crisis months, which were 2.4 times more numerous than in Holland. This experience represented an improvement over the quite desperate conditions of the latter half of the sixteenth century, but it is clear that during the Dutch "golden age" unskilled workers in the eastern provinces remained outside the charmed circle.

The picture brightened markedly by the end of the seventeenth century. Eastern wages remained relatively low, but bread prices did not rise as in Holland, where taxation reached its high point in 1680. Thereafter the eastern crisis months were actually slightly fewer in number than in Holland and in both east and west such episodes were scarce. It is an unexpected finding of this exercise that after 1680 rye bread was financially more accessible to unskilled wage earners in the low-wage east than in the high-wage west. We will examine this puzzling finding in more detail in Chapter 13.

4.   The limited exposure of skilled labor to food crises. Another striking feature of this exercise is the uncovering of a clear social boundary to food insecurity. The wages of journeyman carpenters and masons were higher than those of hod carriers and unskilled construction labor, of course, but Tables 10.1 and 10.2 reveal that the difference was sufficient to shield these skilled workers from distress in all but the most extreme cases. Skilled laborers in Holland faced only eleven months of crisis in the 210-year period 1580–1790, and skilled workers in the east were similarly sheltered. Skilled and unskilled laborers commonly worked side by side, but they faced very different alternatives when bread prices began to climb: the one had to consider unpalatable, if not health-threatening,

---

[13] Cormac Ó Grada, "Making famine history," *Journal of Economic Literature* 45 (2007), 5.

alterations in diet and seek public relief while the other could continue on much as before. When they put down their tools after a day's labor, journeymen and their helpers went home to face sharply different conditions in such times.

5. The return of general food insecurity after 1795. Finally, the crisis of 1795 inaugurated by the fall of the old Republic marks the beginning of a new era in the Dutch standard of living. General price levels had been rising for decades, to be sure, but the combination of war, trade disruption, and heavy taxation that marked the entire "French era" of revolution and Napoleonic rule all but obliterated the distinction I have made thus far between normal and crisis periods of bread accessibility. Four distinguishable periods of crisis accounted for nearly two-thirds of the months between 1794 and 1818 in Holland and three-quarters in the east. In addition, skilled laborers were no longer sheltered from distress in this period. Their higher wages (assuming they were employed) offered some advantage, of course, but bread prices now regularly rose to levels that required them too to adopt austerity measures from which they had been exempted for two centuries. It also compelled many to seek public relief. Yet, in this period of greater need, the available public resources for relief were much diminished. While the populace appears to have been generally quiescent in republican times, this was not always true during the ongoing distress of the early nineteenth century. In June of 1817, at the peak of the severe price rise occasioned by the Tambora volcano-induced harvest failures of the preceding year, food riots occurred in Rotterdam and The Hague, and threats of violence may have been more widespread. For example, on 17 July 1817, at the peak of the price spike, a bread price commissioner from Alkmaar received a crudely lettered note with the following message:[14]

Damnation to you if you do not reduce the bread price and instead let it stand as it is; you can be sure that we will, within two times 24 hours, set fire to your house.

This was the first crisis faced by the centralized government of the new Kingdom of the Netherlands, and while royal decrees and central government financing of relief measures may have promised speedy and

---

[14] "*Slegt en Verdommelen als Gy hed brood niet aflaat slaan En Gy houd de zettings weer in, kan Gy versekert zyn Dat wy binnen den tyd van 2 maal 24 Uren Jou huis in de brand zullen steken.*" R.A. Haarlem, Departementaal Bestuur, no. 461, in a report to the provincial government about the situation in the city of Alkmaar. For unrest more generally, see John D. Post, *The Last Great Subsistence Crisis in the Western World* (Baltimore, Md.: Johns Hopkins University Press, 1977), p. 77.

comprehensive relief, the reality was quite different. No effective replacement yet existed for the town-based initiatives on which the old Republic had relied, with fair success, for over two hundred years.[15] Luckily for the new central government this exercise reveals no further major crises after 1817. But our monthly price data end in 1844, just before the international potato famine of 1845–47 subjected northern Europe to what is often regarded as its last food crisis of the old type.[16]

Appendix A.2 provides details on the crisis periods, showing the monthly course of rye bread prices in each and brief summaries of their causes and impact. But that impact could be mitigated. Town magistrates and provincial authorities could intervene to modify the ordinary workings of the regulatory process. What form did these interventions take?

Mitigation Policies

Lowering Grain Prices

In a period of crisis, or impending crisis, the authorities could intervene in the grain and bread markets in two general ways. The first, and historically most common form of intervention left the bread regulatory regime in place but sought to lower the grain price via distributions from public granaries, prohibitions on grain exports, and the forced release of grain from private stocks. This is how the medieval *annona* regimes of Mediterranean Europe functioned, as well as the grain trade licensing system of the Habsburg Empire. In the Low Countries controls on international trade and orders to release for public sale the holdings of private individuals were much discussed during the periodic grain shortages of the sixteenth century. But, as noted in Chapter 2, both of these policies had significant drawbacks for an economy that depended on imports and private storage for its grain supplies. Interdicts on grain *exports* inevitably discouraged grain *imports*, while public threats to merchants' grain inventories increased the risk of investing in grain and discouraged the international grain trade from using Dutch ports. A commercial people saw more clearly than an aristocratic ruling class the long-run drawbacks of *force majeure* in a society that depended on markets and trade for its prosperity.

Conflict over these trade-destroying practices created an abiding suspicion of Habsburg rule in Holland's port towns. Once the threats of such intervention dissipated, and with the consolidation of Amsterdam as the "granary of Europe," interventions in the grain trade and grain

---

[15] Jessica Dijkman, "Managing food crises," unpublished paper, Utrecht University, pp. 21–30.

[16] For comparative national studies of "the hungry forties," see Eric Vanhaute, Richard Paping, and Cormac Ó Grada, eds., *When the Potato Failed* (Turnhout: Brepols, 2007).

storage quickly shifted from being the first measures considered by public authorities to being a last resort. In the severe crisis of 1595–97 some of Holland's towns forced their most prosperous burghers to release their grain stocks to the market. Alkmaar did this in 1595 and simultaneously prevailed on these same "more or less wealthy" citizens to lay up a supply of grain sufficient for six months of their household's consumption needs.[17] The two directives may appear contradictory to modern readers, but both speak to the common medieval practice of enlisting, under pressure, the cooperation of the wealthy to support the common good of the total urban community. In the food shortage of 1630 Alkmaar again issued similar ordinances. But now they were crafted to affect only a few individuals and, indeed, they proved to be the last of their kind.[18]

Another way in which magistrates intervened in the grain markets was to prohibit the use of grain for a range of "wasteful and unnecessary" purposes, such as brewing strong beer and baking luxury breads and pastries. The aim was to reserve scarce grain for basic nutrition and thereby reduce its price. Thus, as grain prices rose in 1595, Amsterdam's *burgemeesters* forbade the baking of white breads that included luxury ingredients (milk, eggs or butter) "for this is indulgence rather than sober necessity" [*want dat was lekkernije en geen noodruft*]."[19]

The last Dutch example I have found of what had become a rather antique form of crisis management comes from the city of Groningen during the crisis of 1630. On 14 December the *burgemeesters* ordered special measures "because of the great scarcity and expense of bread grain." They went on to observe:[20]

---

[17] Noordegraaf, "Levensstandaard," p. 80. The obligation rested on burghers "of some means" [*"van eenigzins vermogen zijnde"*].

[18] *Ibid.*, p. 82.

[19] Cited in D. J. Coster, *Bijdragen tot de geschiedenis van de keuring der voedingsmiddelen te Amsterdam* (Amsterdam, 1864), p. 47.

[20] G.A. Groningen, Oud Archief, no. 219, Stadsresolutien; Ordonnantie van 14 December 1630. There is later evidence of restriction on "luxury" baking in order to avoid waste, but this seems much more an intervention in cultural practice than a scarcity measure. In 1656 the magistrates of Leeuwarden forbade bakers from preparing special treats for St. Nicholas Eve "for the purpose of suppressing superstition and useless waste." G.A. Leeuwarden, Resolutieboek, 16 September 1656. *"Geen St. Nicolaasgoed te bakken tot wegneeming van superstitie en onnuttige verkwistinge by pene dat de goederen zullen zijn verbeurt."* Yet, much later, in cosmopolitan Amsterdam, the magistrates also found occasion to intervene in St. Nicholas celebrations, this time in order to maintain the peace in a period of scarcity. In the crisis of 1698, which intensified through the final months of that year, an edict of 29 November announced that: "The time is approaching in which it is the custom of Amsterdammers to bake a kind of bread named *deuvekater* as well as other pastries all known as *Sint Nicolaasgoed* which use the finest flour of the wheat meal, such that the coarser parts are mixed into the dough of other breads. Given the current scarcity of grain and its rising price it is most appropriate that [the baking of all such breads be forbidden] and that all bread be baked in the same manner, so that the less well off and the more well off will be equal in this respect." J. G. van Dillen, "De duurte van het jaar 1698," *Onze Eeuw* 17 (1917), 267–68.

At certain times, especially during mid-winter, New Years, Shrove Tuesday, Easter, Pentecost, and such feast days, greater quantities [of wheat] and refined rye are consumed, than are necessary for one's daily maintenance but lead to unnecessary baking, which increases the cost [of grain]. To give relief to the good citizens in a time of costly bread grains, and to abolish unnecessary baking [we order] that no bolted rye or wheat breads may be baked in loaves larger than two pounds.

Lowering Bread Prices

Interventions in local grain markets and private investments became uncommon; by the early seventeenth century they appeared too arbitrary to tolerate, even in times of great social distress. As the grain markets became freer the urban magistrates succeeded in developing the second approach to "crisis management." Instead of intervening in the *grain* markets, the magistrates intervened in the *bread* markets in one or more of four basic ways: by subsidy, by poor relief, by fiat, and by "price smoothing."

Subsidy. The first strategy was to sell publicly purchased grain to the bakers at a below-market price in exchange for their commitment to supply bread at a price below the official *broodzetting*. One can see this as a variant of the very old practice of maintaining public granaries from which supplies are withdrawn in time of distress. In the Dutch case, inventories were largely in private hands and the towns bought their grain from private traders or they commissioned traders to secure grain "in the east" – the Baltic region – on their account.

Already in the fifteenth century, access to an international grain market seems to have encouraged Holland's towns to purchase grain, or commission merchants to purchase on their behalf, for local sale at subsidized rates. Dijkman cites several instances of this in 1437–39. However, she doubts that it had much effect on the grain price level.[21] The very severe crisis of 1556–57 provoked a combination of export controls and international grain purchases, but it may be that only Amsterdam possessed the means materially to affect the terms on which the population secured its bread.

In 1587 Leiden and probably other towns engaged in public grain purchases. On 12 May of that year, in the face of rumors of closure of the Danish Sound and a sharp rise in grain prices, Leiden's magistrates (informed that the supplies via the Sound would soon reappear)

---

[21] Dijkman, *Shaping Medieval Markets*, pp. 297–300.

ordained that the city's bakers could neither stop baking bread altogether nor charge more than 3 stuivers 1 blanc (4 penningen) per 8-pound loaf of rye bread. They could, however, apply to two named regents, who stood ready to supply "city rye" at a below-market price of 51 stuivers per sack.[22] This crisis, based more on rumor than fact, was of short duration, but the scope of the subsidy was broad (all consumers could benefit) and shallow (the price discount was small).

Consider now how the Haarlem town council approached the much more severe crisis of 1630 as it began to take shape. The price of 6-pound loaves of rye bread had ranged between 4.5 and 5.5 stuivers in the 1620s, but rose in 1629–30 to about 6.5 stuivers. When the price rose to 7.75 stuivers by 8 July 1630, the bread price commissioners noted in the margin of their price book the following:[23]

The *burgemeesters* called us to their chambers, instructing us to continue setting bread prices in accordance with the Amsterdam grain market except if they [the *burgemeesters*] decide to distribute [subsidized] rye.

By 4 November, as prices rose further to 9.5 stuivers, double the price that had prevailed in earlier years, the *burgemeesters* took action. They instructed the commissioners "to visit personally all the bakers, and to tell them that from now on they may not bake pure rye bread, but must bake loaves of mixed rye and buckwheat, 50 percent each. The magistrates will supply the bakers with buckwheat at 5 guilders per sack ... " They went on to calculate that such loaves could be sold by the bakers for 8.375 stuivers per loaf instead of the prevailing 9.5 stuiver price for pure rye bread.[24]

Matters only got worse, however, and a week later the *burgemeesters* launched a second subsidy scheme: they told the commissioners to order the lifting of the prohibition on mixing barley with the bread grains, and declared that they would supply barley to the bakers at 5.5 guilders per sack. Bakers now had to choose whether they would continue mixing rye and buckwheat or take up the barley and buckwheat option; they could not do both and the barley–buckwheat loaves had to be branded with a B to protect the consumer from fraud.[25] The price of rye continued to rise until 13 January 1631. By then, the official price of a 6-pound loaf of rye bread stood at a peak value of 10.25 stuivers. Bakers were forbidden

---

[22] G.A. Leiden, Ordonnantie, 12 May 1587.
[23] G.A. Haarlem, Stadsarchief 1581–1795, II 1930a, Broodzettingregisters, 1611–1795 (R412–417)
[24] *Ibid.*, 4 November 1630.
[25] *Ibid.*, 12 November 1630.

from actually producing such bread, however. In its place they could offer subsidized rye–buckwheat bread, at 9.0 stuivers, and barley–buckwheat bread at 7.25 stuivers. By April, when the rye bread price had fallen back to 8.75 stuivers, the commissioners brought the subsidy arrangement to an end; bakers were once again *forbidden* from producing the mixed-grain breads they had so recently been *required* to supply.

The crisis of 1630–31 was severe. Permitting, nay, requiring the "adulteration" of bread with lesser grains violated one of the chief commandments of the regulatory regime, but at least one other city, Alkmaar, also turned to this desperate strategy in 1630. Thereafter the resort to barley and buckwheat mixtures was avoided, as the cities were able to secure sufficient rye and wheat for subsidized distribution to the bakers. The only exception occurred in late 1698, when the expectation that Baltic grain shipments would be long delayed by severe weather raised fears that already high prices would only become higher. Alkmaar then included barley among its purchases of wheat and rye, while in Amsterdam the *burgemeesters* informed the regents of the Almoners' Orphanage that they could avail themselves of grain from whomever they pleased, but that the city stood ready to supply it at 5 to 6 gold guilders below the market price in return for their commitment to bake mixed rye–barley bread.[26] There is no evidence that they imposed the same terms on the public bakers.

Grain purchases by the towns for subsidized distribution to bakers (as in Haarlem in 1630) and to charitable institutions may not always have worked well. Often, the grain arrived after the need had passed. But the towns turned to it several times up to the end of the old Republic – and the end of their financial capacity to conduct such a policy.

Poor relief. The grain-price subsidy strategy lowers the price of all bread and thereby subsidizes all consumers without regard to their economic status. Over time it tended to give way to a more targeted approach. Even before 1630, Leiden, Alkmaar, and Amsterdam acted to distinguish between the respectable community (*goede gemeente*), whose members were expected to pay the going price even in times of crisis, and the poor (*schamele gemeente*) – casual laborers and seamen, unskilled manual laborers, textile workers, hawkers, and petty retailers – who could hope for some reduction from the prevailing bread price when this reached uncommon heights. Amsterdam began this more targeted approach in 1623, when the captains of the civic guard were instructed to identify those necessitous persons in each of the city's wards who

[26] Noordegraaf, "Levensstandaard," pp. 75–76; G.A. Amsterdam, Part. Archief 343, no. 40, correspondence of 31 October 1698, 5 July 1699, and 5 February 1700.

qualified for subsidized bread.[27] By the crisis of 1662, the city had developed a system of *buurtmeesters* (ward captains), who, among their other duties, distributed bread coupons to residents deemed eligible. The city then distributed 50 to 70 lasts of rye every week to the bakers, who sold cheap bread in exchange for the coupons, which they then returned to the city treasury in order to receive restitution.[28]

Fiat. Subsidizing bread prices in times of crisis imposed a heavy financial burden on the cities. The more targeted policy of subsidizing only the bread of the poor reduced the cost but it remained a burden not every city could bear and it became unsustainable by the end of the eighteenth century when crises became more frequent and urban finances more tenuous. So long as bread price regulation existed the magistrates could avail themselves of a third method of lowering the cost of bread, one that cost them nothing: lowering prices by fiat. The existing literature on bread pricing generally assumes that this was a common practice, even an integral feature of the regulatory system. Posthumus, for example, simply assumed that Leiden's price commissioners raised bread prices more slowly when grain prices were rising. By implication, the bakers were forced to absorb their higher costs as a sacrifice to the common good, or perhaps as a deserved punishment for their multiple collective sins – in good times and bad – of adulterating bread, selling underweight loaves, and speculating in grain.[29]

Noordegraaf, who studied price-setting policy in Alkmaar in detail, appears to have assumed that deliberate underpricing in times of crisis was a routine practice. "In times of high prices a self-evident instrument for making the situation of the modest burgher tolerable was to set the price other than in accordance with the price schedule. One could assume

---

[27] The first example I have found of this approach dates from April 1597, when Leiden ordered the city's ward captains to draw up a list of inhabitants eligible for free bread distributions. However, the list was very long, numbering 12,097 individuals or about half the rapidly growing population of that time, and each was to be supplied with six 12-pound loaves per week at no cost. The city calculated that this would require 564 sacks of grain per week, all purchased with public funds, until the crisis passed. This generous and not highly targeted policy may better be classified under the general subsidy strategy. G.A. Leiden, Secretariearchief II, Gerechtsdagboeck, D–E, no. 48–49, 12 April 1597.

[28] Van Dillen, "De duurte van het jaar 1698"; Noordegraaf, "Levensstandaard," pp. 82–83. Alkmaar sold below-market bread to the poor in crisis periods in the seventeenth century, but appears to have left this problem to charitable institutions in the eighteenth. In Amsterdam the *buurtmeesters* were expected to distribute coupons only "after having inquired carefully into the economic distress of applicants [*nae naerstige genomen informatie van ieders nootdruftigheyt*]." Cited in Van Dillen.

[29] Van Schaïk, "Prijs- en levensmiddelenpolitiek," pp. 245–61.

that the government would now set the bread price below its normal relationship to the grain price." But once he had examined the price evidence he had to concede that "This was not the case in Alkmaar."[30] Nor was it generally the case anywhere else in the Dutch Republic. Pricing by fiat did occur, as we will see, but it was rare, brief, and often part of an elaborate arrangement with the bakers designed to compensate them for their losses. Bread price regulation was certainly a politically sensitive matter, but the cities almost always approached it as an economic science rather than a political art.

Consider Haarlem's experience during a run-up of prices in 1661–62. Haarlem normally followed the price trends of nearby Amsterdam, but on 13 May 1662, when prices reached what would be their peak, the *burgemeesters* asked the bread price commissioners – ordered them, in fact – to keep the price of rye bread constant, at 9 stuivers 6 penn., despite a rise in the grain price that normally would have triggered a price increase of 4 penn. This "price freeze" continued until 22 May, when grain prices began to fall and Haarlem's rye bread price again equaled that of Amsterdam. This intervention, as brief as it was modest, is not explained, but market conditions appear to have been highly unusual. On 31 July the commissioners note that "people with ready cash [*met gelt in de handt*] report being unable to secure even one-half last of rye on the market, and a pastry baker said that he has sat for 293 days without being able to buy rye."[31] Rye was physically scarce on the market, yet bread was readily available, suggesting that bakers were producing from inventories presumably purchased at lower prices at an earlier date. Whether for this or other reasons, the *burgemeesters* felt justified in approving another price freeze two weeks later.

But on 5 October the commissioners report on a meeting with the bakers: "[We have listened to] the complaints of the bakers, hearing them out at full length and breadth, and have come to an understanding that the rye bread [price] will follow Amsterdam when the [grain] market rises above the regulated price."[32] That is, the bakers secured a concession from the commissioners to cease these episodes of price suppression.

Memory of this confrontation faded, it seems, for brief episodes are recorded again on 19 October and 28 November 1740 where the city's magistrates again stayed the hand of the bread price commissioners. It is possible, however, that these were not arbitrary actions, but should be

[30] Noordegraaf, "Levensstandaard," p. 83.
[31] G.A. Haarlem, Stadsarchief 1581–1795, II 1930a, Broodzettingregisters, 1611–1795 (R412–417), 31 July 1662.
[32] *Ibid.*, 5 October 1662.

grouped with the several interventions that we might call "self-financed" subsidies of the bread price.

Self-financing. On 8 March 1699, as the rye loaf reached 11 stuivers, Haarlem's *burgemeesters* offered to sell rye to the bakers at 250 gold guilders per last (the market rate was then 260–275) in return for their agreement to lower the loaf price to 10.5 stuivers. This was a public subsidization of bread of the traditional type discussed earlier.[33] But it did not last long, for later in the year, on 28 September, a marginal note in the *broodzetting* account book reveals that the magistrates had shifted the burden of subsidizing rye bread from the city treasury to the population of *wheat bread consumers*. On that date the bakers were allowed to raise the price of wheat bread by 8 penningen per loaf, and to persist in this for six weeks, as compensation for having been forced to charge 8 penningen too little for rye bread over the preceding three months. This was repeated a year later, since the commissioners note the absence of a price increase on 10 January 1701 with this explanation: "no change in price, consistent with our agreement with the bakers concerning the arrears [owed them] for the rye bread, for which the wheat bread price will be one *duit* above the Rotterdam price for five successive weeks." Then, in an *aide mémoire* to themselves, the commissioners add: " Make note here when the arrears are completed."[34]

On 14 July 1709, in the midst of another period of very high prices, the commissioners again held the price of 6-pound rye bread loaves 4 penningen under the level indicated by the grain price. The bakers were offered no immediate compensation, but were given the promise that when grain prices began to fall, they would be allowed to continue charging higher prices (this time, for the same type of bread), until they had recouped the losses incurred at the peak of the crisis.

This strategy of "price-smoothing" via intertemporal transfers between bakers and consumers did not work as smoothly as the commissioners had hoped. Arguments arose with the bakers over just how long they should enjoy the compensatory prices in order to be made whole. The commissioners once again had to hear the bakers out ("in length and in breadth") and, after extending the period of compensatory prices, wrote on 2 October 1711, not without a note of exasperation: "At this time all the arrears due to the bakers definitely have been satisfied, so that there can be no further pretense [to claims for additional compensation]."[35]

[33] *Ibid.*, 13 March 1699.
[34] *Ibid.*, 10 January 1701.
[35] *Ibid.*, 2 October 1711.

A final example comes from 1787, the year of the aborted Patriot Revolution. Bread prices were not unusually high, but after what otherwise would have been a routine price adjustment to a rise in grain prices on 17 November, the Dordrecht commissioners noted the following:[36]

It is resolved … to raise the rye bread price by 4 penningen [the grain price had risen by an amount warranting an 8 penning increase] per 4 pound loaf since a larger increase in this period of unrest strikes the Gentlemen Commissioners as dangerous … but we also wish to state here our intention not to proceed immediately to a lowering of the price when the grain price falls, but to give consideration to damage now being suffered by the bakers.

This should suffice to demonstrate that the task of setting the official bread price was not taken lightly. The commissioners followed with care the price schedules established by their baking trials and investigations of relevant grain prices; they were expected to listen to the bakers and their guild leaders when disputes arose and to come to a common resolution. Only the *burgemeesters* could unilaterally suspend the *broodzetting*, and this they did very rarely.

Public subsidy of grain prices, targeted relief of the poor, and self-financed price smoothing were the three techniques used by Dutch authorities to intervene in the normal operation of bread price regulation. The first became less common over time, while the second and third came to be the main antidote to crisis-level prices.

What are we to conclude from all this? While it will require similar analyses for other countries to be certain, it does seem likely that in the Netherlands the threat of bread being too expensive for employed workers was a problem usually confined to the unskilled. It was a circumscribed problem, and even then the crisis periods were relatively infrequent in the western Netherlands after 1580 and in the eastern Netherlands after the 1660s. Therefore, the bread price commissioners could not have seen their task *primarily* as the protection of consumers from bread price fluctuations.[37] Indeed, to the extent that the regulatory procedures established in the 1590s made high taxes on bread administratively possible (as I argued in Chapter 3), the *broodzetting* was part of the problem more than it was part of the solution, since it brought elevated bread prices in good times and bad.

---

[36] G.A. Dordrecht, Stadsarchief, Bataafse Tijd, no. 387.

[37] Contrast this with the French approach to bread price regulation. Only in 1816 did Parisian regulators concede that it was their task "to accustom the Parisian population to accepting the idea that the price of bread would float up and down with that of commercial wheat and flour," while subsidizing only the bread of the poor. Miller, *Mastering the Market*, pp. 241–45.

How big a problem was the milling excise? Thanks to the systematic character of new system price regulation it is possible to recalculate every bread price without the provincial tax and then to re-estimate the share of earnings needed to purchase 2.2 kg of rye bread per day. With that information in hand we can recalculate the length and severity of crisis periods presented in Table 10.1.

Table 10.3 shows the results of this "counterfactual" exercise. The milling excise had no substantial impact until after 1605, yet for the period

Table 10.3 *The effect of the milling excise on crisis-level bread prices*
Number of months in which the cost of 2.2 kg of rye bread, *excluding the provincial tax*, required 45–49 percent and at least 50 percent of the daily earnings of an unskilled laborer in Holland.

	Percentage of wage in peak month	Months requiring		Total duration in months
		50%+	45–49%	
1595–1600*	47.3	0	4	4
1623–25	53.3	2	0	2
1629–31	**75.3**	**13**	**12**	**25**
1649–51	45.3	0	4	4
1661–63	*51.9*	*2*	*14*	*16*
1692–95	36.3	0	16	16
1697–1700	**57.8**	**8**	**3**	**11**
1708–10	*51.0*	*4*	*6*	*10*
1740–41	40.3	0	0	0
1756–58	39.6	0	0	0
1771–73	*52.9*	*5*	*3*	*8*
1788–90	41.6	0	0	0
1794–96	**77.7**	**12**	**4**	**16**
1799–1807	**67.2**	**87**	**13**	**100**
1811–13	**64.2**	**21**	**6**	**27**
1816–18	**61.3**	**10**	**5**	**15**

Summary	+50%	45–49%	Total duration period in months	% of total
With provincial milling excise (from Table 10.1)				
1580–1675	38	51	89	8%
1676–1790	34	33	67	5
1791–1818	150	35	185	62
Without provincial milling excise				
1580–1675	17	34	51	4%
1676–1790	17	11	28	2
1791–1818	130	28	158	53

The provincial excise is usually expressed in guilders per last. I estimate the excise per kilogram of rye bread by dividing the excise per last by 2,900 kg, nearly the maximum amount of bread that could be produced from a last of rye. Thus these are minimum estimates.

1580–1675 it added sufficient cost to rye bread to increase the number of crisis months by 75 percent. From 1676 to 1790, when taxes reach their high point, they more than doubled the number of crisis months over what they would have been in the absence of the tax. Throughout these two centuries food crises were infrequent, but the excise clearly made them substantially more frequent and more severe than they needed to be. Moreover, were we to perform this exercise for wheat bread – which was taxed at double the rate of rye bread – the measured impact would be greater still.

After 1790, when bread prices are at almost permanent crisis levels, removing the heavy excise from Holland's rye bread prices (which was actually done in 1812–13 and 1817–21) reduces the number of crisis months by only 15 percent. In the period 1790–1818 the milling excise is no longer the culprit, or, rather, the most culpable of the culprits; now it is the chronically high grain prices doing most of the damage. Still, many readers familiar with the long European history of popular protest and rebellion focused on food supply and bread prices will wonder how the Dutch system of price regulation and taxation escaped the wrath of the people. How did this policy survive politically?

Bread and the State: Fear, Violence, and State Building

The act of setting bread prices had more than a purely economic meaning; it also conveyed moral and political signals. Even when the bread price commissioners did nothing but ratify a market outcome, their visible oversight of the market conferred – and was intended to confer – legitimacy to the political authority they represented.

Building State Capacity

It is a commonplace of the theory of state formation in pre-industrial Europe that the most important mechanism for developing public authority and state legitimacy, after maintaining and financing an effective military power, was cultivating the capacity to guarantee the material sustenance of the population. If military might defined the external power of the developing European state, the capacity to protect society from famine and severe economic shocks defined its internal, or domestic power.

But, if the problem was everywhere the same, the policies and institutions developed to address it were not. States faced varied constraints on their actions, both by their objective economic situations and by the nature of their relationships to the social classes of their polities. Charles

Tilly's influential work on European state building began by asking "What difference did the manner and extent of [state] intervention [in the control and distribution of food] make to the subsequent political experiences of the states involved?"[38]

The review of European grain and bread price controls in Chapter 1 gives an impression of the variety of policies pursued by European states, including invasive controls over grain marketing and arbitrary interventions in bread pricing. But it also documented a discernable convergence on bread price regulation as the first line of defense against events that could destabilize society and delegitimize the state.

The Low Countries participated in this broader European development. But the newly independent Dutch Republic took steps, unprecedented in the Europe of its time, to secure a very nearly complete free trade in grain. In this, it relinquished a tool, however dysfunctional in practice, which all other states continued to regard as essential to their domestic state building aims. However, the Republic's retreat was a strategic one. At nearly the same time that it denied itself authority over the grain markets, relinquishing a symbolic tool of paternal regulation, it acted to control the bread markets as never before. The long-established *broodzetting* was transformed in the 1590s into a sophisticated apparatus to set not only maximum prices but minimum prices, to define the allowable bread types, to establish cross-subsidies between those bread types and thereby impose price differentials between them that differed significantly from those that might emerge from market forces. Finally, the authorities used their new price-regulating apparatus to tax bread, lightly at first, but more heavily over time, so that it became one of the primary pillars of state revenue. In short, Dutch bread price regulation became a powerful instrument of public policy, affecting the structures of the milling and baking sectors, the fiscal health of the state, and the wellbeing of consumers.

One might think that such an invasive policy instrument must be the product of a "strong" and centralized state, one capable of imposing its will and withstanding the protests of a population exposed simultaneously to the vagaries of free grain markets and the fiscal and pricing policies of the *broodzetting*. But, of course, the structure of the Dutch Republic was confederal. It was decentralized at the Republic's founding and none of its successes in building military power, developing fiscal potency, or in achieving domestic food security led to the sort of centralizing "state building" that Tilly and other chroniclers of the European nation state had in mind.

---

[38] Tilly, "Food supply and public order in modern Europe," p. 392.

A strong bread price policy was carried out by an institutionally weak state. Indeed, the ultimate responsibility for food supply, prices, and the welfare of the population was usually in the hands of urban magistrates. Only in the nineteenth century did the provinces and then the central government bypass the towns and assume these responsibilities directly. Thus, the institutions charged with oversight of food supply and public order were deeply decentralized, yet we have seen (in Chapter 3) that both in the origins of the new system of bread pricing and in its week-by-week operations, the *broodzetting* achieved a high degree of coordination. An organized complexity of municipal bread price commissioners and provincial milling excise policies somehow produced a coherent system, guided by common principles yet adjusted to local circumstances. This, of course, was a characteristic of many other aspects of Dutch political life. Whether one examines its drainage polders, canals, or the organization of its admiralties and the East and West India Companies, the Republic's political DNA led to decentralized forms that usually cohered and often projected impressive power while it simultaneously disabled any initiatives toward more centralized rule.[39]

A Moral Economy?

The regulatory system's decentralized form did not prevent it from pursuing a coherent set of policies, but sheltering the ordinary consumer from market forces was definitely not its highest priority. On the contrary, the regulatory system enabled the addition of heavy taxes onto every loaf of bread. Periods of food crisis were few, but they were certainly not absent, and tax policy made them much more severe. Yet we observed in Chapter 5 that food riots and tax riots were rare, and those directed specifically at the price of bread were almost entirely absent.

Did the Republic's common people not share with other Europeans the concept of "moral economy" that many historians claim to have detected in the mentality of early modern people? While this concept is not well defined, most who invoke it refer to a broadly shared understanding of traditional rights or customs that legitimated popular intervention in food markets, especially grain and bread markets, when those in authority were judged to have failed in protecting the interests of the local community. The interventions that revealed this "moral economy" mentality generally took the form of seizures of food from millers, bakers,

---

[39] The puzzle of a strong but decentralized state that emphasizes consultation among stakeholders over the top-down exercise of authority is explored in Maarten Prak and Jan Luiten van Zanden, *Nederland en het poldermodel* (Amsterdam: Bert Bakker, 2013), pp. 9–20.

and merchants for distribution by the mob at a price it judged to be fair. England alone experienced over 700 such food riots between 1580 and 1850.[40] Such "direct popular action" or *taxation populaire*, was, it is said, irregular but disciplined. It had clear objectives and could expect the approbation of the broader community. Indeed, such food riots were thought to become numerous precisely because public authorities neglected or abandoned their age-old regulatory obligations.[41]

In the Netherlands such interventions in the movement of foodstuffs have yet to be discovered. Objections to the interregional movement of grain made little sense in most regions since they usually depended on grain imports. Nor was there much space for price-setting actions by mobs in lieu of negligent magistrates since the Dutch bread pricing system, so vital to Dutch fiscal health, continued in full vigor throughout the eighteenth century. The bread price control system was not attacked directly because the institutions of public relief generally sufficed to alleviate distress. So long as this distress remained brief and confined to the lowest classes the system of regulation and taxation was sheltered from attack. But what happened when in the French revolutionary era this system was put under extreme pressure? Even then, somehow, the mix of price setting and public charity persevered. "By whatever miracle, the dykes holding the fabric of Dutch society together did not break" and bread riots never became a significant channel for the expression of political discontent.[42]

An Economy of Fear?

Violence against the state over bread prices is all but absent, but the fear of violence and tumult certainly lived among the Dutch Republic's public authorities. Or, more correctly, it came to do so. If officials of the seventeenth century were confident of their authority despite the weakness of their formal levers of power, a new awareness of the fragility of their position took hold of the regental mind in the course of the

---

[40] Bohstedt, *The Politics of Provisions*.

[41] Thompson and Rudé claimed that such riots became common, indeed endemic, from the late seventeenth century onward precisely as a new liberal economic ideology led English and French authorities to lift controls on grain movements and bread prices. Dekker concurs in this by noting that Holland's first major food riot took place at the same time as food riots in England and France, 1693–94. But the public regulation of bread prices was then an ongoing feature of all three societies. There is little evidence of a move away from a regulatory mindset until after the 1750s. Indeed, in England the old Assize of Bread was revived and more generally enforced with its reformulation in 1709.

[42] Simon Schama, *Patriots and Liberators: Revolution in the Netherlands, 1780-1813* (New York: Alfred Knopf, 1977), p. 654.

eighteenth century, leading to a nervous caution that yielded to naked fear in moments of looming conflict. Curiously, it was not food crises that led to political tension, but the other way around: moments of political tension led to preemptive interventions in the bread economy. The crises of 1747–48 and 1787–89 illustrate this claim.

1747–48. Fear gained the upper hand among magistrates in 1747–48. Beginning in April 1747 the Republic found itself entangled in the War of the Austrian Succession, the devout wish of the States General to persist in its policy of neutrality notwithstanding. With a French army at its door (indeed, already in the vestibule, having occupied States Flanders), popular opinion shifted against the ineffectual leadership of the regental elite and demanded a restoration of the House of Orange to the post of stadholder, which had been kept vacant in the province of Holland since the death of Willem III in 1702. This demand was realized by the end of the year, but by then the public lack of confidence in the political establishment had moved on to focus on an additional grievance. The lesser burghers of the towns, in what sometimes is seen as a first, tentative, articulation of modern democratic sentiments in the Netherlands, led demands for an end to the tax farming regime on which every province relied for the collection of the numerous excises, and, indeed, to demands for the abolition of the excises themselves.

The excise on milling figured prominently in the public agitations of this time of crisis, and the offices of the tax farmers were favorite objects of crowd violence. In this tense environment local officials, uncertain of the loyalty of their town militias (*schutterijen*) were hesitant to act. When the Haarlem bread price commissioners met on 23 June 1748 (ten days after violent protests in the town) they declared simply: "due to the tumult that has arisen our provisional decision is to do nothing." Two days later the new stadholder, Willem IV, declared it to be his wish that both tax farming and the excises should immediately be abolished, and the States of Holland (and most other provinces) did so the following day even though it had no alternative fiscal plan to fill the gaping revenue shortfall that would inevitably follow.

Even this bold, or rather panic-induced, act brought no immediate relaxation of popular tension. Bread prices should have been much reduced after 26 June but in Haarlem a lack of nerve once again brought paralysis. The *burgemeesters* provided no guidance – and the bread price commissioners took no action – until 12 August, when they finally decided to join fully in the spirit of the provincial decision to abolish the milling excise by also abolishing both the city's own excise on milling and its poor relief tax on bread. As a result, the 6-pound loaf of rye bread that had sold for 6 stuivers suddenly plummeted in price to 3.75 stuivers. This might have restored the popularity of the city's magistrates, but the abolition of these taxes clearly was done under duress, and it was seen by many as a sign of weakness. Indeed, the States of Holland's proclamation announcing this decision did nothing to hide the fear and trembling that infected its deliberations.[43]

As we have come to know that the inhabitants of this province have revealed a strong preference for the abolition of the farming of the common [excise] revenues, and to the extent that this [preference] has led to outbursts of an unbounded rage, which even the highly convincing reasons that we expressed in our publication of the 19th of this month – namely that in very difficult circumstance such as these, drastic measures should not be taken until other fiscal solutions are identified and secured – have had no effect, and could not prevent many from taking actions, which if they were to spread would lead to the most sorrowful consequences: We [place our] trust in the reasonableness that upright Hollanders have exhibited through the ages ... and therefore, we have decided that the tax farms will be abolished – however difficult it is, especially in the current circumstances, to do without such an important source of revenue ... But, [we do this] in order to prevent the dangers and disasters that would hang over our heads by continuation of the unrest that has arisen.

The protest movement that led to the installation of a stadholder and the suspension of excise tax collections had not been only negative and violent. At times it articulated a demand to replace the excises with a more equitable tax, and in 1749 Prince Willem IV proposed that the States choose between a new but undefined *familie-hoofdgeld* [a direct tax on income], or the restoration of the excises. Once the magistrates regained their composure and their political footing, they quickly chose the second option, the excise taxes, including the milling tax.[44] On 1 January 1750 the entire edifice of the common means sprang back to life. The tax farms did not return; the ubiquitous excise collectors' offices would henceforth be staffed by provincial officials, but otherwise the changes were minor. Holland, Utrecht, and Friesland lowered slightly the excise on rye, and Friesland also lowered the wheat excise. Otherwise, all the provincial milling excises returned essentially unchanged and would remain so until the fall of the old Republic, and, indeed, beyond, until

---

[43] *GPB van Holland*, vol. VII, 26 July 1748. Publicatie van de Staaten van Holland tot afschaffing van de Pachten der Gemeene Middelen.

[44] For a discussion of the entire episode see Jan A. F. de Jongste, "The restoration of the Orangist regime in 1747: the modernity of a 'Glorious Revolution'," in Margaret Jacob and Wijnand Mijnhardt, eds., *The Dutch Republic in the Eighteenth Century: Decline, Enlightenment, and Revolution* (Ithaca, NY: Cornell University Press, 1992), pp. 32–59.

1806. It is, apparently, exceedingly difficult to be rid of a tax that for generations had proven its capacity to deliver a large, dependable stream of revenue to the state.

The return of the excises and the sudden jump in bread prices on 1 January 1750 went smoothly enough in most places, but the fear and indecision shown by Haarlem's leaders in 1748 appears to have encouraged an enduring spirit of insubordination among the rabble – *het grauw* – and also, more dangerously, among members of the town militias, the *schutterij*:[45] Maintaining order in Haarlem required the unprecedented intervention of States troops, but the milling tax as well as the institutions of the Republic persevered. On the surface little had changed, but the regents were now deeply cognizant of the precarious position they were in. The anonymous author of a 1755 memorial on Holland's difficult financial situation could not have been more forthright.[46]

Taxes on real property are now so high that there is no hope of securing more from this source. The common means have been brought to a higher level than ever before and no further increase can be expected; indeed, one can only hope that the [common means] revenues are maintained [at their current level], and that they do not suffer the fate of the former tax farms. Expecting new sources of tax revenue which, in the past, had bailed out the sinking ship would now be futile, since we have, over time, taxed everything and refined the system [to such a point] that we should be thinking of tax reductions rather than new taxes if we do not wish to strip the citizenry naked [*wil men zig niet de ingezetenen ontblooten*].

1789. Markets, it is said, are governed, alternately, by greed and fear. The year 1789 is definitely one in which fear dominated the grain markets. During the previous year the Amsterdam grain market had been enlivened by large purchases intended for France, where the harvest had been very poor. Prices rose, but only slightly, until March of 1789, when news of political unrest in Paris began to reach the Netherlands. The news sounded disturbingly familiar to Dutch magistrates who had just suppressed, with the help of the Prussian army, their own "Patriot Revolution" of two years earlier.[47] They now anticipated renewed trouble

---

[45] An eye-witness account of civil unrest in Haarlem triggered by the restoration of the excises in 1750 is described in Cornelis Nozeman, *Kort berigt van 't voorgevallene binnen Haerlem in 't begin van den jaere 1750*, cited in R. M. Dekker, *Oproeren in Holland gezien door tijdgenoten* (Assen: Van Gorcum, 1979), pp. 149–50.

[46] ARA Den Haag, 3de afdeling, Financie van Holland, no. 797. Anon., "Memorie of verhandeling om het gene omtrent het stuk van de financiën van de provincie van Holland en West Vriesland van tijd tot tijd is voorgevallen" (1755).

[47] The Patriot movement consisted of burghers and aristocrats who sought democratic reforms and saw the stadholder (the Prince of Orange) and the town regents in league with the stadholder as the chief obstacle to the changes they sought. Their rising in 1787 was suppressed by a Prussian army (Willem V's wife, Princess Wilhelmina, was the sister

and began to prepare precautionary measures. Amsterdam's *burgemeesters* convened a secret meeting on 12 May. "At present," they claimed, "[grain] imports are not equal to the exports, and while there is every reason to expect that before long a considerable supply will come in from the Baltic Sea, caution requires that some measures be taken, in confidence and with all necessary secrecy, so as not to create unrest among the good burghers." The bread price commissioners presented the *burgemeesters* with two alternatives: pay bakers 56 guilders per last of wheat (effectively, a 50 percent discount on the milling excise) in exchange for a reduction of the official bread prices or distribute tokens to the poor with which they could purchase the cheaper bread types at a discounted price. The bakers would then be reimbursed upon return of the tokens to the city treasury. They favored the latter, more targeted, course.

Before they could implement this plan, which had been used several times in the (distant) past, prices rose further in June and July (the storming of the Bastille, of course, took place on 14 July). The bread price commissioners knew that the rising prices were not driven by any actual shortage of grain: "Against all expectations the price of grains has been rising considerably despite the fact that the harvests have been favorable and this city holds inventories as large or larger than ever. We are informed that grain is stacked so high in the attics that it can barely be turned."[48] They recognized that merchants were building inventories in the expectation of large precautionary purchases, and this is precisely what occurred as Amsterdam's *burgemeesters* now faced pressure from the States General to participate in more drastic, national-level action. To forestall any disturbance to the grain trade Amsterdam's *burgemeesters* committed themselves to secretly commission ships and merchants to purchase and transport grain from the Baltic.[49] By 15 June (five days before the Tennis Court Oath at Versailles) the *burgemeesters* convened the city's nearly 600 bakers in order to document the grain stocks they held, purchased 382 lasts of wheat on the Amsterdam market, and began signing agreements with merchants and ship captains to secure an additional 1,300 lasts of grain in Hamburg and Elbing.[50]

---

of the Prussian king, Frederick Wilhelm II, and had been held in custody by a Patriot militia), after which many Patriots fled to France to await developments. They returned to the Netherlands in the wake of a French invasion army in 1795 to help establish the new Batavian Republic.

[48] G.A. Amsterdam, Archief 5028, Archief van de Burgemeesters. Gecommitteerden tot het Zetten en Wegen van het Brood, no. 603.

[49] A.R.A. The Hague, Financiën van Holland, no. 657, Aankoop van Graan, 1789.

[50] G.A. Amsterdam, Archief 5028, Archief Burgemeesteren, Graancommissie, 15 and 26 June 1789. Amsterdam was not alone in taking precautionary measures. Alkmaar's *burgemeesters* began to purchase 30 lasts of rye in July 1789 to prepare for "unhoped for shortages," and acquired authorization to purchase more if the need arose. Noordegraaf, "Levensstandaard," p. 98, n. 61.

In retrospect, their pro-active stance – motivated by fear of the *scha-mele gemeente*, the plebeian community – appears a bit exaggerated. The run-up of prices that concerned them peaked in July, just as they were committing nearly a half million guilders of public funds to building up a store of grain sufficient to feed the *entire* population of Amsterdam for two months. If the *burgemeesters* ever really began distributing this grain at discounted prices, they had ceased to do so by the time the Elbing grain arrived in September. They ordered the newly arrived grain to be sold at auction, where it fetched a price that gave their operation a tidy profit.[51]

Amsterdam was not alone in fretting over the unfolding events in Paris. Indeed, as Amsterdam's magistrates were confidently selling off their recently purchased Baltic wheat, the States of Zeeland prepared a highly unusual intervention in their provinces' grain markets. This major wheat producing and exporting province feared that French orders would drain its own grain reserves. It ordered Zeeland's farmers to sell a defined portion of their wheat harvest to the province at a fixed, below market, price. This amount was judged adequate to secure the food needs of the province's large urban population. In exchange for this, farmers were free to sell their remaining wheat on the open market without restriction. The States of Zeeland were concerned, above all else, to appear visibly as the guarantors of public wellbeing.[52]

The year 1789 was not a year of real crisis in the Netherlands, but it was definitely a year of crisis mentality, particularly among the magistrates. Both the municipally based Dutch system of bread price regulation and its provincial-based system of milling excises depended, as so much else in the Dutch system of government, on the functioning political autonomy of its subsidiary units. That political autonomy was predicated, in turn, on financial autonomy. So long as towns and provinces had the means to secure the wellbeing of their populations in times of economic crisis their authority over bread price regulation and the milling excise – and much more – might be preserved, even in the face of challenges to the civic and local loyalties on which the Republic's venerable institutions depended.

---

[51] The price of wheat in Elbing was 74 percent of the price in Amsterdam, but at the elevated grain prices of the time this amounted to a difference of 95 guilders per last. Transport, insurance, taxes, and other transaction costs amounted to 50 guilders per last while the opportunity cost of capital for the 155,000 guilders tied up in this transaction may have added another 4,000–5,000 guilders, leaving a net profit of 40 guilders per last.

[52] For more on this complex operation, see De Vries, "Production and consumption," pp. 199–219.

Amsterdam's conspicuous demonstration of its intention to protect its inhabitants from scarcity and Zeeland's unprecedented intervention in its grain markets in 1789 can best be explained by the acute awareness of their magistrates that the political legitimacy they long had taken for granted was eroding. They reveal governments with the financial means and the administrative competence to organize complex operations and take decisive action. But, in fact, by that date most Dutch cities no longer possessed the economic capacity to act in such a muscular way. By the time a true bread crisis struck in 1795, Amsterdam once again acted to organize the municipal purchase of grain from abroad.[53] It was the largest, but also the last effort of this kind. These traditional coping mechanisms would be unavailing in sheltering consumers from the price shocks that would come repeatedly after 1795. Already before this crisis questions about the efficacy of the regulatory regime and about the fairness of the milling excise had begun to be raised. Once the old Republic collapsed, the enlightened critics – the Patriots – who had yearned for that day also looked forward to the dismantling of the bread pricing and taxing policies with which the state had been entangled nearly since its inception. A new dawn was breaking – or so they hoped. We turn to the nineteenth-century fate of these policies in Chapter 15. But first we continue with the early modern consumer, shifting our focus from consumer welfare in times of crisis to consumer choice in goods times and bad.

---

[53] In 1795 Amsterdam made direct purchases on a much larger scale than ever before. Altogether 41 ships delivered 2,194 lasts of wheat and 1,597 lasts of rye. The city purchased this grain for 1,995,666 guilders plus an additional 68,575 guilders for freight and other transport costs. G.A. Amsterdam, Archief no. 5028, Archief van de Burgemeesters, no. 603.

11 Choosing What to Eat in the Early Modern Era

This study's chief concern is the consumption of the bread grains and their close substitutes. But these foods are not consumed in a vacuum, and it will be useful to our investigation of consumer choice to begin by examining the place of these basic foodstuffs in the context of total food consumption. There are three distinct approaches to the question of how early modern people chose what to eat: foodways, food hierarchies, and food systems. We will begin by considering the main assumptions undergirding these approaches and then proceed to an investigation of what the Dutch actually ate, how their diet changed over time, and how their choices might be explained.

Foodways, Food Hierarchies, and Food Systems

Foodways

The foodways approach begins with the proposition that food – its acquisition, preparation, and consumption – is culturally embedded. That is, food consumption is not shaped primarily by utilitarian considerations but by such non-economic considerations as power, meaning, and identity.[1] Massimo Montanari's meditation on the meaning of white and dark breads offers a good example of this approach:

The former [wheat bread] was prepared for the upper classes and was decidedly a luxury item. Black bread was for peasants and servants, whether made from rye, spelt, or *mixtura*. A complex typology characterized the relationship between the type of bread and the status of the consumer, whether it was a question of social rank (ruler vs. ruled) or a moral desire for penitence or the humbling of self.[2]

From a foodways perspective the old German saw, *Man ist was man isst* (You are what you eat), might be reversed, for *what* one consumes is

---

[1] Patricia Harris, David Lyon, and Sue McLaughlin, *The Meaning of Food* (Guilford, CT: Pequot Press, 2005).

[2] Massimo Montanari, *The Culture of Food* (Oxford: Blackwell, 1993), p. 31.

deeply implicated in *who* one is – or who one is understood to be and understands oneself to be. All of this suggests that we should expect a great deal of inertia in food consumption. Both personal standing and community culture enforce a strong path dependence on what one eats, where, when, and with whom.[3]

Foodways are part of folkways, and in the context of a pre-industrial society it would seem that there is little room for the exercise of voluntary consumer choice. From this perspective one might approach the variety of food types available in the Netherlands as a matter of geography and of social status: there were rye zones and wheat zones, depending on soil conditions and climate, and there were the distinctive foodways of elite consumers and of peasants, and presumably of yet other social groups.[4] In an influential article on historical Dutch consumption practices the folklore specialist (and novelist) J. J. Voskuil offered a sharp criticism of the concept of foodways, which he saw as dependent on structural if not "racial" determinism. He shared the folklorists' belief that ordinary folk did not regularly exercise consumer choice, but he denied that this was because of their immobilizing embeddedness in established practices of culturally determined consumption. "The great mass of consumers lived so close to the survival minimum that they had no opportunity to establish fixed patterns of consumption ... "[5] In

---

[3] For a vigorous but reasonable defense of the cultural determinants of food consumption, see Victor Magagna, "Food and politics: the power of bread in European culture," in Beat Kümin, ed., *A Cultural History of Food*, vol. IV: *The Early Modern Age* (London and New York: Berg, 2012), pp. 65–86. Magagna emphasizes "commensality," rules of exclusion and inclusion in meal-taking rites, the stratification of food and cooking styles by social class, but also the strong cultural and symbolic meaning of foods: "Food grain and cooked foods such as (and above all) bread were understood by elites and commoners to have a kind of moral power and sanctity that could not be completely reduced to economic logic," p. 69.

[4] "A rye–wheat boundary is located, according to soil and climate suitable for wheat vs. rye, from the province of South-Holland, through Germany to Russia. North of this line, wheat was only eaten by the rich and as a luxury product." Jobse-van Putten, *Eenvoudig maar voedzaam*, p. 83. Likewise, Vermoesen claims that "A 'cereal curtain' came into being, stretching from the North Sea, south of Holland, to as far as Russia. Wheat could be grown south of that line, but not to the north ... This gave rise to a regional distinction in the pattern of bread consumption: rye bread to the north, wheat bread to the south ... " R. Vermoesen, "The Low Countries, 1000–1750," in Van Molle and Segers, eds., *Agro-Food Market*, p. 275. The same "boundary" is found in J. Witteveen, "Rye, a daily bread and a daily treat," in *Proceedings of the Oxford Symposium on Food and Cooking, 1989: Staple Foods* (Oxford: Harlan Walker, 1990), pp. 240–45.

[5] J. J. Voskuil, "De weg naar Luilekkerland," *Bijdragen en mededelingen voor de geschiedenis der Nederlanden* 98 (1983), 466. Voskuil's remarkable seven-volume novel, *Het Bureau*, describes the goings-on in a research institute (in truth, *his* institute, the P. J. Meertens Instituut voor Volkenkunde) where, in the first volume, the researchers are engaged in the (futile) construction of maps laying out folkloric cultural boundaries, including a "rye frontier."

his view, people ate what they could under the circumstances, not what they preferred: they had neither the luxury of choice nor the luxury of habit. Voskuil's critique of the foodways concept may strike a telling blow against anthropologists and folklorists, but it leaves the economist with a puzzle. If people "ate what they could under the circumstances," what, then, did they choose to eat when circumstances were good? To put it another way: were people constrained in their consumption by what could be produced and supplied locally, or did local production change in response to changing demand?[6] Another interpretive framework is needed to address this question, which brings us to the second approach.

Food Hierarchies

The notion of food hierarchies supposes that there is a stable (though not necessarily unvarying) hierarchy of foods; that this hierarchy is broadly (though not necessarily universally) shared; and that individual choice of food is determined primarily by income. People buy the "best" diet they can afford and changes in income lead to a predictable progression or regression through the hierarchy of steadily more or less desired foods. This predictable progression might be thought of as an extension of Engel's law, one of the most durable and dependable regularities of economics, which states simply that as incomes rise, food expenditures decline as a percentage of total income. In other words, the income elasticity of demand for food is less than one.

Engel's law refers to food as a whole, but if we break down this large category of expenditure, further patterns can be found: as income rises consumers upgrade their diet by reducing their intake of carbohydrates, shifting their source of protein from vegetable to animal products, and increasing their intake of fats, especially animal fats, and sugars.[7] All of these marginal shifts increase the per-calorie cost of the diet. Thus, while Engel's law speaks of a shift away from food as a whole, his law does not preclude absolute increases for some foodstuffs and absolute decline for others. That is, the income elasticities of demand for particular foodstuffs vary from above one to less than zero. It is easy

---

[6] The common view that certain soils – thin, sandy soils, for instance – are suitable only for the lesser grains, ignores the fact that soil improvement – through manure, marling, liming, etc. – can loosen this constraint. Sir William Ashley, in *The Bread of Our Forefathers*, pp. 136–45, argues that English arable farming made such a transition as capitalist landowners invested in their lands to cater to the growing demand for wheat.

[7] Maurice Aymard, "Pour l'histoire de l'alimentation: quelques remarques de méthode," *Annales. Économies, sociétés, civilisations* 30 (1975), 431–44.

enough to rank the foods that concern us here by their cost per calorie (see Table 11.1). Their costs per unit of protein or of other dietary requirements will not all yield exactly the same hierarchy, but markets yielded a fairly clear and stable hierarchy of relative prices for the four staples of wheat bread, rye bread, buckwheat and the other boiled grains (*grutten*), and potatoes. In that order, they offered basic calories at progressively lower cost, with the important proviso that the potato was not *consistently* the low-cost supplier of calories. One of its interesting features was a price that was only weakly correlated with that of the bread grains (discussed in more detail below).

Do we then find that these commodities and the economic hierarchies of society sorted themselves out to form distinctive, if not exclusive,

Table 11.1 *Index of cost per kilocalorie, relative to the average cost of the Amsterdam Burghers' Orphanage diet, 1639–1812*

The following index numbers can be understood as follows: The overall average cost of the Amsterdam Burghers' Orphanage (BWH) diet per kilocalorie is set at 1.00. Thus rye bread supplied a kilocalorie at a cost only 44 percent of this average. Cheese supplied a kilocalorie at 172 percent of the average cost of kilocalories. Adding any foodstuff with a relative cost below 1.00 reduces food costs per calorie, while foodstuffs above 1.00 increase those costs.

Potatoes★	0.30
Legumes, groats, buckwheat	0.40
Rye bread	0.44
Potatoes★	0.44
Wheat bread	0.67
Buttermilk★★	0.80
Beer	0.80
BWH diet	**1.00**
Whole milk★★	1.15
Butter	1.47
Cheese	1.72
Fish	2.78
Meat★★★	3.33

★ Potatoes are inserted into this schedule of relative prices using potato prices for 1763–1848. Potatoes appear in two places in this list: one when rye prices are low (below 195 gld per last) and the other when rye prices are high (above 195 gld per last).
★★ The overall index for both types of milk was 0.98. However, whole milk generally cost 80 percent more than buttermilk per liter, while offering 25 percent more calories. I have therefore entered them separately on the basis of this information.
★★★ Pork and beef had comparable costs per kilogram, but pork supplied far more calories per unit of cost.
Note: orphanage bread costs do not include taxes that would elevate the cost of both types of bread relative to the other foodstuffs, and elevate the cost of wheat bread relative to rye bread.

spheres of consumption? Was white bread the food of the rich and buck-wheat the food of the poor? Did the well-off eat no rye bread and urbanites no potatoes? Here supporters of the foodways approach might object that any food hierarchy is subject to non-economic influences. The white bread that may have been held in the highest esteem in 1750 would today be rejected by devotees of healthy artisanal whole-wheat breads. Tastes and nutritional knowledge – or presumed knowledge – can affect demand and, hence, relative prices.[8] This complicates but it does not undermine the notion that consumers made choices shaped by their budget, basic nutritional requirements, and a hierarchy of value, or utility. In short, while the foodways approach denies that people had choices to make, the food hierarchy approach is all about choice, about maximizing utility under an income constraint.

Food Systems

The food systems model integrates elements of the first two approaches: it identifies the utility of a given food within a larger complex of dietary complementarities and substitutions. Thus, certain foods are valued as a *complement* to others (if you eat more of one, you eat more of the other) while others serve primarily as *substitutes*. For example, the bread substitutes barley groats (*gort*) and buckwheat were most commonly served with (butter) milk. If milk becomes more readily available or cheaper, the demand for these bread substitutes will rise also. The potato, which initially may have been valued as a caloric substitute for bread in times of distress, entered the diet more broadly and permanently as an accompaniment to garden vegetables. Coarse wheat bread, on the other hand, was clearly a substitute for rye bread: where the one was widely consumed the other was largely absent. But this substitutability did not apply to the finer grades of wheat bread. None of the lesser breads or bread substitutes possessed the qualities that allowed them to take the place of fresh, warm, white bread. It was in a class by itself. We will return later to the historical evidence for these complementarities and substitutabilities. Here it must suffice to call attention to the complex ways in which income *plus* the price or the private availability of other foods shapes

[8] The state of eighteenth-century nutritional knowledge was succinctly summarized by Collins: "The view gained ground that wheat, being a light fermented foodstuff made with yeast, was the healthiest grain food, and that gruels, being unfermented, were taxing on the stomach and harmful to health. Until recently ... medical opinion came out strongly in favor of wheat as the perfect grain and the raised loaf as the most desirable human grain food." Collins, "Why wheat?," p. 34. On the difficult question of "presumed knowledge" – what we think we know, in this case about nutrition, and how consistently we act on it – see Joel Mokyr, "More work for mother? Knowledge and household behavior, 1870–1945," *Journal of Economic History* 60 (2000), 1–41.

the relative demand for the breads and bread alternatives. Moreover, the existence of these food systems means that few if any types of bread would be consumed *exclusively* by a specific social group: every income and status group would find occasion to purchase nearly every type, even though the specific mix could vary considerably. A food system can be understood as a "structure," as historians of the Annales school used that term. A food system, or dietary regime, evolves very slowly over time and, in the short run, has only limited flexibility. It responds to price signals and other market information, but does so within a fairly well-defined set of complementarities and substitutabilities. Only a major shock can seriously reorganize such a structure.

To be sure, some food systems were rather spartan and simple, offering a limited choice for most people most of the time, and revealing brittleness in times of distress. Others were complex, based on the regular availability of a variety of potential substitutes and complements that enabled a more supple response to distress. The food system of the Netherlands as it took shape, apparently, in the late sixteenth century, is of particular interest because of the unusually broad range of choice it offered consumers relative to other food systems of the early modern era. This complexity is fundamental to understanding both the behavior of consumers and the development of the bread price regulatory system and the associated fiscal regime from the 1590s onward.

The Republican Diet

The Dutch diet in the time of the Republic was a varied one. Several types of breads and bread substitutes were all widely available and broadly consumed, thereby presenting consumers with the possibility for substitutions that could at least partially absorb price shocks. This variety was made possible by a broad access to bakeries and retail suppliers of milled buckwheat and barley, legumes and, as it became available, rice. The Dutch Republic was covered in all but the deepest countryside by networks of mills, bakeries, and shelling and grinding mills that could supply consumers with all of these products.[9] The bakeries were generally required by ordinance to supply both rye and wheat breads. Taken

---

[9] Table 7.1 shows the number of grain mills by province as of 1819. Also shown are the number of *grutterijen*, the mills for barley groats and buckwheat grinding, and the *pelmolens*, the shelling mills for peas, beans, and rice. The former were distributed across the country in comparable numbers to the grain mills. The groats grinding mills were scarce only in Zeeland and Gelderland. In contrast to this, the shelling mills were concentrated in industrial centers. The Zaan region of North Holland and Groningen held nearly half the country's total in 1819.

together, these commodities formed the caloric basis of the diet, but in normal times they did not dominate it as in other pre-industrial societies where the bread grains are often said to account for 70–80 percent of total caloric intake.

Demonstrating this claim requires some knowledge about the Dutch diet as a whole. Historical sources that can shed light on the overall composition of the diet are scarce until well into the nineteenth century, when a nascent social science began conducting budget studies, usually among urban working-class households, and when data on agricultural output and trade become more detailed.[10] Before the mid-nineteenth century we have less to go on, and the temptation is great simply to assume that the sober diets of the poorest of nineteenth-century urban proletarians must have prevailed more generally in early modern times. To check this convenient but ahistorical assumption, the only sources that provide anything approaching a comprehensive picture of the diet are those for "institutionalized" populations: prisoners, seafarers, the inmates of hospitals and almshouses, and orphans. There are obvious objections to reliance on evidence drawn from groups who, by definition, could not choose their own diet but depended on the decisions of others. There are also obvious reasons why the diet provided on board ships sailing the high seas or to those being punished for their crimes should not be regarded as representative for a civilian population.[11] The representativeness of orphanage diets can also be questioned, but of all the available evidence of this type, the orphanage diets are certainly the most useful for our purposes. The Netherlands, in part because of its high level of urbanization and in part because of its nuclear family structure, came to rely on orphanages to house, feed, and educate a substantial number of its children and adolescents. The children left by the death of well-to-do parents were mostly cared for by family, but this left a broad cross-section of the social hierarchy that relied on institutions for the care of orphans, foundlings, and children whose parent(s) could not care for them while away, usually at sea. In the larger towns the municipality usually supported a burghers'

---

[10] General studies include: Burema, *De voeding in Nederland*; Jobse-Van Putten, *Eenvoudig maar voedzaam*; Van Otterloo, *Eten en eetlust*. The most thorough analysis of nineteenth-century budget studies was made by Arthur van Riel, "Prices and industrialization in the Netherlands, 1800–1913: markets, openness and public finance" (Ph.D. thesis, Utrecht University, 2017), appendix E. See also: www.iisg.nl/hpw/brannex.php.

[11] On shipboard diets see Michel Morineau, "Rations militaires et rations moyennes en Hollande au XVIII siècle," *Annales. Économies, sociétés, civilisations* 18 (1963), 521–31; R. Baetens, "De voedselrantsoenen van de zeevarenden: de theorie getoetst aan de werkelijkheid," *Bijdragen tot de geschiedenis van het Hertogdom Brabant* 60 (1977), 273–306. The diet provided to inmates of Amsterdam's prison, *het Rasphuis*, is revealed in G.A. Amsterdam, Thes. Ord. no. 14, resolutieën.

orphanage, for the children left by those possessing burgher status. Orphans who did not qualify for admission to the burghers' orphanage could seek admission to orphanages maintained by the religious denominations and to municipal orphanages for non-burghers.[12]

A combination of municipal pride and inter-denominational competition acted to make Dutch orphanages more central institutions in civic life than one might suppose. A large number of families, and not only the poorest and most marginal, understood that the orphanages might in time be taking care of their children.[13] Can we infer from this that the orphans participated in the dietary practices of the broader society? In some fairly obvious ways, they did not. The orphanage populations were concentrated in the age range 6–18, which affected both the size and composition of the diet; institutional menus tended to be routinized and were slow to introduce new food alternatives. The orphanage directors were probably more conservative than private households in responding to short-term changes in the market environment. But there are good reasons to have confidence that the orphanage records offer a fair picture of broader societal practices: the diet supplied by the orphanages was feasible (that is, a modest household could replicate their feeding practices within its budgetary constraints) and in cases where other types of consumption evidence are available, they are broadly consistent with the orphanage evidence.

We will proceed by reviewing the food budgets and provision of calories for three orphanages in periods stretching from 1581 to 1892.

---

[12] Amsterdam, an extreme case, to be sure, supported two civic orphanages (the Burghers' and Almoners' Orphanages), plus orphanages established by the Reformed, Remonstrant, Walloon Reformed, Roman Catholic, Anabaptist, Lutheran, and Jewish denominations. The civic orphanages for non-burghers went by a variety of names. In Groningen the *rode* (red) *weeshuis* was for the burghers, while the *groene* (green) *weeshuis* was for non-burghers; in Haarlem and Leiden the non-burgher orphans entered the bluntly named *armekinderhuis* (poor children's house); in Utrecht the *Stads-Ambachtskinderhuis* (house for tradesmen's children); in Zutphen the *vreemde weeshuis* (foreigner/outsider orphanage).

[13] There is a substantial literature on Dutch orphanages. The most comprehensive is J. Dane, ed., *Wezen en boefjes: zes eeuwen zorg in Wees- en Kinderhuizen* (Hilversum: Verloren 1997). See also, G. N. M. Vis, *Het Weeshuis van Woerden* (Hilversum: Verloren, 1996); P. J. J.M. van Wees, *Het Burgerweeshuis van Amersfoort* (Amersfoort: Uitgeverij Bekking, 2002); J. T. Engel, *Kinderen van Amsterdam* (Amsterdam: Walburg Pers, 1989); J. P. Vredenberg, *Als off sij onse eigene kijnder weren: het Burgerweeshuis te Arnhem, 1583–1742* (Arnhem: Gemeente Arnhem, 1983); J. M. Fuchs, *Opvangen en opvoeden: Lutherse wezenzorg in Amsterdam, 1678–1978* (Amsterdam: Lankamp en Brinkman, 1978); Aukje Zondergeld-Hamer, *Een kwestie van goed bestuur: twee eeuwen armenzorg in Weesp, 1590–1822* (Hilversum: Verloren, 2006); A. J. M. Kunst, *Van Sint Elisabeths-gasthuis tot Gereformeerd Burgerweeshuis (1485–1814)* (Assen: Van Gorcum, 1956). The most penetrating study of the economics of an orphanage is Anne McCants, *Civic Charity in the Golden Age: Orphan Care in Early Modern Amsterdam* (Urbana and Chicago: University of Illinois Press, 1997).

Two of them have already been introduced: Amsterdam's Burghers' Orphanage (BWH) and the Almoners' Orphanage (AWH). The BWH was a well-endowed institution dating from before the Dutch Revolt that catered for the orphaned children of burghers – especially the artisans and traders that constituted Amsterdam's "middling sort." The AWH was established only in 1666 to care for the orphans of the city's most marginal families: recent immigrants, seafarers, peddlers, and hawkers, etc. It was financed by the city, primarily via an array of dedicated local taxes. The BWH (which cared from between 400 and 900 children at any given time) and AWH (whose population varied between 800 and 2,200, and cared for many additional young children via wet nurses) catered for distinct tranches of Amsterdam's social hierarchy.[14] They also differed in their economic vulnerability to short-term economic changes; the AWH revenues depended on annual tax revenues and contributions, while the BWH drew nearly all of its revenue from its assets (houses, farms, and public bonds). The third institution examined here is Utrecht's Burghers' Orphanage. It was smaller than the others (housing between 70 and 200 orphans) but like Amsterdam's BWH, was supported primarily by endowments of land and urban property.[15]

Table 11.2 presents the food expenditure patterns of the three orphanages, showing the total food cost per orphan and how food expenses were divided among major food categories. Table 11.3 displays the total caloric value of the diet provided and the calorific contribution of the major food categories. These observations stretch from 1581 to 1850 and reveal a long period of impressive stability stretching from the 1640s to 1790s. In this long republican era, the well-endowed BWH of Amsterdam supplied its orphans with a diet that Casparus Commelen described with some pride in 1693: "the meals provided by this house are *burgerlijk*, since at intervals, such as holidays and Sundays, they provide variation in the dishes, such as rice with pudding and mash with prunes and raisins."[16]

---

[14] The occupations for which the male orphans were destined upon their departure from the orphanages shows nicely how the BWH and AWH acted to reproduce the social order. The BWH boys were overwhelmingly destined for skilled work in the building trades, shipbuilding, and a miscellany of artisanal crafts. While in the care of the orphanage, they were apprenticed for this purpose. The AWH also apprenticed its boys, but until the mid-eighteenth century about half of its male "graduates" was destined for service on the ships of the Dutch East India Company. McCants, *Civic Charity*, pp. 70–82; G.A. Amsterdam, P.A. 343, no. 471–75.

[15] Kunst, *Gereformeerd Burgerweeshuis*, pp. 170–72. The Utrecht BWH endowments were a combination of personal legacies and the property of a pre-Reformation abbey. A sharp decline in property values after the French invasion of 1672 placed its finances in a precarious state until 1719, when the city succeeded in restoring its finances by placing in its hands the operation of the municipal pawn bank (*bank van lening*).

[16] Casparus Commelen, *Beschryving der stadt Amsterdam* (Amsterdam, 1693), p. 564.

Table 11.2 Food consumption in three orphanages, 1581–1850 (percentage of total food expenditures for each food category)

Amsterdam AWH

	1683–89	1690–99	1700–09	1710–19	1720–29	1730–39	1740–49	1750–59	1760–69	1770–79	1780–89	1790–95	1799–1807
Bread	18.00	22.40	19.70	21.40	19.80	14.70	17.70	19.30	19.60	21.90	21.20	26.70	33.10
Legumes, groats	13.50	16.40	13.60	14.40	12.40	11.70	12.70	11.90	12.00	16.10	14.30	15.90	20.00
Meat	11.20	12.20	13.50	11.70	13.20	16.60	15.30	15.80	16.70	15.10	13.80	11.00	15.00
Butter	17.90	14.90	14.30	15.60	14.50	15.60	15.80	15.30	15.20	13.10	16.40	15.30	12.70
Cheese and milk	16.70	14.90	16.20	17.30	20.00	20.20	22.00	20.70	19.80	18.80	18.60	17.80	12.00
Beer	11.80	8.90	10.00	8.60	10.00	10.40	7.40	7.50	7.50	6.00	5.90	4.90	4.00
Other	10.90	10.10	12.70	11.00	10.00	10.70	9.10	9.50	9.30	9.00	9.70	8.50	3.20
Total	100.00	99.80	100.00	100.00	99.90	99.90	100.00	100.00	100.10	100.00	99.90	100.10	100.00
Annual cost per orphan	28.73	36.49	36.39	40.08	37.79	35.73	45.65	44.91	46.03	51.61	54.92	52.46	51.46

Amsterdam BWH

	1614–31	1638–49	1650–65	1666–75	1690–1701	1704–58	1761–1812	1816
Bread	23.50	21.60	29.00	19.60	22.20	14.80	18.50	28.30
Legumes, groats	6.40	8.90	8.50	8.10	9.90	4.80	5.30	15.30
Potatoes								2.10
Vegetables								2.90
Meat	22.10	21.40	18.70	20.70	19.50	25.10	24.20	13.20
Fish	5.10	2.30	2.30	2.70	2.70	2.70	2.30	1.00
Butter	18.50	20.60	18.30	20.00	19.00	20.00	15.10	10.10
Cheese	12.90	5.60	4.30	4.70	4.10	4.80	5.70	1.50
Milk	5.00	8.20	7.10	9.70	11.70	14.00	12.40	19.50
Sugar					0.90	1.50	3.30	
Beer	6.50	11.40	11.90	14.40	10.90	12.20	6.80	2.00
Other							6.40	4.10
Total	100.00	100.00	100.10	99.90	100.00	99.90	100.00	100.00
Annual cost per orphan		43.24	41.05	45.65	62.84	67.79	75.11	53.50

Table 11.2 (cont.)

Utrecht BWH

	1581–89	1591–1600	1611–17	1630–42	1650–60	1675–79	1680–1700	1700	1719	1730–32	1750	1800	1850
Bread	33.75	34.45	35.10	36.75	41.08	34.99	35.86	35.01	18.59	24.55	18.58	33.53	27.21
Legumes	1.81	1.76	1.19	1.21	4.39	6.52	4.11	9.64	10.40	6.05	6.07	10.27	5.63
Potatoes												2.55	7.65
Meat	12.01	11.59	16.00	12.69	13.66	9.70	15.85	17.88	16.64	19.66	21.68	19.33	24.62
Cheese and butter	31.74	31.60	26.88	24.68	22.32	31.06	23.90	18.46	20.80	16.50	26.86	17.41	14.66
Milk	5.36	5.35	5.36	8.93	7.37	4.70	6.93	5.10	11.79	7.41	6.52	3.61	5.23
Beer	5.36	5.35	5.36	5.79	6.06	5.30	6.25	4.09	4.16	6.50	6.15	2.48	3.64
All other	9.97	9.89	10.10	9.95	5.12	7.74	7.10	9.82	17.61	19.33	14.13	10.82	11.36
Total	100.00	100.00	100.00	100.00	100.00	100.00	100.00	100.00	100.00	100.00	100.00	100.00	100.00
Annual cost per orphan	21.69	27.66	32.82	43.73	41.65	51.27	35.608	40.75	55.46	37.91	49.64	76.25	67.73

Table 11.3 *Orphanage diets: the source of calories in percentages of the total*

Amsterdam AWH

	1690–1709	1723	1730	1745–54	1757	1772–81	1788–93	1800–02
Bread	41.47	60.70	38.32	45.99	42.68	48.08	46.04	47.59
Legumes, gort	12.57	12.75	9.79	12.19	12.91	14.11	14.54	28.27
Butter	12.92	11.31	10.47	11.82	12.37	8.51	8.67	6.19
Cheese	6.17	4.05	3.12	3.65	3.83	2.13	3.11	2.64
Buttermilk	4.67	4.70	4.30	5.15	5.80	4.64	5.16	2.71
Fresh milk	2.77	2.74	2.38	3.00	5.22	3.24	3.78	1.27
Beef	4.29	4.34	4.84	3.61	3.74	6.05	6.23	2.08
Pork	0.91	0.60	0.52	0.91	0.88	0.66	0.68	1.96
Fish	1.50	1.50	1.31	1.51	1.46	1.63	1.68	0.00
Beer	12.25	11.89	10.07	10.74	9.26	8.90	7.98	4.85
Molasses	0.47	0.62	1.15	1.43	1.85	2.06	2.12	2.45
Calories per day	2211.68	2547.70	2197.45	2203.18	2272.54	2039.23	1977.87	1709.34

Amsterdam BWH

	1639–59	1660–79	1680–99	1700–19	1720–39	1740–59	1760–79	1780–89	1790–1812
Bread	41.20	40.70	38.10	37.50	33.40	32.00	32.30	33.60	34.60
Legumes, gort	12.20	11.60	11.40	11.20	10.90	13.60	12.20	13.10	19.50
Meat	6.70	5.90	6.30	7.50	8.50	7.50	6.70	7.90	7.10
Fish	0.90	0.80	1.10	0.80	0.90	1.20	0.80	0.80	0.60
Butter	13.60	13.90	14.40	14.40	14.00	12.20	13.60	9.70	7.90
Cheese	3.50	3.00	2.60	2.10	3.30	3.00	3.40	3.60	2.80
Milk	7.40	9.20	10.90	11.90	11.80	13.70	13.50	15.40	19.10
Sugar	0.60	0.50	0.90	0.90	2.10	3.40	3.90	4.30	2.70
Beer	13.60	14.00	13.80	13.60	14.60	13.20	13.50	11.40	5.80
Other	0.30	0.40	0.40	0.10	0.30	0.00	0.00	0.00	0.00
Calories per day	2269.00	2153.00	2604.00	3040.00	2662.00	2597.00	2659.00	2741.00	2384.00

Table 11.3 (*cont.*)

Utrecht BWH

	1581–89	1591–1600	1611–17	1630–42	1650–60	1675–80	1680–99	1700	1719	1730–32	1750	1800.00	1850.00
Bread grain	63.144	55.350	60.182	58.730	61.773	55.370	52.629	58.390		51.274	47.951	43.905	30.138
Legumes	3.269	6.089	4.012	4.195	2.552	4.857	5.398	9.239		10.682	10.703	9.470	11.803
Potatoes							0.000					6.685	18.416
Meat	9.559	10.327	10.325	10.796	10.748	13.000	10.419	10.145		11.233	12.781	12.924	13.311
Cheese	5.462	9.133	5.900	4.647	5.538	9.570	6.576	5.975		9.344	10.211	6.762	4.477
Butter	9.845	11.462	10.635	11.252	9.240	6.630	14.531	7.249		7.550	8.246	13.945	13.910
Milk	3.059	2.850	3.304	4.707	4.498	4.315	4.429	3.369		4.275	4.455	3.399	5.046
Beer	5.662	4.755	5.642	5.674	5.651	6.257	5.795	5.634		5.642	5.653	2.911	2.897
Total	2507.849	2691.692	2321.726	2220.532	2141.278	1917.844	2065.992	2520.615	NA	2180.081	2175.754	2164.067	2070.834

Anne McCants' thorough analysis of the BWH confirms Commelen's boast: the orphans received what today would be regarded as calorically and nutritionally adequate meals, apart from a notable vitamin C deficiency, made good only with the adoption of the potato after 1800. The bread grains, which accounted for about 40 percent of those calories in the seventeenth century, supplied 32 percent after 1740, while the assembly of barley groats, buckwheat, rice, and legumes supplied an additional 12 percent throughout the period. Dairy products, meat and fish, beer, sugar, and dried fruits together accounted for a gradually growing percentage of total calories, with butter, cheese, buttermilk, and fresh milk accounting for most of the increase.

What is most striking in the BWH food supply is that bread accounted for no more than 15–21 percent of total food expenditures, with the other grains and legumes accounting for an additional 5–9 percent. The orphanage spent at least as much on meat and fish, and considerably more, 33–39 percent of the total, on dairy products. This is not to say that nothing changed; there was a decline in beer consumption in the eighteenth century and a rise in the use of sugar, mostly in the form of treacle (*syroop*), but certainly the major impression the BWH leaves us is of a stable, adequate, and fairly varied diet in which bread and bread substitutes accounted for no more than half of the calories and a quarter of total food expenditures.

Did comparably placed children and adolescents, living at home rather than in the orphanage, enjoy a similar diet? Were the BWH meals *burgerlijk* in the sense that ordinary burghers ate much the same fare? Direct comparisons are not possible before the nineteenth century, but we can check per capita consumption of certain foodstuffs against taxed consumption levels for the general population. For example, the inhabitants of Beverwijk, a small Holland town, consumed 14.6 kg of taxed butter annually in the period 1760–84, compared to the BWH's 19.5 kg, throughout the period 1639–1779. The BWH supplied its charges with 24 kg of beef and pork annually up to 1699, thereafter the supply jumped to 35 kg in the period 1700–79. The tax on slaughtered livestock (*het beestial*) reveals a per capita consumption for all of Holland in 1801–04 of 28 kg, while from 1808 to 1837 taxed meat consumption in the western provinces averaged 34 kg.[17] The BWH orphans fared well relative to these

[17] The butter and meat consumption data are both from A. M. Van der Woude, "De consumptie van graan, vlees en boter in Holland," *AAG Bijdragen* 9 (1963), 138–43, 149; Hans de Beer, *Voeding, gezondheid en arbeid in Nederland tijdens de negentiende eeuw. Een bijdrage to de antropometrische geschiedschrijving* (Amsterdam: Aksant, 2001), pp. 37–42. Van Zanden sets the national consumption level for dairy products in 1810 at 15.7 kg of "butter equivalent" (this incorporates both butter and cheese consumption). Van Zanden, *Economische ontwikkeling*, p. 106.

benchmarks, although we need to keep their limitations in mind: they refer to taxed consumption, not total consumption, and most of the meat data derive from a period of depressed "luxury" food consumption. We can also note that the orphans were supplied with more (weak) beer than was commonly being consumed in the eighteenth century, but standing against this was an adherence to tradition on the part of the orphanage directors that kept such novelties as potatoes, tea, coffee, and sugar (except in the form of treacle) out of their diet until the nineteenth century.[18] All in all, it is not difficult to accept that the children of parents most of whom as burghers enjoyed a measure of economic security, should themselves have been furnished with something more than a barebones diet.

How did this diet compare with that available to the run of unskilled laborers? Here is where the records of the plebeian Almoners' Orphanage (AWH) can come to our assistance, since it fed the orphaned children of such families. Beginning in 1683 the AWH food budgets and caloric values can be compared directly with those of the BWH.

Neither the pattern of expenditures among the major food categories nor the meals supplied to the orphans of the two institutions differed fundamentally. The AWH orphans' bread was a mix of wheat and rye, but the BWH supplied a bit more wheat in the mix; dairy products weighed heavily in the diet at both, but the BWH offered more whole milk relative to buttermilk; orphans at both houses received meat and fish, but at the BWH this figured in nearly every midday meal, while at the AWH it was limited to Sundays and, usually, two additional days per week, and it was more often pork than beef. Finally, while both institutions fed their orphans barley groats, buckwheat, rice, and legumes, the AWH usually supplied more than twice as much. Via these marginal differences, the AWH managed to offer – roughly – 85 percent of the calories of the BWH at 65 percent of the per-orphan cost – which is roughly the difference in pay between skilled and unskilled workers.[19]

---

[18] Neither coffee nor tea appear as items of regular purchase in Dutch orphanage records before the nineteenth century, but in 1770 Middelburg's orphanage records make the intriguing comment that the orphans could supplement their bread-based breakfast with coffee, tea, or beer "purchased with their own money." Vis, *Het weeshuis van Woerden*, p. 118. In 1801 girls of the Utrecht BWH were accused of trading portions of their food for "adornment and coffee." Kunst, *Gereformeerde Burgerweeshuis*, p. 259.

[19] Weekly menus are available for many Dutch orphanages, and they reveal a prevailing pattern, to which the AWH conformed, of serving meat at the midday meal (the warm meal of the day) at least three days per week. Orphans could be fairly certain of receiving beef for Sunday dinner. Woerden's orphanage supplied beef, pork, and fish (when available) each week in the first half of the seventeenth century. At Haarlem's Anabaptist orphanage in 1681 the orphans were fed beef on Sundays, sausages on Wednesdays and Saturdays, and fish on Friday. At Delft's Holy Ghost home, the 1774 menu featured meat on Mondays, Tuesdays, and Fridays. On Sunday there seems to have been no meat on offer but in its place a dish sweetened by currants, raisins, or prunes. In the same year the routine of Hoorn's burghers' orphanage was to serve pork on Sundays and beef

These two feeding patterns – one for the middling sort, another for plebeians – can be compared to two standards of maintenance defined by Robert Allen: the "respectable" and the "barebones" budgets. It was not Allen's purpose to describe faithfully the diets of specific historical populations, but to establish two benchmarks with sufficient generality that they could be used in many societies to measure the attainability of a survival diet (barebones) and one offering greater variety, more protein, and higher status (respectability). His model budgets set the food component at 80 percent of total expenditure in both cases. Table 11.4,

Table 11.4 *Model diets developed by Robert Allen and average annual food consumption in the BWH (1639–1812), AWH (1683–1795), and Utrecht BWH (1650–1750) (quantities in kilograms unless specified)*

| | Allen model diets | | Orphanage diets | | |
	Respectable	Barebones	BWH	AWH	Utrecht BWH
Bread	182		114	148	121.2
Grain (oats)		170			
Groats, buckwheat, rice		12.6	20.1	*	
Beans and peas	34	20	22.3	19.1	15.6
Meat and fish	26	5	39	25.1	25.4
Butter	5.2	3	19.5	11.7	9.4
Cheese	5.2		9.3	9.1	18.9
Milk (in liters)			210–329	192	82.6
Beer (in liters)	182		309	171	n/a
Eggs (no.)	52				
Treacle		7.5	2.9		
Calories per day	2096	1938	2568	2136	2096
Protein	86 gm	89 gm	115 gm	106 gm	90 gm

* included with beans and peas.
Sources: Robert Allen, "Poverty lines in history, theory, and current international practice" unpublished paper, Nuffield College, Oxford, 2013. Allen presented somewhat different versions of his model diets in "The great divergence in European wages and prices" and *The British Industrial Revolution in Global Perspective* (Cambridge University Press, 2009), pp. 36–37. BWH: McCants, "Monotonous"; G.A. Amsterdam, P.A. 367, no. 591–597, Grootboeken; AWH: G.A. Amsterdam, P.A. 343, no. 85–90, Rekeningen; Utrecht BWH: G.A. Utrecht, Geref. Burgerweeshuis, no. 116, Rekeningen.

or pork on Tuesdays and Fridays. Schiedam's orphans were usually served meat three days per week and could count on fish on a fourth. Vis, *Het Weeshuis van Woerden*, p. 124; Dane, ed., *Wezen en boefjes*, pp. 163–64; G.A. Hoorn, no. 948 (2272), Kinderboekjes; Van der Vlis, *Van wezen to zijn*, pp. 90–91.

which compares Allen's two standards to the provisions of the BWH and AWH, reveals that both orphanages substantially exceed Allen's "respectable" standard, and – of particular relevance for this study – that bread was not the overwhelmingly dominant component of the diet that Allen's standards (reasonably) assume it to have been in most pre-industrial societies.[20] From the perspective of Allen's benchmarks the AWH differed from the BWH more in degree than in kind.

The Pre- and Post-Republican Diets

These generalizations pertain primarily to the period 1640–1790, the era of the classical republican diet. Both before and after this period, matters were rather different.

The available data are more fragmentary for the period before 1640, but they are consistent in showing a diet more dependent on bread, especially rye bread, and less varied than we have just observed. The BWH's records for 1600–32 are not complete, but their grain purchases up to 1623 indicate a per capita bread consumption of 160 kg, some 33–40 percent above its 1640–1780 average level. Utrecht's Burghers' Orphanage supplied even more, 179 kg per annum before 1600; and still 160 kg in 1650 before it, too, reduced its reliance on bread in later decades.[21] This is consistent with other evidence (discussed in the following chapter) that sixteenth- and early seventeenth-century bread consumption was distinctly higher than it would later be.

After 1790, feeding practices change again. Then rising food prices, falling institutional revenues, and new foodstuffs combine to alter the pattern of food expenditures and the sources of calories for burghers and plebeians alike. The plebeians went first, as is well illustrated by the dietary changes at Amsterdam's orphanages. After 1790 the tax revenues and charitable giving on which the AWH depended declined, while the number of orphans and, especially, foundlings, increased sharply. Their total numbers rose from 1,365 in 1782 to 3,482 in 1802. In that year, over 1,300, mostly very young children, were sent out to wet nurses (*minnemoeders*), but this left 2,127 to be squeezed into a building designed in 1666 to house 800.[22] Matters only got worse thereafter, as the AWH in

---

[20] Allen's model diets assume that bread or bread grains accounted for 87 percent of the "barebones" caloric supply and 63 percent of the "respectability" caloric supply. In the BWH diet, bread ranged from 32 to 41 percent of the total caloric supply over the period 1639–1812, while the AWH ranged from 38 to 48 percent over the period 1683–1793.

[21] G.A. Amsterdam, Part. Archief 367, no. 240–41; G.A. Utrecht Burgerweeshuis Archief, no. 116.

[22] In 1802 the regents secured additional space through the purchase of an adjacent building, a warehouse, which they had converted into a sort of barracks, in which bunk beds

1811 had charge of 4,304 orphans, 2,444 of whom somehow found a spot in the orphanage – and somehow were fed there.

The AWH expenditure pattern shifted toward a concentration on the cheapest calories, gradually at first, but with growing urgency in the last years of the eighteenth century. Bread had not claimed more than 20 percent of the food budget for a century, but rose to absorb 33 percent by 1799–1807; groats and legumes, which had absorbed 11–12 percent of the food budget, now rose to 20 percent. Year by year, the AWH orphans received less meat, less butter and cheese, less milk, less treacle, and by 1800 almost no beer.[23] The fate that befell the AWH as the larger economy was pressed to its limits during the Napoleonic era was truly horrific.

As this drama was playing out at the AWH on Amsterdam's Prinsengracht, life for the burgher orphans a few hundred meters away continued more or less as before. The BWH was spared the inundation of foundlings and its stable orphan population was supported by a fairly steady stream of income from its endowment of bonds and real property. But in 1811 the BWH, too, felt the winds of change. Then Napoleon Bonaparte brought an end to the nominally autonomous Kingdom of Holland by incorporating it directly into the French Empire, and thereby brought an end to life as many Dutch burghers had known it by defaulting on the Dutch public debt. Suddenly, the BWH along with many hitherto comfortable burghers faced the need to economize radically. In the case of the BWH, the expenses for bread jumped from under 20 percent to 28 percent of food costs; legumes jump from about 5 to 15 percent; potatoes and vegetables suddenly appeared as a significant element in the diet, and – as at the AWH a decade earlier – purchases of meat, dairy products, and much else were cut back sharply: meat from 29 kg in 1810 to 10 kg per orphan in 1812, cheese from 5.7 kg to 2.2 kg, butter from 6.4 to 4.1 kg, milk from 301 to 231 liters.[24]

The year 1811 struck the already sorely afflicted AWH even harder: the new public authority cut off much of its revenue and ordered the removal of many of its inmates – the foundlings in particular – for placement in rural locations, there to be raised at smaller expense and trained for entry into agrarian occupations. In the following years barge after

---

were stacked to the ceiling and up to three orphans slept in each bed. An 1804 report on conditions in the orphanage claimed the rebuilding was adequate for 1,400 orphans, but conceded that over 2,300 were currently being housed. G.A. Amsterdam, Part. Archief 343, no. 38. See also W. F. van Voorst, *Aalmoezeniersweeshuis en inrichting voor stads-besteledlingen, 1 Januari 1666 – 1 Januari 1916* (Amsterdam: Stadsdrukkerij, 1916), p. 23.

[23] The bread ration did not fall, but the bread appears to have declined significantly in quality. The bread yield per kilogram of grain usually varied between 1.25 and 1.35, but in 1818 the AWH bakery managed to squeeze 1.54 kg of rye bread and 1.64 kg of wheat bread from each kg of grain. G.A. Amsterdam, Part. Archief 343, no. 505.

[24] G.A. Amsterdam, Part. Archief 367, no. 827.

barge, filled with orphans, threaded its way through Amsterdam's canals and set sail across the Zuider Zee. Nearly 2,000 children were sent off in this way to twenty-nine separate locations in the eastern provinces until the orphanage itself was closed in 1825.[25]

Unlike the AWH, the BWH lived on – into the 1960s, in fact – so we can observe that these "emergency" measures were not temporary – they became the "new normal." The sober diet introduced in 1811 remained in place into the 1850s, even after economic conditions improved. Perhaps "burgher status" meant less in the nineteenth century than it had under the old Republic, for the BWH orphans were now fed a diet similar to that provided to the AWH orphans in the eighteenth century: the bread was now predominantly rye; butter, cheese, and meat were far less abundant; and the total caloric provision was reduced. Moderating this deterioration was the appearance of potatoes and vegetables as a regular part of the diet.

It appears, however, that the BWH orphans simply shared in the more spartan diet of the population at large. Table 11.5 shows how

Table 11.5 *Nineteenth-century diets based on household budget studies and orphanage records (percentage of total food expenditures for each category)*

	Budgets	Utrecht BWH	BWH	Budgets	BWH	Budgets
	1853–62	1850	1851–57	1886–97	1886–91	1911–12
Bread	36.3	27.2	32.3	29.3	26.4	23.6
Legumes, gort	11	5.6	12.9	6.1	4.1	7
Potatoes	19.4	7.7	3.5	13.4	5.7	7.9
Vegetables	8.3		8.9	5.9	6.8	10.3
Butter	6.3	14.7	8.4	8.1	10.8	7.4
Cheese	0.3	*	0.8	1.8	1.1	2.9
Milk	3.1	5.2	12	7.3	14.2	11.0
Meat	7.2	24.6	16.2	14.3	23.7	16.3
Fish	1.3	**	0.1	0.8	0.3	1.4
Eggs	0			0.6		1.2
Sugar	2.9			5.2		5.8
Coffee, tea, other	3.9	11.4	3.9	7.2	5.4	5.2
Beer		3.6	1		1.5	
	100	100	100	100	100	100
Food as % of total expenditures	60.8			50.9		48.4

* Cheese included with butter
** Fish included with meat
Sources: Van Riel, "West Netherlands household budgets," www.iisg.nl/hpw/brannex.php
G.A. Utrecht, Geref. Burgerweeshuis, no 116; G.A. Amsterdam, Part. Archief 367.

[25] Van Voorst, *Aalmoezeniersweeshuis*, pp. 23–28. Many of the AWH regents, male and female, opposed the 1811 directive from the new French administration, resigning in

the distribution of food expenditures of the orphanages compared to those reconstructed from household budget studies drawn from the western provinces of the Netherlands. There are some notable differences – the orphans received far fewer potatoes and much more meat and milk in the 1850s – but both sources show a larger expenditure on bread and its substitutes than had been common in the eighteenth century.

This long era of dietary austerity came to an end after the 1850s. By the 1880s the (much smaller) orphanage population ate chiefly wheat bread, along with the population at large, and its meat and dairy product allowances had been restored. Groats, buckwheat and legumes had now definitively given way to potatoes and vegetables, and all of these changes are reflected in the household budgets for this period as well.

The orphanage records offer a fair reflection of food consumption practices in (urban) society generally, and they help situate the place of bread in the Dutch diet. This appears to have been broadly comparable to other European societies in the sixteenth century, but early in the seventeenth century a transition to a new "republican diet" was being completed in which bread accounted for under half of total calories and less than a quarter of total food expenditures. This more varied diet prevailed until a combination of rising prices and falling incomes placed it out of reach, first for the lower classes and then for the middling sort as well. A new, more sober diet prevailed through the first half of the nineteenth century, but it is not one in which bread assumed a notably different place than before. This raises a question that requires a few words of explanation.

The Potato: A New Bread Substitute?

It is often claimed that the diffusion of the potato transformed the northern European diet – that it had revolutionary implications for the long-standing bread-centric foodways of northern Europe, and of the Netherlands. If the potato really acted as a bread substitute – if, as is generally assumed, the rise of its consumption after the mid-eighteenth century came at the expense of bread consumption – this would have posed a mortal threat to Dutch regulatory policies and fiscal structures.

protest. However, the restoration of self-rule did not end this policy. Indeed, one of the new Kingdom's early initiatives was the encouragement of resettlement colonies for urban paupers (and orphans) via the *Maatschappij van Weldadigheid* in Drenthe. The one thing that can be said for this "reform" program is that it reduced very significantly the mortality experienced by the orphans who otherwise would have passed their youth in the insalubrious chambers of the AWH's Amsterdam facility – which, once closed in 1825, was converted to house the city's law courts, a role it fulfills to the present day.

After all, bread was heavily taxed and its price was regulated, while potatoes escaped both taxation and price regulation.[26]

Unlike the bread grains and most boiled grains, whose distribution relied on centralized markets and, often, imports, the potato reached consumers via local fields and gardens, district by district. In time it became ubiquitous, but this does not mean that reliable information about its production, consumption, and price has been easy to come by. The absence of a large, articulated market for this bulky and perishable commodity causes it to remain in the documentary shadows until well into the nineteenth century.[27] Consequently, much about its early diffusion, especially its role in the diet, has been based on surmise.

An important assumption underlying most of the speculation about the rise of the potato is that it offered a cheaper source of calories than the bread grains. But the evidence for this durable assumption is not strong. If we set 3 hectoliters (hl) of potatoes as nutritionally equivalent to one hl of rye, the market price of potatoes was only occasionally below that for the equivalent amount of rye until the 1790s.[28] Moreover, potato prices long showed a much greater spatial variance than did rye. For

[26] A particularly forceful case for the substitution hypothesis was made in Christiaan Vandenbroeke, "Aardappelteelt en aardappelverbruik in de 17e en 18e eeuw," *Tijdschrift voor geschiedenis* 82 (1969), 49–68. In the northern Netherlands, Jobse-van Putten claimed that "the potato apparently formed the principal element of the diet for most social groups by 1800." De Meere made a similar claim. Jobse-van Putten, *Eenvoudig maar voedzaam*, p. 106; J. M. M. de Meere, *Economische ontwikkeling en levensstandaard in Nederland gedurende de eerste helft van de negentiende eeuw* (The Hague: Martinus Nijhoff, 1982), p. 111.

[27] Potatoes are bulky and heavy relative to their caloric and nutritional value. This caused the cost advantages enjoyed by potatoes near their point of production to be quickly undone by distance. Moreover, unlike the bread grains, potatoes cannot be stored over a season and are vulnerable to frost. Lacking supply inventories to smooth consumption over good and bad harvests, potato prices tended to be more volatile than grain prices. For more on the potato's tendency to "decommercialize" the rural economy, see Elizabeth Hoffman and Joel Mokyr, "Peasants, potatoes and poverty: transaction costs in prefamine Ireland," in Gary Saxonhouse and Gavin Wright, eds., *Technique, Spirit and Form in the Making of the Modern Economies, Research in Economic History*, Supplement 3 (1984), pp.115–45.

[28] I have compared the national annual average rye price with an average of available potato prices for Leiden, Alkmaar, Brabant, and, beginning in 1800, a national price series compiled by Van Riel, "Prices and industrialization," Appendix B. Until 1790 3 hl of potatoes cost 95 percent of the price for 1 hl of rye. One hl of rye weighs about 70–72 kg. The weight of 1 hl of potatoes could vary considerably from year to year. Van Zanden set the specific gravity at 61 kg; Noordegraaf set it at 77 kg, while De Meere accepted a nineteenth-century source that set it at 84 kg. I assume here that their weight per hl was 70 kg. My assumption about caloric equivalence is also subject to some margin of error. Noordegraaf and De Meere, following Vandenbroeke, held that potatoes yielded 700 kcal per kg. It took 2.73 kg of potatoes to equal one kg of rye. McCants, relying on FAO/WHO energy tables, set the caloric value of one kg of peeled potatoes at 594, which would require 3.53 kg of potatoes to equal one kg of rye.

example, potato prices on the Alkmaar market exceeded those of Leiden by some 32 percent in the period 1778–1810.

The economic and political crisis beginning in the 1790s dramatically altered the potato's appeal. In an era of chronic trade disruption and volatile grain prices a commodity grown near home and traded locally must have had a strong appeal. Potato markets remained relatively unintegrated, but potato prices had the signal advantage of being only weakly correlated with the prices of the bread grains. Thus, when grain prices rose – as they did to unprecedented heights in 1795 and again in 1800 and most years thereafter until 1817 – potato prices followed their own course. This lack of price correlation is demonstrated in Figure 11.1,

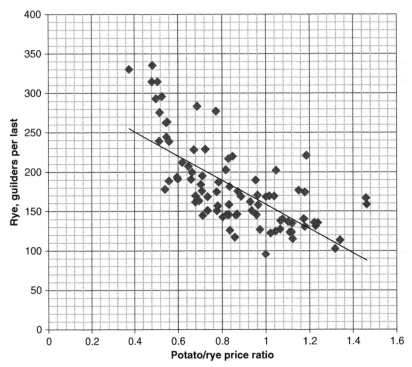

Figure 11.1 Potato/rye price ratio relative to rye price, 1763–1853

Potato prices: 1763–1799, Leiden market prices, Pot, *Arm Leiden*, pp. 309–10; 1800–1853, Van Riel database. National average prices.

Four years have been excluded from these calculations as outliers. 1816–17 and 1846–47 were all years of failure of the potato crop, the first two for weather reasons, the second two, better known, because of the potato blight. In these years, potato prices were no bargain even though rye prices were very high.

which shows the ratio of potato to rye prices as rye prices rose. If potato prices followed the general trend of rye prices, the ratio of these prices would remain constant. Instead, we see that potatoes often were no bargain when grain prices were low (a ratio above 1.0 shows that the per-calorie cost of potatoes exceeded that of rye), but became progressively more attractive as the rye price rose. This was an enduring relationship over the period 1763–1853, although individual years could deviate greatly from this pattern.

The price patterns displayed in Figure 11.1 suggest that we should expect potato consumption to rise as grain and bread prices rise sharply, but to remain a subsidiary element in the diet of most people, since its price advantage was not enduring, disappearing whenever grain prices fell back to normal levels (to which disincentive one must add the year-to-year volatility of potato prices themselves, which introduced an element of risk to a reliance on potatoes).

Once the crisis was over, the potato ceased being a bargain food. It retained its place in the diet as a broad range of consumers came to appreciate its versatility – but that place did not become much larger again until the second half of the nineteenth century.

On the eve of the European potato blight and food crisis of 1845–47 Dutch daily potato consumption was not trivial; a daily consumption of nearly 0.4 kg per capita (perhaps 150 kg per year) fell within the range of other northern European countries, but was only half the level of Belgium and far below Ireland's prodigious average daily intake of 2.1 kg per capita.[29] It had become a significant source of calories, supplying about 8 to 10 percent of average per capita consumption.

Potato consumption rose again after the 1850s.[30] But neither then nor earlier can one speak of a radical substitution of the potato for bread. While it may have replaced bread at certain times of distress, it functioned more commonly as an accompaniment to other vegetables and as a substitute for the lesser grains and legumes that had long been an

---

[29] Eric Vanhaute, "The European subsistence crisis of 1845–50: a comparative perspective," in Eric Vanhaute, Richard Paping, and Cormac Ó Grada, eds., *When the Potato Failed* (Turnhout: Brepols, 2007), pp. 15–40.

[30] "Verbruik van sommige voedings- en genotmiddelen," *Maandschrift van het Centraal Bureau voor de Statistiek* (1913); Patricia Van den Eeckhout and Peter Scholliers, "De hoofdelijke voedselconsumptie in België, 1831–1939," *Tijdschrift voor sociale geschiedenis* 9 (1983), 280–81. The supply of potatoes available in the Netherlands for all purposes (including animal fodder) rose from 177 kg per capita in 1852–56 to 323 kg in 1892–96, before falling back to 245 kg in 1907–11. "Verbruik van sommige voedings- en genotmiddelen," *Maandschrift CBS* (1913). M. Knibbe estimates human consumption in the 1850–1911 period to have averaged about 180 kg per capita, fluctuating between 150 and 210 kg in response to relative prices.

important part of the Dutch diet – the buckwheat, barley groats, peas, and beans discussed earlier.[31]

The "substitution hypothesis" has little to recommend it as a long-term proposition. Bread consumption was no lower in the 1820–50 period than before 1800.[32]. Moreover, as we will see in Chapter 15, the further increase in potato consumption after 1850 was paired with an even faster rise in bread consumption up to the beginning of the twentieth century. Netherlanders then became confirmed potato eaters, but they consumed both more potatoes *and* more bread. The potato came to form a key element in the modern (post-1850) Dutch diet, but its rise did not trigger a decline in bread consumption.

---

[31] Jobse-Van Putten, *Eenvoudig maar voedzaam*, p. 203; Jan van der Maas and Leo Noordegraaf, "Smakelijk eten. Aardappelconsumptie in Holland in de achttiende eeuw en het begin van de negentiende eeuw," *Tijdschrift voor sociale geschiedenis* 9 (1983), 198–200. Buckwheat consumption all but disappears in the course of the nineteenth century, falling from 17 to 4 kg per capita, including use as animal fodder.

[32] Establishing a negative correlation between potato cultivation and bread consumption has also proved difficult elsewhere in Europe. See L. M. Cullen, "Irish history without the potato," *Past and Present* 40 (1968), 72–83.

12   Bread Consumption: A Wheat Bread Revolution?

Consumer Choice within a Distinctive Food System

The aim of this chapter is to measure Dutch bread consumption over the course of the early modern period, with special attention to the relative amounts of wheat and rye bread and the major regional differences. Ideally, one would also wish to know how bread consumption differed by social class, but in practice we will only be able to distinguish between the consumption of charity recipients and the rest of the population.

Since Dutch markets for the bread grains were highly integrated throughout the period under study, consumers in most areas faced a broad choice of bread grains and grain substitutes. As the preceding chapter demonstrates, a large portion of the population usually had access to a diet in which the bread grains were only one among several dietary pillars. Consumers faced choices among several types of bread and bread substitutes just as they faced choices regarding the place of bread within the larger republican diet. Rather than being captive to unyielding, culturally determined, foodways they were participants in a market-based food system.

To many who have studied the social conditions of workers and peasants in the early modern era an emphasis on choice rather than survival will appear as both misdirected and unfeeling for the difficult circumstances in which many people periodically found themselves. The challenge of securing sufficient nutrition was very real in these periods, as discussed in Chapter 10. While these crises rarely led to outright famine in the Netherlands, malnutrition was not unknown, as revealed by the stunted stature of many Netherlanders, especially in the early nineteenth century.[1] But even in difficult circumstances, people made choices that

---

[1] Dutch heights appear to have followed a downward course throughout the medieval and early modern eras. Skeletal remains from the eleventh and twelfth centuries suggest an average adult male height of 173–74 cm. By the fifteenth and sixteenth centuries this had fallen to 169 cm, and a low point was reached in the first half of the nineteenth century: 167 cm. (In 2010, the average height of males at age 20 was 184 cm, making Netherlanders the world's tallest population.) A combination of urbanization, labor

affected the cost and quality of their diet. Moreover, fiscal and regulatory policies both influenced and responded to those choices via the setting of tax rates and in defining the structure of relative bread prices, as shown in Chapter 9. That is, contemporaries were under no illusion that consumer behavior was cocooned in cultural structures or constrained by poverty into a fixed pattern of minimal expenditure.

Measuring the Consumption of the Bread Grains

So, what breads and how much bread *did* the Dutch actually consume over the period 1570–1855? The sources available to estimate the level and composition of bread consumption fall into four broad categories, all of them far from ideal. Thus far we have examined two of them. In Chapter 6 I approached this question from the supply side, attempting a reconstruction of bread grain availability. In most European countries this supply approach would suffice to give a fair picture of consumption, but in the Netherlands, where domestic production was supplemented by large grain imports and exports, the best we can hope for is an approximation of the overall direction of change. We were able to establish that the great bulk of the rye consumed in the western provinces was imported from the Baltic, and that the volume of imports did not rise after the sixteenth century. However, wheat imports did grow. As late as 1574–1629, wheat accounted for only 11 percent of total Baltic grain imports. Thereafter, wheat imports rose both in absolute volume and as a percentage of the total. By 1691–1730 wheat accounted for 26 percent of Baltic grain shipments in Dutch ships, rising to 34 percent in 1731–83.[2] This inflow was supplemented by rising shipments of wheat from England, the Southern Netherlands, and the German lands and, even more importantly, by the rise in domestic wheat production, particularly in Zeeland and adjacent clay-soil districts.[3]

A second source is institutional data. The records of food purchases to feed prison inmates, military personnel, seafarers, and orphans supply quite detailed information, although their representativeness for the civilian population may be questioned. Of these, the orphanage records appear to be most useful for our purposes, and we examined the dietary practices of three orphanages in Chapter 11.

intensification, and dietary change suppressed height attainments in many countries in the first half of the nineteenth century, including Britain and the United States. G. Maat, "Two millennia of male stature development," *International Journal of Osteoarchaeology* 15 (2005), 276–90. For details on the nineteenth century, see Hans de Beer, *Voeding, gezondheid en arbeid in Nederland tijdens de negentiende eeuw: een bijdrage to de antropometrische geschiedschrijving* (Amsterdam: Aksant, 2001), pp. 147–58.

[2] See Table 6.1. See also Faber, "Het probleem van de dalende graanaanvoer," pp. 3–28.

[3] De Vries, "Production and consumption," pp. 199–219.

Table 12.1 assembles estimates of the per capita bread grains provided by the three orphanages studied in Chapter 11 and identifies, where possible, wheat's share in the bread diet. Several features warrant comment. The earliest observations, up to the 1650s, reveal a distinctly higher level of bread grain consumption than thereafter, and wheat then

Table 12.1 *Bread and bread grain consumption in three orphanages, 1562–1899*

	Bread calories % wheat			Quantity of bread grain per capita kg per annum		
	BWH Amsterdam	AWH Amsterdam	GBWH Utrecht	BWH Amsterdam	AWH Amsterdam	GBWH Utrecht
1562	10.8			?		
1582–92			16.3			200–20
1594–1600			11.5			164
1611–17			*			158
1614–32	19.3			137		
1637–42			*			130
1639–59	27.0			120		
1650–60						137
1660–79	27.9			110		
1680–99	39.7	48.3		126	100	
1680–1700						121
1700–19	37.5	32.5		145 (119)***	94	
1719						133
1720–39	44.4	31.9		117	97	
1730–32			*			127
1750						127
1740–59	40.5	36.1		107	108	
1760–79	47.5	41.2		110	112	
1780–89	47.7	44.4		115	95	
1790–1812	44.1			104		
1790–95		39.9			88	
1799–1809		29.1			94	
1800						120
1814–17	26.9**					
1850			57			114
1856–58	23.1**			99		
1886–99	79.6**			88		

Sources: G.A. Amsterdam, Part. Archief 343; Part. Archief 367; G.A. Utrecht, Gereformeerd Burgerweeshuis, Archief 725, no. 116; McCants, "Monotonous," p. 78.

Table 12.1 (*cont.*)

*Utrecht GBWH records do not distinguish wheat (*tarwe*) and rye (*rogge*) after 1610, referring to all grain as "*weit.*" The name suggests that it is wheat, but the prices paid do not. The average price paid per last of *weit* averaged only 84 percent of the market price for wheat in the period 1611–17 and 1637–42. If the orphanage had purchased 20 percent wheat and 80 percent rye in this period, the average grain price would have been approximately 75 percent of the wheat price. This suggests that relatively more wheat was being purchased for the orphanage after 1611 than before – perhaps as much as 50 percent wheat. However, by 1700–01 the records refer specifically to *tarwe*, and the prices appear consistent with the purchase of wheat. By then it appears that this orphanage supplied *only* wheat bread.
**BWH live-in personnel ate in the same building as the orphans, but not at the same table. Their bread supply was 75–80 percent wheat throughout the period 1814–99.
***The high figure for 1700–19 is based on McCants' study of the BWH orphan diet. In this period the orphans received not only an unusually large amount of bread, but of nearly every other foodstuff in their diet, leading to a caloric intake 18 percent above any other twenty-year period. This hints at an underestimation of the orphan population in this period. A reduction of the bread grain consumption by 18 percent leaves 119 kg. The estimation of per capita bread grain consumption is sensitive to the size and composition of the orphan population. The BWH did not admit children below the age of 6. The AWH was the destination for foundlings and other abandoned children, who became numerous by the 1790s. Infants were sent to wet nurses, and I have subtracted them from the total orphanage population, but there remains some uncertainty as to the number of orphans actually resident in the AWH after 1790.

accounted for only a small portion of the total. Thereafter, the consumption level remained fairly constant, at approximately 95–115 kg per year in Amsterdam and somewhat higher in Utrecht. Also noteworthy is the gradually increased place of wheat bread in the orphan diets, from less than 30 percent wheat before 1650, to more than 40 percent after 1720.

The orphanage records are broadly consistent with the directions of change indicated by the evidence of grain supplies, but a question persists about the representativeness of orphans' diets. We know, for instance, that live-in orphanage servants (*suppoosten*) routinely received more wheat bread than did the orphans. A detailed accounting of BWH bread usage in 1812 (preparatory to a major economizing move) showed that wheat bread accounted for 67 percent of the servants' total bread consumption, while it accounted for about 45 percent of the bread fed to orphans. Was wheat bread thought more appropriate for adults, whether for health or status reasons? I suspect status played some role, but this could not be the only consideration, since among the orphans further distinctions were made. At breakfast the adolescent orphans who worked (the boys as apprentices to craftsmen in the city, the girls in the textile workshops within the orphanage) each received 13 slices of bread per week (two per day except Sunday, when they got only one). The boys received only rye bread slices; the girls received 7 slices of rye bread and 6 of wheat. At dinner and supper all orphans received the same mix of wheat and rye bread, but sick orphans received only wheat bread. The orphanage also served bread in the form of chunks (*brokken*) soaked in buttermilk or broth; for some dishes they used wheat bread, for others rye bread was deemed more suitable. These practices led to an overall wheat–rye usage that was about equal for the orphans. The servants ate more wheat in large part because they consumed more bread and less bread-chunk infused porridge.[4]

A third source, tax data, offers what is potentially a very rich source of information. The provincial excises on milled grain date from the 1570s, came to be levied in every province, and continued in effect until 1806, when they were replaced by a uniform national tax. Unfortunately, all that has been preserved systematically from before 1798 are provincial records of total annual revenues. How they can be made to yield insights into the amounts of grain milled for bread-making purposes presents a major challenge.

I begin by reviewing the evidence that is most secure, which is available from 1798 onward and then work backward, via progressively less complete evidence, to estimate bread consumption trends back into the sixteenth century. In making this indirect circuit, I will focus attention initially on Holland but broaden the scope of inquiry to the rest of the country whenever possible.

Bread Consumption, 1798–1855

The first detailed record of bread consumption in Holland dates from 1798. Ten years later, in 1808, data become available not only for Holland (which then had been divided into two provinces), but for the entire Republic – now the Batavian Republic.

The 1798 data show Holland's bread consumption to be low by the European standards of that time, when figures twice as high are often cited, and confirm that Hollanders – both urban and rural – consumed twice as much wheat bread as rye bread. The national data for 1808 confirm the patterns revealed for Holland in 1798, and show that Zeeland and Utrecht shared them. But the data also show that rye bread continued

---

[4] G.A. Amsterdam, P.A. 367, 1812 schaftlijst.

to dominate elsewhere. Overall, wheat accounted for 70 percent of taxed bread grains in the three western provinces but only 15 percent in the eastern and northern provinces. The data also show a significantly lower level of bread consumption in most of these provinces (75 kg in the east and north vs. 108 kg in the west). This may be misleading. Since all our data are based on tax revenue, we need to take into account bread that escaped taxation for both legitimate (charitable) and illegitimate (evasive) reasons. Moreover, since the national bread excise had just been introduced in 1806, and it met with widespread resistance in the eastern provinces, where taxes had earlier been much lower, the low recorded consumption levels there are likely to be incorrect.[5]

This surmise is supported by the next available provincial-level records, which begin in 1834. National taxes were then much lower than before, and, perhaps for this reason, taxed consumption in the east was strikingly higher than it had been in 1808. Indeed it was now, on average, higher than in the west (102 kg in the east and north vs. 96 kg in the west). These differences, shown in Table 12.3, are likely to speak more to changes in the extent of compliance than to changes in the actual consumption levels.

The milling excise revenues from 1798 and 1808 reflect a period of economic volatility and general distress, but they reveal – once their shortcomings are taken into account – a stable consumption pattern that was similar in level to that documented by orphanage diets, and that can

Table 12.2 *Per capita grain consumption in Holland, 1798 (per capita, in kg)*

	Wheat	Rye	Buckwheat	Total
Urban	77.99	26.53	22.59	127.11
Rural	53.40	37.46	17.01	107.87
Total	67.05	31.39	20.11	118.55
Total lasts	24,335	12,547	9,246	46,128

NB In addition, 2,073 lasts of grain were recorded as being subject to the lower taxes levied on grain for brewing and starch making. This was 4.3 percent of total excised grain, but accounted for under 1 percent of excise revenue.
Source: Van der Woude, "De consumptie van graan."

[5] Tom Pfeil, *"Tot redding van het Vaderland": het primaat van de Nederlandse overheidsfinanciën in de Bataafs-Franse Tijd, 1795–1810* (Amsterdam: NEHA, 1998), pp. 451–53. Resistance to the new national tax in Groningen is discussed in some detail in Paping, *Voor een handvol stuivers*, p. 379.

Table 12.3 *Bread grain consumption in the Netherlands, 1808 (excluding Zeeland-Flanders, and Limburg) (by weight)*

	Wheat	Rye	Total	Population	Wheat	Rye	Total	wheat as %
	kg per capita	kg per capita	kg per capita	in thousands	in lasts	in lasts	in lasts	of total
North Holland	69.11	35.87	104.98	394.00	11,838.84	6,729.90	18,568.74	65.83
South Holland	74.19	31.81	106.00	391.00	12,612.30	5,922.72	18,535.02	69.99
Zeeland	74.91	9.38	84.29	114.00	3,712.93	509.20	4,222.13	88.87
Utrecht	70.91	50.10	121.01	103.00	3,175.53	2,457.29	5,632.82	58.60
Friesland	19.82	63.10	82.92	171.00	1,473.57	5,138.14	6,611.72	23.90
Groningen	9.35	56.05	65.40	126.00	512.22	3,363.00	3,875.22	14.30
Drenthe	3.95	73.26	77.21	43.00	73.85	1,500.09	1,573.93	5.12
Overijssel	5.74	47.45	53.19	142.00	354.38	3,208.52	3,562.91	10.79
Gelderland	12.51	44.03	56.54	240.00	1,305.39	5,032.00	6,337.39	22.13
North Brabant	10.32	89.46	99.78	277.00	1,242.89	11,800.20	13,043.09	10.34
Total	41.74	47.91	89.65	2,001.00	3,6301.91	45,661.05	81,962.96	46.56
West	71.94	35.85	107.79	1,002.00	31,411.55	15,654.95	47,066.50	66.74
North and east	11.42	63.15	74.57	999.00	4,962.30	30,041.95	35,004.25	15.31

Source: I. J. A. Gogel, *Memoriën en correspondentiën* (Amsterdam, 1814).

Table 12.4 *Bread grain consumption in the Netherlands, 1834–37 (excluding Zeeland-Flanders and Limburg) by weight*

	Wheat kg per capita	Rye kg per capita	Total kg per capita	Population in thousands	Wheat in lasts	Rye in lasts	Total	Wheat as % of total
North Holland	51.75	37.38	89.13	428.00	9630.00	7618.40	17248.40	58.06
South Holland	77.38	20.25	97.63	505.00	16989.96	4869.64	21859.60	79.26
Zeeland	116.25	5.50	121.75	144.00	7278.26	377.14	7655.40	95.48
Utrecht	53.38	33.25	86.63	138.00	3202.80	2185.00	5387.80	61.62
Friesland	14.13	60.75	74.88	219.00	1345.42	6335.36	7680.78	18.87
Groningen	9.25	64.13	73.38	168.00	675.65	5130.40	5806.05	12.61
Drenthe	5.75	94.38	100.13	69.00	172.50	3101.06	3273.56	5.74
Overijssel	11.00	79.75	90.75	190.00	908.70	7215.48	8124.17	12.12
Gelderland	25.88	80.50	106.38	329.00	3701.97	12611.67	16313.63	24.33
North Brabant	29.63	102.88	132.51	363.00	4676.39	17783.54	22459.93	22.36
Total	43.77	55.31	99.08	2553.00	48581.64	67227.69	115809.32	44.18
West	70.23	26.01	96.24	1215.00	37101.02	15050.19	52151.20	72.97
North & East	19.73	81.89	101.62	1338.00	11480.62	52177.50	63658.12	19.42

Source: J. de Bosch Kemper, *Statistiek van Nederland* (Amsterdam: Weijtingh en van der Haart, 1854), p. 29.

serve as a benchmark for our further investigations. Annual per capita bread consumption stood at approximately 100 kg of taxed bread grain (at least 110 kg of total consumption), a level that did not differ greatly by region. What did differ greatly by region, and consistently so, was the mix of wheat and rye chosen by consumers. In the west wheat accounted for at least two-thirds of the total, while in the east it accounted for about 15 percent.

This is a pattern that persisted throughout the first half of the nineteenth century, with two exceptions. Consumption sank by one-third in the final, desperate years of the Napoleonic era when the country was cut off from Baltic grain and even domestic (Zeeland) wheat. But, after 1817 the old patterns returned. The "Hungry Forties" were another difficult period, but per capita bread consumption changed very little in these years. Instead, consumers shifted a portion of their bread consumption from wheat to rye.

Thus far, we have been able to break down the aggregated data geographically: by province and urban–rural location. What we could not do is distinguish consumption trends by social class. However, it is difficult to reconcile these data with the common assumptions found in earlier literature that most common people consumed rye bread almost exclusively until they had to abandon even this and derive satisfaction from potatoes. Moreover, if manual workers consumed bread near the national average (about 110 kg of bread grain per year, or 140–45 kg of bread) the working-class diet was not founded on a large, monotonous supply of bread, as may have been true of other countries at the time. Nor is there any evidence of a general shift away from bread in favour of the potato. Still, one must recognize that there are clear limits to what aggregated data can reveal about the consumption practices of individuals or even social classes.

Bread Consumption, 1650–1798

We now have a firm benchmark for Dutch bread consumption, and will consider the post-1855 course of bread consumption in Chapter 15, where we examine how the removal of price controls and taxes affected consumer behavior. Now the time has come to look backward. Is it justified to project the pattern of bread consumption just summarized back to the early eighteenth century or even further?

Only fragments of information remain of the municipal-level milling tax administration records, which once must have been voluminous. Table 12.5 summarizes data gathered from several of Holland's cities. Amsterdam's detailed consumption data take us back no further than 1782–86, when consumption was above the 1795–1814 average and

Table 12.5 *Bread grain consumption in Holland cities, 1720–1848 (in kilograms per capita)*
T = taxed; NT = non-taxed (charity bread)

		Wheat	Rye	Total	% Wheat bread grain
Leiden					
1720	T	50.0	23.8	73.8	67.8
	NT	5.1	11.6	16.7	30.5
	total	55.1	35.4	90.5	60.8
1726–29				93.5	
1730–39				94.5	
1740–47				98.6	
1750–54				89.7	
1795–96		44.5	22.9	67.4	66.0
1798		51.9	34.0	85.9	60.4
Haarlem					
1733	T	56.7	19.8	76.5	74.4
	NT	4.6	10.3	14.9	30.9
	total	61.3	30.1	91.4	67.1
1734	T	55.9	19.6	75.5	74.0
	NT	4.9	12.5	17.4	28.2
	total	60.8	32.1	92.9	65.4
1740*	T	67.1	46.1	113.2	59.3
	NT	2.2	4.5	6.7	32.8
	total	69.2	50.6	119.9	57.7
1750		60.0	23.0	83.0	72.3
1751		54.1	26.3	80.4	67.3
1752		55.5	26.6	82.1	67.6
1753		53.4	25.1	78.5	68.0
1798		58.3	31.5	90.2	64.6
Amsterdam					
1698–1700				130	
1771		84.1	27.5	111.6	75.4
1782–86		100.1	24.1	124.7	80.3
1795–98		77.2	23.9	101.1	76.4
1809		82.3	25.4	107.7	76.4
1810–14		91.7	20.3	112.0	81.9
1817–26		69.0	31.9	100.9	68.4
Dordrecht					
1795		95.9	23.1	119.0	80.6
1809		80.9	29.9	110.8	73.0
The Hague					
1790		59.8	27.3	87.1	68.6
Rotterdam					
1789	T				90
	NT				74
1839–48		96.2	25.4	121.6	79.1

* 1740 was a year of high prices, especially toward its end. Haarlem's magistrates spent 169,000 guilders to purchase 604 lasts of grain, partially for distribution to the churches

Table 12.5 (*cont.*)

for charitable distribution, but chiefly for distribution to the bakers for the production of reduced price bread. Overall, this was one-third of all grain consumed in Haarlem in 1740, and it appears – ironically – to have resulted in an usually high level of bread consumption.

Sources:

Amsterdam: Nieuwenhuijs, *Proeve*, vol. I, p.199; Ad Knotter and Hans Muskee, "Conjunctuur en levenstandaard in Amsterdam, 1815–1855," *Tijdschrift voor sociale geschiedenis* 12 (1986), 153–81; Gogel, *Memorieën*, Bijlage F, p. 508; Heijder, *Korenschuur*, p. 83.

Haarlem: G.A. Haarlem, Stadsarchief 1581–1795, R413, K270 (1157).

Leiden: G.A. Leiden, SA II, no. 7829, 7847, 7853, 7875, 7881; G.A. Leiden, Gilden archief, no. 832; Pot, *Arm Leiden*, p. 313.

The Hague: G.A. Den Haag, O.A., no. 5741.

Dordrecht: G.A. Dordrecht, no. 4–387 (grain milled by bread bakers in the first six months of 1795); Gogel, *Memorieën*, Bijlage F, p. 508.

Rotterdam: G.A. Rotterdam, Oud Archief, no. 2125; Anon., "Staat van de jaarlijksche consumptie binnen Rotterdam van 1839–1848, volgens de aangiften van de belastingen," *Staathuishoudkundig jaarboekje* 2 (1950), 309.

weighted even more heavily toward wheat bread – a result that is certainly consistent with the more benign economic environment before 1795. Haarlem and Leiden, industrial cities in decline in the eighteenth century, supply consumption data going back to 1733 and 1720, respectively, and reveal the now familiar pattern of wheat accounting for *at least* two-thirds of the total bread supply. Finally, we can turn back to Amsterdam, for which we have contemporary estimates of aggregate bread grain consumption in 1698–1700 (estimated to deal with the city's needs in a time of looming shortage and high prices). The city's residents were thought to consume 130 liters, or about 100 kg of wheat and rye together.

The Haarlem and Leiden records also offer a glimpse of non-taxed bread grain, intended for charitable distribution. This gives a more complete picture of total bread consumption in the towns, although non-taxed bread should not be confused with bread that has evaded taxation. In both cities some 20 percent of all bread was tax exempt in the early eighteenth century, and the poor beneficiaries received twice as much rye bread as wheat bread – the reverse of the wheat–rye mix chosen by the tax-paying population. However, in more prosperous Rotterdam, the distinction between taxed and untaxed bread was much smaller. Even charity recipients consumed far more wheat bread than rye bread in 1789.[6]

[6] Another glimpse into the bread consumption of charity recipients is provided by the registration books of Delft's municipal Office of Poor Relief [*Kamer van Charitatie*]. These books list the households eligible for distributions of bread and/or cash. In 1645, 61 percent of the 740 poor households received rye bread, 64 percent received wheat bread (nearly half of the households received both kinds), while 23 percent received only cash.

Overall, these fragmentary data from urban Holland support the hypothesis that Holland's late-eighteenth-century consumption pattern, both in level of consumption and in wheat–rye mix, was of long standing, going back at least a century. But they are fragmentary. Can we do better than that? The most comprehensive source of information is the provincial milling excise. In theory, the records of this tax provide annual data on the amount of grain milled for baking from the earliest days of the Dutch Republic.

Holland's fiscal archives (we will consider other provinces later) preserve a record of the annual milling excise revenues from 1650 onward. Before then data for only a few scattered years have been preserved.[7] These are highly aggregated data, providing only an annual lump sum that combines the excises on all milling, including that for non-bread grains. Moreover, before 1750 they are the payments of tax farmers (approximating net revenues), while thereafter they are the gross revenues of provincial tax collectors. Finally, they incorporate excise payments from the countryside, where, in the milling excise's early years, under-collection was endemic, while later, from 1680 in Holland, the excise was converted to a head tax that, by definition, held per capita bread consumption at a fixed level.

Uncovering the course of bread grain consumption from this "noisy" source requires a careful analysis of all the factors that could cause the course of milling excise revenue to deviate from the underlying volume of milling activity. These issues – the size of the difference between gross and net revenues, the amount of non-bread milling (mainly for brewing), the extent of rural tax evasion before 1680 – are complex, and to spare the reader a tedious discourse here, I deal with them in Appendix 3, where my methodology may be inspected in detail. Here I present the findings from that interrogation of the excise tax records.

The results of these adjustments to the original tax data are presented in Figure 12.1, which offers separate estimate of per capita bread grain consumption for Holland's urban and rural populations. This is necessary because the post-1680 capitation policy set rural bread consumption at a fixed, and very low, amount. We simply do not know the *actual* course of bread consumption in the countryside from 1680 to 1795. However, both the revenues before 1680 and, again, in 1798 and after 1806 (shown in Tables 12.2–12.4) show the consumption level set by the capitation policy to have been a fiscal fiction.

Ingrid van der Vlis, *Leven in armoede. Delftse bedeelden in de zeventiende eeuw* (Amsterdam: Uitgeverijen Prometheus/Bert Bakker, 2001), pp. 111–20.
[7] A.R.A. The Hague, Financiën van Holland, no. 826–28; Leisker and Fritschy, *GWF – Holland*, pp. 106–14.

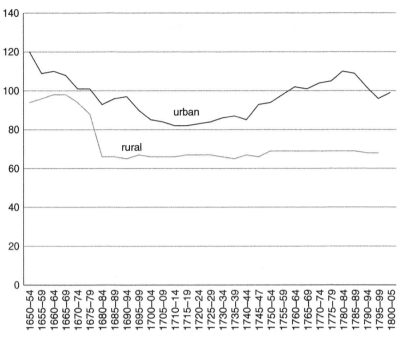

Figure 12.1 Estimated taxed bread grain consumption in Holland, 1650–1805

The limitations of the milling excise revenue records counsel against over-interpretation. But Figure 12.1 offers some support to the hypothesis that both the level and the mix of bread grain consumption in Holland observed in the 1790s had prevailed already in the late seventeenth century. The apparent decline in consumption between 1690 and the 1715 is puzzling. It may reflect an increase in tax evasion but, whatever its cause, it was largely undone by the 1740s. Before 1680, consumption levels appear to have been higher than in the eighteenth century. In 1650 per capita excise revenues were about 20 percent above the 1680–1798 level. Just how much higher actual bread consumption then was depends sensitively on the wheat–rye consumption mix, which we have assumed thus far to be fixed at the eighteenth-century level. But the place of wheat was almost certainly much smaller early in the seventeenth century, and this will require some further adjustment to the estimates we have just made.

Bread Consumption before 1650

I have uncovered only scattered information on Holland's milling excise revenues before 1650. These fragments offer no secure basis for estimating consumption levels but do send one clear message: the assumption that Hollanders consumed twice as much wheat bread as rye bread cannot be valid before 1650. Under that assumption consumption calculations remain fairly flat, even declining in the earliest years. Yet every other type of evidence we have for the sixteenth and early seventeenth centuries argues for much higher levels of bread consumption. The only conclusion one can draw is that the wheat–rye mix in the 1590s and early 1600s had been much more heavily weighted toward rye than it was by the early eighteenth century. In between, a substantial shift in diet must have occurred, from a large level of bread consumption dominated by rye bread to a smaller level of bread consumption dominated by wheat bread.

Many historians, invoking a variety of sources, have claimed that the consumption of the bread grains in pre-Revolt Holland was well above the level we have established for the eighteenth century (100–10 kg). Table 12.6 assembles observations of many sorts, but all based on archival evidence. The data from Leiden and Haarlem are particularly relevant. In 1599–1605 the population of Leiden consumed 82 percent more bread than in 1726–54. By 1626 consumption had fallen substantially, but was still 45 percent above Leiden's eighteenth-century level. Haarlem's bread price commissioners had two occasions to attempt estimates of the volume of bread prepared by their bakers in the 1660s and 70s. In both cases, they set annual production at about 20 percent above the level recorded in the excise tax records of 1733–53 displayed in Table 12.5.

We can be confident of the *direction* of change before 1650 but we have little certain knowledge about the *amount*. Can the milling excise data come to our help here? On the face of things, matters do not look promising. The surviving records suffer from the interpretive difficulties we grappled with for the 1650–1798 period plus two additional shortcomings. We no longer have annual observations, but only data for isolated years, and the further back in time we go the more we must worry that only a portion of the population paid the tax – or paid it into the provincial treasury.

The first problem – scattered observations – can be partially remedied by the comforting fact that the milling excise was raised at fairly long intervals and that revenues were a fairly consistent percentage of the total common means in those intervals. Since we do have annual data for the

Table 12.6 *Estimates of per capita annual bread grain consumption,*
1500–1850

Civilian populations	
1537 Idaarderadeel, Friesland,[a] elderly couple	165 kg
c. 1550 Amsterdam[b]	200 kg
1570 Friesland,[c] Rienck Hemmema servants	191 kg of rye
1599–1605, Leiden,[d] taxed bread grain	166 kg
1626 Leiden,[d] taxed bread grain	122 kg
Seafarers	
1565–1648[e] Average of French, English, and Dutch shipboard rations	179 kg
Southern Netherlands	
1526, 's-Hertogenbosch, charitable distribution	186.5 kg
1557, Antwerp, total population[f]	137 kg (60% rye)
1577–1601, Antwerp, Godshuis der Meerseniers en St. Anna[f]	172–204 kg (75% rye)
1591, Antwerp, Maagdenhuis[f]	133 kg
1594–1600, Antwerp, skilled laborers[f]	250 kg (84% rye)
16th–17th century, Flanders, rural population[g]	235–325 kg
1557–1601 Flanders, total population[h]	243 kg
1648–92 Flanders, total population[h]	250 kg

Sources:
[a] *Charterboek van Friesland*, vol. II, p. 694.
[b] Unger, "Hollandsche graanhandel," pp. 243–69; 337–86; 461–507.
[c] B. H. Slicher van Bath, "Robert Loder en Rienck Hemmema," *It beaken* 20 (1958), 116.
[d] G.A. Leiden, SA II, no. 7829, 7847, 7853, 7975.
[e] R. Baetens, "De voedselrantsoenen van de zeevarenden: de theorie getoetst aan de werkelijkheid," *Bijdragen tot de geschiedenis van het Hertogdom Brabant* 60 (1977), 273–306.
[f] Scholliers, *Levensstandaard*, pp. 173–74, 200–09.
[g] A. Wijffels, "De betekenis van de niet-vrije rente en broodprijzen voor de sociaal-economische geschiedenis," *Tijdschrift voor geschiedenis* 70 (1957), 329–39.
[h] Vandenbroeke, "Aardappelteelt," p. 59.

common means as a whole beginning in 1626, this allows for an indirect estimation of milling excise revenues.

The second problem – limited compliance – was most acute in the sixteenth century, as the provinces struggled to secure agreement to impose the milling excise in the countryside, but it lingered on as a problem of rural enforcement. The evidence points in the direction of assuming that the sixteenth-century milling excise revenues was drawn primarily from the urban population.

Table 12.7 assembles the available milling excise data for Holland and offers a sketch of the possible course of per capita consumption. It calculates per capita consumption under four alternative mixes of wheat and rye consumption (ranging from a 67–33 wheat–rye mix to a 33–67 wheat–rye mix) and two assumptions about the portion of the population that actually paid the milling excise in this period (full compliance and payment by three-quarters of Holland's population).

Two things seem clear: the pre-1650 revenues were never sufficient to be consistent with full compliance, and the 67–33 wheat–rye mix that characterized Holland's bread grain from the late seventeenth century onward could not have prevailed in the late sixteenth and early seventeenth centuries. The most plausible interpretation of the surviving tax records is this: the milling excise was paid primarily by the urban population, certainly in the earliest years, and the consumption of wheat was then much smaller than later, probably only one-third of total bread grain use before 1600. Under these assumptions, the data are consistent with a per capita consumption of 150–70 kg in the 1599–1629 period, and a gradually declining consumption thereafter, converging on the 120–30 kg level in the 1650s, declining further to the 110 kg level that seems to have prevailed by the 1680s.

Bread Consumption in Other Provinces

This interpretation finds support in the milling excise evidence from the Republic's other provinces. The milling excise was levied in all provinces although, of course, each province went about this task in its own way. In several the surviving data for the pre-1650 period are more complete than for Holland and they offer useful information concerning the course of the overall level of bread grain consumption.

Friesland, the best-documented province, reveals a rather high consumption level in the 1630s, 158 kg per capita, which falls to the 135–115 kg range from the 1650s through the 1790s.[8] In Zeeland, where most surviving records refer only to the chief island of Walcheren, bread grain consumption from 1610 through the 1640s exceeded 165 kg per capita, but by the 1690s it had fallen to 120 kg.[9] Both of these provinces show high bread grain consumption levels in the early seventeenth century (158–65 kg) that then decline to a level near that of eighteenth-century Holland.

---

[8] Trompetter, *GWF – Friesland*, pp. 94–101, 143. These estimates assume that the wheat–rye consumption ratio was near the level found in 1808: 25% wheat – 75% rye.

[9] Veenstra, *GWF – Zeeland*, pp. 158–60, table III 4.1a. As a wheat-producing and exporting province, Zeeland consumed little rye bread, no more than 20 percent, in the eighteenth century. I have assumed this was also true in the seventeenth century in estimating the volume of taxed bread grain. To the extent that the lower-taxed rye was then more important, the estimates here understate the true level of bread grain consumption.

Table 12.7 *Model of bread consumption before 1650*

| | Milling excise | | Excise per lasts of grain | | Holland |
| | net revenue | gross revenue | Wheat | Rye | Total population |
			guilders per last		
1599	216.00	248.40	12.00	6.00	570.000
1608	698.10	802.82	32.40	16.20	605.000
1621	848.00	975.20	32.40	16.20	680.000
1625–29	1141.00	1312.15	40.50	20.25	700.000
1630–34	1136.00	1306.40	47.70	23.85	720.000
1635–39	1344.00	1545.60	63.60	31.80	740.000
1640–44	1439.00	1654.85	63.60	31.80	760.000
1645–49	1580.00	1817.00	63.60	31.80	780.000
1650–54	1703.00	1958.45	63.60	31.80	800.000
1655–59	1640.00	1886.00	63.60	31.80	815.000

Estimated per capita bread grain consumption under four wheat–rye mixes, assuming full compliance

	67–33	55–45	40–60	33–67
1599	86.11	92.78	102.72	**107.86**
1608	97.12	127.48	115.85	**121.64**
1621	104.96	137.78	**125.20**	131.46
1625–29	109.75	118.24	**130.92**	137.46
1630–34	90.20	97.18	**107.60**	112.97
1635–39	77.87	83.90	**92.89**	97.54
1640–44	81.18	87.47	**96.84**	101.68
1645–49	86.85	**93.58**	103.60	108.78
1650–54	91.27	**98.34**	108.88	114.32
1655–59	86.28	**92.96**	102.92	108.06

Estimated per capita bread grain consumption, assuming 3/4 of population was subject to milling excise

	67–33	55–45	40–60	33–67
1599	114.82	123.71	136.96	**143.81**
1608	129.49	169.98	154.46	**162.18**
1621	139.94	183.70	**166.93**	175.28
1625–29	146.33	157.65	**174.56**	183.28
1630–34	120.27	129.57	**143.46**	150.63
1635–39	103.83	111.87	**123.86**	130.05
1640–44	108.24	116.62	**129.12**	135.58
1645–49	115.80	**124.77**	138.14	145.04
1650–54	121.70	**131.12**	145.17	152.43
1655–59	115.04	**123.95**	137.22	144.09

Per capita bread grain consumption is estimated by determining the taxed lasts of grain (gross revenue, which is 15 percent more than net revenue, divided by the weighted average of the wheat and rye taxes) and dividing by the population. I assume throughout that 10 percent of milling excise revenue is attributable to non-bread milling.
Bold: probable course of consumption.

The long-term evolution of bread grain consumption in most of the Netherlands is from a relatively high sixteenth-century level to a much lower one by the early eighteenth century; only in the western region, most notably in Holland and Utrecht, was there a simultaneous evolution from a bread diet composed principally of rye to one dominated by wheat. This claim is broadly accepted; the chief issues concern the details: when and why did the decline in consumption take place and when, and with what intensity, did the shift from rye to wheat occur?[10]

The Views of Contemporaries

Contemporary observations (more often about the types of bread consumed than the quantity) form our final body of evidence. Given the limitations of the quantitative evidence reviewed thus far, it is comforting to note that literary evidence is consistent with the view that Hollanders became a predominantly wheat-eating people in the course of the seventeenth century. The folklore specialist J. J. Voskuil addressed this matter in an influential article. After noting that sixteenth-century visitors to Holland did not fail to comment on the universality of rye bread consumption, he proceeded to trace the diffusion of a new expression: *wittebroodskinderen*, literally, "white bread children." The term was

---

[10] Two recent studies have attempted to answer these questions. Van Zanden and Van Leeuwen, in their effort to calculate national income for Holland in the period 1510–1800, estimate per capita grain consumption (excluding beer) *c.* 1500 at 200 liters (*c.* 145 kg). They believe this level of consumption remains constant until *c.* 1750, when rising potato consumption drives grain consumption down by 15 percent, i.e., to about 170 liters (*c.* 125 kg). They also estimate the share of wheat in these totals as rising from 10 percent in the early sixteenth century to 70 percent by 1808. Jan Luiten van Zanden and Bas van Leeuwen, "Persistent but not consistent: the growth of national income in Holland, 1347–1807," *Explorations in Economic History* 49 (2012), 119–30. The sixteenth-century estimates are defended in Jan Luiten van Zanden, "Taking the measure of the early modern economy: historical national accounts for Holland in 1510/14," *European Review of Economic History* 6 (2002), 3–36.

Milja van Tielhof reviews the entire grain economy of the region, and concludes, tentatively, that per capita grain consumption may have been nearly 200 liters (equivalent to approximately 145 kg of bread grain) in the sixteenth century, and that it fell in the course of the seventeenth century to 130 liters (95 kg). Milja van Tielhof, *The Mother of All Trades: The Baltic Grain Trade in Amsterdam from the Late 16th to the Early 19th Century* (Leiden: Brill, 2002), pp. 86–87. She is more circumspect than Van Zanden and Van Leeuwen concerning the scope of the shift from wheat to rye: "One cannot rule out that wheat was consumed at a relatively high level in sixteenth-century Holland, although one cannot, of course, simply project the eighteenth-century situation back by two centuries." Van Tielhof, *De Hollandse graanhandel*, p. 125.

introduced in the early seventeenth century as an expression of disapproval of a younger generation's new taste for white bread. By 1641 the Dordrecht playwright Peter van Godewijcx had written a play on this theme with the explicit title: *Wittebrootskinderen, of bedorve jongelingen* [White bread children, or spoiled youth]. This expression of social disapproval of what had begun as an elite fashion was reinforced by medical disapproval: then (as now) doctors warned their patients away from bolted wheat bread.[11]

It seems unlikely that the consumption of wheat bread could have been as novel in the early seventeenth century as Voskuil suggests, since the orphanages, which are unlikely to have coddled and spoiled their charges with luxurious fare, already included at least some wheat bread in the diet they supplied. It may be that the issue that most concerned the critics cited by Voskuil was not wheat bread, *per se*, but refined, bolted white bread. But the orphanage records do reveal a gradual tendency away from rye and toward wheat bread in all its forms in the course of the seventeenth century. Thus, while we cannot suppose that wheat bread had no place in the non-elite diet of sixteenth-century Hollanders, it does appear highly likely that it was a much smaller place than we find by the end of the seventeenth century.

In this chapter I have been engaged in the assembly of a jigsaw puzzle with many missing pieces. The placement of some pieces seems obvious; that of others is more tentative. Pending the discovery of more of the missing pieces, Table 12.8 is presented as the most consistent arrangement of the available evidence on the course of bread consumption in the Netherlands.

On the basis of these estimates of per capita bread grain consumption, the regional mix of grains, and the discussion in Chapter 6 of grain availability (from domestic production and net imports), I have made estimates of total national bread grain use for several benchmark years, broken down by region and grain type. The trade data reviewed in Chapter 6 also permits estimates of the role of imports in total Dutch consumption.

These estimates, especially those for the seventeenth century, are no more than approximate, but they are, I believe, sufficiently reliable to support the following generalizations about the Dutch bread grain economy:

[11] J. J. Voskuil, "Op weg naar luilekkerland," *Bijdragen en mededelingen voor de geschiedenis der Nederlanden* 98 (1983), 460–82. Voskuil refers to the sixteenth-century travel accounts of Chrysostomos Neapolitanus, Ludovico Guicciardini, and Alonso Vásquez, which date from the 1560–70s, p. 475.

Table 12.8 *Summary estimates of bread grain consumption in the Netherlands, 1580–1850*

	West		East				National average	
	Bread grain kg	Wheat–rye mix	Bread grain kg	Wheat–rye mix	% of pop in west	Total pop (in thousands)	Bread grain kg	Wheat–rye mix
1580–1608	130–40 kg	33–67	150–70	15–85	55%	1,322	146	25–75
1608–34	125	40–60	130	15–85	59	1,528	127	30–70
1650–59	115	55–45	120	15–85	60	1,700	118	35–65
1660–1810	110	67–33	120–10	15–85	60>50	1,750>1,950	113	43–57
1810–14	85	62–38	85	15–85	48	2,000	85	38–62
1815–50	110	67–33	100	15–85	47	2,025>2,850	104	42–58

First, the growth of population in the seventeenth and early nineteenth centuries was paired with a decline in consumption, resulting in only modest growth in total demand for grain for bread consumption purposes. Second, the shift toward wheat in the western provinces was such that total rye consumption was no more than stable over long periods. In contrast to this stability, the aggregate demand for wheat doubled in the seventeenth century. Third, and finally, at least 40 percent of the demand for rye was met by imports throughout this 250-year period, while the growing demand for wheat was met by an even faster rise in domestic production, leading to a large overall decline in the role of imports over the course of the seventeenth and eighteenth centuries. By the early nineteenth century domestic production satisfied some 90 percent of the demand for wheat, but throughout the period 1600–1850 domestic production satisfied only about 60 percent of the demand for rye.

Bread Consumption in an International Context

Dutch and other European consumers alike purchased bread in regulated markets. But the Dutch differed from them in the form of the regulatory regime they faced (the new system), the heavy taxation of bread they endured, and the small role of self-provisioning. Did these differences lead to a distinct bread-consuming behavior in the Netherlands? Did neighboring countries also exhibit the decline in per capita consumption documented above for the Netherlands in the seventeenth and eighteenth centuries? Did they also display a growing preference for wheat bread?

Table 12.9 *Estimated consumption of bread grains in the Netherlands plus net grain imports, 1600–1850*
The following tables are constructed with the use of several assumptions, summarized below, concerning the level of per capita bread grain consumption and the proportions of wheat and rye consumed in each region.

	Assumed per capita kg bread grains		Assumed wheat–rye proportions	
	West	East	West	East
1600	140	150	33–67	15–85
1680	110	120	67–33	15–85
1808	110	110	67–33	15–85
1834–37	110	110	67–33	15–85
1850	110	100	62–38	15–85

Estimated bread grain use and net grain imports by grain type and region, in lasts per annum
c. **1600**

	Wheat	Rye	Total
West	14.7	32.5	47.2
East	5.8	36.1	41.9
Total	20.5	68.6	89.1
Net imports	10.0	25.0	35.0
Imports as % of total use	49	36	39

c. **1680**

	Wheat	Rye	Total
West	33.6	18.2	51.8
East	5.5	34.0	39.5
Total	39.1	52.2	91.3
Net imports	12.5	25	37.5
Imports as % of total use	32	48	41

1808

Grain use	Wheat	Rye	Total
West	32.0	17.3	49.3
East	7.2	44.5	51.7
Total	39.2	61.8	101.0
Net imports 1803–09	5.2	21.4	26.6

These estimates may be compared to evidence compiled by contemporaries (Gogel and Alphonse) based on the national milling excise presented in Table 6.3 and the estimates for 1804–09 by Van Riel and presented in Jansen, *Industriële ontwikkeling*, pp. 342–45.

1806–09 estimate	37.4	48.3	85.7
1802–09 estimate	42.0	53.9	95.9

Sources: 1806–09 data from Alphonse, *Aperçu sur la Hollande*, p. 457.
1802–09 data from Van Zanden, *Economische ontwikkeling*, p. 373; Jansen, *Industriële ontwikkeling*, pp. 342–43.

Table 12.9 (*cont.*)

1834–37

	Wheat	Rye	Total
West	37.1	15.1	52.2
East	11.5	52.2	63.7
Total	48.6	67.2	115.8
Net imports (1831–44)	9.9	26.8	36.7
Imports as % of total use	20.2	39.9	31.7

Source: imports, Van Zanden, *Economische ontwikkeling*, p. 373; De Bosch Kemper, *Statistiek van Nederland*, p. 29

c. 1850

	Wheat	Rye	Total
West	37.8	25.2	63.0
East	10.5	59.6	70.1
Total	48.3	84.8	133.1
Total from other sources			
Van Riel (1845–49)	48.4	94.5	142.9
Van Zanden	53.0	110.0	163.0
Heijder	51.6	86.4	138.0
Net imports	3.1	39.4	42.5
Imports as % of total use:	6.4	46.5	31.9

The Netherlands: All provinces except Limburg, in order to render this table comparable to estimates for earlier dates. Grain use, 1846–50; imports, 1851–60.
Sources: Net imports: Van Zanden, *Economische ontwikkeling*, p. 373. Estimates of grain consumption: Jansen, *Industriële ontwikkeling*, pp. 342–43; Heijder, *Korenschuur*, p. 290; De Bosch Kemper, *Statistiek van Nederland*, p. 29.

My estimate of per capita bread consumption in the Netherlands before the 1590s is not precise, but if it stood in the vicinity of 140–150 kg it is almost certainly below levels found elsewhere in Europe. Sixteenth-century estimates for Flanders and Brabant exceeded 200 kg of bread grain per capita; indeed, Unger's survey of grain provisioning in the fifteenth-century Low Countries towns settled on 250 kg for an average figure.[12] More secure estimates for the eighteenth century generally set bread consumption at similarly high levels. Vandenbroeke estimated consumption in the Southern Netherlands at 244 kg in 1710, while contemporary English observers set bread grains of all sorts at one quarter, or 200–220 kg, in the first half of the eighteenth century. Herr placed eighteenth-century rural Spanish consumption at 240 kg, while French estimates – made by both

---

[12] Unger, "Feeding Low Countries towns," pp. 329–58. Prevenier and Blockmans estimated a similar consumption level – 3.2 kg per household per day – for the sixteenth century. For a household of five, this amounts to 234 kg per person per year. Blockmans and Prevenier, "Armoede in de Nederlanden," pp. 502–03. The exception is supplied

contemporaries and modern historians – vary between 2 and 3 *setiers* of grain, or 234 to 350 kg of bread grain.[13] Finally, we can note that Robert Allen's "respectability" basket of goods, designed to calculate the cost of a common pre-industrial standard of living, sets per capita bread consumption at 182 kg, accounting for 63 percent of a 2,100 calorie diet.[14]

Bread consumption in other western European countries was probably higher than in the Netherlands already in the sixteenth century; it certainly was so in the seventeenth and eighteenth centuries when the Dutch diet became more diversified and bread consumption declined. However, there is substantial evidence that a more muted decline took place, although its onset was later, usually only after 1750. Table 12.10 assembles bread consumption estimates for four countries. In the Southern Netherlands, consumption fell by one-third in the period 1710–1791; in Germany, Saalfeld measures a 25 percent decline in the first half of the nineteenth century; in England, a similar decline in bread consumption stretched out over the 1750–1830 period. France may have escaped this development, although this has been a subject of debate. However, nowhere in the surveyed countries did per capita bread consumption fall to the level that appears to have prevailed in most of the Netherlands from the late seventeenth century to the 1850s.

The Wheat Bread Revolution in Northwestern Europe

Today nearly all European bread is wheat bread. Other grains have made something of a comeback in recent decades among advanced consumers, but this has dented only slightly the total dominance of wheat among the bread grains, a dominance completed in the course

by Scholliers' bread consumption estimate for Antwerp in 1557, 171.6 kg of bread or about 130–35 kg grain. However, he offers higher estimates elsewhere, and concludes his study with a hypothesized household budget providing for 240 kg of bread per capita. Scholliers, *Levensstandaard*, pp. 60–61, 173–76.

[13] Vandenbroeke, "Landbouw in de Zuidelijke Nederlanden," pp. 73–101; Richard Herr, *Rural Change and Royal Finances in Spain* (Berkeley: University of California Press, 1989), p. 192; George Grantham, "Professional and occupational specialization in pre-industrial France," *Economic History Review* 46 (1993), 478–502; J.-C. Toutain, "Food rations in France in the eighteenth and early nineteenth centuries: a comment," *Economic History Review* 48 (1995), 769–73; George Grantham, "Food rations in France in the eighteenth and early nineteenth centuries: a reply," *Economic History Review* 48 (1995), 774–77; Cormac Ó Grada and Jean-Michel Chevet, "Famine and market in Ancien Régime France," *Journal of Economic History* 62 (2002), p. 719.

[14] Allen, "The great divergence in European wages and prices." Elsewhere Allen revised his respectability diet to increase the supply of calories. He achieves this goal by increasing the assumed consumption of bread, to as high as 250 kg. Allen, *The British Industrial Revolution in Global Perspective*, pp. 36–37.

Table 12.10 *Per capita bread consumption in four European countries, 1700–1914*

Southern Netherlands/Belgium, 1710–1914		
	% wheat	Total bread consumption
Vandenbroeke's estimates:		
1710		244 kg
1740		232 kg
1781–91		162 kg
1800–10	39%	162 kg
Blomme's estimates:		
1800–10 Flanders		145 kg
Wallonia		187 kg
Eeckhout and Scholliers' estimates:		
1845–49	53%	171 kg
1850–59	54%	167 kg
1913–14	74%	290 kg
Germany, 1800–1913		
		Bread consumption
1502–1517	Nürnberg	380–209 kg
1558–1631	MünsterMagdalenenhospital	342–275 kg
1707	Schwäbish Gmund, hospital	368 kg
German national population		
Abel's estimate:		
Early modern era		270 kg
"standard model"		
Saalfeld's estimates:		
1800	12%	205 kg
1850	17%	150 kg
1910–13	44%	125 kg
Teuteberg and Wiegelmann's estimates:		
1850–54	29%	97.5 kg
1855–59	29%	105 kg
1875–79	35%	138 kg
1900–04	49%	133 kg
Eeckhout and Scholliers' estimates:		
1850–59	31%	93 kg
1904–13	50%	131 kg
France, 1781–1914		
Morineau's summary of local studies:		
1690s		292 kg
1750s		285 kg
1833		246 kg
Toutain's estimates:		
1781–90	68%	257–202 kg

Table 12.10 (cont.)

	France (cont.)	
	% wheat	Total bread consumption
1825–34	72%	223 kg
1845–54	73%	261 kg
1905–14	77%	301–267 kg
Grantham's estimate:		
1700–1840		250–215 kg
	England and Wales, 1688–1870	
1688	20%*	
1764	50%*	
Petersen's estimates:		
1700–50		218 kg
1770–79	53%	193
1800–09	66%	174
1830–39	74%	164
1869–70	85%	153

Sources:

Belgium: Vandenbroeke, "Aardappelteelt," p. 59; Vandenbroeke, "Landbouw in the Zuidelijke Nederlanden," pp. 84, 90; Blomme, "Werk in uitvoering," pp. 401–15; Van den Eeckhout and Scholliers, "De hoofdelijke voedselconsumptie," pp. 273–301.

Germany: Thomas Rahlf, *Getreide in der Social- und Wirtschaftsgeschichte vom 16. bis 18. Jahrhundert: das Beispiel Köln im regionalen Vergleich* (Trier: Auenthal Verlag, 1996), pp. 33–35; Wilhelm Abel, *Agrarkrisen und Agrarkonjunktur im Mitteleuropa vom 13. bis zum 19. Jahrhundert* (Berlin: Parey, 1966), pp. 147, 245; Diedrich Saalfeld, "Methodische Darlegung zur Einkommensentwicklung und Sozialstruktur, 1760 bis 1860," *Schriften des Vereins für Socialpolitik* 83 (1975), 242; Hans J. Teuteberg and Günter Wiegelmann, *Unser tägliche Kost* (Münster: Coppenrath, 1986); Van den Eeckhout and Scholliers, "De hoofdelijke voedselconsumptie," pp. 273–301.

France: J.-C. Toutain, "La consommation alimentaire en France de 1789 à 1964," *Économies et Sociétés* 5 (1971), 1919–23; Collins, "Why wheat?," pp. 37–38; Michel Morineau, "Budgets populaires en France au XVIII siècle," *Revue d'Historie Économique et Sociale* 50 (1972), 203–37, 449–81; George Grantham, "Food rations in France in the eighteenth and early nineteenth centuries: a reply," *Economic History Review* 48 (1995), 774–77.

England: Gregory King, *Natural and Political Observations* (London, 1696 [1973]); Sir Charles Smith, *Three Tracts on the Corn-Trade and Corn-Laws* (London, 1766), p. 182; Petersen, *Bread*, pp. 135, 145–46, 193–95, 208–12.

*King and Smith's estimates are based on their view that consumers in each region of England consumed a single grain exclusively. The characterization of Britons as wheat-eaters, barley-eaters, etc., suggests an exclusivity of grain diet that must be moderated by the fact that breads made of the lesser grains often were mixed with wheat. For an overview of these practices see Ashley, *The Bread of Our Forefathers*.

of the first half of the twentieth century. This marked the culmination of a very long transition. It can be said to begin in the late Middle Ages when bread (of whatever grain) emerged as the everyday food of Europeans (especially, northern Europeans), gradually replacing boiled grains of barley, millet, emmer, spelt, and buckwheat. Rye and mixed grains played a very large role in the early emergence of bread, but over time consumers came to recognize the raised wheat loaf as the most desirable of the staple grain foods and medical opinion overcame an initial skepticism to bolster this public preference by endorsing wheat as the most perfect grain.[15]

Large parts of Europe began this transition only in the nineteenth century. Table 12.10 shows wheat's share in total bread consumption in four countries. Germany stands out for wheat's small share in 1800. The Scandinavian countries and lands further east were similar. By 1900 much had changed and wheat bread accounted for half of total German consumption, a figure that would continue to rise thereafter. But Germany was a late adopter: in 1900 wheat's market share in Germany was one that other countries – the Netherlands, Belgium, France, and Britain – had reached around 1800 or even earlier.

Of course, every country had its regional differences. In France these must have been at least as substantial as in England. Toutain found wheat to account for only two-thirds of total French bread consumption as late as 1830, yet whole tomes have been written about the Parisian wheat baguette of the eighteenth century and Fernand Braudel confidently declared that "the French led the way … on the matter of wheat bread." He described wheat bread as a luxury product, confined to elites and special occasions, until the coming of a revolution:[16]

The real revolution in wheat bread only occurred between 1750 and 1850. At that period wheat took the place of other cereals (as in England) and bread was increasingly made from flours that had most of the bran removed. At the same

---

[15] The advice of Johan Christophorus Ludeman was particularly influential. His *Burger Huys-Schat, of Heylzaame Waarnemingen* (The Hague, 1760) declared freshly baked bolted wheat bread, not more than one day old, to be most healthy. He recommended coarser grains only for their laxative properties.

[16] Fernand Braudel, *Civilization and Capitalism, 15th–18th Centuries*, vol. I: *The Structures of Everyday Life* (New York: Harper, 1981), pp. 137–38; Toutain, "La consommation alimentaire en France," p. 1919. See also Kaplan, *Provisioning Paris*, p. 44, who described wheat as "the exclusive bread grain" of Paris (and of most cities) in the eighteenth century. Parisian bread was then whiter than elsewhere, but, he claims, a darker bread had prevailed in the seventeenth century.

time the view gained ground that only [wheat] bread, a fermented food, suited the health of the consumer.

The revolution Braudel wrote of was largely confined to northern France, and especially Paris, just as the shift toward wheat bread in England first identified by Sir William Ashley was concentrated in the south, and especially London.[17] In 1688 Gregory King estimated wheat consumption at only 20 percent of total English bread grains. When Charles Smith turned to the matter in 1764 he opined:

It is certain that bread made of wheat is becoming much more generally the food of the common people since 1689 than it was before that time, but is still far from being the food of the people in general.

Smith proceeded to divide England and Wales into six regions with quite distinct wheat-eating propensities. In southeast England wheat was already dominant, accounting for 89 percent of total bread consumption; the southwest was close behind (75 percent); and the Midlands stood at 67 percent. But further north wheat accounted for no more than 30 percent, and in Wales only 11 percent. Overall, he concluded that "half the people feed on wheat bread."[18] In a modern overview, Petersen, following Collins, sets wheat bread consumption at 53 percent of the total in 1770 and 66 percent by 1792–94. (Adding Scotland, a land of oat eaters where wheat accounted for only 10 percent of bread grain consumption as late as 1800, reduces the *British* wheat proportion to 58 percent.) But the difficult years that followed saw a retreat, such that the level of the 1790s was not surpassed until 1836–47, when English wheat bread reached 77 percent, and by 1870, 85 percent of total bread consumption.[19]

Both northern France and southern England, led by their large and growing capital cities, experienced a decisive shift toward wheat bread consumption in the course of the eighteenth century. In France, Braudel's "wheat bread revolution" had to pause for the real revolution, but in the nineteenth century, especially its second half, it resumed. Belgium joined

[17] Sir William Ashley's *The Bread of Our Forefathers*, based on his Ford Lectures of 1923, argued that England's shift from lesser grains to wheat extended over a long period, but with an acceleration in the eighteenth century.

[18] Charles Smith, *Three Tracts on the Corn-Trade and Corn-Laws*, 2nd edn. (London, 1766), Supplement, ch. 4, p. 182.

[19] Petersen, *Bread*, pp. 201–12. E. J. T. Collins, "Dietary change and cereal consumption in Britain in the nineteenth century," *Agricultural History Review* 23 (1975), 97–115. It is worth noting here that the British government resolved in 1795 that all wheaten flour should henceforth be mixed at least by one-third with barley, oats, or rye. From then until 1818 it is probable that the English person's white loaf was more a product of adulteration (the admixture of alum, a whitener) than of actual bolted wheat flour. Webb and Webb, "Assize," p. 209.

in the process of substituting wheat for rye and other lesser grains, until by the early twentieth century wheat had become very nearly synonymous with "bread."

In the Netherlands the wheat revolution occurred nearly a century earlier than the one announced by Braudel. It was confined to the western provinces and was over – perhaps had been brought to a premature halt – at about the time (1688) that the English were just beginning to "lose their rye teeth" and increase their wheat bread consumption.[20] By then a ceiling had been reached in Holland that would not be broken through until after 1855. This ceiling was imposed more by taxation than by either changing consumer preferences or declining purchasing power. The interplay of consumer preferences and tax policy described in Chapter 5 led to a major increase in tax revenues until a point of equilibrium was reached in which consumer preferences were held in check, as it were, by differential tax rates. This equilibrium, was decisively disrupted beginning in 1855, a year that saw the simultaneous cessation of bread price regulation in the Netherlands and the abolition of the national excise on milling. This "big bang" to the Dutch bread sector ushered in the second and final stage of the Dutch wheat bread revolution, to which we will turn in Chapter 15.

---

[20] A Nottinghamshire laborer, when asked why he persisted in consuming wheat bread when grain prices rose during the Napoleonic period, is said to have responded that he "had lost his rye teeth." Cited in T. S. Ashton, "The standard of living of the workers in England, 1790–1830," in F. A. Hayek, ed., *Capitalism and the Historian* (University of Chicago Press, 1954), p. 154.

13 Measuring the Standard of Living: A Demand-Side Approach

Regional Standards of Living: Did a "Little Divergence" Develop within the Dutch Republic?

We examined food crises – their frequency and intensity – and the public policies used to address them in Chapter 10. There our concern was "impact" – the impact of bread prices on purchasing power. Consumers were assumed to remain passive – at least in their purchasing behavior. However, in Chapters 11 and 12, where we examined food consumption more broadly, we discovered that the Dutch diet generally and bread preferences specifically underwent changes over the course of time. We turn now to the larger issue of the standard of living – how well the Dutch population lived over the 260 years they were subject to the bread price regulatory system and its associated fiscal regime. In doing so it will be necessary to depart from the conventions of historical standard of living measurement in order to incorporate the behavior of consumers, especially their changing demand for bread, into the analysis. We begin by examining regional differences in the standard of living.

Prices and Wages

By the standards of its time the Dutch Republic formed a well-integrated market economy. Goods from the port towns penetrated to nearly every provincial market town at low cost, just as agricultural commodities and rural manufactures flowed readily in the opposite direction.[1] This is not to say that the Dutch Republic had abolished all impediments to internal trade. Far from it. Its decentralized political structure established numerous local tolls for the support of the transport infrastructure and maintained even more for the protection of particularistic urban and provincial economic interests.[2] In addition, the provinces found ways

---

[1] De Vries and van der Woude, *First Modern Economy*, pp. 179–92.
[2] Jan de Vries, "Van centrum naar periferie. Transport en infrastructuur in het Noorden en Oosten van Nederland tijdens de Republiek," in J. N. H. Elerie and P. H. Pellenbarg, eds., *De welvarende periferie* (Groningen: Regio-Project Uitgevers, 1998), pp. 11–22.

to legislate against a wide range of "outside" goods entering their local markets. Thus, the milling excises levied by city and province stood as a mighty barrier to the development of any interprovincial trade in flour. Particularism flourished in the Netherlands, imposing a cost on the economy that probably grew over time, but it did not undo the essential achievement nor did it prevent the Republic from functioning as the heart of a larger economic zone extending in many ways beyond the Republic's borders into the surrounding North Sea region. Labor, capital, and (most) commodities moved across this northwest European space with relative ease. As a consequence, commodity prices across the Republic showed a high level of integration and price level differences were small. With wages matters were different.

Nominal wages were remarkably uniform throughout Holland and most of its western neighbors. There was no consistent difference between the wage rates paid in large cities and small, or even between urban and rural locations.[3] But wages in the Republic's eastern and northern provinces were distinctly lower than in the west, and also showed somewhat greater heterogeneity. Wages were usually higher in Friesland and Groningen than in the eastern provinces, and rural wages in the east (for which evidence is sparse) may have been significantly lower than in the eastern towns.[4]

Figures 13.1–2 display the average daily wage rates in both regions for six types of construction labor for the period 1550–1820, while Figure 13.3 shows eastern wages as a percentage of wages in the west. A substantial nominal wage gap is present already in the 1550s and persisted nearly 300 years later.[5] One may be tempted to explain it as the

---

[3] Jan de Vries, "The labour market," *Economic and Social History in the Netherlands* 4 (1992), 55–78.

[4] Fairly comprehensive data from 1819 show urban and rural wages to have varied as follows (cents per day, summer wages):

	Crafts in municipalities of 5,000 and more		Agriculture in municipalities of below 5,000 population	
	Range	Avg.	Range	Avg.
West*	110–100	104	87–72	81
East **	90 – 71	80	64–47	56

*North Holland, South Holland, Zeeland, Utrecht.
**Groningen, Drenthe, Overijssel, Gelderland, and North Brabant. (Friesland wages are excluded from these averages.)
De Meere, *Economische ontwikkeling*, p. 72.

[5] In the course of the nineteenth century this east–west wage gap narrows. The weakness of the urban economies of Holland and Zeeland accounted for much of this before 1850, while the growth of industry in provincial regions did so thereafter. By 1913 eastern wages stood, on average, at 86 percent of the average of North Holland, South Holland, and Utrecht.

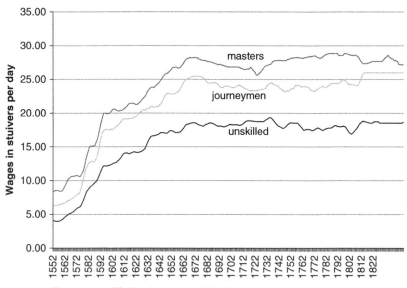

Figure 13.1 Holland wages, 1550–1822

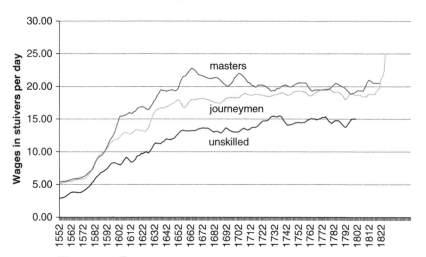

Figure 13.2 Eastern wages, 1550–1822

consequence of the north and east's peripheral and rural character, but this oversimplifies matters. If we could track the wage records back to, say 1450, we may then uncover a time when the wage gap was small or even non-existent. Many of the commercial towns on the numerous channels of the Rhine and Maas were then economically vigorous, while the industrial towns and seaports of the west were just beginning to provide

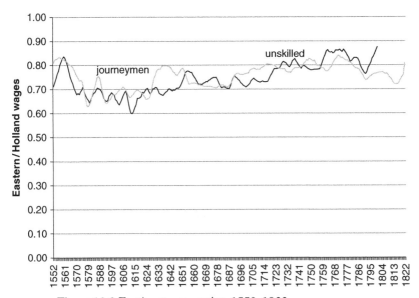

Figure 13.3 East/west wage ratios, 1550–1822
*For clarity, the east/west ratio for masters is omitted.

productive employment to the rural migrants crowding into them.[6] But by the 1550s eastern wages were only 75 percent of those in Holland, and that gap increased in the turbulent decades of the Revolt. Eastern wages reached a low point in the period 1580–99, when they were only two-thirds the level of now vigorously growing Holland.

Military activity in the new Republic's eastern and southern borderlands disrupted economic life in these years, but eastern wage rates recovered somewhat after 1600 and generally stood at approximately 75 percent of Holland's wage level for the next two centuries. The eastern provinces were more agrarian than Holland, to be sure, yet they were more urbanized than all but a handful of European regions. None of their cities were truly large ('s-Hertogenbosch, Leeuwarden, and Groningen, the largest, had populations of 15,000–20,000 through most of the period), but eastern cities were numerous, accounting, as Table 13.1 shows, for nearly 30 percent of the region's population in the seventeenth century, falling to 24 percent by the early nineteenth century (when population growth tended to concentrate in proto-industrial districts rather than the established cities). But, more importantly, nominal

[6] Bas van Bavel and Jan Luiten van Zanden, "The jump start of the Holland economy during the late medieval crisis, c. 1350 – c. 1500," *Economic History Review* 57 (2004), 503–32.

Table 13.1 *Regional urbanization in the Netherlands, 1550–1840*
(percentage of total population residing in cities of at least 5,000 population)

	Holland	Zeeland Utrecht	Friesland Groningen	Overijssel Drenthe Gelderland North Brabant	National average
1550	47				
1580	49	44	31	29	42
1620	57	54	30	29	45
1680	63	52	29	28	48
1750	66	48	29	24	42
1795	64	40	27	24	42
1840	59	34	24	24	38

Sources: Calculated from data in De Vries, *European Urbanization*; Piet Lourens and Jan Lucassen, *Inwoneraantallen van Nederlandse steden, ca. 1300–1800* (Amsterdam: NEHA, 1997).

wages in the Republic's east were comparable to, if not above, those in the rest of northwestern Europe, the large capital cities excepted.

The wages paid in the Republic's largest city, Amsterdam, were representative of a larger zone, both urban and rural, embracing three provinces and at least half the Dutch population. This was a well-integrated zone with a high overall level of urbanization.[7] In contrast to this, the payment of London wages did not extend for any distance beyond the metropolis; on leaving the city one entered immediately into a profoundly rural zone with distinctly lower wages.[8] Wage rates throughout southern England were broadly similar to those of the eastern provinces of the Netherlands, while wages in northern England until the beginnings of modern industrialization in the late eighteenth century were lower still, comparable, perhaps, to wage levels in the German and Scandinavian zones and in France outside the Paris region. Table 13.2 reveals the

---

[7] This point deserves to be emphasized. Pre-industrial European wages were nearly always higher in towns than in the countryside, and higher in the largest cities than in smaller places. These nominal wage differentials are generally accounted for by a combination of factors: low labor productivity in agriculture, urban disamenities (high mortality) requiring a compensating wage premium to attract migrants, and high urban living costs (related to congestion, greater commercialization, and taxation). In the western Netherlands agricultural productivity was high, such that wage differentials did not power a major, ongoing migration stream to the towns. Both urban and rural economies in the west relied on migration, seasonal and permanent, from beyond the region. Consequently, differential wage rates did not distinguish Amsterdam or the other chief cities of Holland from the surrounding rural districts; rather, the wage fault line separated the entire western region, urban and rural, from the inland provinces.

[8] In southern England (counties south of a line drawn from the Trent to the Severn) cities of at least 10,000 inhabitants accounted for 24 percent of the total population in 1700 and 26 percent in 1750. When London is removed, the remaining cities of this large region accounted for no more than 3 percent of the population as late as 1750.

Table 13.2 *Silver wages for unskilled labor as a percentage of wages in the western Netherlands, 1500–1799*

	1500–24	1525–49	1550–74	1575–99	1600–24	1625–49
ZONE A						
London, revised	1.00	0.79	0.99	0.84	0.88	0.94
Southern Netherlands	0.74	0.85	0.99	0.93	1.06	0.89
Paris	0.70	0.76	1.03	1.08	0.85	0.73
ZONE B						
Eastern Netherlands	0.52	0.65	0.74	0.68	0.65	0.69
Southern England	0.81	0.70	0.78	0.68	0.62	0.54
England, agricultural labor	0.60	0.58	0.67	0.55	0.51	0.49
ZONE C						
Northern England	0.75	0.76	0.60	0.51	0.47	0.47
Germany – North Sea – Baltic					0.46	0.52
France ex. Ile-de-France	0.66	0.69	0.85	0.69	0.58	0.55
France, agricultural labor	0.77	0.82	0.91	0.75	0.71	0.60

	1650–74	1675–99	1700–24	1725–49	1750–74	1775–99
ZONE A						
London, revised	0.84	0.91	0.92	0.96	1.03	1.11
Southern Netherlands	0.81	0.81	0.73	0.73	0.71	0.73
Paris	0.75	0.70	0.67	0.46	0.54	0.66
ZONE B						
Eastern Netherlands	0.74	0.70	0.74	0.80	0.82	0.80
Southern England	0.61	0.65	0.67	0.73	0.78	0.95
England, agricultural labor	0.53	0.52	0.52	0.54	0.62	0.75
ZONE C						
Northern England	0.57	0.58	0.58	0.58	0.64	1.06
Germany – North Sea – Baltic	0.53	0.56	0.50	0.47	0.52	0.54
France ex. Ile-de-France	0.51	0.56	0.51	0.38	0.43	0.47
France, agricultural labor	0.52	0.58	0.55	0.43	0.44	0.45

The data summarized in this table are drawn from the following locations:
London: London data primarily from Gilboy, corrected following Stephenson.
Southern England: Cambridge, Dover, Exeter, Lincoln, Maidstone, Oxford.
Northern England: Carlisle, Chester, Hull, Newcastle.
Western Netherlands: Alkmaar, Alphen a/d Rijn, Amsterdam, Goes (Zeeland), Haarlem, Hoorn, Leiden, Medemblik, Waterland (North Holland), Spaarndam.
Eastern Netherlands: Arnhem, Franeker, Groningen, Harlingen, 's-Hertogenbosch (Den Bosch), Kampen, Nijmegen, Zutphen, Zwolle.

Table 13.2 (*cont.*)

Southern Netherlands: Antwerp, Brussels, Ghent, Lier.
Germany – North Sea – Baltic: Cologne, Copenhagen, Danzig, Emden, Hamburg, Ribe, Stockholm.
France ex. Ile-de-France: pooled wage data from many locations beyond the Ile-de-France.
Sources: West and east Netherlands: De Vries wage database. Southern Netherlands: Christiaan Vandenbroeke, "Prijzen en lonen als social-economische verklaringsvariabelen (14e – 20e eeuw)," *Handelingen der Maatschappij voor Geschiedenis en Oudheidskunde te Gent* 36 (1982), 103–37; Etienne Scholliers, "Le pouvoir d'achat dans les Pays-Bas au XVIe siècle," in Jan Craeybeckx, ed., *Album aangeboden aan Charles Verlinden* (Ghent: Universa, 1975), pp. 305–30; Charles Verlinden *et al.*, eds., *Dokumenten voor de geschiedenis van prijzen en lonen in Vlaanderen en Brabant* (Bruges: De Tempel, 1959–73). England: Elizabeth W. Gilboy, *Wages in Eighteenth-Century England* (Cambridge, Mass.: Harvard University Press, 1934); L. D. Schwarz, "The standard of living in the long run: London, 1700–1860," *Economic History Review* 38 (1985), 24–41; Donald Woodward, "The determination of wage rates in the early modern north of England," *Economic History Review* 47 (1994), 22–43; Gregory Clark, "The long march of history: farm wages, population and economic growth, England 1209–1869," *Economic History Review* 60 (2007), 97–136; Judy Stephenson, "Real wages? Contractors, workers and pay in London building trades, 1650–1800," *Economic History Review* 71 (2018), 1–26. Germany and Scandinavia: Christiaan van Bochove, *The Economic Consequences of the Dutch: Economic Integration around the North Sea, 1500–1800* (Amsterdam: Aksant, 2008), pp. 66–69. France: Leonardo Ridolfini, "L'histoire immobile? Six centuries of real wages in France from Louis IX to Napoleon III: 1250–1860," Scola Superiore Sant' Anna, Pisa, Italy, Working Paper 2017/14, June 2017. Ridolfini's estimates for France exclude the Île-de-France, the region surrounding Paris.

general pattern of nominal wage decline emanating from London and the western Netherlands.[9] It identifies a "core" zone A (London, the western Netherlands, and, until the mid-seventeenth century, the Southern Netherlands and Paris); zone B (the eastern Netherlands and southern England) where wages stood at 67–75 percent of the core level; and zone C with even lower nominal wages.[10] Figure 13.4 displays the course of

---

[9] London wages are "revised" from earlier published data. The index in Table 13.2 represents an effort to correct the published London builders' wage data for a probable error in the interpretation of the main source for these estimates, building contractors' invoices for payment. The wage costs cited in these invoices appear to incorporate a substantial fee paid to the contractor. Consequently, the builders themselves received less than the stated payment per day of work. The revised series reduces the published data by 20 percent after 1650, following the critique of Judy Stephenson, "'Real wages?' Contractors, workers and pay in London building trades, 1650–1800," *Economic History Review* 71 (2018), 106–32.

[10] The regional pattern of nominal wages revealed in Table 13.2 cautions us against making blanket statements about the economy of England or northwestern Europe on the basis of data from the capital cities alone. This is a stricture of particular importance to studies of the English standard of living, where London often stands as a proxy for England as

Figure 13.4 Average wages for unskilled labor in northern Europe
relative to the western Netherlands, 1500–1799
Source: Table 13.2.

silver wages for unskilled labor relative to those prevailing in the western
Netherlands for each zone.

We established in Chapter 6 that the eastern provinces acquired the
bread grains at prices very similar to those prevailing in Holland. In a
conventional analysis of the purchasing power of labor, such as that conducted in Chapter 10, it must follow that wage laborers in the eastern
Netherlands were, and remained, significantly less well off than their
counterparts in Holland: they earned 66 to 75 percent of the western
wage, but faced nearly identical grain cost, which determined the largest
single expenditure of laboring households. Their other commodity costs
(peat, dairy products, meat, clothing) were also likely to be approximately

a whole. For a particularly thorough and forceful exposure of the distortions that arise
from allowing London construction wages to stand for wages in all of England see Paolo
Malanima, "When did England overtake Italy? Medieval and early modern divergence in
prices and wages," *European Review of Economic History* 17 (2013), 45–70.

equal to those in Holland leaving only housing and local services as items of expenditure on which they might hope to pay significantly less.[11] The commodity market integration of east and west had its counterpart in labor market integration. Workers in the east could migrate to the towns of Holland to capture the higher wages on offer there, and we know that they did so in large numbers. Holland's port cities recruited labor from an international zone that extended from the Republic's northern provinces to embrace the German North Sea coast and the Scandinavian lands; its industrial cities were first the refuge of Flemish textile workers and later the destination of craftsmen from Liège and the Rhineland and builders and artisans from the eastern provinces and Westphalia; Holland's hay meadows, linen bleaching grounds, brick yards, and harvest fields attracted tramping seasonal agricultural and industrial workers from a zone stretching from the eastern provinces deep into the north German plain.[12]

The eighteenth-century records of new residents in the city of Utrecht, standing at the threshold of the western employment centers and a destination for industrial craftsmen in its own right, give a fair picture of the migration flow. Table 13.3 shows that more of Utrecht's migrants came from Brabant, Gelderland, and Overijssel, the low wage provinces to its east, than from the immediate provincial environs of the city, and that more came from the German lands yet further east

Table 13.3 *Birthplace of brides and grooms in Utrecht, 1721–1800*

Province of Utrecht	20.0
Holland–Zeeland	19.1
Friesland–Groningen	1.3
Eastern–southern provinces	30.6
Germany	21.1
Other countries	8.5

Source: Ronald Rommes, *Oost-west, Utrecht best? Driehonderd jaar migratie en migranten in de stad Utrecht (begin 16e – begin 19e eeuw)* (Amsterdam: Stichting Amsterdamse Historische Reeks, 1998) p. 105.

[11] Before the nineteenth century price data for the eastern provinces are too scarce to construct region-specific cost of living estimates. However, Van Riel has constructed province-level cost of living indexes beginning with the 1820s. They show that eastern wages were, as before, only 71 percent of the average of the western provinces, while the eastern cost of living was 83 percent of that in the west. Van Riel, "Prices and industrialization," p. 292.

[12] Van Bochove, *Economic Consequences of the Dutch*; Jelle van Lottum, *Across the North Sea: The Influence of the Dutch Republic on International Labour Migration* (Amsterdam: Aksant, 2007), ch. 1.

than from Holland, whose boundaries lay within a few miles of the city of Utrecht. Migration was most intense in Holland, and, within Holland, in the North Sea metropole of Amsterdam. Table 13.4 provides a summary of the geographical reach of Amsterdam's marriage market in the period 1601–1800. Overall, only about half of all the men and women who married in Amsterdam in this period were Amsterdam born. The city's reliance on newcomers was intense but, unlike most European cities of the age, its own region (the western provinces of Holland, Zeeland, and Utrecht) supplied only a small and diminishing portion of the new brides and grooms. It was the more distant inland provinces and, even more, the eastern hinterland of German states that supplied the bulk of immigrants. Their share of all newcomers rose from 61 to 68 percent from the seventeenth to eighteenth century. Based on varied sources, Lucassen estimates that between 12 and 18 percent of Holland's total population was foreign-born throughout the seventeenth and eighteenth centuries, and, to judge from Amsterdam's marriage records, migrants from the Republic's inland provinces added substantially to the percentage.[13]

Table 13.4 *Migration to Amsterdam as revealed by the marriage records, 1601–1800*

Birthplace of brides and grooms	1601–1700		1701–1800	
Amsterdam	119,193	42.5%	193,363	52.5%
Elsewhere	161,419	57.5	175,104	47.5
Total	280,612		368,467	
Of those born elsewhere:				
Holland, Zeeland, and Utrecht	37,432	23.2%	32,907	18.8%
All other Dutch provinces	33,621	20.8	49,510	28.3
Foreign countries:				
Western Germany and Scandinavia	63,814	39.5	71,344	40.7
Other countries	26,552	16.4	21,323	12.2

Source: Simon Hart, *Geschrift en Getal* (Dordrecht: Historische Vereniging Holland, 1976), pp. 136–72.

[13] Jan Lucassen, "Immigranten in Holland: een kwantitative benadering," CGM working paper 3 (Amsterdam, 2002); Jan Lucassen, "The Netherlands, the Dutch, and long distance migration in the late sixteenth to early nineteenth centuries," in Nicholas Canny, ed., *Europeans on the Move: Studies on European Migration, 1500–1800* (Oxford University Press, 1994); Jan Lucassen, "Labour and early modern development," in Davids and Lucassen, eds., *A Miracle Mirrored*, pp. 368–73; De Vries and van der Woude, *First Modern Economy*, pp. 72–74.

An ongoing flow of migrant labor from east to west played a critical role in keeping the towns of Holland supplied with artisans and servants and the merchant marine and fishing and whaling fleets supplied with crews. Indeed, a steady stream of German migrants continually replenished Amsterdam's corps of bakers' apprentices and journeymen.[14] But this ongoing movement of labor did not erode the nominal wage gap, which remained nearly as large in 1820 as it had been in 1550. In a conventional model of labor supply and demand one would expect that the regular movement of workers from low-wage A to high-wage B would, over time, cause labor to become more scarce in A and more abundant in B, reducing the wage gap until some equilibrium is reached between the two labor markets.[15] Perhaps no such adjustment occurred here because the migrants' destinations, primarily the cities and ports of Holland and Zeeland, were "urban graveyards," places whose high mortality (whether in the cities themselves or on board the ships that sailed from many of them) prevented the migrant streams from being translated into later population growth via natural increase.[16] If the labor demand in the western cities persisted despite ongoing migration, there is no reason for the gap in nominal wages to diminish; the same would be expected if the supply of lower-wage labor were literally "unlimited" in the large international zone from which it was recruited.[17]

[14] In the seventeenth century the master bakers of Amsterdam appear to have been predominantly Amsterdam-born, supplemented by migrants from Holland, especially sons-in-law of these bakers. But their apprentices and journeymen were recruited overwhelmingly from the Republic's inland provinces and, even more, from western German lands. Some 77 percent of men marrying in Amsterdam who declared the occupation of baker (including baker's apprentice) had been born in this vast eastern zone. The large capital investment needed to establish a bakery, plus the costs of acquiring burgher rights and guild membership, placed a substantial barrier in the way of immigrant bakery workers who sought to become masters in their own right. But, whether through marriage or independently, many migrants to the city did eventually enter the ranks of masters, especially in the eighteenth and nineteenth centuries. The 1903 report on the baking industry of the city speaks of the German predominance in the past tense, but in between, for at least two centuries, a continual migration of German bakers' servants made their way to Amsterdam and other Dutch cities to work for a shorter or longer period and put their stamp on the industry. Kuijpers, *Migrantenstad*, p. 242; Van Zanden, *The Rise and Decline of Holland's Economy*, p. 53.

[15] Such a model is applied to the intercontinental migration of the nineteenth century to assess the impact of mass migration on wages in Europe and North America. See Tim Hatton and Jeffrey G. Williamson, "What drove the mass migrations from Europe in the late nineteenth century?" *Population and Development Review* 20 (1994), 1–27.

[16] Jan de Vries, "Urban historical demography: graveyards, migrants, and the demographic transition" (Cambridge Group Fiftieth Anniversary Conference, unpublished paper, 2014).

[17] W. Arthur Lewis, "Economic development with unlimited supplies of labor," *Manchester School of Economic and Social Studies* 22 (1954), 139–91.

Real Wages

The nominal wage gap persisted, but what about the *real* wage, the purchasing power of labor? Did a gap in the real wage also persist throughout this period? I asserted above that the integrated commodity markets of the Netherlands would suggest that the gap in nominal wages (eastern wages were 67 percent of western wages in 1580–1619) should translate into a purchasing power gap nearly as large. An examination of bread prices in the first years of the seventeenth century confirms this expectation.

Our best evidence in the first years of new system bread prices comes from Leiden and Haarlem in Holland and Kampen and Deventer in Overijssel. The two Holland cities were large and growing rapidly in 1600, while the two eastern towns on the IJssel River were then neither large nor particularly prosperous. But their bread price commissioners faced similar grain prices and they assessed the constant costs faced by their bakers to be much the same.[18] It follows, then, that the price of rye bread should also be similar. Kampen's prices for these years have not survived but those of Deventer have, and they show that from 1596 through 1604 Leiden's rye bread prices – where bakers in these years must have paid much more for rent and labor than in the IJssel towns – were only 6.8 percent higher than Deventer's: 1.376 stuivers per kg in Leiden; 1.289 stuivers in Deventer.

The similarity observed around 1600 is likely to reflect a pattern of long standing. Bread prices were rarely recorded before the introduction of new system regulation, so we do not know with certainty how prices compared between east and west before 1596. But, since old system pricing closely tracked the grain price, and our evidence points to the widespread use of a pound-of-bread per pound-of-grain criterion for determining the expected bread yield, it is very likely that rye bread prices in Holland and Overijssel had not differed by much under the old system.

Bread was relatively costlier for eastern wage earners than for those in Holland, and their relative disadvantage only grew between 1550 and 1596 as nominal wages in Holland rose more rapidly than in the eastern towns. In the 1550s, a decade with several severe food crises, unskilled laborers needed to spend 47 percent of their daily wage to supply their family with 2.2 kilograms of rye bread, while eastern laborers had to part with 62 percent. As Table 13.5 shows, workers in both regions became significantly better off by the 1580s, but eastern wage earners still spent

[18] Leiden's 1596 baking trials led the commissioners to set constant costs for the baking of a last of rye at 41.28 guilders, which they raised in small steps to 44.35 guilders by 1599. In 1600, Kampen's commissioners set their constant costs at 40.50 guilders.

Table 13.5 *Indicators of rye bread costs in west and east*

	Price of 1 kg rye bread/ price of 1 kg rye		Purchasing power of wage labor Percentage of daily wage needed to purchase 2.2 kg of rye bread per day		
	West	East	West	East	West as % east
1550–79	1.000*	1.000*	0.460	0.631	0.729
1580–95	1.000*	1.000*	0.324	0.479	0.652
1596–1604	0.996	0.919	0.356	0.506	0.704
1605–19	1.219	1.044	0.316	0.421	0.751
1620–39	1.172	1.000	0.372	0.438	0.849
1640–59	1.268	1.035	0.352	0.382	0.921
1660–79	1.351	1.094	0.328	0.345	0.951
1680–99	1.566	1.159	0.340	0.352	0.966
1700–19	1.494	1.072	0.346	0.322	1.075
1720–39	1.704	1.172	0.292	0.249	1.173
1740–59	1.528	1.037	0.321	0.283	1.134
1760–79	1.458	1.028	0.355	0.308	1.153
1780–99	1.401	1.003	0.415	0.384	1.081
1800–19	1.348	1.001	0.530	0.570	0.930
1820–39	1.442	1.094			
1840–54	1.389	1.101			

*A bread price to grain price ratio of 1.00 reflects the rule of old system pricing that prevailed before 1596. See Chapter 3 for discussion.

40–50 percent more of their income than workers in Holland in order to secure the same amount of bread.

In the first years of new system bread pricing this relationship persisted, but matters soon changed fundamentally. As we have seen, the new system provided magistrates with opportunities to determine both the level and the distribution of non-grain costs to be incorporated in the bread prices prevailing in their towns and districts. They had a new policy tool at their disposal, and it soon became apparent that the policy objectives in the maritime west differed significantly from those in the eastern provinces. The *broodzetting* soon confronted consumers with regionally distinct absolute and relative prices.

Table 13.5 shows the details of the unfolding regional divergence. The first two columns reveal the extent to which rye bread came to be burdened with costs that exceed the norm prevailing before the introduction of the new system (which was that the price of a kilogram of bread should equal the price of a kilogram of grain). As additional constant costs – non-grain costs such as taxes, labor, capital, fuel – come to be added to the price of bread, this ratio rises above 1.00. In Holland and its western neighbors the ratio rises rapidly and continuously, exceeding

1.5 by 1680. Thereafter it rises and falls primarily with changes in the grain price (the denominator of the ratio). In the east policy makers sheltered rye bread from these cost and tax increases, and the ratio rises only slightly above 1.00.

At any given price for rye, rye bread in the east came to sell at much lower prices than in the west, and the consequences for the purchasing power of unskilled workers is revealed in columns 3, 4, and 5 of the table. There we draw upon the analysis of workers' ability to afford a supply of 2.2 kilograms of bread per day presented in Chapter 10. The method used was to assume that 250 days of annual labor at the unskilled worker's summer daily wage constituted the family's annual income and then to measure how much of that income was needed to buy 2.2 kilograms of bread per day, month-by-month. Here, only the annual percentages are used, grouped into twenty-year averages.

In the long run, such families became better off in both regions throughout the seventeenth century until they attained a peak of bread–purchasing power in the period 1720–39. But, while the bread-purchasing power of unskilled workers improved in both regions, that of workers in the east improved faster. In 1596–1619 western workers spent only 75 percent as much of their earnings on bread as eastern workers (the same advantage they had enjoyed fifty years earlier), but by the 1660s their rye bread had become relatively more expensive. Their higher nominal wages no longer translated into a higher bread-purchasing power, and by 1700 it was the eastern workers who could more easily afford to supply their families with rye bread. Their nominal wages remained only 75 percent of the unskilled wage in Holland, but their "rye bread wage" was now 10 to 20 percent greater than that in the west!

The Dutch Republic's standard of living gap – its "little divergence," if you will – was clearly in evidence around 1600. Did it dissolve in the course of later decades, such that living standards were no higher in golden age Holland than in the quiet provincial towns and villages of the inland provinces? If so, what motivated those many migrants who continued to leave these very places and tramped westward in search of a better life? Were they destined for places where their higher nominal earnings would be taxed away by the state and appropriated by the bakers, both aided and abetted by the policies of bread price commissioners, those ostensible guardians of the interests of common folk?[19]

---

[19] This was the suspicion of Van Zanden: "The workers in prosperous Holland appear, certainly until 1750, to have been worse off than those in poor Overijssel." Van Zanden, "Kosten van levensonderhoud," p. 315; reprinted in Van Zanden, *Arbeid tijdens het handelskapitalisme* (Bergen: Octavo, 1991), p. 145. English translation: *The Rise and Decline of Holland's Economy*.

On the face of things, nominal wages were at least one-third higher in Holland than in the eastern provinces while grain prices were equal in the two regions. In the sixteenth century Hollanders enjoyed the benefit of their higher wages in higher real earnings: They could consume more bread, better bread, more of other goods, or some combination of all three. But by the mid-seventeenth century, during the boom times of the golden age, Hollanders had lost this advantage. Under the new regulatory system rye bread prices rose faster in Holland than in the east, resulting, ultimately, in the disappearance of the benefit conferred by the western region's higher nominal wage. Their real wage increased in the long run, but it fell behind the real wage rise in the eastern provinces, which experienced no comparable economic transformation. This was certainly a perverse golden age.

Does Consumer Choice Reveal Something Important about the Dutch Standard of Living?

Most studies of real wages in pre-industrial societies stop at this point, but it is the wrong place to stop, certainly if our interest is the standard of living rather than simply the purchasing power of the reward for a day's work. The wage rate is not the same thing as household income, since it takes no account of un- and under-employment or the earnings of other family members. Nor, of course, is a quantity of grain, or even an amount of rye bread, the full measure of consumption. We can, to be sure, calculate (adult male) purchasing power via a full basket of consumables rather than focus only on grain or bread (and will do so later in this chapter), but all of these variants on the standard methodology used by economic historians fall short of capturing the element of consumer choice in shaping the standard of living.

Here we will proceed to an alternative approach. Instead of defining a budget constraint and asking how much of x, or x+y+z, a wage earner could buy, we will examine the cost of what actually was purchased. From this knowledge of what consumers *chose* to purchase we can work backward to consider what this might say about purchasing power and, hence, income levels. We do not have sufficient information to conduct this investigation into consumer choice at the household level, or even at the level of social class, but the sharp east–west differences noted above can serve as a point of entry to consider choice at the regional level. Consumers in east and west not only received different nominal wages and faced different relative bread prices, but they also chose to consume very different mixes of the available bread types. Moreover, these two regimes did not exist in isolation from each other. As we just noted, every year thousands of inhabitants of the eastern provinces moved west, settling primarily in the cities of Holland, where they left one "food system" and voluntarily entered another. Do their choices reveal something important about the level of economic wellbeing available in the two regions?

The base line of our analysis is formed by the evidence introduced earlier in Table 13.5. Column 5 shows that eastern unskilled wage-earning households consuming only rye bread could improve their wellbeing substantially by moving west. In 1600 their higher wages allowed them to purchase 40 percent more rye bread than in the east. But the same column reveals that this advantage was eroded over time; by the eighteenth century such a migrant found his higher nominal wage sufficient for only 85 percent of the bread he could have commanded with the lower wages prevailing in the east. Why then, did the migration stream persist?

In fact, the puzzle before us is more challenging still. In Chapter 12 we learned that consumers in Holland, and also Utrecht and Zeeland, consumed twice as much wheat bread as rye bread from the late seventeenth century onwards. This mix is an average for the total population, to be sure, but evidence was presented in support of the view that most households, even the poor and institutionalized, consumed a mix of both types of bread. The mix varied, but wheat and rye were definitely not an either/or proposition in the western Netherlands. Moreover, western consumers revealed a shift in preferences in favor of wheat bread in the course of the first three-quarters of the seventeenth century – that is, in the same period in which we have just seen that their rye-bread-purchasing power advantage over the eastern provinces disappeared. In contrast, eastern consumers in this period revealed no detectable change in their bread consumption preferences: rye bread remained overwhelmingly dominant from beginning to end, accounting in large regions for some 85 percent of the total.

Not only did Hollanders eat rye bread that became progressively more expensive than in the east, but they ate more of the even costlier wheat bread, which sold at a large premium to the already high rye bread price, and they intensified this preference for wheat bread in the face of a pricing structure (described in Chapter 9) that seemed increasingly to discourage, even to penalize, its consumption.

The standard of living actually experienced by those living in the Dutch Republic is revealed not simply by the movement of wages and prices for a fixed basket of goods but by the choices made by consumers to alter the composition of the basket itself. Economists maintain that maximizing consumers choose "the most preferred bundle from their budget sets," that is, they choose the best bundle of goods they can afford.[20] Their "revealed preferences" say something important about what they value as well as about what they can afford.

What did an "average" household in each region spend on bread over the course of time? Table 13.6 offers estimates based on a simple model of bread expenditures relying on the estimated mix of wheat and rye bread presented in Chapter 11 and an assumed annual household consumption of 803 kg (2.2 kg per day). In the east, the assumed bread mix is 15 percent wheat and 85 percent rye. In the west the assumed bread mix is 33 percent wheat and 67 percent rye in 1596–1619, rising to 67 percent wheat and 33 percent rye by 1660–79.

Using these assumptions, columns 1 and 2 display the annual cost in guilders of 803 kg of bread in each region. Regional bread prices had not yet diverged greatly in the first period, 1596–1619, but the higher consumption of wheat bread caused Hollanders – on average – to spend 30 percent more on bread than easterners. This is a reasonable starting point, since Holland's nominal wages were higher by about that same amount. But in the following decades Hollanders' bread expenditures rose sharply. Column 9 shows that their bread expenditures rose in every twenty-year period until by the 1680s they spent more than twice as much as easterners in order to secure an 803-kg bread supply, and this enormous difference persisted throughout the eighteenth century.

The cost of an 803 kg breadbasket doubled from 71 guilders in 1596–1619, when it was two-thirds rye bread, to over 140 guilders by 1680–99, when it was two-thirds wheat bread. Meanwhile, the eastern basket, after rising initially from 55 to 72 guilders, remained at or below 70 guilders per annum until the 1780s.

Part of the higher cost in the west was *imposed*: consumers faced higher production costs and much higher taxes no matter what type of bread they might choose to eat. We can identify this "inescapable" component of the expenditure differential by measuring the cost to the western consumer of the eastern bread mix (15 percent wheat – 85 percent rye) but at the prices prevailing in the west. Column 3 shows the result of this calculation. This factor accounts for about one-third of the extra expenditures throughout. If migrants from the east chose to persist in an "eastern" consumption pattern in their new homes, this is the premium they would have paid for the privilege of enjoying the west's amenities.

One might expect that this burden placed on bread consumption in the western provinces encouraged Netherlanders to eat less of it. It

[20] Hal R. Varian, *Intermediate Microeconomics: A Modern Approach*, 6th edn. (New York: W. W. Norton, 2003), p. 73.

Table 13.6 *Annual household bread costs in east and west, 1596–1839*

	West	East	West at east bread mix	Cost difference in guilders			% of additional west bread cost		West/east cost	Cost of east mix in west as % of east cost
				imposed	chosen	total	Imposed	Chosen		
1596–1619	70.98	54.65	60.01	5.37	10.97	16.33	0.33	0.67	1.30	1.10
1620–39	107.44	71.21	84.24	13.04	23.20	36.24	0.36	0.64	1.51	1.18
1640–59	124.20	72.75	89.12	16.37	35.09	51.46	0.32	0.68	1.71	1.23
1660–79	136.72	71.89	89.29	17.39	47.43	64.82	0.27	0.73	1.90	1.24
1680–99	143.89	67.88	92.58	24.70	51.31	76.01	0.32	0.68	2.12	1.36
1700–19	140.98	66.17	92.99	26.82	47.99	74.81	0.36	0.64	2.13	1.41
1720–39	131.94	56.90	84.26	27.36	47.68	75.04	0.36	0.64	2.32	1.48
1740–59	141.25	60.54	88.62	28.09	52.63	80.71	0.35	0.65	2.33	1.46
1760–79	156.41	68.95	96.35	27.40	60.06	87.46	0.31	0.69	2.27	1.40
1780–99	174.50	79.65	110.68	31.04	63.81	94.85	0.33	0.67	2.19	1.39
1800–19	200.92	108.42	137.29	28.87	63.63	92.49	0.31	0.69	1.85	1.27
1820–39	137.85	75.53	99.80	24.26	38.06	62.32	0.39	0.61	1.83	1.32

Wheat bread price: average of coarse wheat and fine white bread prices.

did, and we surveyed the bread substitutes and the roles they played in Chapter 11. We might also expect the majority of consumers to avoid the costlier wheat bread as its price rose both absolutely and relatively. But here our expectations are confounded: consumers in the west did just the opposite. Wheat bread consumption rose in spite of the impediments placed in its way, and it is this growing difference in bread consumption patterns that accounts for two-thirds of the difference between bread costs in west and east. That is, by their behavior at the bakery counters consumers in the west voluntarily *chose* to spend more on bread than they had in the past.

At the beginning of the seventeenth century consumers in both regions faced similar bread prices. Consumers in the west used a part of their higher earnings to purchase a superior mix of wheat and rye breads. Even at the 40%–60% wheat–rye mixture of 1620–39 they spent a smaller portion of a day's wage on bread than did their eastern counterparts who consumed at a 15%–85% wheat–rye mix. Thereafter, as westerners continued to increase their consumption of wheat bread such that it came to account for two-thirds of the total, their bread expenditures, on average, rose to more than twice the amount spent in the east for the same quantity of bread.

This increased cost was primarily a choice rather than an imposition, but it was not a choice everyone could make. There must have been many in Holland who could not follow this path toward more costly wheat bread consumption. And what of the numerous migrants from the east who found that their "bread-purchasing power" was no higher in the high-wage west than it had been in their home region of low wages? As we have just seen, Hollanders who resisted the temptation to consume wheat bread did not escape all of the rising costs. If they consumed the eastern bread mix (but paying the higher western prices), they would have spent about the same percentage of their earnings on bread as those in the east up to 1700–19, but thereafter even such sober, "traditional" consumers had to relinquish a larger portion of their earnings than did easterners for the same breadbasket (measured in column 10).

Clearly, the attractions of life in Holland did not include cheap bread. The migration pattern and the bread consumption patterns would appear less puzzling if the east did not offer full employment and the west did, or if the west offered superior supplementary employment possibilities for family members. Much as an astronomer might predict the existence of an as yet undiscovered planet from observation of the movements of visible ones, I hypothesize from the voluntary behavior of migrants and consumers the existence of higher western household *incomes* than can be measured from observable daily *wages*. This remains to be confirmed, of course, but what I have uncovered here in the form of regional differences in bread consumption also existed as social class differences within a single region and, most important, as a gradual, economy-wide development over time, the "wheat bread revolution." This process, in which the western Netherlands participated as an early adopter, was economically more consequential than is generally recognized. It is simultaneously an important factor in the accurate measurement of the cost of living and a key development in the emergence of a commercialized consumer-focused economy.

Bread, Deep Commercialization, and the Cost of Living

It is well known that the cost of living can vary enormously according to the range of comforts and conveniences that are regarded as belonging to a socially acceptable living standard. This has given rise to debates about the correct composition of the basket of consumables used in measuring the cost of living. An evasion of these difficulties – and when sufficient price information is unavailable, a necessary simplification – is to use nothing more than the price of grain as the measure of the cost of living. It is, after all, the largest single portion of that cost for all but elite consumers. Indeed, there are scholars who prefer a "grain wage" as a proxy for the real wage even when more comprehensive cost of living indexes are feasible because it assures a comparison of like-with-like.[21] Unfortunately, this simplification is an oversimplification – one that can generate highly misleading comparisons both across societies and over time.

Measuring the cost of this most basic element of the cost of living has its own complications. The specific form in which a household secures its basic dietary standard of carbohydrates, protein, and calories can lead to large differences in monetary cost. A household that purchases grain of whatever type, or raises it on its own land, generally could not efficiently digest its grain without subjecting it to milling (in the case of wheat and rye) or breaking and husking (in the case of oats, barley, and buckwheat). This processing step involved an expense of time and money. The household could then prepare the milled or husked grain in one of two basic ways: baking or boiling. We have been concerned in this study primarily with wheat and rye, the baked grains, but barley, oats, and buckwheat were consumed usually in a boiled form – as porridges, gruels, or, when mixed with more glutinous grains, in the form of pancakes. Baked bread required access to an oven, while a boiled grain could be produced with

---

[21] Stephen Broadberry and B. Gupta, "The early modern great divergence: wages prices and economic development in Europe and Asia, 1500–1800," *Economic History Review* 59 (2006), 2–31.

equipment likely to be available at the family hearth. The cost of an oven plus the greater expertise required to prepare baked goods led to the rise of a specialized profession of bakers.

This brief account suffices to reveal the successive stages of processing and preparation that stand between the *bare expense of grain* and the *full cost of the consumed food*. Some of those steps can be performed by the household's own labor and capital (kitchen equipment), while others are more demanding. Consider the following alternative ways in which European households fed themselves:

1. Purchased barley, oats, and buckwheat – themselves considerably cheaper per liter and per unit of caloric value than the baking grains – could be processed and boiled for ultimate consumption at little additional monetary cost. (The household labor involved in these processes might be considerable, but our concern for now is with monetary costs.) The cost of the consumed food in this case may be only 5 to 10 percent more than the bare cost of the grain.

2. Purchased rye or wheat, which are more costly grains, needs to be milled. The household could prepare the resulting flour plus yeast, salt, etc. into dough, but needs access to an oven for baking. A large farm household may invest in such an item of capital equipment, a lord may make one available to his serfs or tenants at a price, or a professional baker may lease space in his oven to self-baking householders. The consumed food will cost significantly more than in case 1 since the milling and baking are more capital intensive and require more skilled labor than the preparation of boiled grains.

3. The household could dispense with purchasing grain and transforming it into a consumable product and instead purchase bread from a professional baker. In the Dutch Republic nearly all urban households had taken this step by the period that is our chief concern. Rural households' practices were more varied, but the absence of grain production in large areas and the ready access to towns and villages caused self-baking to become a distinctly minority pursuit already in the seventeenth century. Consequently, a large majority of households purchased bread rather than grain, and its price incorporated the value-added of the processing and preparation stages plus the costs of retail distribution. Under the old system bread-pricing regime that prevailed throughout Europe before the seventeenth century basic rye bread and unbolted wheat bread cost approximately 50 percent more than the grains from which they were made.

4. Finally, the household could rely even more on the expertise of the baker in order to purchase wheat breads made from refined flour and

costly ingredients such as eggs and milk. The grain now undergoes additional processing in the form of bolting and sifting which reduces the bread yield per kilogram of grain, and the flour is transformed into white loaves and rolls requiring an expertise that home bakers rarely possessed. By the mid-eighteenth century consumers in northern France and southern England had joined those of the western Netherlands (and many in the Southern Netherlands) to regard white bread as a necessary part, though not necessarily the only part, of their total bread consumption.

These four bread grain consumption scenarios form stages in which the consumer purchases steadily more costly grains. But even more significant is the choice to purchase products in which progressively more "value added" is inserted between the cost of the basic commodity and the cost of the consumed product. These stages were not mutually exclusive; they could live side by side for centuries within the same society. To some extent they represented regional adaptations to ecological and commercial constraints (oats in Scotland, barley in northern England, wheat in the south); to some extent they represented the income constraints of social classes (more rye bread for the poor, more wheat for the well-off). But over the course of many centuries, from the late Middle Ages to the mid-nineteenth century, the regions and social classes of western Europe moved at least part way though these stages, some faster and farther than others.

As the "normative" form of bread grain consumption in a society passed through these stages the "base line" expense of the bread grain element of the diet rose substantially and *independently of the underlying price trends of the grains themselves*. Figure 13.5 offers Dutch price evidence to illustrate how consequential the movement through these steps could be. It shows the cost for calorically equivalent amounts of the grains and breads (810 liters of grain; 803 kg of bread) in successive twenty-year periods. In 1596–1619 a household could survive on buckwheat at an average annual cost of 21.53 guilders (the cost of the grain plus 10 percent for tax and grinding costs) or they could feast on fine white bread from the baker at 129.68 guilders – nearly six times as much. Over time these cost differentials only grew.

We have seen in earlier chapters that Dutch households rarely consumed only one type of grain or bread. Thus, to better capture the actual consumption strategies of Dutch social classes over the course of time Table 13.7 uses the grain and bread costs shown in Figure 13.5 to calculate the cost of six "bundles," each representing 810 liters of grain or 803 kg of bread per year, designed to capture in a stylized way the consumption practices of various Dutch class and regional populations in the early modern era.

Table 13.7a *Annual cost of "bread bundles," 1550–1839*

	Barebones	Simple and sober	Basic	Basic plus	Republican	Wheat bread Standard
1550–59	12.87	18.53	21.53	26.98	32.97	38.21
1560–79	20.18	28.73	33.39	41.92	51.23	59.38
1580–99	27.51	39.22	45.59	57.34	70.08	81.23
1596–1619	29.21	41.09	55.45	72.41	91.50	111.82
1620–39	43.10	58.24	74.55	94.78	118.86	143.14
1640–59	45.16	62.68	82.33	105.43	134.40	163.61
1660–79	41.89	60.74	78.37	102.04	136.41	166.82
1680–99	41.91	61.55	82.60	109.35	143.56	176.46
1700–19	43.59	62.92	83.65	110.23	140.67	171.44
1720–39	35.44	54.81	73.20	98.09	131.64	162.21
1740–59	39.30	58.23	78.05	103.17	140.91	174.65
1760–79	43.16	63.02	86.73	114.59	156.02	194.53
1780–99	51.15	74.44	98.69	128.64	174.09	215.00
1800–19	74.55	102.96	129.83	159.23	200.51	241.30
1820–39	46.87	73.88	85.36	106.04	137.61	162.01

Table 13.7b *Annual cost of "bread bundles," 1550–1839, as percentage of earnings of journeymen builders*

	Barebones	Simple and sober	Basic	Basic plus	Republican Standard	Wheat bread Standard	Avg. path
1550–59	0.16	**0.23**	0.27	0.34	0.41	0.48	**0.23**
1560–79	0.20	**0.29**	0.33	0.42	0.51	0.59	**0.29**
1580–99	0.14	0.21	**0.24**	0.30	0.37	0.43	**0.24**
1596–1619	0.13	0.18	**0.24**	0.31	0.39	0.48	**0.24**
1620–39	0.15	0.20	0.25	**0.32**	0.41	0.49	**0.32**
1640–59	0.14	0.19	0.25	**0.33**	0.42	0.51	**0.33**
1660–79	0.12	0.17	0.22	0.28	**0.38**	0.46	**0.38**
1680–99	0.12	0.18	0.24	0.31	**0.41**	0.51	**0.42**
1700–19	0.13	0.18	0.24	0.32	**0.41**	0.50	**0.41**
1720–39	0.10	0.16	0.22	0.29	**0.38**	0.47	**0.38**
1740–59	0.12	0.17	0.23	0.30	**0.41**	0.51	**0.41**
1760–79	0.13	0.18	0.25	0.34	**0.46**	0.57	**0.46**
1780–99	0.15	0.21	0.28	0.37	**0.49**	0.61	**0.50**
1800–19	0.21	0.29	0.36	**0.45**	0.56	0.68	**0.45**
1820–39	0.13	0.20	0.23	0.28	**0.37**	0.43	**0.37**

Table 13.7b (*cont.*)

In bold: proposed most common bread bundle in each period, tracked as "average path" in Figure 13.6.

Bread bundles:

Barebones:	50% buckwheat, 50% rye
Simple and sober:	33% buckwheat, 67% rye bread
Basic:	33% buckwheat, 33% rye bread, 33% unbolted wheat bread
Basic plus:	50% rye bread, 50% unbolted wheat bread
Republican standard:	33% rye bread, 33% unbolted wheat bread, 33% white bread
Wheat bread standard:	50% unbolted wheat bread, 50% white bread

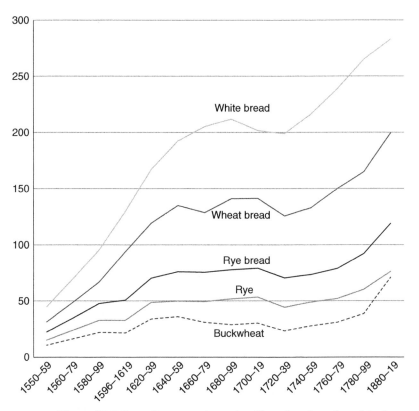

Figure 13.5 Cost of an annual supply of bread grain or bread in the western Netherlands, 1550–1819

1. **Barebones**. Only grain: 50% buckwheat, 50% rye. This represents a subsistence level standard of living in which the household subsists on boiled grain and coarse home-baked bread.
2. **Simple and sober**. Grain and bread: 33% buckwheat, 67% rye bread. This represents a diet that may have been characteristic of poor households both urban and rural. It depended primarily on purchased bread of the cheapest kind plus porridge.
3. **Basic**. Grain and bread: 33% buckwheat, 33% rye bread, 33% unbolted wheat bread. This is a diet that became more common, particularly in urban environments, as wheat bread consumption spread.
4. **Basic plus**. Only bread: 50% rye bread, 50% coarse wheat bread. This more costly diet depends entirely on purchased bread.
5. **Republican standard**. Only bread: 33% rye bread, 33% coarse wheat bread, 33% fine white bread. This diet represents the approximate average bread consumption pattern of the western provinces in the eighteenth century.
6. **Wheat bread standard**. Only wheat bread: 50% coarse wheat bread, 50% fine white bread. This diet, depending entirely on wheat breads, represents an idealized version of the consumption pattern of the well-to-do who could dispense with both boiled grain and rye bread. Of course, an even higher consumption standard is possible, in which only bolted wheat breads are consumed.

Table 13.7 shows that "upgrading" one's "bread bundle" became progressively more costly between the advent of new system price regulation in the 1590s and the mid-eighteenth century. Before 1600 bundle 6 cost three times as much as bundle 1, but between 1720 and 1779 it cost 4.5 times as much. Most consumers chose among bread bundles 2 through 5, but here, too, the cost premium rose from 80 percent in the sixteenth century to 2.4-fold in the eighteenth. The bread price regulators did not make it easy for consumers to act on their preferences. They paid a hefty price. Yet the choices made by consumers that led to this "extra expense" are invisible to historians who approach the measurement of the standard of living via a fixed basket of consumables. This invisibility is aided by the fact that theory teaches us to expect something quite different: a decline in basic food expenditures as incomes rise – whether for a society over time or for households in the cross-section.

This expectation is known as Engel's law, a venerable and generally reliable law, as social laws go. But the conventional understanding of Engel's law fails to make a distinction that is essential to understanding what was guiding Dutch – and other northwest European – consumption behavior in the seventeenth and eighteenth centuries. The necessary distinction – which lies at the heart of the stylized model of consumption alternatives introduced above – is between the purchase of agricultural commodities (farm crops as they are sold on the market) and the purchase of commercial commodities ready for direct consumption (the retail sale of bread, in this case).

That is, *final food consumption* is the product of two kinds of consumption:[22]

$F = F_a + F_b$, where:
F_a = consumption of agricultural commodities, and
F_b = consumption of food product enhancements provided by transport, processing, and marketing.

If this distinction is accepted, then the income elasticity of demand for any foodstuff is the sum of two elasticities, one for the basic agricultural product and one for the subsequent processing services:

$\eta = \eta_a + \eta_b.$

The first, η_a, is what Engel's law is held to refer to and its demand elasticity is usually low; but η_b is a demand for something else, not food *per se*, but labor-saving convenience, superior quality, taste, status, and health. The demand elasticity for this can be quite high.

In an earlier work I argued that early modern consumers in northwestern Europe experienced an industrious revolution, a simultaneous intensification of market-oriented work effort and increase in the purchase of consumer goods.[23] I argued that this revolution was propelled by an intensified desire for new goods, especially those that economized on the use of household labor in the transformation of purchased goods into that which was ultimately consumed. The goods that could incentivize such behavior included tropical commodities, such as sugar, tobacco, tea, and coffee; Asian manufactures, such as cotton textiles and porcelain; and a variety of European manufactures, such as distilled spirits and home furnishings.

One is naturally inclined to look for powerful commercial novelties to push forward so dramatic a transformation of the inner workings of the household economy. Profound changes must have profound causes. Yet one of the quantitatively most important of the "incentive goods" of this era was nothing more exotic than wheat bread – hidden in plain sight, as it were. Over the course of the seventeenth and eighteenth centuries, wheat bread changed – first in the western Netherlands, followed by southern England and northern France – from holding a modest

---

[22] This discussion is based upon Gregory Clark, Michael Huberman, and Peter Lindert, "A British food puzzle, 1770–1850," *Economic History Review* 48 (1995), 215–37.

[23] De Vries, *The Industrious Revolution*, esp. ch. 4.

place in the common diet to a position of dominance, accounting for at least two-thirds of total bread grain consumption. As the sketch of bread consumption stages in Table 13.7 reveals, this shift, invisible from the highly aggregated perspective of most cost of living studies, required households to greatly increase their cash expenditures. This expenditure increase was even greater in the Netherlands than in the other participating regions of the "wheat bread revolution" because state policy was alert to changing consumer preferences and acted early on to harness them to the Republic's fiscal needs.

Households that switched to successively richer bread bundles faced higher money costs and, hence, required higher incomes. We could treat the source of higher household incomes as an exogenous factor, beyond our immediate concern here, but that would cause us to pass over an important aspect of the process whereby the commercialization of early modern economic life was "deepened," which, in turn led to rising household incomes. That is, the deepening of the market economy and the rise in household incomes were endogenously linked, and they were linked via the processes of the industrious revolution.

Each successive bread bundle required higher cash expenditures, but it also required distinctly different amounts of household labor, usually the labor of the wife, ranging from substantial in the preparation of boiled grains, even more substantial in home baking, to very little in the case of bakery-supplied breads. Just how much household labor was thus tied up is difficult to quantify, but the productivity of household labor in bread production will certainly have been much lower than that of professional bakers. This household labor had an opportunity cost – its value in alternative forms of production or in leisure – and where market labor opportunities offered higher productivity than offered by home baking, the resulting redeployment of a portion of the household's labor generated two simultaneous results: a higher monetary income for the household and a greater dependence on market-supplied goods, in this case bread from the baker. In short, rising household income was not only an "exogenous" force, but one influenced by decisions made internal to the household, usually concerning the labor of the wife.

The Economic Historian Confronts the Aspirational Consumer

So, did Hollanders become economically worse off or better off in the course of the seventeenth century, their golden age? The conventional approach, as noted at the beginning of this chapter, measures the amount of a basket of goods, or of grain, that can be purchased by the daily wage of an unskilled laborer.[24] A variant of this methodology, developed by Robert Allen, measures purchasing power as a "welfare ratio." Allen established two standard "baskets" of consumption (see Table 11.4 for details of each basket's composition) that were sufficiently general to be of use for international comparison. Each basket contains sufficient calories and non-food items to sustain a household – one on a "respectable" standard; the other at a "barebones" standard. Figures 13.6a and b display the welfare ratio for Holland using Allen's "respectability basket," prices in Holland, and unskilled builders' wages. A ratio of one reveals earnings just sufficient to supply a household of two adults and three children at the respectability standard. Higher ratios reveal greater prosperity; ratios below one indicate an inability to meet the standard. Figure 13.6a, which covers the period 1550–1689, shows a long-term rise in purchasing power but it assumes – as all such indexes do – that householders consumed a fixed quantity of rye bread throughout the period. Figure 13.6b, which covers the period 1690–1799, shows a decline in purchasing power, especially after 1730. It too assumes an unchanging consumption of rye bread.

But, as we have seen, consumers had choices in how they satisfied the bread component of their diet, and we have just established that they experienced a major upgrade of their bread bundles, particularly in the century ending in 1680–99. Table 13.8 shows the relative price changes that stood before Dutch consumers over the course of this period: a buckwheat diet became relatively less expensive by a quarter, while a self-baking household could secure rye for nearly 10 percent less of its earnings than a century earlier. The purchaser of rye bread suffered a small deterioration of purchasing power, while those who purchased the wheat breads found costs rising faster than their wages by about a quarter. Thus the purchasing power of laborers rose significantly if they held to a diet of boiled grains and self-baked rye bread, but declined significantly if they shifted toward wheat bread. Yet many households appear to have made precisely this change over the course of the period. Following the standard methodology of calculating purchasing power,

---

[24] Several efforts to measure Holland's standard of living in this way are now available and, while they differ in details, they agree on the overall course of development. The most comprehensive cost of living index, presented as the Van Zanden – Van Riel – De Vries index, is available in Jan Luiten van Zanden, "Prices and wages and the cost of living in the western part of the Netherlands, 1450–1800." www/iisg.nl/hpw/brenv.php. Other estimations of purchasing power are found in De Vries and van der Woude, *First Modern Economy*, p. 628; De Vries "How did pre-industrial labour markets function?"; Jan Luiten van Zanden, "What happened to the standard of living before the Industrial Revolution? New evidence from the western part of the Netherlands," in Robert Allen, Tonny Bengtsson, and Martin Dribe, eds., *Living Standards in the Past* (Oxford University Press, 2005), pp. 173–94.

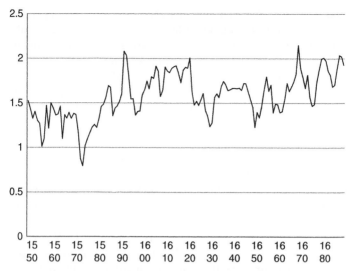

Figure 13.6a Welfare ratios for unskilled labor in
Holland, 1550–1689

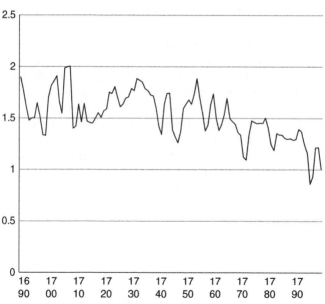

Figure 13.6b Welfare ratios for unskilled labor in
Holland, 1690–1799

Table 13.8 *Index of an unskilled laborer's real cost of acquiring bread and bread grains in 1680–99 relative to 1580–99*

		1680–99/1580–99
Buckwheat	810 kg	76
Rye	810 kg	91
Rye bread	803 kg	104
Coarse wheat bread	803 kg	122
Fine white bread	803 kg	128

the rise shown in Figure 13.6a would have been undone if account could be taken of the average change in the basket of consumables.

If consumers are given no choice to alter their diet, we can measure an increase in their purchasing power over the course of the Dutch golden age, but if we follow the apparent evolution of food expenditures over this period, most consumers appear to have chosen breads that increased their expenditures faster than their incomes rose – *as measured by the daily wage rate*. Incomes differed, of course, and not all consumers made the same choices. Clearly, the unskilled laborer faced a more constrained range of options than the statistical "average" consumer. Still, the problem remains that the consumption evidence reveals a rise in bread expenditures that cannot be accommodated by the available income assumed by the standard approach to measuring purchasing power.

We can achieve a rough idea of the costs facing households as they sought to upgrade their bread consumption by returning to the bread bundles and calculating the proportion of annual income each required over time. In this exercise we will measure annual income by the wage rates of skilled construction laborers in Holland, standing for the "average" consumer.

Figure 13.7 presents this information, and traces a path that Dutch consumers, *in the aggregate*, appear to have followed over the course of the 1550–1819 period. The elusive average consumer, who in the sixteenth century needed some 30 percent of income to acquire a bread bundle in which rye bread predominated, shifted to a bread bundle dominated by wheat bread in the course of the seventeenth century. At first rising wages kept pace with the additional cost of the preferred diet – it continued to require about 30 percent of annual wage earnings – but from the 1680s through the 1750s it usually required 40 percent. As we have seen, the rise of Holland's milling excise in 1680 accounts for most of this increase in real cost. After 1760 matters became even worse: the "average" bread bundle now required up to 50 percent of the laborer's earnings.

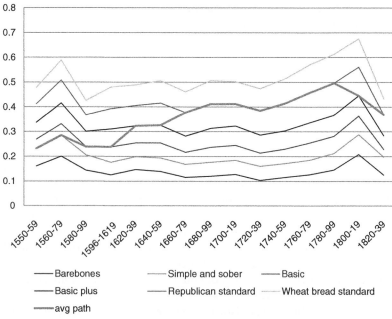

Figure 13.7 Percentage of journeymen's earnings required for six "bread bundles" plus hypothesized average path of consumption,1550–1839

How can we resolve the puzzle of consumption trends whose costs exceed the realm of possibilities as revealed by the wage evidence? There are three possibilities:

1. **Consumers pursued their preferences for wheat bread, but reduced their total bread consumption.** The household that purchased 803 kg of bread, mainly rye bread, in 1580, purchased much less bread, mainly wheat bread, by 1680. In Chapter 12 I showed that this is precisely what happened. But it removes, at best, only a small part of the gap between earnings and expenditures. Total caloric intake does not appear to have declined. Thus, this reduction in bread consumption was made good in large part by increased consumption of even more costly sources of calories, such as dairy products and meat. Only in a later phase, after 1750, did the consumption of legumes and potatoes begin to weigh more heavily in the overall diet, and allow for a reduction in total expenditures.

2. **The "average" consumer after the mid-seventeenth century, eating two loaves of wheat bread for every loaf of rye bread, was actually a statistical fiction.** Income inequality was far too great for national averages to have much meaning. There were, of course, social class

differences in the bread bundles consumed, but we have seen in Chapters 11 and 12 that these were differences of degree rather than of kind. After all, the richest 20 percent of consumers could not consume enough wheat bread to cause its consumption among lower social groups to be negligible.[25] Most social groups moved to a "higher," costlier, bread bundle over time, even though they did not all rise to the most wheat-intensive bundles. This argument, like the first, can resolve only a small part of our problem.

3. The daily wage is a poor guide to annual household incomes. We have already discussed the shortcomings of setting annual household earnings equal to the daily wage multiplied by a fixed number of days of labor. The number of days in the Dutch work year almost certainly rose between the 1580s and 1620s and later, especially after 1760, wage accounting practices understate the earned wage in some – perhaps many – cases.[26] When one adds to this the earnings of wives and children there is strong reason to believe that household earnings rose faster than is indicated by daily male wage rates alone.

Did Household Incomes Really Rise Faster than Has Long Been Thought?

This third argument has the potential to explain much more than the first two and deserves further exploration, which we can do by reversing the standard approach to standard of living studies. Instead of calculating how much bread one can purchase with an assumed income, we can calculate the average income required in order to purchase the bread bundles prevailing at various times across the seventeenth and eighteenth centuries. Figure 13.8 displays the results of this exercise. For successive twenty-year periods it shows the household income needed to purchase the prevailing bread bundle (as identified in Figure 13.7) under the assumption that one-third of income is devoted to the bread grains. This consumption-based approach to estimating average household income

---

[25] After about 1680 about 67 percent of total bread consumption consisted of wheat bread. If per capita bread consumption were equal across income groups and the richest 20 percent of households consumed wheat bread exclusively, the remaining 80 percent would have consumed, on average, 57 percent wheat bread and 43 percent rye bread.

[26] The most consequential of these practices was the payment of "extra *schoften.*" The workday was commonly divided into periods between meal breaks. Except in the short winter days there were four such *schoften.* Wages could be raised (without revealing this as a general wage increase) by paying a fifth *schoft* for what remained a standard workday. This was a common practice in the last decades of the eighteenth century. De Vries, "How did pre-industrial labor markets function?," pp. 39–63: De Vries, "An employer's guide to wages and working conditions in the Netherlands," pp. 47–63.

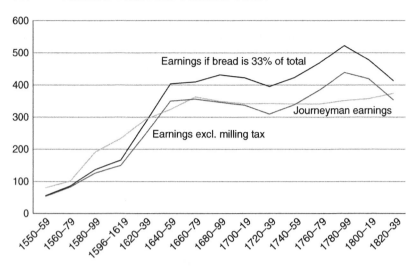

Figure 13.8 Journeymen's annual earnings compared to earnings needed to purchase "average" bread bundle using 33 percent of earnings, with and without taxes, 1550–1839

can then be compared to the conventional income-based approach, the annual earnings of skilled laborers (journeymen construction workers) assumed to work 250 days per year before 1600 and 287 after 1620. These earnings comfortably exceed the amount required to purchase the prevailing bread bundle until 1620–39. However, from 1640 to 1760 the required earnings, 400–430 guilders per year, exceed the skilled labor wage by approximately 25 percent. After 1760 the required income rises further, peaking at 500 guilders around 1800 – nearly 50 percent above the wage rate – before declining in the 1820s to a level only slightly above the skilled labor wage. It is interesting to note here that the cost of the same bread bundles would not have exceeded the 33 percent of income norm in any period up to 1760 if bread had not been taxed. But, of course, it *was* taxed, and Figure 13.8 helps identify the "missing" household earnings needed to account for the observed behavior of consumers.

Could average household income in Holland and its western neighbors have been this much higher than the wage-based earnings estimates? One hint that they may have been is provided by the earnings of *salaried* employees. The historical course of salary incomes is an understudied topic.[27] But it is a potentially important supplement to wage data. Just as

[27] Scholars have avoided salary data for several good reasons. To begin with, salaried occupations are heterogeneous, making generalization from specific examples hazardous. Second, many salaried occupations in early modern times were not full-time jobs,

the comparison of piece rate payments and daily wage rates can reveal changes in work intensity, or industriousness, so the comparison of salaries and wage rates – even when they do not refer to the performance of the same tasks – can reveal changes in the expected, or normative, length of the work year.[28]

Figure 13.9 shows the long-term trend of the ratio of annual salaries in the western Netherlands to daily wage rates for skilled construction labor. Wage earnings – assuming a constant number of days worked per year – declined relative to annual salaries continually over the seventeenth and eighteenth centuries. The sharp deterioration recorded at the beginning of the seventeenth century may exaggerate the actual course of events, but even if the implied doubling of annual salaries relative to wage earnings over the entire time period might be doubted, the long-term persistence of the trend in favor of salaried workers offers an intriguing piece of evidence for the reconciliation of consumer behavior with income evidence.

The salary evidence is consistent with a second and more comprehensive body of evidence in support of my claim that daily wage data are likely to understate the rise of household earnings: the course of gross domestic product (GDP). A well-founded time series of Dutch GDP begins with 1807. Another GDP time series, but limited to Holland, is available for the period 1511–1807.[29] Moreover, these Dutch estimates

complicating the interpretation of their absolute level. Third, many salaries were supplemented by additional income derived from the right to levy fees, by room and board, and by other perquisites whose monetary value is either unquantifiable or unstable over time, or both. These are all potentially serious sources of mis-measurement. In the index of Dutch salaried incomes used in Figure 13.8, I have excluded all occupations known to provide room and board and have included only salaried occupations where supplemental earnings appear not to have been the dominant source of income.

[28] Salaried positions included occupations requiring special training – doctors, schoolmasters, clergymen – but also included such occupations as windmill operators, watchmen, lamplighters, sewage haulers, and scribes at the town gates. The comparison of piece rates and daily wages in agriculture is carried out in Gregory Clark, "The long march of history: farm wages, population and economic growth, England 1209–1869," *Economic History Review* 60 (2007), 97–136. For an examination of English daily wages and annual salaries (in this case, chiefly the salaries of farm servants) that uncovers the same general pattern as I find here, see Jane Humphries and Jacob Weisdorf, "The wages of women in England, 1260–1850," *Journal of Economic History* 75 (2015), 405–47; Jane Humphries and Jacob Weisdorf, "Unreal wages? Real incomes and economic growth in England, 1260–1850," CEPR Discussion Paper no. 11999, April 2017.

[29] Jan-Pieter Smits, Edwin Horlings, and Jan Luiten van Zanden, *Dutch GNP and its Components, 1800–1913*, Monograph Series no. 4 (Groningen Growth and Development Centre, 2000); De Vries and van der Woude, *First Modern Economy*, pp. 701–07; Jan Luiten van Zanden and Bas van Leeuwen, "Persistent but not consistent: the growth of national income in Holland, 1347–1807," *Explorations in Economic History* 49 (2012), 119–30.

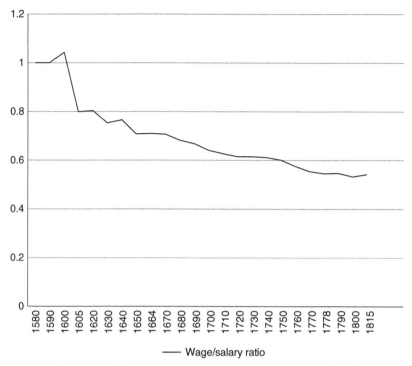

— Wage/salary ratio

Figure 13.9 Wage/salary ratio, western Netherlands, 1580–1815

can now be compared to more detailed GDP estimates for Britain and several other countries.[30]

Earlier in this chapter I argued that earnings-based calculations of the standard of living should be supplemented by an expenditure, or consumption-based approach. This, indeed, is one of the three standard methods used to estimate GDP in modern economies.

Expenditure based GDP = consumption + investment + government spending + net exports.

Unfortunately, the necessary data, especially for consumption and investment, are rarely sufficient to carry out expenditure-based GDP estimates. A second approach is income-based GDP.

[30] Broadberry et al., British Economic Growth. Pre-1800 GDP estimates have also been made recently for Spain and Tuscany. C. Álvarez-Nogal and L. Prados de la Escosura, "The rise and fall of Spain (1270–1850)," Economic History Review 66 (2013), 1–37; Paolo Malanima, "The long decline of a leading economy: GDP in central and northern Italy, 1300–1913," European Review of Economic History 15 (2011), 169–219.

Income based GDP = labor income (average wage * days worked) + capital income (rate of return * capital stock) + land income (rent * improved land area)

Data on wages, interest rates, and land rents are sufficiently abundant to make this a viable estimation procedure for earlier centuries. However, since labor income is by far the largest component part of this approach the results are highly sensitive to the assumed volume of the economic labor supplied, expressed in person-days per year. That is, income-based GDP estimates encounter the same problem we are seeking to circumvent: the use of daily wages as a proxy for annual earnings.

This leaves output-based GDP estimation, which is based on physical production data and output prices in each sector of the economy.

Output-based GDP = value added in agriculture + industry + services

In theory, the summation of value added in each sector should equal the income streams flowing to the factors of production, which should equal the total of all expenditures. For periods before the nineteenth century the GDP studies done to date have preferred the output-based approach. Figure 13.10 displays the course of real GDP per capita (in

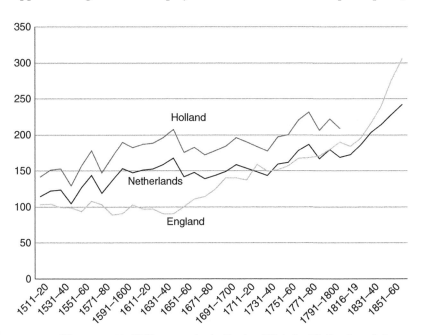

Figure 13.10 GDP per capita in England/Britain, Holland, and the Netherlands, 1511–1870 in 1700 guilders

1700 guilders) for both Britain (England) and the Netherlands (Holland) over the period 1510–1870. The very long-term growth trends in the two countries are similar: 0.20% per annum in England vs. 0.15% per annum in Holland over the period 1510–19 – 1790–99. Dutch growth was concentrated in the 1510–1650 period when English real income actually declined; England's growth was concentrated in the 1650–1720 period, when it caught up with the slower-growing Netherlands. In the late eighteenth century, when Britain embarked on its Industrial Revolution, the data show – surprisingly – rather similar per capita growth trends in the two countries.

The Dutch real wage trends introduced above do not lead us to expect these results, certainly not in the eighteenth century, when daily wages were flat and real wages declining. Indeed, a ratio of the skilled construction wage to Dutch GDP per capita, shown in Figure 13.11, reveals

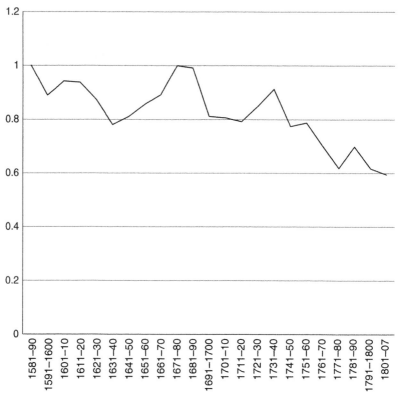

Figure 13.11 Ratio of skilled construction wages to GDP per capita, 1581–1807

a persistent long-term deterioration of the wage rate relative to GDP by nearly half – echoing the deterioration of wages relative to salaries discussed earlier (and broadly replicating the same pattern of wage rate decline relative to per capita GDP found in England in the same period).[31]

There is much more to be learned about the factors that could cause daily wages and annual household earnings to diverge. But the single most important factor underlying the trends we have uncovered in the long-term ratios of wages to salaries and wages to GDP is the growth over time of the supply of labor, whether through increases in hours worked per day, days worked per year, or participation of household members in the market-oriented labor force.

What do these issues in the measurement of macro-level economic performance have to do with the price of bread and consumers' bread preferences? They help us make sense of the behavior of the early modern consumer. The puzzle is one I first pondered when studying consumer expenditures as revealed by probate inventories (showing ownership of consumer durables such as clothing and home furnishings) and import data for colonial groceries (such as coffee, tea, sugar, and tobacco). Households whose earnings as measured by wage rates did not rise rapidly, if at all, somehow managed to purchase growing amounts of these items in the seventeenth and eighteenth centuries.[32] For most consumers, these new "luxury" expenditures formed only a small part of their total budgets. But the puzzle intensifies as we contemplate consumer spending on bread, which was easily the largest single expense of most households

The "wheat bread revolution" that unfolded in northwestern Europe in the seventeenth and eighteenth centuries involved a major increase of expenditure by the households that participated in it, and in the Dutch Republic this expense grew even more because of its unique policy of heavy taxation on bread. Could it be that the new, costlier bread bundles served to incentivize the deepening of commercial relations and the intensification of household economic activity even more than did the new colonial groceries of the same era? At the very least, we appear to be justified in concluding from this exploration of changes in consumer preferences within the bread economy that the industrious revolution had both a domestic and a colonial point of origin.

---

[31] Broadberry et al., British Economic Growth, pp. 257–60; L. Angeles, "GDP per capita or real wages? Making sense of conflicting views on pre-industrial Europe," Explorations in Economic History 45 (2008), 147–63.

[32] See Jan de Vries, "Between purchasing power and the world of goods: understanding the household economy in early modern Europe," in John Brewer and Roy Porter, eds., Consumption and the World of Goods (London: Routledge, 1993), pp. 85–132; De Vries, Industrious Revolution, pp. 154–85.

Part IV

Perspective and Demise

14 Dutch Bread Price Regulation in International Perspective

Bread price regulation was a pan-European phenomenon. This study began with an account of the development of broadly shared regulatory practices labeled the "old system." It then proceeded to focus on a departure from general European practice in the Dutch Republic – the "new system" – and has dedicated many chapters now to exploring its workings and identifying its consequences. But what of the rest of Europe? Did it persist with old system regulation or follow Dutch practice? Did other states also discover the pleasures and benefits of bread taxation or reject it as an antisocial horror? And, finally, how did regulated bread prices elsewhere compare with those in the Netherlands? Did the Dutch have the privilege of eating Europe's most expensive bread?

Answering these questions is hindered by a scarcity of bread price data. While grain prices are abundant, bread prices are not. Indeed, it was this scarcity that first motivated me to begin an investigation into Dutch bread prices as a means to improve the quality of cost of living indexes. While we now know much more about Dutch bread prices, our ability to compare them with prices elsewhere in Europe remains limited. In what follows, I will focus on a handful of locations where sufficient information is available to see just how the regulation of bread prices elsewhere differed from Dutch practice, and what difference this made.

Did the "New System" of Bread Price Regulation Spread beyond the Dutch Republic?

Recall that the key new system innovations were, first, to make a clear distinction between variable costs (grain) and constant costs (all others, including labor, capital, milling, fuel, and ingredients), and, second, to establish an expected bread yield close to the maximum attainable, thereby reducing to a practical minimum the extra loaves that had served as the chief source of revenue under the old system. Consequently, old system price regulation can easily be identified by the absence of these features and it remained dominant in most areas well into the eighteenth century. In some cities magistrates introduced the new system, but they did so half-heartedly. They accepted the first principle, the distinction between variable and constant costs, but they did not fully embrace the second. That is, they did little to track the bakers' non-grain production costs and continued to provide for ample extra loaves, which remained the chief source of the bakers' income – just as under the old system.

Antwerp provides a good example of a tentative and incomplete transition to new system bread price regulation. It continued to follow old system practices until 1621. In that year Antwerp conducted baking trials, identified the constant costs of production, and drafted new bread weight schedules.[1] The new schedules provided explicitly for the bakers' costs and labor (27 stuivers per *viertel* of grain for both wheat and rye, or 52.65 guilders per last). This was the first step in establishing the new system. The constant cost identified in 1621 was small and it remained unaltered until at least 1787, but this was perhaps not so important to the bakers since Antwerp's magistrates had not taken the second step necessary for the new system. They continued to allow the bakers to enjoy a generous allotment of extra, or "advantage" loaves. Their price schedules set the expected bread yield per *viertel* (77 liters) of rye at 53 kg of bread. Since the *viertel* actually yielded closer to 68 kg, they allocated nearly 30 percent of the bread as advantage loaves to defray the baker's non-grain costs, including the millers' fee, which continued to be paid with a portion of the grain. In short, Antwerp's 1621 bread regulations assumed a new system form but continued to breathe the spirit of the old system throughout the early modern era.

Cologne, up the Rhine from the Dutch Republic, made use of a similarly half-hearted new system bread-pricing formula. Its assignment of constant costs was even smaller than Antwerp's and its allocation of extra loaves (*Backpfunde* in German) even larger. Indeed, the Cologne city fathers retained the old rule of thumb that one pound of grain should yield one pound of bread, when in fact it generally yielded more like 1.4 pounds.[2]

---

[1] Antwerp's policies, including the 1621 reforms, are described in detail in Scholliers, *Levensstandaard*, pp. 25–33.

[2] The Cologne price schedule adopted the following formula:
Rye bread price per loaf of 7.25 *pfund* = $(A + B)/32$
Where A = rye price per *malter;* B = constant cost per *malter*
32 = loaves of bread per *malter* of rye.
All prices in *albus* (24 *albus* per *gulden*). The regulators expected 32 * 7.25 = 232 pfund, or 108.51 kg of rye bread per *malter.* The *malter* contained 143.5 liters, which would equal a rye weight of 101–103 kg, which, in turn, would yield 141–144 kg of bread. In short, Cologne bakers could actually secure a yield not of 32 but of 42 loaves per *malter* of rye. This 32 percent difference went to the bakers as their advantage loaves.
Dietrich Ebeling and Franz Irsigler, *Getreideumsatz, Getreide- und Brotpreise in Köln, 1368–1797*, 2 vols. (Cologne and Vienna: Böhlau-Verlag, 1977), p. xviii. My discussion

Denmark introduced the first true new system regulatory regime I have found outside the Republic – in Copenhagen, in 1683. The parallel with the Dutch move to the new system in the 1590s is quite striking. If the growing importance of excise taxation hovered in the background of the Dutch transition, it was openly acknowledged in the Danish decision.

In 1660 the Danish crown (newly endowed with absolutist powers in the wake of a costly military defeat at the hands of the Swedes) introduced excises on foodstuffs, including a milling excise. These taxes were levied in all the Danish towns, but were higher in the capital than elsewhere, and they quickly gave rise to bakers' complaints about the pressure the milling excise placed on their profit margins under the prevailing old system bread price controls. Small changes were made in response but a more radical revision of bread pricing waited on the recommendations of a commission appointed in 1672. This led to the new regulations of 1683, where a clear distinction was made between variable and constant costs, the extra loaves allowed as a baker's allowance were sharply reduced, and a municipal commission took charge of setting bread prices on a quarterly basis.[3]

The English assize of bread, a national law that guided local officials – town aldermen and county justices of the peace – in the regulation of bread (and beer) prices, dated from the thirteenth century.[4] Historians are of the view that by the seventeenth century its old system rules, discussed in Chapter 1, were widely neglected and/or misapplied.[5]

This and the immediate threat of famine and disorder in 1709 spurred the English Parliament to reform the venerable assize and introduce new system rules.[6] At the heart of the reformed assize was an increase in

---

draws on this source for data, and, for analysis, on Dietrich Ebeling, *Bürgertum und Pöbel: Wirtschaft und Gesellschaft Kölns im 18. Jahrhundert* (Cologne and Vienna: Böhlau-Verlag, 1987). However, I have not followed them in their claim that the city's standard grain measure, the *malter*, contained 164 liters. It appears to have been 143.5 liter. For the silver value of the *albus* I follow Rainer Metz, *Geld, Währung und Preisentwicklung: der Niederrhein-raum im europäischen Vergleich* (Frankfurt: Knapp, 1990), pp. 366–95.

[3] Astrid Friis and Kristof Glamman, *A History of Prices and Wages in Denmark, 1660–1800* (London: Longman, 1958), vol. I, pp. 143–51. Commercial contacts between Copenhagen and the Dutch Republic had long been intense. It would be interesting to know with certainty what one can at present only suspect: that the 1672 commission drew on Dutch precedents in drafting its recommendations.

[4] London's assize was set by the Lord Mayor and the Court of Aldermen every Tuesday on grain price information supplied by corn meters, meal weighers, and corn factors on all grain delivered the previous week in London. The new price took effect on Thursdays. Edlin, *Treatise*, p. 116.

[5] Davis, "Baking," p. 493; Petersen, *Bread*, pp. 99–101.

[6] "Alarmed by the threat of famine and disorder in 1709, Parliament chose to rescue the assize of bread from desuetude." Petersen, *Bread*, p. 99. Webb and Webb, "Assize," p. 199; Edlin, *Treatise*, p. 104.

the expected bread yield from 326 pounds per quarter to 434 pounds for "standard wheaten bread" (less for high-quality "wheaten" bread (413 pounds); more for basic "household" bread (468 pounds), and an instruction to local governments to establish an appropriate "bakers' allowance" to replace the bakers' advantage loaves. It took years, even decades, for the localities to revise, or re-establish, their regulatory machinery, but from then until 1815–36, when the assize was abolished in stages, England's bread was subject to price regulation according to the new system, at least in the established corporate towns.[7]

Figure 14.1 shows how London bread prices were linked to the cost of wheat in fundamentally different ways before and after the 1709 reform. A regression of seventeenth-century London bread on grain prices reveals that wheat bread prices, while fairly irregular, approached zero as the price of wheat approached zero and the implicit expected bread yield was 344 pounds per quarter. After 1709 the same regression method shows that the expected yield jumped by 50 percent to 524 pounds,

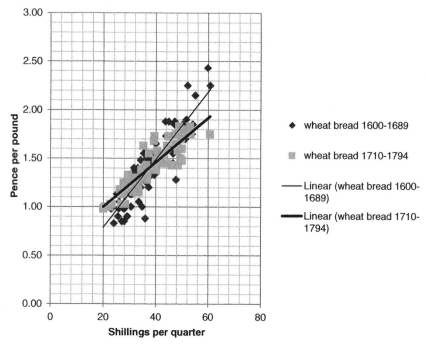

Figure 14.1 London wheat bread prices in relation to wheat prices, 1600–89 and 1710–94

[7] Petersen, *Bread*, pp. 112–16; Davis, "Baking," p. 494; Webb and Webb, "Assize."

while a constant cost was introduced of 0.543 pence per pound of bread, or nearly 24 shillings per quarter (£12.8 or 144 guilders per last).[8] The bakers' allowance (i.e., constant costs) incorporated into English bread prices was modest by Dutch standards. In London it rose from 80 guilders per last in 1709 to 93.38 guilders in 1797, which was always less than the excise tax alone in Holland; in Oxford it rose from 36 guilders per last in 1733 to 72 guilders from 1776 to 1804, which was well below the constant costs for rye bread in the Republic's eastern provinces.[9]

In Berlin, the Prussian kings placed an understandably high priority on securing low and stable bread prices for their seat of government and the site of their largest military garrisons. As noted in Chapter 1, their preferred method was to maintain subsidized granaries, from which supplies could be released strategically in order to dampen fluctuations in the grain markets. This policy did not usually have the desired effect, certainly not when Berlin became a city of over 100,000 inhabitants. This may explain Frederick the Great's new interest in revising the Prussian bread-pricing system (*Brottaxe*) in the mid-eighteenth century.

Baking trials and revised ordinances (in 1744 and 1766) culminated in 1774 in a fundamental change from old to new system bread pricing, or as the ordinance explicitly put it, from a *Backpfunde* [bakers' loaves] to a *Backlohn* [bakers' fee] system.[10] From then on, Berlin's rye bread consumers enjoyed lower prices – about 10 percent lower – at any given grain price. They did so in part because the city's wheat bread consumers now paid more than they had before. A substantial tax, introduced in 1766, weighed only on wheat bread (while a small, older, tax on rye bread was abolished), and the bakers' fee for wheat bread, now 62 percent higher than that for rye bread, suggests some cross-subsidization of rye bread consumers.[11]

Tracking a shift from old to new system bread price regulation in France is frustrated by the highly political character of this branch of public administration under the *ancien régime*. The supply of bread in France has attracted the attention of historians as in no other country, with major modern contributions by Steven L. Kaplan and Judith A.

---

[8] The data for 1600–1689 form the following equation: $X = 0.0348Y + 0.096$. For the period 1710–94 the equation is $X = 0.0229Y + 0.543$. $X =$ price in pence of wheat bread per pound and $Y =$ price of a quarter of wheat in shillings.

[9] Petersen, *Bread*, p. 108; W. Thwaites, "The assize of bread in eighteenth century Oxford," *Oxoniensia* 51 (1986), 171–81; Edlin, *Treatise*, p. 104. Conversions from shillings per quarter to guilders per last were made using the following values: 10.66 Winchester quarters per last; 11.25 guilders per pound sterling.

[10] Stalweit, *Die Getreidehandelspolitik*, p. 313

[11] A detailed, but dispersed account of this reform is found in the four volumes of Naudé, *Getreidehandelspolitik*.

Miller. All this attention has familiarized us with the practices of the *police* (the regulators), their conflicts with the bakers' guilds, and the policy debates among higher-level authorities. But many basic questions remain unanswered.

Perhaps the place to start is with the influential work of Nicolas Delamare, whose *Traité de la Police* of 1707, a treatise on the proper execution of what we can call civil administration, included a detailed discussion of the proper regulation of bread prices, including the results of baking trials Delamare conducted as a councilor of the king and commissioner of the city of Paris in 1693. His treatise also reproduces a 1700 price schedule for bread that guided Parisian bread pricing for the next forty years.[12]

Delamare's discussion bears comparison to the writings of the Dutchman Cornelis François Eversdijck, introduced in Chapter 3. Both Eversdijck, whose work, published in 1663, was based on empirical research reaching back to the 1620s, and Delamare, whose empirical work appears to date from 1693–1700, began by extending their inquiries back to the earliest medieval regulations. Eversdijck, as we have seen, expressed dissatisfaction verging on contempt for all that had gone before, dismissing it as unsystematic and arbitrary. He was a convinced advocate for the new system. Delamare was very different, insisting on his deep respect for the wise laws of the early French kings and describing the regulatory process as one of an admirable organic development.[13]

These laws [concerning the regulation of grain and bread], which began with the study of wheat and bread, were gradually perfected in the course of time; experience and new information has improved and changed their provisions as new insights are acquired, such that large numbers of them today are found to be so useful that they remain the largest, most extensive and, one can add without doubt, the most popular parts of the *droit public* [the administrative law] of each nation.

Delamare's sensibilities were gradualist and perhaps complacent. He also exhibited a different attitude toward enforcement of the bread price schedules, whatever their design. For Eversdijck (and, indeed, Dutch bread price commissioners generally) price regulation was, or should be, a science, yielding results to be applied with unstinting rigor week in and week out – at all times. Delamare's approach (again, mirroring French *police* practice generally) was to enforce the rules selectively: in times of abundance, let the market prices fall; in normal times apply benign neglect of the regulations; in times of dearth apply the schedules with

---

[12] Delamare, *Traité de la Police*, esp. vol. II, book 5, "Le pain." Delamare's work is discussed in detail in Kaplan, *Bakers of Paris*, pp. 503–20.

[13] Delamare, *Traité*, book 5, p. 36.

vigor and in times of famine, ignore the schedules in favor of a highly visible social and political intervention.[14]

From a Dutch perspective there was something both arbitrary and antique about French policy, but this is not to say that the French price schedules ignored the constant costs of bread production. Delamare's influential baking trial of 1700 explored these costs explicitly, and identified a substantial amount of constant expense, but it is not clear that he actually incorporated his findings into his bread price schedule.[15]

After Delamare, a succession of officials, including police chiefs, a procurator general, and at least three controllers general, tried their hands at drafting new price schedules. Table 14.1 summarizes the chief

Table 14.1 *Constant costs identified in Parisian bread price regulations*

	Livres tournois per *setier*	Neth. guilders per last	Assumed pounds per *setier*
1700 Delamare	7.88*	114.94	197
1700 Delamare	6.38	93.73	
1740 Joly de Fleury	5.30	47.29	232**
1767 Sartine/Necker	4.84	43.59	222.5
1769 "Assembly of Police"	7.70	68.52	216
1770s Terray, Turgot, Necker	5.00***	32.63	240
1780s "Paris Model"	5.00–7.00	44.54–62.36	202
1725 Rouen	6.35	48.54	200–4

Paris *setier* = 156.1; liter = 240 pounds of wheat; Paris pound = 491 grams.
Rouen *setier* = 182 liters; Rouen pound = 509 grams.
* Delamare offers a detailed itemization of constant costs, which correspond to the figures cited in the table. However, his price schedule, which was intended to implement these cost findings, does not provide for more than 1.35–2.50 *livres tournois*, depending on the quality mix of the breads produced.
**Joly de Fleury's schedule abolishes the baking of *pain blanc*, the finest bread, in order to maximize total bread yield.
*** The bread price schedules endorsed by these Controllers-General set 4 denier per pound of bread as a fair "constant cost" for Paris. They regarded 3 denier as adequate outside Paris. This would generate 4 *livres tournois* per *setier* if the bread yield were 240 pounds, which appears to be their assumption. They also supposed the sale of bran would add one *livre* of income, for a total of 5 *livres tournois* per *setier*.
Sources: Kaplan, *Bakers of Paris*, pp. 510–16; Miller, *Mastering*, p. 263.

[14] Kaplan, *Provisioning Paris*, pp. 31–33; Kaplan, *Bread, Politics*, vol. I, pp. 78–80.
[15] In the *Traité* he sets these costs at 7.88 *livres tournois* per *setier* (156 liter) of wheat (or 151.75 *livres tournois* per last). This equaled 115 Netherlands guilders per last in 1700. It remained in effect after the French currency devaluation of 1724–27, when it amounted to only 70 guilders. At 115 guilders, the constant costs assigned to Parisian bakers were at the low end of Dutch constant costs for wheat bread; at 70 guilders they were far below Dutch costs.

features of several of them, plus Kaplan's understanding of common practice in Paris, what he called the "Paris Model." They all provided for constant costs, although the values they assigned to these costs, besides being very low, seem to vary arbitrarily over time.[16] Indeed, even as high officials drafted these new system price schedules others continued to insist on the old medieval standard: bread should cost as many deniers per pound as the *setier* costs in *livre tournois*.

All these efforts were inconsistent in actually incorporating constant costs into the calculation of bread prices. Kaplan, after reviewing these proposed schedules, paused to ask himself whether a "basic production cost" could be said to have existed. "Apparently not," he concluded, "for the bakers profit [that is, revenue after paying for the grain] is related to the price of flour [and grain], i.e., it is not fixed."[17] What Kaplan was observing, of course, was the core feature of old system bread pricing, where the baker's revenue rose and fell with the price of the grain. The one piece of direct evidence we have, Paris bread prices for 1745–88, confirms his intuition. Table 14.2 shows the estimated revenue available to the baker, after subtracting the price of the wheat, at successively higher prices of wheat. Under new system pricing, this revenue should not vary; under old system pricing it would rise with rising grain prices.

The average revenue left to the bakers (constant costs) is close to the constant costs referred to in the various proposals described in Table 14.2, but instead of being "constant" it varied with the grain prices. Indeed, the "constant costs" showed more variation year-to-year than either the prices of grain or bread.

An explicit proposal to establish the bread price schedules on a more consistent new system basis came only in 1781, when Mathieu Tillet submitted a report to the Academy of Sciences proposing a "scientific" approach to this contentious issue. His "Projet d'un tariff" received the endorsement of Controller General Calonne and was distributed to towns across the country. But Calonne's accompanying letter of recommendation revealed him to be a bread science denier: "An infinity of motives and circumstances can make inadmissible the arithmetic calculation that serves as a base [of these bread price schedules]."[18]

---

[16] Kaplan, *Bakers of Paris*, pp. 509–16. By the 1760s a recurring criticism of Delamare's price schedules was that he was overly generous in his assessment of the bakers' constant costs. By then the *livre tournois* had been devalued by some 40 percent, making this a surprising complaint. One might have expected the French to hold new baking trials. But they continued to rely on Delamare's 1700 trials, and when the head of police proposed new ones in 1767, the idea was rejected as an inquiry into matters "best left to the men of the métier." Kaplan, *Bread, Politics*, vol. I, p. 336.

[17] Kaplan, *Bakers of Paris*, p. 515.

[18] *Ibid.*, pp. 496–98.

Table 14.2 *Estimation of constant costs allowed to Paris bakers, 1745–88, based on actual average annual bread prices*

Price of wheat	N	Baker's revenue
Livres tournois per *setier*		*Livres tournois* per *setier*
13	1	0.6
15–19	4	4.1
20–24	10	7.4
25–29	12	8.2
30–34	4	7.6
35–36	2	11.1
Total	33	7.6

Total revenue is estimated under the assumed yield of 204 pounds of bread per *setier*.
Source: Paris bread prices: Henri Hauser, *Recherches et documents sur l'histoire des prix en France de 1500 à 1800* (Paris, 1936).

By the eighteenth century new system bread pricing was not unknown beyond the borders of the Dutch Republic. But in most places, and most strikingly in France, a large gap remained between the theoretical acceptance of this method and its practical application. True new system regulatory practices long remained highly exceptional.

Did Others Tax Bread?

Here we can be brief. The taxation of bread, which generally took the form of taxing the milling of grain intended for bread making, was not altogether unique to the Netherlands, but nowhere else were these taxes so high, so long lasting, and so comprehensive, applying to all types of bread. Such taxes were not levied at all in either France or England while in the Southern Netherlands they existed only as minor town excises (which, of course, is how they had begun in the north).[19]

In the German lands bread taxes are occasionally encountered in the cities. Cologne levied a *Mahl Akzise* (milling excise) as early as 1605. At 6 *albus* per *malter* of rye, or about 5 guilders per last.[20] The city raised the

---

[19] Municipal bread taxes are discussed in Brecht Dewilde and Johan Poukens. "Bread provisioning and retail dynamics in the southern Low Countries: the bakers of Leuven, 1600–1800," *Continuity and Change* 26 (2011), pp. 411, 416. Antwerp imposed an excise on wheat bread in 1621 (about 25 guilders per last), but not on rye bread. Scholliers, *Levensstandaard*, p. 32. In 1798, while under direct French rule, municipal-level excises were introduced, but the *octrois communaux de bienfaisance* was applied to the bread grains in ony three towns. Yves Segers, "Oysters and rye bread: polarising living standards in Flanders, 1800–1860," *European Review of Economic History* 5 (2001), 301–36.

[20] There were 24 *albus* per German *gulden*. The *malter* equaled 143.5 liters. Metz, *Geld, Währung und Preisentwicklung*, table A3, pp. 366–95.

excise in stages to 32 *albus* in 1646, where it remained for over a century until being raised slightly, to 36 *albus*, in 1756. In the mid-seventeenth century the excise amounted to about 20 guilders per last, which fell with the declining value of the local currency to about 15 guilders a century later – well below the lowest milling excise found in any of the Dutch provinces.

In the Prussian capital of Berlin we first encounter the *Accize sur Mühle* in 1744, when two *Groschen* was levied per *Scheffel* of grain,[21] or about 8 Netherlands guilders per last. In 1766 this milling excise was replaced by the *Fabriquesteuer*, which exempted rye bread altogether, but subjected wheat bread consumers (only 30 percent of Berlin's bread was made from wheat in this period) to what was regarded as a luxury tax equal to 30 Netherlands guilders per last.

After Waterloo, the expanded Prussian state established a national *Mahlsteuer* that was levied only in the cities. When phased out in 1873-76 flour prices fell by 2.4 percent for rye and 5.2 percent for wheat. The Prussian milling tax was not trivial and endured for a long time, but it was always far below the Dutch level.

Finally, we can take note of the bread taxes of Copenhagen. There, as already mentioned, the introduction of new system price regulation was closely linked to the introduction of excise taxes, known as the *consumption*. From 1683 until the beginning of the nineteenth century consumers paid 7.2 *rigsdalers* per last of rye, or about 15.5 Netherlands guilders. Wheat consumers initially paid double the rate on rye, and after 1688 somewhat more, 18 *rigsdalers* per last, of nearly 39 guilders.

All of these instances of bread taxation are found in large cities. Unlike the Netherlands, small towns and rural areas were always exempted and the taxes are all at or below the lowest milling excises found in the Dutch Republic. The lowest Dutch taxes were nearly always found in the province of Overijssel, where from 1688 to 1805 the excise on wheat stood at 36 guilders, and the rye excise was half that amount, 18 guilders. Moreover, consumers in the cities of Overijssel paid an additional 6 to 12 guilders per last. While I cannot claim to have found every case of bread taxation in Europe,[22] this brief survey confirms the exceptional

---

[21] There were 24 *Groschen* per *Reichsthaler*. The *Scheffel* equaled 53 liters.

[22] An unexpected case of fairly heavy bread taxation is found in Papal Rome. The Roman *annona* sought to keep bread prices constant and went to great and often costly lengths to do so. Yet, beginning in 1644, the Papal administration levied a tax on both coarse and luxury loaves, which was raised in 1689 and again in 1716. By then the tax equaled about 14 percent of the price of grain. It is possible that the Papal treasury used this tax to recapture from the bakers windfall profits that the policy of price stability granted them. In an era of low grain prices, stable bread prices were actually far too high. Rather than lower them for the benefit of consumers, the Papal administration imposed a tax to benefit the state. Reinhardt, *Überleben*, pp. 251–52.

character of Dutch practice. In most of Europe, and all of rural Europe, bread remained untaxed. Those cities that followed the Dutch in levying excises, did so at rates at or below the very lowest rates found in the Dutch provinces.

Were Dutch Bread Prices Higher than Elsewhere in Europe?

This appears to be a straightforward factual question, and even before we begin assembling bread price data the answer would appear quite obvious: Dutch bread prices must have been higher, probably much higher. After all, the major cost of bread is the grain from which it is prepared and we know that the neighboring countries (Germany, France, the Southern Netherlands, and England) all sent grain to Dutch markets for at least part of the period that concerns us. This is a good sign that prices were generally higher in Dutch grain markets than elsewhere. Of course, Amsterdam functioned as "Europe's granary," which means that it regularly re-exported grain to markets with even higher prices. But the export destinations varied with the harvests while the Netherlands' own demand for imports was constant. As a rule, the Dutch consumer faced higher prices for grain than consumers in neighboring countries and far higher prices than the eastern European regions that regularly sent their surpluses via the Baltic ports. The overall pattern is revealed in Table 14.3a, which assembles rye prices from across northern Europe for a specific time period, while Table 14.3b analyzes the Amsterdam–Danzig price differentials for both wheat and rye across the seventeenth and eighteenth centuries. A quite persistent price gap of 50 guilders per last separated the two markets, which defined "transaction costs" in what was certainly Europe's single most important international grain trade corridor.

High grain prices imply high bread prices. But, as we have seen, the Dutch Republic differed from neighboring countries in two important respects: the new system of bread pricing and the milling tax. The first allowed Dutch regulators to calibrate bread prices more closely to actual production costs, and we have seen that this moderated bread prices, especially when grain prices were higher than average. It also allowed regulators to shift costs among the various types and grades of bread. That is, the structure of bread prices faced by Dutch consumers may have offered some types of bread at lower prices (and others at higher prices) than were faced by consumers in countries that persisted with old system pricing.

But this possible advantage must be set against the more certain disadvantage of Dutch taxation. In the Netherlands every loaf of bread

Table 14.3 *Rye prices in northern Europe*
a. Rye prices, Netherlands guilders per last, 1765–87

West Netherlands average	155.40
Antwerp	153.69
Brussels	152.34
South Netherlands average	151.98
East Netherlands average	151.78
Xanten	136.14
Strasbourg	133.83
Würzburg	132.45
Augsburg	129.80
Berlin	125.75
Cologne	125.73
Düren	122.08
Frankfurt/Oder	115.22
Kustrin	110.19
Stettin	108.22
Halberstadt	106.65
Magdeburg	104.19
Halle	100.74
Danzig	99.22
Vienna	96.25

b. Amsterdam–Danzig relative prices

	Amsterdam rye (Polish rye) as a percentage of Danzig rye	Amsterdam wheat (Polish wheat) as a percentage of Danzig wheat
1602–19	1.47	
1620–39	1.55	
1640–59	1.54	
1660–79	1.58	
1680–99	1.65	
1700–19	1.74	1.31
1720–39	1.56	1.24
1740–59	1.56	1.27
1760–79	1.56	1.31
1780–99	1.48	1.33
1800–15	1.46	1.68

Sources: Gdansk prices: Allen data set; Amsterdam prices: Posthumus and this study. Stalweit, *Die Getreidehandelspolitik*, p. 666; Rahlf, *Getreide in der Social- und Wirtschaftsgeschichte*; Verlinden *et al.*, eds., *Dokumenten*, vol. IV, p. 119.

included a tax that, as we have just seen, had no real parallel elsewhere in Europe and by the late seventeenth century accounted for about a quarter of the total cost of every loaf of bread sold in the Republic's western provinces.

With these preliminary considerations out of the way, it is time to look at the actual bread price data. But which data? Do we simply compare the prices of the same type of bread, or the prices of the most commonly consumed bread? Even if we can settle this issue, we are often constrained by the general scarcity of bread price data of any kind. Long time series of bread prices exist for only a handful of places. In what follows I generally compare rye bread prices in several countries to Dutch rye bread prices and international wheat bread prices to Dutch wheat bread prices – all prices converted to Dutch currency per kilogram of bread via silver equivalences. This allows us to make direct comparisons of the price levels for each bread type. But this is not the same as comparing the cost of bread actually paid by consumers across countries. Their incomes differed, of course, but so did the selection of bread types – rye versus wheat, coarse wheat versus fine white, etc. I will call attention to this issue at several points in what follows, but the chief aim here is simply to compare the monetary cost of basic bread types across countries.

Southern Netherlands. Before the Dutch Revolt, the Low Countries grain markets were fairly well integrated around the metropole of Antwerp and the trading center of Amsterdam. After the division of the Low Countries into the Dutch Republic and the southern or Spanish Netherlands the regions quickly began to differ. The movement of grain across the new border between the Republic and the Spanish Netherlands became costlier and subject to blockage. As a result, short-term price fluctuations came to differ significantly, but the coefficients of correlation between southern and northern grain markets were usually only slightly lower than those prevailing among northern markets and the overall grain price levels in the two regions remained similar.[23] It was policy, not grain prices, that drove divergence; the millers and bakers in the Southern Netherlands faced regulatory and cost environments in the seventeenth and eighteenth centuries that came to differ significantly from those of their colleagues in the Republic.

The impact of these differences on bread prices must, unfortunately, be read from fragmentary time series for only two cities, Antwerp and

---

[23] Coefficients of correlation, Amsterdam and Antwerp markets, on first differences of average annual prices:

	1600–49	1650–99	1700–49	1750–99
Rye	0.667	0.960	0.817	0.776
Wheat	0.741	0.923	0.840	

Brussels.[24] In the first half of the seventeenth century consumers in these cities faced prices for both wheat and rye bread that were usually about 10 percent higher than in Holland. Thereafter bread prices fell to the Holland level and after 1680 they fell further, averaging about 10 percent below the price levels of Holland (see Figures 14.2 and 14.3).

For most of the eighteenth century the data are insufficient to track relative prices, but from the 1770s Antwerp bread prices are much lower; 75

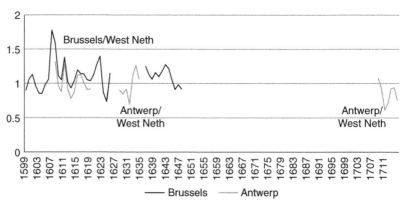

Figure 14.2a Southern Netherlands/Western Netherlands rye bread price ratios, 1599–1711

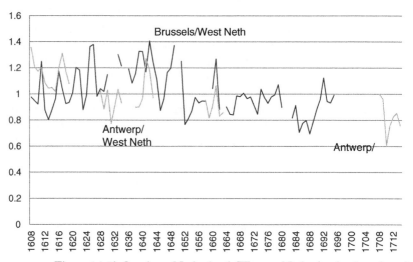

Figure 14.2b Southern Netherlands/Western Netherlands wheat bread price ratios,1608–1712

[24] Price data are drawn from Scholliers, "De Antwerpse merkuriale," pp. 350–58; Jan Craeybeckx, "Brood en levensstandaard," *Bijdragen tot de prijzengeschiedenis*, 3 (1958), 133–62; Jan Craeybeckx, "De Brusselse 'Terminatieboeken'," *Bijdragen tot de prijzengeschiedenis* 2 (1957), 66–68; Jan Craeybeckx, "De prijzen van graan en van brood te Brussel," in Verlinden *et al.*, eds., *Documenten*, vol. I, pp. 481–522.

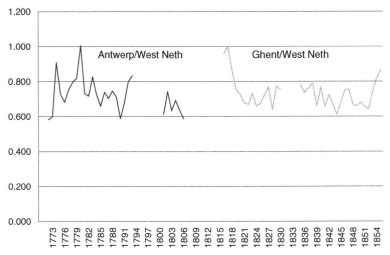

Figure 14.3a Southern Netherlands/Holland rye bread price ratios,
1772–1855

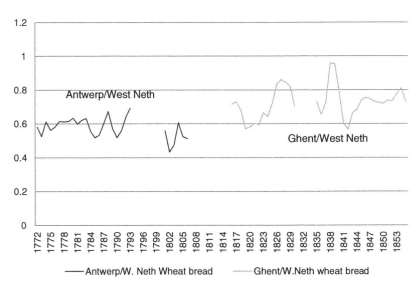

——— Antwerp/W. Neth Wheat bread   ········ Ghent/W.Neth wheat bread

Figure 14.3b Southern Netherlands/Holland wheat bread price ratios,
1772–1855

percent of Holland's rye bread price level and only 60 percent of Holland's
wheat bread price level. Later, in the 1815–55 period, if Ghent's prices are a
safe guide to the Southern Netherlands as a whole, both wheat and rye bread
cost 75–80 percent as much as in the western provinces of the Netherlands.

Over the entire period 1599–1855 consumers in the Southern
Netherlands cities for which data are available enjoyed a gradual decline of
bread prices relative to those prevailing in Holland. The absence of heavy

taxation in the south must have influenced this development, but at least as important was the gradual devaluation of the south's guilder relative to the Dutch guilder. The two regions began with a common currency but the silver content of the southern unit of account declined to 92 percent of the Dutch guilder by 1700 and 85 percent by 1749. These devaluations lowered all southern prices in silver terms, but, of course, they also lowered the silver value of southern wages. Southern producers thereby gained a competitive advantage relative to the north, but southern consumers did not actually experience a real decline in the price of their bread.

Cologne. The Rhineland city of Cologne, the nearest large German city to the Netherlands, used what on the face of it was a system of bread price regulation very similar to the Dutch new system. But, as noted above, there was something half-hearted about Cologne's embrace of new system regulation. Thus, while Cologne had the advantage of lower grain prices than the Netherlands (on average, Cologne grain prices were 5 percent below the Utrecht market) plus lower taxes and constant costs, this did not lead to bread prices below the levels found in the nearby towns of the Netherlands' eastern provinces (such as Nijmegen, Arnhem, Deventer, Zwolle, and Kampen). In fact, Cologne's consumers paid on average slightly more for rye bread than did these eastern Dutch towns: 1.375 stuivers per kg vs. 1.366 stuivers per kg over the period 1658–1757, for which Cologne price data are available. Figure 14.4, which

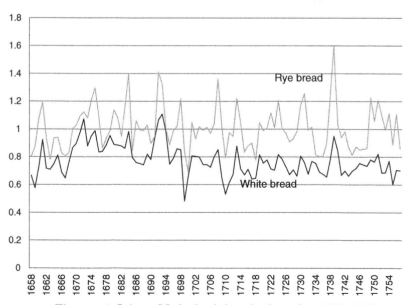

Figure 14.4 Cologne/Netherlands bread price ratios, 1658–1757

shows the long-term equality of rye bread prices in Cologne and the eastern Netherlands, also shows that Cologne's consumers enjoyed lower prices for fine white bread (*Semmelgen*) than did consumers in the Dutch east, where cross-subsidy policies made those prices higher than even in the western Netherlands. However, rye bread is the relevant comparison since, just as in the nearby Dutch provinces, it formed 85 percent of Cologne's bread consumption through most of our period.[25]

The puzzle of why Cologne's rye bread was as costly as in the eastern Netherlands despite its sizeable cost advantages is revealed by a decomposition of the costs allowed, implicitly or explicitly, by the two regulatory systems, shown in Table 14.4. Cologne tolerated an old system slack in the bread yield used in its pricing formula. As a consequence, Cologne bakers profited more per unit of rye than did bakers in the Netherlands.[26] On the other hand, bakers in the eastern Netherlands profited more per unit of wheat, where bread price regulators saw to it that fine white bread

Table 14.4 *Rye and wheat bread costs in Cologne and the eastern Netherlands, 1658–1757*

	Cologne		Eastern Netherlands	
Total revenue and cost	Guilders	% of total	Guilders	% of total
Semmelgen/white bread				
Total revenue	332.06		412.55	
1.Cost of wheat	174.28	52.5%	198.12	48.1%
2.Excise tax	34.88	10.5	46.07	11.2
3.Constant costs*	42.89	12.9	148.70	36.0
4.Extra loaves	80.01	24.1	19.66	4.8
Total bakers' revenue (3+4)	122.90	37.0%	168.36	40.8
Malterbrot/rye bread				
Total revenue	206.46		206.20	
1.Cost of rye	129.10	62.5%	135.59	65.9%
2.Excise tax	17.44	8.4	21.00	10.2
3.Constant costs*	7.88	3.8	27.91	13.6
4.Extra loaves	52.04	25.2	20.70	10.1
Total bakers' revenue(3+4)	59.92	29.0%	48.60	23.7%

*Constant costs include milling costs, fuel, and all non-grain ingredients.
Sources: Ebeling and Irsigler, *Bürgertum und Pöbel;* bread price registers for cities in Overijssel and Gelderland.

[25] Ebeling, *Bürgertum und Pöbel*, p. 160.
[26] Cologne's policies also resulted in greater year-to-year variation in bread prices. Over the century 1658–1757 the average price of rye bread in Cologne and the eastern Netherlands was nearly equal, but the coefficient of variation was higher in Cologne: 26.6 percent vs. 21.6 percent in the eastern Netherlands.

sold for an average of 3.93 stuivers per kg while in Cologne, the equivalent *Semmelgen* sold for 3.02 stuivers. Wheat bread accounted for only about 15 percent of total bread consumption in both places, but the Cologne consumers paid 2.2 times the rye bread price for fine wheat bread while the consumer in the eastern Netherlands paid 2.9 times as much. Cross-subsidization helped keep the Dutch rye bread price low.

Copenhagen. Grain prices in Copenhagen were ordinarily well below those prevailing in the Republic. After all, much of the Republic's supply sailed past Copenhagen and through the Danish Sound on its way to Amsterdam. Grain prices in Copenhagen averaged about 70 percent of Amsterdam prices in the period 1684–1719, and 80 to 90 percent of Amsterdam in the period 1740–99.[27]

In view of these lower costs and the similar price-setting procedures – recall that Copenhagen adopted a full-blown new system regulatory policy in 1683 – it cannot come as a surprise that Copenhagen's bread prices were lower than those prevailing in the Republic. What is surprising is the small size of Copenhagen's bread price advantage.[28]

Basic rye bread prices in Copenhagen, certainly after 1720, were not lower than those in the eastern Netherlands, where taxes were comparable, but they always remained far lower than rye bread prices in Holland, home of large cities that might be compared to Copenhagen. Here the high milling excises had their effect, but another factor of importance was Copenhagen's cross-subsidization strategy.[29]

---

[27] Friis and Glamann, *History of Prices*, pp. 152–58. All conversions to metric measurements, lasts, and Netherlands guilders make use of the following: volume grain measure: *tonde* = 139.1 liters; 21.6 *tonde* per last. Danish *pund* = 496 grams. Danish *rigsdaler*: the *rigsdaler* (consisting of 96 *skilling*) had two variants, a specie system and a *kurant*, or current system. Bread and grain prices made use of the current system, which had a silver content of 20.64 grams until 1737. Thereafter, the introduction of banknotes complicates the conversion, but the *rigsdaler* depreciated only slightly, to 19.50 grams after 1770.

[28] Denmark produced its own rye, but apparently imported a portion of its wheat, which was subject to a significant duty until the 1850s. Denmark's Corn Laws may, therefore, account for its elevated grain prices.

[29] The new system regulatory regime allowed Copenhagen's magistrates to shift costs among bread sorts, which they did in two ways: by altering the assumed bread yield (the number of pounds of bread per measure of grain) for wheat and rye and by allocating the bakers' costs disproportionately to wheat. When the new pricing regime was introduced in 1684 bread prices were set by dividing the bakers' total constant costs by an assumed bread yield of 1,672 kg of wheat bread and 2,507 kg of rye bread. Later (the exact date is unclear) the assumed bread yields were altered to 1,493 kg of wheat bread – a 17 percent reduction – and 2,871 kg of rye bread – a 15 percent increase. This had the effect of raising the price of every loaf of wheat bread (and granting the bakers additional loaves of "advantage bread") and of reducing the cost of rye bread (and reducing the loaves of "advantage bread" closer to zero). In addition, the constant costs assigned in 1684 were never raised for rye bread but became 54 percent higher for wheat bread in the eighteenth century.

Table 14.5 *Relative prices of Copenhagen bread types* (coarse rye bread = 100)

	1684–1712	1713–75	1776–99
Coarse rye bread	100	100	100
Fine rye bread	211	231	263
Wheat bread	287	282	315

Source: Friis and Glamman, *History of Prices.*

Copenhagen's bakers supplied three basic types of bread: coarse rye bread, fine rye bread, and bolted wheat bread. It appears that the coarse rye bread was, indeed, very coarse, while the wheat bread was, indeed, quite fine: the price differential between these two was large, and, as a result of cross-subsidization, became larger, as Table 14.5 shows.

A distinctive feature of Copenhagen's relative bread prices is that the fine rye bread (a bolted rye bread, probably mixed with some wheat) was priced much closer to fine wheat bread than to coarse rye bread, which shows every sign of having been a product intended specifically for the very poorest Danes.[30] For this reason, Figure 14.5 also includes a comparison of Copenhagen's fine rye bread prices with western Netherlands unbolted wheat bread prices. Here the Danish price advantage was small and, after 1740, non-existent. Overall we can observe that public policy in Copenhagen sought to make the basic coarse rye bread "affordable," but forced consumers to pay dearly for higher-quality breads. This may help explain why wheat bread accounted for only one-third of total bread consumption in Copenhagen in the 1740s, and even less by the 1790s.[31] By the final decades of the eighteenth century Danish bread prices were equivalent to those in the Netherlands, despite its lower grain prices.

Berlin and other German cities. Continuing eastward, beyond the river Elbe one enters the heartland of northern European grain production.

---

[30] The coarse rye loaves were large and available only through direct purchase from the baker. They were not sold by retail distributors (which added to the allowable price). Friis and Glamann note that contemporaries viewed it as a provision for the poorest inhabitants (p. 143), and Khaustova and Sharp, in their calculation of a cost of living index for Denmark, chose to use the prices for fine rye bread, presumably because it was widely consumed by ordinary wage earners. Ekaterina Khaustova and Paul Sharp, "A note on Danish living standards using historical wage series, 1731–1913," *Journal of European Economic History* 44 (2015), 143–74.

[31] These estimates are based on data provided in Poul Thestrup, *The Standard of Living in Copenhagen, 1730–1800* (Copenhagen: G. E. C. Gads Forlag, 1971), appendices 2.1111–2.1123.

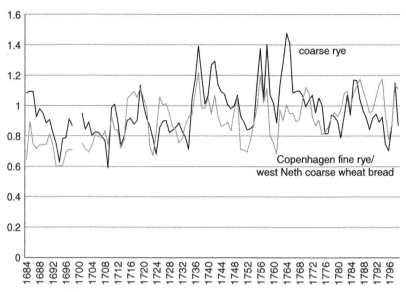

Figure 14.5 Copenhagen/Netherlands bread price ratios,1684–1799

Mecklenburg, Pomerania, and Brandenburg-Prussia exported large amounts of grain via their Baltic ports. It follows that the cities of this large region, foremost among them the growing Prussian capital of Berlin, had access to wheat and rye at much lower prices than the Low Countries.

Monthly price data for both grain and bread in Berlin are available for only the brief period, 1757–1805, but they allow us to examine the effects of the 1774 reform, when the city began setting bread prices following the new system. The variance in annual bread prices, and even more in the revenue a baker held over from the sale of bread from a measure of grain, fell immediately with the 1774 reform. This is precisely what one would expect. Before then, the baker's revenue rose and fell with the price of grain; thereafter bakers received a rather steady 55 gulden per last of rye and 150 gulden per last of wheat, no matter what the price of grain.

Berlin's basic rye bread (*Hausbackbrot*) was not cheaper than the eastern Dutch rye bread so long as the Prussian state continued with old system prices, but once the 1774 reform was introduced a significant price gap opened up. Berlin's price fell to 86 percent of the eastern Netherlands average, and even lower after 1795.

Berlin's wheat bread consumers, certainly after 1774, faced some of the discouragements that had long characterized the Netherlands – taxes and cross-subsidization in favor of rye bread – but it still comes as a

Table 14.6 *Berlin grain and bread prices in comparison with the Netherlands, 1757–1805*

	Wheat Berlin/Neth avg.	Wheat bread Berlin/West Neth avg.	
1757–74	1.004	1.044	
1775–94	0.719	0.847	
1795–1805	0.762	0.957	
1757–1805	0.830	0.942	
	Rye Berlin/Neth avg.	Rye bread Berlin/East Neth avg.	Rye bread Berlin/West Neth avg.
1757–74	1.051	1.045	0.743
1775–94	0.799	0.860	0.620
1795–1805	0.802	0.820	0.589
1757–1805	0.889	0.916	0.656

Conversions:
Reichsthaler = 16.70 g silver; guilder = 9.61 g silver
Reichsthaler = 1.738 Netherlands guilders
Prussian *Pfund* = 0.470 kg
Scheffel = 53 liters (1 last = 55.58 *Scheffel*)
Source: Stalweit, *Die Getreidehandelspolitik.*

surprise to find wheat bread was no cheaper than in Holland up to 1774, and only slightly cheaper after 1795, even though the price of grain in Berlin was often 25 percent lower.[32]

In addition to the two German cities discussed so far, time series for rye bread prices are also available for several other places, widely scattered through the German lands: Braunschweig, Bremen, Chemnitz, and Strasbourg.[33] Their overlapping time series permit us to calculate an average annual price for rye bread in the period 1745–1839. The resulting average can be considered only as a provisional effort to measure this price for such a large and varied zone, but it allows for a rough

[32] Berlin was a large city by the late eighteenth century, but remained primarily rye bread consuming. In 1786 Berlin's population annually consumed 163 kg of bread grain, 32 percent of which was wheat. For Prussia as a whole (the "old provinces," not including its western German and Silesian territorial acquisitions) the mostly rural population consumed 210 kg per capita, 90 percent of which was rye. Naudé, *Getreidehandelspolitik*, vol. III, p. 314; vol. IV, p. 110.

[33] Chemnitz was known from 1953 to 1990 as Karl-Marx-Stadt. Strasbourg is, of course, in France, and was also part of France in the period considered in Table 14.7. It is included among the German towns because its municipal autonomy allowed it to pursue German-style price regulatory practices rather than the French *police* tradition described below.

Table 14.7 *"Average German" rye bread prices compared with the western and eastern Netherlands, 1745–1839*

	Rye bread, stuivers per kg			Price ratios	
	Germany	West Neth.	East Neth.	Germany/ West Neth.	Germany/ East Neth.
1745–59	1.25	1.79	1.25	0.711	1.012
1760–79	1.47	1.97	1.42	0.759	1.054
1780–99	1.48	2.30	1.66	0.644	0.898
1800–19	2.46	2.96	2.25	0.838	1.099
1820–39	1.80	2.08	1.56	0.863	1.160

The German price is the unweighted average of annual prices for Strasbourg, Cologne, Emden, Bremen, Braunschweig, Berlin, and Chemnitz.

Sources: Rudolph Strauss, "Löhne sowie Brot- und Kartoffelpreise in Chemnitz, 1770 bis 1850," *Jahrbuch für Wirtschaftsgeschichte* 62/4 (1962), 144–90; Stalweit, *Die Getreidehandelspolitik*; Ebeling and Irsigler, *Getreideumsatz*; A. Hanauer, *Études économiques sur l'Alsace ancienne et moderne* (Strasbourg, 1878); Otto Aden, *Entwicklung und Wechsellagen ausgewählten Gewerbe in Ostfriesland* (Aurich: Verlag Ostfriesische Landschaft, 1964) pp. 168–70; Hans-Jürgen Gerhard and Karl Heinrich Kaufhold, eds., *Preise im vor- und frühindustriellen Deutschland* (Stuttgart: Frans Steiner, 2001).

Conversions

	Grams per *Pfund*	Grams silver per currency unit
Emden	496 g; 1820: 494 g	*Ostfriesische gulden* 6.1867 g
Bremen	499 g	*Reichsthaler* 25.944 g (72 *grot* per *Reichsthaler*)
Braunschweig	467 g	*Reichsthaler* 16.704 g (36 *Mariengroschen* per *Reichsthaler*)
Chemnitz	467 g	*Pfennig* = 0.0609 g
Cologne	467.7 g	See discussion in text.
Berlin	470 g	*Reichsthaler* 16.704 g (25 *Groschen* per *Reichsthaler*)

Strasbourg: Hanauer converted all data to nineteenth-century French francs of 4.5 grams. Unfortunately, there are apparent errors in his conversions, although the more serious ones are for periods before 1745.

comparison with Dutch bread prices over a considerable period. Table 14.7 summarizes the results of this effort and reveals that German rye bread generally cost from 15 to 30 percent less than in the high-cost western Netherlands, but was no cheaper – usually more costly – than rye bread in the Netherlands' eastern provinces. The lower grain and labor costs and the lower taxation of the German lands did not usually translate to comparably lower bread prices.

Paris. The French devoted a great deal of thought to the regulation of bread prices, but they did not leave much of a record of actual prices. At any rate, I have found only one published time series of French bread prices of any length, regarding Paris in 1745–88.[34] Grain-bread price schedules, actual and proposed, are fairly abundant and some were described in Table 14.1, above. In order to gain some insight into French bread prices I have supplemented the single time series we have with two "virtual" time series, constructed by applying the bread price schedules developed by Delamare for Paris in 1700 and another adopted by Rouen in 1725 and calculating the "official" bread prices they specify from average annual wheat prices in these cities. Actual prices may have varied from those prescribed in the *tarifs*, but my procedure should serve as an "upper bound" estimate: presumably the frequent political interventions worked to set actual prices below the *tarif* level, not above.[35] I then compare the resulting bread price estimates (for *pain bourgeois*, the middle grade and, apparently, the most widely consumed type) to the prices for unbolted wheat bread in the western Netherlands, with the currencies converted according to their silver value.

The results of this procedure, shown in Table 14.8, are quite remarkable. Throughout the period 1727–88 the price for Parisian (bolted) wheat bread was far lower than the price for (unbolted) wheat bread in the western Netherlands – usually between two-thirds and three-fourths of the Dutch price. In the large provincial city of Rouen, prices were even lower, little more than half the Dutch price level. Parisians and, presumably, French consumers generally, paid substantially less for wheat bread than consumers in any of the other markets surveyed in this work. Could it be that France, the epicenter of dissatisfaction with the bread prices, actually enjoyed Europe's lowest prices?

We might also wonder whether this Parisian bread price advantage had also existed earlier. We have no time series for bread prices before 1745, and cannot reasonably apply the eighteenth-century price schedules to periods before they were devised. The remaining possibility is to proceed as suggested by Robert Allen, who has fitted a regression equation that

---

[34] Hauser, *Recherches et documents*. Hauser's data are included in a database of Parisian prices and wages compiled by Philip Hoffman. The time series is far from ideal. A single bread price is cited, without specifying the quality. It is likely that it refers to the highest quality, *pain blanc*. Observations are available for only 34 of the 44 years of the time series.

[35] Delamare's 1700 price schedule is published in his *Traité*. Rouen's 1725 schedule is described in Miller, *Mastering the Market*, pp. 35–40. The grain prices are taken from Micheline Baulant, "Le prix des grains à Paris de 1431 à 1788," *Annales: Économies, sociétés, civilisations* 23 (1968), 520–40.

Table 14.8 *French bread prices relative to those of the western Netherlands,*
1724–88

French *pain bourgeois* relative to Holland's coarse wheat bread		
	Paris–Hauser	Delamare	Rouen
1727–44		0.59	0.43
1745–59	0.62	0.65	0.51
1760–79	0.73	0.68	0.59
1780–91	0.77	0.65	0.53
French *pain bourgeois* relative to Holland's rye bread		
1727–44		1.01	0.74
1745–59	1.21	1.13	0.89
1760–79	1.31	1.23	1.08
1780–91	1.36	1.15	0.94

Sources: See this chapter, fn. 35.

makes the bread price a function of grain prices, and wages (as a proxy for constant costs).[36] The regression equation estimates the bread yield rate and coefficients that determine the weight of the constant costs. His estimates of annual average prices are expressed in grams of silver per kilogram of wheat bread, and I display them together with comparable prices for London (discussed below) and the western Netherlands, in Figures 14.6 and 14.7. Once again, the results are striking.

First, this comparison confirms the result just reported in Table 14.8: after 1727 Parisian bread prices were distinctly lower than in either London or the western Netherlands. But before 1727 this Parisian price advantage is nowhere in evidence. Parisian bread prices appear actually to have been higher than either Dutch or London prices up to 1680 and only slightly lower in the following forty years. Over the period 1608–79, the Parisian wheat bread price was, on average, 4 percent above that in

---

[36] Allen, "The great divergence in European wages and prices." For the annual data used by Allen in this study see:
www.economics.ox.ac.uk/members/robert.allen/Wages Files/labweb.xls
Allen's influential calculations of "welfare ratios," which he proposed as a more flexible measure of consumer purchasing power than conventional consumer price indexes, required bread prices. Since such prices are unavailable for most places, he estimated the bread price using a regression equation with the form:
Pb = constant $+a\ Pg + (b+c)\ W$.
Where Pb = price of bread, per kg
Pg = price of grain (wheat or rye) per liter
W = wage rate
a = bread yield: kg bread per liter of grain
b and c = coefficients

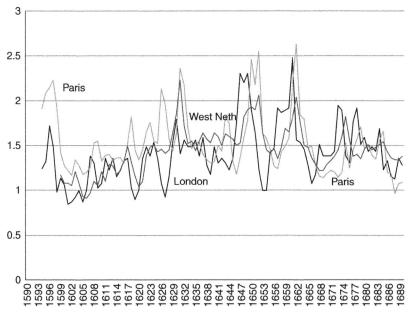

Figure 14.6 Wheat bread prices: London, Paris, and Holland, 1594–1689 (wheat bread in grams silver per kg)

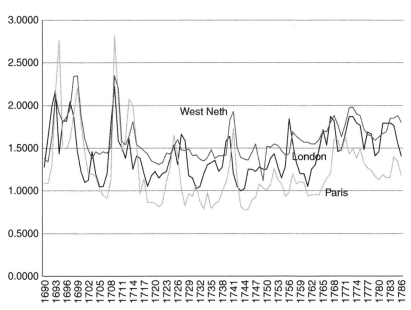

Figure 14.7 Wheat bread prices: London, Paris, and Holland, 1690–1786 (wheat bread in grams silver per kg)

Holland and 18 percent above London. From 1680 to 1717 the Paris price was 10 percent below Holland's, but still 1 percent above London. Once stability returned to the *livre tournois* in 1727 the price of Parisian wheat bread stood at only 64 percent of the Holland price and 81 percent of the London price – and there it remained, on average, until 1789.

What can account for the large reversal of French bread prices relative to those of its neighbors? Obviously, the absence of a tax on milling (in either England or France) can account for part of this difference. It may also be that French milling in the eighteenth century led to a higher yield of flour per pound of grain, and hence a lower bread quality, even for the relatively costly white bread that urban consumers appear to have favored.[37] But more important than these possibilities surely was the large and sudden currency devaluation undertaken by the French state in the wake of the failure of John Law's financial innovations in the Mississippi Bubble of 1720. By 1727 the *livre tournois* was restabilized at a silver value only 64 percent of that prevailing before 1717.[38] This sudden and permanent change in the exchange value of the French currency had a profound impact on price levels denominated in silver. In modern economies domestic prices tend to inflate after a currency devaluation, especially the prices of internationally traded goods, but in eighteenth-century France – which by itself still accounted for a quarter of Europe's total population – this process of convergence was very, very gradual; it was far from complete at the outbreak of revolution in 1789.

The currency devaluation in France was sudden and large. We observed earlier that the Southern Netherlands guilder was also devalued, but this was gradual and cumulatively much smaller – a 15 percent loss in silver value by 1750. In neither case did consumers benefit from cheaper bread since their wages were also devalued in silver terms.[39] However, from a Dutch employer's perspective matters were different: eighteenth-century currency devaluations had made the "wage good" cheaper in the Southern Netherlands and cheaper still in France, and this could be

---

[37] Kaplan, *Provisioning Paris*, pp. 393–465.

[38] The silver content of the *livre tournois* had declined gradually in the seventeenth century, from 8.69 grams of silver in 1637 to 6.94 in 1717. After the currency disorders of the next decade, the *livre tournois* was restabilized at 4.454 grams of silver. There it remained until the Revolution.

[39] Before 1717 wages in Paris (for unskilled construction laborers) were substantially lower than in Holland or London – only 70 percent of Holland's wage rate in 1680–1717. After the currency devaluation, Parisian wages rose in nominal terms, from 16 to 18.6 sou per day, but this only softened slightly the blow of the sharp reduction in the silver content of the wage, which fell to 68 percent of its pre-1720 level. After 1727 Parisian unskilled laborers earned – in silver terms – only half the wage of their counterparts in Holland.

expected to make goods from these countries more competitive relative to the Dutch – and the English.

London. Bread costs in England are of particular interest, since it was the chief economic rival of the Dutch Republic in the seventeenth century and its economic advance in the eighteenth century is often ascribed, in part, to its high real wages.[40] Money wages were comparable in London and Holland (and, at a lower level, in England beyond London and the eastern Netherlands). Given the importance of bread in the household budgets in both countries, a significant difference in bread prices would have had a major impact on the cost of living, and hence on the purchasing power of labor.

We are better informed on most historical prices in England than anywhere else in the world, but this data richness does not extend to bread prices. There is only one available long time series, but a very important one, for London, stretching for 300 years from the mid-sixteenth century.[41] This series presents annual average prices for 4-pound loaves of wheat bread. The grade of this bread is left unspecified, but it is assumed to be the lowest grade, wheaten, or household bread. In Figure 14.8 the London prices (converted to guilders at the silver values of the pound sterling) are expressed as a ratio of the price for unbolted wheat bread in the western Netherlands.

Wheat bread was almost always costlier in the Dutch Republic than in London. London's advantage was fairly small in the seventeenth century, averaging 8 percent, but by 1700 it had become much larger, averaging 24 percent until 1770, whereafter London's advantage tended to diminish until the onset of the French Wars. Then the relative cost positions of

---

[40] This is the chief message of Allen, *The British Industrial Revolution.*

[41] Petersen provides a detailed review of all sources for bread price data in *Bread*, appendix 11, pp. 276–83. Apart from the London time series, all pertain to brief periods of the late eighteenth and nineteenth centuries. In addition, a bread time series for "Britain" is available beginning in 1770. It usually tracks the London series very closely, suggesting it, too, is essentially based on London observations. B. R. Mitchell, *British Historical Statistics* (Cambridge University Press, 1988), pp. 769–70. London bread prices are said to "relate to wheaten or household bread." Similar data are provided in Jeremy Boulton, "Food prices and the standard of living in London in the 'century of the revolution,' 1580–1700," *Economic History Review* 53 (2000), 480–83 and, for the period 1735–1801, in T. S. Ashton, *Economic Fluctuations in England, 1700–1800* (Oxford University Press, 1959), p. 181. Outside England, there are eighteenth-century time series for Glasgow and Dublin. Wheat bread was not the primary bread grain in Scotland, and wheat bread prices in Glasgow (1788–1815) averaged 18 percent higher than in London. In Dublin (1745–1855) wheat bread usually sold for 80–90 percent of the London price. Terence R. Gourvish, "A note on bread prices in London and Glasgow, 1788–1815," *Journal of Economic History* 30 (1970), 854–60; Dublin prices in Mitchell, *British Historical Statistics*, p. 771.

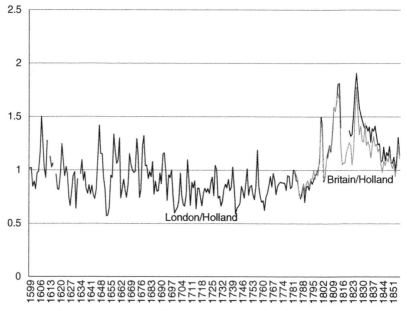

Figure 14.8 London/Holland wheat bread price ratio,1599–1855

London and Holland reversed; after 1797 London's wheat bread sold, on average, for 20 percent more than Dutch wheat bread, an advantage to Dutch consumers that persisted into the 1840s. Thus, during the era of the British Industrial Revolution, 1760–1830, wheat bread was only significantly cheaper in London than in Holland in the first decade and it was significantly more costly than in Holland from the 1790s onward.[42]

Of course, the industrial transformation of Britain began and was long centered in districts far from London. What can be said about British bread prices outside the metropolis? The assize was a national law, but provided for variation in local application. While we have no useful price data for provincial locations, we know that the constant costs incorporated into bread prices were significantly lower outside London. In the 1730s the bakers' allowance set by regulators in Oxford was less than half of the London allowance. It rose to 79 percent by 1805. Worcester

[42] The Dutch consumer who chose rye bread (which was not generally available from London, or most English, bakers) never paid as much as 70 percent of the London wheat bread price, and in the nineteenth century paid only half the London wheat bread price. Thus, a "typical" consumer in the western Netherlands, whose total bread purchases were two-thirds wheat bread and one-third rye bread, paid less for bread than a wheat-eating Londoner at all times except 1700–69, when he/she paid, on average, only 6 percent more.

data, available only from 1779, shows a bakers' allowance even lower than Oxford's and only two-thirds of the London level.[43]

These fragments of information are not enough to form the basis for firm generalizations, but they hint at a pattern of prices akin to the large difference in rye bread prices we found between the western and eastern provinces of the Dutch Republic. This counsels caution in accepting the information we have for London as a proxy for England as a whole, which is a stricture that deserves to be heeded in many comparative studies of England and other countries.

The closure of the gap between London and Holland wheat bread prices, followed by the rise of London prices far above those in Holland is an unexpected finding, given England's lower constant costs and, of course, the absence of excises. One cannot rule out the possibility that some of this change in relative prices was the result of a change in bread quality. In both countries bakers felt a pressure to increase their bread yields per unit of grain, which reduced quality, but it is far from obvious that the Dutch bread deteriorated more than the English.[44]

More important than differences in bread quality was the evolving differential in the price of grain. We have had several occasions to note the high degree of grain market integration in the Netherlands, thanks to Amsterdam's key position in the international grain trade. The grain markets of Britain were also highly integrated, thanks to the dominant position of London. However, this does not mean that prices on the chief English and Dutch markets were highly correlated with each other. Usually they were not.

Although not highly correlated year-to-year, the long-term levels of wheat prices in the two markets were equal in most of the seventeenth century. Thereafter the English price level began to rise above the Amsterdam market. The Dutch bought their wheat for 6 percent below the London price in 1690–1769. Yet it was just at this time that England began to be a significant exporter of wheat and barley, particularly to the Dutch Republic. How could a region of high prices export to one with lower prices?

Throughout the period 1690–1760 Parliament pursued a policy of encouraging the export of grain via corn bounties. By clearing the domestic market of a portion of the grain produced it hoped to raise domestic

---

[43] Petersen, *Bread*, pp. 282–83.
[44] Petersen, *Bread*, pp. 108–09; Webb and Webb, "Assize," pp. 206–10. In 1757 Parliament sought to lower the quality of the lesser grades of wheat bread; as consumers avoided these bread types, Parliament acted in 1772 to abolish sale of the finest "wheaten" bread. In 1795 it required bakers to mix at least one-third part of barley, oats, or rye to nominally wheat bread and, in 1801, acted to incentivize a permanent shift toward coarser bread.

price levels. Its goal was to counteract the downward pressure on prices in a period of population stagnation and rising grain production and in this it succeeded. Sufficient grain was exported to raise domestic prices by 19 percent over international levels, making English wheat prices usually the highest in Europe.[45] The English policy held the decline in wheat prices between 1650 and 1700 to 16 percent, while in the Netherlands, over the same period, they fell by 30 percent.[46]

As British domestic demand rose after 1760, grain exports and the bounty program ended; Britain began its long history as a grain importer.[47] In this new economic environment Parliament was concerned to encourage domestic production by protecting it from lower-cost foreign grains, and to this end it periodically adjusted its Corn Laws in an effort to maintain domestic prices above the international price level. Figure 14.11 shows the course of wheat prices in England and Holland.

Parliament abolished the Corn Laws in 1846 after a lengthy campaign waged by the Anti-Corn Law League, which argued that its sliding scale of tariffs on imported grains acted as an indirect tax on bread by maintaining domestic grain prices above the international level. The beneficiaries of such a policy were landlords, whose farms could be let for higher rents if grain prices were high. The victims of the Corn Laws, they continued, were workers, whose real earnings were eroded by the artificial elevation of the price of the "wage good" (bread), and employers, for whom the cost of labor was elevated for the same reason, eroding the competitiveness of British exports.[48]

There has never been much disagreement about the Corn Law's intentions, but there has long been disagreement about its efficacy. Did it really succeed in maintaining a significant differential between domestic and international grain prices? The current consensus view is that it did, indeed, make a difference, at least until revisions to the laws moderated

---

[45] J. A. Chartes, "The marketing of agricultural produce," in Joan Thirsk, ed., *Agrarian History of England and Wales*, vol. V, part 2 (Cambridge University Press, 1985), pp. 448–54; Ormrod, *English Grain Exports*, pp. 49–52.

[46] Abel, *Agrarkrisen und Agrarkonjunktur*, pp. 152–53.

[47] From 1760 until 1846 Britain was a grain importer, on net, but not a large one. As late as 1837–46 it appears to have imported only 10 percent of domestic grain consumption. Susan Farlie "The Corn Laws and British wheat production, 1829–76," *Economic History Review* 22 (1969), 88–116; see also Mette Ejrnaes, Karl Gunner Persson, and Søren Rich, "Feeding the British: convergence and market efficiency in the nineteenth-century grain trade," *Economic History Review* 61 (2008), 140–71.

[48] For skeptical views of the effects of the Corn Laws, see D. C. Moore, "The Corn Laws and high farming," *Economic History Review* 18 (1965), 544–61; Patrice Bertail and Jean-Michel Chevet, "The effects of the customs duty sliding scale on the wheat prices in England, 1828–1850," in Clara Eugenia Núñez, ed., *Integration of Commodity Markets in History. Proceedings of the Twelfth International Economic History Congress, Madrid, August 1998* (University of Seville, 1998), pp. 65–77.

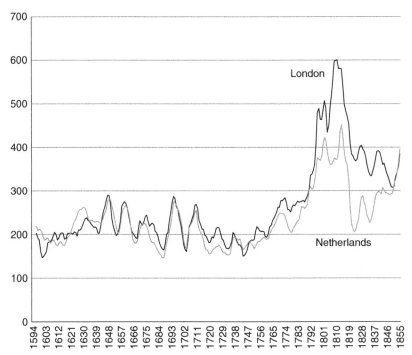

Figure 14.9 London and average Netherlands wheat prices, 1594–1855 (guilders per last)

its impact in the decade before repeal.[49] British policy appears to have succeeded in maintaining grain prices above the level of the Amsterdam market. We noted earlier that London wheat prices rose above the Amsterdam level after 1770, averaging 16 percent higher in 1770–97. This became 35 percent higher in 1800–46, which could not fail to have had a major effect on relative bread prices in the two countries.

Conclusion

In the early modern era grain prices varied considerably, usually by at least 50 percent between the low-cost eastern regions and northwestern Europe. Nominal wages, likewise, were up to 40–50 percent lower in the peripheries relative to the urbanized core of northwestern Europe. Yet

[49] Susan Farlie, "The nineteenth-century Corn Law reconsidered," *Economic History Review* 18 (1965), 562–75; Jeffrey G. Williamson, "The impact of the Corn Laws just prior to repeal," *Explorations in Economic History* 27 (1990), 123–56.

regulated bread prices varied by considerably less than either nominal wages or the bread grains from which they were produced. Rye bread prices across Germany (and in Copenhagen) were rarely more than 10 percent below the price levels prevailing in the eastern Netherlands. They were always well below rye bread prices in the western Netherlands, however, usually ranging between 65 and 75 percent of the latter's price level. Basic wheat bread prices varied within a narrower range, at least in the seventeenth century. Prices in London, Paris, Antwerp, Brussels, and Copenhagen (when data are available in the 1680s) were then generally within 10 percent above or below the level prevailing in the western Netherlands. Thereafter, wheat bread prices nearly everywhere fell below the Dutch level, most spectacularly in France, where currency devaluation pushed the silver price of wheat bread to 65–70 percent of prices in the western Netherlands. Prices in Copenhagen and Berlin (where price data become available only in the 1770s) were comparable to Holland and London's prices; they converged on the Dutch level toward the end of the eighteenth century before rising above it in the nineteenth.

Earlier chapters revealed a Dutch regulatory regime that developed into an invasive force used by the Republic's provinces and cities to achieve multiple objectives. Keeping bread cheap seems not to have been one of them. But this survey of bread prices elsewhere in Europe reveals a surprisingly positive situation. Dutch prices for the basic breads were among the highest in Europe, to be sure, but not as high as the costs of grain, labor, and taxes lead us to expect. Input costs were not wholly determinative of bread prices; pre-industrial production and distribution systems were capable of achieving efficiencies, and a well-designed regulatory system could serve to stimulate this capability.

15 Bread Price Regulation Renewed and Abolished, 1776–1855

The *broodzetting*, the regulation of bread prices, and *het gemaal*, the milling excise, were distinct policies governed and administered by separate organs of government. Price regulation was essentially a municipal affair, while taxation was primarily a provincial matter. Yet the two policies were joined at the hip: the viability of provincial tax policy depended on town regulation; any attack on the principle of bread price regulation would have to begin with a fundamental redesign of the Republic's fiscal system, since, as we have seen, the milling excise stood at its very heart. It was the largest single source of public revenue in a state that taxed its population more heavily than any other in Europe, and probably in the world.

Once it took definitive form in the late seventeenth century (in Holland, with the increased rates and shift in rural collection practices of 1680) this linked fiscal-regulatory regime continued in force without major changes for over a century. The political crisis of 1747–48 brought change to the *manner* of excise collection, abolishing the tax farmers, but otherwise left matters as they were. Altered consumer preferences, which increased the purchase of costly wheat breads, must have increased public dissatisfaction with the pricing policies of the regulators, but there is very little evidence of public grievance directed at price regulation as such.

This fiscal-regulatory regime, burdensome and invasive though it was, met with a response of puzzling quietude. But this changed after the mid-eighteenth century as the long-term trend in grain prices began to creep upward. As this trend accelerated in the 1770s, maintaining the achieved wheat bread diet became a challenge for growing numbers, and with the fall of the old Republic in 1795 it threatened to fall out of reach for nearly everyone as the Netherlands – and Europe as a whole – entered a twenty-year period of nearly constant crisis-level food prices. The Dutch had experienced nothing remotely like this for over 200 years. In this harsh new economic environment the operation of the regulatory system attracted a new critical scrutiny.

Besides the obvious concern of consumers over high prices, a new criticism emerged, directed at the organization of production held in place by the regulatory regime. In neighboring countries, especially in large cities such as London and Paris, a trade in flour emerged as large millers introduced new grinding techniques. Bakers could now purchase various grades of flour rather than grain, simplifying their operations, and millers entered a competitive market that rewarded efficient operations. None of this was possible in the Netherlands. The pioneer in a free grain trade was now a laggard in introducing a free flour trade, which was explicitly forbidden in order to protect the integrity of the milling excise collection system.

The town bakers were organized in guilds, and while they regularly butted heads with the regulatory bodies they also benefited from the suppression of internal competition enforced by those same regulators. As long as the guilds were seen as a pillar of stability and harmony in the urban communities, the *broodzetting* could be viewed as a desirable instrument for reconciling the interests of consumers and producers, and for binding these artisans to the regental order that governed the towns. But once the guilds were regarded primarily as instruments for rent seeking and the subordination of the consumer interest, the *broodzetting* came to be seen in a more negative light. This, indeed, was how the "enlightened public" saw them, and once the guilds were formally abolished, in 1798, the regulatory regime increasingly stood exposed as antiquated – enforcing a guild-like organization on an industry that supposedly had been freed of guilds.

In retrospect, it is apparent that the milling and baking sectors and the fiscal system were locked in an immobilizing embrace. A fiscal-regulatory regime that could be respected – if not admired – for its practical benefits in the seventeenth century, lived on to limit the adaptability of the economy to changed circumstances by the late eighteenth century. The first major criticisms focused on the milling excise.

The Bread Tax and the Classical Economists

Beginning in the 1770s what was by then a venerable pillar of Dutch fiscalism began to attract new attention. If, during the Dutch "golden age," consumer preferences for wheat bread encouraged the Republic's provincial governments to raise milling excises, step by step, to very high levels, now, in a period of high wages, declining industry, and structural unemployment, the milling excise began to be seen as a conspicuous obstacle to economic prosperity.

Adam Smith raised the issue in *The Wealth of Nations*, and he did not mince his words:[1]

> In Holland the money price of the bread consumed in the towns is supposed to be doubled by means of such taxes [excise taxes on the necessities of life] ... These and some other taxes of the same kind, by raising the price of labour, are said to have ruined the greater part of the manufactures of Holland.

Within the Republic Smith's critique was soon taken up by the political economist Elie Luzac. In *Hollands Rijkdom* [The Wealth of Holland] of 1783, he wrote:[2]

> Taxes on the food consumption of the common man raise the cost of living of the workers, and therefore a worker has to earn more than otherwise ... [Therefore] it will be clear that the taxes are the cause of the high wages ...

Supporters of the excise quickly came to its defense, rejecting Smith and Luzac's key claim. Laurens van der Spiegel, who would become the Republic's last Grand Pensionary, not only denied that the Dutch economy was in a ruinous state but denied that high wages and high taxes were causally linked, noting that wages in his home province of Zeeland were every bit as high as in Holland while its excises were significantly lower. Zeeland's wheat excise was, in fact, 73 percent of Holland's rate in the 1780s.[3] Van der Spiegel, Luzac, and Smith launched a debate that has continued to attract academic attention for well over two centuries. But this academic debate also became a political one.

The chief political opposition to the Republic's two-century long rule by the town regents and the stadholders supplied by the House

---

[1] Smith, *Wealth of Nations*, ed. Cannon, book V, ch. 2, p. 159. A generation later David Ricardo also found occasion to dwell on this theme. In arguing against Smith's view that the abundance of capital explained the low interest and low profit rates of Holland, he wrote: "Holland was obliged to import almost all the corn which she consumed, and by imposing heavy taxes on the necessities of the labourer she further raised the wages of labour." David Ricardo, *Principles of Political Economy and Taxation* ed. R. H. Hartwell (Harmondsworth: Penguin, 1971), p. 291n.

[2] Elie Luzac, *Hollands rijkdom* (Leiden, 1783), vol. IV, p. 82. Luzac's book is an annotated translation of the 1778 work of Jacques Accarias de Sérionne, *La Richesse de la Hollande*. These comments appear to be added by Luzac.

[3] L. P. van de Spiegel, *Over de armoede en de bedelaary, met betrekkinge tot de provintie van Zeeland* (Goes, 1780), pp. 21–23. Another defender of the excises was G. K. van Hogendorp. Unlike Van de Spiegel, he conceded that the excises on basic commodities drove up wages, but he defended high wages as preferable to the most likely alternative. He reasoned that the higher wages depressed the profits of the rich, the employers of labor. Better, he argued, that the rich should face lower profits than confiscatory taxation on their income and wealth, since they could more easily avoid such taxes by sending their capital abroad or leaving the country altogether. G. K. Van Hogendorp, *Gedagten over 's Lands finantiën* (Amsterdam, 1802), p. 79.

of Orange was a political movement known as the Patriots. They had imbibed liberal critiques of economic regulation and advocated, among other measures, the abolition of guilds and the ending of the Republic's elaborate structure of excise taxes. The milling excise attracted their particular scorn; more than any other single tax it acted to burden the ordinary burgher with regressive taxes while sheltering rich merchants and *rentiers*. Far from being a clever example of optimal taxation it appeared to them as emblematic of the profound unjustness of the Dutch *ancien régime* as a whole.[4]

The Patriots' first attempt to stir up a revolutionary movement in opposition to the institutions of the old Republic in 1787 failed ignominiously. But after the successful revolution in France, they came to power in 1795 in the wake of an invading French army. Their newly proclaimed Batavian Republic embarked on a far-reaching program of institutional change. It abolished all guilds in 1798 and announced an intention to abolish the excise taxes as well: indeed, the first draft of the Batavian Republic's constitution (which was voted down) declared flat out that taxes "should never be placed on goods that form the primary means of subsistence."[5]

Yet the longer the Patriots pondered the matter – and the more pressing became the need to raise ever more revenue in support of their French sponsors – the more necessary these taxes appeared.[6] The constitution of 1801, which did take effect, abandoned the old ideals and simply stated: "taxes shall remain as before, as they existed in each province." This disappointing news was compounded in 1806, when finance minister Isaac Gogel finally revealed to the Batavian *citoyen* the fruits of his herculean labors in crafting a new unitary system of taxation: not only would the tax on bread be retained, but it would extend to the entire country the high milling excise that previously had been levied only in Holland and its maritime neighbors.[7] Gogel, like most Patriots, had initially supported abolition of the milling excise.[8] But after entering

---

[4] John Pocock, "The problem of political thought in the eighteenth century: patriotism and politeness," *Theoretische geschiedenis* 9 (1982), p. 323.

[5] Cited in Fritschy, *Patriotten*, p. 142.

[6] The Dutch state ran an enormous structural deficit in these years of war and stagnant trade, made more severe by its obligation to pay the French a 100-million-guilder "indemnity" in 1795, followed by additional large subsidies in later years.

[7] From the fall of the old Republic to very nearly the end of the Kingdom of Holland (in 1810), the central figure in refashioning the old federal fiscal system into a unified national one was Isaac Gogel. Schama, *Patriots and Liberators*, pp. 494–524, provides a spirited and very positive account of his leadership. His accomplishments are discussed in a more nuanced way in Fritschy, *Patriotten*, and Pfeil, *Tot redding van het vaderland*.

[8] When he was about to take up the task of reforming the tax system, Gogel wrote in *De Democraten*, no. 40, 9 February 1797, of the evils of the excises, especially those on bread and beer. Fritschy, *Patriotten*, p. 145.

the new Batavian government as finance minister and becoming familiar with the urgency of the new state's financial situation he changed his mind. Already in 1799 he wrote:[9]

Were it possible to abolish this [the milling excise] and similar taxes, or if the governing bodies actually advanced [such legislation], we would not advise in favor, since the situation as it is does not allow for the destruction of such a major source of revenue.

The nation's financial straits and the difficulties of unifying what had always been a highly decentralized federal fiscal system caused a decade of delay in wrapping up the practices of the old Republic and introducing a new unitary national tax system. Indeed, the implementation of this new system was the Batavian Republic's last major act. Within months of its introduction, Napoleon installed one of his brothers, Louis Bonaparte, as king of a successor state, the Kingdom of Holland. But this did not interrupt implementation of the new fiscal regime of 1806, which abolished the provincial milling excises in favor of a single national rate of 108 guilders per last for wheat and 45 guilders for rye. Not only had Gogel not abolished the milling excise, he had increased the rates for nearly everyone, as Table 15.1, which lists the provincial rates prevailing until then, makes clear.

Table 15.1 *Final provincial milling excise rates (1795–1805) and the new national rates introduced in 1806–7 (guilders per last)*

	Wheat	Rye
Holland	104.9375	42.35
Utrecht	115	53.75 (urban only)
Zeeland	77	38.65
Friesland	72	39.60
Groningen	82.5	24.75
Gelderland (Nijmegen)	45	21
(Zutphen and Veluwe)	30	14
Overijssel	36	18
North Brabant*	24	12
National rates		
1806	108	45
1807	108	21.60

*The city of 's-Hertogenbosch (Den Bosch) levied higher rates: 47 guilders per last for wheat and 23.85 for rye. This may include a municipal surcharge, which is not included in the other provincial data.

[9] Quoted in *ibid.*, p. 145.

This unwelcomed innovation met with immediate resistance, especially in the inland provinces, where rye taxes had always been much lower.[10] Recognizing the impolitic nature of the new tax, the new king of Holland responded quickly to adjust its most objectionable feature by using his royal powers to lower the rye tax to only 21.60 per last, one-fifth of the tax on wheat, in 1807.[11] The national excise on rye was now close to what the eastern provinces were accustomed to. Thus, from 1807 the entire country paid a low, eastern-type rye excise but continued to pay a high, western-type wheat excise. This sudden shock to a tax regime that had changed very little for over a century could be expected to encourage increased tax evasion (the incentive was now greater) and to discourage wheat bread consumption everywhere.

Measuring the extent of evasion is difficult (since our chief source of information about bread grain consumption is derived from the tax records themselves), but the evidence of province-level excised grain use in 1808 (see Table 12.3) shows consumption levels in most eastern provinces that are implausibly low. Despite this, the overall result of Gogel's 1806 unification of the Dutch fiscal system was impressive – if you take the side of tax collectors in such matters. In the face of a stagnant economy (at best), the new fiscal regime increased central government revenues from 34–35 million in the period 1799–1805 to 42.7 million in 1806 and 44.6 million in 1807.[12] The results of the new milling excise were also impressive, the outcry against it notwithstanding. The old provincial levies, taken together, rarely raised over 3.9 million guilders while the national excise, in its first year, raised 5.46 million, a 40 percent increase. Even after the radical lowering of the excise on rye in 1807, revenues continued to exceed the pre-reform level by 19 percent.

Despite this achievement, the new tax administration had left a large amount of potential revenue uncollected. King Louis' good deed of sharply reducing the excise on rye, while a large concession to consumers in the eastern provinces, led, at best, to only a marginal improvement in compliance. The state had given up much more revenue by lowering the rate than it had gained in improved compliance.[13]

Substantial resistance to the national milling excise continued until the excise was suspended in 1812, with the incorporation of the entire nation

---

[10] Pfeil, *Tot redding van het vaderland*, pp. 451–53; Schama, *Patriots and Liberators*, p. 513.
[11] Pfeil, *Tot redding van het vaderland*, p. 452.
[12] Gogel, *Memoriën en correspondentiën*, pp. 131, 510–11.
[13] While the average tax on the bread grains in 1807 (weighted by their relative consumption) fell to 82 percent of its 1806 level, revenue in 1807 fell by only slightly less, 85 percent of its 1806 level.

into the French empire. Still, Gogel's unified milling excise had secured a much greater fiscal contribution from the provincial periphery than had ever occurred under the old Republic. The average per capita milling tax revenue, shown in Table 5.8, rose slightly in Holland (from 3.21 guilders per annum before 1806 to 3.40 guilders in 1807), and by rather more (22 percent) in the other western provinces, but in the eastern provinces it nearly doubled (from 0.60 guilders before 1806 to 1.10 guilders in 1807). As a result, the share of the national milling excise revenue paid by Holland (shown in Table 5.7) fell from 65 percent before 1806 to 58 percent in 1807, the share of the other western provinces remained almost unchanged, and the share of the eastern provinces rose substantially, from 12 to 18 percent.

The Batavian Republic faced an urgent need to increase tax revenues. It intended to do so via a radical revision of the fiscal regime that would secure much more revenue from the rich than had been customary under what it regarded as the corrupt and unfeeling practices of the old regime. But in practice the regressive, anti-social milling excise retained the critical place it had held for so long: it continued, as before, to account for 10 to 12 percent of total tax revenues – and total revenues were now much greater than before. Enlightened thought had put the tax on the defensive, but the Batavians learned through experience what Adam Smith had suspected: that excises, however objectionable on theoretical grounds, offer an efficient way to raise revenue. Throughout this era the public, now national, debt was the elephant in the room of Dutch politics. We began this section with Smith's influential theoretical critique of Dutch excise taxes, but we must end it with his less often cited comment, later in *The Wealth of Nations*, of a more practical nature:[14]

Such taxes [excises], though they raise the price of subsistence, and consequently the wages of labour, yet they afford a considerable revenue to government, which it might not be easy to find in any other way. There may, therefore, be good reasons for continuing them.

Taxing Bread under the Kingdom of the Netherlands

The rigorously unitary approach to excise taxation imposed by Isaac Gogel survived the Batavian-French era to live on under the "restored" Dutch state of 1814, which now took the form of a Kingdom of the Netherlands. The new government presented itself as a "restored" Dutch state, but this certainly did not extend to the revivification of the old

---

[14] Smith, *Wealth of Nations*, p. 404, book V, ch. 2, p. 158.

Republic's decentralized institutions. The provinces were now distinctly subordinate administrative units, and the chartered cities that had loomed so large under the old Republic now held legal powers no different, at least in theory, from any other municipalities. But the new state made concessions to local conditions that altered profoundly the workings of the milling excise as crafted by Gogel. In a series of steps, all highly ad hoc in character, the new kingdom moved toward the creation of a milling excise that shared many pre-1806 characteristics. The fragility of the new state's institutions was such that the details of the milling excise were almost constantly under revision. To assist the reader Table 15.2 offers a timeline of the major nineteenth-century policy changes to both the milling excise and the operation of the bread price regulatory authority.

The new United Kingdom of the Netherlands – "united" because it incorporated the Southern Netherlands – did not attempt to impose its peculiar institution of a milling excise on its new southern provinces, but in the north, it was restored immediately as a central government tax with rates nearly equal to those of 1806–10. The new state also allowed municipalities to levy substantial surcharges (*opcenten*) on the central excise rates to generate funds for local use on the condition that they first secure approval from the Ministry of Internal Affairs and that these local levies not exceed 50 percent of the central government excises.

The national milling excise of 1814 was prudentially suspended in 1817, a year of scarcity and very high grain prices.[15] It was restored in 1822, but at much reduced rates. At the same time the central government devolved responsibility for both tax collection and bread price regulation to the provinces. The poor results of this move led to a reassertion of central government oversight and a rise in rates in 1826, but the revolt of the Belgians in 1830 and the ensuing war mobilization provoked a second suspension of the milling excise. This was a gesture to mollify a restive populace, but it also allowed the state to come to the assistance of the many financially strapped municipalities (chiefly the larger cities of the maritime provinces), which were now, in 1831, permitted to raise local excises without limit and without central government review.

The central government milling excise returned in 1833 at higher rates than before. These rates and the numerous – and often very high – municipal surcharges on these rates then continued with little change until 1855, when the entire edifice of bread price regulation

---

[15] The eruption of the Indonesian volcano Tambora in 1815 led to atmospheric changes around the world; as the "year without a summer," 1816 witnessed crop failure in many areas. The resulting high grain prices became most severe during the following year. John D. Post, *The Last Great Subsistence Crisis in the Western World* (Baltimore, Md.: Johns Hopkins University Press, 1977).

Table 15.2 *Changes in the milling excise (guilders per last) and the bread price regulatory system from 1806 to 1865*

	Wheat	Rye
The Batavian-French era		
1806	108.00	45.00
1807–10	108.00	21.60
1811	72.00	21.60
1812–13	0	0

The Dutch state is incorporated into the French Empire. The milling excise is abolished. Bread prices are set at the municipal level, as before.

The Kingdom of the Netherlands

1814–16	108.00	21.60

Municipal surcharges require central government approval. They may not exceed 50 percent of the national tax. Bread pricing remains a municipal responsibility.

1817–21	0	0

The central government tax is abolished. Municipal excises remain and are raised.

1822–25	42.00	12.00

Municipal surcharges continue. The milling excise becomes a provincial responsibility, as does bread pricing.

1826–29	51.60	15.00

By Royal Decree of 25 July 1826 bread pricing is to be guided by provincial rules. Price controls are now limited to establishing maximum prices. Bakers are free to sell at prices below the regulatory maximum. The central collection of the milling excise is restored, and introduced to the Southern Netherlands.

1830–32	0	0

Revolt of Belgium. The milling excise is temporarily abolished; municipal excises remain. In 1831 the central government transfers to the provinces its oversight of municipal taxes. Municipal excises now face no hard limit.

1833–55	60.00	18.00

Uncapped municipal surcharges remain. 1843 By Royal Decree of 15 April 1843 municipalities are free to exercise local option in the enforcement of the *broodzetting* on some or all bread types.

1855	0	0

The national milling excise is abolished together with the regulation of bread prices. Municipalities retain for ten years the right to levy local milling excises; 379 (of 1,134 municipalities) do so.

1865 The remaining municipal excises, still levied in 70 municipalities, are now abolished.

and milling excise was dismantled. Only the municipal excises, some of them, remained for another decade. By 1865 the last remnants of an institution that had served for over 250 years as a major pillar of Dutch fiscalism disappeared.

The milling excise in the 1814–55 period was an odd duck. Under the old Republic it had been primarily a provincial levy with small municipal surcharges that was enforced and collected locally in the numerous urban-based tax districts. The Batavian Republic replaced this with a unitary national levy enforced and collected by a new centralized fiscal apparatus. After 1814 this centralized apparatus was retained, but the municipal surcharge could now become very substantial, and, after 1831, even larger than the central excise. This complicates our efforts to assess the overall burden placed on consumers but it also imposed a complex and contradictory set of incentives and constraints on the new kingdom's millers, bakers, consumers, and local authorities.

Municipalities that exercised their new authority now, just as before 1806, had a strong incentive to restrict interlocal trade in flour and bread. Protecting local millers and bakers also protected a newly strategic source of municipal revenue.[16] But, by the 1820s and 30s, the Batavian-inspired move away from local protectionism was increasingly difficult to roll back.[17] There was an incoherence at the heart of excise taxation in this period. Centralization of taxation, begun in 1806, encouraged a more integrated and competitive economy, a policy strongly endorsed by the new monarch of 1814, Willem I; but the new municipal taxing powers initiated in 1814, and strengthened in 1831, encouraged a revived local particularism in order to enforce the sharply different official bread prices of neighboring municipalities. Ironically, it was not the rural or remote areas that cultivated local protectionism most assiduously but the large cities of the nation's commercial core, whose financial salvation now required the strengthening of barriers to regional and national trade.

Did the milling excise under the Kingdom continue to weigh as heavily on the consumer as it had in earlier times? The central government rates were much lower from 1822 onward, raising no more than half the revenue of the milling excise in 1807–11. Moreover, rate adjustments after 1806 acted to shelter rye bread consumers from the heaviest taxation. Under the old Republic the milling of rye had faced excises that were typically 50 percent of the rate for wheat and the new centralized

---

[16] Van Zanden and Van Riel, *Strictures of Inheritance*, pp. 144–46.

[17] The erosion of town and village authority to shelter local markets from outside suppliers is nicely illustrated in Tom Nieuwenhuis, *Keeshonden en Prinsmannen: Durgerdam, Ransdorp en Holisloot, 1780–1813*, Amsterdamse Historische Reeks 11 (Amsterdam: Historisch Seminarium van de Universiteit van Amsterdam, 1986). He describes how local bakers in the villages near Amsterdam, who had long enjoyed monopoly control of their markets, had to tolerate merchants bringing in rye bread produced in Gelderland after 1805, since village protective measures were now overridden by higher authority. The best the local authorities could do was to require that all "outside" bread be sold at a special site. They selected the village burial grounds (p. 55).

rates imposed in 1806 taxed rye at nearly that rate. The 1807 reduction set the rate on rye at only 20 percent of the wheat rate, and later excise rates never again rose above 30 percent of that rate. Thus, the central government's milling excises were somewhat less objectionable from the perspective of equity than they had been under the old regime. But the central state's forbearance was directly linked to a newly aggressive use of the milling excise by municipalities.

The Municipal Milling Excise

Assessing the overall burden of the municipal milling excise is not easy. Two-thirds of the nation's 1149 municipalities declined to levy a local excise at all, but the remaining third included all of the cities and at least two-thirds of the population, and the rates they settled on varied enormously. We can begin with the case of Amsterdam, which was home to one of every ten Netherlanders in most of this period. From 1829 to 1853 the city of Amsterdam collected, on average, 3,045,000 guilders per year in tax revenues; nearly two-thirds of this amount came from excises, and the municipal milling excise was by far the largest of these, generating 613,000 per year for the city.[18] Before 1806 an "average" Amsterdammer could expect to pay – via purchases of bread – at least 3 guilders per year in milling excise to the provincial government plus an additional 10–15 percent to the city for a total of perhaps 3.5 guilders. After 1822 he or she enjoyed the benefits of a national milling tax that had been lowered to about 1.5 guilders per year, but now faced a municipal tax that amounted to 2.5 guilders, on average, for a total of about 4.0 guilders.

Amsterdam was exceptional in many ways, but in this it pursued a policy common to several other cities, especially in Holland. Many more levied charges only slightly lower than Amsterdam. Table 15.3 offers a few examples of the evolution of the central and local milling excises. It is not comprehensive, but serves to illustrate two patterns: first, the municipal milling excise on wheat was a minor addition to the provincial/central government levy until 1814; thereafter it grew over time, often to become much larger than the central government tax; second, the municipal excise on rye did not rise comparably. Municipalities followed the lead of the central government in keeping the excise on rye modest, rarely more than 20 to 30 percent of their tax on wheat.

---

[18] Marco van Leeuwen, *Bijstand in Amsterdam, ca. 1800–1850* (Zwolle: Waanders, 1992), pp. 173–76.

Table 15.3 *Examples of the central government and municipal milling taxes (guilders per last)*

		Wheat		Rye	
		Central	Municipal	Central	Municipal
Utrecht	1751	115.00	8.75	53.75	8.75
	1806	108.0	27.00	45.00	6.30
	1811	72.00	25.25	21.60	2.31
	1833	60.00	34.35	18	9.00
Amsterdam	1733	104.95	16.20	42.35	5.40
	1807	108.00	27.00	21.60	5.40
	1815		21.60		10.80
	1816	104.95	45.10		
	1849	60.00	105.90	18.00	13.50
Haarlem	1659	63.60	5.40		
	1843	60	135.13	18.00	12.75
Alkmaar	<1748	104.95	10.80		
	1755	104.95	16.20		
Zwolle	1744	36.25	12.00	18.00	6.00

1826 survey data

		Wheat	Rye
National tax:		51.60	15.00
Municipal tax:			
	Haarlem	124.80	13.50
	Leiden	84	24
	The Hague	63	9
	Delft	42	12
	Rotterdam	81	18
	Dordrecht	107.10	12
	Gouda	42	12
	Utrecht	42	12
	4 smaller Holland towns	63.90	16
	3 Overijssel cities	11.4	2

The municipal excise was primarily an urban affair, but even very small cities took part. Table 15.4 shows how the incidence of all excises (of which the milling excise was the largest, accounting for 25–35 percent of the total) varied by the size of municipality in the province of North Holland in 1849.[19] Amsterdam shows up as the most heavily taxed place,

[19] Holland had been officially divided into the modern provinces of North and South Holland in 1840, although its division into two entities can be dated to the Kingdom of Holland of 1807, when they were named, in the French Revolutionary tradition of riparian Department-naming, Amstelland and Maasland, respectively.

Table 15.4a *Municipal taxation in North Holland, 1849 (guilders per capita)*

Pop. of municipality	N	Total population	Direct taxes	Indirect taxes	Total
< 1,000	72	41,422	2.48	0.54	3.02
1,000–1,999	40	56,609	1.69	0.80	2.49
2,000–4,999	24	67,428	1.52	3.63	5.15
5,000–9,999	6	44,873	0.70	6.43	7.13
Zaandam	1	11,542	0.76	5.38	6.14
Haarlem	1	25,969	0.61	9.04	9.65
Amsterdam	1	211,349	0.44	10.50	10.94
9 largest towns			0.51	9.55	10.06
all other municipalities			1.82	2.38	4.20
Weighted average North Holland			0.98	6.97	7.95

Table 15.4b *Total municipal tax revenue, 1849 (in thousands)*

	Population	Direct tax rev.	Indirect tax rev.	Total revenue
9 largest towns	293.7	149.0	2804.6	2953.6
all other municipalities	165.4	300.9	393.9	694.8
Total North Holland	459.1	449.9	3198.5	3648.4

Source: Richard Griffiths, "The role of taxation in wage formation in the Dutch economy in the first half of the nineteenth century," in Johan de Vries, ed., *Ondernemende geschiedenis* (The Hague: Martinus Nijhoff, 1977), p. 268.

but the excises were only slightly less burdensome in the smaller cities, even those of no more than 5,000 inhabitants. All nine such towns faced excises that were over four times higher than those charged in the remaining 136 villages and small towns. The rural areas paid higher direct taxes, mainly real property levies, but they largely escaped the excises: the rural 36 percent of North Holland's population paid only 12 percent of the municipal excises collected in the province.

If we turn to the country as a whole, an 1849 report on municipal finances reveals that all local taxes raised 11.5 million guilders in revenue, 72 percent of which came from the excises. The amount accounted for by the milling excise is not revealed, but almost everywhere it was the largest single source of excise revenue. In five Holland cities it accounted for 27 percent of total excise revenues. Just as Table 15.4 reveals the uneven incidence of the excises within a province, Table 15.5 reveals the highly uneven incidence of municipal excises among the provinces and provides a rough estimate of the total amount raised by the milling excise. The bottom panel of Table 15.5 shows how much the municipal milling excise had become a western and urban phenomenon: western municipalities as a whole paid twice as much tax as those in the east, but they paid five times as much excise tax per capita and nearly ten times as much milling excise.

The municipal milling excise in 1849 generated approximately 2.1 million guilders in annual revenue. At that time the central government milling excise raised approximately 4.4 million. The national excise rates were, of course, everywhere the same. Only regional differences in the relative consumption of wheat and rye caused consumers in the eastern provinces to pay less, about 35–40 percent of the western rate on a per capita basis. But the municipal tax, as we have seen, could vary

Table 15.5 *Municipal taxes in 1849: average annual taxes in guilders per capita*

	Total	Excises	Estimated share raised by milling	Estimate of milling excise per capita	Total milling revenue in thousands of guilders
North Holland	7.90	7.01	27%	1.87	983*
South Holland	5.58	4.10	27	1.11	579
Zeeland	3.71	2.39	25	0.60	96
Utrecht	3.58	2.77	25	0.69	103
Friesland	4.64	2.96	20	0.59	146
Groningen	2.65	1.25	15	0.19	36
Overijssel	1.99	0.95	15	0.14	33
Gelderland	1.75	1.01	15	0.15	56
North Brabant	1.63	0.66	15	0.10	42
Drenthe	1.60	0.65	15	0.10	9
Limburg	0.96	0.59	0	0	0
Total revenue (in thousands of guilders)					
West	7,963	7,043			1,907
East	3,574	1,218			176
Total	11,537	8,261			2,083
Per capita taxation by region					
West	5.37	4.10		1.19	
East	2.62	0.80		0.12	
National	3.83	2.74		0.69	

NB: these averages include municipalities that levied no local excise taxes.
*Amsterdam's municipal milling excise alone accounts for 600,000 of this amount.
Source: Total and excise tax data from Richard Griffiths, *Industrial Retardation in the Netherlands, 1830–1850* (The Hague: Martinus Nijhoff, 1979), p. 59.

from 0 to over 100 guilders per last of wheat. On a provincial basis, the western provinces paid nine times as much in milling excise as the eastern provinces, although, of course, there were many households in the west that escaped this municipal excise and some in the east who paid substantially. Overall, the sharp provincial differences in tax burden that

Table 15.6 *Estimated milling excise revenues, 1807–49 (millions of guilders per annum)*

	Central	Municipal	Total
1807–10	4.9	0.7	5.6
1814–16	4.8	0.7	5.5
1822–25	2.2	0.8	3.0
1826–29	3.1	1.0	4.1
1833–39	3.9	1.6	5.5
1840–49	4.2	1.8	6.0

Per capita milling excise revenue by region, 1807–49 (in guilders per capita)

	Holland	Z-U-F	Other	National avg.
1807–10	3.82	3.23	1.63	2.76
1814–16	3.72	3.15	1.60	2.65
1822–25	1.93	1.62	0.76	1.39
1826–29	2.37	2.00	0.96	1.68
1833–39	3.08	2.32	1.13	2.10
1840–49	3.08	2.32	1.13	2.07

Estimation method: First, maximum central government milling excise revenue was estimated by applying the prevailing excise rates to the total population in each time period. Following the per capita bread grain consumption estimates described in Chapter 12, I set per capita consumption at 1/20th of a last (*c.* 110 kg), 45 percent wheat and 55 percent rye.

The total municipal revenue was set at 15 percent of the central revenue in 1807–16, rising to 40 percent in 1833–55. These totals were then compared to direct evidence of the central milling revenue for 1807, 1815, and 1849 and my estimate of total municipal milling excise revenues for 1849. The maximum estimates generally exceeded the available data by approximately 20 percent. I reduced all estimates by this percentage to achieve a best-fit estimate of probable total revenues.

I estimated the regional burden of the milling excises by assigning the total central government revenue according to population size and the prevailing grain mix in each region, and assuming the average of municipal excises added 10 percent to total revenue in the eastern provinces, 33 percent in Friesland, Utrecht, and Zeeland, and 67 percent in Holland.

Sources: Griffiths, *Industrial Retardation*, p. 58; R. van der Voort, "Gemeentelijke financiën," in Tom Pfeil *et al.*, eds., *Steden en dorpen in last: historische aspecten van locale belastingen en financiën* (Amsterdam: NEHA, 1999), pp. 141–55.

had characterized the old Republic had been recreated under the new Kingdom, though now at the municipal level. In the western provinces, combined milling excises averaged about 3 guilders per capita, but urban residents certainly paid more than this, closer to 4 guilders. In the eastern provinces, combined milling excises averaged 1.2 guilders, and rural residents closer to 1 guilder per capita.[20]

Finally, the milling excise revenue information for benchmark dates (1806–07, 1814, 1849) can be added to information about the central excise rates and our estimates of the average municipal rates in order to estimate the overall central and municipal milling excise revenues over the period 1807–49, and to break this down by region (Table 15.6). These revenue estimates can be compared to the pre-1806 estimates displayed in Table 5.6 and 5.8. Overall, the rise of municipal-level taxation fully compensated for the reduction of central government taxation. Consumers in the eastern provinces had been forced to pay heavier central milling excises, while most of those in the west continued to pay at least as much as before. The milling excise remained as burdensome as ever – and became even more meddlesome.

The Liberal Debate

The pressing need to raise revenue during the desperate years of the Napoleonic Wars overshadowed, even obliterated, the Enlightenment debate over the milling excise. It is also likely that revisions to the excise rates that lowered the burden on rye bread consumers blunted the edge of the critique. But a conjuncture of factors revived the debate in the 1840s. The rising tax rates (via the municipal surcharges), the rising grain prices combined with the potato blight of 1845–47, the arguments popularized by the British Anti-Corn Law League, and the growing conviction that Dutch industry was structurally uncompetitive relative to surrounding countries all brought renewed attention to the excises in general and the milling excise in particular.

Another factor of importance was the changing fiscal condition of the Dutch state. The Batavian Republic had inherited – and sought to honor – the vast public debt incurred by the province of Holland under

[20] Estimated total milling excise revenue by region, 1849 (millions of guilders):

	East	West	Total
Municipal	0.18	1.91	2.09
Central	1.50	2.90	4.40
Total	1.68	4.81	6.49
Per capita total (guilders)	1.18	3.00	2.15

the old Republic, and while French rule brought about a de facto default on what by 1811 had become a far larger centralized debt, the new Kingdom of 1814 held out the hope of redeeming that deferred debt. For decades thereafter the state labored under this burden. The shadow cast by this debt (1.7 billion guilders in 1814, or 3.6 times GDP) was lifted in 1843 when Finance Minister Floris van Hall succeeded in engineering a massive debt conversion. A growing flow of remittances from the Dutch East Indies (the so called *batig slot*) and low interest rates made this refinancing possible, and once it occurred debates about future fiscal policy enjoyed a new degree of freedom.[21] If the debt problem could be resolved, perhaps other problems, such as an oppressive reliance on indirect taxes, could now be tackled also.

The new attack on the excise taxes was led by political liberals such as the clergyman O. G. Heldring and publicist J. L. de Bruyn Kops, who were convinced that the excise stood in the way of the development of a competitive industrial economy. Heldring estimated that all excises together took up one-seventh of a poor householder's income – thus reducing demand for industrial products.[22] But, just as in the eighteenth century, the excises continued to have their defenders. A leading political economist, J. de Bosch Kemper, estimated that the most conspicuously anti-social of these taxes, the milling excise, placed on consumers an annual burden of (only) 1.5 guilders per capita. Most of the other excises he could defend because they suppressed socially undesirable

---

[21] The willingness of the Amsterdam capital market to purchase the new low-interest bonds was encouraged by the implicit threat that the failure of voluntary purchases would lead to forced lending, but, all-in-all, Van Hall's reorganization of the public debt must rank with Gogel's reorganization of taxation as a key step in establishing a viable new state on the ruins of the old. Van Zanden and Van Riel, *Strictures of Inheritance*, pp. 171–73.

[22] O. G. Heldring, *Noodkreet over de belasting op het gemaal en den hoogen prijs van het brood* (Amsterdam, 1846); J. L. de Bruyn Kops, *Over indirecte belasting als middel van plaatselijke inkomsten: eene staathuishoudkundige proeve* (Leiden, 1851). An earlier work on this theme was A. H. Van der Boon Mesch, "Over het Nederlandsche fabrijkswezen en de middelen om hetzelve te bevorderen en in bloei te doen toenemen," *Tijdschrift ter bevordering van nijverheid* 7 (1843), 524–86. Heldring's pamphlet was emotional in tone, but conveyed a rather subtle argument. He reasoned that the poor consumer of rye bread suffered in two ways: directly via the excise on rye bread and indirectly via the effect of the much higher wheat excise on the price of rye. The high wheat excise, he argued, shifted demand toward rye, thereby increasing the price of rye relative to wheat, and diverted the poorest quality wheat from human consumption to animal fodder (since the price of such bread, once the tax was added, made it uncompetitive with rye bread). By his reckoning, the tax added 7.5 cents per 10-pound loaf of rye bread, while the indirect effects added another 10 cents. A household of seven went through three "10-pounders" per week, he reckoned, and thus spent an additional 0.175 *3 * 52 = 27.30 guilders per year. An unskilled laborer in the Betuwe, the rural eastern district where Heldring served as pastor, could not hope to earn even 200 guilders per year; hence his claim that such a household parted with one-seventh of its income because of the milling excise.

consumption (the tax on spirits), fell primarily on the well-to-do (taxes on meat and wine), or were simply trivial in total weight (beer, soap, salt, vinegar, peat). When all was said and done, he concluded, the excises remained as close as one could get to optimal taxation.[23]

In this second round of debate it was not only the excises that came under scrutiny but also the regulation of bread prices itself. The erosion of town autonomy brought about by both constitutional changes and economic developments had done much to render enforcement of bread price regulations less effective, and the state's decision to shift this authority to the provincial governments did not improve matters. A Royal Decree of 1826 limited the regulatory authorities to the setting of *maximum* prices, and signaled the first retreat from the comprehensive controls that had always characterized the Dutch regulatory system. This was followed by a further Royal Decree in 1843 that gave municipal governments the right to restrict price regulation to only some of the types of bread or even to cease regulating bread prices altogether.

The 1843 decree brought little immediate change.[24] Price regulation still appeared to be an unbreakable habit. Moreover, many suspected that the benefits of deregulation would flow to unsympathetic schemers and investors rather than to honest artisans and consumers. An article of 1830 put it as follows:[25]

It is all well and good to stimulate industrial progress, but it is no less admirable to honor the interests and recognized rights of established citizen-artisans, who bear heavy civic duties and who should not be thoughtlessly sacrificed to the interests of project developers and outside fortune-seekers.

But the experience of the "hungry forties" unleashed a flurry of publications subjecting the *broodzetting* to a renewed attack, and while the revolutionary atmosphere of 1848 did not lead to the upheavals that roiled France and the German lands, it did persuade the monarchy to make concessions that led to the introduction of a new liberal constitution.[26] This emboldened the liberals, who now presented the *broodzetting*

[23] J. de Bosch Kemper, *Geschiedkundig onderzoek naar de armoede in ons vaderland* (Haarlem, 1851).
[24] Price regulation appears to have ended in Overijssel shortly after the 1843 decree. Among major towns only Rotterdam is said to have acted on the new opportunity.
[25] "Het geheele afschaffing der broodzetting," *De Weegschaal* 12 (1830).
[26] G. E. van Nooten, *Beschouwingen omtrent de broodzetting* (Schoonhoven, 1845); M. M. von Baumhauer, "De broodzetting," *De Gids* (May 1848), pp. 586–605; J. van Kuijk, *De broodzetting. Onnut, schadelijk, ongeoorloofd* (Amsterdam, 1852); P. N. Muller, "Iets over de broodzetting," *De Economist* (1853), pp. 52–61. The remainder of this paragraph summarizes the chief arguments for abolition made in these publications.

as a relic surviving from an earlier age. If it had made sense in a world of guilds and paternalistic, regental rule, and if its continuation when the guilds had been abolished, fifty years earlier, seemed prudent given the uncertainties of those times, it no longer served any purpose in the modern age now dawning.[27] It violated the principle that the state should not intervene in the voluntary contracts between consumers and suppliers, and its claim that regulation balances the interests of all parties was laughable (only the free market can do that). Moreover, the fear that deregulation would unleash the greed of the bakers and lead to higher prices was unfounded: recent experience in Belgium, France, and even the Kingdom of Sardinia supplied "natural experiments" that demonstrated the price-reducing effects of open competition. In short, it was now time to clean the Augean stables, to guide Dutch society into the modern age of individual freedom and responsibility promised by its new constitution.

The 1848 constitution equipped Liberals to act on their long-held views. While the franchise was extended only modestly, power was now vested in Parliament and a new ministerial cabinet. The liberal cabinet of J. R. Thorbeke immediately acted to scale back (but not abolish) the milling excise and, after seven years and a great deal of parliamentary maneuvring, Thorbeke's successor, Frans van Hall, secured abolition.[28] Getting rid of the *broodzetting* was then a fairly simple matter, but ending the milling excise was not. If the milling excise originally could grow to importance after 1596 because of the new regulatory system, by the nineteenth century it was the importance of the excise that propped up the regulatory regime.

In the world of bakers and millers, 1855 became the year of the "big bang," the year in which an encompassing regulatory embrace and an invasive tax regime that had been a centerpiece of Dutch fiscalism since the earliest days of the Dutch Revolt suddenly came to an end – with one exception. Municipal milling excises could continue by local option (which 379 of the country's 1,134 municipalities elected to do), but by 1865 they too were abolished.[29]

---

[27] G. C. Nicola, J. F. R. Nievergeld, and G. Keller, *Jaarboekje voor broodbakkers* (The Hague: K. Fuhri, 1856), p. 87.

[28] The parliamentary history of this achievement is extremely complicated. See Christianne Smit, *Omwille der billijkheid: de strijd over de invoering van de inkomstenbelasting in Nederland* (Amsterdam: Wereldbibliotheek, 2002), pp. 94–103.

[29] Almost abolished. Seventy municipalities received permission to continue levying local excises for a while longer. Bert Altena and Dirk van der Veen, "Een onbekende enquête naar broodconsumptie in Nederland," *Tijdschrift voor sociale geschiedenis* 12 (1986), 135–52.

The Big Bang: What Difference Did it Make?

These dual events would seem to bring this study to an end. The objects
of our attention had been abolished; henceforth bakers could compete
with each other on price, millers could produce and sell flour without
restriction, and consumers could purchase bread at market prices unburdened by excise taxes. But this new situation, as close as one gets to a
"big bang" in historical reality, deserves a moment of our attention, since
it permits us to investigate three large outstanding questions:

First, did the free market bring about a substantially different structure
of bread prices than had been enforced for so long by the *broodzetting*?
Were consumers now able to act on their preferences without the distorting intervention of the regulators?

Second, did the sudden abolition of the milling excise and the release
of the milling and baking sectors from comprehensive regulation lead
to a reorganization of these sectors and the achievement of greater
productivity?

Third, and most important, did deregulation and the removal of taxes
stimulate economic growth? Had the old regulatory regime really acted
as an obstacle to the growth of the national economy by inflating bread
prices, forcing up wage rates, undermining industrial competitiveness
and reducing demand for industrial products? That is, did the Dutch
economy after 1855 enjoy a "deregulation dividend" that could confirm
the validity of the claims made by Smith, Ricardo, and Dutch liberals?

1. *Did the structure of bread prices change when price controls were lifted?*
The introduction of competitive markets should have altered the relative prices of the various types of bread. Defenders of the old regulatory
regime expressed doubts that bakers would actually compete with each
other. Indeed, bakers in some towns formed cartels; they replaced the
municipal pricing commissioners with their own agents, who continued
to announce weekly bread prices on their own authority.[30] Who now
would protect the consumer from the greed of the bakers?

In fact, neither formal cartels nor informal price leadership were
able to prevent a decline in bread prices and a major revision of the
long-prevailing structure of bread prices. Chapter 9 revealed that bread
price commissioners engaged in a persistent and often very pronounced
intervention in relative bread prices – price differentials that cannot
be explained by grain and production costs. Right up to the 1850s

---

[30] Post-1855 price setting is described for Haarlem and Utrecht in Nicola *et al.*, *Jaarboekje*,
pp. 40–41. "Six months after abolition [of price regulation] very little has changed ....
This has led some to demand a return of the *broodzetting*, but there is nothing to be
gained by restoring obsolete institutions." *Wetenschappelijke Bladen* 2 (1856), 317–18.

consumers paid twice as much for a kilogram of coarse wheat bread as for rye bread, and over three times as much for fine white bread. The removal of price regulation and taxation led to major reductions in those differentials. Figure 15.1 shows the overall trend of price differentials after 1840 based on national average bread prices, while Figure 15.2 shows the convergence of the long-distinct eastern and western price structures. Within a decade after deregulation in 1855 consumers in the east ceased to face punitive wheat bread price differentials and consumers everywhere enjoyed much lower wheat bread prices.

Consumers facing a changing price structure within a category of goods can be expected – *ceterus paribus* – to shift a portion of their demand toward the items that are becoming relatively cheaper. In earlier chapters we observed what appears to be a violation this dictum. In the course of the seventeenth century west Netherlands consumers shifted a portion of their bread consumption from rye to wheat *in the face of* rising relative prices for the wheat breads. Cross-subsidization by regulators and taxation by the state combined to raise the relative prices of wheat breads, yet consumers in the aggregate substituted wheat for rye bread until wheat bread accounted for two-thirds of total bread consumption. This

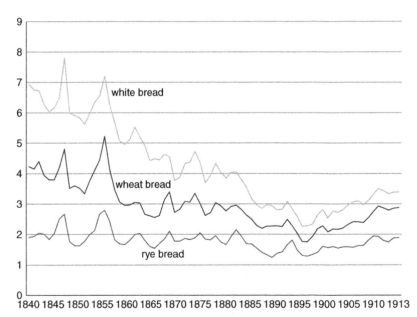

Figure 15.1 White bread, wheat bread, and rye bread stuivers per kg, 1840–1913

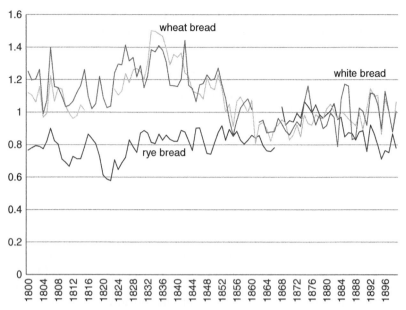

Figure 15.2 East/west price ratios for rye bread, coarse wheat bread, and white bread, 1800–99

"apparent" violation is just that, because in this period other things were not equal: *ceterus paribus* conditions did not apply. Consumers faced a price structure that discouraged purchasing wheat bread, but their rising incomes and personal preferences (their acquired tastes) countervailed, and more, to generate a net shift toward wheat bread.

Where might this have led had incomes continued to rise or had bread taxation not been radically increased in 1680? It appears that a sort of equilibrium was reached between consumer preferences and the structure of relative prices imposed by the regulatory system, and that this equilibrium persisted – although disturbed by price and income shocks in the Napoleonic era – until 1855. Thereafter, the new liberal era brought with it a major change in relative prices that allowed Dutch consumers to "resume," as it were, a long-term shift toward wheat bread, especially the bolted white bread, which they had initiated in the seventeenth century.

Figure 15.3 displays the prices of breads and grains relative to the price of rye bread. It shows clearly how the threefold difference in the prices of rye bread and fine white bread of the 1850s had been reduced to a twofold difference by the 1870s, and the 100 percent difference between coarse wheat bread and rye bread prices had fallen to 50 percent. But

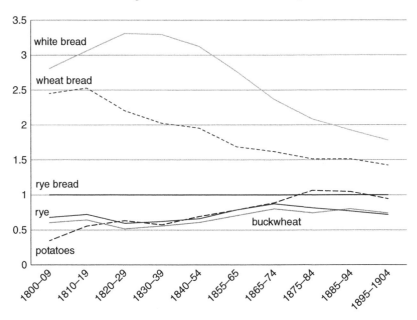

Figure 15.3 Price of grains, bread, and potatoes relative to the price of rye bread, 1800–1904

this was not the only shift in relative prices taking place in the second half of the nineteenth century. Just as wheat breads became more affordable relative to rye bread the important bread substitutes, buckwheat and potatoes, lost their price advantages. Potato consumption continued to be important – another piece of evidence to show that it did not function as a true substitute for bread in the diets of most people – but buckwheat disappeared from the diet in the same period that rye bread was driven to the margins. By the early twentieth century wheat bread had come to dominate the diets of consumers throughout the country.

2. *Did deregulation bring about a reorganization of the milling and baking sectors, leading to significant productivity gains?*

Milling. Our investigation of the grain millers (in Chapter 7) revealed an industry that had been placed in a peculiar position. The regulatory regime had intervened in the operation of grain mills in a particularly invasive way, forcing millers to operate far below their maximum efficiency. In addition, regulation greatly restricted the commercial side of the miller's business, forbidding a trade in flour, side businesses such as animal fattening, and the integration of milling and baking activities.

Standing against these restraints on the entrepreneurship of the millers was the second legacy of the centuries of regulation. Because the grain mills had long furnished the strategic point of enforcement for the milling excise every province pursued a policy of restricting the number of mills. This policy encouraged wind-powered mills of large size by the standards of the early modern era. The large average scale of milling operations plus the large increases in the millers' fees granted after 1800 placed the millers, certainly the larger millers, in a strong position.

But, in matters of scale of operation and technology, all things are relative. An industrial sector that was positively progressive in 1650 and still relatively efficient in 1790, came to be viewed soon thereafter as a technological laggard and a commercial dinosaur. By the early nineteenth century the steam engine made possible a much larger scale of production than could be reached by either wind- or water-driven grain mills and liberal commercial policy began to take aim at the regulations that prevented a free trade in flour. New vistas now opened up for the entrepreneurial miller.

But the millers, whose ancestors had chaffed at being stripped of their entrepreneurial role as traders in grain and flour, now expressed little interest in adopting technologies and commercial practices that could radically reduce their costs. Long held in the encompassing embrace of both the municipal *broodzetting* and the republican fiscal regime, their instinct – reinforced by their guilds – was to defend the cosseted position to which they had grown accustomed.[31]

In Amsterdam, where the potential for large-scale milling was most obvious, the millers responded to such liberal threats, real and perceived, by replacing their abolished guild with a cartel. This was immediately struck down by royal decree of Louis Bonaparte, but the millers revived their cartel under the new Dutch Kingdom in 1817. Under agreements renewed periodically until 1852 the millers cooperated in a central collection of all millers' fees. Each miller received a portion of this fee immediately while the remainder (first 30, later 44 percent of the total) was placed in a central fund, to be divided annually among all millers according to their ownership share in the grain mills. This removed any individual's incentive to seek a larger scale of production at the same time that it prevented any miller from secretly working under the cartel price. The cartel also allowed the millers to present a united front against

---

[31] The obstacle formed by the milling excise to the adoption of technological innovations and cheap, commercially available flour proved to be the strongest argument of the liberals in the parliamentary debates leading to abolition. D. H. "Ons dagelijksch brood. Voorheen en thans," *De economist* 19(1870), 225–26.

any outsider who might invest in a high-capacity steam-powered grain mill. By temporarily lowering the millers' fee, the cartel could prevent such a venture from reaching the scale of operation needed to achieve profitability, a strategy it used with success in 1828 to defeat the first steam-powered mill in Amsterdam, established by Lodewijk Cantillon.[32] Between 1838 and 1843 others tried their luck where Cantillon had failed, but the millers' cartel, aptly named *Eendragt maakt magt* [In unity there is strength], prevailed, thwarting all effort to introduce the new milling technology.[33] To be precise, the millers together with the tax and price regulations of public authorities thwarted the innovators. Only after the provincial milling excise and the regulation of bread prices were both eliminated, in 1855, was the path effectively cleared for a radical restructuring of the milling industry.[34]

The first step in this restructuring was taken that same year by Samuel Sarphati. He was more a philanthropist than an entrepreneur, but the firm he established, the *Maatschappij der Meel- en Broodfabrieken* [Flour and bread factory company] was an immediate success, bringing the millers' cartel to an end. Sarphati and his followers combined their steam-powered mills with industrial bakeries causing millers' fees and bread prices to fall quickly and sharply.

[32] H. W. Lintsen, *Molenbedrijf en meelfabriek in Nederland in de negentiende eeuw* (The Hague, 1989); H. W. Lintsen, "Stoom als symbol van de Industriële Revolutie," *Jaarboek voor de geschiedenis van bedrijf en techniek* 5 (1988), 109–37. A critique of Lintsen's analysis of the difficulties of early steam-powered grain mills is found in J. L. van Zanden, "De introductie van stoom in de Amsterdamse meelfabricage 1828–1855: over de rol van marktstructuren, ondernemersgedrag en de overheid," *Jaarboek voor de geschiedenis van bedrijf en techniek* 8 (1991), 63–80. For a summary account of the difficult transition to steam power in Amsterdam, see Van Zanden and Van Riel, *Strictures of Inheritance*, pp. 144–50.

[33] Van Zanden, "De introductie," p. 72. See also Diedriks, *Een stad in verval*, pp. 202–05.

[34] Attempts to establish large-scale steam-powered flour mills in London also failed, even though millers were free of the restrictions imposed by the Dutch milling excise and the assize of bread had been abolished there in 1815. The London market appeared well suited to this innovation, given the lack of wind- and water-driven mills in the vicinity of the metropolis. The firm of Boulton and Watt participated in the first such mill, which began operation in 1786. Known as the Albion Mill, it pioneered in the use of a reciprocal-action steam engine, but to no avail. The owners soon found that coal prices in London were still too high for competitive operation against traditional competitors who – like the Amsterdam millers – could temporarily lower their prices to prevent the new entrants from achieving the necessary economies of scale. A second attempt soon thereafter met a similar fate; indeed, the explosion of the Albion's steam engine in 1791 served for decades as a cautionary tale, a very useful one for the owners of wind and water mills. It was only at the end of the 1840s (just a few years before Amsterdam), that steam-powered grain mills took hold in London. Chartres summarizes this slow diffusion by noting: "by 1850 steam had not displaced the larger and more efficient urban watermills ... [they were] principally confined to London and the larger [industrial] towns." John Chartres, "British Isles, 1750–2000," in Van Molle and Segers, eds., *Agro-Food Markets*, p. 109; Petersen, *Bread*, pp. 60–66.

Sarphati was a hero to nineteenth-century Amsterdammers, who named a street and a park in his honor, and one would like to conclude this account by describing how an efficient, steam-powered milling industry quickly emerged everywhere in the Netherlands once the artificial restraints on rationalization were removed. In fact, the transition was a slow one: in 1880 there were more wind-powered grain mills than ever before. The steam-powered mills added by that date were, on average, far larger than the windmills, but together they accounted for only 20 percent of total milling output.[35]

It is clear from the experience of Amsterdam that public policy (shaping market structure) and the business culture of a long-regulated industry stood as a formidable obstacle to productivity-increasing technical innovation in grain milling. But public policy had also shaped the wind-based milling sector to consist of fairly large mills, which allowed them – once challenged by new competitors and released from old constraints – to achieve substantially higher levels of productivity.[36] In the new, post-1855 environment, relative factor prices were such that the new technology replaced the old only gradually outside the largest cities.

Baking. The reorganization of milling was gradual, stretched out over the entire second half of the nineteenth century; the bakers faced a more immediate challenge. We have seen that factory-scale bread production in Amsterdam began immediately after the lifting of price controls, and other large cities soon followed Amsterdam's lead. A contemporary advocate of bread factories attributed the 23 percent fall in price of bolted wheat bread in Leiden in 1868 entirely to the establishment of such a factory in 1866.[37] The new factories did not sweep away the numerous local bakeries. Some bakers became distributors of bread produced off-site; others, especially where the new competition had not yet penetrated, formed local cartels to preserve something of the old regulatory regime, but most learned to compete with the factory bakeries.[38]

---

[35] De Jonge, *De industrialisatie in Nederland*, pp. 217–22; H. W. Lintsen, "Meel," in H. W. Lintsen, ed., *Geschiedenis van de techniek in Nederland* (Zutphen: Walburg Pers, 1992), vol. I: *Techniek en modernisering: landbouw en voeding*, pp. 70–101. Steam-powered flour mills grew from 20 in 1850 to 232 in 1883, but over the same period wind-powered mills grew from 1,920 to 2,350. Only after the 1880s, when the actual milling technology (as opposed to the source of power) was transformed, did the milling sector experience a true restructuring.

[36] The slow diffusion of steam-powered milling in a country of relatively efficient wind-powered grain mills can be compared to the slow diffusion of railways in a country of numerous canals. Both illustrate the "penalty of the pioneer" [*wet van de remmende voorsprong*] phenomenon: early investment in an obsolete technology can slow the diffusion of a more advanced technology. See Jan de Vries, *Barges and Capitalism: Passenger Transportation in the Dutch Economy, 1632-1839*, AGG Bijdragen 21 (Wageningen: Afdeling Agrarische Geschiedenis, 1978), pp. 187–218.

[37] D. H. [Hartevelt], "Ons dagelijksch brood," *De economist* 18 (1869), 913–24.

[38] Anon., "Een woord over broodfabrieken en den goeden ouden tijd," *De economist* 17 (1868), 257–64. The unknown author observes that the success of the *Haagsche*

The bakers' fee that had been incorporated in the regulated bread prices before 1855 now disappeared, of course, and my reconstruction of bakery finances shows that free market prices pressed down drastically on their revenues. The estimated net bakers' revenue per last of grain is displayed in Table 15.7. The sharp price inflation of the French Revolutionary era caused the bread price commissioners to grant substantially higher bakers' fees. These may not have sufficed to cause bakers' real earnings to rise in this period, but they certainly did so after 1818, as price levels fell while bakers' fees remained as before.

Table 15.7 *Estimating bakery revenue in the nineteenth century*
a. Estimated net revenue of bakers per last of grain (guilders per last)

	West		East		National	
	Rye	Wheat	Rye	Wheat	Rye	Wheat
1700–79	73.12	151.97	34.53	156.35		
1780–99	84.55	177.69	29.28	187.46		
1800–19	89.47	195.83	42.59	246.74	70.85	187.50
1820–39	85.70	201.34	45.90	211.68	67.03	193.11
1840–55	77.05	142.01	39.55	200.40	60.30	177.88
1856–65	55.34		33.13		43.65	116.29
1866–75					31.11	64.81
1876–85					38.18	71.78
1886–1913					59.71	77.90

West and east: based on data derived from municipal and provincial sources; see Table 8.9. National: based on national average prices in Van Riel database.

b. Estimated net revenue per "average" bakery, with an output of 15 lasts of bread grain
Western bakeries are assumed to produce 10 lasts of wheat and 5 lasts of rye; eastern bakeries process 2.5 lasts of wheat and 12.5 lasts of rye in every period.

	West	East
1700–79	1,885.30	822.51
1780–99	2,199.65	834.65
1800–19	2,405.65	1,152.22
1820–39	2,441.90	1,102.95
1840–55	1,805.35	995.38
1856–65	1,381.15	836.35
1866–75	803.65	550.90
1876–85	908.70	656.70
1886–1913	1,077.55	941.13

Broodfabriek had undermined the viability of many bakeries, but that it was the policy of the bread factory "to appoint its distributors from among those bakers who were willing to do so; which were, of course, those whose bakeries had not prospered and who had the most to fear from the new competitor." These bakers-turned-distributors, according to the author, now throve as they never had thriven before.

This changed suddenly and radically with deregulation. Except for rye bread in the first deregulated years, we can track the changes in average net revenue only at the national level after 1855, but the picture is clear: by the 1860s bakers could earn only a fraction of the amount per last of grain that they enjoyed before 1855. Moreover, the large price differentials in favor of wheat bread quickly became a thing of the past once bread prices were determined by market forces rather than regulators. Deregulation brought to an end the cross-subsidization policy that had pressed on the bakers' margins for rye bread while it offered them relief via the more generous prices allowed for wheat breads. After 1855 the margins for all bread types – rye, coarse wheat, and fine white breads – converged.

As a consequence, the net revenue of a bakery at a given scale of production fell in the west by about half in the two decades after 1855 and by at least a quarter in the east. As shown in Table 15.7b, the "typical" west Netherlands bakery working up 15 lasts of grain per year (10 lasts of wheat, 5 lasts of rye) could expect to take in about 1,900 guilders per year in the eighteenth century. This revenue needed to cover the cost of labor (hiring a journeyman baker and perhaps an apprentice), capital (the cost of owning or renting the bakery and the oven), and the baker's own compensation and profit. From our investigation of these costs in Chapter 8 it appears that this net revenue allowed the baker a personal income comfortably above the 600-guilder-per-year level. Shortly after deregulation a bakery of this size could expect only 800–900 guilders in net annual revenue. Since both labor and capital costs rose after this date, it is unlikely that much if any income remained to compensate the baker. In the east, where bakery earnings had been much lower, net revenues also declined after deregulation to the 550–650 guilder range.

How did the bakers survive? These estimates of the net revenues of an average bakery assume that the wheat–rye mix purchased by consumers remained constant at the levels observed before deregulation. But we have just noted that the change in the price structure of breads led to a major increase in wheat bread consumption. Unfortunately for the bakers, this shift no longer offered the economic relief that it had under regulation, which routinely granted bakers much greater revenues from wheat bread than from rye. After 1855 the bakers' net revenues from the various bread types gradually converged. Consequently, even a bakery selling exclusively wheat and white breads could earn only 7 to 10 percent more than the estimates shown in Table 15.7b.

Only a major increase in the scale of production and a significant improvement in labor productivity could preserve the viability of the artisanal bakery after deregulation. A 1901 survey of the baking sector in Amsterdam confirms that this is indeed what happened. In the century and more before 1855 Amsterdam was a city of some 220,000 inhabitants and about 500 bakeries. By 1901 the city's population had reached 500,000, but the number of bakeries had shrunk to 323.[39] Two of them were bread factories each employing over 100 workers and 38 were large bakeries with an average of 16 employees each. This left 283 traditional bakeries (no more than five workers) which, with an average of 3.2 employees, operated on a much larger average scale than the 500+ bakeries of the pre-1855 era.[40] Of course, Amsterdam was hardly typical of the country as a whole, and small towns and villages long retained many small bakeries. Overall, the productivity of bakeries increased substantially.[41] Setting aside the handful of bread factories, which employed new technologies, this increased productivity was achieved by a combination of increased scale, harder work (fewer employees), and the introduction of ancillary trades (selling other products in the bakery). In short, higher productivity was achieved by methods that had long been available, but had not been necessary as long as the *broodzetting* had remained in place. Were it not for price regulation, much of the post-1855 rationalization of the baking sector would have occurred earlier.

Overall, the decades after 1855 altered the bread economy for both producers and consumers in fundamental ways. Given the size of the bread economy, these changes alone could have had a substantial impact on the economy as a whole. But contemporaries often foresaw a larger benefit to the dismantling of the old regulatory and tax regimes, one that would transform the macro-economy of the Netherlands – even restore its lost economic glory.

3. *Had bread price regulation and bread taxation acted to undermine the Dutch economy? Did their removal provide a "deregulation dividend," helping to "jump-start" the Dutch economy?*

Millstone. Time has not eroded support for the analysis of the founders of classical economics. An earlier generation of Dutch economic historians – whether champions of social democratic ideals[42] or defenders of the liberal critique of Dutch stagnation before the introduction of the constitution of 1848[43] – were in broad agreement that the excise taxes in

---

[39] The number of bakeries fell sharply from 514 in 1859 to 400 in 1865 and 230 in 1882 as a few large bread factories quickly gained market share. Ad Knotter, *Economische transformatie en stedelijke arbeidsmarket* (Zwolle: Uitgeverij Waanders, 1991), pp. 196–97.
[40] *Het bakkersbedrijf* (Amsterdam, 1903), pp. 49–51.
[41] Van Zanden and Van Riel, *Strictures of Inheritance*, pp. 225–26.
[42] I. J. Brugmans, *Paardenkracht en mensenmacht* (The Hague: Martinus Nijhoff, 1961), pp. 66–199; Brugmans, *De arbeidende klasse in Nederland*.
[43] W. J. Wieringa, *Economische heroriëntering in Nederland in de 19e eeuw* (Groningen, 1955); P. W. Klein, *Traditionele ondernemers en economische groei in Nederland, 1850–1914* (Haarlem, 1966). See also Charles Wilson, "Taxation and the decline of empires: an unfashionable theme," *Bijdragen en Mededelingen van het Historisch Genootschap* 77 (1963), 10–23.

general, and the milling excise in particular, were inefficient and unjust: they caused wages to be too high, suppressed discretionary income available for manufactures, and weighed inequitably on the ordinary people.

In 1976 Joel Mokyr took up this issue, and sought to measure the impact of the milling excise on nineteenth-century wages. Mokyr agreed that Dutch wages were higher than those of neighboring countries, but was dubious about the impact of the excises on the wage level. He brought a bit of economic theory to his analysis. It is not enough, he noted, to measure the absolute size of the milling tax and assume that this must "explain" a rise in wages by that full amount; one must first calculate supply and demand elasticities in order to determine the extent to which the milling tax would be "passed through" to bread prices, and bread prices "passed through" to wage rates. Mokyr did not attempt to actually estimate the relevant elasticities since this seemed unnecessary. The national milling tax – which after 1822 was significantly lower than before – was, he concluded, quite insufficient, even if "pass through" were complete, to be more than a very minor factor in explaining the unquestionably high nominal wages prevailing in the Netherlands.[44]

If Mokyr's position is reminiscent of De Bosch Kemper in the debate of the 1840s, he was soon challenged by the successor to Heldering and De Bruyn Kops in the person of Richard Griffiths. Griffiths conceded the importance of demand elasticities but faulted Mokyr for neglecting the complicating role of the municipal milling taxes. We have considered these taxes in some detail because of their large, and locally variegated impact on consumers; Griffiths concluded that the pattern of municipal milling excises accounted for much of the large observable wage differential between the urban maritime provinces and the more rural inland provinces. Wages in the western provinces were high, he concluded, in order to compensate for the burden of indirect taxes on the income of urban workers.[45] This burden was heavier than Mokyr had suspected because of the impact of municipal surcharges.

Adam Smith appears to have been vindicated after all. Yet a very long-term perspective on this issue leads one to wonder if the direction of causation assumed by all participants in this debate (from taxes to prices

---

[44] Joel Mokyr, *Industrialization in the Low Countries, 1795–1850* (New Haven, Conn.: Yale University Press, 1976), pp. 192–93.

[45] Griffiths, "The role of taxation," pp. 266–67; Griffiths, *Industrial Retardation.* Also in support of this view: Van Zanden and Van Riel, *Strictures of Inheritance,* p. 150. Van Riel went on to study the effect of the nineteenth-century excises as a whole, and concluded that: "municipal excises ... must be considered a critical factor in raising the nominal wage as well as in explaining wage differences in the Netherlands itself." Van Riel, "Prices and industrialization," p. 298.

to wages) should be reversed? The division of the Netherlands into high-and low-tax zones did not date from the 1840s, nor from the 1770s, when Enlightenment critics first examined the issue. Its origins are to be found in the period 1600–80, as Holland and its maritime neighbors constructed a fiscal system based on high excise taxes while the more rural inland provinces kept their excises relatively low. If high taxes necessarily push up wages, this is the period in which one should seek a growing wage differential between east and west. But regional wage data summarized in Figure 13.3 show that the large differentials of 1840 and 1770 were already at least as large in the 1600–80 period. Indeed, they pre-date the emergence of the excises as heavy provincial levies.

The excises did not force up the wage rates; rather, the excises rose where wages were already high. This is a more fruitful starting point for any analysis of the relationship between taxes, food prices, and high wages. The Dutch excises exploited the sizeable purchasing power of the population. In those provinces where a growing discretionary income led to changing consumer preferences, the milling excise rose, and it is this income characteristic that made the milling excise an efficient tax and an example of optimal taxation.

A second factor that is often neglected in discussions of the wage-increasing effect of the milling excise is the fact that excises on wheat always accounted for the bulk of total revenues. Until 1805 rye bread consumers paid no more than half as much tax as wheat bread consumers, and this proportion declined thereafter, to no more than 30 percent as much. Municipal milling excises in the nineteenth century followed the same course. In 1826 the municipal excises on rye ranged from 18 to 29 percent of the wheat excise. Overall in the period 1800–55, wheat bread in the west accounted for about 65 percent of total bread consumption, about 75 percent of total bread expenditures, and 85 percent of milling excise revenue (see Table 15.8). In the eastern provinces wheat bread remained a special taste, but those who indulged in it were made to pay: from 1806 onward wheat accounted for 15 percent of total bread consumption, but 35 percent of excise revenues. Wheat bread eaters, concentrated in the eastern towns, paid a hefty premium for their preference.

This does not quite dispose of the matter, since I have demonstrated in earlier chapters that the Dutch population, certainly in the western provinces, could not be divided cleanly into wheat-bread and rye-bread eaters; most people consumed both, albeit in varying mixes. Perhaps the best way to describe the weight of the milling excise burden in the nineteenth century is via the simple exercise displayed in Table 15.9. There, I have calculated the per capita excise tax burden depending on whether the consumer lived in a municipality that levied a local surcharge on

Table 15.8 *Wheat as a percentage of total grain consumption, total bread expenditure, and total milling tax revenue, 1804–50*

	Wheat as a percentage of:		
	total bread grain consumed	total bread expenditure	total milling excise revenue
Holland			
1798	66.0	76.2	80.4
Western Netherlands			
1800–19	59.4	72.8	83.0
1820–39	64.5	78.1	88.9
1840–55	64.6	75.9	88.8
Eastern Netherlands			
1800–19	13.7	28.2	33.0
1820–39	13.7	28.1	35.8
1840–55	13.7	25.8	35.2
Netherlands total			
1806–09	43.8	66.7	74.9
1810–14	40.6	63.5	68.5
1815–19	43.9	66.7	80.9
1820–29	42.3	65.2	76.9
1830–39	40.0	61.9	74.5
1840–49	34.1	55.5	66.9

Source: Netherlands total calculated from data assembled in Van Riel database; Jansen, *Industriële ontwikkeling*, pp. 340–45. Excise revenue refers to central government revenues only.

the national tax, and depending on whether the household consumed the bread grains at the western average (67 percent wheat – 33 percent rye), the national average (approximately 50–50), or the eastern average (15 percent wheat – 85 percent rye). The per capita tax is based on an assumed annual per capita consumption of 110 kilograms of bread grain in all cases. Two-thirds of municipalities, overwhelmingly rural, levied no local surcharges. Of the remainder, the surcharges varied, but for this exercise I have assumed a municipal excise of 80 guilders per last for wheat and 15 guilders for rye. This approximates the average of eight large cities of Holland.

Table 15.9 reveals very clearly that the weight of the milling excise on households in the 1814–55 period could vary fourfold between consumers of the rural east and the urban west. Thus, the household of an unskilled laborer in the west could see 8 to 10 percent of its income flow, via the baker, to the public coffers. The unskilled laborer's household in the east earned less, but the milling excise claimed only 3 to 4 percent of its income. Even this latter amount is not trivial for a poor

Table 15.9 *Per capita milling excise for 110 kg of bread grain per year under various wheat–rye mixes, 1833–55 (guilders per head per year)*

Wheat–rye mix	67–33	50–50	33–6	15–85
High municipal tax	5.20	4.33	3.43	2.45
No municipal tax	2.30	1.95	1.60	1.22

household, but the western burden was truly striking. Of course, the poor western household could soften the blow by consuming mainly rye. This could cut its milling excise tax bill nearly in half and, indeed, the milling excise records show that consumers substituted away from wheat bread in 1810–14, and again in 1845–47. But these shifts were temporary, induced by extreme adversity; once bread prices moderated, consumption patterns snapped back to their long-established norms.

Table 15.9 shows schematically that the milling excise remained a serious burden in the nineteenth century for the urban population and some rural western areas. Since many of the cities of Holland and Zeeland had long ago lost their economic prosperity, the milling excises then stood as a significant impediment to any revival. In this sense, Griffiths' critique of Mokyr was valid, just as liberals' arguments against De Bosch Kemper had been in the 1840s. But neither Griffiths nor the nineteenth-century liberals, nor Adam Smith and the Classical economists appear to be correct in arguing that wages in the western Netherlands had been driven to their high levels *because of* the excises. The high western wages pre-dated the seventeenth-century rise of the milling excise to its high levels, just as the east–west wage differential pre-dated the emergence of large regional differences in the excise burden.

The excises were raised in the course of the seventeenth century to take advantage of *existing* high wages and the developing preference for wheat bread that they supported. I have argued that the milling excise was an efficient tax and an example of optimal taxation. But its persistence into the first half of the nineteenth century must be seen as an unfortunate example of path dependence, the strategic adjustments of King Louis Bonaparte and his successors notwithstanding. So many institutions – fiscal as well as commercial, involving the very structure of the milling and baking sectors – had adjusted themselves for so long to life within the embrace of the *gemaal* and the *broodzetting* that a disruption to these familiar arrangements appeared very risky at a time in which the entire society already faced unprecedented challenges. Better, it must have seemed at the time, to stick with the devil you know.

Bread Prices in International Perspective

But have we set the cart before the horse? One question none of the participants to these debates asked – probably because the answer appeared to be only too obvious – is whether bread prices in the Netherlands actually were higher than those faced by consumers elsewhere. This is really what is at stake in the classical-liberal critique of the milling excise: costly bread, given its centrality to the budgets of most households, will harm the economy one way or another; it may force up wages, thereby reducing the international competitiveness of the economy, especially its labor-intensive industrial sectors; it may reduce purchasing power for discretionary consumer goods of all kinds, thereby limiting domestic demand for industrial products.

Thus far we have considered two questions: was the milling tax large enough to have a significant effect on wages and industrial competitiveness? (yes, at least in the urban west); and is there any evidence that Dutch wages rose as the excises rose? (no, they rose earlier). But this takes as given the assumption that bread prices in the Netherlands were actually substantially higher than in other European countries. *Ceterus paribus* this must have been the case – nowhere else were such heavy taxes levied on bread – but were other things really equal in fact?

Chapter 14 was devoted to answering this question. There I assembled detailed bread price data from across western and central Europe, converted those prices to a Dutch guilder standard via the silver value of the relevant currencies, measured the difference in price levels, and sought to explain the differences revealed.

The results were surprising. To be sure, the basic rye and wheat breads in the Netherlands were generally among the most expensive in Europe. Especially in the period 1700–70 wheat bread prices were distinctly higher than nearly anywhere else. But throughout the period 1600–1850 rye bread in countries to the east of the Netherlands rarely sold for much less than in the eastern Netherlands, while in Britain, the Netherlands' most formidable economic rival, wheat bread actually became more expensive throughout the key decades of the Industrial Revolution. In Belgium and France bread prices fell well below Dutch levels in the course of the eighteenth century, but this was driven primarily by currency devaluations. The effect was real, but the cause cannot be laid at the feet of the regulatory–excise complex.

How was this surprisingly favorable result achieved? How did a country facing high grain prices manage to make bread consumers contribute at least 10 percent of an enormous public revenue over some 250 years while keeping most bread prices at or near the price levels prevailing in countries where grain was cheaper, labor was cheaper, and taxes were small or, more commonly, non-existent?

We can search for the answer in three directions. First, the principles of new system regulation were not embraced elsewhere until much later and, even then, they were often not fully embraced or consistently applied. Old system regulation generally led to an inefficient bread sector.

Could Dutch millers and bakers really have been sufficiently more efficient than their foreign counterparts to cancel out much of the extra costs imposed upon them by the state? This result could be achieved if the new system regulatory regime succeed in setting millers' fees and bakers' fees closer to true costs, thereby denying these artisans the large profits often available under the crude old system price setting common to most neighboring countries. If regulated prices pressed on producers' margins they created an inducement to seek greater operating efficiencies. This possibility was explored in Chapter 8 where the regulatory process that established the constant costs of bread production was examined in some detail. There we could dismiss the contrary claim that the regulators set constant costs at unreasonably high levels in order to enrich the bakers. But in most places the regulators stopped well short of pushing the bakers toward the sort of consolidation that would have allowed for major economies of scale. Their interest in preserving the viability of small bakeries kept any such policy in check.

What we can say, however, is that the new system of price regulation, when carefully managed, secured over the long run a lower average bread price than did the rules of thumb that governed the old regulatory system. This "careful management" required that regulators minimize the number of "advantage loaves" left to the baker and secure a low milling fee. While these measures did not revolutionize the baking sector, they did suffice in securing a degree of efficiency and price moderation that most of Europe's regulatory regimes failed to achieve.

Second, consumers in Netherlands faced a wider variety of bread types, and a wider range of prices, than consumers in most other parts of Europe. Consequently, there was more scope for cross-subsidization within the Dutch regulatory regime than elsewhere. Only Copenhagen appeared to have anything like it. As a consequence, the basic breads were cheaper in the Netherlands than they could have been under an old system form of regulation. However, "basic bread" is not necessarily synonymous with "most consumed bread." Over time, many consumers upgraded their bread consumption bundles, which exposed them to higher costs. A comparison of bread prices, loaf per loaf, is not the same thing as a comparison of bread expenditures, household per household, across countries.

The third element of our answer is of particular relevance to the important comparison of bread prices in England and the Netherlands. Taxes are not the only way the state can impose costs on bread consumers. In Chapter 14 we noted the effect of England's bounty policy (subsidizing grain exports) and, especially its Corn Laws (taxing the import of grain) on wheat prices. Both policies raised the domestic price level above the international level.

English public policy caused bread prices to incorporate (via high grain prices) a payment to the nation's landlords, while Dutch bread prices included (via the milling excise) a payment to the state. Both nations raised artificially the cost of the "wage good." This equivalence did not escape the attention of Adam Smith. As we have already noted, he had few kind words for the Dutch practice of taxing bread via its milling excise.[46]

Such taxes [excises on necessities], when they have grown up to a certain height, are a curse equal to the barrenness of the earth and the inclemency of the heavens ... Holland is the country in Europe in which they abound most, and which from peculiar circumstances continues to prosper, not by means of them, as has been most absurdly supposed, but in spite of them.

But Smith saw the British corn bounty of his time as an equivalent evil:[47]

The bounty upon the exportation of corn, so far as it tends in the actual state of tillage to raise the price of that necessary article, produces all the like bad effects [like unto the Dutch milling excise]; and instead of affording any revenue, frequently occasions a very great expence to government.

It is interesting to speculate on the further macro-economic consequences of these two forms of intervention. In the eighteenth century, a quarter of the price of every loaf of bread in Holland went to the public treasury, where about 70 percent of all revenues was devoted to paying interest on the enormous public debt.[48] Dutch bread consumers thereby supported the state's creditors, who were disproportionately the regental families that dominated the Republic's political life. English consumers supported their landowners via export bounties and the Corn Laws. Public policy in both countries funneled income drawn from the multitude of bread consumers into the hands of a small and favored class: Dutch *rentiers* and British landowners.[49]

[46] Smith, *Wealth of Nations*, book IV, ch. 2, p. 36.
[47] *Ibid.*, book V, ch. 2, p. 404.
[48] For a fuller discussion of the Dutch fiscal system, see De Vries and Van der Woude, *First Modern Economy*, pp. 113-29.
[49] What economic effects could one expect from the removal of the public policies that enforced these market distortions? This is precisely the question that motivated David

This leads to a final question, which we can only touch on here. What did the beneficiaries of these fiscal regimes do with the revenues that flowed into their coffers? In the Dutch case we can be fairly certain that by the eighteenth century most *rentiers* reinvested a large percentage of their income in additional bonds, especially foreign government bonds, making Amsterdam Europe's foremost international capital market.[50] British landowners also invested in the public debt, primarily domestic bonds, but appear to have invested more in their estates and other domestic enterprises. Public policy in both countries used grain and bread pricing to concentrate income in the hands of a favored class, but the consequences for domestic investment and consumption were quite different.

By the 1840s the British state had gone far to rid itself of these practices, as venerable as they were objectionable. The last vestiges of the assize were gone by 1835 and the Corn Laws, of course, succumbed to a mighty campaign of abolition in 1846. The Kingdom of the Netherlands, by this time, had engaged only in half measures. Both the price controls and the excises continued in force more or less as they had for 250 years. All of this changed in 1855.

Jump start. The abolition of the milling excise and the end of bread price regulation occurred together. They suddenly changed the rules of the game governing the organization of the milling and baking sectors and had an immediate effect on the disposable income of consumers. Of course, these reforms also occurred in close temporal proximity to a number of other

Ricardo's seminal *Essay on the Influence of a Low Price of Corn on the Profit of Stock*. Using the British Corn Laws as his example, he analyzed how relative price changes would induce investors to reallocate resources among the sectors of the economy, putting resources to a higher use. In the British case, Ricardo predicted that the resulting decline in domestic grain production would be paired with a rise in manufacturing output. Growing industrial exports would pay for the rise in grain imports, while domestic labor and capital would be put to more productive uses. Ricardo's allegiance to the labor theory of value precluded him from considering the role of consumer demand in channeling this structural shift, but this cannot be so easily ignored in the Dutch case. There it was fiscal and regulatory policy at the "retail" level rather than tariff policy at the "wholesale" level that would set the reallocative process in motion. Domestic grain producers would not be directly affected, as in Britain. If there were to be a release of labor and capital from agriculture, it would have to come through the channel of the consumer. But could one be confident that the removal of the bread tax – which would reduce bread prices suddenly and substantially – would lead to a shift of consumer expenditure *away* from bread and toward industrial goods? On the Ricardian model that stood behind Liberal arguments against the milling excise see: Ronald Findlay, "Relative prices, growth and trade in a simple Ricardian system," *Economica* 41 (1974), 1-13.

[50] James C. Riley, *International Government Finance and the Amsterdam Capital Market, 1740-1815* (Cambridge University Press, 1980); De Vries and van der Woude, *First Modern Economy*, pp. 139-47.

major economic changes in the Dutch economy, such as the conversion of the public debt, an influx of colonial remittances from the Netherlands East Indies via the operation of the *Cultuurstelsel*, and the introduction of a liberal constitution. This complicates the identification and measurement of the economic stimulus that the liberal reformers so confidently expected would flow from the lifting of these economic shackles. But we now know that bread prices fell sharply after 1855. The cost of the prevailing bread consumption bundles of nearly every income group in every region fell, putting money in people's pockets. Liberal critics expected many good things to come from this fact, not least a reinvigoration of the manufacturing sectors of the domestic economy. In this they echoed the same arguments made by the British reformers urging removal of the Corn Laws.

Were the consumer savings of the reforms of 1855 in fact very large, and where did they go? We can identify these savings by decomposing the per-last costs of bread production before and after the abolition of bread taxes and regulation. Table 15.10 presents these costs for the period 1840–55, the final years of bread taxes and regulations; 1856–65, immediately after the abolition of price controls and of central government taxes; and 1866–85, when the bread economy was freed of all remaining excises. Overall, deregulation and tax abolition removed nearly two-thirds of total non-grain costs from the price of wheat bread, and over half from the price of rye bread. The total reduction in wheat bread costs, approximately 220 guilders per last, exceeds the abolished milling taxes (60 guilders national tax plus approximately 40 guilders in municipal tax). The difference, over 100 guilders per last, can be attributed to new competition, industrial reorganization, and the demise of cross-subsidization. The reduction of non-grain costs from rye bread production was less dramatic. Since the milling tax on rye bread weighed less heavily by the 1840s, its removal had a smaller effect on bread prices. The abolition of the 18 guilder national tax plus approximately 5–8 guilders of municipal tax accounts of only about half of the 50 guilders in cost reduction per last of rye. Moreover, economies introduced by heightened competition and scale economies in baking were partially undone by the removal of the subsidy offered in many places by cross-subsidization.

Overall, these are not trivial savings for a commodity on which especially poor and middling householders spent a large portion of their income. If Dutch consumers had persisted in the bread consumption habits of the 1840–55 period, a typical household of four would have saved 23.48 guilders per year by 1866–75 and 29.49 guilders by 1876–85, as shown in Table 15.11. However, this is a national average; western households – more heavily invested in wheat bread – would have saved considerably more. Panel B shows annual savings of nearly 40 guilders by 1876–85 as wheat bread

Table 15.10 *The cost of bread, per last of grain, 1840–85*
a. Wheat bread

	Grain cost gld per last	All other costs gld per last	Non-grain costs as % of total	Bread price gld per kg
1840–55	286.65	300.32	51.2	0.245
1856–65	292.41	166.29	36.3	0.191
1866–75	330.51	79.76	19.4	0.171
1876–85	287.04	83.27	22.5	0.154
Index (1840–55 = 100)				
1840–55	100	100		100
1856–65	102.0	55.4		78.0
1866–75	115.3	26.6		69.8
1876–85	100.1	27.7		62.9

b. Rye bread

	Grain cost gld per last	All other costs gld per last	Non-grain costs as % of total	Bread price gld per kg
1840–55	207.86	100.31	32.6	0.103
1856–65	207.18	65.66	24.1	0.091
1866–75	238.83	48.11	16.8	0.096
1876–85	213.30	55.14	20.5	0.089
Index (1840–55 = 100)				
1840–55	100	100		100
1856–65	99.7	65.5		88.3
1866–75	114.9	48.0		93.2
1876–85	102.6	55.0		86.4

fell in price more rapidly than rye bread. Even 25 guilders per household multiplied by more than 800,000 households amounts to about 4 percent of total private consumer expenditures in the 1860s.[51] This sudden and ongoing infusion of consumer spending would not have gone unnoticed.

But this is all hypothetical. In fact, bread consumption habits did not remain unaltered in the face of the "big bang." Consumers responded to the changing price structure of bread. Unfortunately, the abolition of the milling excise also abolishes our best source for tracking the level and mix of bread consumption. After 1855 we must rely on estimates of grain availability (domestic production + net imports), and make adjustments for the non-bread uses of grain (brewing and animal fodder, among others).

[51] Private consumer expenditures in current prices are estimated at 519 million guilders in 1860, rising to 656 million by 1869. Smits *et al.*, *Dutch GNP and its Components*, table E.1.

Table 15.11 *Model of consumer expenditures, 1841–80 (guilders per year per household of four)*
a. National model: If bread consumption remained as in 1841–55: 40% wheat; 128 kg bread per capita

	Wheat bread	Rye bread	Total cost	Saving relative to 1851–54
1841–46	53.29	30.29	83.58	
1846–50	52.92	31.33	84.25	
1851–55	53.80	34.84	88.64	
1856–60	44.76	28.94	73.70	-14.94
1861–65	39.38	27.62	67.00	-21.64
1866–70	36.86	28.29	65.16	-23.48
1871–75	35.41	27.99	63.40	-25.24
1876–80	31.47	27.68	59.15	-29.49

b. Western model: If bread consumption remained as in 1841–55: 62% wheat, 128 kg bread per capita

	Wheat bread	Rye bread	Total cost	Saving
1841–46	82.64	19.17	101.81	
1846–50	82.07	19.83	101.90	
1851–55	83.43	22.04	105.48	
1856–60	69.41	18.31	87.72	-17.75
1861–65	61.07	17.48	78.55	-26.93
1866–70	57.17	17.90	75.07	-30.41
1871–75	54.91	17.71	72.62	-32.86
1876–80	48.80	17.52	66.32	-39.16

c. National model: Actual course of bread consumption: 1841–55: 40% wheat, 128 kg bread; 1856–65: 45% wheat, 144 kg bread per capita; 1866–75: 54% wheat, 156 kg bread per capita, 1876–80: 65% wheat, 165 kg bread per capita

	Wheat bread	Rye bread	Total cost	Savings
1841–46	53.29	30.29	83.58	
1846–50	52.92	31.33	84.25	
1851–55	53.80	34.84	88.64	
1856–60	56.65	29.84	86.49	−2.15
1861–65	49.84	28.48	78.32	−10.31
1866–70	60.65	26.44	87.09	−1.55
1871–75	58.26	26.15	84.41	−4.23
1876–80	65.92	20.81	86.73	−1.91

In what follows I am guided by the estimates of Knibbe and Van Riel, whose individual attempts to estimate the volume of domestically consumed bread grains are shown in Table 15.12. Their calculations are in agreement that per capita bread grain consumption rose substantially after 1855 – by 40 percent – to levels not seen since the sixteenth century. At the same time, consumers replaced their rye bread with wheat bread, such that wheat accounted for 80 percent of the bread grains by the beginning of the twentieth century. Not shown in Table 15.12, but helping account for the large rise in bread consumption, was the virtual disappearance in this period of the boiled grains, especially buckwheat.

These are reliable, but necessarily national-level estimates. Some town-level data allow for a more detailed view of the changes afoot after 1855. Leiden was by no means a flourishing town in the nineteenth century, but Table 15.13 shows bread consumption shifting decisively toward the wheat breads – especially the costliest wheat breads – after 1855. Amsterdam data also show a shift toward the costliest wheat bread, but illustrate a second feature of the late nineteenth century, the definitive displacement of rye bread by coarse wheat bread. Both of these shifts – from rye to wheat and from coarse breads toward fine, bolted breads, involved a rise in cost, but, of course, a far smaller rise in cost than had faced consumers during the preceding two centuries.

Table 15.12 *Bread grain consumption in the Netherlands, 1580–1993 (in kg per capita)*

	Bread grain	Wheat/rye ratio
1580–1608	146 kg	25–75
1608–34	127	30–70
1650–59	118	35–65
1660–1810	113	43–57
1810–14	85	38–62
1815–50	97	42–58
1860s	114	47–53
1870s	118	56–44
1880s	135	67–33
1890s	145	75–25
1900s	138	78–22
1910s	137	82–18
1951	102	
1962	80	98–2
1993	60	99–1

Source: 1580–1850: from Table 12.8.
1860–1950: Van Riel database; Merrijn Knibbe, "De hoofelijke beschikbaarheid van voedsel en de levensstandaard in Nederland," *Tijdschrift voor sociale en economische geschiedenis* 4 (2007), 71–107; Merrijn Knibbe, *Agriculture in the Netherlands, 1851–1950* (Amsterdam: NEHA, 1993), pp. 97–98.
1951–93: Jobse-van Putten, *Eenvoudig maar voedzaam*, pp. 322–23.

Table 15.13 *Changing bread preferences after 1850*
a. Amsterdam bread consumption, 1851–1900, as percentage of bread type

	1851		1900
	Original	Revised	
White bread	52	52	70
Unbolted wheat bread	0*	10	30
Rye bread	48	38	0

Sources: Voskuil, "De weg naar Luilekkerland," p. 468; E. C. Büchner, "Over de voornaamste voedingsmiddelen te Amsterdam verbruikt in het jaar 1851," *De economist* 2 (1853), 175. Büchner based his estimate of the consumption of unbolted wheat bread on the opinion of city officials who stated that the inhabitants' consumption of unbolted wheat bread was, for whatever reason, "next to nothing." In the second column I have adjusted the estimates, based on the modest assumption that "next to nothing" was not actually zero but 10 percent of bread consumption.

b. Leiden bread consumption, 1850–67, as percentage of bread type

	1840–55	1868	1883
Bolted wheat bread		64	68
Raisin bread		8	9
Unbolted wheat bread		9	12
All wheat breads	63	81	89
Rye bread	37	19	11
Total in grams per day	220	330	n/a
Annual bread consumption	*c.* 80 kg	120.5 kg	

Sources: D. H. [Hartevelt] "Ons dagelijksch brood," *De economist* 18 (1869), 913–24; D. de Loos, "Ons dagelijksch brood," *De economist* 33 (1884), 581–90; Pot, *Arm Leiden*, p. 313.

These local data and the national consumption estimates reveal the existence of a "pent-up" demand for wheat bread that was unleashed by the "big bang" of 1855. Liberal reformers anticipated a diversion of household expenditures from bread, now that it was cheaper, to manufactures. But Table 15.11c shows what actually occurred. At the aggregate level, the absolute household expenditure for bread barely declined; instead, consumers spent their "savings" on an upgrading of their bread diet. They purchased more bread, more wheat bread, and more fine wheat bread.

It is worth pausing at this finding for a moment. What does it reveal about the social impact of the taxes and regulations that had shaped the Dutch bread markets for so long? At first glance, the dedication of the entire "deregulation windfall" to an increase in bread consumption (per capita bread consumption rose by 40 percent between 1850 and 1890) seems to reveal an undernourished population whose first order of business was finally getting enough to eat. But this conclusion, while certainly relevant to the poorest consumers, ignores the fact that the entire rise in bread consumption consisted of wheat bread, mostly the costly white bread. The consumption of rye bread fell absolutely (while that of buckwheat fell to nearly zero). It was not the caloric intake that rose so much as the quality, or perceived quality, of the diet. Consumers after 1855 were driven more by aspiration than desperation.

This shift in preferences bears comparison to the shift described in Chapter 13 that occurred in the western provinces during the seventeenth century. Then rising real incomes allowed consumers to shift from rye to wheat breads, despite the rise in the relative cost of the preferred bread. This shift was brought to a standstill when income growth slowed while bread taxes reached their apogee. The shift resumed after 1855 when both income growth and declining bread prices put wind into the sails of consumer preferences.

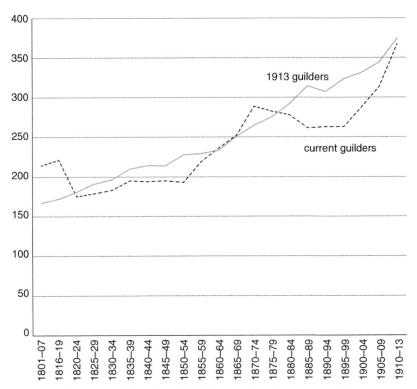

Figure 15.4 Netherlands GDP per capita, in current and constant (1913) guilders

The Dutch finally became the nation of wheat bread eaters they had aspired to be since the seventeenth century – they completed their "wheat bread revolution." To be more precise, it was the broad middle ranks of Dutch society that nurtured these aspirations most strongly. It was this broad middle that had been most severely affected by the old regulatory regime, which had placed a fuller transition to wheat bread out of their reach for nearly two centuries while it harnessed them to the fiscal wagons of state.

The "big bang" had clear, measurable consequences for the organization of the milling and baking sectors and it affected the behavior of consumers even more dramatically. But what of its macro-economic effects? These are hard to isolate since deregulation took place in a period crowded with events and policy changes that affected the economy's growth. However, it is undeniable that the Dutch economy embarked on an impressive growth spurt in the two decades after deregulation. This acceleration of the economy had once been seen as a turning point, a transition from a long stagnation stretching back to the eighteenth century, if not before, to the era of modern industrial development. But recent efforts to measure the economic performance of the Netherlands in the nineteenth century have removed some of the drama from these years. The economy actually had grown smartly, or recovered, for a time after the Napoleonic era came to an end. However, this growth was not long sustained. The liberal reforms we are concerned with were debated and enacted in an extended period of economic retardation that began in 1840 – the "hungry forties" of pan-European distress – and continued into the early 1850s with the elevated commodity prices associated with the Crimean War. Per capita GDP barely rose in the 1840s and 50s. But the three decades that followed the "big bang" saw a sharp acceleration; from 1860 to 1889 GDP per capita grew at 1.3 percent per annum. Perhaps these years can no longer be interpreted as a "take off," but it does seem fair to conclude that the "big bang" of 1855 contributed significantly to the larger mid-nineteenth-century renovation of the industrial organization, fiscal system, and institutions of the Netherlands that led to sustained improvement in its long-run economic performance.

Conclusion

When the Dutch towns revised their bread price regulatory practices in the 1590s they were modernizing an ancient and ubiquitous European institution. The "new system" brought basic economic principles to the task of establishing a proper bread price for a given grain price and revealed a still uncommon appreciation of the power and legitimacy of market forces. It made a sharper distinction than did the regulatory regimes of other countries between *monitoring* the economics of bread pricing and *guaranteeing access to* bread in times of distress. The first was illuminated with unusual clarity by the regulators, while the second could now more clearly be separated and addressed by targeted social policies.

The "new system" was market-focused and required administrators who were systematic in their work and highly numerate. But its very sophistication endowed the regulatory system with new powers not only to *reflect* the market but also to *shape* it. It accommodated a policy of bread taxation, via a milling excise incorporated into the price of every loaf of bread sold in the Netherlands, and it enabled policies of cross-subsidization, whereby purchasers of certain types of bread absorbed a portion of the cost of producing other types. These two policies could not have been conducted, certainly not on the scale they eventually attained, without a broad commercial market and the instrument of new system regulation.

Thus, the Dutch *broodzetting* migrated from being a device to render more transparent the market forces affecting bread pricing toward becoming a highly invasive regulatory institution, an instrument of social engineering. Over the course of 260 years it extracted from bread consumers at least 10 percent of all public revenues raised in the Netherlands, the most heavily taxed country in Europe; it established and enforced restrictions on millers and bakers that shaped the structure of their industries; it imposed on consumers a unique set of relative prices for breads that altered the composition of the Dutch diet and shaped the pace of the "wheat bread revolution," the west European shift toward wheat breads, in which Dutch consumers were in the forefront.

451

In the early decades of the new regulatory system its impact seems to have been primarily positive. In periods of high grain prices its technical superiority set bread prices below what they would have been under the "old system" procedures still common elsewhere in Europe. It encouraged concentration in the milling sector and the capture of economies of scale. It raised an enormous public revenue for a nation under nearly constant attack from its European neighbors, and it did all this via a carefully structured tax code that answers well to the characteristics of "optimal tax policy." Finally, the bread pricing policy supported the development of a varied diet, the "republican diet" in which bread consumption was fairly modest, legumes and vegetables were common, and meat and dairy products accounted for a large portion of total caloric intake.

Whether by design or not, bread pricing policy had the effect of strengthening both state and society. The apparatus of municipal regulation and provincial taxation was not the product of central direction or coordination, but it contributed to the development of an impressive state capacity, one honed over time by the regular, disciplined, administrative work of gathering and assessing market information, setting rules and policies, and monitoring and enforcing the entire regulatory and fiscal regime. That enlarged state capacity came "from below"; it came from urban administrations renovating an already venerable practice that, in turn, responded to a broadly shared public demand. In a market society ordinary people sought some sort of official commitment of protection against the self-interested actions of merchants and producers. Public authorities accepted this responsibility – not, perhaps, because they actually believed they could shelter the population from market forces but because they recognized the political importance of appearing to act in the public interest. In most of Europe this somewhat cynical bargain led to the often ineffectual and sometimes corrupt old system bread price regimes described in Chapters 1 and 14. In the urbanized and market-oriented environment of the Netherlands, matters took a different turn.

The reformers of the bread regulation in 1596 may not have consciously intended everything that unfolded in the decades thereafter. However, they were determined to turn the ancient practice of bread price regulation into a much more precise tool for economic, social, and fiscal purposes. The new system encouraged a major step toward enhanced governmentality, but enhanced governmentality can, and in this case did, lead to a structure of controls and an administrative capacity that went far beyond the ostensible goal of protecting consumers from unreasonable prices.

What if these reformers had embraced a more radical approach? What if they had decided that price regulation was futile and counterproductive, and consumers would better be served by targeted relief in times of crisis (which, in fact, became common practice), or by limiting price regulation to the most basic bread, rye bread.[1] This counterfactual proposition is, of course, not raised in order to imagine a preferred "alternative history" but to help us see more clearly the full import of the path actually taken.[2]

We can explore this counterfactual by breaking it down into three related questions: 1. How would bread prices have differed in the absence of the regulatory machinery? 2. Could the milling excise have existed without price regulation? 3. Was price regulation essential to maintain social peace? That is, would consumers have tolerated a free market in bread prices in the early modern context?

1.The first question is not as difficult as one might suppose. The Dutch new system *broodzetting* was not designed to force bread prices downward. Its purpose was to identify the true long-run equilibrium price of the main bread types. In a competitive market, this is the price that would have prevailed – in the long run – without regulation. Thus our problem comes down to this: did bakers operate in a competitive environment? Did they compete for customers and did most consumers have practical access to competing bakers?

The assumption of competitive markets seems unreasonable where most bakers were organized in local guilds. On the other hand, the ability of guilds to discipline their members and enforce their monopoly would have been much reduced in the absence of the regulatory regime. Yet even imperfectly competitive bread markets would not have been capable of maintaining the characteristic Dutch pricing structure that artificially inflated the prices of wheat bread and white bread. In the absence of regulation most consumers of the wheat breads – those with sufficient income – would almost certainly have been better off in the long run.

But, one might object, in the long run the more vulnerable portion of the population could face malnutrition and even starvation during the

---

[1] Confining price regulation to rye bread was not unheard of. We noted earlier that when Leiden introduced its new system regulation of rye prices in 1596 it also drafted a schedule for wheat prices. But there is no evidence of its operation until 1648. Earlier, in 1546, Delft set prices for wheat bread, but with respect to rye bread it confined itself to an insistence that rye loaves weigh either 4 or 8 pounds. Further "one and all may sell rye bread for as much as it shall please them, until and unless it is decided otherwise." *"Een ijegelicken 't Roggenbroot zoe diere verkoopen sal moegen als t selve hem gelieven sal, ten waere dat anders geordonneert ende geset worde."* Mr. J. Soutendam, *Keuren en ord. der stad Delft, 1500–1536* (Delft, 1870).

[2] On the concept of counterfactual history, see Philip Tetlock, Richard Ned Lebow, and Geoffrey Parker, eds., *Unmaking the West: "What-if?" Scenarios that Rewrite World History* (Ann Arbor: University of Michigan Press, 2006); Martin Bunzl, "Counterfactual history: a user's guide," *American Historical Review* 109 (2004), 845–58; Paul David, "Transportation innovation and economic growth: Professor Fogel on and off the rails," *Economic History Review* 29 (1976), 82–100.

periodic short-term periods of grain shortage and high prices. Here our counterfactual exercise has no difficulty in predicting how such periods of distress would have been handled. After all, the ordinary operation of the Dutch *broodzetting* did nothing to shield consumers from price spikes. In such periods succor came to those in distress not from the bread price regulators, but from the suspension of their work and the intervention of subsidy schemes organized by the towns and churches.

2. In the absence of the new system bread price regulatory system the imposition of heavy taxes on bread would have been impossible. The milling excise would have been much harder to enforce if bakers competed with each other on price since the incentive to evade taxation would have been powerful and the opportunities to do so extensive. Thus, our counterfactual would need to assume that the milling excise was a choice rather than a necessity – that the Dutch Republic could have relied on others of its myriad taxes to generate over 10 percent of its revenue over this long period of time. This would not have been technically impossible, but the Republic's experience with efforts to shift toward direct taxes on income and wealth shows that it certainly would have posed a major political challenge.

3. The ubiquity of price controls on bread throughout Europe suggests that these institutions were essential to the maintenance of political legitimacy in the early modern era. It is a challenge to find a place where the authorities did not act to regulate bread prices, although there were many places where it was done poorly and inconsistently. In this era legitimacy in the eyes of the public often depended on being able to give at least the appearance of monitoring the economy for the public benefit.

But this act of oversight could be done lightly (controlling the prices of only the most basic type of bread, setting only maximum prices, doing so only in periods of rising prices) or comprehensively and invasively. The latter was the path chosen by the Dutch. Moreover, while price regulation may have seemed inevitable in 1600, this may no longer have been true in, say, 1750.

As it happens, a political crisis that shook the foundations of the Republic's regental rule in 1747–48 led to a sudden abolition of the excise taxes. Critics of the Republic's political elite advocated a new tax system, one based more on direct taxes than on excises, and it would not have been too large a step to go on to abolish or loosen the price regulations as well. As we have seen, radical fiscal changes were then earnestly discussed. But they were not pursued; within eighteen months the old policies were restored with only minor adjustments. What other road might have been taken at that juncture?

Here our counterfactual exercise encounters the realm of unknowability. We can point to developments in France and England, where the modernization of milling led to a growing trade in flour that was impossible for Dutch millers to follow, given the fiscally driven restrictions on their operations. We can point to the "pent up demand" for wheat bread that could have been unleashed by a deregulation of prices. And we can point to the potential for greater economies of scale in urban bakeries that deregulation could have stimulated. In short, many of the developments observed soon after the "big bang" of 1855 could plausibly have stimulated greater efficiency in the bread sector a century earlier.

But what we cannot conjure is a political force able and willing to tackle the intertwined institutions of urban regulation and provincial taxation that simultaneously sustained the political elites and constrained economic innovation. Even decades later, the combined power of liberal ideology and the French army failed at this task. The institutions that had done much to strengthen state capability and discipline the citizenry in the course of the seventeenth century now stood as a mighty bulwark against the renovations whose need began to be apparent already in the eighteenth.

Historians are now inclined to locate the origins of modern Dutch society neither in the revolutionary era that brought the old Republic to an end and led to the current Kingdom, nor in the economic, religious, and cultural efflorescence of the Dutch Revolt and golden age, but in the painful and sometimes inglorious century from 1750 to 1850.[3] It took this entire century to bring the old regulatory regime to an end. But one reason it took so long was that this regime had been constructed with care and possessed a great resilience. It was not wholly suited to a modern market economy, but neither was it medieval. It was a distinctly early modern achievement. But in another sense, it was an early modern achievement with an abiding relevance to modern societies that seek to temper and channel the market economy via regulation. The regulatory task of the Dutch *broodzetting* was ambitious and its methods sophisticated, but this could not save it from creating major distortions, private windfalls, and inefficiencies. And these undesired features, once established and routinized, came to be protected and legitimized by the regulatory institutions themselves. If there is a lesson to be learned from this study of regulatory behavior it is simply to be careful what you wish for.

---

[3] Paul Brusse and Wijnand W. Mijnhardt, *Towards a New Template for Dutch History: De-urbanization and the Balance between City and Countryside* (Utrecht: Uitgeverij Waanders/ Universiteit Utrecht, 2012).

Appendix 1

Old System Bread Price Schedules

This appendix describes five medieval bread price schedules from France, Switzerland, and the Low Countries. Each has distinctive features, but all illustrate the basic characteristics of old system price regulation.

Geneva, 1458

Geneva's 1458 price schedule remained in use, with only slight alterations, until 1747. In that year Geneva introduced a new price table founded on new system principles. The 1458 price schedule provides the baker with revenue that is 10 percent in excess of the grain cost. This is similar to the French schedule discussed in Chapter 1 (Figure 1.1) in that it defines the baker's revenues as a percentage of the cost of grain.

Underlying assumptions: The coup = 77 liters = approx. 100 livres (55.2 kg) of grain = approx. 88 livres (48.57 kg) of flour after removal of bran and rough materials.

Each coup yields 88 livres of wheat bread. Bread was sold by weight in Geneva. Figure A1.1 converts the official weights into a bread price per livre of bread. These prices generated revenue per coup that consistently exceeded the grain price by 10 percent. Thus, at a grain price of 20 gros per coup, the baker took in 22 gros of revenue; at 40 gros the baker earned 44 gros.

Utrecht, 1374

In Utrecht an ordinance of 1374 established weight-variable schedules for the sale of white bread and coarse wheat bread. Figure A1.2 displays these schedules after converting the bread weights to prices per pound. Both schedules are consistent with the old system: at a notional wheat price of zero, the bread prices are approximately zero.

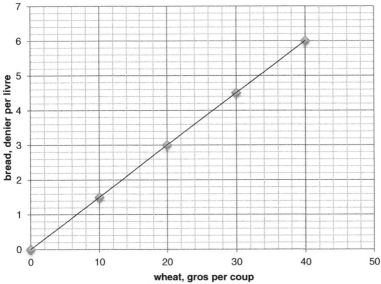

Figure A1.1 Geneva wheat bread price schedule, 1458
Source: Blanc, *La Chambre des Blés de Genève.*
Grain measure: coup = 77 liters
Weight measure: livre = 18 onches = 552 grams
Currency: gros (sou) = 12 deniers

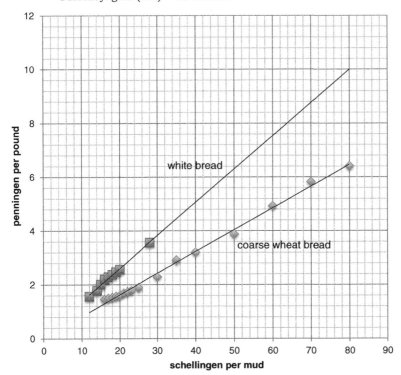

Figure A1.2 Utrecht wheat bread price schedules, 1374
Source: S. Muller Fz., *De middeleeuwsche rechtsbronnen der stad Utrecht*
(The Hague, 1883).

Groningen, 1404, 1589

The price schedules for rye and wheat bread introduced in 1404 continued in use until 1589, when it was repromulgated. The 1404 schedule only contemplated grain prices rising to 30 stuivers per *mud* of rye and 38 stuivers for wheat; by 1589 the intervening price inflation led the magistrates to extend their tables to 130 stuivers per *mud* of rye and 168 stuivers for wheat. Otherwise it remained virtually unchanged. The grade of wheat bread is not specified. It was priced consistently at just over double the cost of rye bread, suggesting it was a bolted wheat bread. As Figure A1.3 shows, both are classic old system price schedules.

Figure A1.4 shows the 1404–1589 price schedule for rye bread and the first new system schedule preserved in the archives. It dates from 1679 but was in force from an unspecified earlier date. The new system

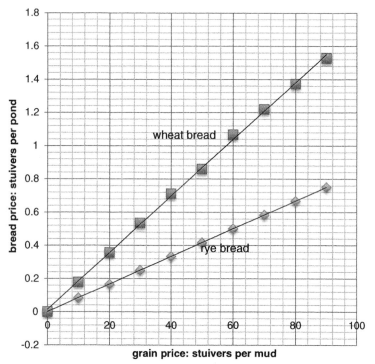

Figure A1.3 Groningen wheat and rye bread price schedules, 1404, 1589
Sources: Groningen Oorkondenboek, no. 1168. De overheid der stad Groningen stelt eene verordening vast omtrent den prijs van het brood, 1404; G.A. Groningen, Archief no. 293, Gilden Archief, no. 11.

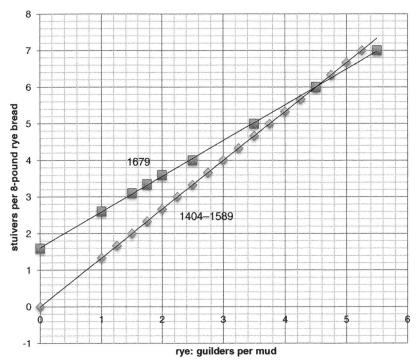

Figure A1.4 Groningen rye bread prices: old system and new system, 1404, 1589, 1679

schedule required bakers to supply 37 percent more rye bread per unit of grain, but provided for 1.62 stuivers per 8-pound loaf as a constant cost provision by way of compensation.

Grain measure: *mud* = 91.2 liters
Weight measure: *pond* = 468 grams
Currency: guilder = 20 stuivers = 320 penningen;*
* 1404 prices are converted from *kromstaarten, plakken,* and *grootkens* to stuivers.

Brielle, 1530

In 1530 the magistrates of the small Holland city of Brielle announced the following rule for setting the price of rye bread:

When a sack of rye costs 24 stuivers, then the bakers sell a 2-pound rye bread loaf for 3 *duiten* (6 penningen).

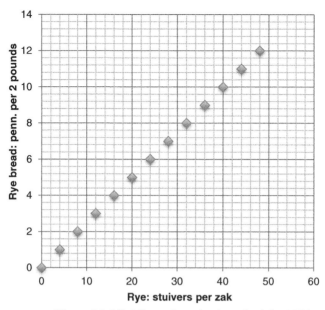

Figure A1.5 Brielle rye bread price schedule, 1530

For every 4-stuiver rise or fall in the price of a sack of rye, the bakers may charge 1 penning more or less per 2-pound rye bread loaf.

For every 2-stuiver rise or fall, the bakers may charge ½ penning more or less.

For every 1-stuiver rise or fall, the bread price will remain unchanged, at the discretion of the breadweighers.

Because a 1 penning rise in a 2-pound loaf must generate 4 stuivers, it follows that the magistrates assumed a bread yield of 128 *pond* per sack, or 4,928 *pond* and 2,311 kg per last.

Figure A1.5 shows this classic old system price schedule.

Grain measure: last = 38.5 sacks (*zakken*); the sack = 78 liters
Weight measure: *pond* = 469 gram
Currency: guilder = 20 stuivers = 320 penningen

Brielle's magistrates also promulgated rules to govern the price of the wheat breads, which were sold by weight. They specified the weight in *loden* (32 *loden* per pound) for white bread, a middle grade, and coarse wheat bread, at a wide range of possible wheat prices. Unlike the simple rule for rye bread, this was a tedious exercise, but produced a consistent schedule, which Figure A1.6 reproduces with the weights transformed into the equivalent prices per pound. Given the yield for each grade of bread assumed by the magistrates, the revenue generated just sufficed to cover the cost of the wheat. As was the custom with all old system price schedules, the assumed yield was far below the actual yield, which

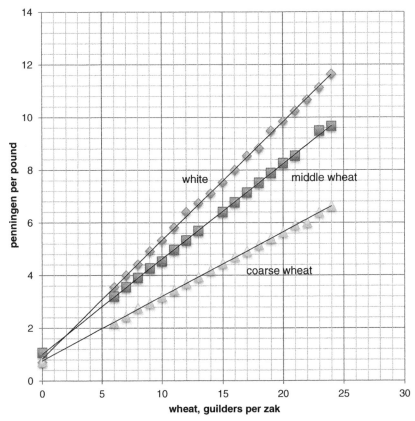

Figure A1.6 Brielle wheat bread price schedules, 1530
Source: H. de Jager, *De Middeleeuwsche keuren der stad Brielle* (The
Hague: Martinus Nijhoff, 1901) Werken der Vereeniging tot uitgave
der bronnen van het Oude Vaderlandsche Recht, Tweede reeks, no. 2.
Ordonnatie van 't gebacken rogghenbroot, 1530, pp. 272–75.

provided for extra loaves to supply the bakers with revenue to cover their
other costs.

Antwerp, 1588

Antwerp's 1588 price schedule assumed rye bread output to be 140–
145 pounds (67–68 kg) per *viertel*. It reveals old system practice, with
preparation costs expressed as a percentage of the grain price, which
causes bakers' revenue to rise faster than the cost of grain. The final
column of the table below shows how the expected revenue to be generated by the sale of bread fails to fully cover grain costs at very low grain

Table A1.1 *Antwerp rye bread schedule, 1588 (in stuivers)*

Price of rye per viertel	Rye bread price per kg	Revenue per viertel	Revenue as percentage of grain price
0	−0.160		
16	0.208	13.94	0.87
26	0.438	29.34	1.13
36	0.668	44.76	1.24
40	0.773	51.79	1.29
50	1.001	67.07	1.34
60	1.217	81.54	1.36
70	1.449	97.08	1.39

Grain measure: *viertel* = 77 liters = 53–55 kg (112–116 pounds of grain)
Weight measure: *pond* = 470 grams
Currency: guilder = 20 stuivers

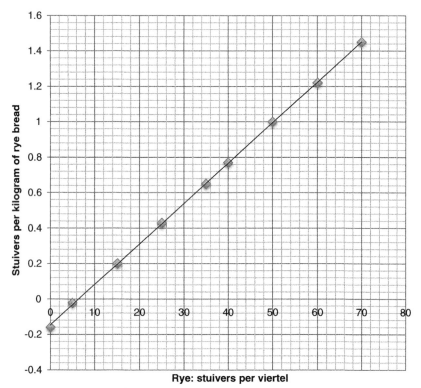

Figure A1.7 Antwerp rye bread price schedule, 1588
Source: Scholliers, *Levensstandaard.*

prices, but rises from 13 percent in excess of the grain cost when the grain price is 26 stuivers per *viertel* to 39 percent in excess when grain costs 70 stuivers.

Appendix 2
Crisis Periods

The nine most serious episodes of high bread prices between 1600 and 1820 are described here together with details of the prices set by the commissioners.

1629–31

The food crisis of 1629–31 was both exceptionally severe and prolonged. Prices rose rapidly in the summer of 1629, leveled off at a high level, and rose further in the summer of 1630. By December a 12-pound rye loaf in Leiden cost over 20 stuivers, more than double the price prevailing in 1624–28 and again beginning in 1632. As a consequence an unskilled laborer needed to devote three-quarters of his income to acquire 2.2 kg of bread per day during three consecutive months in the winter of 1630–31. This left too little to purchase the other foodstuffs that would round out anything like an adequate diet. The crises did not begin to recede significantly until May 1631. Thus an unskilled worker faced 29 months in which bread absorbed at least 45 percent of income. The strategies of makeshift – food substitutions, reduced consumption, borrowing, and sale or pawn of assets that might tide a family over for a short period – would not have availed for such an extended period of distress. As this food crisis unfolded town governments throughout the Republic responded with measures to address the pressing need: As shown in Chapter 10, they purchased grain for subsidized distribution to the bakers, lifted prohibitions on mixing inferior grains into the breads, introduced new prohibitions on "luxury" breads, and expanded bread distributions to the poor. In its combination of severity and duration this was the greatest food crisis experienced in the Netherlands between 1580 and 1800.

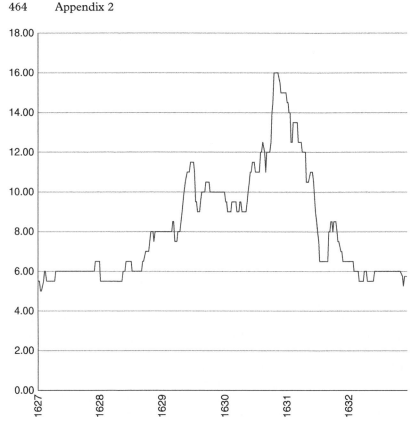

Figure A2.1 Leiden rye bread prices, 1628–32 (stuivers per 12-pound loaf)

1649–53 and 1661–63

The Dutch Republic faced price spikes again in 1649–53 and 1661–63. The first, compounded by war with England, was of long duration – 41 months of elevated prices – but not of great intensity. Bread never required as much as 50 percent of the unskilled laborer's income. The second, caused by short Baltic supplies that led Danzig to impose a total prohibition on grain exports, saw prices rise in two stages, beginning in September 1661 and culminating in May 1662. By then bread claimed 56 percent of the unskilled laborer's income. The most severe phase of this crisis passed quickly; prices began to decline again in August 1662, although it took over a year for prices to return to normal levels.

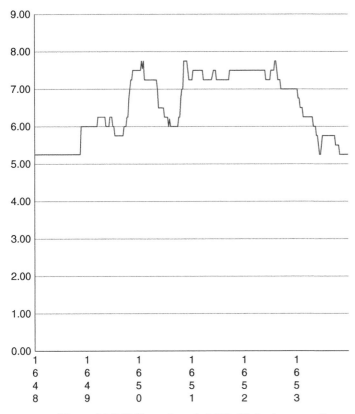

Figure A2.2 Delft rye bread, 1648–53 (stuivers per 8-pound loaf)

1698–1700 and 1708–10

The elevated prices of 1661–63 marked a turning point in the long-run trend of grain prices. Grain prices declined thereafter, reaching a low point in a long period of price stability in the 1720s–30s. This extended European-wide period of favorable grain prices was interrupted by two severe famines. Harvest failure and widespread military action brought famine conditions to much of Europe in 1693–94. France was particularly hard hit, suffering the death of over a million people, or 6 percent of the population. One detects nothing more than a faint echo of this disaster in the market prices of the Netherlands (two months of high prices), but five years later, in 1698, disruptions in Baltic grain supplies sent prices rising rapidly from September until December, when the unskilled laborer needed to part with 65 percent of his wage to secure

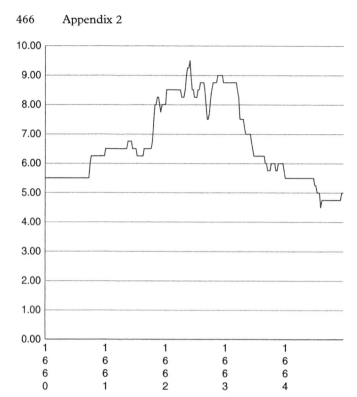

Figure A2.3 Delft rye bread, 1660–64 (stuivers per 8-pound loaf)

2.2 kg of bread per day. The crisis was severe, sending town magistrates into action for the first time – in most cases – since 1630–31. Amsterdam subordinated its commercial interest in free trade long enough to urge the States of Holland to declare a prohibition on grain exports. Once this was enacted, in October, they felt the need to intervene in the futures markets for grain, forcing settlement prices on participants whose market expectations had so rudely been disturbed. Shortly thereafter, on 5 November, Amsterdam's *burgemeesters* turned to the effects of rising bread prices on the *kleine gemeente*, the common folk, fearing they might "descend to excessive acts and deeds that would bring great confusion and disorder to the city."[1] As in 1662, they did not intervene in the bread prices but ordered the *wijkmeesters* to distribute coupons to necessitous

[1] Van Dillen, "De duurte van 1698," p. 266.

residents, which gave them a 2-stuiver discount on the price of a 6-pound rye loaf.[2]

The prospect of no new grain supplies until well into 1699 led Amsterdam's magistrates not only to a prohibition on grain exports, but also to a careful monitoring – and rationing – of grain shipments to other cities within Holland. Fortunately, their worst fears were not realized. The winter of 1698–99 was mild, allowing shipments to arrive much earlier in the new year than normally was the case. This broke the upward price movement and clarified the future supply situation. Prices began to descend in July 1699, reaching normal levels by the end of that year.

The crisis of 1709–10 was, even more than that of a decade earlier, a pan-European event. The winter of 1708–09, known in France as *Le Grand Hiver*, was the most frigid of the little ice age.[3] The resulting

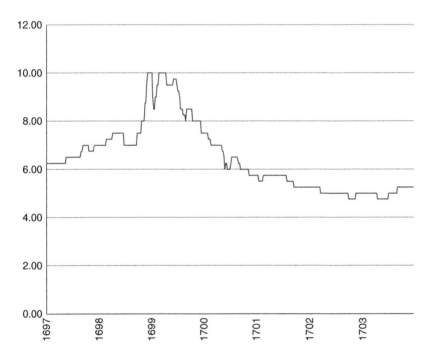

Figure A2.4 Delft rye bread, 1697–1703 (stuivers per 8-pound loaf)

---

[2] The use of bread coupons for the poor was an efficient and targeted approach to the problem at hand, but was not without problems. A month after its introduction the city issued a new ordinance imposing heavy fines on citizens who claimed larger families than they had and/or sold their coupons for brandywine, and on bakers who demanded more than one coupon for a discounted loaf. *Ibid.*, p. 268.

[3] Monahan, *Years of Sorrow, passim*; Ó Grada and Chevet, "Famine and market in Ancien Régime France."

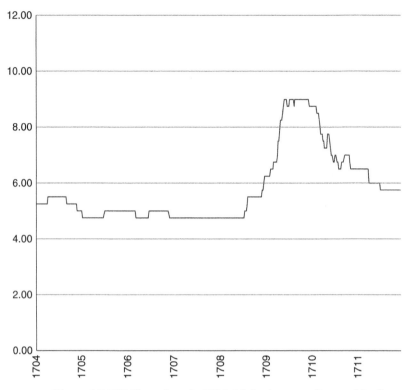

Figure A2.5 Delft rye bread, 1704–11 (stuivers per 8-pound loaf)

famine led to the premature deaths of 600,000 French people. Warfare (the War of the Spanish Succession, and especially, the Great Northern War in the Baltic region) and a final outbreak of plague in the Baltic compounded the effects of extreme weather, sending grain prices sharply higher from March through September 1709, when our standard bread ration claimed 58 percent of the unskilled laborer's wage. This was sufficient to trigger the various interventions chronicled in Chapter 10: bread coupon distribution to the poor and "price smoothing" organized by the bread price commissioners. Prices remained very high through the winter, declining only after March 1710.

1740–41 and 1770–73

After 1709 grain prices declined, reaching a low and stable level that lasted throughout the 1720s and 30s. This extended era of food abundance was interrupted in 1740 by harvest shortfalls induced by poor weather. It did not lead to a statistically impressive crisis in the Netherlands – unskilled laborers allocated over 45 percent of their earnings for bread in only two months – but it came as a shock that provoked much commentary from a society that had experienced nothing remotely like it for over a generation.

The price disturbance of 1740–41 also marked a turning point in the long-term price trend, which thereafter tended to creep upwards over time. The only period of crisis between 1741 and 1795 occurred in 1770–73. Poor harvests sent prices rising from September of 1770. The rise was gradual, but by December 1771 prices reached levels not seen since 1709. Bread claimed over 50 percent of the unskilled laborer's wage, under our assumptions, for five consecutive months in early 1772, but declined rapidly thereafter.

1794–96

The short but severe crisis of 1795 is associated with the political crisis that brought the United Republic to an end and installed a new regime, the Batavian Republic. Poor harvests and trade disruptions had already

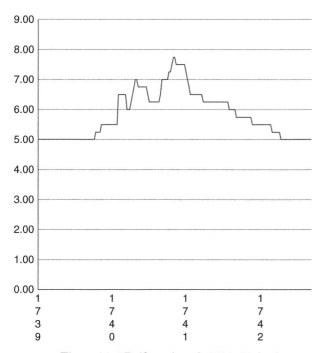

Figure A2.6 Delft rye bread, 1739–42 (stuivers per 8-pound loaf)

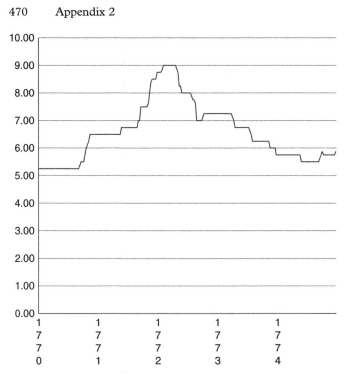

Figure A2.7 Delft rye bread, 1770–74 (stuivers per 8-pound loaf)

forced prices up in 1794, but the French invasion of January 1795 brought uncertainties to the market that led quickly to an unprecedented price spike. By the end of 1795 our unskilled laborer needed to devote 83 percent of his earnings to acquire 2.2 kg of rye bread per day.

As the market uncertainties dissipated, prices fell, but they took all of 1796 to return to more normal price levels. But "normal" prices were now higher than those of fifty years earlier, and beginning in 1799 the Napoleonic Wars disturbed both agricultural production and international trade to such an extent that crisis-level prices became the norm, with only brief interruptions, for the following seventeen years.

1800–17

Figure A2.9 provides an overview of bread price trends in this tumultuous era. Bread prices reached unprecedented price levels in 1800–02 followed by another peak in 1806–07. Prices were lower in 1808–10, but still far above pre-1799 levels, and rose to a new peak during the death spasms of the French Empire. Peace in 1815 brought only a brief respite

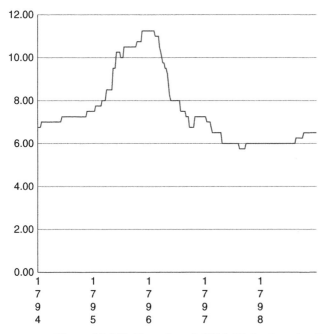

Figure A2.8 Delft rye bread, 1794–98 (stuivers per 8-pound loaf)

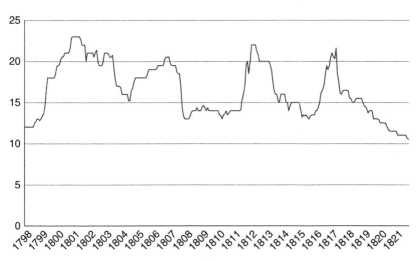

Figure A2.9 Leiden rye bread price, 1798–1821 (stuivers per
12-pound loaf)

as the climate-induced distress of 1816–17 imposed a final, intense price
spike. Only after 1817 did prices drift lower for an extended period –
until the era of the potato famine in 1845–47.

Appendix 3

Estimating Bread Consumption from Tax Records

The annual revenues generated by Holland's milling excise have been preserved from 1650 until 1805, when the provincial excise was superseded by a national milling excise. Unfortunately, the surviving data are highly aggregated: a lump sum of payments made by the tax farmers who collected the milling excise in Holland's many tax districts. In order to make these data reveal the volume of taxed bread grain a number of adjustments must be made. The taxes on wheat and rye accounted for the great bulk of total revenues, but not all. And the amount representing other milled grains changed over time. Some of the necessary adjustments are fairly straightforward while others are not. The steps made to convert the raw data into estimates of per capita bread grain consumption are revealed in Table A3.2. My methodology and justifications for the assumptions made are presented below.

From Net Revenue to Gross Revenue

Until 1748 these data reveal what tax farmers paid for the rights to collect the milling tax in Holland's tax districts. The milling excise was suspended then and when it was restored, in 1750, it was collected directly by fiscal agents. Then the documents reveal the gross revenues collected by the fiscal authorities. How large was the difference between gross and net tax receipts?

By examining revenues for the years directly before and after 1748–50 we have an opportunity to investigate this matter. Table A3.1 shows the annual receipts from the excise on milling and receipts for all the other excises that made up the common means in the years immediately before the abolition of tax farming and for the first years after the introduction of direct collection. Gross receipts for the milling excise averaged 13.3 percent higher than the net revenues offered by the tax farmers in 1745–47. The reinstated milling tax of 1750 brought a 20 percent reduction to the tax on rye, which caused tax receipts from 1750 onward to be about 4 percent lower than they otherwise would have been. When this is taken into account, direct collection appears to have increased receipts by 17.7 percent. These estimates fall into a range that appears fairly reasonable. When Holland's treasury assumed responsibility for direct collection in 1750 it reported collection costs of 825,650 guilders for all of the common means, or 7.9 percent of the gross revenue of 10.5 million guilders.[1] To this one must add the *rantsoenpenning* (allowance money), an additional 5 percent charge imposed by the province on tax farm revenues. This fee generated a sum earmarked for the support of the salaries of the Reformed clergy, poor relief, and the cost of administering the tax farms. Together, the tax farmers seem to have incurred costs amounting to 13 percent of their gross receipts.

Direct collection made a much larger difference to the revenues of the rest of the common means excise taxes. Taken together, these revenues rose by nearly 30 percent! Here, too, adjustments must be made to insure that one is comparing like with like, but these do little to change the overall picture: the milling tax, which was in 1750 by far the largest single excise, was either less costly to collect (more efficient) and/or the bidding was more competitive in comparison with the other excises. As for the other excises, the reform of the common means clearly was long overdue. In Table A3.2 I inflate all pre-1750 tax revenues by 15 percent, representing a global approximation of the revenues retained by the tax farmers to defray their costs and as profit.

Non-bread Grain Revenues

The annual milling tax revenues available to us incorporate not only the taxes levied on the bread grains but also on lesser grains for human consumption, brewers' and distillers' grains and starch makers' grain. The tax rates on all the other milled grains were much lower than the rates

---

[1] A.R.A. The Hague, Financiën van Holland, no. 826–28. Liesker and Fritschy set collection costs at 750,000 in the 1750s and 850,000 by the early 1790s, or 8–9 percent of gross revenues. A report of 1788 subtracted 1,590,000 guilders from the gross common means revenues of 11.75 million guilders, or 15.6 percent. Of this, 590,000 represented the *rantsoenpenning*, while collection costs must account for the remaining 1,000,000 guilders. Liesker and Fritschy, *GWF – Holland*, pp. 62, 113–14. The *rantsoenpenning* began in 1581 as a 2 percent tax on tax farm contracts and was earmarked for the support of the salaries of the Reformed clergy. Tracy, *Founding*, p. 178.A report on collection costs prepared by Friesland in 1787 offers a detailed look into what it took to administer the milling excise. The province appointed 30 "general collectors" (one in each of the cities and rural jurisdictions) who supervised 187 "collectors" charged with taking payment from bakers and individuals and providing them with a certificate of payment. An additional 188 "contrarollers" patrolled the grain mills, checking the certificates. Their salaries plus some incidental charges amounted to 11.1 percent of the gross milling excise receipts in 1787–88. Trompetter, *GWF – Friesland*, pp. 63–68.

Table A3.1 *Net and gross revenues of the milling excise and the other common means, 1745–53 (in guilders per year)*

	Milling excise	Common means (except milling excise)
1745–47 (net)	2,174,500	6,241,433
1750–53 (gross)	2,458,650	8,045,725
Adj. for tax rate change	2,559,053	
% change	13.3% (adj. 17.7%)	28.9%

Source: Liesker and Fritschy, *GWF – Holland*, pp. 239, 248–51.

on wheat and rye for baking. Thus, while buckwheat accounted for 20 percent of taxed grain in 1798, it accounted for only 3 percent of tax revenue. But before 1680 buckwheat was relatively more heavily taxed; if its consumption was proportionately as great then, it would have accounted for 6 percent of total milling tax revenue.

The most important of the subsidiary contributors to the milling excise, barley and other grains milled for brewing, will have played an even bigger role. Revenue from this source declined enormously after 1650 for we know that per capita beer consumption in Holland fell from approximately 200 liters per year in 1650 to one-fifth of this level by the 1790s, about 40 liters.[2] The excise tax on beer traces this general pattern of the decline of beer consumption. The tax on grain milled for brewing was reduced by more than half in 1750 in the hope of bringing the decline of consumption (and of the tax revenue from the excise on beer) to a halt. We do not know precisely the share of brewing in total milling tax revenue in 1650. I estimate it at 12 percent of total revenue in the period 1650–70, after which it declines in step with the decline in beer consumption revealed by the excise tax on beer. Beginning in 1750 the excise on the milling of brewers' grain is reduced by more than half, and this, too, is incorporated in the estimated portion of total revenue that did not pertain to the bread grains.

Rural Bread Consumption and Tax Evasion

The milling excise began as an urban levy, and its imposition on the countryside was both delayed and incomplete. Even in 1650 it is likely that rural evasion of the tax was significant. In response to this ongoing

---

[2] Richard Yntema, "The brewing industry in Holland, 1300–1800: a study in industrial development," unpublished Ph.D. thesis, University of Chicago, 1992; Unger, *History of Brewing in Holland*, pp. 222–44.

problem, Holland revised the milling excise significantly in 1680, when a major increase in the rates was combined with a change in the manner of collection in rural areas. Outside the cities and their immediate environs, households were now taxed on a capitation basis. This revision in the method of collection, which also was adopted by other high-tax provinces, was intended to reduce the scope for tax evasion where monitoring was particularly difficult, and Chapter 5 offers evidence that Holland's reform succeeded in increasing revenue very substantially. The new capitation tax, if fully collected, could have raised net revenue (paid to the tax farmers) of about 600,000 guilders, which suggests that the capitation system, by itself, increased rural revenue by a minimum of 33–45 percent.

This exercise allows us to conclude that excise tax revenues before 1680 suffered from a very substantial rural non-compliance, or non-enforcement, reducing revenue at 1680 capitation rates by 200,000 to 270,000 guilders annually. It also alerts us to the fact that from 1680 onward, the milling excise does not accurately measure rural bread consumption, but sets it at the permanent – and very low – capitation level of 65 kg per annum.

In 1680 the rural population of Holland stood at approximately 328,000. If this population was taxed for 58 percent at the rate for wheat and 42 percent at the rate for rye (the wheat–rye mix consumed by Holland's rural population in 1798), and if 76 percent were taxed as adults (above age 10) and 14 percent as children (aged 4–10), total revenue could have reached 808,000 guilders. Tax-exempt charity cases and people claiming reduced payments because of prolonged absence (as sailors, for example) would reduce this amount by at least 10 percent, This reduced amount could have been collected by the tax farmers, but their actual payments to Holland's treasury (based on their bids to farm these tax revenues) will have been about 15 percent less. Thus the net revenue from Holland's rural capitation could not have much exceeded 600,000 guilders.

Estimating Bread Consumption

We are now ready to apply the adjustments discussed above to the original time series. Table A3.2 starts with the original (net) milling excise data in column 1, which is then converted to gross receipts in column 2. Columns 3 and 4 supply estimates of Holland's total and urban populations. The estimated milling excise collected for lesser grains, primarily buckwheat, and for brewers' grain are shown in columns 5 and 6, respectively. Column 7 shows the approximate revenue derived from taxing the bread grains, our chief concern. It subtracts from column 3 the quantities in columns 5 and 6.

This could be the end of the necessary adjustments, were it not for the introduction in 1680 of taxation by capitation to Holland's rural districts. From 1680 onward, the rural milling revenue was capped at a fixed and artificially low level of consumption. Therefore, from 1680 onward our data can only hope to measure urban consumption. But the transition to the capitation system revealed that rural collections before 1680 had suffered from substantial evasion. My analysis in Chapter 5 of this situation immediately before the shift to capitation supplies an estimate of rural revenue (column 8) and of rural underpayment (column 9). These necessarily approximate estimates for before 1680 are replaced thereafter by estimates of capitation revenues that vary only with changes in the size of the rural population. Column 10 shows the tax revenue collected in urban Holland (column 7 minus rural revenue from columns 8 and 9). Before 1680 it incorporates the sensitive assumption that rural revenues were no more than 350,000 guilders per year.

Now we can proceed to estimate the total and per capita volumes of taxed bread grains. By dividing the gross revenue by the tax per last, we derive an estimate of the lasts of taxed grain milled in Holland. But, since we do not know how much of this grain was wheat and how much was rye, we must first make an assumption about the wheat–rye mix. As stated above, we begin our exploration of these data by assuming that Hollanders always consumed two lasts of wheat for every last of rye. Column 11 shows the average tax per last of grain in each period (the weighted average of the tax on wheat and rye). By dividing the tax revenue by the average tax per last, we generate estimates for the total lasts of grain taxed for bread consumption, for Holland as a whole (column 12), the urban sector (column 13), and the rural sector (column 14). Note that rural grain consumption in the period 1650–79 is wholly dependent on the assumption discussed above concerning columns 8 and 9. Columns 15 and 16 convert the total grain volumes into per capita bread grain consumption (using the population data from columns 3 and 4 and the kilogram weights of wheat and rye per last) in the urban and rural sectors, respectively.

Table A3.2 Adjusted model of bread consumption in Holland

	Milling excise revenue in 000s	Adjusted gross milling revenue	Population of Holland Total in 000s	Population of Holland Urban in 000s	Non-bread rev Milling tax on buckwheat	Non-bread rev Milling tax on brewing	Revenue after deduction of non-bread tax	Rural capitation revenue estimate	Rural under payment	Urban revenue	Tax per last 67% wheat 33% rye	Lasts of grain Total	Lasts of grain Urban	Lasts of grain Rural	Kg bread grain per cap Urban	Kg bread grain per cap Rural
1650–54	1,703	1,958	800	495	100	100	1,758	350	285	1,408	53	39,413	26,513	12,900	120	94
1655–59	1,640	1,886	815	515	100	100	1,686	350	285	1,336	53	38,057	25,157	12,900	109	96
1660–64	1,688	1,941	830	535	100	95	1,746	350	285	1,396	53	39,187	26,287	12,900	110	98
1665–69	1,685	1,938	840	545	100	90	1,748	350	285	1,398	53	39,225	26,325	12,900	108	98
1670–74	1,625	1,869	860	555	100	85	1,684	350	285	1,334	53	38,020	25,120	12,900	101	94
1675–79	1,624	1,868	883	555	100	80	1,688	350	285	1,338	53	38,095	25,195	12,900	101	88
Urban/rural capitation																
1680–84	2,328	2,677	883	555	85	75	2,517	690		1,827	79		23,012	9,705	93	66
1685–89	2,505	2,881	870	540	85	75	2,721	690		2,031	87		23,225	9,705	96	66
1690–94	2,484	2,857	860	530	85	75	2,697	680		2,017	87		23,065	9,564	97	65
1695–99	2,315	2,662	840	520	78	65	2,519	680		1,839	87		21,030	9,564	90	67
1700–04	2,180	2,507	830	510	78	60	2,369	670		1,699	87		19,429	9,423	85	66
1705–09	2131	2451	820	500	78	55	2318	670		1648	87		18845	9423	84	66
1710–14	2,044	2,351	810	490	78	50	2,223	670		1,553	87		17,759	9,423	81	66
1715–19	2,055	2,363	800	490	78	50	2,235	660		1,575	87		18,011	9,283	82	67
1720–24	2,074	2,385	800	490	78	50	2,257	660		1,597	87		18,262	9,283	83	67
1725–29	2,092	2,406	800	490	78	50	2,278	660		1,618	87		18,502	9,283	84	67
1730–34	2,102	2,417	800	485	78	45	2,294	660		1,634	87		18,685	9,283	86	66
1735–39	2,103	2,418	800	480	78	45	2,295	660		1,635	87		18,697	9,283	87	65
1740–44	2,061	2,370	790	480	78	40	2,252	660		1,592	87		18,205	9,283	85	67
1745–47	2,175	2,501	783	475	78	35	2,388	650		1,738	87		19,875	9,142	93	66

Table A3.2 (*cont.*)

| | Milling excise revenue in 000s | Adjusted gross milling revenue | Population of Holland | | Non-bread rev | | Revenue after deduction of non-bread tax | Rural capitation revenue estimate | Rural under payment | Urban revenue | Tax per last 67% wheat 33% rye | Lasts of grain | | | Kg bread grain per cap | |
			Total in 000s	Urban in 000s	Milling tax on buckwheat	Milling tax on brewing						Total	Urban	Rural	Urban	Rural
1750–54	2,455	2,455	783	475	75	20	2,360	675		1,685	84		20,055	9,494	94	69
1755–59	2,514	2,514	783	475	75	20	2,419	675		1,744	84		20,758	9,494	98	69
1760–64	2,595	2,595	783	475	75	15	2,505	675		1,830	84		21,781	9,494	102	69
1765–69	2,567	2,567	783	475	75	15	2,477	675		1,802	84		21,448	9,494	101	69
1770–74	2,616	2,616	783	475	75	12	2,529	675		1,854	84		22,067	9,494	104	69
1775–79	2,645	2,645	783	475	75	12	2,558	675		1,883	84		22,412	9,494	105	69
1780–84	2,734	2,734	783	475	75	12	2,647	675		1,972	84		23,471	9,494	110	69
1785–89	2,706	2,706	783	475	75	12	2,619	675		1,944	84		23,138	9,494	109	69
1790–94	2,566	2,566	783	470	75	10	2,481	675		1,806	84		21,496	9,494	102	68
1795–99	2,465	2,465	783	470	75	10	2,380	675		1,705	84		20,294	9,494	96	68
1800–05	2,442	2,442	783	450	75	10	2,357	675		1,682	84		20,020	9,494	99	64

Bibliography

Archival Sources

A.R.A. Den Haag (Nationaal Archief)

Financiën van Holland
657–58   Rekeningen betreffende den aankoop van graan, 1789–92
796–98
826–29   Gemene Middelen

Gecommitteerde Raden van de Staten van Holland en Westfriesland, 1621–1795
4020
4031

Tweede afdeling. Binnenlandse zaken, Binnenlands bestuur B
1366–67   Staten van de Broodzetting in Oost en West-Vlaanderen, Luik, Luxemburg, Henegouwen, Zuidholland, Utrecht, en Overijssel, 1827

Ministerie van Financiën, 1795–1813
853

Ministerie van Binnelandse Zaken, 1813–64

R.A. Haarlem (Provincie Noord-Holland)

Gewestelijk Bestuur
587   1807 rapport
Departementaal Bestuur
461   Graan voorhanden, 18 dec 1816 in Noordholland

G.A. Alkmaar

Stadsarchief voor 1815

1326   Grain sold at Alkmaar market, 1757–59
1969   Ordonnantie op het Bakken, 1697

G.A. Amsterdam (Stadsarchief Amsterdam)

Archief vande Burgemeesters, no. 5028, Stukken betreffende de broodzetting, Gecommitteerden tot het zetten en wegen van het brood
60   Register, 1789
603

480   Bibliography

Algemene Zaken (no. 5181)
3237–38

Part. Archief 5243
3   Broodcommissie
4   Broodcommissie, broodzetting 1847–52

Part. Archief 367, Burgerweeshuis
90
164   Uitgaven, 1562–1614
165   Uitgaven, 1626–28
193   Journal, 1631–38
226
240–41   Uitgaven, 1647–66
242–88   Uitgaven, 1667–1756
591–97   Grootboeken
822–27
829   Groenten, 1799–1805

Part. Archief 343, Almoezeniersweeshuis
8   Propositie tot oprichten van een weeshuis, c. 1665
12   Berigt wegens het AWH der Stad Amsterdam, 1731
15   1784 report over lichaamelijke voeding
29–38   Resoluties notulen, 1667–1825; Rapport betreffende het AWH
         door zes regenten geschreven, 1804
40   Resolutien, 1698–1709, met klapper op zaken
60–83   Boekhouding, 1633–1822
85–90   Korte rekening van onfangh en uitgaaf, 1672–1795
90   Uitgaven, 1800–03
309
371   Register van opgenomen vondelingen
418–19   Jongens naar Oost Indië
444   Doodboek
471–75   Register van bevolking
504   Leveranties en verbruik van levensmiddelen, 1708–89, 1817–18
505   Levering van graan, 1818
509   Calculation of taxes due in 1805 if AWH were subject to taxes
561–65   Register van ontvangsten en uitgaven, 1791–1825
586

G.A. Arnhem

Oud archief der gemeente Arnhem
3679   "Policy-boekje," midden 18de eeuw
3680   Toezicht op het bakken van brood, 1757
3697   Register, prijzen van brood, enz. 1812–14

Archieven der Gasthuizen en Fundatiën, Gilden, Schutterijen en Vendels

1513   Stukken op den broodzetting, 1693

G.A. Delft

Stadsarchief

980	Broodzettingsboek, 1640–1801
996	Broodzetting over Delfland
1028	Memorie van broodwegers Edmond Coolhaes en Jan van Koeverden, 21 dec. 1773
2030	Broodkeure

G.A. Den Haag

Oud Archief der gemeente 's-Gravenhage, 1313–1815

4965	St. Oberts- of bakkersgilde, 1631–1797
4966	Naamlijsten, 1751–1797
5741	Ordonnantien, publicatien van de Magistraat en andere stukken betreffende de broodzetting en het bakken van brood, 1693–1814
5742–44	Register van broodzetting, 1650–1811, 3 delen

Archief 1811–52

879	Gemaal, 1817
1394–95	Broodbakkers
1407	Prijzen voor granen, boter en aardappelen, 1839–51

G.A. Deventer

Middeleeuws archief

297	Ordonnatie van 1545 over het bakkersgilde
299	Ordonnantie van 1509 over het backen van brood
300	Broodzettingboeken

Archief Republiek

278–80	Broodzettingboeken

Archief Franse tijd

692	Broodzettingboeken

G.A. Dordrecht

Stadsarchief, Tijd van de Republiek, 1572–1795 (3)

387	Resolutieboek over de broodzetting, 1786
4762–63	Register houdende aantekeningen van de broodzetting, 1709–95
4764–67	Resolutiën over het platteland

Bataafse Tijd, 1795–1813 (4)

387–88	Ordonnantien op de broodzetting, 1804

Stadsarchief 1813–51 (5)

738	Register van de broodzetting, 1803–17
738–743	Aantekeningen van de broodzetting. 1813–55
741	Koninklijk besluit rapport van 1826
748	

482   Bibliography

G.A. Groningen

Oud Archief,
219 r na R, no. 14
1314 r na R, no. 200
394, no. 659. Resolutien van de regering der stad Groningen, 1605–1816

G.A. Haarlem

Stadsarchief, 1581–1795
1142 (K257)   Grain purchased by city for distribution, 1698–99
1157 (K270)   Grain sold by city for distribution, 1740
1298   Commissie van de broodzetting
1830 (O.261)   Grain milled in Haarlem, 1750

Restant Enschedé doos 62
II-1925   Aanschrijvingen, 1661–1795
II-1926   Memoriën en rapporten, 1644–1795
II-1930a   Broodzettingregisters, 1611–1795 (R412–417)
III-597a, 595–600   Stukken betreffende de Broodzetting
III-1931 (R418)   Prijzen der granen

Gilden Archief
2068   Broodbakkersgilde. Stukken betreffende de broodzetting, 1593–
        1676 (proefbakken Amsterdam en Haarlem)

Stadsarchief Franse Tijd

Commissarissen over de Broodzetting
268–70   Registers, 1764–1837
Nieuw Archief
189   Losse stukken voor 1826; proeve op de tarieven van de brood en
          meelzetting
190

G.A. Hoorn
948   Kinderboekjes (2272)

G.A. Kampen

Oud Archief
2206   1606–1661, ordinances op brood
2207   Broodzettingregister, 1661–1821
2208   "Resultaten van proef wegens het verbakken van een mudde rogge,
        en een mudde tarwe," 12 April 1826

G.A. Leeuwarden

Bakkersboek (F6040, M 506), 1542–1802, pp. 693–706
Leeuwarden Resolutieboeken van Agtbare Magistraat of Magistraat en
Vroedschap der Stede Leeuwarden

G.A. Leiden (Regionaal Archief Leiden)

Stads archief, 1574–1816. Secretarie archief

15–16	Aflezingsboeken
48	Gerechtsdagboeken
2099–2102	Registers van de broodzetting, 1596–1843; Staet dienende tot de brootsettinghe, 1597 (also numbered 2536–39)
2542	Voorraden graan, 1699
2546–47	Aantekeningen en bijgehouden stukken in het register van de broodzetting (midden 18e eeuw)
2548	Aantekeningen omtrent broodzetting in Rotterdam, Utrecht, en Amsterdam (1795)
2549	Stukken betreffende aardappelen (1795)
2550	Concept rapport van de Kamer van Wethouders omtrent verhoging van de zetting v. h. brood en v. h. maalloon, 1803

Gilden archief: Bakkers

158–80	Broodzetting dokumenten
2248	Keuren, resoluties en requesten betreffende de broodbakkerij, 1506–1742
2249	Register en lijsten van bakkers
2250	Stukken betreffende de vergunningen van bakkerijen, 1804, 1806

G.A. Nijmegen

Oud-archief der gemeente Nijmegen

3113	Politsie Boeck der Stadt Nijmegen. Register, prijzen van het brood, 1600–05, 1660–1700.
3114	Politsie Boeck, 1623–1690

Gilden archief

27	Politsie Boeck, prijszettingen, 1632–1757

G.A. Rotterdam

Oud Stadsarchief

2121–27	Broodzetting, 1609–12, 1648–1843

G.A. Utrecht

Oud Archief: Stadsarchief III

461, deel 1, no. 8	Backersgilde ordonnantie, 1626
2023–25	Rijdingboek, 1599–1818

Archief Geref. Burgerweeshuis

116	Rekeningen, 1580–1979
118	Acquitten tot de rekeningen
723–34	Weeskinderen
798	Weekelykse keukenrekeningen

Nieuw Archief

674   · Rijdingboek

G.A. Zaltbommel (Streekarchief Bommelerwaard)

Oud Archief

19–1226	Ordonnantie op de zetting van brood, 1820
20–2079–80	Broodzettingsregisters; Culemborg broodzetting, 1658
127–301	Regelement op de broodzetting in het Schoutambt Kerkrijk, 1821

G.A. Zwolle

Oud Stadsarchief

484	Verkogte granen op de markt te Zwolle, 1811–12
488–92	Rekening van Roggenbrood, z.d., 17th c., Besluiten van de Keurmeesters, 1651–1822
490	Roggebrood zetting van 1773
491–92	Tarwebrood bij dispositie van de Maire, 1811–20
495	Register van Vaststelling van Broodprijzen, 1682–1795
4427–48	Maandstaten verwerkte weit
6058	

Published Sources and Publications before 1820

Alphonse, F. J. B. d', *Aperçu sur la Hollande* (1811). Reprinted in Centraal Bureau voor de Statistiek, *Bijdragen tot de Statistiek van Nederland*, n.s., 1 (The Hague, 1900).

Blok, P. J., et al., *Oorkondenboek van Groningen en Drenthe*, 2 vols. (Groningen, 1896–99).

Boretius, A. *Capitularia Regum Francorum* (Hanover, 1897), vol. I.

Commelen, Casperus. *Beschryving der stadt Amsterdam* (Amsterdam, 1693).

Craeybeckx, Jan. "Brood en levensstandaard,"*Bijdragen tot de prijzengeschiedenis* 3 (1958), 133–62.

"De Brusselse 'Terminatieboeken'," *Bijdragen tot de prijzengeschiedenis* 2 (1957), 66–68.

"De prijzen van graan en van brood te Brussel," in Charles Verlinden, ed., *Documenten voor de geschiedenis van prijzen en lonen in Brabant en Vlaanderen (XVIe–XIXe E.)*, vol. I (Bruges: De Tempel, 1959), pp. 481–522.

Daamsma, D., J. M. M. de Meere, and L. Noordegraaf, eds. *Statistieken van de Nederlandse nijverheid uit de eerste helft der 19e eeuw*, supplement, Rijks geschiedkundige publicatiën, Grote serie, 168 (The Hague: Martinus Nijhoff, 1979).

Delamare, Nicolas. *Traité de la Police*, 4 vols. (Paris, 1707).

Dillen, J. G. van. *Bronnen tot de geschiedenis van het bedrijfsleven en het gildewezen van Amsterdam, 1512–1672*, Rijksgeschiedkundige publicatiën, 78 (The Hague: Martinus Nijhoff, 1933).

Edlin, A. *A Treatise on the Art of Bread-Making* (1805) (London: Prospect Books, 2004).

Ent, L. van der, and V. Enthoven. *Gewestilijke financiën ten tijde van de Republiek der Verenigde Nederlanden: Groningen, 1594–1795*, vol. III (The Hague: Instituut voor Nederlandse Geschiedenis, 1998). Cited as *GWF – Groningen*.

Ent, L. van der, and Wantje Fritschy. *Gewestilijke financiën ten tijde van de Republiek der Verenigde Nederlanden: Drenthe, 1602–1795*, vol. II (The Hague: Instituut voor Nederlandse Geschiedenis, 1998). Cited as *GWF – Drenthe*.

Eversdijck, Cornelis François. *Paste-boeck vanden Broode* (Middelburg 1663). *Tafelen vande Wanne-mate* (Middelburg, 1655).

Friis, Astrid, and Kristof Glamman. *A History of Prices and Wages in Denmark, 1660–1800* (London: Longmans, 1958).

Fritschy, Wantje. *Gewestilijke financiën ten tijde van de Republiek der Verenigde Nederlanden: Overijssel, 1604–1795*, vol. I (The Hague: Instituut voor Nederlandse Geschiedenis, 1996). Cited as *GWF – Overijssel*.

Gerhard, Hans-Jürgen, ed. *Löhne im vor- und frühindustriellen Deutschland* (Göttingen: Schwarz, 1984).

Gibson, A. J. S., and T. C. Smout. *Prices, Food and Wages in Scotland, 1550–1780* (Cambridge University Press, 1995).

Gogel, I. J. A. *Memoriën en correspondentiën betreffende den staat van 's Rijks geldmiddelen in den jare 1820* (Amsterdam, 1844).

Graswinckel, Dirck. *Placcaten, ordonnantien ende reglementen op 't stuck vande lijftocht*, 2 vols. (Leiden: Elseviers, 1651).

Groot Placaatboek de Staaten 's Lands van Utrecht mitsgaders van de Stad Utrecht tot het jaar 1728 ingelsoten, Johan van de Water, 3 vols. (Utrecht, 1729). Cited as *GPB – Utrecht*.

Groot Placaatboek van de Staten Generaal der Verenigde Nederlanden, de Staten van Holland en Westvriesland, mitsgaders van de Staten van Zeelandt, Cornelis Cau, et al., 9 vols. (The Hague, 1658–1796). Cited as *GPB – Holland*.

Handvesten van Amsterdam (Amsterdam, 1748), pp. 882–93.

Hauser, Henri. *Recherches et documents sur l'histoire des prix en France de 1500 à 1800* (Geneva, 1936).

Jager, H. de. *De Middeleeuwsche keuren der stad Brielle* (The Hague: Martinus Nijhoff, 1901).

Kemper, Johannes de Bosch. *Statistiek van Nederland* (Amsterdam: Weijtingh en van der Haart, 1854).

Knoop, J. H. *Tegenwoordige staat van Friesland* (Leeuwarden, 1763).

Liesker, R., and Wantje Fritschy. *Gewestilijke financiën ten tijde van de Republiek der Verenigde Nederlanden. Holland, 1572–1795*, vol. IV (The Hague: Instituut voor Nederlandse Geschiedenis, 2004). Cited as *GWF – Holland*.

Ludeman, Johan Christophorus. *Burger Huys-Schat, of Heylzaame Waarnemingen* (The Hague, 1760).

Luzac, Elias. *Hollands rijkdom*, 4 vols. (Leiden, 1783).

Mitchell, B. R. *British Historical Statistics* (Cambridge University Press, 1988).

Mitchell, B. R., and P. Deane. *Abstract of British Historical Statistics* (Cambridge University Press, 1962).

Muller Fz., S. *De Middeleeuwsche Rechtsbronnen der Stad Utrecht* (The Hague: Martinus Nijhoff, 1883).

Nederlandsche Jaarboeken (1750, 1756).

Nieuwe Nederlandsche Jaarboeken (1789, 1790).

Nieuwenhuijs, Cs. Js. *Proeve eener geneeskundige plaatsbeschrijving der stad Amsterdam*, 2 vols. (Amsterdam, 1816).

Oldewelt, W. F. H. *Kohier van de personele quotisatie te Amsterdam over het jaar 1742*, 2 vols. (Amsterdam, 1945).

Posthumus, N. W. *An Inquiry into the History of Prices in the Netherlands/ Nederlandse prijsgeschiedenis*, 2 vols. (Leiden: E. J. Brill, 1943/1946, 1964).

Ricardo, David. *Principles of Political Economy and Taxation*, ed. R. H. Hartwell (Harmondsworth: Penguin, 1971).

Scholliers, E. "De Antwerpse mercuriale van granen en brood (1576–1583)," in Charles Verlinden, ed., *Prijzen en lonen in Brabant en Vlaanderen* (XVIe–XIXe E.), vol. III (Bruges: De Tempel, 1972), pp. 350–58.

Sillem, J. A. "Tabellen van markt-prijzen van granen te Utrecht, 1393–1644," *Verhandelingen der Koninklijke Akademie van Wetenschappen, Afd. Letteren,* n.s., vol. 3 (Amsterdam, 1901).

Smith, Adam. *Inquiry into the Causes of the Wealth of Nations* (1776), ed. Edwin Cannon (London, 1904).

Smith, Charles. *Three Tracts on the Corn-Trade and Corn-Laws* (1758) (2nd edn. London, 1766).

Soutendam, J., *Keuren en ordinantiën der stad Delft, 1500–1536* (Delft, 1879).

Statistieke beschrijving van Gelderland van 1808, vol. I: *Kwartier van Arnhem*; vol. II: *Kwartier van Zutphen*; vol. III: *Kwartier van Nijmegen* (Arnhem: Vereniging Gelre, 1986).

Swinden, J. H. van. *Vergelijkings-tafels tusschen de Hollandsche koorn-maten en de hectoliter met het nodige onderright over dezelve maten* (Amsterdam, 1812).

Tegenwoordige Staat van Drenthe, vol. I (Amsterdam, 1795).

Tegenwoordige Staat van Friesland, vol. IV (Amsterdam, 1785–89).

Trompetter, Cor. *Gewestelijke financiën ten tijde van de Republiek der Verenigde Nederlanden. Friesland, 1587–1795*, vol. VI (The Hague: Instituut voor Nederlandse Geschiedenis, 2004). Cited as *GWF – Friesland.*

Tijms, W. "Prijzen van granen en peulvruchten te Arnhem, Breda, Deventer, 's-Hertogenbosch, Kampen, Koevorden, Maastricht, Nijmegen," *Historia Agriculturae*, 11 (Groningen: NAHI, 1977).

Groninger graanprijzen: de prijzen van agrarische producten tussen 1546 en 1990. Historia Agriculturae 31(2000), entire issue.

Veen, J. S. van. *Rechtsbronnen van Tiel* (The Hague: Martinus Nijhoff, 1901).

Veenstra, Wietse. *Gewestelijke financiën ten tijde van de Republiek der Verenigde Nederlanden*, vol. VII: *Zeeland 1573–1795* (The Hague: Instituut voor Nederlandse Geschiedenis, 2009). Cited as *GWF – Zeeland.*

Verrijn Stuart, C. A. "Marktprijzen van Granen te Arnhem in de jaren 1544–1901," *Bijdragen tot de Statistiek van Nederland*, n.s., 26 (1903), 19–25.

Verstegen, S. W. *Gewestelijke financiën ten tijde van de Republiek der Verenigde Nederlanden*, vol. V: *Utrecht 1579–1795* (The Hague: Instituut voor Nederlandse Geschiedenis, 1998). Cited as *GWF – Utrecht.*

Wagenaar, Jan. *Amsterdam, in zijne opkomst, anwas, geschiedenissen ...* 4 vols. (Amsterdam: Isaak Tirion, 1760–67).

Digital Sources

Allen, Robert C. "European wages and prices." www.economics.ox.ac.uk/ members/robert.allen/Wages Files/labweb.xls

Allen, Robert C., and Richard W. Unger. "Database: European commodity prices, 1260–1914." www.history.ubc.ca/unger/htm_files/new_grain.htm www.gcpdb.info/data.html

Fritschy, Wantje et al. "Provincial finances of the Dutch Republic." www .resources.huygens.knaw.nl/gewestelijkefinancien

Riel, Arthur van. "Prices of consumer and producer goods, 1800–1913." www .iisg.nl/hpw/data.php#netherlands

Vries, Jan de. "Bread and grain prices, 1594–1855." www.iisg.nl/hpw/data .php#netherlands

Zanden, Jan Luiten van. "Prices and wages and the cost of living in the western part of the Netherlands, 1450–1800." www.iisg.nl/hpw/brenv.php

Zanden, Jan Luiten van, and Bas van Leeuwen, "Reconstruction: national income accounts of Holland, 1510–1807." www.cgeh.nl/ reconstruction-national-accounts-holland-1500–1800–0

Bibliography, Published after 1820

Anon. "Staat van de jaarlijksche consumptie binnen Rotterdam van 1839–1848, volgens de aangiften van de belastingen," *Staathuishoudkundig jaarboekje* 2 (1850).

Anon. "Verbruik van sommige voedings- en genotmiddelen," *Maandschrift van het Centraal Bureau voor de Statistiek* (The Hague, 1913).

Abel, Wilhelm. *Agrarkrisen und Agrarkonjunktur im Mitteleuropa vom 13. bis zum 19. Jahrhundert* (Berlin: Parey, 1966).

Massenarmut und Hungerkrisen im vorindustriellen Europa: Versuch einer Synopsis (Hamburg and Berlin: Parey, 1974).

Aden, Otto. *Entwicklung und Wechsellagen ausgewählter Gewerbe in Ostfriesland* (Aurich: Verlag Ostfriesische Landschaft, 1964).

Alan S. C. "The Assize of Bread," *Economic History Review* 9 (1956), 332–42.

Alfani, Guido. *Calamities and Economy in Renaissance Italy: The Grand Tour of the Horsemen of the Apocalypse* (Basingstoke: Palgrave, 2013).

"Famines in late medieval and early modern Italy: a test for an advanced economy," Working Paper no. 82, Dondena Centre, Università Bocconi, Milan, 2015.

Allen, Robert. *The British Industrial Revolution in Global Perspective* (Cambridge University Press, 2009).

"The great divergence in European wages and prices from the Middle Ages to the First World War," *Explorations in Economic History* 38 (2001), 411–47.

"Poverty lines in history, theory, and current international practice," unpublished paper, Nuffield College, Oxford, 2013.

Allen, Robert, Jean-Paul Bassino, Debin Ma, Christine Moll-Murata, and Jan Luiten van Zanden. "Wages, prices, and living standards in China, 1739–1925: in comparison with Europe, Japan, and India," *Economic History Review* 64 (2011), 8–38.

Allen, Robert, and Richard Unger. "The depth and breadth of the market for Polish grain, 1500–1800," in J. Ph. S. Lemmink *et al.*, *Baltic Affairs* (Nijmegen: Instituut voor Noord en Oosteuropese Studies, 1990), pp. 1–18.

Altena, Bert, and Dirk van der Veen. "Een onbekende enquête naar broodconsumptie in Nederland," *Tijdschrift voor sociale geschiedenis* 12 (1986), 135–52.

Angeles, L. "GDP per capita or real wages? Making sense of conflicting views on pre-industrial Europe," *Explorations in Economic History* 45 (2008), 147–63.

Appleby, Andrew. *Famine in Tudor and Stuart England* (Liverpool University Press, 1978).

Ashley, William. *The Bread of Our Forefathers: An Inquiry into Economic History* (Oxford University Press, 1928).

Ashton, T. S. "The standard of living of the workers in England, 1790–1830," in F. A. Hayek, ed., *Capitalism and the Historian* (University of Chicago Press, 1954), pp. 123–55.

Aten, Diederik. *"Als het gewelt comt ...": politiek en economie in Holland benoorden het IJ* (Hilversum: Verloren, 1995).

Aymard, Maurice. "Dietary changes in Europe from the 16th to 20th century, with particular reference to France and Italy," in Henri Baudet and Henk van der Meulen, eds., *Consumer Behavior and Economic Growth in the Modern Economy* (London: Croom Helm, 1982).

"Pour l'histoire de l'alimentation: quelques remarques de méthode," *Annales. Économies, sociétés, civilisations* 30 (1975), 431–44.

Baars, C. *De geschiedenis van de landbouw in de Beijerlanden* (Wageningen: Centrum voor landbouwpublikaties en landbouwdocumentatie, 1973).

Baetens, R. "De voedselrantsoenen van de zeevarenden: de theorie getoetst aan de werkelijkheid," *Bijdragen tot de geschiedenis van het Hertogdom Brabant* 60 (1977), 273–306.

Balani, D. *Il vicario tra città e Stato: l'ordine pubblico e l'annona nella Torino del Settecento* (Turin: Deputazione Subalpina di Storia Patria, 1987).

Basini, Gian Luigi. *L'uomo e il pane: risorse, consumi e carenze alimentari della populazione modenese nel cinque e seicento* (Milan: Dott. A. Giuffrè Editore, 1970).

Baulant, Micheline. "Le prix des grains à Paris de 1431 à 1788," *Annales. Économies, sociétés, civilisations* 23 (1968), 520–40.

Baulant, Micheline, and Jean Meuvret. *Prix de céréals extraits de la mercuriale de Paris (1520–1698)*, 2 vols. (Paris: SEVPEN, 1962).

Baumhauer, M. M. von, "De Broodzetting," *De Gids*, May 1848, pp. 586–605.

Bavel, Bas van, and Jan Luiten van Zanden. "The jump start of the Holland economy during the late medieval crisis, c. 1350 – c. 1500," *Economic History Review* 57 (2004), 503–32.

Beer, Hans de. *Voeding, gezondheid en arbeid in Nederland tijdens de negentiende eeuw: een bijdrage to de antropometrische geschiedschrijving* (Amsterdam: Aksant, 2001).

Bernados-Sanz, Jose Ubaldo. "Libertad en el abastecimiento de trigo a Madrid," in Martin and Voirlouvet, eds., *Nourrir les cités*, pp. 369–88.

Bertail, Patrice, and Jean-Michel Chevet, "The effects of the customs duty sliding scale on the wheat prices in England, 1828–1850," in Clara Eugenia Núñez *et al.*, eds., *Integration of Commodity Markets in History. Proceedings of the Twelfth International Economic History Congress, Madrid, August 1998* (University of Seville, 1998), pp. 65–77.

Bieleman, Jan. *Boeren in Nederland: geschiedenis van de landbouw, 1500–2000* (Amsterdam: Boom, 2008).

Blanc, Hermann. *La Chambre des Blés de Genève, 1628–1798* (Geneva: Impr. du Journal de Genève, 1939).

Blockmans, Wim, *Metropolen aan de Noordzee* (Amsterdam: Bert Bakker, 2012).

Blockmans, Wim, and Walter Prevenier. "Armoede in de Nederlanden van de 14e tot het midden van de 16e eeuw: bronnen en problemen," *Tijdschrift voor geschiedenis* 88 (1975), 501–38.

Blomme, Jan. "Werk in uitvoering: de hoofdelijke broodgraan consumptie in België, 1850–1939," *Tijdschrift voor sociale geschiedenis* 12 (1986), 401–15.

Bochove, Christiaan van. *The Economic Consequences of the Dutch: Economic Integration around the North Sea, 1500–1800* (Amsterdam: Aksant, 2008).

Boer, D. E. H. de. *Graaf en grafiek: sociale en economische ontwikkelingen in middeleeuws "Noordholland" tussen 1345 en 1415* (Leiden: New Rhine Publishers, 1978).

Bohstedt, John. *The Politics of Provisions: Food Riots, Moral Economy, and Market Transition in England, c. 1550–1850* (Farnham: Ashgate, 2010).

Bonke, Hans. *De kleyne mast van de Hollandse coopsteden: Stadsontwikkeling in Rotterdam, 1572–1795*, Amsterdamse Historische Reeks, no. 32 (Amsterdam: Stichting Amsterdamse Historische Reeks, 1996).

Boulton, Cynthia. *The Flour War: Gender, Class, and Community in Late Ancien Régime French Society* (University Park, Pa.: Pennsylvania State University Press, 1993).

Braudel, Fernand. *Afterthoughts on Capitalism and Material Civilization* (Baltimore, Md.: Johns Hopkins University Press, 1977).

Civilization and Capitalism, 15th–18th Centuries, vol. I: *The Structures of Everyday Life* (New York: Harper, 1981).

The Mediterranean and the Mediterranean World in the Age of Philip II, 2 vols. (New York: Harper, 1972).

Broadberry, Stephen, and B. Gupta. "The early modern great divergence: wages prices and economic development in Europe and Asia, 1500–1800," *Economic History Review* 59 (2006), 2–31.

Broadberry, Stephen, Bruce M. S. Campbell, Alexander Klein, Mark Overton, and Bas van Leeuwen. *British Economic Growth 1270–1870* (Cambridge University Press, 2015).

Brouwer Ancher, A. J. M. *De Gilden* (The Hague: Loman en Funke, 1895).

Brugmans, H. "Statistiek van den in- en uitvoer van Amsterdam, 1 Oct 1667 – 30 Sept 1668," *Bijdragen en mededelingen van het Historisch Genootschap* 19 (1898), 125–83.

Brugmans, I. J. *De arbeidende klasse in Nederland in de negentiende eeuw*, 2nd edn. (The Hague: Martinus Nijhoff, 1929).

Paardenkracht en mensenmacht (The Hague: Martinus Nijhoff, 1961).

Statistieken van de Nederlandse nijverheid uit de eerste helft der 19e eeuw, Rijks geschiedkundige publication, Grote serie, 98–99 (The Hague: Martinus Nijhoff, 1956).

Brunt, Liam, and Edmund Cannon. "A grain of truth in medieval interest rates? Re-examining the McCloskey–Nash hypothesis," Working Paper, University of Bristol, Department of Economics, 1999.

"Variation in the price and quality of English grain, 1750–1914: quantitative evidence and empirical implications," *Explorations in Economic History* 58 (2015), 74–92.

Brusse, Paul. *Gevallen stad: stedelijke netwerken en het platteland. Zeeland, 1750– 1850* (Zwolle: Waanders, 2011).

Overleven door ondernemen: de agrarische geschiedenis van de Over-Betuwe, 1650–1850, AAG Bijdragen 38 (Wageningen: Afdeling Agrarische Geschiedenis, 1999).

Brusse, Paul, and Wijnand W. Mijnhardt, *Towards a New Template for Dutch History: De-urbanization and the Balance between City and Countryside* (Utrecht: Uitgeverij Waanders/Utrecht University, 2012).

Bruyn Kops, J. L. de. *Over indirecte belasting als middel van plaatselijke inkomsten: eene staathuishoudkundige proeve* (Leiden, 1851).

Büchner, E. C. "Over de voornaamste voedigsmiddelen te Amsterdam verbruikt in het jaar 1851," *De economist* 2 (1853), 174–82.

Burema, L. *De voeding in Nederland van de middeleeuwen tot de twintigste eeuw* (Assen: Van Gorkum, 1953).

Chartres, John. "British Isles, 1750–2000," in Van Molle and Segers, eds., *The Agro-Food Market*, pp. 99–132.

"The marketing of agricultural produce," in Joan Thirsk, ed., *Agrarian History of England and Wales*, vol. V, part 2: *1640–1750* (Cambridge University Press, 1985), pp. 406–502.

Coclanis, Peter. *The Shadow of a Dream: Economic Life and Death in the South Carolina Low Country, 1670–1920* (Oxford University Press, 1989).

Coeckelberghs, H. "Lonen en levensstandaard te Brussel in de 16e eeuw," *Bijdragen tot de geschiedenis* 58 (1975), 169–207.

Coenen, Ann. *Carriers of Growth? International Trade and Economic Development in the Austrian Netherlands* (Leiden: Brill, 2015).

Collins, E. J. T. "Dietary change and cereal consumption in Britain in the nineteenth century," *Agricultural History Review* 23 (1975), 97–115.

"Why wheat? Choice of food grains in Europe in the nineteenth and twentieth centuries," *Journal of European Economic History* 22 (1993), 7–38.

Corritore, Renzo Paolo. *La naturale "abbondanza" del Mantovano: produzione, mercato e consumi granari a Mantova in età moderna* (Università di Pavia, 2000).

Coster, D. J. *Bijdrage tot de geschiedenis van de keuring der voedingsmiddelen te Amsterdam* (Amsterdam, 1864).

Crafts, Nicholas. "Income elasticities of demand and the release of labor by agriculture during the British Industrial Revolution: a further appraisal," in Joel Mokyr, ed., *The Economics of the Industrial Revolution* (Totowa, NJ: Rowman and Allenhead, 1985), pp. 151–63.

Cruyningen, P. J. van. *Behoudend maar buigzaam: boeren in West-Zeeuws-Vlaanderen, 1650–1850*, AAG Bijdragen 40 (Wageningen: Afdeling Agrarische Geschiedenis, 2000).

"Farmers' strategies and the West-Zeeland-Flanders grain trade, 1648–1794," in Piet van Cruyningen and Erik Thoen, eds., *Food Supply, Demand and Trade* (Turnhout: Brepols, 2012), pp. 161–72.

Cullen, L. M. "Irish history without the potato," *Past and Present* 40 (1968), 72–83.

Dane, J., ed, *Wezen en boefjes: zes eeuwen zorg in Wees- en Kinderhuizen* (Hilversum: Verloren, 1997).

Dardel, Pierre. *Navires et marchandises dans les ports de Rouen et du Havre au XVIIIe siècle* (Paris: SEVPEN, 1963).

David, Karel. "Innovations in windmill technology in Europe, c. 1500–1800," *NEHA-Jaarboek* 66 (2003), 43–63.

Davis, James. "Baking for the common good: a reassessment of the assize of bread in medieval England," *Economic History Review* 57 (2004), 465–502.

Dawson, J. A. *Retail Geography* (London: Croom Helm, 1980).

Dekker, R. M. *Holland in beroering: oproeren in de 17de en 18de eeuw* (Baarn: Ambo, 1982).

Oproeren in Holland gezien door tijdgenoten (Assen: Van Gorcum, 1979).

"Oproeren in de provincie Holland, 1600–1750: frequentie en karakter, relatie met de conjunctuur en repressie," *Tijdschrift voor sociale geschiedenis* 3 (1977), 299–329.

Delumeau, Jacques. *Vie économique et sociale de Rome dans la seconde moitié du XVIe siècle* (Paris: De Boccard, 1966).

Desportes, Françoise. *Le pain au Moyen Âge* (Paris: Oliver Orban, 1987).

Deursen, A. Th. van, *Een dorp in de polder: Graft in de zeventiende eeuw* (Amsterdam: Bert Bakker, 2006).

Plain People in a Golden Age (Cambridge University Press, 1991).

Dewez, W. J., "De landbouw in Brabants Westhoek in het midden van de achttiende eeuw," *Agronomisch-historisch bijdragen* 4 (1958), 1–65.

Dewilde, Brecht, and Johan Poukens. "Bread provisioning and retail dynamics in the southern Low Countries: the bakers of Leuven, 1600–1800," *Continuity and Change* 26 (2011), 405–38.

Dictionnaire du Commerce, 2nd edn. (Brussels, 1840).

Diederiks, Herman. *Een stad in verval: Amsterdam omstreeks 1800* (University of Amsterdam, 1982).

Dijkman, Jessica. "Coping with scarcity: a comparison of dearth policies in three regions in northwestern Europe in the fifteenth and sixteenth centuries," *Tijdschrift voor sociale en economische geschiedenis* 14 (2017), 5–30.

"Managing food crises," unpublished paper, Utrecht University, 2016.

Shaping Medieval Markets: The Organization of Commodity Markets in Holland, c. 1200–c.1450 (Leiden: Brill, 2011).

Dillen, J. G. van. "De duurte van het jaar 1698," *Onze eeuw* 17 (1917), 250–73.

"Dreigende hongersnood in de Republiek in de laatste jaren der zeventiende eeuw," in J. G. van Dillen, *Mensen en achtergronden* (Groningen: J. B. Wolters, 1964).

"Stukken betreffende den Amsterdamschen graanhandel omstreeks het jaar 1681," *Economisch-historisch jaarboek* 3 (1917), 221–30.

"Termijnhandel te Amsterdam in de 16e en 17e eeuw," *De economist* 76 (1927), 503–23.

Van rijkdom en regenten: handboek tot de economische en sociale geschiedenis van Nederland tijdens de Republiek (The Hague: Martinus Nijhoff, 1970).

Dupâquier, Jacques. "Demographic crises and subsistence crises in France, 1650–1725," in John Walter and Roger Schofield, eds., *Famine, Disease and the Social Order in Early Modern Society* (Cambridge University Press, 1989), pp. 189–200.

Dwyer, G. P., and C. M. Lindsay. "Robert Giffen and the Irish potato," *American Economic Review* 74 (1984), 188–92.

Ebeling, Dietrich, and Franz Irsigler. *Bürgertum und Pöbel: Wirtschaft und Gesellschaft Kölns im 18. Jahrhundert* (Cologne and Vienna: Böhlau-Verlag, 1987).

Getreideumsatz, Gretreide- und Brotpriese in Köln, 1368–1797, 2 vols. (Cologne and Vienna: Böhlau-Verlag, 1977).

Eeckhout, Patricia Van den, and Peter Scholliers. "De hoofdelijke voedselconsumptie in België, 1831–1939," *Tijdschrift voor sociale geschiedenis* 9 (1983), 271–301.

Eichholz, P. M. A., and M. A. J. Theebe: "Zo vast als een huis," *Economisch-statistisch berichten* 84 (1999), 132–34.

Ejrnaes, Mette, Karl Gunner Persson, and Soren Rich. "Feeding the British: convergence and market efficiency in the nineteenth-century grain trade," *Economic History Review* 61 (2008), 140–71.

Engel, J. T. *Kinderen van Amsterdam* (Amsterdam: Walburg Pers, 1989).

Epstein, Stephan R. "Craft guilds, apprenticeship, and technological change in preindustrial Europe," *Journal of Economic History* 58 (1998), 684–713.

Freedom and Growth: The Rise of States and Markets in Europe, 1300–1750 (London: Routledge, 2000).

Epstein, Stephan R., and Maarten Prak, eds. *Guilds, Innovation and the European Economy, 1400–1800* (London: Routledge, 2008).

Faber, J. A. *Drie eeuwen Friesland*, AAG Bijdragen 17, 2 vols. (Wageningen: Afdeling Agrarische Geschiedenis, 1972).

"Het probleem van de dalende graanaanvoer uit de Oostzeelanden in de tweede helft van de zeventiende eeuw," *AAG Bijdragen* 9 (1963), 3–28.

Farlie, Susan. "The Corn Laws and British wheat production, 1829–76," *Economic History Review* 22 (1969), 88–116.

"The nineteenth-century Corn Law reconsidered," *Economic History Review* 18 (1965), 562–75.

Fogel, Robert William. *The Escape from Hunger and Premature Death, 1700–2100* (Cambridge University Press, 2004).

"Second thoughts on the European escape from hunger: famines, chronic malnutrition, and mortality rates," in S. Osmani, ed., *Nutrition and Poverty* (Oxford University Press, 1992), pp. 243–86.

Fritschy, J. M. F. *De patriotten en de financiën van de Bataafse Republiek* (The Hague: Stichting Hollandse Historische Reeks, 1988).

Fritschy, Wantje. "The efficiency of taxation in Holland," in Oscar Gelderblom, ed., *The Political Economy of the Dutch Republic* (Farnham: Ashgate, 2009), pp. 55–84.

"A 'Financial Revolution' reconsidered: public finance in Holland during the Dutch Revolt, 1568–1648," *Economic History Review* 41 (2003), 57–89.

Fuchs, J. M. *Opvangen en opvoeden: Lutherse wezenzorg in Amsterdam, 1678–1978* (Amsterdam: Lankamp en Brinkman, 1978).

Galloway, James, and Margaret Murphy. "Feeding the city: medieval London and its agrarian hinterland," *The London Journal* 16 (1991), 3–15.

Garber, Peter. *Famous First Bubbles: The Fundamentals of Early Manias* (Cambridge, Mass.: MIT Press, 2000).

Goubert, Pierre. *Louis XIV et vingt millions de Français* (Paris: Fayard, 1966).

Gourvish, Terence R. "A note on bread prices in London and Glasgow, 1788–1815," *Journal of Economic History* 30 (1970), 854–60.

Grab, A. *La politica del pane: le riforme annonarie in Lombardia nell' età teresiana e giuseppina* (Milan: Franco Angeli, 1986).

Grantham, George. "Food rations in France in the eighteenth and early nineteenth centuries: a reply," *Economic History Review* 48 (1995), 774–77.

"Professional and occupational specialization in pre-industrial France," *Economic History Review* 46 (1993), 478–502.

Greif, Avner, Paul Milgrom, and Barry Weingast. "Coordination, commitment and enforcement: the case of the merchant guild," *Journal of Political Economy* 102 (1994), 912–50.

Grendi, E. "Genova alla metà del Cinquecento: una politica del grano?," *Quaderni Storici* 13 (1970), 106–60.

Griffiths, Richard. *Industrial Retardation in the Netherlands, 1830–1850* (The Hague: Martinus Nijhoff, 1979).

"The role of taxation in wage formation in the Dutch economy in the first half of the nineteenth century," in Johan de Vries, ed., *Ondernemende geschiedenis* (The Hague: Martinus Nijhoff, 1977), pp. 260–71.

Guenzi, Alberto. "Un mercato regolato: pane e fornai a Bologna nell' età moderna," *Quaderni Storici* 13 (1978), 370–97.

"La politica annonaria in età moderna," in Cristina Papa, ed., *Il pane: antropologia e storia dell' alimentazione* (Milan: Electa Editore Umbri, 1992).

Guerreau, Alain. "Mesures du blé et du pain à Mâcon (XIVe–XVIIIe siècles)," *Histoire et Mesure* 3 (1988), 163–219.

Hanauer, A. *Études économiques sur l'Alsace ancienne et moderne* (Strasbourg, 1878).

Hanlon, Gregory. *Early Modern Italy, 1550–1800* (Basingstoke: Macmillan, 2000).

Harris, Patricia, David Lyon, and Sue McLaughlin, *The Meaning of Food* (Guilford, Conn.: Globe Pequot Press, 2005).

Hart, Simon. *Geschrift en getal* (Dordrecht: Historische Vereniging Holland, 1976).

't Hart, Marjolein C. *In Quest for Funds: Warfare and State Formation in the Netherlands, 1620–1650*, Ph.D. thesis, University of Leiden, 1989.

The Making of a Bourgeois State: War, Politics and Finance during the Dutch Revolt (Manchester University Press, 1993).

"The merits of a financial revolution: public finances, 1550–1700," in Marjolein 't Hart *et al.*, eds., *A Financial History of the Netherlands* (Cambridge University Press, 1997), pp. 11–36.

Harten, J. D. H. "De verzorging van het platteland van de Zeeuwse eilanden in de Franse Tijd," *Bulletin Geografisch Instituut Rijksuniversiteit Utrecht* 3 (1971), 31–73.

Hartevelt, D. "Ons dagelijksch brood," *De economist* 18 (1869), 913–24. "Ons dagelijksch brood. Voorheen en Thans," *De economist* 19 (1870), 215–31.

Hatton, Tim, and Jeffrey G. Williamson. "What drove the mass migrations from Europe in the late nineteenth century?" *Population and Development Review*, 20 (1994), 1–27.

Heijden, Manon van der. *Geldschieters van de stad: financiële relaties tussen stad, burgers en overheden, 1550–1650* (Amsterdam: Bert Bakker, 2006).

Heijder, M. *Amsterdam, korenschuur van Europa* (Stadsdrukkerij van Amsterdam, 1979).

Heldring, O. G. *Noodkreet over de belasting op het gemaal en den hoogen prijs van het brood* (Amsterdam, 1846).

Herr, Richard, *Rural Change and Royal Finances in Spain* (Berkeley and Los Angeles: University of California Press, 1989).

Hirschman, Albert O. *Exit, Voice, and Loyalty* (Cambridge, Mass.: Harvard University Press, 1970).

Hoek Ostende, J. H. van den. "Een prijsregeling van de 15e tot de 19e eeuw: de broodzetting," *Maandblad Amstelodamum* 55 (1968), 131–34.

Hoffman, Elizabeth, and Joel Mokyr. "Peasants, potatoes and poverty: transaction costs in pre-famine Ireland," in Gary Saxonhouse and Gavin Wright, eds., *Technique, Spirit and Form in the Making of the Modern Economies, Research in Economic History*, supplement 3 (1984), pp. 115–45.

Hoffman, Philip. *Growth in a Traditional Society* (Princeton University Press, 1996).

Holthuis, Paul. *Frontierstad bij het scheiden van de markt. Deventer: Militair, Demografisch, Economisch, 1578–1648* (Deventer: Arko Uitgeverij, 1993).

Horlings, Edwin. *The Economic Development of the Dutch Service Sector, 1800–1850: Trade and Transport in a Premodern Economy* (Amsterdam: NEHA, 1995).

Howell, Martha. *Commerce before Capitalism in Europe, 1300–1600* (Cambridge University Press, 2010).

Hufton, Olwen. "Social conflict and the grain supply in eighteenth-century France," *Journal of Interdisciplinary History* 14 (1983), 303–31.

Humphries, Jane, and Jacob Weisdorf. "Unreal wages? Real incomes and economic growth in England, 1260–1850," CEPR Discussion Paper no. 1999, April 2017. "The wages of women in England, 1260–1850," *Journal of Economic History* 75 (2015), 405–47.

Israel, Jonathan I. "The phases of the Dutch *straatvaart* (1590–1713): a chapter in the economic history of the Mediterranean," *Tijdschrift voor geschiedenis* 99 (1986), 1–30.

Jager, J. L. de. *Volksgebruiken in Nederland* (Utrecht: Het Spectrum, 1981).

Jansen, Michael. *De industriële ontwikkeling in Nederland, 1800–1850* (Amsterdam: NEHA, 1999).

Jansen, P. C. "Armoede in Amsterdam aan het eind van de achttiende eeuw," *Tijdschrift voor geschiedenis* 88 (1975), 613–25.

Jasny, N. *Competition among Grains* (Stanford University, Food Research Institute, 1940).

Jobse-van Putten, Jozien. *Eenvoudig maar voedzaam: cultuurgeschiedenis van de dagelijkse maaltijd in Nederland* (Nijmegen: SUN, 1995).

Jonge, J. A. de. *De industrialisatie in Nederland tussen 1850 en 1914* (Amsterdam: Scheltema en Holkema, 1968).

Jongste, Jan A. F. de. "The restoration of the Orangist regime in 1747: the modernity of a 'Glorious Revolution'," in Margaret Jacob and Wijnand Mijnhardt, eds., *The Dutch Republic in the Eighteenth Century: Decline, Enlightenment, and Revolution* (Ithaca, NY: Cornell University Press, 1992), pp. 32–59.

Kaplan, Steven L. *The Bakers of Paris and the Bread Question, 1700–1775* (Chapel Hill, NC: University of North Carolina Press, 1996).

Bread, Politics and Political Economy in the Reign of Louis XV, 2 vols. (The Hague: Martinus Nijhoff, 1976).

Provisioning Paris: Merchants and Millers in the Grain and Flour Trade during the Eighteenth Century (Ithaca, NY: Cornell University Press, 1984).

Kappelhof, Ton. "Laverend tussen Mars en Mercurius," in A. Voss, ed., *'s-Hertogenbosch: de geschiedenis van een Brabantse stad, 1629–1990* (Zwolle: Waanders, 1997), pp. 55–78.

Kemper, J. de Bosch. *Geschiedkundig Onderzoek naar de Armoede in Ons Vaderland* (Haarlem, 1851).

Kernkamp, J. H. *De handel op den vijand, 1572–1609*, vol. II (Utrecht, 1931).

Khaustava, Ekaterina, and Paul Richard Sharp. "A note on Danish living standards using historical wage series, 1731–1913," *Journal of European Economic History* 44 (2015), 143–72.

Klein, Peter W. "Kwantitatieve aspecten van de Amsterdamse roggehandel in de 17e eeuw en de Europese economische geschiedenis," in Johan de Vries, ed., *Ondernemende geschiedenis* (The Hague: Martinus Nijhoff, 1977), pp. 75–89.

Traditionele ondernemers en economische groei in Nederland, 1850–1914 (Haarlem, 1966).

Klooster, Wim. "An overview of Dutch trade with the Americas, 1600–1800," in Johannes Postma and Victor Enthoven, eds., *Riches from Atlantic Commerce: Dutch Transatlantic Trade and Shipping, 1585–1817* (Leiden: Brill, 2003), pp. 365–83.

Knibbe, Merrijn. *Agriculture in the Netherlands, 1851–1950* (Amsterdam: NEHA, 1993).

"De hoofelijke beschikbaarheid van voedsel en de levensstandaard in Nederland," *Tijdschrift voor sociale en economische geschiedenis* 4 (2007), 71–107.

Knotter, Ad. *Economische transformatie en stedelijke arbeidsmarkt* (Zwolle: Waanders, 1991).

Knotter, Ad, and Hans Moskee. "Conjunctuur en levenstandaard in Amsterdam, 1815–1855," *Tijdschrift voor sociale geschiedenis* 12 (1986), 153–81.

Köllmann, Wolfgang. *Bevölkerung in der industriellen Revolution* (Göttingen: Vandenhoeck & Ruprecht, 1974).

Komlos, John, and David Landes. "Anachronistic economics: grain storage in medieval England," *Economic History Review* 44 (1991), 36–45.

Koopmans, Caroline. *Dordrecht 1811–1914* (Hilversum: Verloren, 1992).

Kopsidas, Michael. "The creation of a Westphalian rye market, 1820–1870: leading and following regions; a co-integration analysis," *Jahrbuch für Wirtschaftgeschichte* 2 (2002), 85–112.

"Peasants and markets: market integration and agricultural development in Westphalia, 1780–1880," in Piet van Cruyningen and Erik Thoen, eds., *Food Supply, Demand and Trade* (Turnhout: Brepols, 2012), pp. 189–215.

Kopsidas, Michael, and Klaus-Joachim Lorenzen-Schmidt. "North-west Germany, 1000–1750," in Van Molle and Segers, eds., *The Agro-Food Market*, pp. 261–92.

Korthals Altes, W. L. *Van £ Hollands tot Nederlandse f: de geschiedenis van de Nederlandse geld eenheid* (Amsterdam: Boom, 1996).

Kuijk, J. Van. *De broodzetting: onnut, schadelijk, ongeoorloofd* (Amsterdam: J. H. Gebhard en Comp., 1852).

Kuijpers, Erika. *Migrantenstad: immigratie en sociale verhoudingen in 17de-eeuws Amsterdam* (Hilversum: Verloren, 2005).

Kula, Witwold. *Measure and Men* (Princeton University Press, 1986).

Kunst, A. J. M. Van. *Sint Elisabeths-gasthuis tot Gereformeerd Burgerweeshuis (1485–1814)* (Assen: Van Gorcum, 1956).

Kuppers, Willem, and Remi van Schaïk. "Levensstandaard en stedelijke economie te Zutphen in de 15de en 16de eeuw," *Bijdragen en mededelingen "Gelre"* 72 (1981), 1–45.

Kuttner, Erich. *Het hongerjaar, 1566* (Amsterdam: Amsterdamsche Boek- en Courantmaatschappij, 1949).

Kuys, Jan, and Hans Bots, eds. *Nijmegen: geschiedenis van de oudste stad van Nederland*, 2 vols. (Nijmegen, n.d.).

Labrousse, C.-E. *La crise de l'économie française à la fin de l'Ancien Régime et au début de la Révolution* (Paris: PUF, 1943).

Esquisse du mouvement des prix et des revenues en France au XVIII siècle (Paris: Dalloz, 1933).

Lane, Frederic C. *Venice: A Maritime Republic* (Baltimore, Md.: Johns Hopkins University Press, 1973).

Lebrun, François. "Les crises démographiques en France aux XVIIe et XVIIIe siècles," *Annales. Économies, sociétés, civilisations* 35 (1980), 205–34.

Leeuwen, Bas van, and Jan Luiten van Zanden. "The character of growth before 'modern growth'? The GDP of Holland between 1347 and 1807," Center for Global Economic History Working Paper no. 4, www/cgeh.nl/working-paper-series/

Leeuwen, Marco van. *Bijstand in Amsterdam, ca. 1800–1850* (Zwolle: Waanders, 1990).

De rijke Republiek, 1500–1800, vol. I, and *De eenheidsstaat, 1800–1890,* vol. II,
in Jacques van Gerweren and Marco van Leeuwen, *Zoeken naar zekerheid:
risicos preventive, verzekering en andere zekerheids regelingen in Nederland,
1500–2000* (The Hague and Amsterdam: NEHA, 2000).

Lesger, Clé. *Het winkellandschap van Amsterdam: stedelijke structuur en
winkelbedrijf in de vroegmoderne en moderne tijd, 1550–2000* (Hilversum:
Verloren, 2013).

Huur en conjunctuur (Amsterdam: Historisch Seminarium van de Universiteit
van Amsterdam, 1986).

"Patterns of retail location and urban form in Amsterdam in the mid-
eighteenth century," *Urban History* 38 (2011), 24–47.

Lewis, W. Arthur. "Economic development with unlimited supplies of labor,"
Manchester School of Economic and Social Studies 22 (1954), 139–91.

Lintsen, H. W. *Molenbedrijf en meelfabriek in Nederland in de negentiende eeuw*
(The Hague: 1989).

"Stoom als symbol van de Industriële Revolutie," *Jaarboek voor de
geschiedenis van bedrijf en techniek* 5 (1988), 109–37.

Loos, D. de. "Ons dagelijksch brood," *De economist* 33 (1884), 581–90.

López Losa, Ernesto, and Santiago Piquero Zarauz. "Spanish real wages in the
north-western European mirror, 1500–1800: on the timing and magnitude
of the little divergence in Europe," AEHE Working Paper, 2016.

Lourens, Piet, and Jan Lucassen. *Inwoneraantallen van Nederlandse steden, ca.
1300–1800* (Amsterdam: NEHA, 1997).

Lucassen, Jan. *Immigranten in Holland, 1600–1800: een kwantitatieve benadering*
(Amsterdam: CGM, 2002).

"Labour and early modern development," in Karel Davids and Jan
Lucassen, eds., *A Miracle Mirrored* (Cambridge University Press, 1995), pp.
368–73.

"Loonbetaling en muntcirculatie in Nederland (1200–2000)," *Jaarboek voor
munt- en penningkunde* 86 (1999), 1–70.

"The Netherlands, the Dutch, and long-distance migration in the late
sixteenth to early nineteenth centuries," in Nicholas Canny, ed., *Europeans
on the Move: Studies on European Migration, 1500–1800* (Oxford University
Press, 1994).

"Zeevarenden," in L. M. Akveld *et al.,* eds., *Maritieme geschiedenis der
Nederlanden,* vol. II (Bussum: De Boer Maritiem, 1977), pp. 131–32.

Maas, Jan van der, and Leo Noordegraaf. "Smakelijk eten:
aardappelconsumptie in Holland in de achttiende eeuw en het begin van de
negentiende eeuw," *Tijdschrift voor sociale geschiedenis* 9 (1983), 188–220.

Magagna, Victor. "Food and politics: the power of bread in European culture,"
in Beat Kümin, ed., *A Cultural History of Food,* vol. IV: *The Early Modern
Age* (London and New York: Berg, 2012), pp. 65–86.

Malanima, Paolo. "When did England overtake Italy? Medieval and early
modern divergence in prices and wages," *European Review of Economic
History* 17 (2013), 45–70.

Marglin, Stephen. "What do bosses do? The origins and functions of hierarchy
in capitalist production," *Review of Radical Political Economy,* 6 (1974),
60–112; 7 (1975), 20–37.

Marin, Brigitte. "Organisation annonaire, crise alimentaire et réformes," in Marin and Virlouvet, eds., *Nourrir les cités*, pp. 389–417.

Marin, Brigitte, and Catherine Virlouvet, eds. *Nourrir les cités de Méditerranée: Antiquité – Temps modernes* (Paris: Maisonneuve & Larose, 2003).

Martinat, Monica. "Le blé du pape: système annonaire et logiques économiques à Rome à l'époque moderne," *Annales. Histoire, sciences sociales* 54 (1999), 219–44.

Le juste marché: le système annonaire romain aux XVIe et XVIIe siècles (Rome: École Française de Rome, 2004).

Marx, Karl, *Capital*, vol. I (1867; London: Penguin, 1967).

Matthey, T. B. M. *Westeremden: het verleden van een Gronings terpdorp* (Groningen, 1975).

Mattozzi, I., *et al.* "Il politico e il pane a Venezia, 1570–1650: camieri e governo della sussistenza," *Società e Storia* 20 (1983), 271–303.

McCants, Anne. *Civic Charity in the Golden Age: Orphan Care in Early Modern Amsterdam* (Urbana and Chicago: University of Illinois Press, 1997).

"Monotonous but not meager, the diet of burgher orphans in early modern Amsterdam," *Research in Economic History* 14 (1992), 69–116.

McCloskey, D. N., and J. Nash. "Corn at interest: the extent and cost of grain storage in medieval England," *American Economic Review* 74 (1984), 174–87.

Meere, J. M. M. de. *Economische ontwikkeling en levensstandaard in Nederland gedurende de eerste helft van de negentiende eeuw* (The Hague: Martinus Nijhoff, 1982).

Meuvret, Jean. "Les crises de subsistance et la démographie de la France d'Ancien Régime," *Population* 1 (1946), 643–50.

Le problème des subsistances à l'époque de Louis XIV (Paris: Mouton, 1977).

Metz, Rainer. *Geld, Währung und Preisentwicklung: der Niederrheinraum im europäischen Vergleich* (Frankfurt: Knapp, 1990).

Meyer, Jean. *La noblesse bretonne au XVIIIe siècle*, 2 vols. (Paris: SEVPEN, 1966).

Miller, Judith A. *Mastering the Market: The State and the Grain Trade in Northern France, 1700–1860* (Cambridge University Press, 1999).

"Politics and urban provisioning crises: bakers, police, and parlements in France, 1750–93," *Journal of Modern History* 64 (1992), 227–62.

Mokyr, Joel. "Industrialization and poverty in Ireland and the Netherlands," *Journal of Interdisciplinary History* 10 (1990), 429–59.

Industrialization in the Low Countries, 1795–1850 (New Haven, Conn.: Yale University Press, 1976).

Molle, Leen van, and Yves Segers, eds. *The Agro-Food Market: Production, Distribution and Consumption* (Turnhout: Brepols, 2013).

Monahan, W. Gregory. *Years of Sorrows: The Great Famine of 1709 in Lyon* (Columbus: Ohio State University Press, 1993).

Montanari, Massimo. *The Culture of Food* (Oxford: Blackwell, 1993),

Moore, D. C. "The Corn Laws and high farming," *Economic History Review* 18 (1965), 544–61.

Morgan, Kenneth. "The organization of the colonial American rice trade," *William and Mary Quarterly* 52 (1995), 433–52.

Morineau, Michel. "La pomme de terre au XVIII siècle," *Annales. Économies, sociétés, civilisations* 25 (1970), 1767–84.

"Rations militaires et rations moyennes en Holland au XVIII siècle," *Annales. Économies, sociétés, civilisations* 18 (1963), 521–31.

Muldrew, Craig. "The importance of the food trade in urban credit networks in early modern England: the example of King's Lynn," in Piet Van Cruyningen and Erik Thun, eds., *Food Supply, Demand and Trade* (Turnhout: Brepols, 2012), pp. 173–87.

Muller, P. N. "Iets over de broodzetting," *De economist* (1853), 52–61.

Murphey, Rhoads. "Provisioning Istanbul," *Food and Foodways* 2 (1988), 217–63.

Nash, R. C. "South Carolina and the Atlantic economy in the late seventeenth and eighteenth centuries," *Economic History Review* 45 (1992), 684–85.

Naudé, W. *Die Getreidehandelspolitik und Kriegsmagazinverwaltung Preussens* (Berlin: Paul Parey, vol. I, 1896; vol. II, 1901; vol. III, 1910).

Neal, Larry. *The Rise of Financial Capitalism* (Cambridge University Press, 1990).

Nederlandse vereniging van meel fabrikanten. *Het broodverbruik in Nederland* (The Hague: Martinus Nijhoff, 1963).

Nicola, G. C., J. F. R. Nievergeld, and G. Keller. *Jaarboekje voor broodbakkers* (The Hague: K. Fuhri, 1856).

Nieuwenhuis, Tom. *Keeshonden en Prinsmannen: Durgerdam, Ransdorp en Holisloot, 1780–1813*, Amsterdamse Historische Reeks 11 (Amsterdam: Historisch Seminarium van de Universiteit van Amsterdam, 1986)

Noordegraaf, Leo. "Levensstandaard en levensmiddelenpolitiek in Alkmaar vanaf het eind van de 16de tot in het begin van de 19de eeuw," in M. van der Bijl *et al.*, eds., *Van Spaans beleg tot Bataafse tijd: Alkmaars stedelijk leven in de 17 de en 18 de eeuw*, Alkmaar Historische Reeks 4 (Zutphen: De Walburg Pers, 1980), pp. 55–100.

Nooten, G. E. van. *Beschouwingen omtrent de broodzetting* (Schoonhoven, 1845).

Ó Grada, Cormac. "Making famine history," *Journal of Economic Literature* 45 (2007), 5–38.

Ó Grada, Cormac, and Jean-Michel Chevet. "Famine and market in Ancien Régime France," *Journal of Economic History* 62 (2002), 706–33.

Offermans, P. H. M. G. *Arbeid en levensstandaard in Nijmegen omstreeks de reductie (1550–1600)* (Zutphen: De Walburg Pers, 1972).

Ogilvie, Sheilagh. "The economics of guilds," *Journal of Economic Perspectives* 28 (2014), 169–92.

Oldewelt, W. F. H. "De Hollandse imposten en ons beeld van de conjunctuur tijdens de Republiek," *Jaarboek Amstelodamum* 47 (1955), 48–80.

Olson, Mancur. *The Rise and Decline of Nations: Economic Growth, Stagflation, and Social Rigidities* (New Haven, Conn.: Yale University Press, 1982).

The Theory of Collective Action: Public Goods and the Theory of Groups (Cambridge, Mass.: Harvard University Press, 1965).

Ormrod, David, *English Grain Exports and the Structure of Agrarian Capitalism, 1700–1760* (Hull University Press, 1985).

The Rise of Commercial Empires (Cambridge University Press, 2003).

Otterloo, Anneke H. Van. *Eten en eetlust in Nederland, 1840–1990* (Amsterdam: Bert Bakker, 1990).

Outhwaite, R. B. "Dearth and government intervention in English grain markets, 1590–1700," *Economic History Review* 34 (1981), 389–406.

"Dearth, the English crown and the 'crisis of the 1590s'," in Peter Clark, ed., *The European Crisis of the 1590s* (London: George Allen & Unwin, 1985).

Overvoorde, J. C., and J. G. Ch. Joosting. *De Gilden van Utrecht tot 1528* (The Hague: Martinus Nijhoff, 1896).

Özveren, Eyüp. "Black Sea and the grain provisioning of Istanbul in the *longue durée*," in Marin and Virlouvet, eds., *Nourrir les cités*, pp. 223–49.

Paping, Richard. *Voor een handvol stuivers* (Groningen: NAHI, 1995).

Parziale, Lavinia. "Aspetti della politica milanese in materia annonaria," in Marin and Virlouvet, eds., *Nourrir les cités*, pp. 321–48.

Perks, W. A. G. *Zes eeuwen molens in Utrecht* (Utrecht: Het Spectrum, 1974).

Perlairet, Michael. "The descent into a dark age: Byzantine Europe, c. 400–800 A.D.," in Philipp Robinson Rössner, ed., *Cities – Coins – Commerce* (Stuttgart: Franz Steiner Verlag, 2012), pp. 1–24.

Persson, Karl Gunnar. *Grain Markets in Europe, 1500–1900: Integration and Deregulation* (Cambridge University Press, 1999).

"On corn, Turgot, and elasticities: the case for deregulation of grain markets in mid-eighteenth century France," *Scandinavian Economic History Review* 41 (1993), 37–50.

"The seven lean years, elasticity traps, and intervention in grain markets in pre-industrial Europe," *Economic History Review* 49 (1996), 692–714.

Petersen, Christian. *Bread and the British Economy, c. 1770–1870* (Aldershot: Scolar Press, 1995).

Peuter, Rogier de. *Brussel in de achttiende eeuw* (Brussels: VUB Press, 1999).

Pfeil, Tom. *"Tot redding van het Vaderland": het primaat van de Nederlandse overheidsfinanciën in de Bataafs-Franse Tijd, 1795–1810* (Amsterdam: NEHA, 1998).

Post, John D. *The Last Great Subsistence Crisis in the Western World* (Baltimore, Md.: Johns Hopkins University Press, 1977).

Posthumus, N. W. *De geschiedenis van de Leidse lakenindustrie*, 3 vols. (The Hague: Martinus Nijhoff, 1908–39).

Pot, G. P. M. *Arm Leiden: levensstandaard, bedeling en bedeelden, 1750–1854* (Hilversum: Verloren, 1994).

Prak, Maarten. "Corporate politics in the Low Countries," in Maarten Prak, ed., *Craft Guilds in the Early Modern Low Countries: Work, Power and Representation* (Aldershot: Ashgate, 2006), pp. 74–106.

Gouden Eeuw: het raadsel van de Republiek (Amsterdam: Boom, 2012).

Prak, Maarten, and Jan Luiten van Zanden. *Nederland en het poldermodel* (Amsterdam: Bert Bakker, 2013).

Priester, Peter. *De economische ontwikkeling van de landbouw in Groningen, 1800–1910*, AAG Bijdragen 31 (Wageningen: Afdeling Agrarische Geschiedenis, 1991).

Geschiedenis van de Zeeuwse landbouw circa 1600–1910, AAG Bijdragen 37 (Wageningen: Afdeling Agrarische Geschiedenis, 1998).

Pult Quaglia, Anna Maria. "Controls over food supplies in Florence in the late
XVIth and early XVIIth centuries," *Journal of European Economic History* 9
(1980), 449–57.

"Per provvedere ai popoli": il sistema annonario nella Toscana dei Medici
(Florence: Leo S. Olschki Editore, 1990).

Rahlf, Thomas. *Getreide in der Social- und Wirtschaftsgeschichte vom 16. bis 18.*
Jahrhundert: das Beispiel Köln im regionalen Vergleich (Trier: Auenthal Verlag,
1996).

Ramsey, F. P. "A contribution to the theory of taxation," *The Economic Journal*
37 (1927), 47–61.

Reddy, William. *The Rise of Market Culture* (Cambridge University Press, 1984).

Reinhardt, Volker. *Überleben in der frühneuzeitlichen Stadt: Annona und*
Getreideversorgung in Rom, 1563–1797 (Tübingen: Max Niemeyer Verlag,
1991).

Revel, Jacques. "A capital city's privileges: food supplies in early modern
Rome," in Robert Forster and Orest Ramum, eds., *Food and Drink in*
History (Baltimore, Md.: Johns Hopkins University Press, 1979), pp.
37–49 [first published in *Annales. Économies, sociétés, civilisations* 30 (1975),
563–74].

"Le grain de Rome et la crise de l'Annone dans la seconde moitié du XVIIIe
siècle," *Mélange de l'École française de Rome* 1 (1972), 201–81.

Ridolfini, Leonardo. "L'histoire immobile? Six centuries of real wages in France
from Louis IX to Napoleon III: 1250–1860," Scola Superiore Sant' Anna,
Pisa, Italy, Working Paper 2017/14, June 2017.

Riel, Arthur van. "Trials of convergence: prices, markets and industrialization in
the Netherlands, 1800–1913," Ph.D. thesis, Utrecht University, 2018.

Riley, James C. *International Government Finance and the Amsterdam Capital*
Market, 1740–1815 (Cambridge University Press, 1980).

Ringrose, David. *Madrid and the Spanish Economy, 1560–1850* (Berkeley and
Los Angeles: University of California Press, 1983).

Roeck, Bernd. *Bäcker, Brot und Getreide in Augsburg* (Sigmaringen: Jan
Thorbecke Verlag, 1987).

Roessingh, H. K. "Beroep en bedrijf op de Veluwe," *AAG Bijdragen* 13 (1965),
181–274.

Inlands tabak, AAG Bijdragen 20 (Wageningen: Afdeling Agrarische
Geschiedenis, 1976).

Romani, M. A. *Nella spirale di una crisi: popolazione, mercato e prezzi a Parma tra*
Cinque e Seicento (Milan: Giuffrè, 1975).

Rommes, Ronald. *Oost-west, Utrecht best? Driehonderd jaar migratie en migranten*
in de stad Utrecht (begin 16e – begin 19e eeuw) (Amsterdam: Stichting
Amsterdamse Historische Reeks, 1998).

Root, Hilton L. *The Fountain of Privilege: Political Foundations of Markets in*
Old Regime France and England (Berkeley and Los Angeles: University of
California Press, 1994).

Roover, Raymond de. "The concept of just price: theory and economic policy,"
Journal of Economic History 18 (1958), 418–34.

Ross, Alan S. C. "The Assize of Bread," *Economic History Review* 9 (1956),
332–42.

Rössner, Philipp Robinson. "Mercantilism as an effective resource management strategy," in Moritz Isenmann, ed., *Mercantilismus: Wiederaufnahme einer Debate* (Stuttgart: Fritz Steiner Verlag, 2014), pp. 39–64.

Royen, P. C. van. "The first phase of the Dutch Straatvaart (1591–1605): fact and fiction," *International Journal of Maritime History* 2 (1990), 69–102.

Zeevarenden op de koopvaardijvloot omstreeks 1700 (The Hague: De Bataafse Leeuw, 1987).

Rudé, Georges. *The Crowd in History: A Study of Popular Disturbance in France and England, 1738–1840* (New York: Wiley and Sons, 1964).

Saalfel, Diedrich. "Methodische Darlegung zur Einkommensentwicklung und Sozialstruktur, 1760 bis 1860 am Beispiel einiger deutscher Städte," *Schriften des Vereins für Socialpolitik* 83 (Berlin, 1975), 227–59.

Sargent, Thomas J., and François R. Velde. *The Big Problem of Small Change* (Princeton University Press, 2003).

Schaïk, Remi van. "Marktbeheersing: Overheidsbemoeienis met de levensmiddelenvoorziening in de Nederlanden (14de–19de eeuw)," in Clé Lesger and Leo Noordegraaf, eds., *Ondernemers en bestuurders* (Amsterdam: NEHA,1999), pp. 465–89.

"Prijs- en levensmiddelenpolitiek in de Noordelijke Nederlanden van de 14e tot de 17e eeuw: bronnen en problemen," *Tijdschrift voor geschiedenis* 91 (1978), 214–55.

Schama, Simon. *Patriots and Liberators: Revolution in the Netherlands, 1780-1813* (New York: Alfred Knopf, 1977).

Scholliers, E. *De levensstandaard in de XVe en XVIe eeuw te Antwerpen* (Antwerp: De Sikkel, 1960).

"Peilingen naar het consumptiepatroon in de pre-industriële samenleving," in J. Hannes, ed., *Consumptiepatronen en prijsindices* (Brussels: Centrum voor Hedendaagse Sociale Geschiedenis, 1981), pp. 9–16.

"Le pouvoir d'achat dans les Pays-Bas au XVIe siècle," in Jan Craeybeckx, ed., *Album aangeboden aan Charles Verlinden* (Ghent: Universa, 1975), pp. 305–30.

Scholliers, E. and Christiaan Vandenbroeke. "Structuren en conjuncturen in de Zuidelijke Nederlanden, 1480–1800," *Algemene geschiedenis der Nederlanden* (Haarlem: Fibua-Van Dishoek, 1980), pp. 252–310.

Schumpeter, Joseph. *History of Economic Analysis* (New York: Oxford University Press, 1954).

Scott, James C. *The Moral Economy of the Peasant* (New Haven, Conn.: Yale University Press, 1976).

Scott, Tom. *The City-State in Europe, 1000–1600* (Oxford University Press, 2012).

See, Henri. "Le commerce des Hollandais à Nantes pendant la minorité de Louis XIV," *Tijdschrift voor geschiedenis* 41 (1926), 246–60.

Sella, Domenico. *Crisis and Continuity: The Economy of Spanish Lombardy in the Seventeenth Century* (Cambridge, Mass.: Harvard University Press, 1979).

Serrurier, L., *et al. Het bakkersbedrijf te Amsterdam* (Amsterdam, 1903).

Shammas, Carole. "The eighteenth-century English diet and economic change," *Explorations in Economic History* 21 (1984), 254–69.

Sharp, Buchanan. *Famine and Scarcity in Late Medieval and Early Modern England: The Regulation of Grain Marketing, 1256–1631* (Cambridge University Press, 2016).

Sharp, Paul R. "1846 and all that: the rise and fall of British wheat protection in the 19th century," Discussion paper 06–14, Department of Economics, University of Copenhagen, 2006.

"Malta and the nineteenth-century grain trade: British free trade in a microcosm of Empire?" in J. Chircop (ed.), *Colonial Encounters: Maltese Experiences of British Rule 1800–1970s* (Rabat, Malta: Horizons, 2015), pp. 1–13.

Sickenga, Folkert Nicholaas. *Bijdrage tot de geschiedenis der belastingen in Nederland* (Leiden, 1864).

Slicher van Bath, B. H. "Een landbouwbedrijf in de tweede helft van de zestiende eeuw," *Agronomisch-historisch bijdragen* 4 (1958), 67–188.

"Robert Loder en Rienck Hemmema," *It beaken* 20 (1958), 89–117.

Smit, Christianne. *Omwille der billijkheid: de strijd over de invoering van de inkomstenbelasting in Nederland* (Amsterdam: Wereldbibliotheek, 2002).

Smits, Jan-Pieter, Edwin Horlings, and Jan Luiten van Zanden. *Dutch GNP and its Components, 1800–1913*, Monograph Series no. 5 (Groningen: Growth and Development Centre, 2000).

Solar, Peter, and Jan Tore Klovland. "New series for agricultural prices in London, 1770–1914," *Economic History Review* 64 (2011), 72–87.

Soltow, Lee, and Jan Luiten van Zanden. *Income and Wealth Inequality in the Netherlands, 16th – 20th Century* (Amsterdam: Het Spinhuis, 1996).

Stalweit, August. *Die Getreidehandelspolitik und Kriegsmagazinverwaltung Preussens, 1756–1806* (Berlin: Paul Parey, 1931).

Stephenson, Judy. "Real wages? Contractors, workers and pay in London building trades, 1650–1800," *Economic History Review* 71 (2018), 106–32.

Stern, W. M. "The bread crisis in Britain, 1795–96," *Economica* 31 (1964), 168–87.

Stigler, George. "The theory of economic regulation," *The Bell Journal of Economics and Management Science* 2 (1971), 3–21.

Stone, Richard D. *The Interstate Commerce Commission and the Railroad Industry: A History of Regulatory Policy* (New York: Praeger, 1991).

Stouff, Louis. *Ravitaillement et alimentation en Provence aux XIVe et XVe siècle* (Paris: Mouton, 1970).

Strauss, Rudolph. "Löhne sowie Brot- und Kartoffelpreise in Chemnitz, 1770 bis 1850," *Jahrbuch für Wirtschaftsgeschichte* 62/4(1962), 144–90.

Studer, P. *The Oak Book of Southampton of c. A.D. 1300* (Southampton, 1910–11)

Tassenaar, Vincent. *Het Verloren Arcadia: de biologische levensstandaard in Drenthe, 1815–1860* (Capelle a/d Ijssel: Labyrint Publications, 2000).

Teall, John. "The grain supply of the Byzantine Empire, 330–1025," *Dumbarton Oaks Papers*, 13 (1959), 87–139.

Teeuwen, D. "A penny for the poor: the widespread practice of monetary charitable donations in Dutch towns, 17th–18th century," *Tijdschrift voor sociale en economische geschiedenis* 11 (2014), 15–38.

504   Bibliography

Tellingen, B. D. H. "Het verbruik van tarwe en rogge in de stad Groningen in de jaren 1821 en 1822, en in de jaren 1827–1856," *Staathuishoudkundig jaarboekje* 9 (1857), 320–21.

Teuteberg, Hans J., and Günter Wiegelmann. *Unser tägliche Kost: Geschichte und regionale Prägung* (Münster: Coppenrath, 1986).

Thestrup, Poul. *The Standard of Living in Copenhagen, 1730–1800* (Copenhagen: G. E. C. Gads Forlag, 1971).

Thompson, E. P. "The moral economy of the English crowd in the eighteenth century," *Past and Present*, 50 (1971), 76–136.

"The moral economy reviewed," in *Customs in Common* (New York: W. W. Norton, 1991), pp. 259–351.

Thwaites, Wendy. "The assize of bread in eighteenth-century Oxford," *Oxoniensia* 51 (1986), 171–81.

Tielhof, Milja van. "Grain provision in Holland, ca. 1490 – ca. 1570," in Peter Hoppenbrouwers and Jan Luiten van Zanden, eds., *Peasants into Farmers? The Transformation of Rural Economy and Society in the Low Countries (Middle Ages – 19th Century) in Light of the Brenner Debate* (Turnhout: Brepols, 2001), pp. 202–19.

De Hollandse graanhandel, 1470–1570: Koren op de Amsterdamse molen, Hollandse Historische Reeks 23 (The Hague: Stichting Hollandse Historische Reeks, 1995).

The "Mother of All Trades": The Baltic Grain Trade in Amsterdam from the Late 16th to the Early 19th Century (Leiden: Brill, 2002).

"Stedelijke regulering van diensten op de stapelmarkt: de Amsterdams korengilden," in Clé Lesger and Leo Noordegraaf, eds., *Ondernemers en bestuurders* (Amsterdam: NEHA, 1999), pp. 491–523.

Tilly, Charles. *Coercion, Capital, and European States, AD 990–1990* (Oxford: Blackwell, 1990).

The Contentious French (Cambridge, Mass.: Harvard University Press, 1986).

"Food supply and public order in modern Europe," in Charles Tilly, ed., *The Formation of National States in Western Europe* (Princeton University Press, 1975), pp. 380–455.

Tilly, Louise A. "Food entitlement, famine and conflict," *Journal of Interdisciplinary History* 14 (1983), 333–49.

"The food riot as a form of political conflict in France," *Journal of Interdisciplinary History* 2 (1971), 23–57.

Toutain, J.-C. "La consommation alimentaire en France de 1789 à 1964," *Économies et Sociétés* 5 (1971), 1909-23.

"Food rations in France in the eighteenth and early nineteenth centuries: a comment," *Economic History Review* 48 (1995), 769–73.

Tracy, James D. *The Founding of the Dutch Republic: War, Finance, and Politics in Holland, 1572–1588* (Oxford University Press, 2008).

"Habsburg grain policy and Amsterdam politics: the career of Sheriff Willem Dirkszoon Baerdes, 1542–1566," *The Sixteenth Century Journal* 14 (1983), 293–319.

"Holland's new fiscal regime, 1572–1576," in Oscar Gelderblom, ed., *The Political Economy of the Dutch Republic* (Farnham: Ashgate, 2009), pp. 41–54.

Tussenbroek, Gabri van, *Amsterdam in 1597: kroniek van een cruciaal jaar* (Amsterdam and Antwerp: L. J. Veen, 2009).

Unger, Richard. "Feeding Low Countries towns: the grain trade in the fifteenth century," *Revue Belge de philologie et d' histoire* 77 (1999), 329–58.

A History of Brewing in Holland, 900–1900: Economy, Technology and the State (Leiden: Brill, 2001).

Unger, Willem Sbrand, *De levensmiddelenvoorziening der Hollandschen steden in de Middeleeuwen* (Amsterdam, 1916).

Usher, Abbot Payson. *The History of the Grain Trade in France* (Cambridge, Mass.: Harvard University Press, 1913).

Vandenbroeke, Christiaan. "Aardappelteelt en aardappelverbruik in de 17e en 18e eeuw," *Tijdschrift voor geschiedenis* 82 (1969), 49–68.

Landbouw in the Zuidelijke Nederlanden, 1650–1815," in *Algemene geschiedenis der Nederlanden*, vol. VIII (Haarlem: Van Dishoek, 1979), pp. 73–101.

"Prijzen en lonen als social-economische verklaringsvariabelen (14e–20e eeuw)," *Handelingen der Maatschappij voor Geschiedenis en Oudheidkunde te Gent* 36 (1982), 103–37.

Vanhaute, Eric. "The European subsistence crisis of 1845–50: a comparative perspective," in Vanhaute, Paping, and Ó Grada, eds., *When the Potato Failed*, pp. 15–40.

Vanhaute, Eric, Richard Paping, and Cormac Ó Grada, eds., *When the Potato Failed* (Turnhout: Brepols, 2007).

Varian, Hal R. *Intermediate Microeconomics: A Modern Approach*, 6th edn. (New York: W. W. Norton, 2003).

Verlinden, C., and E. Scholliers, eds., *Dokumenten voor de geschiedenis van prijzen en lonen in Vlaanderen en Brabant*, 4 vols. (Bruges: De Tempel, 1959–73).

Vermeesch, Griet. *Oorlog, steden en staatsvorming: de grenssteden Gorinchem en Doesburg tijdens de geboorte-eeuw van de Republiek (1570–1680)* (Amsterdam University Press, 2006).

Vermosen, E. "The Low Countries, 1000–1750," in Van Molle and Segers, eds., *Agro-Food Market*, pp. 199–224.

Vis, G. N. M. *Het Weeshuis van Woerden* (Hilversum: Verloren, 1996).

Vlis, Ingrid van der. *Van wezen to zijn: vier eeuwen zorg voor kinderen* (Zutphen: Walburg Pers, 2005).

Voort, R. van der. "Gemeentelijke financiën," in Tom Pfeil *et al.*, eds., *Steden en dorpen in last: historische aspecten van locale belastingen en financiën* (Amsterdam: NEHA, 1999), pp. 141–55.

Voskuil, J. J. "Op weg naar luilekkerland," *Bijdragen en mededelingen voor de geschiedenis der Nederlanden* 98 (1983), 460–82.

Vredenberg, J. P. *Als off sij onse eigene kijnder weren: het Burgerweeshuis te Arnhem, 1583–1742* (Arnhem: Gemeente Arnhem, 1983).

Vries, Jan de. *Barges and Capitalism: Passenger Transportation in the Dutch Economy, 1632-1839*, AGG Bijdragen 21 (Wageningen: Afdeling Agrarische Geschiedenis, 1978).

"Between purchasing power and the world of goods: understanding the household economy in early modern Europe," in John Brewer and Roy

Porter, eds., *Consumption and the World of Goods* (London: Routledge, 1993), pp. 85–132.

The Dutch Rural Economy in the Golden Age, 1500–1700 (New Haven, Conn.: Yale University Press, 1974).

"An employer's guide to wages and working conditions in the Netherlands, 1450–1850," in Carol Leonard and Boris Mironov, eds., *Hours of Work and Means of Payment: The Evolution of Conventions in Pre-industrial Europe Proceedings of the XI International Economic History Congress, Milan, September 1994* (Università Bocconi, 1994), pp. 47–63.

European Urbanization 1500–1800 (London: Methuen, 1984).

"How did pre-industrial labor markets function?" in George Grantham and Mary MacKinnen, eds., *The Evolution of Labour Markets* (London: Routledge, 1994), pp. 39–63.

The Industrious Revolution: Consumer Behavior and the Household Economy, 1650 to the Present (Cambridge University Press, 2008).

"The labour market," *Economic and Social History in the Netherlands* 4 (1992), 55–78.

"Peasant demand patterns and economic development: Friesland, 1550–1750," in William N. Parker and Eric L. Jones, eds., *European Peasants and their Markets* (Princeton University Press, 1975), pp. 205–66.

"Playing the market: grain prices, inventory formation, and speculation in the Dutch Republic," unpublished paper.

"The production and consumption of wheat in the Netherlands, with special reference to Zeeland," in B. de Vries, ed., *Het platteland in een veranderende wereld: Boeren en het process van modernisering* (Hilversum: Verloren, 1994), pp. 199–219.

"The Republic's money: money and the economy," *Leidschrift* 13 (1998), 7–30.

"Urban historical demography: graveyards, migrants, and the demographic transition," paper presented at the Cambridge Group Fiftieth Anniversary Conference, 2014.

"Van centrum naar periferie: transport en infrastructuur in het Noorden en Oosten van Nederland tijdens de Republiek," in J. N. H. Elerie and P. H. Pellenbarg, eds., *De welvarende periferie* (Groningen: Regio-Project Uitgevers, 1998), pp. 11–22.

Vries, Jan de, and Ad van der Woude. *The First Modern Economy: Success, Failure and Perseverance of the Dutch Economy, 1500–1815* (Cambridge University Press, 1997).

Vries, Johan de. "De statistiek van in- en uitvoer van de Admiraliteit op de Maaze, 1784–1793," *Economisch-historisch jaarboek* 29 (1961), 188–259; 30 (1963), 236–310.

Wagner, Ulrich, ed. *Geschichte der Stadt Würzburg*, vol. II (Stuttgart: Konrad Weiss Verlag, 2004).

Wallerstein, Immanuel. *The Modern World System*, vol. I (New York: Academic Press, 1974).

Webb, Sidney, and Beatrice. "The Assize of Bread," *Economic Journal* 14 (1904), 196–218.

Weber, Max. *General Economic History* (London: Allen Unwin, 1927 [1923]).

Wee, Herman van der. *Growth of the Antwerp Market and the European Economy*, 3 vols. (The Hague: Martinus Nijhoff, 1963).

Wees, P. J. J. M. van. *Het Burgerweeshuis van Amersfoort* (Amersfoort: Uitgeverij Bekking, 2002).

Weir, David R. "Markets and mortality in France, 1600–1789," in John Walter and Roger Schofield, eds., *Famine, Disease and the Social Order in Early Modern Society* (Cambridge University Press, 1989), pp. 201–34.

Werveke, Hans van. "Les villes belges: histoire des institutions économiques et sociales," in *La ville*, vol. II: *Institutions économiques et sociales* (Brussels: Éditions de la Librarie Encyclopédique, 1955).

Wesoly, Kurt. *Lehrlinge und Handswerksgesellen am Mittelrhein*. Studien zur Frankfurter Geschichte 18 (Frankfurt am Main: Verlag Waldemar Kramer, 1985).

Weststrate, Job, *In het kielzog van moderne markten: handel en scheepvaart op de Rijn, Waal en Ijssel, ca. 1360–1560* (Hilversum: Verloren, 2008).

Wieringa, W. J. *Economische heroriëntering in Nederland in de 19e eeuw* (Groningen, 1955).

Wijffels, A. "De betekenis van de niet-vrije rente en broodrijzen voor de soicaal-economische geschiedenis," *Tijdschrift voor geschiedenis* 70 (1957), 329–39.

Wilde, Brecht De, and Johan Poukens. "Bread provisioning and retail dynamics in the Southern Low Countries: the bakers of Leuven, 1600–1800," *Continuity and Change* 26 (2011), 405–38.

Willems, Bart. *Leven op de pof: krediet bij de Antwerpse middenstand in de achttiende eeuw* (Amsterdam: Aksant, 2009).

Williamson, Jeffrey G. "The impact of the Corn Laws just prior to repeal," *Explorations in Economic History* 27 (1990), 123–56.

Wilson, Charles. "Taxation and the decline of empires: an unfashionable theme," *Bijdragen en Mededelingen van het Historisch Genootschap* 77 (1963), 10–23.

Witteveen, J. "Rye, a daily bread and a daily treat," in *Staple Foods: Proceedings of the Oxford Symposium on Food and Cookery, 1989* (Oxford: Harlan Walker, 1990), pp. 240–45.

Working, H. "The theory of price of storage," *American Economic Review* 39 (1939), 1254–66.

Woude, A. M. van der. "De consumptie van graan, vlees en boter in Holland op het einde van de achttiende eeuw," *AAG Bijdragen* 9 (1963), 127–53.

Het Noorderkwartier, AAG Bijdragen 16, 3 vols. (Wageningen: Afdeling Agrarische Geschiedenis, 1972)

Wrigley, E. A. *People, Cities, and Wealth* (Oxford: Blackwell, 1987).

Yildirim, Onur. "Bread and empire: the workings of grain provisioning in Istanbul," in Marin and Virlouvet, eds., *Nourrir les cités*, pp. 251–72.

Yntema, Richard. "The brewing industry in Holland, 1300–1800: a study in industrial development," unpublished Ph.D. thesis, University of Chicago, 1992.

Zanden, Jan Luiten van. *Arbeid tijdens het handelskapitalisme* (Bergen: Octavo, 1991). English translation: *The Rise and Decline of Holland's Economy* (Manchester University Press, 1993).

De economische ontwikkeling van de Nederlandse landbouw in de negentiende eeuw, 1800–1914, AAG Bijdragen 25 (Wageningen: Afdeling Agrarische Geschiedenis, 1985).

"De introductie van stoom in de Amsterdamse meelfabricage 1828–1855:
over de rol van marktstructuren, ondernemersgedrag en de overheid,"
Jaarboek voor de geschiedenis van bedrijf en techniek 8 (1991), 63–80.

"Kosten van levensonderhoud en loonvorming in Holland en Oost-
Nederland, 1600–1815: de voorbeelden van Kampen en Alkmaar,"
Tijdschrift voor sociale geschiedenis 11 (1985), 309–23.

"Taking the measure of the early modern economy: historical national
accounts for Holland in 1510/14," *European Review of Economic History* 6
(2002), 3–36.

"A third road to capitalism? Proto-industrialization and the moderate nature
of the late medieval crisis in Flanders and Holland, 1350–1550," in Peter
Hoppenbrouwers and Jan Luiten van Zanden, eds., *Peasants into Farmers?*
CORN Publication Series 4 (Turnhout: Brepols, 2001), pp. 85–101.

"What happened to the standard of living before the Industrial Revolution?
New evidence from the western part of the Netherlands," in Robert Allen,
Tonny Bengtsson, and Martin Dribe, eds., *Living Standards in the Past*
(Oxford University Press, 2005), pp. 173–94.

Zanden, Jan Luiten van, and Bas van Bavel. "The jump-start of the Holland
economy during the late medieval crisis, c. 1350- c. 1500," *Economic
History Review* 57 (2004), 503–32.

Zanden, Jan Luiten van, and Bas van Leeuwen. "Persistent but not consistent:
the growth of national income in Holland, 1347–1807," *Explorations in
Economic History* 49 (2012), 119–30.

Zanden, Jan Luiten van, and Arthur van Riel. *The Strictures of Inheritance: The
Dutch Economy in the Nineteenth Century* (Princeton University Press,
2000).

Zanetti, Dante. "Contribution à l'étude des structures économiques:
l'approvisonnement de Pavie au XVIe siècle," *Annales. Économies, sociétés,
civilisations* 18 (1963), 44–62.

Problemi alimentari di un'economia preindustriale (Turin: Boringhieri, 1964).

Zondergeld-Hamer, Aukje. *Een kwestie van goed bestuur: twee eeuwen armenzorg
in Weesp, 1590–1822* (Hilversum: Verloren, 2006).

Zylbergeld, Léon. "Contribution à l'étude des ordonnances du pain du XIIIe
siècle de la *Brodtaxe* de Lübeck (1255)," *Revue belge de philologie et d'histoire*
60 (1982), 263–304.

"Le prix des céréales et du pain à Liège dans la première moitié du XIIIe
siècle," *Revue belge de philologie et d'histoire* 51 (1973), 271–98; 761–85.

"Les regulations du marché du pain au XIIIe siècle en Occident et l'Assize
of Bread de 1266–1267 pour l'Angleterre," in Jean-Marie Duvosquel and
Alain Dierkens, eds. *Villes et campagnes au Moyen Âge: mélanges Georges
Despry* (Liège: Éditions du Perron, 1991), pp. 791–814.

Index

advantage loaves, 30, 35–36, 213, 378
Allen, Robert, 297, 328, 361, 397
Almoezeniers Weeshuis (AWH), *see*
  Almoners' Orphanage
Almoners' Orphanage of Amsterdam, 266,
  290
  crisis years, 298
Annales school, 287
annona, 7–15, 262
  definition, 9
  Italian, 8
  Maltese, 13
  Papal Roman, 10, 13
  Roman, 7
  Spanish, 14
  Venetian, 12
Anti-Corn Law League, 404, 422
Ashley, Sir William, 4, 332
assize, *see* bread price regulation
Assize of Bread, 16, 22, 36, 233, 275,
      377–79, 487, 491, 501, 504, 506
  repealed, 443

Bäckpfunde, *see* advantage loaves
baked grains
  preparation costs, 353
baker's dozen, 96, 189
bakeries
  capital costs of, 182
  density in other countries, 191
  density of, 190–93, 434
  earnings, 217, 220
  earnings after 1855, 433–34
  location of, 194–95
  oven capacity, 182, 200
  rural density of, 108
  scale of production, 194, 201
  size distribution of, 195–99
  specialized in wheat or rye, 210
bakers
  as tax collectors, 188
  beneficiaries of regulation?, 221

coinage problems of, 112
  credit practices, 113
  foreign-born, 344
  grain purchase strategies of, 99
  suppressing competition among, 97
bakers' fee, 83, 180, 190, 195
  efforts to calculate, 183
  historical reflections on, 202
  removal of, 433
  wheat-rye differential,
bakers' guilds, 65, 67, 73, 74
  as recipients of rents, 188
  concept of scale, 200
baking trials, 72, 81, 82, 88, 178, 234
bakloon, *see* bakers' fee
bakproef, *see* baking trials
Baltic grain trade, rise of, 42
barebones food budget, 297, 361
Batavian Republic, 410, 411, 413, 469
  food insecurity in, 261
  millers' fee policies, 178
  milling excise under, 416
beer excise, 140–41
Belgium, *see* Southern Netherlands
Betuwe, *see* Gelderland river region
Black Death, 40, 41
boiled grains, 54–55, 138
  decline of, 331, 447
  preparation costs, 353
bran, 82, 165, 172, 227
Braudel, Fernand, 3, 331
bread bundles, 355–58, 441
bread consumption
  assumed level, 257
  in Holland, 475–77
  rural areas, 475
bread factories, 432, 435
bread grain availability, 307
bread grain consumption
  after 1855, 446
  alternative forms of, 354–55
  by social class, 314

bread grain consumption (*cont.*)
  charity distribution, 316
  compared to other countries, 325–30
  decline in, 364
  from Holland tax data, 317–18
  Holland before 1650, 319–21
  in Friesland, 321
  in Holland cities, 314–17
  in Zeeland, 321
  milling excise data, 310–21
  national totals, 324
  orphanage data, 308–9
  place in pre-industrial diet, 288
  regional differences, 311
bread price commissioners, 65, 81, 84, 85,
      93, 180, 184, 270
  as creators of economic rents, 186
  concept of modal bakery, 199
  of Haarlem, 71
  policy objectives of, 247
  rye prices used by, 160
  weekly price announcements, 228
bread price regulation, 15–22
  abolished, 425
  Antwerp, 1588, 461
  Brielle, 1530, 459
  definition, 17
  diffusion of new system, 375
  effects of removal, 435
  Geneva, 1458, 456
  Groningen, 1404, 1589, 458
  in Antwerp, 376
  in Berlin, 379
  in Cologne, 376
  in Copenhagen, 377
  in England, 377–79
  in France, 379–82
  in medieval England, 22
  in medieval France, 22
  in medieval Netherlands, 23
  in rural areas, 107
  invasive character of, 451
  limited to maximum prices, 424
  medieval origins, 16
  movement to abolish, 424
  new system in Deventer, 56
  new system in Holland, 56
  new system in Nijmegen, 56
  new system origins, 55–60
  new system rules, 65–68
  old system rules, 23–26
  pan-European, 1
  social consequences of, 37
  Utrecht, 1374, 456
bread prices
  announcement of, 67
  Dutch compared to Europe, 406

evasion practices, 96
  in Berlin, 393–95
  in Britain beyond London, 401
  in Cologne, 390
  in Copenhagen, 392
  in Europe, 387
  in German cities, 395
  in international perspective, 440
  in London, 401–5
  in Paris, 397–401
  in Southern Netherlands, 387–90
  maximum and minimum prices, 94
  regional price structures, 245
  rural differentials, 106
  sensitivity to grain prices, 93-94
  structure after 1855, 239, 426–29
  structure before 1596, 239
  structure of, 229–32, 236, 238, 451
  structures abroad, 243
  without regulation, 453
bread quality
  in France, 400
bread riots, 19
bread substitutes, 138
bread yield, 225
  disputes concerning, 78–81
  Eversdijck estimates, 90
  in Cologne, 391
  in Copenhagen, 392
  in England, 377
  in new system regulations, 60, 66, 84
  in old system regulations, 29, 38
broodwegers, see bread price commissioners
broodzetters, see bread price commissioners
broodzetting, see bread price regulation
brottaxe, see bread price regulation
buckwheat
  a food of the poor?, 286
  a pseudo-grain, 54
  decline of, 301, 449
  in crisis of 1630, 265
  lowest cost bread grain, 355
  milling excise, 138, 474
  price advantage lost, 429
budget studies, 288, 301
Burghers' Orphanage of Amsterdam,
  crisis years, 299
  nineteenth-century diet, 300
Burghers' Orphanage of Utrecht,
  290

calmiere, see bread price regulation
Cantillon, Lodewijk, 431
capitalism, 2
capitation tax, 119, 124
  beyond Holland, 125, 128
Charlemagne, 8

circulation of money, 111
coinage, Dutch, 110, 111
Collins, E. J. T., 332
Commelen, Casparus, 290
common means, 62–65, 116, 139, 473
  Holland's review of, 116
  outside Holland, 125, 127
  proposals for reform, 277
  reform of 1680, 143
congiegeld, see grain export licences
constant costs of baking, 81–83, 180
consumer behavior, 135, 137, 139, 140,
    141–42, 371
  response to deregulation, 427
consumer choice, 2, 306, 348–49, 352
  after deregulation, 448
  and standard of living, 361
  constrained by taxation, 333
  criticism of, 283
  of bread bundles, 358
  preference for wheat bread, 236
consumer credit, 113–14
consumer demand
  influence of bread price structure, 232
consumer price index, 220
consumer protection, 251
consumer savings, 444
Continental System, 161
coordination failure, 18
corn bounties, British, 404, 442
Corn Laws, British, 404, 442
cost of living, 220
  definition, 353
counterfactual history, 453
credit risk, 113
crisis of 1596, 58–59
crisis of 1629–31, 266, 463
crisis of 1698–1700, 465–67
crisis of 1708–10, 467
crisis of 1747–48, 276–78, 407, 454
crisis of 1789, 278–80
crisis of 1795, 469
crisis of 1845–47, 304, 422
crisis of Napoleonic era, 470
crisis periods, 254–60, 274, 453
  forced sale of grain, 263
  intervention in grain markets, 262–63
  price lowering strategies, 264–70
  prohibition of luxury baking, 263
  regional differences, 260
cross-subsidization, 208–10, 221, 229,
    392, 393, 434, 441, 451
Cultuurstelsel, 443
currency devaluation, 440
  in France, 400
  in Southern Netherlands, 389

Dekker, Rudolf, 136
Delamare, Nicolas, 380–81, 397
demand elasticities for foodstuffs,
    284
demand elasticity for beer, 140
demand elasticity for bread, 37, 119, 124,
    134, 359
deregulation
  effect on baking, 432–35
  effect on bread prices, 427
  effect on consumers, 443–49
  effect on milling, 429–32
  effect on wheat bread consumption,
    445
  macroeconomic effects, 435–39, 450
  removal of costs, 444
Dutch bread types, 49–54
  relative price adjustments to, 233

economies of scale, 441, 455
  in baking, 182, 434
efficiency, of millers and bakers, 441
elasticities of supply and demand, 436
Engel's law, 223, 284, 358
England
  bread consumption in, 328
  wheat bread revolution in, 332–33
Eversdijck, Cornelis Françoiszoon, 85–91,
    93, 202, 245, 380
expenditure patterns for food,
  BWH compared to AWH, 296
  BWH compared to civilians, 295–96
  nineteenth-century diet, 300–1
  post 1790, 298–300

Fagel, Gaspar, Grand Pensionary of
    Holland, 118
famine of 1693–94, 465
fixed costs, 180, 182
flour trade
  in other countries, 408
  prohibition of, 165, 175
food hierarchies, 284–86
food riots
  in Dutch Republic, 275
  in England, 274
food systems, 286–87
foodways, 282–83
foundlings, 298
France
  bread consumption in, 328
  wheat bread revolution in, 331
French Empire
  controls on grain trade, 161
  Netherlands incorporated into, 413
Friesland grain production region, 157

Gelderland river region grain production, 156

gemaal, het, impost of, *see* milling excise

gemene middelen, see common means

Germany
  bread consumption in, 328
  bread taxes in, 383

Godewijcx, Peter van, 324

Gogel, Isaac, 410, 412

grain
  re-export of, 149

Grain Exchange of Amsterdam, 149

grain export licences, 43

grain markets
  rye price integration, 160
  speculation, 46
  wheat price integration, 162, 163–64

grain mills
  horse-powered, 170
  steam-powered, 430

grain price differentials, 225

grain prices
  determination of, 68–72

grain production, domestic, 154–58, 162

grain re-exports, 161

grain storage, 47, 99

grain trade
  Baltic supplies, 41, 58, 69, 147, 152, 279
  Baltic wheat, 161
  English supplies, 153
  German supplies, 154
  intervention in, 262
  medieval, 40–42
  Southern Netherlands supplies, 153
  state intervention, 44, 280, 466
  with Italy, 44

grain turners, 149

Granary of Europe, Amsterdam, 148

Graswinckel, Dirk, 45–48

Great Northern War, 152

Griffiths, Richard, 436

Groningen grain production region, 157

Gross Domestic Product (GDP), 450
  in Britain, 369
  in the Netherlands, 370
  methods of measurement, 368

guilds
  abolition of, 410
  theories of, 187–88

Habsburg Empire, 43, 262

Hall, Floris van, Minister of Finance, 423

Harberger triangle, 134

height of Netherlanders, 306

Heldring, O. G., 423

herengeld (Gentleman's tax), 117

home baking, 108, 193

household expenditures for bread, 350–52, 448
  long-term changes, 355

household income, 365–71
  based on GDP, 367–70
  consumption-based approach, 365

household labor, 360

Huguenot refugees, 96

incentive goods, 359

income inequality, 364

industrial structure
  baking, 200–1
  milling after 1855, 432
  milling in north and south, 167
  milling in Prussia, 167
  milling, influence of tax policy on, 165

industrious revolution, 3, 359–60, 371
  agent of market deepening, 360

information asymmetry, 185

institutionalized populations, 288

just price, 9–10, 18, 31, 84

Kaplan, Steven L., 379, 382

Kemper, J. de Bosch, 423, 436

King, Gregory, 332

Knibbe, Merrijn, 446

koekbakkers, see pastry bakers

Kops, J. L. de Bruyn, 423, 436

Korenbeurs, see Grain Exchange of Amsterdam

korfstok, see tally stick

labor costs
  wheat vs. rye, 201–3

law of one price, 162

Le Grand Hiver 1708–09 , 467

Lesger, Clé, 195

liberal constitution of 1848, 424

little divergence, within Netherlands, 347

location theory, 194

Louis Bonaparte, King of Holland, 411, 430, 439

Luzac, Elie, 409

maalloon, see millers' fee

market integration
  impediments to, 334

Marktzwang, 8

Marx, Karl, 195

McCants, Anne, 295

meat, place in diet, 296
migration to Amsterdam, 343
migration to Republic, 59, 204, 342
migration within Republic, 342, 347
  influence of cost of living on, 352
Miller, Judith A., 380
millers
  earnings of, 175–79
  official suspicions of, 171
  restrictions on, 165
millers' cartel, 430
millers' fee, 30, 165
  in England, 174, 179
  in France, 175
  in kind, 172
  monetized, 173
  setting the level of, 171–74
  under Batavian Republic, 178
millers' guilds, 167, 169, 178
milling
  entrepreneurial character of, 175, 430
  large-scale milling, 430
  large-scale milling in England, 431
  productivity of, 166
  rural regulation of, 104–5
  technology of, 170
milling excise, 82, 165, 451
  abolition, 425
  after unification of rates, 412
  as cause of high wage rates, 436
  basis for consumption estimates, 472
  conversion to capitation, 119–22
  differential rates per grain, 138
  example of optimal tax, 144
  growing dissatisfaction, 407
  in Copenhagen, 384
  in Germany, 383
  in Rome, 384
  on brewers' grain, 474
  outside Holland, 125–28
  rates charged, 63
  reform of 1680, 117, 144, 407, 428, 474
  restoration in 1750, 278
  revenue from, 129–32
  role in crisis periods, 271
  rural enforcement, 104, 107, 119
  suspension of 1748, 276
  suspension of 1817, 414
  suspension of 1830, 414
  under Kingdom of the Netherlands,
    414–15
  uniform rates introduced, 412
  wheat-rye differentials, 437
  without price regulation, 454
milling excise revenue

  in 1849, 420
  regional tax burden, 413, 420
Mokyr, Joel, 436
Montanari, Massimo, 282
moral economy, 2, 19, 21, 135, 274–75
municipal surcharges, 414–16, 417–22,
    436, 438
  uneven incidence of, 418

Nahrungsprinzip, 19
Netherlands, Kingdom of, 413
  food insecurity in, 261
  milling excise under, 416
new system introduction, 57, 76
numeracy, 92, 451
nutritional value of grains, 226

Ogilvie, Sheilagh, 187
optimal tax theory, 133–37, 139, 437,
    452
orphanage diets
  place of wheat in, 309, 324
  representativeness of, 288–89
orphanages, 288–89
overbroden, see advantage loaves

P. J. Meertens Instituut, 109
pastry bakers, 176, 191–93
path dependence, 439
Patriot Revolution, 270, 278, 410
Patriots, 281
penalty of the pioneer, 4, 432
Personele Quotisatie, 177, 191, 195, 217
Petersen, Christian, 332
Polanyi, Karl, 1
political legitimacy
  role of bread price controls, 454
  role of grain policy, 281
poor relief, 266
Posthumus, N. W., 251
potato famine, 262
potatoes, 139, 429
  a bread substitute?, 301, 305
  complement or substitute?, 286
  consumption levels, 304
  relative price of, 285, 302–4
  source of vitamin C, 295
pound for pound rule, 25, 28
price control by fiat, 267
price control by self-financing, 269–70
price revolution, 58
price smoothing, 269, 468
prices
  Danzig–Amsterdam grain price gap, 385
  of grain in Europe, 385–86

production costs of bread types, 225–28
provisionment policies, 8, 46, 103
Prussian granaries, 14
public debt, 422
public disorder, fear of, 275–81
public granaries, 13
public subsidy of bread prices, 264
purchasing power, 254

quality of bread, 97
    in England, 403

Ramsey, F. P., 133
rantsoenpenning
    charge on tax farm receipts, 473
real wages, 348
    regional differences, 345–46
    reversal of fortunes, 347
regional tax burdens, 129, 437
regulatory capture, 185–87, 190, 220
respectable food budget, 297, 361
revealed preferences, 350
    revealed by migration, 352
revenue
    baking sector,
        as portion of GDP, 222
    milling sector, 176
Revolt of the Belgians, 414
Revolutions of 1848, 424
Ricardo, David, 405, 409
Riel, Arthur van, 446
rosmolens, see grain mills, horse-powered
rural bakers
    competition from, 103
    toleration of, 103–4
rye bread
    bakers' earnings, 221
    place in the diet, 49
    production costs, 201–3
    setting bakers' fee, 203–5
    varieties of, 50, 229
rye bread consumption
    after 1855, 447, 449
    before 1640, 323
    in Burghers' Orphanage, 309
    regional divergence, 346–48
rye bread price
    based on Amsterdam market, 69
    based on old and new systems, 60
    frequency of change, 93
    subsidized by wheat bread consumers,
        209
rye bread, place in diet, 49–51
rye prices
    in northern Europe, 385

influence of Baltic supplies, 160
    regional variation of, 160
    relative to potato prices, 303
    relative to wheat prices, 225
rye–wheat boundary, 283

Sarphati, Samuel, 431
scale of milling, 169
    in England and France, 170
small coin problem, 32, 78, 109–11
Smith, Adam, 47, 409, 413, 436, 442
Smith, Charles, 332
Sound Toll Registers, 149
Southern Netherlands, 87, 103, 153, 161,
        167, 170, 387
    bread consumption in, 328
    within Kingdom of the Netherlands,
        414
speculation in grain, 98–100
Spiegel, Laurens van der, 409
St. Nicholas celebrations, 263
standard of living, 348–49
    influence of consumer choice, 349,
        361–63
state capacity, 2, 452
state formation
    puzzle of Dutch Republic, 273
    role of bread price regulation in, 273,
        452
    theory of, 20, 272–74
States Flanders, 276
    grain production, 156
    wheat shipments from, 161
stranded assets, 169
subsidy schemes, 11
subsistence crises, 58

tally stick, 113
tax du pain, see bread price regulation
tax evasion, 119, 122, 128, 165, 311, 412,
        474
tax farmers, 121, 122, 135, 166, 317, 472
    abolition, 277
    collection costs of, 472
tax reforms proposed, 454
tax revenues
    central government, 412
    rural under-collection, 105
tax riots, 136
taxation of bread
    defenders of, 423
    elsewhere in Europe, 383–85
    Liberal critique of, 422–23
    views of Classical economists, 408–9
    views of Patriots, 409–10

taxation, seasonal, 189
tea and coffee, 140, 296
tiende verhoging (10-percent surcharge), 117, 124
Tillet, Mathieu, 382
Tilly, Charles, 273
trade barriers
    erected by milling excise, 416–17

Unger, Richard, 327
Union of Utrecht, 63, 64
unitary tax system, 410
urban graveyard, 344
urbanization
    of eastern provinces, 158
    regional differences, 337

value added, 355, 369
Vandenbroeke, Christiaan, 328
verschietsters, see grain turners
Voskuil, J. J., 283, 323

wage gaps, regional, 344
wage good, 2, 442
wage rates, 254, 363
    and household earnings, 365
    effect of milling excise on, 436
    in England, 338
    in western Europe, 340
    regional differences, 335–37
warfare, 116
weights and measures, 85
    monitoring,
weight-variable system, 31–35, 110
    algebraic problem, 32
    reasons for, 32
welfare ratios, 361

wet nurses, 298
wheat bread
    as incentive good, 359
    place in diet, 51
    varieties of, 52–54, 229
wheat bread consumption
    after 1855, 447
    before 1650, 318
    contemporary observers on, 323–24
    in England, 332
    in face of rising cost, 352
    regional differences, 349
    relative to rye, 310, 439
wheat bread prices
    based on Rotterdam market, 70
    frequency of changes, 94
    price differentials, 232–33
wheat bread revolution, 3, 331–33, 353, 371, 449, 451
    resumed, 428
wheat imports, 160, 307, 325
wheat prices
    regional variation of, 164
wheat, varieties of, 162, 163
white bread
    consumer preferences for, 236
    medical opinion of, 286
    premium prices for, 244
Willem I, King of the Netherlands, 416
wine and brandy excise, 117
work year
    length of, 257, 365

yield rate, *see* bread yield

Zanden, Jan Luiten van, 184, 188
Zeeland grain production, 154